TRIBONIAN

TRIBONIAN

Tony Honoré

Regius Professor of Civil Law
in the University of Oxford

Duckworth

First published in 1978 by
Gerald Duckworth & Co. Ltd.
The Old Piano Factory
43 Gloucester Crescent, London NW1

© 1978 by Tony Honoré

ISBN 0 7156 1131 3

Printed in Great Britain
by W & J Mackay Limited, Chatham

Contents

TO THE MEMORY OF MY FATHER

Known and proposed dates

(proposed dates in italics)

25 August	450	Accession of Marcianus (east)
8 October	451	Council of Chalcedon, first session
16 March	455	Death of Valentinian III (west). Collapse of imperial rule in the west
June	455	Capture of Rome by Gaiseric, king of the Vandals
26 January	457	Death of Marcianus
7 February	457	Accession of Leo I (east)
1 February	460	Certificate of legal instruction required of practitioners at praetorian bar
	468	Leo's unsuccessful attempt to reconquer North Africa
	471	Acacius patriarch of Constantinople
3 February	474	Death of Leo I
9 February	474	Accession of Zeno
	481	Zeno's edict (*Henotikon*)
	482	Beginning of the Acacian schism
9 April	491	Death of Zeno
11 April	491	Accession of Anastasius I
17 November	*500*	*Iohannes quaestor*
	505	Truce with Persia
	513	Revolt of Vitalian
20 July	514	Hormisdas pope
8 July	518	Death of Anastasius I
9 July	518	Accession of Justin I
after 18 September	518	Correspondence of Justinian with pope Hormisdas
1 Dec.	*518*	*Proclus quaestor*
	519	End of Acacian schism
25 February	520	Epiphemius patriarch of Constantinople
July	520	Murder of Vitalian
	521	Consulship of Justinian
6 August	523	Death of Hormisdas
before 19 November	*524*	*Death of empress Euphemia*
not after	*525*	*Marriage of Justinian and Theodora*
1 April	527	Justinian I Augustus
1 August	527	Death of Justin I
	528–9	Persecution of pagans, heretics and homosexuals

13 February	528	C. HAEC. First Law Commission under John of Cappadocia
		Thomas quaestor. Menas praetorian prefect
7 April	529	C. SUMMA. Promulgation of first Codex Iustinianus
17 September	*529*	*Tribonian quaestor.* Demosthenes praetorian prefect
18 March	530	Julianus praetorian prefect
June	530	Victory of Belisarius over Persians at Daras
1 August	*530*	*Series of Fifty Decisions begins*
15 December	530	C. DEO AUCTORE. Second Law Commission under Tribonian
30 April	*531*	*Last of series of Fifty Decisions.* John of Cappadocia praetorian prefect
13 January	532	Nika rebellion breaks out
14 January	532	Dismissal of Tribonian and John of Cappadocia
18 January	532	Massacre in hippodrome. End of Nika rebellion
spring	532	Peace with Persia ratified
c. 9 July	*532*	*Excerpting for Digest completed*
18 October	*532*	John of Cappadocia again praetorian prefect. *Tribonian drafting constitutions*
2 January	533	John II pope
c. March	*533*	*First draft of Digest complete*
June	533	North African expedition leaves Constantinople
13 September	533	Battle of ad Decimum. Collapse of Vandal kingdom
21 November	533	C. IMPERATORIAM. Promulgation of Justinian's Institutes
		Tribonian *magister officiorum*
16 December	533	C. OMNEM (new law syllabus) and TANTA /ΔΕΔΩΚΕΝ (promulgation of *Digest*)
25 March	534	Pope John II endorses Justinian's declaration of faith
16 November	534	C. CORDI (second edition of *Codex Iustinianus*)
1 January	*535*	*Tribonian again quaestor*
16 March	535	Hermogenes *magister officiorum*
15 April	535	Reform of provincial appointments
13 May	535	Agapetus I pope
June	535	Anthimus (monophysite) patriarch of Constantinople
	535	Dalmatia and Sicily reconquered
12 March	536	Deposition of Anthimus

Abbreviations

Appendix	*Corpus Iuris Civilis* vol. III, ed. Schoell-Kroll appendix II. Appendix constitutionum dispersarum. 6th ed. 1954
Background	A. M. Honoré, 'The background to Justinian's Codification', *Tulane Law Rev.* 48 (1974) 859
Barker	J. W. Barker, *Justinian and the Later Roman Empire* (1966)
Bluhme	F. Bluhme, 'Die Ordnung der Fragmenten in den Pandektentiteln', *Zeit. f. gesch. Rechtswissenschaft* 4 (1820) 256
Browning	R. Browning, *Justinian and Theodora* (1971)
Buildings	Procopius, *De aedificiis* = *Buildings*
Bury	J. B. Bury, *History of the Later Roman Empire*, Dover ed. 2 vols (1958)
C.	*Constitutio* (*Deo auctore* etc.)
Collectio	*Collectio Avellana*, ed. O. Guenther, *Corpus Scriptorum Ecclesiasticorum Latinorum* vol. 35
CJ	*Codex Iustinianus. Corpus Iuris Civilis* vol. II, ed. P. Krueger, 13th stereotype ed.
Collinet	P. Collinet, *Histoire de l'école de droit de Beyrouth* (1925)
Commissioners	A. M. Honoré and Alan Rodger, 'How the *Digest* commissioners worked', 87 *ZSS* (1970) 246
CTh	*Codex Theodosianus. Theodosiani libri XVI cum constitutionibus Sirmondianis*, ed. Th. Mommsen (1905)
CTh/N	*Codex Theodosianus*, Sirmondian constitutions and *Novels* of Theodosius II and later emperors up to Majorian. The latter are in *Leges Novellae ad Theodosianum pertinentes*, ed. P. M. Meyer (1905)
D.	*Iustiniani Digesta. Corpus Iuris Civilis* vol. I, ed. Th. Mommsen—P. Krueger, 13th stereotype ed.
Daube	D. Daube, 'The marriage of Justinian and Theodora, legal and theological reflections', 16 *Catholic University of American Law Rev.* (1967) 380
Distribution	A. M. Honoré and Alan Rodger, 'The distribution of *Digest* texts into titles', 89 *ZSS* (1972) 351
Edict	*Corpus Iuris Civilis* vol. III, ed. Schoell-Kroll, appendix 1. Iustiniani XIII edicta quae vocantur. 6th ed. 1954
Editing	A. M. Honoré, 'The editing of the *Digest* titles', 90 *ZSS* (1973) 262
Gibbon	E. Gibbon, *The History of the Decline and Fall of the Roman Empire*, ed. J. B. Bury (1909–1914)

Gradenwitz   O. Gradenwitz, *Heidelberger Index zum Theodosianus* (1925);
                  Ergänzungsband zum Heidelberger Index zum Theodosianus
                  (1929)

Holmes   W. G. Holmes, *The Age of Justinian and Theodora* (2nd ed.
                  1912)

Inst.   *Iustiniani Institutiones*, ed. P. Krueger,
                  Corpus Iuris Civilis vol. 1 13th stereotype ed.

Jones   A. H. M. Jones, *The Later Roman Empire 284–602*, 3 vols
                  (1964)

Justinian   A. M. Honoré, 'Some constitutions composed by
                  Justinian', 65 *Journ. Rom Stud.* (1975) 107

Lydus   J. L. Lydus, *De Magistratibus Populi Romani*

Oracle   *The Oracle of Baalbek—The Tiburtine Sibyl in Greek dress*, ed.
                  P. J. Alexander (1967)

N.   *Iustiniani Novellae*, ed. R. Schoell—G. Kroll. *Corpus Iuris
                  Civilis* vol. III. 6th ed. 1954

Pal.   O. Lenel, *Palingenesia Iuris Civilis* 2 vols. 1889, reprinted
                  1960

Progress   A. M. Honoré, 'Justinian's *Digest*—work in progress
                  (1971)', = 88 *Law Quar. Rev.* (1972) 30

Rubin   B. Rubin, *Das Zeitalter Justinians* (1960)

Schulz   F. Schulz, *History of Roman Legal Science* (1946)

SH   Procopius, *Historia Arcana* = *Secret History*

Stein   E. Stein, *Histoire du Bas-Empire* 2 vols. 1949, 1959

Stein, *Deux questeurs*

                  E. Stein, 'Deux questeurs de Justinien et l'emploi des
                  langues dans ses novelles', *Bulletin de la classe des lettres de
                  l'Académie royale de Belgique* 5è série xxiii (1937) 365

Trail   A. M. Honoré, 'Justinian's *Digest*: following the trail',
                  88 *Law Quar. Rev.* (1972) 530

Vasilev   A. A. Vasilev, *Justin the First* (1950)

VCJ   *Vocabularium Codicis Justiniani* 2 vols, ed. R. von Mayr and
                  M. San Nicolò (1923, 1925)

Wars   Procopius, *Bella* = *Wars*

Wenger   L. Wenger, *Die Quellen des römischen Rechts* (1953)

Preface

This is the first book to be devoted solely to the career, work and personality of Tribonian. For nearly thirteen years (529–542) in the reign of Justinian (527–565) Tribonian was his chief legal adviser and during most of it his 'quaestor', that is to say his Minister for Legislation and Propaganda. In various capacities Tribonian composed about three-quarters of Justinian's legislation (or what has survived). He also directed Justinian's Second Law Commission which in 530–4 compiled the three-volume restatement of Roman law, the *Digest*, the *Institutes* and the second edition of the code of imperial constitutions. These volumes, together with the *Novels* of Justinian, constitute the bulk of the texts from which our knowledge of Roman law is derived. They are also the texts which in the middle ages became the substance of advanced legal study and formed the mind of generations of lawyers.

It is a curiosity of Latin culture that in poetry, history and law the figures who summarise and bring to a close the authentic tradition appear centuries after that tradition has apparently withered, and come from a Greek background or ambience. This is true of Tribonian as it is of Claudian and Ammianus. Where Tribonian differs from the others is in the major role he played in the transmission of the classical legal tradition.

Yet the career, style, outlook and personality of the man who so strongly shaped the legal edifice of Europe have attracted little attention. One can but speculate why. Scholars both in law and history have been unclear about the respective parts of Tribonian and his emperor in the codification. The tendency of Roman legal science has long been to fuse the lawyers of the sixth century, together with Justinian himself, into a single Byzantine figure, the counterpart of the 'classical' jurist whose uniform and unchanging pen supposedly filled the rolls of the law from Augustus to Alexander Severus. Hence the books of Romanists are full of descriptions of what 'Justinian' thought or decreed—a manner of speaking which is technically correct but which ignores the fact that Justinian was no more a lawyer than Napoleon.[1]

Another influence in diverting attention from Tribonian has been pre-occupation with the classical. This, natural enough in a sense, has led to false emphases and wrong methods of inquiry. The discontinuity of the legal tradition has been over-stressed, despite the fact that, for example, the Beirut law school lasted from the classical age to the middle of the sixth century, and sustained through its students an intellectual and professional tradition which was rooted in the Roman republic. Seen in the focus of an

[1] Cf. G. G. Archi, *Stud. biz. e neoellenici* 8 (1953) 277, 279 n. 1.

over-sharp contrast between the classical and the post-classical, Tribonian appears as a destroyer, mutilating the authentic texts, rather than as the last great Roman jurist. Thus in Kunkel's admirable study of the origins and social status of the jurists Tribonian, from whom we have more legal texts than anyone apart from Ulpian,[2] is not included.

One reason for this is that legal work done for the state, such as the drafting of imperial constitutions, does not appear to the classically-oriented mind as creative lawyerly work. Yet Papinian, Ulpian and Modestinus held the secretaryship *a libellis* and in that capacity composed imperial rescripts. They did not become puppets of the Severan monarchy when they expressed their view of the law on the emperor's behalf rather than in their own name; they simply worked within a constitutional framework by which imperial constitutions were the most authoritative source of law.

In the later empire the constitutional pre-eminence of the ruler was such that no place remained for private legal writing. A lawyer who wished to make a positive contribution to his discipline did so either as a teacher or as a lawyer in government. Tribonian, composing laws as quaestor or as chairman of Justinian's Second Law Commission, was the last of a long line of scholars who sought in the public service to maintain the tradition they had been taught. He was unusual in the degree to which, under the intellectual influence of Gaius and the political direction of Justinian, he was prepared to criticise and reform.

Once the illusions—that Justinian compiled the codification,[3] that Byzantine lawyers were a uniform crew and that a lawyer in government service is not a real lawyer—are dissipated, the way is clear to a study of Tribonian in his own right and as successor to Julian, Gaius, Papinian and Ulpian. It is then that technical problems have to be surmounted. In order to identify the constitutions composed by the quaestor and to unravel the scheme which he adopted for compiling the *Digest*, the *Institutes* and the *Codex*, I have resorted to simple numerical calculations. In two contexts these can usefully supplement the customary sorts of evidence. Given a methodical man, such as Tribonian, the programme can, so to speak, be

---

[2] Taking as the unit a line the length of that in Lenel's *Palingenesia Iuris Civilis* (1889) the figures are:
  a. Ulpian 46150 (*Digest* only; something must be added for the rescripts drafted by him as secretary *a libellis* in 202–9: Honoré, 'Private rescripts & their authors': *Aufstieg und Niedergang de römischen Welt* (ed. Temporini) 2.14.
  b. Tribonian 30983 (in the Codex Iustinianus 10468, in the Novels 20515. For this purpose the constitutions falling within his two quaestorships are attributed to him, together with those constitutions falling outside it which bear the marks of his style).
  c. Paul 19434.
  d. Papinian 6802 (same reservations as for Ulpian, but the addition does not amount to more than 300 lines).
The basic statistics for the *Digest* are tabulated in [1972A] *Cambridge Law Journal* 280, 293.

[3] Still maintained by F. Amarelli: *Labeo* 21 (1975) 238f.

deduced from the output. It is thus that it has been possible to reconstruct the way in which he organised the work of the Second Law Commission and in particular the production of the *Digest* in the short space of three years. Scattered elements of the story have been published before, but they are here drawn together and summarised in Chapter 5.

Simple arithmetic is also in place when it comes to the study of style. The authors of legislation can be settled only if the various styles of composition can be marked off from one another. For purposes of this book it was necessary to list the norms of style not only of Tribonian but of Justinian, who is said by Procopius to have written some laws himself, and of Tribonian's forerunners and successors in the quaestorship, since the exact limits in time of his activity must be settled. Justinian's style has been elucidated in an article not here reproduced (see 1975 *JRS* 107), though its conclusions are summarised in Chapter 1. Tribonian's Latin is the topic of Chapter 3 and forms the core of the present book. The other sixth-century quaestors appear in Chapter 8.

Though the identification of styles is in the ultimate analysis dependent on the trained judgment of the scholar, an attempt has been made to introduce an element of discipline into the investigations.

In its general form the method involves five steps. First, a document or set of documents is provisionally identified as the work of a particular author. Secondly, a document or set of documents is chosen to represent the language or sub-language to which the first set belongs: for example, Latin, or official Latin. Thirdly, the first set is analysed in order to list characteristics which appear in it with considerably greater frequency than in the second set. Fourthly, the list is whittled down by the elimination of those items in it which do not appear in the first set of documents with considerably greater frequency than they do in the writings of any contemporary authors who are available for comparison. The fifth and last step is to use the reduced list to settle the authorship of documents of disputed paternity.

In applying this method no claim is made to statistical purity. What counts as a 'considerably greater' frequency is settled by trial and error. Nor are the criteria applied with unbending rigour. They are intended to supplement, not to supplant, other forms of evidence.

Chapters 3 and 8 give examples of the application of the technique. Thus in Chapter 3 the constitutions dated between 17 September 529 and 14 January 532 are provisionally identified as Tribonian's. The vocabulary of the *Codex Iustinianus* is chosen to represent official legal Latin. The initial list of marks of style is set up on the basis that the words or constructions listed must appear at least three times more frequently in the texts provisionally identified than in the *Codex* as a whole. Then the list is reduced by the elimination of those marks which occur more than once in the texts of the thirty-eight years up to A.D. 529 or in the ecclesiastical Latin writings and letters of the emperor himself. The revised list is used to identify the author of some disputed constitutions, for example those issued when

Tribonian was temporarily out of office, also the prefaces to the *Digest*, together with certain passages in the *Institutes* and the second edition of the *Codex*.

The disciplined pursuit of norms of style seems to me a fruitful technique in any context where authorship is in question. Roman legal history is only one such context, albeit one where the yield is copious and in the main unmistakeable.

To the method adopted some scholars are likely to oppose lively scepticism. On the one hand, they will be bemused by the picture of a uniform Byzantine or Justinianic way of writing, just as earlier the supposedly pure and uniform classical style stood in the way of those who wanted to look at each classical writer in and for himself.

In the sixth century there are some features of legal Latin which can be put down to the practice of the age, the tradition of the quaestor's office or the insistence of the emperor. Beyond these common features, however, are others which mark out one quaestor from another, officials from law professors, Beirut from Constantinople and the emperor from them all. It is useless to deny the existence of these features before the search for them has been put in train. It was precisely because Tribonian composed with an eloquence and splendour which his contemporaries could not match that he gained and held Justinian's esteem and died in office despite the corruption of which he was, perhaps justly, accused.

A different objection, perhaps more acutely felt in regard to the classical lawyers than to their Byzantine successors, is that the texts have undergone such mutilations, through copying, shortening and editing, that the original manner can no longer be discerned. Even for the texts of Justinian's age it must be conceded that many of them passed through the hands of two law commissions, the first under John of Cappadocia in 528–9 and the second under Tribonian in 530–4. Unlike the later *Novels*, the versions of Justinian's constitutions we possess in the *Codex Iustinianus* are not original. They have been shortened and edited, even revised retrospectively. Is this not inconsistent with a successful search for the idiosyncrasies of the various composers?

The doubt is misconceived. If despite all the changes which, for example, Volterra[4] postulates in the text of the imperial constitutions it remains possible, reading them chronologically, to find a deposit of consistent style for successive periods of time, the changes, whatever their nature and extent, have demonstrably not had the obfuscating effect which the critics fear. The proof of the eating is in the eating. Norms of style, once listed, can be used to criticise the texts and identify bits which do not fit in with the bulk. The jagged edges are not to be made into an excuse for tearing up the regular pattern to which they are attached.

The book begins with a sketch of the background: the personality of Justinian, the place of law in Roman society and the optimism which

[4] F. Volterra, 'Il problema del testo delle costituzioni imperiali', *Atti ll cong. int. soc. it. stor. dir.* 1971.

marked the early sixth century. It then turns to Tribonian's career and his Latin and Greek style. Next his part in the elaboration of the *Digest*, *Institutes* and *Codex Iustinianus* and his chairmanship of Justinian's Second Law Commission are studied. Finally, after a contrast with the styles of six other quaestors of the age, I try to assess Tribonian as a lawyer, scholar and propagandist.

Except where problems of style make reference to Latin and Greek inevitable I have told the story in translation and cited in the footnotes only those of the original texts which are not readily accessible.

The book makes no attempt to be definitive. It seeks rather to present solutions to a limited set of problems which seem to be crucial to further advance in Roman legal science. The detailed study of the interpolations made by the compilers in the classical or post-classical texts is left for future attention. The idea that this form of criticism could make progress without an understanding on the one hand of the methods of Justinian's commissioners and on the other of the individual styles of the classical writers is an illusion which has cost Roman legal science a century of largely wasted effort and returned it after a vast detour to its starting point. Perhaps it will now be possible to begin again under better auspices.

Nor have I been able, as I should have preferred, to assess the place of the central figure in the cultural setting of the sixth-century movement, much wider than the law, which sought to husband the treasures of antiquity before the darkness fell. It was an age of anthologists and epitomisers: Boethius, Johannes Stobaeus, Stephanus of Byzantium, Dionysius Exiguus, Cassiodorus. Their world was dissolving, but in the golden years of the 530s the siege was lifted for a moment as Byzantium sallied forth to conquer. In the optimism of those years there exuberated Tribonian.

Many friends have aided *ope consiliove* during the eight years these researches have so far occupied. In particular I am grateful to Robert Ireland, Patrick Wormald, Michael Wallace-Hadrill, Averil Cameron, Cyril Mango, Robert Feenstra and John Barton for their help. I am indebted to Gwen Bryant for coping with messy manuscripts and ancient tongues. But my chief debt is to Alan Rodger. As explained in Chapter 5 he set me on the path which led to the discovery, or what I believe to be the discovery, of the methods employed by the *Digest* commissioners in excerpting the ancient works. In the laborious counts and checks which preceded the publication of our joint articles in 87 and 89 ZSS his rigour and sympathetic understanding of the new methods lightened and hastened an obsessional task. Parts of these and of other articles concerning the compilation of the *Digest* have been drawn together in Chapter 5 in order to present in detail for the first time the story of a remarkable feat of organisation.

CHAPTER ONE

The Master, the Art and the Hope

This chapter is an introduction to the story of Tribonian and the part he played in Justinian's reign.[1] It will necessarily be selective and idiosyncratic. Of the many possible themes from the history of early sixth-century Byzantium I have chosen three as peculiarly appropriate to my tale: the character of the emperor, so different from what is generally supposed, who in the rest of the story is to be projected as a background presence, forever prodding the lawyers to do more and better; the law itself, the highest Roman achievement, in its intellectual, practical and professional aspects; and the efflorescence in the sixth century, especially the 530s, of a hope which briefly escalated into unlimited expectation. For if Justinian was Tribonian's master, to whom he owed his career, the law was his profession and his love, and the thirties were the age when in partnership the team carried through the programme of law reform and codification which leaves its mark on us still.

At the turn of the century it was by no means clear that what lay ahead was *les grandeurs et misères de la victoire*. Anastasius (491–518) had been for eight years on the throne.[2] For the last fifty, since the collapse of the imperial rule in the west,[3] the eastern authorities had been saddled with responsibility for millions of western subjects for whom they could do little, since the western provinces were under Vandal, Visigothic or Ostrogothic rule and their rulers acknowledged in varying degrees a Byzantine suzerainty that in the nature of things could seldom be of practical effect. The auspices for reconquest were not favourable. In 468 the emperor Leo[4] had sent an expedition of, it was said, over 1000 ships and 100,000 men to retake Vandal North Africa.[5] It was an ignominious failure.

---

[1] Of the general histories of the period the best from a lawyer's point of view are E. Gibbon, *The History of the Decline and Fall of the Roman Empire* (ed. Bury 1909–14); J. B. Bury, *History of the Later Roman Empire* (Dover edition 2 vols 1958); E. Stein, *Histoire du Bas-Empire* (2 vols 1949, 1959), the latter being outstanding on administrative detail. A. H. M. Jones, *The Later Roman Empire* 284–602 (3 vols 1964) is indispensable from the point of view of information.

[2] He reigned from 11 April 491 to 8 July 518. He was chosen by the empress Ariadne, widow of Zeno (9 Feb. 474 to 9 April 491) who herself lived on until 515.

[3] Although this cannot be precisely dated, the death of the general Aetius on 21 Sept. 454 (*magna occidentalis reipublicae salus*) and Valentinian III on 16 March 455 (last male descendant of the house of Theodosius) marked the end of serious prospects of military and political survival in the west: Bury 1.300.

[4] Leo was emperor from 7 Feb. 457 to 3 Feb. 474.

[5] Marcellinus, *Chron.* sub anno 468; Procopius, *Wars* 3.6.

The religious situation was hardly better from the viewpoint of those to whom true belief was a condition of salvation for the individual and unity of belief a necessity for the empire–Romania, as it was now coming to be called.[6] Such of the east Germans as had accepted Christianity appear mostly to have been converted to Arianism and therefore believed that Jesus was not eternal but was created by the Father from nothing:[7] he was at most similar to, not identical in substance with, the Father. The western Romans living under barbarian rule mostly accepted the authority of the Roman see and the decrees of the Council of Chalcedon (451) which had been summoned and addressed by Marcianus 'best of emperors'.[8] They believed that while Christ's humanity is not separable from his divine *person*, so that, for example, the Virgin is rightly called the Mother of God, his divine and human *natures* are not to be confused. The eastern Romans were divided. Many, far more than one would a priori expect, adhered to the western, Chalcedonian view, but a substantial force called monophysites, as opposed to the Chalcedonian diphysites, held, especially after the patriarchate of Dioscurus (444–51) in Egypt, that Christ had a single nature and that a divine one.[9] Beyond the eastern limits of the empire there flourished a fourth view, that of the Nestorians who believed that the incarnate Son consisted of two persons, not one.[10]

It would be unfair to stigmatise these disputes as futile cavillations. Granted the initial paradox of Christianity, which goes back at the latest to the late first century, viz. that Christ was not merely the Messiah but a God and, indeed, an element in the only true God, intellectual inquiry must either cease or controversy rage. To delineate so unique a being obvious analogies fail, and one must necessarily have recourse to what seems far-fetched.

Whatever view one held, there was a sharp contrast in religious outlook between the rigorous, the lax and the pragmatic. To the first-named group heretical or dissenting views were non-Christian, the officials who expounded them not priests, the places where they were celebrated not churches. Their adherents were the religious equivalent of barbarians. Such, for example, was Justinian's view of the Arians, as we can see from

[6] R. L. Wolff, 'Romania: the Latin empire of Constantinople', 23 *Speculum* (1948) 1–34.

[7] G. Bardy, *Recherches sur S. Lucien d'Antioche et son école* (1936).

[8] Marcianus (emperor 25 Aug. 450 to 26 Jan. 457) is so described in Just. *N.* 105 pr. (28 Dec. 537). He and his officials dominated the council and imposed the views of pope Leo on the eastern bishops: de Ste Croix, 'Political elements in the persecution of and by the early Christians' (forthcoming).

[9] Eutyches (died 454) whose views were upheld at Ephesus in 449 but, after the accession of Marcianus, condemned at Chalcedon in 451, was the leading exponent of these views in the fifth, Severus of Antioch (*c.* 465–538) in the sixth century—see W. H. C. Frend, *A History of the Monophysite Movement* (1972) ch. 7.

[10] Nestorius, who was briefly patriarch of Constantinople (428–431) was supported by the emperor Theodosius II (10 Jan. 408 to 28 July 450) but condemned by the council of Ephesus (431).

the constitutions which he himself composed after the reconquest of Vandal North Africa.[11]

The lax, like Procopius,[12] thought that we cannot know the nature of God and had better not waste time speculating about it. The pragmatic approach was in effect, though not in motivation, similar. There was an empire to be governed, and it was a matter of political necessity to avoid confrontation, especially between Chalcedonians and monophysites. One might pay lip-service to the notion of a single truth and yet define it loosely enough to envelop a wide spread of opinion. In 481 the emperor Zeno by his *Henotikon* attempted just this.[13] Roundly condemning the Nestorians who were for the most part safely outside the imperial boundaries, he inaugurated a *détente* with the monophysites by defining orthodoxy in terms of the fourth-century councils and avoiding mention of Chalcedon and of Christ's nature or natures.

Anastasius was, and was known before his election to be, of stricter theology.[14] He inclined strongly to a monophysite position, and though before his coronation he signed a written declaration of orthodoxy, the Chalcedonians were disquieted. Their concern seemed vindicated by the outbreak of the Persian war in 502, in which the Romans suffered grave defeats in 502 and 503.[15] The Oracle of Baalbek,[16] vaticinating probably in 503 or 504, presents a Chalcedonian view of present and impending disasters.

This apocalyptic version of Roman and divine history is a revision of an earlier apocalypse written under the impact of the defeat and death of the emperor Valens at Adrianople in 378.[17] The revisionist Sybil, like the original, divides history into nine generations. In the sixth Constantine renames Byzantium (A.D. 330) but 'do not boast, city of Byzantium, you will not hold imperial sway for thrice sixty of your years'—not, that is, beyond 510.[18] In the eighth, under Leo (457–74), an 'emperor named after a wild beast', the birth pains of the world begin: 'There will be no one to administer or to manage Romania.'[19] Later in the same generation comes

[11] *CJ* 1.27.1.pr.-4 (534).

[12] *Wars* 5.3.5–6; 7.35.1; cf. *Buildings* 4.3.12 (childish pretence that once a strange race of men existed compounded of the nature of two creatures). The historian was perhaps a Christian of monophysite tendencies, impatient of theological niceties. For another view (perhaps not radically different) see A. and A. Cameron, *Class. Quar.* 14 (1964) 317; Averil Cameron, *Historia* 15 (1966) 466; J. A. S. Evans, *Procopius* 116–18. Bonfante, *BIDR* 41 (1933) 283, makes him a heretic; B. Rubin, *Das römische Recht in Osten Byzanz*: *Propyläen Weltgeschichte: Eine Universalgeschichte*, ed. G. Mann and A. Hens (1963) 4. 641, a Syrian or Jew.

[13] Evagrius, *Hist. eccl.* 3.14. It is important to remember that the *Henotikon* was an edict of Zeno and so, while from Zeno's point of view designed to secure political unity, from that of the Roman see it embodied a claim to define Christian doctrine by imperial enactment.

[14] Theophanes anno 5982–3. On Anastasius see Stein II.157f.

[15] Procopius, *Wars* 1.7.

[16] *The Oracle of Baalbek: The Tiburtine Sibyl in Greek Dress*, ed. P. J. Alexander (1967).

[17] *Oracle* 63f.   [18] *Oracle* lines 94–5.   [19] *Oracle* lines 136–40.

Anastasius: 'He is bald, handsome, his forehead is like silver, he has a long right arm, he is noble, terrifying, high-souled and free, and hates all beggars. He will ruin many of the poor, either lawfully or unlawfully, and will depose those who observe godliness. The Persians will arise in his times and will overturn with the sword the cities of the east together with the multitudes of the soldiers of Romania. And he will be king for 31 years.'[20] After him, in the ninth generation, wars, bloodshed and (notable feature) tax exemptions announce the Second Coming.[21]

The Oracle's gloom was exaggerated. True, the time when an emperor would arise from the east, grant exemption from public tax and restore all the people of the east and of Palestine was not at hand. But neither was the empire to be overwhelmed by the Persians. In late 503 and 504 the war turned in favour of the Romans, and 505 saw a truce which lasted for over twenty years.[22] The year 510 passed with Byzantium imperial and intact. Though Anastasius did not rule for 31 years, he lasted for over 27, into the summer of 518. Whether his economies pressed more heavily on the poor than the rich is debated.[23] At all events, he filled the treasury, reduced taxes and bequeathed to the next dynasty a financial springboard.[24] He also left behind a religious confrontation. In old age he veered from the path of compromise represented by the *Henotikon* towards open support for the monophysites and their candidates for the patriarchal sees.[25] To the chant 'Holy, holy, Lord God of Hosts' the addition 'who was crucified for us'— implying that Christ's single divine nature suffered on the cross—was flaunted in St Sophia.[26] Revolt simmered, but the personal piety of the emperor saved the day when in November 512 he appeared before the people in the hippodrome, offered to abdicate, and provoked the crowd to beg him resume the crown.[27] The next year, however, a revolt by Vitalian, Count of the Federates, led from Thrace, took an ideological turn when Vitalian offered himself as the champion of the Chalcedonian party against the monophysites.[28] In 514 it seemed that a compromise might be reached between Anastasius, Vitalian and pope Hormisdas.[29] But both sides were intransigent. Hormisdas, reversing a concession of pope Anastasius II (496–8)[30] insisted that the name of the patriarch Acacius of Constantinople (471–89) should be struck from the diptychs.[31] From his point of view Zeno's edict and Acacius as its supporter had been engaged in an attempt to substitute the emperor for the Roman see as the arbiter of dogmatic truth. The emperor, on the other hand, said that he would

[20] *Oracle* lines 165–72.   [21] *Oracle* lines 173f., esp. 188–9, 206–8.
[22] Lydus 3.53; Bury II. 10–15.   [23] Literature in *Oracle* 96–7, nn. 75–8.
[24] Bury I. 441–7, esp. 446.
[25] Bury I. 438; P. Charanis, *The Religious Policy of Anastasius* I (1939).
[26] On 4 Nov. 512 (Stein II. 177).
[27] Marcellinus anno 512; *Chron. Pasch.* anno 507; Evagrius 3.44.
[28] Bury I. 448; Stein II. 177–85.
[29] Victor Tonnensis anno 514; Theophanes anno 6006.   [30] Bury I. 440.
[31] On Acacius see G. Bardy, *Fliche-Martin* iv (1945) 290–320.

tolerate insults but not orders.[32] He would not sacrifice the living to the dead by risking the disturbances such a rewriting of history would provoke.[33] Loyalty to truth was pitted against duty to govern.

The civil war resumed. Vitalian suffered a naval defeat in 515 but remained lurking off-stage for the last three years of Anastasius.[34] On 8 July 518, when the octogenarian emperor died, Vitalian was not in Byzantium. His sincerity may have been suspect.[35] At any rate, in the election which ensued the Chalcedonian party had other candidates.

JUSTINIAN

Perhaps because of his unpopularity in his later years, the relatives of Anastasius, including three nephews who had been prominent in public life,[36] were not seriously considered for the succession. An elaborate intrigue was mounted.[37] The election of 9 July 518 required the consent of the high palace officials, the senate and the army, represented by the Excubitor and Scholarian guards. One of the officials, the chamberlain Amantius, hoped to secure the throne for a puppet and to that end gave money to Justin, commander of the Excubitors, to bribe the troops. Instead, Justin's agents inspired the Excubitors to put forward a number of other candidates, including Justin's nephew Justinian, none of whom secured the vote of the palace and senate. Nor did the candidate of the Scholarians. In the deadlock the senate chose Justin, and the Excubitors and people in the hippodrome accepted him, the Scholarians being constrained to concur.

Justin, a firm Chalcedonian, was about 66.[38] He was a Latin-speaking Illyrian or Thracian[39] peasant from Bederiana, near Skoplje in Yugoslav Macedonia, about equidistant between Rome and Byzantium. He had come to Constantinople to join the army and make a career. He fought with distinction in the wars of Anastasius, including the civil war against Vitalian, and, though uneducated—Procopius says illiterate[40]—was a reasonable stop-gap choice for the party interested in improving relations with Rome. The reunion with Rome followed speedily. The 'Acacian schism' was ended, the *Henotikon* of Zeno abandoned, the canons of Chalcedon accepted as a starting point of dogmatic thought.

[32] *Collectio Avellana* ep. 138 (11 July 516: *iniuriari enim et adnullari sustinere possumus, iuberi non possumus*).

[33] *Collectio* ep. 125.   [34] Malalas 405; Evagrius 3.43; Cyril, *Vita S. Sabae* 340.

[35] Bury 1. 448 n. 4.

[36] Probus, Pompeius and Hypatius, of whom only Probus managed to remain out of reach of the imperial purple in Jan. 532 at the time of Nika.

[37] Constantine Porphyrogenitus, *Ceremonies* 1.93; Malalas 410; *Chronicon Paschale* anno 518; Marcellinus anno 519.

[38] A. A. Vasilev, *Justin the First* (1950); Stein II. 219–73. 66: Mal 424B: perhaps 68 years old: *Chron. Pasch.* 617B.

[39] Browning 39 and I. Popescu-Spineri, *3e cong. int. étud. byz.* (1930) 344–7, emphasise the Thracian elements. Sources in Vasilev, 52 n. 25.

[40] *SH* 6. 10–16, but the fact that Justin signed his name with a stencil does not prove illiteracy.

The real leader of the pro-Roman and Chalcedonian party was the emperor's nephew Justinian, who was briefly a candidate of the Excubitors in the election of July 518. My temerity in adding to the many attempts to depict the character and outlook of the most famous of Byzantine emperors is explained by a number of considerations. No historian, I believe, has hitherto properly taken account of the division of responsibility between emperor and quaestor insofar as the drafting of legislation is concerned.[41] Nor have historians been sufficiently concerned to set Procopius' *Secret History* alongside the legislation and ask how far each confirms or rebuts the other. In the result not enough attention has been paid either to Justinian's style or to his psychology.[42]

Justin, then, brought his nephew Petrus Sabbatius, along with other relatives, to Byzantium—we do not know when—and the young man took the name Iustinianus, the form of which suggests that he was adopted by his uncle.[42a] Justinian was much abler than Justin. A staunch Chalcedonian,[43] yet more flexible than his uncle, his forceful character and capacity for attention to detail were soon noticed. In July 518 he was a

[41] Eg. Rubin (below, n. 42) 150, 167 and n. 374; Schubart 43f., 78; G. G. Archi, *Giustiniano legislatore* (1970). The latter sees the difficulties but lacks the means to solve them.

[42] *CIL* 5.8210.3. The history of Justinian remains to be written, despite much ink. B. Rubin, *Das Zeitalter Justinians* (1960) is a compilation. C. Diehl, *Justinien et la civilisation byzantine* (1901) is elegant but romantic. See also W. G. Holmes, *The Age of Justinian and Theodora* (2nd ed. 1912); E. Grupe, *Kaiser Justinian* (1923); H. Erman, *Zu Justinian: Festschrift Koschaker* 1 (1939) 157; W. Schubart, *Justinian und Theodora* (1943); P. N. Ure, *Justinian and his Age* (1951); G. Ostrogorsky, *Geschichte des byzantinischen Staates* (1952); R. Browning, *Justinian and Theodora* (1971); J. W. Barker, *Justinian and the Later Roman Empire* (1966); G. W. Downey, *Constantinople in the Age of Justinian* (1960); J. P. von Ludwig, *Vita Justiniani atque Theodorae necnon Triboniani* (Halle 1731: interesting). But on the whole the works of Gibbon, Bury, Stein (above, n. 1) and Vasilev (above, n. 38) are the most useful.

Of the ancient writers I have freely used Procopius and treated his *Secret History*, with allowance for bias and exaggeration, as a reliable source. The divergence between the *Wars*, the *Secret History* and the *Buildings* is of tone and emphasis rather than fact. Not a professional historian but a lawyer who liked writing history, Procopius followed the ordinary career of an ambitous lawyer: law school (*CJ* 2.7.11), bar (Agathias praef. and 2.19 = *CSHB* 11.9, 14.7, 105.6: ὁ ῥήτωρ), assessor to Belisarius (σύμβουλος: *Wars* 1.1.3, 1.12.24; πάρεδρος: 3.14.3), and prefect (below n. 124). He knows the law well and understands evidence. It must be remembered that his three works belong to different genres (classical historiography, satire, panegyric) and that despite his legal experience and literary talent Procopius was twice passed over for the quaestorship, in 542 and 548 (for the dates see ch. 8 below) in favour of inferior writers with little or no legal talent or experience at the bar (*SH* 20.17–23).

I have used Justinian's legislation with due regard to the fact that nearly all the constitutions which throw light on his outlook were composed by Tribonian (chs 3, 4 below) who was, however, expert in presenting Justinian's point of view.

[42a] Alan Cameron, 'Theodorus τρισέπαρχος', *Greek, Roman and Byzantine Studies* 17 (1976) 269, 282.

[43] E. Schwartz, 'Zur Kirchenpolitik Justinians', *Sitz. der bayer. Akad. der Wiss. zu München,* Phil- hist. Abt. 1940 n. 2 p. 32–81; J. Meyendorff, *Dumbarton Oaks Papers* 22 (1968) 43.

candidatus, a member of the emperor's personal bodyguard.[44] In his uncle's reign he rose to be master of soldiers in presence and, in 521, consul.[45]

The scenario of 9 July 518, with its elaborate feints and manipulations, has an air of Justinian's devising.[46] He could be both forceful and subtle. He was not prepared to suffer the barbs which sophisticated Greek intellectuals directed against that rough Thracian, his uncle. He studied assiduously and mastered Christian theology, a discipline largely conducted in Greek, which demanded all the refinements of which the Greek mind was capable. No sooner was his uncle established on the throne than Justinian was conducting in parallel with the emperor a correspondence with pope Hormisdas about the doctrinal basis of reunion.[47] Such parallel diplomacy, which he was later to practise in harness with Theodora,[48] was typical of his method. Justinian's letters differ in tone and manner from those of Justin. The emperor's correspondence was, it seems likely, composed by Proclus, his senior law minister, the 'quaestor of the sacred palace'.[49] Justin's style is, in consequence, elegant and restrained. Justinian, on the other hand, wrote his own letters.[50] They give evidence of a Latin rhetorical education, but rough, colloquial turns of phrase keep obtruding, and the author is guilty of repetition and anti-climax.[51] While showing the pope respect—indeed exasperated deference in questions of doctrine—Justinian, though neither emperor nor Caesar, has no patience with what he sees as papal procrastination or timidity. In 521 he writes to Hormisdas that, with reunion agreed, 'no further religious controversy will we allow in our republic, nor is it appropriate for your holiness to listen to those who indulge in superfluous disputes'.[52]

'Our republic.' Justinian's manner affords support to the claim of Procopius that, though Justinian *reigned* only from 527, he *ruled* from his uncle's accession in 518.[53] But Procopius exaggerates a little both in point of date and power. After Justin's elevation Amantius and his puppet candidate for the throne had to be removed. They were killed, says Procopius, after 'Justinian had been in power scarcely ten days', viz. in July 518.[54] The historian says that Amantius was charged with having spoken hastily against the patriarch John. This trivial complaint may have been the pretext, but given Justin's deception of Amantius during the election, he could hardly be allowed to survive.

[44] Const. Porph., *Cer.* 1.86; *CJ* 12.33.5.4 (25 Dec. 524); A. H. M. Jones 2.613; Gosse, *Römische Militärgeschichte* (1925) 96.

[45] *Collectio Avellana* ep. 154, 162, 230; *CJ* 6.22.8 (1 June 521).

[46] But Vasilev 74-5, 81 rejects the notion of an intrigue.

[47] Preserved in the *Collectio Avellana*, printed in *Migne, Patr. Lat.* 63. 430, 450, 475, 476A, 476C, 485, 496, 507, 508, 510 = O. Guenther *CSEL* vol. 35 ep. 147, 162, 187, 188, 191, 193 (attributed by G. to Justin, wrongly in my opinion), 196, 200, 235, 243. The earliest is dated 7 Sept. 518, the latest antedates the death of Hormisdas on 6 Aug. 523.

[48] *SH* 10. 13-14.   [49] Ch. 8 nn. 87-94.   [50] *Justinian* 107.

[51] *Justinian* 39-49, 134-40, 148-65.

[52] *Patr. Lat.* 63. 509B (*ultra non patiemur a quoquam controversiam religionis in republica nostra moveri, nec vestram sanctitatem convenit audire superflua concertantes*).

[53] *Wars* 3.9.5; *Buildings* 1.3.3; *SH* 6.19, 11.5, 12.29.   [54] *SH* 6.26; c. 2 n. 181.

The ex-rebel Vitalian was a more difficult problem.[55] He was recalled to
Constantinople on Justin's accession, made master of soldiers in presence
and consul for the year 520.[56] He was a serious rival to Justinian, since he
had treated with the pope as leader of the Chalcedonian party and sustained a prolonged civil war against Anastasius. He was senior to Justinian,
and became both master of soldiers and consul before him. In July 520 the
consul Vitalian was murdered.[57] The killing perhaps occurred in the
course of rioting by the circus partisans, the Blues and Greens.[58] These
names were given to the two most prominent of the guilds which in
origin provided horses and stables for the chariot races and, later, other
forms of public entertainment such as mimes, and to their supporters,
whose noisy enthusiasm, rivalry and proclivity for violence anticipated
those of modern football fans. Despite their involvement the responsibility for Vitalian's death is, no doubt rightly, pinned by both Procopius
and Victor Tonnensis on Justinian.[59] For Justinian, a fervent Blue, used
that faction as the nucleus of a private force of personal supporters in the
cities of the empire.[60]

The rival thus liquidated, Justinian soon succeeded to his offices and
showered the citizens with brilliant displays in celebration of his consulship of 521.[61] But the taste of Vitalian, with whom Justinian had shared
the holy sacraments,[62] was not erased. In 532 at the time of the Nika
revolt the crowd in the hippodrome showed it had not forgotten.[63]

Powerful though Justinian's position remained thereafter, there was
until near the end of Justin's reign another substantial figure who,
according to Procopius, handled much government business for the aged
soldier.[64] This was Proclus, quaestor of the sacred palace, whom we have
met as the presumptive draftsman of Justin's letters to Hormisdas.[65] A man
of high reputation for just dealing, his conservatism led to the rejection of
a proposal by the Persian king Cabades that Justin should adopt the king's
son Chosroes.[66]

The quaestor of the sacred palace—the office is not connected with the
republican quaestorship but originated some time during the fourth-
century—had the duty of composing laws and, more generally, of acting
as the emperor's spokesman.[67] He was a legal adviser, draftsman and

---

[55] Above, nn. 28–35.   [56] Malalas 411.   [57] *SH* 6.27–8.

[58] Malalas, *de ins.* 43. On the partisans see Alan Cameron, *Porphyrius the Charioteer*
(1973); *Circus Factions* (1976); Vasilev 77.

[59] N. 57 above and Victor Tonnensis anno 523.

[60] *SH* 7; Evagrius, *Hist. eccl.* 4.32; Malalas 416; Gibbon ch. 40 n. 46. Among other
misdemeanours their clothes were too flashy and they refused to cut their hair. *SH* ibid.

[61] Marcellinus anno 521.   [62] *SH* 6.27.   [63] *Chron. Pasch.* anno 532.

[64] *SH* 6.13.   [65] Ch. 8 nn. 87–94; *Greek Anthology* 16.48; Stein 2.245–6.

[66] Ch. 8 nn. 74–8; Stein ii. 268–9.

[67] *Not. Dig. Or.* xii, *Occ.* x 'sub dispositione viri illustris quaestoris: leges dictandae,
preces': Jones iii. 74 n. 3; Noailles, *Les collections de novelles de l' empereur Justinien* (1912)
4, 25; N. 53.2 (1 Oct. 537 τὸν κοαίστωρα τὸν τοῖς θείοις ἡμῶν ὑπηρετούμενον γράμμασιν);
Stein i. 111–12; G. Wesener, *RE* 24.1.801 (1963); Corippus, *In laudem Iustini* 1.16
(*compositor morum, iuris, legumque sacerdos*).

propagandist. 'The quaestorship necessarily involves close familiarity with the sovereign's ideas, so that the holder can correctly express what he knows the latter feels. He sets aside his own views and clothes himself in the sovereign's, so that his words seem to proceed from the latter.'[68] The quaestor had judicial as well as literary and legal functions, and was expected, if necessary, to initiate law reform, but it would be misleading to describe him as the minister of justice. The administration of the central government offices concerned with law was in the hands of the master of offices,[69] who had under him three offices or *scrinia*—records,[70] letters,[71] petitions with imperial trials[72]—which among other duties serviced the quaestor's department.[73] The leading court, short of the emperor's consistory, was that of the praetorian prefect,[74] who possessed the most influential bar in the capital and was responsible for giving effect to new laws, except when they were specially addressed to some other authority.

The functions of justice were therefore divided, so that, in broad terms, legislation fell to the quaestor, legal administration to the master of offices and the *scrinia*, and the execution of laws to the praetorian prefect.

It was legislation that Justinian needed for the crucial step he now proposed to take. He wished to marry an ex-actress, reputedly also an ex-prostitute, despite the law forbidding senators to marry present or past actresses.[75] For the country lad had become deeply attached to Theodora, whose kinky sexual accomplishments Procopius pruriently records.[76] The empress Euphemia, Justin's slave-born wife,[77] opposed the match but died some time before 19 November 524.[78] The validity of Justin's marriage to Euphemia, as Daube has shown, depended on a grant to her not merely of freedom but of free birth, i.e. of a retrospective annulment of her period of slavery.[79] A similar technique was adopted for Theodora. The reforming

---

[68] Cassiorodus, *Varia* 6.5.

[69] *Magister officiorum*: *Not. Dig. Or.* xi, *Occ.* ix; Lydus 2.26; Priscus 7; Cassiodorus, *Varia* 6.6; Jones I. 368–9; A. E. R. Boak, *The Master of Offices: Two Studies in Later Roman and Byzantine Administration* (1924).

[70] Under the *magister memoriæ*, who was responsible for rescripts (*adnotationes*): *Not. Dig. Or.* xix, *Occ.* xxxvii *magister memoriae adnotationes omnes dictat et emittit et precibus respondit*), Jones I. 367–8, 504–5, III. 73–4.

[71] Under the *magister epistularum* who handled references to the emperor by judges (*consultationes, relationes*), Jones I. 349, 504.

[72] Under the *magister libellorum et sacrarum cognitionum* who was responsible for preparing trials for hearing by the emperor in consistory, Jones I. 504.

[73] *Not. Dig. Or.* vii, *Occ.* x; Noailles, *Novelles* 25f.

[74] *CTh.* 11.30.16 (331); Just. *N.* 23 (3 Jan. 535; Stein II. 805f); Jones I. 481–3, 512–13.

[75] *D.* 23.2.44 (Paul I leg. Iul. et Pap.); *CJ* 5.27.1 (336); *CJ* 5.5.7.2 (454).

[76] *SH* 9.10–26; cf. *N.* 74.4 pr. (4 July 538; nothing is more vehement than erotic passion). On Theodora see C. Diehl, *Théodora, Impératrice de Byzance* (1938); for a more realistic view John of Ephesus, *Lives of the Eastern Saints*, ed. E. W. Brooks, is revealing.

[77] *SH* 6.9; Victor Tonnensis anno 518; Theodore Lector 2.37.

[78] *SH* 9.27; *CJ* 5.4.23 (Demostheni pp., see n. 80 below).

[79] D. Daube, 'The marriage of Justinian and Theodora: legal and theological reflections', 16 *Catholic Univ. of America LR* (1967) 380, 385–6.

law of between 520 and 524 (*CJ* 5.4.23), composed by Proclus, provides that a penitent actress can apply for an imperial grant of marriage privileges, upon the grant of which a man of whatever dignity may validly marry her, provided there is a written marriage settlement.[80] It was not, however, on this provision alone that Justinian and Theodora relied. The future empress had been raised to the highest social rank, the patriciate, before Euphemia's death.[81] The reform law went on to provide that in the case of a woman thus spontaneously raised by the emperor, without petition, to a dignity such as this, 'any other blemish, which serves as a bar to marriage with certain persons, is eradicated'.[82] This Daube rightly interprets as a subtle method of meeting in advance any objection to the legitimacy of the future offspring based on the assertion that their mother had been not merely an actress but a prostitute.[83] At the same time the text did not open the door to any general right of senators or patricians to marry whores.[84] The drafting technique is highly expert, and speaks for a working understanding between Justinian and Proclus.

The marriage should be dated not later than 525. Justinian was nearing 43, old enough.[85] Theodora's age is uncertain.[86] That her early life was dissolute and that she bore at least one child before her association with Justinian is clear.[87] That her interest in sex should have dwindled and her concern with religion and public affairs correspondingly waxed is by no means as incredible as Bury, for example, thinks.[88] Her loose life made her conversion into a chaste Christian consort all the more remarkable and all the more appealing to Justinian, to whom it was evidence of God's providential power.[89] The reforming constitution, *CJ* 5.4.23, begins with an eloquent exordium. 'We (Justin) believe that we should, so far as is possible to our nature, imitate the benevolence of God and the great clemency to the human race of Him who deigns always to forgive the day-to-day sins of men, to receive our penitence and bring us to a better state. And if we delay doing the same for our subjects we shall deserve no pardon.'[90] That is close to Justinian's thought also. His Christianity had

---

[80] *CJ* 5.4.23.1 (Iustinus A Demostheni pp., undated, *pro tanto* amending *CJ* 5.27.1 pr. (21 July 336), 5.5.7.2 (3 Apr. 454). Demosthenes was praetorian prefect on 1 June 521 (*CJ* 6.22.8) but not on 19 Nov. 524 (*CJ* 1.3.40–6.23.23).

[81] *SH* 9.30; *Joh. Eph. Comm.* 68.

[82] *CJ* 5.4.23. 4 (*ex qua dignitate aliam etiam omnem maculam, per quam certis hominibus legitime coniungi mulieres prohibentur, aboleri penitus oportet*). The words *aliam etiam omnem maculam* are typically Proclan: below, ch. 8 n. 68.

[83] Daube, 392–3.   [84] As asserted by *SH* 9.51.

[85] Said to have been 45 in 527 (Zonaras 14.5.40); hence born about 482.

[86] A. Nagl, 'Theodora', *PW* 2. 5. 1776–91.

[87] *SH* 4.37; John of Ephesus 3.5.1 (the latter, a monophysite, says she came from a brothel: unless to try and palliate this unassailable testimony to her dissolute youth). *SH* 17.16 mentions a second child, a son.

[88] Bury II. 29. The empress's chastity is vouched for by Procopius, who would have retailed misdemeanours had there been any (*SH* 16.11).

[89] Cf. *C. Deo auctore* 15 (15 Dec. 530).   [90] *CJ* 5.4.23 pr.

radical implications. In Christ there was neither male nor female bond nor free.[91] His marriage was an affront to polite Byzantine society, even more than Justin's ex-slave Lupicina,[92] and he was no more forgiven than the Pharaoh Ahkenaton for his marriage to Nefertiti.

What is less to be expected is that he should have chosen a monophysite bride. For there is no doubt that Theodora consistently supported that viewpoint and protected monophysite divines from persecution.[93] But Justinian, as noted,[94] liked parallel diplomacy. He also appreciated the need to conciliate moderate monophysites. At heart a Chalcedonian rigorist, he thought that the requirements of good government could be met consistently with regard for truth, not by taking refuge in a vague formula like that of the *Henotikon*, but by a careful analysis of the theological problems involved. Such an analysis would reveal that the differences between Chalcedonians and monophysites were largely verbal. No one, he thought, was better qualified than himself to discover a formula which would be both true and generally acceptable.[95] This self-confident conviction carried him along the twisting theological paths of the next thirty years to formal success at the Second Council of Constantinople (553). In substance, however, his effort ended in failure, and it is doubtful if anyone who believed in the need for universal acceptance of a single theological truth could have done better. It was not so much that west and east, Latin and Greek thought, had come to diverge, but that in the east cultural diversity, Syriac and Coptic as well as Greek, and centuries of philosophical speculation, in which intellectuals had become attuned to diverse schools of thought, resisted all attempts to impose a uniform belief.

Justinian's Sisyphean efforts to find a formula of reconciliation probably owe something to the influence of Theodora and reflect one of the redemptive dimensions of his marriage.

The children who figure prominently in *CJ* 5.4.23 failed to appear. Theodora devoted herself to politics, carved out an independent position,[96] and at times thwarted her husband more than she supported him.[97] Her influence can be discerned in Justinian's legislation in favour of equality

---

[91] *N.* 5.2. pr. (17 March 535: slaves can become monks).

[92] On the empress's barbarian origin and capture as a slave see Victor Tonnensis anno 518; *SH* 6.17 (also concubine of previous purchaser).

[93] Bury II. 31f. Note for example the incident mentioned by Daube, op. cit. 389, when in 530 the orthodox abbot Sabas declined to entreat God to grant her a child lest it might 'suck of the tenets of Severus [Monophysite patriarch of Antioch 512–18] and trouble the church worse than Anastasius', citing Kyrillos von Skythopolis, ed. Schwartz, *49 Texte und Untersuchungen zur Geschichte der Altchristlichen Literatur* 4th ser. pr. 2 (1939) 173f.; Nagl, 'Theodora', *RE* (2nd 1934) 5.1782.

[94] Above, nn. 47–52.

[95] E. Stein, II. 279–80; M. V. Anastos: *Dumb. Oaks Papers* 6 (1951) 125.

[96] Economic independence: *SH* 9.31; *Buildings* 1.4.1; 1.10.4; *N.* 28.5.1 (6 July 535), 29.4 (16 July 535), 30.6 pr. (18 March 536).

[97] Bury II. 33; Stein II. 238 (biased on the religious issue).

between the sexes,[98] in measures against the traffic in prostitutes[99] and in favour of the underprivileged.[100] In her early travels she had been the mistress of the governor of Libya and had stayed in Alexandria.[101] Here, in the stronghold of the monophysite belief, her theology may have been formed, and here too, perhaps, this clever, beautiful and dangerous woman became interested in provincial administration.[102] At any rate the reform of provincial government in 535 is partly credited to her advice[103] and the *Novel* which provides for it includes an oath to be taken by governors to her as well as Justinian.[104] From a formal point of view this is the high point of her imperial status. Her influence, rising since she saved the day by her resolute defiance at the time of Nika in January 532,[105] peaked in 535. In June of that year, after the failure of Justinian's attempt to conciliate the monophysites by way of the 'theopaschite' doctrine,[106] she was allowed her head and procured the election of a monophysite, Anthimus, to the see of Constantinople, only to see him deposed at the insistence of pope Agapetus on 12 March 536.[107] Theodora's positive influence was never thereafter as great, but she remained a destructive force,[108] *secunda inter pares*, until she died of cancer in 548,[109] leaving her husband seventeen years a widower.

Such was Justinian's choice for a wife in the 520s. On 1 April 527 he became co-emperor, and on 1 August 527 Justin died, leaving him sole ruler. It will become clear from other instances that Justinian's talents included that of spotting the talent of others. Emancipated from the snobbery of birth and letters which dominated the outlook of Procopius and his like, Justinian found and raised a brilliant team of helpers.[110] John of Cappadocia[111] came from Caesarea and, from a clerk in the office of one

---

[98] *N.* 18.4 pr. (1 March 536: since each contributes to propagation), 21 pr. (18 March 536); 89.12.5 (1 Sept. 539); Diehl 63f.; E. Gianturco, *Studi Fadda* (1906) 6.1; Duquesne, *NRH* 32 (1908) 254f; J. E. Spruit, *Opstellen over Recht en Cultuur aangeboden aan Prof. Pitlo* (1970) 109.

[99] *SH* 17.5–6; Malalas 440–1; *N.* 14 (1 Dec. 535).

[100] *Wars* 7.31.14; Lydus 3.69.   [101] *SH* 9.27.

[102] *SH* 10.11; *Buildings* 1.11.8 emphasises her beauty, Lydus 3.69 her intelligence, Procopius again her lethal qualities (e.g. *SH* 15.39–17.4).

[103] *N.* 8.1 (15 April 535).   [104] *N.* 8, Oath (15 April 535).   [105] *Wars* 1.24.33–8.

[106] Viz. that one of the Holy Trinity suffered in the flesh—perhaps subtly distinguishable from the version of the Trisagion chant which offended under Anastasius (above, nn. 25–6). Justinian's version, approved by pope John II, was that Christ was *passibilem carne, eundem ipsum impassibilem deitate* (*CJ* 1.1.8.7–24, 6 June 533; approved by John, *CJ* 1.1.8.25–39, 25 March 534); cf. 1.1.5.2–3 (c. 527), 1.1.6.6.8 (15 March 533) which propound the same formula in Greek.

[107] Zacharias of Mytilene 9.15–19; Bury II. 376–7. *N.* 42 (6 Aug. 536) banished Anthimus but Theodora concealed him in her apartments: John of Ephesus 247–8.

[108] E.g. John of Cappadocia (below, n. 118), pope Sylverius (below, n. 184).

[109] Malalas 484; *Wars* 7.30.4; Victor Tonnensis anno 549.

[110] *Buildings* 1.1.25–6 is closer to the truth than *SH* 21.9–14.

[111] Unfavourable portraits in *Wars* 1.24.11–15, 25; 2.30.49–54; 3.13.12–20; Lydus 57f.; C. N. Tsirpanlis, 'John Lydos on the imperial administration', *Byzantion* 44 (1974) 479.

of the masters of soldiers, rose to be logothete (*inspecteur des finances*) under the praetorian prefect of the east. Said by Procopius to be the boldest and cleverest man of the time,[112] he was expert in raising taxes and suggesting economies, without which Justinian's ambitious programmes would have foundered, since Justin's praetorian prefects had squandered the accumulated surplus inherited from Anastasius.[113] In February 528 Justinian made him chairman of the First Law Commission,[114] that which composed the first code of constitutions (*Codex Iustinianus*). Thereafter as praetorian prefect from 531 to January 532,[115] and again from October 532 to May 541,[116] he had the main responsibility for putting Justinian's reforming legislation into effect. His rivalry with Tribonian is touched on later.[117] Most of the administrative measures of the decade 531 to 541 bear his imprint, and Justinian achieved nothing notable in this sphere after John's dismissal through an intrigue of Antonina, the wife of Belisarius, and Theodora in 541.[118]

John's low birth, poor education, avarice, bluntness and debauchery offered a target to wealthy aristocrats and intellectual snobs. Procopius and Lydus find nothing too harsh to say of him.[119] He was an excellent administrator who foolishly tried to precipitate a breach between Justinian and Theodora.[120] He became a scapegoat for the disaster, not of his making, of 540, when the Persians invaded the eastern provinces and captured Antioch.[121] So the ablest woman secured the downfall of the ablest man of the time, but his death she could not contrive, and, outliving her, he returned from exile to end his days in Byzantium, an unwilling priest still dreaming, says Procopius, of glory.[122]

The list of Justinian's distinguished protégés is long: in engineering Anthemius of Tralles, designer of the rebuilt St Sophia,[123] in literature Procopius of Caesarea,[124] in the army Belisarius,[125] and Narses,[126] in law

[112] *Wars* 3.10.7. Cf. 1.24.13 'excellent at seeing what was needed and finding a solution to difficulties'.

[113] Lydus 3.51.   [114] *C. Haec* 1 (13 Feb. 528).

[115] From 30 April 531 (*CJ* 6.27.5–6.46.6 etc.) to 14 Jan. 532 (dismissal at Nika: Malalas 475; *Chron. Pasch.* anno 532; *Wars* 1.24.11f.).

[116] From 18 Oct. 532 (*CJ* 6.20.21 etc., *Wars* 1.25.1) to 7 May 541 (*N.* 109, *Wars* 1.25).

[117] Ch. 2 nn. 44–51, 159–173, ch. 4 nn. 87f.

[118] The reform of the Egyptian administration (Justinian Edict xiii) though undated should be attributed on grounds of style to Tribonian's quaestorship and so to John's prefecture; Schoell-Kroll, *Corp. Iur. Civ.* 3,795 n. 3; ch. 4 n. 71.

[119] Above, n. 111.   [120] *Wars* 1.25.4, *SH* 17.38.   [121] *Wars* 2.8.20f.

[122] *Wars* 1.25.31–44, 2.30.49–54, *SH* 17.38–45.

[123] *Buildings* 1.1.24 (Anthemius was the most erudite engineer not just of his contemporaries but including all who had preceded him for a long time past); cf. 1.1.50. For Justinian's alleged intervention to solve a technical problem which baffled Anthemius and Isidore see *Buildings* 1.1.70.

[124] One may infer that Justinian commissioned the buildings (*Buildings* 1.3.1. The work is to be dated before the collapse of the dome of St Sophia on 7 May 558, perhaps in 554; Stein II. 837; Averil Cameron, *JRS* 63 (1973) 298; B. Rubin, *RE* 23. 354–5; contra J. A. S. Evans, 'Procopius 45–6', *Class. Phil.* 64 (1969) 29, who favours 558–60

Tribonian.[127] But *la carrière ouverte aux talents* was closed to high-born mediocrity. This caused resentment and explains why the Nika rioting of January 532, of which an outline is given in the next chapter,[128] turned to rebellion and nearly cost Justinian his throne. For by 532 it had become clear that Justinian was a radical.[129] In the eyes of the conservative Procopius 'he was not interested in preserving established institutions, but always wanted to innovate in everything'.[130] 'When Justinian took over the empire he at once brought confusion on everything. He introduced into the state what had previously been forbidden, he tore down all existing and customary institutions, as if he had put on the imperial robes on the condition that he redressed everything else. He abolished existing offices and created new ones to take charge of affairs. He did the same with laws and army establishments, not out of respect for justice or utility but so that everything might be new and called after himself. If there was anything which he could not change at a stroke he at least put his name on it.'[131]

In the *Secret History* the mercurial historian is at his most hostile. Writing in 550–1,[132] before the definitive conquest of Italy by Narses,[133] he sees the emperor as a malign destroyer.[134] Yet he is mistaken neither about Justinian's desire for change nor about his obsessive concern with his own personality and role in history.

On Justin's death the wind of change blew first in the direction of rigorous law enforcement. The laws against heretics, pagans[135] and male

---

and so places the *Secret History* which foreshadows *Buildings* (*SH* 18.38) too late also. We do not know Justinian's attitude to the *Wars* (seven books 545–50, the eighth 553), though their point of view is that of Belisarius. Procopius became prefect of the city (Theophanes anno 6055 = 562 A.D. mentions a Procopius in that office and John of Nikiu, *Chronicle* 92.20, tr. R. Charles (1916), says 'he was a man of intelligence and a prefect whose work is well known'). There are many examples of a man changing his views in later life in order to secure high office before it is too late (e.g. Aneurin Bevan) and in this connection it should be remembered that, even on the basis of the *Wars*, Procopius had some explaining to do.

[125] *Wars* passim, esp. 7.1.1–16.   [126] *Wars* 8.26. 14.17.

[127] 'Best educated man of the age' (*Wars* 1.24.16), 'very learned' (Lydus 3.20, see below, ch. 2 n. 25).

[128] Ch. 2 nn. 119–27.

[129] Stein 'ce grand conservateur' (II. 276) is misled through attributing Tribonian's classicism to Justinian: so also Barker, 82, 93, 167, 172–5.

[130] *SH* 6.21. This passage is significant since it, along with the emperor's proclivity for murder and confiscation, comes in Justinian's first appearance in the *Secret History*.

[131] *SH* 11.1–2.   [132] Ch. 8 n. 205.

[133] Recorded in book 8 of the *Wars*, which was written after the *Secret History* and published in 553: Bury II. 420 n. 2.

[134] E.g. *SH* 6.20, 18.1–9.

[135] *CTh* 16.5 *de haereticis* has 66 laws between 1 Sept. 326 and 3 Aug. 435, to which can be added *CJ* 1.5.6 (435), 1.5.7 (438), 1.5.8 (455), 1.5.10 (Leo), but the tactics employed are largely those of monetary penalties, transfer of assets to orthodoxy, censorship and disqualification.

homosexuals[136] were of long standing and, in the former case, frequently renewed. But no serious attempt had hitherto been made to purge the central or local administrations of officials with unorthodox beliefs or sexual tastes, still less to rid the empire of them altogether. Justinian did not view either of these classes of dissenters with tolerance. On the contrary, he thought that laxity or delay in enforcing the rigour of the law would bring God's wrath on himself and the empire.[137] Dereliction of duty by emperor or pope brings speedy retribution. Justinian therefore launched an attack on both groups but allowed monophysite bishops and monks, exiled under Justin, to return.[138] To him they were potentially orthodox.

The campaign against homosexuals and the public mutilation of episcopal pederasts belongs, it seems, to 528.[139] In this year also, or early in 529, successive purges were directed against pagan practices and pagan office holders, including public teachers.[140] A Christian republic means a Christian state, not a semi-pagan one.

Even given that the persecution was not aimed at monophysites, whom Justinian hoped to reconcile and who in Egypt and Syria were too plentiful to be eliminated, these measures provoked shock. They seemed to Procopius insensitive and in their application arbitrary.[141]

But Justinian was not a city sophisticate. His beliefs were not diluted by indulgence to the privileged or acceptance of human weakness. His was the solid, bitter creed of the countryman and the soldier, learned early and not forgotten.

The measures of 528 and 529 against pagans, Manichees and homosexuals are important because the first measures of a new régime are always close to the ruler's heart. If they are not payoffs to those with whose support he has come to power, they reveal what has most gnawed his susceptibilities during the period of opposition or subordination. Justin's reign

---

[136] Theophanes anno 6021; *SH* 11.16; Zonaras 14.7; Cedrenus 645; Gibbon ch. 44 nn. 203–5; Diehl 553–7; for earlier provisions see Mommsen, *Strafrecht* 703–4.

[137] God's anger: *CJ* 1.11.10 pr. 4, *N.* 77.1 pr. (Constantinopolitanis), 141 pr. (15 March 559). Delay: cf. *CJ* 5.4.23 pr. (Justin), *Patr. Lat.* 69.37B (Justinian to Hormisdas: *cum enim qui de recta fide interrogatur diu protrahit nihil aliud est nisi abnegatio rectae confessionis.* This is a good example of Justinian's ugly but forceful style.)

[138] John of Ephesus 11.469; Zacharias, *Myt.* 9.15.

[139] Cedrenus 645 (second year of reign); Theophanes anno 6021 = A.D. 528; Browning 97. Justinian returns to the theme in *N.* 77 (?535, 538/9: Schoell-Kroll 3.383 n.), *N.* 141 (15 March 559). On Justinian's recourse to mutilation as a punishment in general see *N.* 30.8.1 (18 March 536 amputation of hand), 42.1.2 (6 Aug. 536 same), 128.20 (6 June 545), 134.13 (1 May 556 restriction to amputation of one hand); *SH* 11.36; Malalas 436, 451, 483, 488; Zonaras 14.7; Theophanes anno 5951, 6053, 6055; Agathias 4.8. Mutilation was not a punishment in classical Roman criminal law: T. Mommsen, *Strafrecht* (1899) 981–3.

[140] Ch. 2 nn. 56f.; *CJ* 1.11.10 pr., 2; Theophanes anno 6022.

[141] *SH* 11.14–36, 19.11. Sexual and theological dissent were closely associated in the mind of Procopius as they were in that of Justinian, for reasons which lie beyond my present scope.

had not simply been Justinian's in disguise. The old emperor was cautious, not least about advancing his nephew to the status of Caesar or Augustus.[142] The narrow rectitude of Proclus was a brake.[143] With them removed Justinian could ride free. Impatience, rigour and irenics combine. The first shows in the short period allowed for conversion, the second in the draconian penalties against those outside the church, the third in the attempt to reach a settlement with the monophysites.

Another measure of 528–9 reveals Justinian's conception of the imperial office, though not yet the measure of his ambitions. On 13 February 528 *C. Haec* set up a law commission under John of Cappadocia to prepare a new code of imperial laws which would replace the *Codex Gregorianus*, the *Hermogenianus* of the reign of Diocletian, and above all the *Theodosianus*, enacted in 438, and form a complete authoritative collection in one volume. The Theodosian code, in force in the empire, was also the principal element in the code which Alaric the Visigoth had granted his Roman subjects in a moment of stress in 506.[144] It was the duty of the emperor of Romania to do better, and an opportunity for Justinian to mark out a place in history.

Procopius is right about the emperor's concern to propagate his name.[145] *C. Haec*'s first sentence provides for the composition of a code 'under the happy designation of our name'[146] and the theme returns at the end of the text.[147] It is important to appreciate that, thus early in his reign, Justinian is conscious of living in the age of Justinian.

He was to plaster his name everywhere. The three volumes of laws are called after him, the first-year law students are no longer to be 'two-pounders' but 'Iustiniani novi'.[148] A site, perhaps Caričin Grad, near his birthplace in Macedonia, was renamed Iustiniana Prima and made a metropolitan see.[149] Lipljan (Ulpiana) became Iustiniana Secunda.[150] The governor of Pisidia became the praetor Iustinianus, the vicarii of that

---

[142] Vasilev 94. The statement of Victor Tonnensis (anno 525) that Justinian was created Caesar is belied by the inscriptions to the constitutions *CJ* 7.39.7 (1 Dec. 525) and 9.19.6 (1 Dec. 526). He was made *nobilissimus* before 527 (Marcellinus Comes anno 527), at the entreaty of the senate.

[143] G. Bassanelli, *SDHI* 37 (1971) 119 shows that the procedural reforms of Justin's reign were not the work of Justinian.

[144] *Lex Romana Visigothorum*, ed. G. Haenel (1849 reprint 1962). On Justinian's desire to surpass these codes see Collinet, *Etudes historiques sur le droit de Justinien* 2 (1912) 29–30.

[145] Above, n. 131; Diehl 20.

[146] *C. Haec* pr. (13 Feb. 528 *uno autem codice sub felici nostri nominis vocabulo componendo*). This echoes *CTh* 1.1.5 (26 March 429 [codex] *qui nostro nomine nuncupatus sequenda omnibus vitandaque monstrabit*), with a significant addition.

[147] *C. Haec* 3 (13 Feb. 528). The 'Germanic' construction is due to the quaestor Thomas: ch. 8 nn. 106, 120, 122, 131.

[148] *C. Omnem* 2 (16 Dec. 533 *non . . . dupondios appellari sed Iustinianos novos nuncupari*). The old name perhaps means 'lightweights'.

[149] *N.* 11 (14 April 535); *Buildings* 4.1.19.

[150] *Buildings* 4.1.29. Stein (II. 277) says that at least 27 cities were given his name.

province the comites Iustiniani;[151] other provinces likewise.[152] In Pontus, Petra was granted the status of a city and the honour of being called Iustiniana.[153] The emperor even refers to himself in the third person, speaking of a law found 'in Justinian's code'.[154] It is true that one can point to precedents of Augustus and Trajan, but given such self-absorption, he was at times the victim of servile flattery.[155]

The name Iustinianus symbolises the just man. Petrus Sabbatius, adept from youth at killing two birds with one stone, has chosen it for that and for its association with Justin, so that the name is appropriate to the person and so that the person can be the living name. Its endless repetition expresses a monomania[156] which both reflects the slights Justinian and his family had endured and serves as an instrument of unity in a diverse and divided society.

The years 527 to 529 were the years of appeasement.[157] God was to be reconciled (θεραπεύειν)[158] by a strict observance on the emperor's part of his duties, for kingship is not far removed from priesthood.[159] Thereafter He would reward the just ruler.[160] The emperor looked for a sign that the time had come to demonstrate that with God all things are possible. The transition from repentance and reconciliation to glory can, perhaps, be placed in the year 530. The victory of Belisarius over the Persians at Daras occurred in June of that year.[161] Within the next few months Justinian decided to set up the Second Law Commission under Tribonian and entrusted him with the task, impossible as it seemed, of compiling a comprehensive anthology of ancient legal writers to be called the *Digest* or *Pandects*.[162] *C. Deo auctore* of 15 December 530 by its initial words and its explicit record of Justinian's train of thought shows that even the most desperate enterprises then appeared possible.[163] This is the flowering of the age of hope.

---

[151] N. 24.4.5 (18 May 535); cf. 25.1 (18 May 535, same for Lycaonia), 26.1.1. (18 May 535, Thrace), 28.3 (16 July 535 Helenopontus), 29.2 (16 July 535 Paphlagonia), 30.5 (18 March 536 Cappadocia), 31.1.2 (18 March 536 Armenia), 50 inscription (1 Sept. 537).

[152] Above, n. 151.   [153] N. 28 pr. (16 July 535).   [154] N. 66.1.1. (1 May 538).

[155] *SH* 13. 10–13, 30.30; below, ch. 2 nn. 231–2.

[156] 'Vanité inconsciente mais sans bornes' (Stein II. 277).

[157] *CJ* 1.3.41 pr. (1 March 528).

[158] The use of a word which also means 'heal' is significant: sin and defiance wound God. N. 3.3 (16 March 535); edict of 551 on the Three Chapters (below, n. 271).

[159] N. 87.2.1 (15 April 535); F. Dvornik, *Early Christian and Byzantine Political Philosophy* vol. II (1966).

[160] N. 6 pr. (16 March 535); N. 14.1 (1 Dec. 535: chastity and territorial expansion); St Sabas (*Vita Sabae*, ed. Schwartz 1956, ch. 72) is said to have predicted that God would restore the Roman empire to its limits in the reign of Honorius (note the historical limit of vision) if the emperor adhered to orthodoxy and destroyed Arianism and other heresies: see generally Dvornik, op. cit., 712f.

[161] Theophanes anno 6022; *Wars* 1.13.9–14. 55; Bury II. 82–5.

[162] Ch. 2 nn. 75–82, ch. 5 nn. 17–23.

[163] *C. Deo auctore* 2. Overlooked by P. R. L. Brown, *The World of Late Antiquity* (1971) 150f., thereby setting Justinian's pursuit of glory too late. The same author invents a

It was interrupted by the Nika rebellion of January 532.[164] Through Theodora's resolution and the ruthless butchery meted out to the crowd by Belisarius and Mundus, Justinian survived. A narrow shave can be interpreted as a confirmation of one's historical mission.[165] Nika served only to strengthen the emperor's radicalism, by demonstrating how little the bulk of the senatorial aristocracy esteemed him and his wife. After Nika, the impossible architecture of the new Hagia Sophia was soon planned.[166] In 533, with the *Digest* nearing fruition, there came the invasion, against military and civil advice, of Vandal North Africa.[167] The question is often posed whether from the start of his reign Justinian planned the reconquest of the western provinces. The answer is not difficult, and it bears on the genesis of the *Digest* project. It was plainly, as he saw it, the emperor's duty to retake the lost territories if he could, since his Roman subjects were constantly at risk and some of the businessmen among them at least favoured a policy of intervention.[168] That the western rulers were Arians made the emperor's duty doubly strong. Justinian saw an analogy between the rescue of western Romans from barbarian rule and the emancipation of slaves.[169] Nor was this wholly far-fetched, since according to Roman law conquest resulted in the enslavement of the conquered population. The reality was no doubt different. The barbarian kings looked on the emperor in a filial light. His subjects were not, at least in general, enslaved. Their condition varied. The Vandals treated them and their churches badly. Under the Ostrogoths many flourished and accommodated themselves to foreign military power, which by the sixth century was hardly a novelty. Justinian, if he was informed of it, would not tolerate such backsliding.

> It was out of enthusiasm for this [liberty: the context is the emancipation of slaves] that we undertook such extensive wars in Africa and the west, both for right belief about God and for the freedom of our subjects.[170]

But he must await time and circumstance. The replacement of the tolerant Hilderic in 530 or 531 by the less transigent Vandal king Gelimer threatened the bodies and souls of the Romans in the Vandal kingdom.[171] The peace with Persia, ratified in the spring of 532,[172] made a western war conceivable. That would still not have been enough, had not signs of God's favour

---

second edition of the *Digest* and supposes that John of Cappadocia was on the Second Law Commission (p. 153).

[164] Ch. 2 nn. 119–27.

[165] E.g. Hitler after the plot of 20 July 1944; A. Bullock, *Hitler* (1952) 682.

[166] *Buildings* 1.1.20–78.   [167] *Wars* 3.10.1–21.   [168] *Wars* 3.20.5–6.

[169] *Inst.* 1.3.4. The analogy breaks down only insofar as the barbarians are excluded from the category of enemies (*hostes*) or states lacking in peaceful relation with Romania (*amicitia, hospitium, foedus*) by virtue of their vague recognition of Roman suzerainty. *D.* 49.15.5.1–2 (Pomponius 37 ad Q.Mucium).

[170] *N.* 78.4.1 (18 Jan. 539); cf. 89 pr. (1 Sept. 539 policies favouring emancipation and legitimation), *CJ* 7.24 pr. (Justinianus Hermogeni mo.).

[171] *Wars* 3.9.6–26.   [172] *Wars* 1.22.16, 3.9.26–3.10.1; Malalas 477.

pressed Justinian towards his rash victory. One such sign (*dei omnipotentis providentiae argumentum*)[173] was the successful compilation of the *Digest*.

The *Digest* was finished[174] and the Vandals conquered in 533.[175] The second edition of the *Codex Iustinianus* belongs to 534.[176] Administrative reform, including much reorganisation of the provinces, continued from 535 to 539.[177] A programme of law reform, especially in the spheres of marriage and the family, was hurried through in the 530s,[178] Dalmatia and Sicily were retaken in 535,[179] Rome occupied in December 536,[180] Auximum in 539,[181] Ravenna in the spring of 540.[182] The rebuilt Hagia Sophia was inaugurated on 26 December 537.[183] Though there were military setbacks, and though no progress was made with the religious reconciliation between orthodox catholics (as one may now term the re-united church) and monophysites,[184] hope abounded. In March 536, after the reconquest of Sicily, *Novel* 30 proclaims that 'we have good hope that God will grant us to rule over the rest of what, subject to the ancient Romans to the limits of both seas, they later lost by their easygoing ways'.[185]

This was the culmination of the time of hope. Justinian was in his fifties, Theodora, John, Tribonian, Belisarius and Anthemius at the height of their powers. At this point a linguistic excursus may be helpful.

[173] *C. Deo auctore* 14.

[174] The first draft was complete about March 533: ch. 5 nn. 179–80.

[175] The expedition left Constantinople in June 533, and won the battle of Ad Decimum, outside Carthage on 13 Sept. 533 (Procopius, *Wars* 3.18).

[176] *C. Cordi* promulgated the *Codex Repetitae Praelectionis* on 16 Nov. 534.

[177] N. 8 (17 April 535 general reform of provincial administration); N. 24, 25, 26, 27 (18 May 535 Pisidia, Lycaonia, Thrace, Isauria), 28, 29 (16 July 535 Helenopontus, Paphlagonia), 23 (3 Jan. 536 appeals), 20 (23 March 536 appeals), 30, 21, 31 (18 March 536 Cappadocia, Armenia), 102 (27 May 536 Arabia), 103 (1 June 536 Palestine), 75 = 104 (Nov.–Dec. 537 Sicily), Ed. 13 (between 1 Sept. 538 and 31 Aug. 539, Egypt).

[178] N. 2 (16 March 535 second marriages), 22 (18 March 535 general), 12 (16 May 535 incestuous marriages), 19 (16 March 536 position of children born before marriage settlement), 61 (1 Dec. 537 property comprised in husband's settlement inalienable), 68 (25 May 538 protection of children of first marriage), 74 (4 June 538 legitimation of children), 89 (1 Sept. 539), 91 (1 Oct. 539 preference for family of first marriage), 97 (17 Nov. 539 equality of wife's and husband's settlements), 100 (20 Nov. 539 non-payment of dowry), 98 (16 Dec. 539 interests of children in marriage settlements); cf. 109 (7 May 541 heretical women deprived of privileges in relation to dowry).

[179] Bury II. 169–72.

[180] 9 Dec. 536 (*Wars* 5.14.14; Evagrius, *Hist. eccl.* 4.19).

[181] Marcellinus anno 539; *Wars* 6.27.34.   [182] About May 540: Bury II. 213.

[183] Theophanes anno 6030. That Justinian on this occasion said 'Solomon, I have outdone thee' (*Diegesis in script. origin. Constant.*, ed. T. Preger (Leipzig 1901) is not certain.

[184] After the deposition of Anthimus from the see of Byzantium in March 536 (above, n. 107) Justinian launched a persecution of monophysites (Zacharias, *Myt.* 10.1; John of Ephesus 111, 134, 221) while Theodora tried to advance the monophysite cause by securing the deposition of pope Sylverius and the election of Vigilius in his place (29 March 537, Lib. Pont., *Vita Silverii* 29–3; *Wars* 5.25.13; *SH* 1.14.27), but without success, as Vigilius reverted to the doctrines of Chalcedon.

[185] N. 30.11.2 (18 March 536); cf. 8.10.2 (15 April 535), *C. Tanta* 19 (16 Dec. 533), *C. Omnem* 11 (16 Dec. 533); N. 40 ep. (18 May 536); 14.1 (1 Dec. 535).

In the imperial codices we can study the history of words connected with a sense of possibilities. Most people would be surprised to learn that the word *possibilis* does not appear until the law of Justin's reign which permitted the marriage of Justinian and Theodora.[186] There are in all twenty-four occurrences of *possibilis* in the *Codex Iustinianus* up to the end of 534, of which the one mentioned comes from the quaestor Proclus, another from Thomas (528–9)[187] and the remaining twenty-two from Tribonian.[188] *Possibilitas*, it is true, is found earlier, once in 385,[189] once each in *Novels* of Valentinian[190] and Majorian,[191] and then again in 533.[192] *Impossibilis*, which one would expect to be fairly common (after all, lawyers discussed impossible conditions in wills and contracts) is found three times under Diocletian,[193] once in 412,[194] thrice in Valentinian and Majorian,[195] and then eleven times in 528–34,[196] of which two come from Thomas and nine from Tribonian's quaestorship. *Impossibilitas* occurs only in 531.[197]

These linguistic clues to the thought of the time are not to be despised, especially as they occur in texts not specifically designed to radiate optimism. The forward-looking climate of these years cannot entirely be dissociated from the personality of the emperor himself. His hopes reached a peak in the 530s. But at the turn of the decade[198] came the end of the age of hope. Justinian's limitless ambition had been noticed. The speech which Procopius puts into the mouth of leading Persians expresses their apprehension at Roman expansion not merely in the west but in southern Arabia and the Crimea during the seven years since the peace of 532.[199] 'The whole earth is not enough for him. He surveys the sky and investigates places hidden beyond the oceans, to acquire for himself a new world.'[200] The Persian king Chosroes, whom Justin had declined to adopt,[201] invaded the eastern provinces in 540, 541, 542 and 544.[202] He captured and plundered Antioch in

---

[186] *CJ* 5.4.23 pr. (Iustinus).   [187] *CJ* 4.20.18 pr. (1 June 528).

[188] *CJ* 8.53.34.2a, 4a, 6.61.6.3 (30 Oct. 529), 4.21.21.2 (20 Feb. 530), 3.1.14.4, 7.62.39.2 (29 March 530), 3.33.12 pr., 1, 8.37.13.1 (1 Aug. 530), 5.70.7.6a, 1.4.27.2 (1 Sept. 530), 7.4.14 pr. (1 Oct. 530), *C. Deo auctore* 4 (15 Dec. 530), 4.18.2.1, 1c (20 Feb. 531), 3.28.34.1, 6.27.5.1 (29 July 531), 7.47.1 pr. (1 Sept. 531), 7.2.15.1 (531–2), *C. Tanta* pr. bis, 8 (16 Dec. 533).

[189] *CJ* 11.60.1 pr. (385).   [190] N. Val. 13.15 (445).   [191] N. Maj. 2.14 (458).

[192] *C. Tanta* pr. (16 Dec. 533).   [193] *CJ* 4.58.3.1 (286), 4.6.8, 8.38.7 (294).

[194] *CTh* 11.13.3 (412).   [195] N. Val. 10.32 (441), 15.18 (444/5), Maj. 2.7 (458).

[196] *CJ* (Thomas) 6.41.1.1 (1 June 528), 7.17.1.2 (11 Dec. 528), (Tribonian) 4.21.21.2 (20 Feb. 530), 7.40.1 pr. (18 March 530), 4.38.15.2 (1 Aug. 530), 5.70.6.1, 6.2.21.5 (1 Sept. 530), *C. Deo auctore* 2 (15 Dec. 530), *CJ* 8.37.15 pr. (18 Oct. 532), *C. Tanta* 13, 17 (16 Dec. 533). For the authorship see chs. 3, 8 below.

[197] *CJ* 7.47.1.1 (1 Sept. 531).

[198] Stein II. 282. Procopius sees a portent and beginning of bad times in the weather of 536–7; *Wars* 4.14.5–6.

[199] *Wars* 2.3.32–41. Through the mouths of Persian nobles Procopius develops the criticism of Justinian which was to figure prominently in his *Secret History*: 'Is there anything previously forbidden which he has not done? Is there anything well settled which he has not disturbed?' (ibid. 38).

[200] *Wars* 2.3. 42–3.   [201] Above, n. 66.

[202] *Wars* 2.5–14, 15–19, 20–1, 26–7. Bury II 93–113.

540.[203] In 541 a devastating plague, of the dimensions of the Black Death eight hundred years later, began in Egypt.[204] It reached Byzantium in 542,[205] Italy in 542–3.[206] In Italy Totila counterattacked in 541–3. He recaptured Rome in December 546,[207] and again in January 550.[208] In the 540s the great lieutenants fell. John was disgraced in 541,[209] Tribonian died in 542,[210] Theodora in 548,[211] Belisarius was recalled from Italy, after years of futile campaigning, in 549.[212]

Through the harsh forties Justinian endured. At the age of sixty he was seriously ill from the plague, but recovered.[213] He asked himself the reasons for God's displeasure[214] and resolved to define more closely the path of orthodoxy. This he did in two edicts, one in 542 condemning the views of Origen[215] or the Origenists, bordering on pantheism, and a second in 543 or 544, designed to conciliate the monophysites by attacking their worst enemies, especially Theodore of Mopsuestia, who was regarded as the spiritual father of the Nestorian heresy.[216] This was the peculiar theological offensive known as the 'Three Chapters', an expression which attached originally to the three chapters of Justinian's edict, but later to the opinions condemned in them.

In the 550s the tide turned again. Narses pacified Italy.[217] After many theological twists and turns the Second Council of Constantinople endorsed Justinian's views about the Three Chapters.[218] Even pope Vigilius was constrained to agree.[219] When this apparent triumph merely provoked a schism in the west Justinian, now in his eighties, moved towards an extreme brand of the monophysite view.[220] He died in 565.[221]

[203] *Wars* 2.8.
[204] *Wars* 2.22.6; below, ch. 2. nn. 193f.   [205] *Wars* 2.22.9–10; below, ch. 2 nn. 200–2.
[206] Marcellinus anno 524–5; below, ch. 2 n. 214.
[207] Marcellinus anno 546–7; Bury II 229–44.   [208] 16 Jan. 550 (Bury II 250).
[209] Above, n. 118.   [210] Ch. 2 nn. 193–225.   [211] Above, n. 109.
[212] *Wars* 7.35.1, 2; *SH* 5.1–6.17.   [213] *Wars* 2.23.20.
[214] After a certain relaxation in the 530s, if it can be so termed (*N.* 17.11, 16 May 535 governors to restrain abuses by those persecuting heresy; *N.* 45, 18 Aug. 537 heretics, Jews and Samaritans may hold office as decurions without the privileges normally attaching to the office), except for monophysites (*N.* 42, 6 Aug. 536 against Anthimus, Severus of Antioch etc., above, n. 102), civil disabilities increase in the 540s = *N.* 109 (7 May 541 heretic wives forfeit dotal privileges), 115.3.14, 4.8 (1 Feb. 542 orthodox parents and children can disinherit heretic children and parents), 132 (4 Apr. 544 heretics may not assemble in Constantinople), 131. 14 (18 March 545 heretics may not buy or hire from churches).
[215] Edict *in Patr. Gr.* 86.1.946–91; F. Diekamp, *Die origenistischen Streitigkeiten im sechsten Jahrhundert und das fünfte allgemeine Konzil* (1899).
[216] Below, n. 271.
[217] The fifth capture of Rome (*Wars* 8.33.27) and the battles of Busta Gallorum (ibid. 8.29–32) and Mons Lactantius (8.35.15–38) occurred in 552. The Franks were defeated in 554. But Brescia and Verona fell only in 562.
[218] It assembled on 5 May 553 and ultimately confirmed Justinian's decree condemning the Three Chapters: Mansi ix (1743) cols. 157–658.
[219] By a letter of 8 Dec. 553 (Mansi ix.413f.; *Patr. Lat.* 69.121f.) the effect of which was to cause a schism in the west without healing the schism in the east.
[220] Below, n. 276.   [221] On 14 Nov. 565 (*Chron. Pasch.* anno 565).

What sort of man was it whose nerve broke only once in fifty years of public life, when at the time of Nika he was ready to leave for the Asian shore and Theodora shamed him into staying in Constantinople?[222] What was he like to work for? His megalomania and ruthlessness have been noted already. The positive side of the coin, apart from his political skill and shrewd eye for talent, lay in unflagging industry and determination. Looking back to the disasters of the fifth century, he sees the Christian emperors who preceded him as lax, easygoing, not to say downright lazy.[223] They have allowed the republic to decay. 'This benefit from God [the reconquest of North Africa] our predecessors failed to merit; not only were they not permitted to liberate Africa but they saw the capture of Rome by the Vandals and the transfer of the imperial ornaments to Africa.'[224] He does not propose to imitate them.[225] On the contrary, he is determined to outdo them, for he is driven by insatiable ambition.[226] To repair by incessant vigilance the ravages of a century of neglect and to create a truly Christian republic is the core of his task. 'No good will come of idleness.'[227]

Justinian liked his labours to be noticed. He worked long hours and, presumably suffering from insomnia, often at night.[228] Sleepless so that his subjects might sleep,[229] he took on himself their cares that they might live without care.[230] The aristocratic ideals of leisure and elegance he did not share. Himself austere, he expected others to work hard,[231] produce results and abstain from enriching themselves.[232] Not suffering fools gladly,[233] Justinian hurried and chivvied his associates.[234] The analysis of his Latin prose style brings into prominence expressions connected with haste: *festinare*,[235] *accelerare*,[236] *celerrimo*,[237] *cum omni alacritate*,[238] *absque quadam dilatione*.[239] *Nec expedit diutius causam vitae protrahi sempiternae*,[240] he pleonastically reproaches pope Hormisdas.

---

[222] Above, n. 105; below, ch. 2 nn. 123–4.

[223] N. 30.11.2 (18 March 536) above, n. 185, N. 80.10 pr. (10 March 539).

[224] *CJ* 1.27.1.6 (534). Critical attitude: N. 7 pr. (15 April 535 Anastasius).

[225] N. 8.11 (15 April 535).

[226] Outdoing Augustus (*Inst.* 2.23.12 *nuper et nos eundem principem superare contendentes*).

[227] N. 133.6 (16 March 539); cf. C. *Cordi* pr. (16 Nov. 534).

[228] *Wars* 7.32.10; *Inst.* 2.20.2; N. 37 pr. (1 Aug. 535); 8 pr. (15 Apr. 535).

[229] *SH* 13.28,33; 15.11; *Buildings* 1.7.7–11; Lydus 2.15; 3.55; N. 30.2 (18 March 536), or die in peace: N. 1 epil. (1 Jan. 535).

[230] N. 114 pr. (1 Nov. 541); cf. 1 pr. (1 Jan. 535), 8 pr. (15 April 535), 13 epil. (15 Oct. 535), 18 epil. (1 March 536), 46 pr. (15 Aug. 537), 86 pr. (17 April 539), 82 epil. (8 April 539), 98 pr. (16 Dec. 539), 116 pr. (9 April 542).

[231] N. 17.3 (16 April 535 provincial governors to hear cases themselves, not through their indolence allow their provincials to come to the capital and harass the emperor).

[232] For a distorted version of this see *SH* 13.23–7, for the other side N. 8 (15 April 535: reform of provincial administration).

[233] Stupid and wilful misinterpretation of previous legislation N. 19 pr. (17 March 536); 54 pr. (1 Sept. 537).

[234] N. 8.10.2 (15 April 535).   [235] *Justinian* n. 66.   [236] Ibid. n. 73.

[237] Ibid. n. 75.   [238] Ibid. n. 76.   [239] Ibid. n. 77.   [240] Ibid. n. 80.

Iter arripere[241] is a striking metaphor in one of his letters. But he did not 'hit the road'. Mentally active, he remained immured in Constantinople for virtually the whole of his reign.[242] He neither campaigned in nor inspected the provinces. He did not visit the reconquered territories, not even Rome.[243] Personally affable, quiet and even-tempered,[244] he was geographically remote from most of his subjects, who learned about him from laws, churches, inscriptions, prayers and coins. His solicitude was genuine. No problem was too detailed or trivial to deserve his attention:[245] the mischievous overestimation by the market-gardeners of Constantinople of the value of vegetables is solemnly noted and a remedy proposed.[246] But as the suppliants press in, the emperor feels harassed and overworked.[247] He tries to reduce the burden by enacting general laws to cover the most usual grounds of petition[248] and thereby avoid the reproach of discrimination in favour of those who are close enough to the court to put their case.[249] Yet the emperor's sympathy had sharp edges, for he would not tolerate the half-hearted, and clear boundaries; for those outside the pale, Arians, Goths or pagans, were lucky to be left alive.[250] 'He did not consider it murder if the victims were not of his own faith.'[251] The earth was better rid of them, and without showing his feelings, he would quietly give orders for their death or the confiscation of their property.[252]

He was not, despite the murder of Vitalian,[253] harsh to personal as opposed to ideological enemies. He pardoned Probus, the nephew of Anastasius,[254] and Artabanes, who plotted to kill him after Theodora's death.[255] The defeated Vandal king Gelimer was given an estate in Galatia.[256] The tribute of Procopius to the emperor's personal clemency is deserved.[257]

Romans expected their rulers to be accessible. Justinian was a good listener. 'He sits unguarded in some lobby to a late hour of the night, and enjoys unrolling the Christian scriptures in the company of very old priests.'[258] Good in an informal situation, he lacked style. Procopius

---

[241] Ibid. n. 82.

[242] The only constitutions issued elsewhere than at Constantinople are those of 18 Sept. 539 (Chalcedon), 22 Oct. 529 (the seventh milestone from the capital), 17 Nov. 529 (Chalcedon), 24 June 530 (Chalcedon), N. 85 (25 June 538 Chalcedon), N. 118 (16 July 543 seventh milestone), *Appendix* 9 (August 558 Chalcedon).

[243] 'Fatherland of laws, fount of priesthood' (N. 9 pr. 14 April 535).

[244] *SH* 13.1–2, 15.11–12.

[245] N. 15 ep. (13 Aug. 535), ed. 13 pr. (538–9). Cf. N. 64.2 (19 Jan. 538), N. 147 pr. (15 April 553).   [246] N. 64 (19 Jan. 538).

[247] N. 30.9 (18 March 536), 68.1.2 (25 May 538), 18.5 (1 March 536).

[248] N. 68.1.2 (25 May 538).   [249] N. 18.5 (1 March 536).

[250] *SH* 6.22–8; N. 37 (1 Aug. 535, 6 *cum sufficit eis vivere, non etiam sibi aliquam auctoritatem vindicare*: 8 Jews, pagans, Donatists, Arians and other heretics to celebrate no church rites in Africa, 10 violators of the Christian faith not entitled to sanctuary); 45.1 (18 Aug. 537).

[251] *SH* 13.8.   [252] *SH* 13.2.   [253] Above, nn. 55–60.   [254] Malalas 438.

[255] *Wars* 7.32.51.   [256] *Wars* 4.9.13–14; Gibbon ch. 43 nn. 111f.

[257] *Buildings* 1.1.10,16.   [258] *Wars* 7.32.9.

complains that he neither possessed nor cultivated the qualities appropriate
to the imperial office. He was in speech, dress and thought a barbarian. Yet he
took it on himself to do work which fell within the province of some other
official. For example, he would settle documents himself instead of instruc-
ting the quaestor to do so.[259] In other words, Justinian drafted his own
legislation.

This hostile assessment, taken from the *Secret History*, can be checked if
Justinian's Latin style is analysed according to the methods explained in
Chapter 3.[260] It turns out to be exaggerated, but not unfounded: the view of
an intellectual snob, not a liar. Justinian's style is a curious mixture of the
pretentious and the vulgar. It is repetitive[261] and emphatic[262] and descends
into anticlimax.[263] Writing to the pope about a bishop whose visit to Rome
had been delayed because of illness, 'Still,' he says, 'with the favour of the
deity we will soon send him off, for he is now better, since the problems
which have given rise to a difference of interpretation are not difficult, and
it is not advisable to prolong them to eternity, in case with delay greater uncertainty arises.'[264] This sentence encapsulates much of the emperor's style
and outlook: impatient, colloquial (*iam melius habet* for 'he is better'), loosely
constructed (there is no causal connection between the bishop's recovery
and the problem's being soluble), yet forceful. Or again, 'It has always been
our concern to safeguard to the greatest extent the discipline of the past,
which we have never disdained, except to improve it, especially when the
question concerns ecclesiastical affairs, and is settled by the authority of the
fathers, indeed by inspiration from on high, since it is settled that the
decrees of the apostolic authority are the decisions of heaven.'[265] It is not
difficult to catch the quiet, repetitive tone, the solecisms (*in melius augeremus*
confuses size and quality; if you improve something you do not disdain it),
the urge to explain the self-evident, the anxiety to disclaim radical intentions. One last example, the flavour of which is stronger in the Latin. 'Let
them (the inhabitants of North Africa) know from what most severe
captivity and barbaric yoke they have been freed and what great freedom
they have gained under our happy rule.'[266]

---

[259] *SH* 14.2–3.   [260] Ch. 3 nn. 7–25.   [261] *Justinian* nn. 148–65.

[262] Ibid. nn. 39–48 (use of *semper* in opening sentences).

[263] Ibid. nn. 134–40 (often with *quoniam, quia* or *quatenus* in final clause).

[264] *Patr. Lat.* 63.507A (Justinian to Hormisdas, after 13 Sept. 520 *eum tamen mox
dimittemus favente divinitate, quia iam melius habet, quoniam nec difficilia sunt quae ceciderunt
in ambiguitatem, nec expedit diutius causam vitae protrahi sempiternae ne dilatis temporibus
aliquid nascatur incertius*).

[265] *Appendix* 3 (Schoell-Kroll 3.797, 29 Oct. 542 *semper nostrae serenitati cura fuit
servandae vetustatis maxime disciplinae, quam nunquam contempsimus, nisi et in melius augeremus,
praesertim quotiens de ecclesiasticis negotiis contingit quaestio, quae patrum constat regulis
definita, immo adventu superni numinis inspirata, quia constat esse caelitus constituta quicquid
apostolica decernit auctoritas*). On the authorship see *Justinian* nn. 263–75.

[266] *CJ* 1.27.1.8 (534 *cognoscant eius habitatores quam a durissima captivitate et iugo barbarico
liberati in quanta libertate sub felicissimo nostro imperio degere meruerunt*). '*Quam durissima*' is
a solecism: the self-satisfaction is considerable. For the authorship see *Justinian* nn.
186–225.

Pedestrian, not to say pedantic, he refers back a great deal to 'what has been said previously'.[267] His reading has been in the Christian fathers and the constitutions: religious and bureaucratic, not literary, sources. Of more than 300 Latin constitutions of his reign, half a dozen can with some confidence be ascribed to his hand.[268] They are exclusively concerned with two topics, Christian dogma and the affairs of liberated North Africa. The first was a 'reserved topic'. In dogmatic theology he was an expert[269] (the Roman See did not agree) and, subject to papal approval, he thought his views, expressed in legislative form, the equivalent of the definitions of the oecumenical councils. The task of drafting these laws and confessions of faith could not be left to anyone else, however gifted. But it should be noted that laws dealing with church discipline and organisation were composed by the quaestor.[270]

As to North Africa, it is not altogether surprising that he should have wished to deal personally with the details of the administration, civil, military and ecclesiastical, of the reconquered territories. The liberation was in large measure his own work, and the language of the area was Latin. When Tribonian was in office, however, he was allowed to compose laws for Africa as for the remainder of the empire.[271] It was in the absence of Tribonian that Justinian trusted to himself in this sphere.

Latin is described as Justinian's language, not just the traditional language of the Roman law and administration but his own.[272] He enjoyed speaking it. But he could compose in both official languages. For, unlike any predecessor since Marcus and Julian, Justinian was a writer. His Greek edict against Origen,[273] his various writings in both languages[274] on the Three

[267] Ibid. nn. 141–7.

[268] *CJ* 1.1.8.7–24 (25 March 534), 1.27.1 (534), 1.27.2 (12 April 534), N. *Appendix* 3 (29 Oct. 542), 6 (6 Sept. 552), 9 (22 Sept. 558): *Justinian* 116–21.

[269] Apart from *CJ* 1.1.8.7–24 (above, n. 222) one can list among definitions of faith in the form of constitutions *CJ* 1.1.5 (perhaps 527), 1.1.6 (15 March 533), 1.1.7 (26 March 533).

[270] E.g. *CJ* 1.2.19 (528, Thomas); 1.2.21–3 (529 to March 530, Tribonian), 1.3.48–51 (23 Aug. to 1 Nov. 531, Tribonian). Cyrillus of Skythopolis (above, n. 93 at p. 178) records Justinian as 'busy' with Tribonian (τοῦ . . . βασιλέως ἐν τούτοις ἀσχολουμένου μετὰ Τριβουνιανοῦ τοῦ κυέστορος) in connection with a constitution about maintenance for St Sabas and for certain monasteries in Palestine.

[271] *N.* 36 (1 Jan. 535), 37 (1 Aug. 535).

[272] *N.* 13.1.1 (15 Oct. 535 τῇ μὲν ἡμετέρᾳ φωνῇ *praetores plebis*); cf. *N.* 7.1 (17 May 535 τῇ πατρίῳ φωνῇ), 15 pr. (13 Aug. 535 τῇ πατρίῳ φωνῇ), 13 pr. (15 Oct. 535 ἡ πάτριος ἡμῶν φωνή), 22.2 (15 April 536 κατὰ τὴν ἀρχαίαν καὶ πάτριον γλῶτταν); H. J. Roby, *An Introduction to the Study of Justinian's Digest* (1888) 86; contra Rubin 423. The πάτριος φωνή can, as Stein II. 276 n. 1 says, be taken as the traditional state language, but 'our tongue' means Justinian's own.

[273] Above, n. 216.

[274] Edict of 543–4 (Greek, fragments in von Pewesin, 'Imperium, Ecclesia universalis, Rom', *Forschungen zum Kirchen und Geistesgeschichte* 11 (1937) 150f.); treatise of 549/June 550 (Greek, *Patr. Gr.* 86.1041; E. Schwartz, *Drei dogmatische schriften Iustinians*, 2nd ed. 1973, 47); edict of July 551 (Greek, *Patr. Gr.* 86.993; Schwartz 73; *Patr. Lat.* 69.226); decree of 4 May 553 (Latin, *Patr. Lat.* 69.30–8).

Chapters[275] and doubtless the lost edict of his old age which advocated aphthartodocetism[276] are either articles or short books, mostly in legislative form, much as if Henry VIII had been able to publish his treatises against Martin Luther as an Act of Parliament. Though they are technically edicts,[277] they have little in common with Zeno's *Henotikon*, but like modern papal encyclicals are theological treatises designed to convince doubters.

'Trying inappropriately to appear learned, he disturbs the church by inventing problems,'[278] hints a hostile observer. It is important to appreciate that the emperor's desire to shine as a theorist and an author is connected with his lowly social origin and vulgarity. To the sophisticated style and manners of the cosmopolitan Greek he can oppose expertise in the intricate tangles of Christian theology.

Though the emperor wrote freely on Christian dogma and composed an occasional law on an administrative topic, Procopius is wrong in giving the impression that he regularly usurped the function of the quaestor's office.[279] There is nothing to show that he had any technical competence, as opposed to interest in the law. His relation to the codification which stands in his name is to be conceived as similar to that of Napoleon to the French *Code civil*: lively interest, political authorship, constant harrying of those entrusted with the task, but rarely or never actual composition.[280] The theory of the omnicompetent overseer who solves problems which have baffled the experts[281] is a myth. So is the picture, found even in careful historians, of an emperor versed in history and antiquities.[282] The references in Justinian's laws to the pagan past all come from Tribonian. Outside the quaestorships of the latter, one will search in vain for any precise reference to the laws and institutions of the ages before Constantine.[283] The emperor may not have been the cleverest man of the age, only the most determined. But he could pick those who were the ablest in their field.

Tribonian, who knew how to amplify his master's voice, makes plain in the constitutions of his two quaestorships the extent to which Justinian was conscious of his own personality.[284] How he extended the range of expressions hitherto considered appropriate to the description of imperial thought

---

[275] Evagrius, *Hist. eccl.* 4.39–40; Theophanes anno 6057; John of Nikiu, *Chron.* 94; Eustratius, *Hist. eccl.* 4, 5; Michael Mel. *Chron.* 9.34. To these writings on theology can be added the letter against the monphysites addressed to Alexandrian monks *c.* 540: Schwartz 6; *Patr. Gr.* 86.1104.

[276] The belief, propagated by Julian bishop of Halicarnassus (deposed *c.* 518), that from the incarnation Christ's body was incorruptible. R. Draguet, *Julien d'Halicarnasse et sa controverse avec Sévère d'Antioche sur l'incorruptibilité du corps du Christ* (1924).

[277] *Drei dogmatische Schriften Iustinians* (ed. Schwartz, 2nd ed. M. Amelotti 1973).

[278] Facundus, *Pro defensione trium capitulorum lib. 12, Patr. Lat.* 67. 844C (*si quis igitur ...cum videri doctus appetit importune ac nulla utilitate suadente spontaneis quaestionibus ecclesiam turbat, hic non dispensator familiae dominicae sed dissipator est*): noted by Gibbon ch. 47 n. 80.

[279] We have at least 276 Latin constitutions drafted by Tribonian alone (ch. 3 nn. 549–697), against 6 attributable to Justinian.

[280] Stein II. 281.   [281] *Buildings* 1.1.70–2.

[282] Jones 1.270; Rubin 1.89; even Stein II. 276.   [283] Ch. 3 nn. 28–63.

[284] Above, nn. 51, 131, 145–53.

and action is made clear in Chapter 3.[285] Unlike anything earlier, the laws of this period present to us an emperor conscious of how he has legislated in the past[286] and anxious to tell us not merely of the reasons for his present measures but of the motives which inspire him,[287] the way in which an abuse has come to his notice,[288] his incredulity when first informed,[289] his past mistakes,[290] his shame,[291] his constant efforts to improve[292] and his surprise that his previous legislation has not been adequate.[293] The picture of the mischiefs to be corrected is refreshingly candid. Officials in Thrace are for ever bickering.[294] It is time the Cappadocians stopped pestering us with petitions.[295] Governors, before our salutary reform, were 'forced to steal'.[296] The oaths taken by mothers that they will not remarry are nearly always false.[297] The need for continual change arises from 'variety' (ποικιλία): since human affairs are so various and unpredictable,[298] since nature sports, the conscientious emperor must ceaselessly try to adapt the laws to new situations.[299] He must approach his task empirically, take account of how laws work in practice[300] and adapt them to the infinite variety of events.[301] It is no disgrace to change one's mind and amend one's own legislation,[302] but to leave any situation in a state of confusion[303] or disorder,[304] to pass over an item on the agenda without taking action, is intolerable.[305] To the resulting charge, made explicit by Procopius, of innovation, he at times pleads a denial,[306] at others confesses and justifies his interventionism on the ground of nature's variety,[307] the analogy between

285 Ch. 3 nn. 64–154.

286 E.g. *N.* 5.5 (17 March 535), 24.5 (18 May 535), 22 pr., 45.1 (18 March 536).

287 *N.* 108 pr. (1 Feb. 541).   288 *N.* 2 pr. (21 March 535), 90 pr. (1 Oct. 539).

289 *N.* 154 pr. (probably 535/6 incest in Osroene); cf. 3 pr. (16 March 535).

290 *N.* 82.11.1 (8 April 539), 94.2 (11 Oct. 539 oaths), 111 pr. (1 June 541 prescription).

291 'We blush' (ἐρυθριῶμεν) *N.* 18.5 (1 March 536; cf. 18.1), 30.5.1 (18 March 536), 39.2 pr. (17 April 536).

292 *N.* 22 pr. (18 March 536); cf. 18 pr. (1 March 536); 39 pr. (17 April 536), 78 pr. (10 March 539).

293 *N.* 52 pr. (18 Aug. 537).   294 *N.* 26 pr. (18 May 535).

295 *N.* 30.9 pr. (18 March 536).   296 *N.* 28 (16 July 535); cf. 8.1 (15 April 535).

297 *N.* 94.2 (11 Oct. 539).

298 *N.* 7.2, *C. Tanta* 18 (16 Dec. 533), *C. Cordi* 4 (16 Nov. 534); cf. *N.* 2. pr. pr., 2.4 (21 March 535), 39 pr. (17 April 536), 49 pr. (18 Aug. 537), 73 pr. pr. (4 June 538 'nature innovates'), 74 pr. (4 June 538), 84 pr. pr. (18 May 539), 98 pr. (16 Dec. 539).

299 *N.* 60 pr. (1 Dec. 537).

300 *N.* 82.11.1 (8 April 539), 127.2 (1 Sept. 548), ed. 8 pr. (17 Sept. 548).

301 *N.* 73 pr. 1 (4 June 538).

302 *N.* 22 pr. (18 March 536), 98 pr. (16 Dec. 539), 111 pr. (1 June 541), 127 (1 Sept. 548); cf. 18 pr. (1 March 536).

303 *N.* 21 (18 March 536 contrast of σύγχυσις and νομοθεσία), 82 pr. (8 April 539).

304 1.1.1 (1 Jan. 535).   305 *N.* 43 pr. (17 May 537).

306 *N.* 78.5 (retroactive effect of emancipation of slaves: precedent of Antoninus Pius and Theodosius II), *Inst.* 2. 14 pr.; *N.* 80. 10 pr. (10 March 539); cf. the frequent use of οὐδὲν καινίζομεν etc. *N.* 28.2 (16 July 535), 22.1 (18 March 536), 49.1.1 (18 Aug. 537), 98.2.2 (16 Dec. 539), 56.1 (3 Nov. 537).

307 Above, n. 278.

legislation and medicine,[308] the value of second thoughts,[309] or the wisdom of piecemeal reform. Indeed, he often finds it advisable to take one step at a time, to proceed piecemeal, to change course suddenly, and to conceal his ultimate goals,[310] as he conceals his intention to obliterate the Ostrogothic kingdom.[311] 'This was our initial intention but we deferred putting it into effect to begin with and tested opinion, since we saw that men were moving and inclining towards that point of view; we now accordingly amend the earlier law.'[312] The subject is advancements made by parents to children, the drafter is Tribonian, and the confession bears out Procopius who noticed in the emperor a combination of guile and naiveté.[313] But the passage illuminates Justinian's tactics and conception of his office. The meddlesome peasant, forever uprooting established institutions, is also the crafty, sleepless father of his people.[314]

The portrait I have drawn of Tribonian's master might be left to carry whatever conviction it may, with the help of the sources referred to, be capable of sustaining. The depiction may draw colour, however, from comparison with that of a ruler who achieved supreme power in a similar society fourteen centuries later; from the parallel, that is, between Sabbatius-Iustinianus and Djugashvili-Stalin.[315] In both cases a man of humble birth from the periphery of an empire makes his way by steady effort and careful attention to the details of administration,[316] coupled with a thorough if pedestrian mastery of the official ideology, to the centre of power. Djugashvili's parents were born serfs.[317] From the age of fourteen this voracious reader spent five years at the theological seminary of Tiflis.[318] His formation was in eastern Christianity, and he learned the meaning of orthodoxy, a framework which he proceeded to fill with a Marxist content. 'Eaten up by a vain desire to become a well-known theoretician',[319] according to a hostile colleague, he made himself a competent Marxist[320] and an expert, under Lenin's guidance, on certain questions such as that problem of nationalities, on which he wrote freely.[321] Strongly attached to his status as a philosopher

[308] *N.* 111 pr. (1 June 541).   [309] *N.* 98 pr. (16 Dec. 539).

[310] *SH* 22.30–31; 29.1–12; below, n. 312.   [311] Stein II. 340–1.

[312] *N.* 92.1 pr. (10 Oct. 539).   [313] *SH* 13.10–12, 14.11, 22.29.

[314] *N.* 98.2.2 (16 Dec. 539 ὁ μετὰ θεῶν κοινὸς ἅπασι πατήρ—φάμεν δὲ ὁ τὴν βασιλείαν ἔχων). The need to explain slightly spoils the effect.

[315] I have made free use of I. Deutscher, *Stalin, a Political Biography* (1961); ed. R. Conquest, *The Great Terror* (1968, Pelican ed. 1971); M. Djilas, *Conversations with Stalin* (1962); R. A. Medvedev, *Let History Judge* (tr. C. Taylor 1973). The future Stalin was born on 21 Dec. 1879 (Deutscher 2). Gibbon ch. 43 nn. 112–13 suggests a parallel with Philip II of Spain, which is also instructive.

[316] Conquest 114.

[317] Deutscher 10–11, 24. His father was a cobbler, his mother worked as a washerwoman.

[318] Oct. 1894 to May 1899 (Deutscher 9: 'The mind of this atheistic dicatator was cluttered with biblical images and symbols'; ibid. 327).

[319] Bukharin, cited by Conquest 109.   [320] Conquest 109.

[321] His pamphlets and articles are collected and translated in *Marxism and the National and Colonial Question* (London 1936), the first, 'Marxism and the National Question', being

and historian of socialism[322] he found in it compensation for the fact that 'almost all the other leaders of the revolution came from quite different walks of life, from the gentry, the middle classes or the intelligentsia'.[323] Circumstance bred in him a sense of inferiority,[324] and a boundless ambition,[325] which he concealed behind an affable, approachable manner,[326] an unpretentious personal life,[327] a willingness to drudge at boring administrative tasks[328] and an artful moderation.[329] He was a master of piecemeal advance.[330] His conception of himself and his role was revealed in the name which, in 1913,[331] he selected to symbolise his character and mark out his chosen course. The name of Stalin was to label the régime and all its works: the towns of Stalingrad, Stalinbad, Stalino and the rest, the Stalin constitution, the Stalin canal, the theory of Stalinism, the Stalin plan for the transformation of nature.[332] The megalomaniac[333] habitually referred to himself in the third person.[334]

His hatred of class enemies was as natural and unforced as Justinian's loathing for heretics.[335] To both, their destruction was a necessity for one who takes dogmatic truth seriously and not, like the intellectual or sophisticate, as something half-believed. From that point of view the collectivisation of agriculture,[336] whatever the cost, was as necessary as the purge of central and local administration and the liquidation of wrong believers to his Byzantine forerunner. Through the terrible years of famine and coercion in 1929–33 Stalin's faith held fast.[337] The cost is still being counted.

Stalin was no orator,[338] and his writings, though clear, are repetitive and dreary.[339] With his Georgian accent and crude manners,[340] his power of dissimulation and taste for detail, his colourless style, he must have seemed to his rivals inferior and barbaric, a real son of a serf. But through his patience and persistence he was in time able to pick them off one by one, for to personal enemies or possible contenders his attitude was that of the vindictive Theodora rather than the clement Justinian.[341]

Like Justinian he is said to have faltered once, in the first days of the

---

written in Vienna in Jan. 1913, at the age of 32. For a hostile assessment see Medvedev 508–22 (exaggerated).

[322] Deutscher 364–8.   [323] Deutscher 24.   [324] Deutscher 26.

[325] Medvedev 324.   [326] Deutscher 273–4.

[327] Conquest 106; Medvedev 329–30.

[328] Deutscher 228–34; Medvedev 3. 'Never refuse to do the little things, for from the little things are built the big' (cited by Conquest, 114).

[329] Conquest 111.   [330] Conquest 111–12; Medvedev 329–30.

[331] The name was used for his essay on the national question (above, n. 321).

[332] Medvedev 490.   [333] Medvedev 508, 565.   [334] Conquest 113.

[335] Deutscher 25–6.   [336] Deutscher 317–32.

[337] 'Only an absolute ruler, himself ruled neither by nerves nor by sentiments, could persist in this staggering enterprise in the face of so many adversities.' Deutscher 332.

[338] Deutscher 26; Medvedev 17 (Caucasian accent).

[339] Deutscher 366–8; Medvedev xix.   [340] Deutscher 26; Conquest 110–11.

[341] The interpretation in Deutscher 357–63 errs, perhaps, in giving too much weight to external and too little to personal factors.

German invasion.[342] Apart from this lapse, if it occurred, he kept his nerve, remaining in Moscow, an invisible presence, when the government moved east as the Germans threatened in late 1941.[343] Once in power he remained in the Kremlin, fearing a coup, and directed armies and enterprises he never visited.[344] The night was his favourite work time,[345] to which ministers and foreign embassies must needs adjust. Like Justinian he combined tactical and administrative expertise with simple, long-term views of policy and interest.

Neither had a polycentric outlook. To Stalin the task was to build socialism in one country.[346] To Justinian, with all his deference to the historical status of antique Rome, it was to build a truly Christian republic with one emperor under God, and one capital, the city of Constantine.[347]

No historical parallel is exact. Justinian's ruthlessness was on the whole confined to theological enemies, Stalin's extended to his closest supporters. With all its defects Christianity is a more humane moral guide than Marxism. But neither is the comparison gratuitous. Soviet Russia is a neo-Byzantine society. It inherited the Byzantine conception, which Justinian did more than anyone to shape, of an absolute and omnicompetent ruler whose authority extends to matters of doctrine, and whose duty it is to remove from the scene anyone who in faith or practice deviates from the truth. In other respects the two societies differed. In the Soviet Union economic policy was important, and 'Stalin' connotes, besides toughness, concern with heavy industry. 'Iustinianus', on the other hand, is a name appropriate to a society in which legal policy is regarded as a central concern of government. It is to this aspect of the Roman world that I now turn.

THE LAW

That the administration of justice should be one of the two major concerns of government seems odd to us, to whom class conflicts and national struggles are the focus of social dissension. But older societies conceive social conflict in terms of the antagonism of families, clans or small groups. Law, often invested with divine authority, is one, often the main, agent by which these dissensions can be regulated and the persons or bodies which are at loggerheads reconciled. Its main content is impartial rules, that is rules appropriate to equals who might each at different times be in a given situation vis-à-vis the other. The ruler's main duty, so far as internal affairs are concerned, is to see to the firm and fair administration of the law, which is conceived of, in the words of the early-second-century Roman lawyer Iuventius Celsus, as the technique of justice, the good and equal: *ius est ars*

---

[342] Medvedev 455–9.   [343] Deutscher 468–9.   [344] Deutscher 469.
[345] Conquest 99n.   [346] Deutscher 284–93.

[347] The pragmatic sanction *Pro petitione Vigilii* (13 Aug. 554) contains no suggestion that Rome was to receive an emperor or become in any real sense a capital. Ravenna continued the seat of government in Italy until it was lost to the empire in the eighth century. Justinian was no antiquarian.

boni et aequi.[348] The phrase is of course to be taken conjunctively. The search is for solutions which are both good in themselves and appropriate to a society of equals. The ruler has the duty also, if laws are lacking, or deficient in certain areas, or insufficiently good or equal, of filling the gaps and correcting the shortcomings. He is, secondarily, a legislator.

This conception of the place of law in government applied with special force to Rome. All sophisticated societies, even the People's Republic of China, have laws, but not all are law-oriented. Rome was. A special caste of men regarded themselves, in Ulpian's words, as priests of justice, charged with declaring the good and equal, separating the just from the unjust, the permitted from the forbidden, trying to make men good not just by fear of sanctions but through the promptings of desire for honours, and aspiring to a true rather than a sham philosophy.[349] This is high-flown indeed. Tribonian's version combines the service of justice with duty to the state. The *Digest* is the 'temple of justice',[350] law graduates are to be 'leaders in advocacy, acolytes of justice, athletes and helmsmen of the courts'[351] or 'the ministers of justice and the state'.[352] The young are to approach the arcane beauties of the law in the spirit of postulants[353] and in the hope that, when the initiation is complete, they will have mastered the art which, alone of all arts, has, at least in Justinian's codes, a marvellous completeness.[354] Nor is intoxication absent from the remarks of St Gregory Thaumaturgus who studied at Beirut in the third century: 'I refer to the admirable laws of the *prudentes*, by which the affairs of the subjects of the Roman empire are now regulated, and which are neither composed nor learnt without difficulty. They are wise, exact, varied and admirable and, in a word, thoroughly Hellenic'[355] (viz. intellectually reputable). The sense of intellectual excitement, of membership of an élite, of a secular religion even, was of course confined to initiates. To laymen Roman lawyers often seemed no less preoccupied by a trivial and second-rate discipline than do their modern counterparts to their modern critics,[356] and some lawyers found law a boring distraction from more interesting pursuits such as history.[357] There was a long tradition of hostility between lawyers and orators, which in the republic and early empire went hand in hand with a division of function by which lawyers were consultants and orators advocates.[358] To the lawyer the orator was a contemptible creature, concerned not with the truth but with winning cases, prepared to argue both ways or none according to his interest, larding his speech with irrelevant and meretricious ornament, and sharpening his wits by frivolous debates conducted on far-fetched hypotheses. He himself, on the other hand, was a wise consultant, never deviating

---

[348] *D.* 1.1.1. pr. (Ulp. 1 inst.).   [349] *D.* 1.1.1.1 (Ulp. 1 inst.).
[350] *C. Tanta* 20 (16 Dec. 533).   [351] *C. Summa* 6 (16 Dec. 533).
[352] *C. Omnem* 11 (16 Dec. 533).   [353] *C. Tanta* 11 (16 Dec. 533).
[354] *C. Omnem* 5 (16 Dec. 533).
[355] Gregory Thaumaturgus, *In Originem* 1 (*Patr. Gr.* 10. 1052-3).
[356] Libanius, *Orationes* 2.44, 4.18.   [357] Agathias, *Histories* 3.1 (*CSHB* 3.138).
[358] Schulz, *Roman Legal Science* (1946) 43-5.

from his true opinion, expressing himself in the clearest and plainest language, treating of cases which either were real disputes or, if hypothetical, were debated in a serious spirit of inquiry and guidance.

There is no need to enter into the merits of this debate between disciplines, which in any case becomes blurred in the later empire once lawyers, as at the present day, are commonly also advocates and so equally open to reproach for prostituting their oratorical talents. But the pre-eminence of the Romans in law, and the importance of that pre-eminence in their internal and external relations, will not be understood unless we remember that in Rome, in contrast with Greece, there was a legal profession, a body of initiates, conscious of its moral worth, with a continuous history from the pontifical college of the republic to Tribonian's commission and the bar of John of Cappadocia's praetorian prefecture. It was this corporation, composed for the most part of upper-class Romans prominent in public life, that conceived itself as the guardian of the rule of law, the living justification of Rome's claim to rule.

The existence of a legal profession in Rome is often overlooked because the Greeks had no occasion to depict the qualities of an ideal lawyer, in contrast to a poet, an orator, a king or a philosopher. In Greek νόμος meant both custom and law, in Latin *mos* and *consuetudo* are set apart from *ius* and *lex*. Greek had νομοθέτης and νομογράφος for a legislator or drafter of laws but (in classical culture) no word for a lawyer. The New Testament uses νομικός, but is reproducing a Jewish, not a Greek, concept. In the empire a νομικός (if not simply a translation from the Latin) is usually a a notary,[359] a man of low rank who drafted documents, kept records, and might at most aspire to become a decurion. Greece had legislators, drafters and notaries but no lawyers, and since Roman literary genres are derivative, there is hardly any discussion of them in Latin either.

Yet they existed. To accept the traditional account,[360] which is what matters in this context, from the *XII Tables* onwards there was a group of specialists, originally members of the pontifical college, who were concerned with two topics in particular, the interpretation of the law[361]—viz. in the first instance of the *XII Tables*—and with appropriate procedures and forms of action (*legis actiones*).[362] When in due course knowledge of these arcane matters spread beyond the pontiffs[363] their study remained a specialised one. It could not be mastered in a few months, and besides meticulous attention to problems of interpretation and procedure, it called for practical wisdom and long apprenticeship. In the course of time the materials to be interpreted greatly extended; the exegesis of the urban praetor's edict, in particular, became a central concern of the legal specialist, and the interpretation of private documents, such as wills, stretched his talent. New procedures, no less complex and intractable than the old, replaced the *legis actiones* and continued to form a focus of legal expertise.

[359] *CTh* 9.19.1, 12.1.3 (30 Jan. 316), P. Cairo 67283; Jones II. 515.
[360] *D.* 1.2.2. (Pomponius 1 enchir.).   [361] *D.* 1.2.2.5.   [362] *D.* 1.2.26.
[363] W. Kunkel, *Römische Rechtsgeschichte* (6th ed. 1972) 2.3; 7.1.

The body of specialists which had grown out of the pontifical college became self-perpetuating.[364] Each generation handed its traditions and skills to the next. An extensive literature was published, read and subjected to comment. In time schools of law were established to preserve in greater security the deposit of learning.[365]

In this way the Romans, like the Jews and the Irish but unlike the Germans or Chinese, acquired a legal profession. It was a profession in the sense not that, originally at least, it afforded a living, but that legal skill rested on a distinct discipline with its own apparatus of concepts, its distinctive methods of argument, its accumulated store of casuistry, its unadorned style, its painfully acquired classifications, its slowly emergent general principles, above all its integrity as an independent branch of learning and practical wisdom.[366] Hence the Roman *iuris prudentes*, *iuris consulti*, or *iuris conditores* formed an intellectual and practical brotherhood persisting from the period following the *XII Tables* (if Pomponius is right) to the age of Justinian.

From the legal historian's account—and he was in a good position to absorb the traditions current in the profession—one may infer that the *XII Tables* and the legal profession were regarded as guarantors of the political revolution which was thought to have taken place when the Etruscan kings were expelled and the republic established. In the private as in the public sphere there was a demand for laws publicly declared as the only technique for securing limited, aristocratic government and, within the community of heads of families, a free and equal society.

In its political function the law (using that dangerously misleading expression to mean the laws together with the lawyers dedicated to their elaboration, enforcement and perpetuation) in Rome may therefore usefully be compared with the law in the United States of America, except that the change from aristocracy to democracy extends the range of the units conceived as free and equal. As a guarantor of political freedom within a limited circle, Roman law in the end failed. The republican constitution could not be preserved. But neither was it obliterated. It was rather subordinated to the discretionary and often arbitrary rule of one man, the *princeps* (ultimately) *legibus solutus*, the untrammelled legislator who ought, paradoxically, to consider himself bound by existing laws, and to whose proceedings the law formed a republican and at times an ill-fitting backcloth. The ideal of government according to law survived, and the constitutional theory which underlies it is expressed by the ancient historian who best understood the place of law in the Roman polity. 'Thus the venerable city,' says Ammianus, 'after humbling the proud necks of savage nations, and making laws, the everlasting foundations and moorings of liberty, has, like

---

[364] *D.* 1.2.2.35f.; Wieacker, *Vom römischen Recht* (2nd ed. 1961) 128f.

[365] *D.* 1.2.2.47f.

[366] So far as I can see no instances of corruption in giving legal opinions are recorded. The independence of the lawyer is recognised by Modestinus in *D.* 49.14.10 (1 praescr. *non puto delinquere eum qui in dubiis quaestionibus contra fiscum facile responderit*).

a thrifty, prudent and wealthy parent, entrusted the management of her estate to the Caesars as to her children.'367

Before the end of the republic lawyers had acquired an important moral function which may again be loosely compared with that of American courts as interpreters of the Bill of Rights. Notions such as those of good faith or decent conduct (*bona fides*)368 had been incorporated in the formulae of civil actions, and it was an accepted part of the lawyer's duty to spell out in detail and in relation to the facts of a particular dispute the implications of such moral notions. There was a felt need for authoritative guidance in many spheres which other societies do not handle in legal terms. Thus, the performance of gratuitous services for a friend (*mandatum*) and the making of gratuitous loans (*mutuum, commodatum*) attracted discussions which are in effect attempts to codify the notion of friendship. The law about partnership, again, is not conceived as a branch of business relations but primarily as the enterprise of giving concrete form to the notion of fraternal dealing. Guardianship (*tutela*) was a public duty to be undertaken for nothing, and its content and limits also were spelled out in detail, though guardians were in the nature of things usually close relatives. There was a minute regulation of the property, though not of the personal, relations of husband and wife. In a society in which many public and private services are to be rendered free of charge one can understand that their limits and content can either be left, as traditionally in England, to social convention (though trusteeship is here an exception) or written out precisely. One of the functions of a Roman lawyer was to specify the content of what would in the England of past generations often have been a gentlemen's agreement. The legification of social convention of course adds a dimension to the law. Modestinus in a famous text says that all law is created by consent, necessity or custom.369 How mystifying! Which of the three accounts for the extension of citizenship to free inhabitants of the empire by Caracalla's *constitutio Antoniniana*? But the writer is here thinking of *ius* as the product of lawyerly discussion which gives to ill-defined social obligations an exact shape. It is these social obligations which arise by consent, necessity or custom.

It is not however enough to point to the legification of social *mores* as a feature of Roman law. What accounts for such a tendency? Two factors may perhaps help to explain it. One is that lawyers were upper-class Romans, at least until with the empire we encounter some, like Sabinus and Gaius, who began as teachers or writers rather than consultants. They belonged to the property-owning group whose affairs they were asked to interpret or regulate, and were well-acquainted with their *mores*. Their opinions (*responsa*) were based on a knowledge of the relevant texts and casuistic literature, but in the end there remained an element of sheer experience and wisdom (reflected in the term *responsa prudentium*)370—an appeal to the view of 'one of us' and one whom we trust.

367 Ammianus Marcellinus (*c.* 330–95) 14.6.5.
368 M. Kaser, *Das römische Privatrecht* (2nd ed. 1971) I 178, 180, 200.
369 D. 1.3.40 (Mod. 1 *reg.*).   370 Gaius, *Inst.* 1.7; Justinian, *Inst.* 1.2.8.,

The second element which may be significant is concerned with the association of Roman law with Roman religion, a connection which was whittled down but not abrogated with the loss by the pontifical college of its monopoly of formula and interpretation. Roman religion was largely prophylactic. It was a question of finding the appropriate procedures for averting the gods' anger and eliciting from them the desired responses. If the performance of obligation towards the gods is conceived as consisting in the precise fulfilment of observances which will preserve the state and family, how natural to think of obligations to one's fellows in similar terms and to suppose that the peace of the polity rests on a precise attention to the requirements of social duty. Emerging from its pontifical cocoon, the law concentrates on techniques of social harmony, on the appeasement of men rather than gods.

With these political roots, moral functions and religious attitudes, then, Roman law, once embodied in a professional group, could not fail to represent a source of strength, pride and irritation. Ensconced in a professional tradition, interpretations and procedures changed but slowly, so that the influence of the law and lawyers was conservative. Ideologically, though not politically, lawyers formed a republican island in an autocratic empire, whose science presupposed the play of free and equal units[371] transferring property, making contracts, committing wrongs, intermarrying, each an emperor in his own household and an equal citizen in his external relations. Such a conception was acceptable to the upper classes in the areas which the Roman armies successively subjugated, and its continuation formed the essence of the bargain by which they were willing to participate in the government of a racially and linguistically alien state.[372] That the Roman state rested on arms and the law was more than a figure of speech.[373]

Rome gave civilisation the law—that is to say a certain professional conception of laws as the cement of society—and the arch. Both reach their apogee under Justinian. Both are load-bearing devices. By scrupulously specifying the conditions in which people have obligations, commit wrongs or are subject to liabilities, a legally-oriented society seems, in comparison with one loosely governed by custom, to invite disobedience or social delinquency. But this apparent weakness is compensated by the specification of remedial procedures, which tend to ensure that defined wrongdoing is established and vindicated, while that conduct which falls outside it constitutes an area of freedom reserved to the citizen. 'Inviting

---

[371] C. R. Noyes, *The Institution of Property: A Study of the Development, Substance and Arrangement of the System of Property in Modern Anglo-American Law* (1936), brings out this point very well.

[372] Dionysius of Halicarnassus 2.16; Aelius Aristeides, Εἰς ʿΡώμην, ed. J. H. Oliver, *The Ruling Power* (1953) 3.100; Ammianus Marcellinus 14.6.5; Orosius, *Hist. Adv. Pag.* v. 2.1–8.

[373] Aurelius Victor, *De Caes.* 41.17; Claudian, *De Cons. Stil.* 3.136; *Gesta Senatus Romani de Theod. Publicando* 5 (*per vos arma, per vos iura* Dictum xx); Cassiodorus, *Varia* 4.12; *C. Summa* pr. (8 April 529); *C. Deo Auctore* pr. (15 Dec. 530); *C. Imperatoriam* pr. (21 Nov. 433); *C. Tanta* pr. (16 Dec. 533).

stress, it provides a mechanism for resisting it.'[374] Legal technique, at least if it is relatively sophisticated, concentrates on problems of interpretation and categorisation. Lawyers are concerned not to order people about, but to analyse the conditions in which obligations exist, on the assumption that citizens are disposed to fulfil them and to abstain from wrongdoing. This has an important intellectual consequence. The centre of gravity of legal science is not, despite what some theorists suppose, human conduct, but the existence or non-existence, validity or invalidity of those artificial entities on which the legal position of persons, their rights, duties and liabilities, depend: contracts, marriages, wills, offices, interests in property, rules themselves. Legal learning revolves first round problems of validity, interpretation, proper constitution, modes of creation and extinction. The entities which people this area of discourse constitute the esoteric legal universe, neither natural nor supernatural but secular and artificial. Only secondarily from a disciplinary, though primarily from a social, point of view is law concerned with the consequences to be drawn from the existence or non-existence of these entities in terms of what people may or must not do. What sorts of person (i.e. personal status) may exist, and what sorts of legally recognised thing (property or asset)? How are they acquired and lost? What procedures (actions) are available for persons to pursue things or other persons? Between the study of constituents, interpretations and remedial procedures there is of course an interstice where citizens obey or disobey, but to concentrate on conditions and consequences is to draw some of the sting from the orders and threats to which we are all brutally subject, if we gaze at our social predicament with unblinking eyes.

If law was always a central concern of Roman society and government the standing of the law and lawyers varied from age to age. On the whole lawyers were not critical of legal institutions, but Gaius, the second-century writer and teacher, is an exception.[375] His work has a strongly historical and rational orientation which betrays Greek intellectual influence. Christian opposition to the imperial government opened an avenue of criticism which finds its culmination under Justinian, himself an enthusiastic reformer. Otherwise it is mainly the workings of the legal process, not the content of the laws, which suffer denigration. The laws are excellent, if the emperor Valens had not been distracted from administering them,[376] or if oriental barristers had not developed tricky techniques of argument,[377] or if the rich did not by influence and bribery exploit them to the ruin of the

[374] Honoré in *Oxford Essays in Jurisprudence* (2nd series), ed. Simpson (1973), 9.

[375] D. Nörr, *Rechtskritik in der römischen Antike* (1974) 92f.

[376] Ammianus Marcellinus 30.4.1.

[377] Ibid. 30.4.4. Readers of the historian's brilliant polemic against lawyer-advocates and the corruption of justice should remember his firm attachment to the rule of law and constitutional government. See especially 14.6.5 (above, n. 367) and 14.4.3, 17.12.18, 27.4.10, 31.2.10 (contrast with barbarians who lack law), 26.10.10, 29.1.27, 28.1.11, 29.1.18, 31.14.6 (emperors and officials who disregard their duty to administer justice impartially), 16.5.1, 26.7.5, 29.2.10 (emperor should consider himself bound by law), 16.8.6, 22.9.9., 27.6.14, 22.10.6, 21.13.11 (contrast with arbitrary exercise of power).

poor.[378] The degree to which the administration of the law was corrupt at any given period is hardly to be measured by the number of imperial constitutions denouncing abuses, which are testimony more to the acuity of a sense of injustice than to the prevalence of injustice itself. What is more easily measurable is the standing of lawyers and their influence in the counsels of the emperor. They were trained largely in private law, up to and including the period of Justinian's reforms, and imperial constitutions, let alone criminal and public law, had little part to play in legal education.

The privatistic outlook of these men is likely to be reflected in the output of constitutions, and of this a rough, no doubt selective, guide is to be found in those which survived in Justinian's *Codex*. One way of tracing the graph of legal prestige is to count the number of lines from imperial constitutions in the *Codex Iustinianus* reign by reign and calculate the percentage in each devoted to private law, which for this purpose is taken to comprise books 2 to 8 of the *Codex*. This calculation[379] shows that, if we disregard reigns from

[378] Priscus of Panium at Attila's court in 449, *Frag. Hist. Byz.* in L. Dindorf, *Hist. Gr. Min.* 1 (1870) 305–9; Jones 1. 516, 11. 866, 1061; Salvian (*c.* 400–480), *De gubernatione dei* 7.21.

[379] Best set out as a table (senior Augusti only apart from 395 to 455):

Emperor	Lines in *CJ*	Lines from books 2–8 (private law)	Percentage of private law
Hadrian	6	6	100
Pius	51	47	92
Marcus	59	59	100
Pertinax	13	13	100
Severus	1335	1242	93
Antoninus (Caracalla)	1674	1365	81
Antoninus (Elagabal)	7	7	100
Alexander	3135	2709	86
Maximimus	15	15	100
Gordianus III	2034	1685	83
Philippus	489	412	84
Decius	49	44	90
Gallus	12	12	100
Valerianus	659	516	78
Gallienus	35	30	86
Claudius II	8	8	100
Aurelianus	36	25	69
Probus	25	25	100
Carus	125	99	79
Carinus	62	45	73
Diocletianus	8586	7504	87
Constantius I	32	32	100
Constantinus I	2330	1234	53
Constantinus II	100	64	64
Constantius II	587	159	27
Iulianus	157	80	51
Iovianus	9	0	0
Valentinianus I	1329	326	25
Valens	269	68	25

which less than one hundred lines survive, the private law content exceeds eighty per cent up to and including Diocletian, with slight exceptions for Valerian and Carus. Under Constantine the private and public law material is approximately equal in volume. Beginning with his successors private law falls and remains consistently under a third of the total, apart from the short reign of Julian, until Zeno. A movement towards private law then begins and is continued under Justin and Justinian. The reign of Anastasius reverts, however, to the earlier pattern.

The crude picture is therefore one of a decline of imperial interest in private law which begins with Constantine and is reversed in the late fifth-century. Perhaps, as the exception of Julian suggests, this movement owed something to the association of lawyers with paganism. By the middle fifth-century this connection had become dimmed, and with the loss of the western provinces the demand in the east for officials competent in law and Latin increased. This is why Leo insisted on professional qualifications for practice at the bar[380] and why he was willing to equate barristers with soldiers and to call legal practice a type of *militia*.[381] The movement towards private law under Zeno shows that, as the number of legally trained barristers increased, many of them took up administrative careers, for example as assessors to magistrates.[382] In due course they became provincial governors, thereby giving Rome for the first time a substantial number of professional judges, or occupied posts in the central administration, where they were able to influence the content of imperial constitutions. Some lawyers became praetorian prefects, and I would assume that at this period quaestors were always legally qualified.

The avenue to promotion was via the bar. Barristers seem to have been recruited from the middle ranks of society, from persons who could afford

Emperor	Lines in *CJ*	Lines from books 2–8 (private law)	Percentage of private law
Gratianus	1093	347	32
Valentinianus II	1390	303	27
Theodosius I	378	77	20
Arcadius/Honorius	1853	419	23
Honorius/Theodosius II	1761	521	30
Theodosius II	270	84	31
Theodosius II/Valentinian III	2775	903	33
Valentinian III/Marcianus	442	36	8
Marcianus	88	17	19
Leo I	1900	586	31
Leo II	139	32	23
Zeno	1576	800	51
Anastasius	1621	456	28
Iustinus I	996	600	60
Iustinianus I (to 534)	16888	10926	65

380 *CJ* 2.7.11 (1 Feb. 460).   381 *CJ* 2.7.14 (28 March 469); cf. *CTh* 1.29.1 (368?).
382 For this and what follows see Jones I. 500–1, 507–15.

the expense of the four-year course at Berytus or Constantinople, and to whom the prospect of advancement on merit was attractive.

It was possible also for a law professor to aspire to an administrative post, as is shown by the example of Leontius, who taught at Beirut in 487 or 488 and became praetorian prefect of the east under Anastasius.[383] There was indeed a reservoir of talent at the bars and universities on which an emperor bent on law reform and codification could draw. It is not too fanciful to suppose that the intellectual élite, at least in Beirut, was more favourably disposed towards Justin and Justinian than to Anastasius. Beirut was Chalcedonian.[384] The school was oriented towards private law and the study of Latin texts. Anastasius, as we saw, was a monophysite, his constitutions mainly concern public law and the proportion of Greek in them, which had been increasing since Leo, now exceeds thirty per cent.[385] In all these respects we find a reaction under Justin and Justinian, at least up to 534, after which Greek becomes the predominant language of legislation. From Justinian's point of view the lawyers were natural allies. Determined to modernise the law, to reduce it to orderly and manageable proportions, to shorten trials, simplify complexities and eradicate injustices, he needed their expertise and cooperation. At this point professional tradition unites with the Christian spirit of renewal and the Greek bent for rational ordering. The pious but rustic dynasty benefits from the lustre of an association with a learned coterie of scholars, trained in the classical Latin texts. Middle-class lawyers, oriented not just by education but by class to esteem due process of law, and hopeful of preferment, are eager to collaborate. Tribonian, barrister, quaestor, lover of ancient learning,[386] presents in the great codification the confluence of a threefold tradition.

---

[383] Collinet (1925) 141–54.   [384] Collinet 307.

[385] Percentage of lines from constitutions in Greek: Leo 1900 lines 76 Greek 4 per cent; Zeno 1576 lines 363 Greek 23 per cent; Anastasius 1621 lines 502 Greek 31 per cent; Justin 996 lines 222 Greek 22 per cent; Justinian (to 534) 16888 lines 3687 Greek 22 per cent.

[386] N. 30 pr. (18 March 536) οἱ τῆς ἀρχαίας πολυμαθείας ἐρασταί.

CHAPTER TWO

Tribonian

An effort is made in this chapter to set out the known facts and reasonable conjectures about Tribonian's life. The assessment of his work and personality is left to the last chapter of the book.

The main sources used are the *Corpus Juris Civilis* and Procopius. They can be relied on,[1] but a warning is called for insofar as favourable references to Tribonian in the former are concerned. If these appear during Tribonian's terms of office as quaestor, or even sometimes outside them, they have been drafted by Tribonian himself, though of course endorsed by Justinian. They cannot count as unsolicited testimonials.[2]

Justinian's right-hand lawyer is generally called Tribonianus,[3] sometimes Tribunianus,[4] in Greek respectively Tribounianos and Tribônianos.[5] The name may be derived from Trebonius or Tribunus, both good Latin roots. Not many Tribonians are known. There is a bishop of Aspendos or Primupolis who attended the Council of Ephesus in 431.[6] Aspendos is in Pamphylia, on the south coast of modern Turkey. Isidore of Pelusium, an ascetic and exegete who died about 450, wrote a letter to a bishop Tribunianus who may be the same bishop.[7] The Suda, the tenth-century

---

[1] On Procopius see above, ch. 1 n. 42, and B. Rubin, *RE* 23. 273–599 = *Prokopios von Kaisereia* (1954); J. A. S. Evans, *Procopius* (1972). On Tribonian see B. Kübler, *RE* 2.12. 2419; Stein, 'Deux questeurs de Justinien et l'emploi des langues dans ses novelles', *Bulletin de la classe des lettres de l'Académie royale de Belgique* 5e série xxiii (1937) 365; Ludewig, above, ch. 1 n. 42. Stein's article is in effect the only serious study of Tribonian up to now.

[2] Overlooked even by acute scholars, e.g. Diehl op. cit. 250, Stein op. cit. 369 (comparison of warm tributes to Tribonian in Justinian's laws with more distant references to John of Cappadocia): *C. Haec.* 1 (13 Feb. 528), *C. Summa* 2 (7 April 529), *CJ* 7.63.5 (17 Nov. 529), *C. Imperatoriam* 3, 4 (21 Nov. 533), *C. Omnem* 2, 6 (16 Dec. 533), *C. Tanta* pr., 9, 11 (16 Dec. 533), *C. Cordi* 2 (16 Nov. 534), *N.* 35 (23 May 535), *N.* 23 (3 Jan. 535/6), *N.* 75 (Nov./Dec. 537). The truth was seen by Ludewig, *Vita Justiniani* (ch. 1 n. 42) 186.

[3] *N.* 35 (23 May 535), 75 (Nov.–Dec. 537), *C. Imperatoriam* 3, 4 (21 Nov. 533), *C. Deo auctore* inscr. (15 Dec. 530), *C. Omnem* 2 (16 Dec. 533), *C. Tanta* pr. 9. 11, 17 (16 Dec. 533).

[4] *N.* 17 (16 April 535).

[5] Τριβουνιανός: Edict 9 (undated), *Wars* 1.24.11,16; 1.25.1, 2; Malalas 475B. Τριβωνιανός: *C. Δέδωκεν* pr, 9,11,17 (16 Dec. 533); *SH* 13.12; 20.16, 17; *Suidae Lexicon*, below, n. 8, τ.956,957; Lydus 3.20. In *Chron. Pasch.* 621D the quaestor dismissed at the time of Nika is called Rufinus. This is just a slip. On Rufinus, envoy to Persia, see *Wars* 1.11.24, 38; 1.13.11; 1.16.1f, 10; 1.22.1, 7, 9, 12, 13, 14, 15, 16; 1.17.44; 2.7.15.

[6] *RE* 2.12. 2426 (W. Ensslin); Mansi 4.1125E, 1217B, 1365A.

[7] *Patr. Graec.* 68, 281D (ep. 149).

lexicon, mentions a second Tribonian of Justinian's age, a writer and barrister from Side,[8] in Pamphylia, of whom more later.[9] Justinian's Edict 9 is addressed to 'Tribonian, prefect of the city', possibly a third Tribonian of this age. Then there is Tribunus, a Palestinian doctor who cured the Persian king Chosroes of a serious illness. In 545 Justinian sent him back to the Persian court at Chosroes' request. He was kept there for a year and on leaving secured the release of 3000 Roman prisoners of war.[10] Unlike Procopius and the Suda, Zacharias Scholasticus, the monophysite divine, lawyer and bishop apparently calls the doctor Tribonian.[11]

Though there is nothing to show a connection between Tribunus and Tribonian, the medical or some similar profession—doctors, architects, lawyers, engineers, surveyors, combining empirical and scholarly interests— may well have made up Tribonian's background. The family was from Pamphylia. Tribonian was not, at least in the early stages of his career, a patrician, and there is no indication that he had a connection with the senatorial aristocracy.

We can only guess the date of his birth. He was junior in rank to John of Cappadocia.[12] It is not certain that he was also junior in age, but probably he was not much, if at all, senior. Tribonian attained the quaestorship in 529;[13] so he was presumably born before 500, perhaps in the last fifteen years of the fifth century.

Procopius calls Tribonian a Pamphylian by origin.[14] The Suda says that the second Tribonian (the writer, not the quaestor) came from Side,[15] which is in Pamphylia. The bishop Tribonian held a see in Pamphylia.[16] The name is clearly associated with this area of what is now the south coast of Turkey. But this does not tell us a great deal. It would be interesting to know Tribonian's home tongue. Writers often assume that it was Greek.[17] This is likely, since Pamphylia was not an area of extensive Roman settlement.[18] But since the Latin of the eastern empire was influenced by the Greek environment, it cannot be said that Tribonian's Latin, in itself correct and idiomatic,[19] betrays a Greek-speaking home. Indeed, so far as one can hazard a judgment, his Latin is more eloquent than his Greek. The text of the Latin *C. Tanta*, drafted, as we shall see,[20] by Tribonian, has only to be compared with the Greek *C. Δέδωκεν*, a Greek draft by Tribonian or by

---

[8] *Suidae Lexicon* (ed. A. Adler, Leipzig 1935) IV T.957.   [9] Below, n. 262.

[10] *Wars* 2.28.8, 9; 8.10.11f.; *Suidae Lexicon* (ed. Adler IV. 587), s.v. Tribounos.

[11] Bury II. 112–13.   [12] *C. Haec* I (13 Feb. 529), *C. Summa* 2 (7 April 529).

[13] Pamphylia: W. Ruge *RE* 18.3. 354–407; A. H. M. Jones, *Cities of the Eastern Roman Provinces* (2nd ed. 1971) 123f.

[14] *Wars* 1.24.11.   [15] Above, n. 8.   [16] Above, n. 6.

[17] E.g. Kübler, *RE* 2.12. 2422.

[18] The only Roman colony was Attaleia: W. Ruge *RE* 18.3.386.

[19] Kübler, *RE* 2.12. 2422 speaks of grammatical mistakes. I have not found any construction for which there are no respectable precedents. See below, ch. 3 nn. 362f. Rubin, n. 374, finds *Küchenlatein* and *Überladene Gräzität* in the constitutions. These authors pass directly from the third to the sixth century, ignoring the space between.

[20] Below, ch. 3 nn. 635–48.

another hand, to show that the quaestor preferred Latin at least for composing laws. The opening sentences may be set out in illustration. Both
versions thank God for the Persian peace, the victories in North Africa and
the refurbishing of ancient laws, but their tone is very different:

Tanta pr. (16 Dec. 533) Tanta circa nos divinae humanitatis est providentia ut semper aeternis liberalitatibus nos sustentare dignetur. post bella enim Parthica aeterna pace sopita postque Vandalicam gentem ereptam et Cathaginem, immo magis omnem Libyam Romano imperio iterum socia- tam et leges antiquas iam senio praegravatas per nostram vigilantiam praebuit in novam pulchritudinem et moderatum pervenire compendium.

Δέδωκεν pr. Δέδωκεν ἡμῖν ὁ θεὸς μετὰ τὴν πρὸς Πέρσας εἰρήνη, μετὰ τὸ κατὰ Βανδίλων τρόπαιον καὶ τὴν ὅλην Λιβύης κτῆσιν καὶ τὴν τῆς ὀνομαστοτάτης Καρχηδόνος ἐπανάληψιν καὶ τὸ τῆς ἐπανανεώσεως [τῶν παλαιῶν νόμων ἔργον] εἰς πέρας ἀγαγεῖν.

The Greek version does not match the Latin in splendour, nor is it a literal
translation of the Latin. Ebrard however advanced strong arguments
for the view that the Greek text represents a draft of which the official Latin
text, though not a translation, is an adaptation.[21] He supposed the Greek to
have been compiled partly from the records of the Second Law Commission, under Tribonian's chairmanship, by the Greek professors serving
on it. It is doubtful, however, whether Tribonian would have entrusted the
making even of a draft constitution, especially one of such significance as
Tanta / Δέδωκεν, to a law professor. It is not yet possible to say whether
Δέδωκεν is by the hand of Tribonian or another, since the necessary concordance to the Greek *Novels* is not available. If, however, it should turn
out to be his, this would show that his working language was Greek, and
since Justinian must clearly have seen the draft before the final revision, that
he communicated with the emperor in Greek. On the other hand Tribonian's preference for Latin as the language of the law cannot be denied. Even
when in 535 a radical linguistic change was made and constitutions addressed
to the praetorian prefect of the east were henceforth composed in Greek, he
still represents Justinian as addressing the quaestor (i.e. Tribonian himself)
in Latin.[22] Hence there is some doubt whether Tribonian and Justinian
conversed in Greek or Latin, which was the emperor's first official language.[23] As for Tribonian, the balance of probabilities—no more—favours
Greek as his first official language. In neither case can we be sure of the home
language, which may have been respectively a Thracian or Pamphylian local
dialect.

[21] F. Ebrard, *Das zeitliche Rangverhältnis der Konstitutionen De Confirmatione Digestorum, Tanta und Dedôken*, 40 ZSS (1919) 113–35; Wenger, *Quellen* 579 n. 28; Kübler, *RE* 2.12.2422.

[22] N. 17 (16 April 535), 35 (23 May 535), 23 (3 Jan. 535/6), 75 (= 104), Nov.–Dec. 537.

[23] Rubin, op. cit., 86, 423; to which add N. 13.1.1 (15 Oct. 535), ch. 1 n. 269.

Tribonian was well-educated. Procopius says that the quaestor, whom he contrasts with John of Cappadocia, 'possessed natural ability and was as well-educated as any of his contemporaries'.[24] Lydus describes him as 'very learned'.[25] But it is not easy to say exactly where or by whom he was instructed. His Latin style resembles that of the secretary of pope John II,[26] but this shows no more, perhaps, than the relative uniformity over the Mediterranean of Latin rhetorical education. Further investigation might reveal something more specific of his Greek tutors. As to the law, he must have attended a law school in order to practise before the court of the praetorian prefect of the east, as required by the constitution of Leo.[27] The law school can hardly have been Alexandria or Caesarea, which were to be so harshly criticised in *C. Omnem*,[28] but rather Constantinople or Beirut, which retained their status as recognised law schools after Tribonian's reforms.[29] Of the two the preference must be for Beirut. Tribonian's great interest in classical law would have been more appropriately nourished at Beirut, which was the most famous of all law schools[30] and which had its roots, if not its actual origin, in the age of classical jurisprudence.[31] Beirut, in Phoenice, is reasonably accessible from Pamphylia. Finally, for those at least who see a connection between the career of the second-century writer Gaius and the law school of Beirut, Tribonian's devotion to Gaius, whom he makes Justinian call 'Gaius noster' on three occasions,[32] speaks to his own connection with Beirut. Indeed if the arguments advanced later about the identity of the different members of Tribonian's commission are accepted,[33] we have the following balance among the six main *Digest* commissioners in excerpting the works of Gaius and Paul respectively:

(a) Lines per book

		for Gaius	(b) for Paul	(a) / (b)
A	(Tribonian)	57.3	44.9	127.6
B	(Dorotheus)	94.9	66.7	142.3
C	(Theophilus)	35.6	66.8	41.8
D	(Anatolius)	54.0	70.7	76.4
E	(Constantinus)	26.1	76.6	34.1
F	(Cratinus)	33.4	54.7	61.1

These results depend on a number of hypotheses, but if correct they show that the two Beirut professors, Dorotheus and Anatolius, tended to favour Gaius as against Paul to a greater extent than the two, Theophilus and

[24] *Wars* 1.24.16.

[25] *De Mag.* 3.20. The passage is a lament for the days of the praetorian prefect Sergius (517), and the quaestors Proclus (518–26) and Tribonian.

[26] *CJ* 1.1.8 pr. –6, 25–39 (25 March 534).   [27] *CJ* 2.7.11 (1 Feb. 460).

[28] *C. Omnem* 7 (16 Dec. 533).   [29] Ibid.

[30] P. Collinet, *Histoire de l'école de droit de Beyrouth* (Paris 1925).

[31] Honoré, *Gaius* (Oxford 1962) 85–96.

[32] *Inst.* 4.18.5, *C. Imperatoriam* 6 (21 Nov. 533), *C. Omnem* 1 (16 Dec. 533); ch. 3 n. 766.

[33] Ch. 5 nn. 111f.

Cratinus, from the capital. If the preferences of the two officials also indicate their law-school affiliation, then Tribonian should be assigned to Beirut and Constantinus to Constantinople. But this is only a speculation.

Was Tribonian's learning primarily legal, or do Procopius and Lydus mean to speak more generally? The lawyer will be struck by Tribonian's close acquaintance, as revealed in the constitutions he composed, with the legal sources of every age and kind, private jurists, imperial constitutions, classical and post-classical, pagan and Christian alike. Apart from this he clearly had a good knowledge, for the period, of classical antiquity in general—the institutions and history of the Roman republic and early empire, the history of the eastern Mediterranean. It is a more delicate matter, and beyond my competence, to recognise specific allusions to early Latin and Greek authors outside the law and legal history. The elaborate figure of the temple of justice in *C. Tanta* might be a reminiscence of Ovid[34] or might come from another source. All that can and need be said is that competence in Latin and Greek grammar and rhetoric and in the classical legal sources is an indication of at least a superficial acquaintance with the classical writers in both languages.

The Suda says that Tribonian the quaestor practised before the court of the praetorian prefect (viz. of the east).[35] This was the normal way for an ambitious lawyer who had been through law school to begin his career. The praetorian prefect of the east had an important ordinary and appellate jurisdiction and, if the imperial consistory is left out of account, his court was the leading jurisdiction from the point of view of the matters which came before it, especially fiscal, and of the opportunities for barristers to earn high fees and draw attention to themselves as candidates for political preferment.

Tribonian is next heard of as a member, the sixth senior, of the commission of 13 February 528, set up under John of Cappadocia to draft a code of constitutions to replace the existing three (the *Gregorianus*, *Hermogenianus* and *Theodosianus*) and include the *Novels* (new laws) of Theodosius and his successors to date.[36] He is here described as 'endowed with magisterial dignity *inter agentes*'.[37] This expression means that he was not actually in office but was considered as intermediate in rank between an actual office holder and a merely honorary one. In the terminology of A. H. M. Jones, he was a 'titular' office holder (*vacans*, or *inter agentes*[38]). In any given rank (e.g. the *illustres*) the actual office holders ranked first in order of appointment, followed by the titular holders with a subdivision into those who had received the honour at court and in absence, and then by the honorary

---

[34] *Ex Ponto* 3.6. 23f.

[35] Lexicon τ. 956 (ἀπὸ δικηγόρων τῶν ὑπάρχων). On practice at the bar see Lydus 2.17; Agathias 3.1; Procopius, *SH* 14.11f., 26.1–4.

[36] *C. Haec* (13 Feb. 528).

[37] Ibid. 1 (*virum magnificum magisteria dignitate inter agentes decoratum*).

[38] Jones II. 530–5; *CTh* 6.10.4, 6.22.8 (425), *CJ* 12.18.2 (441), 12.7.2 (Zeno); Koch, *Die byzantinischen Beamtentitel von 400 bis 700* (Jena 1903) 34–45.

appointees with a similar grading. There were exceptions for titular officers, who were given a special commission, and who ranked as active: a complicated system which had grown up over more than a century.

Kübler takes Tribonian to have been *magister officiorum*, master of offices, i.e. active in February 528;[39] Stein also makes him active: *magister memoriae* (master of records) or *magister epistularum* (master of letters).[40] This conclusion Stein reaches by a process of elimination. Constantinus, who is mentioned in *C. Haec* also, was at the time master of petitions and imperial trials (*magister libellorum et sacrarum cognitionum*)[41] and Hermogenes master of offices.[42] But if Tribonian held one of the active civil masterships (offices, records, petitions or letters), why is the specific office not mentioned, as it is for Constantinus? The inference is rather that, at the time of the First Law Commission under John of Cappadocia, Tribonian's magistracy was like the rank held by Constantine, 'count of (imperial) expenditure *inter agentes*',[43] titular, not active. If so, Tribonian was not the only member of the commission not to hold active office at the time: John of Cappadocia, the chairman,[44] and Basilides, number four, are in the same posture:[45] while Thomas, number five, was in office as quaestor of the imperial palace, and Theophilus, number eight, was a professor in Constantinople. Numbers two and three, Leontius[46] and Phocas,[47] are both described as masters of soldiers. This probably implies that both were in active office at the time.

This has some bearing on Tribonian's career, as it has on John's. Both were raised by Justinian, perhaps in his uncle's reign, to high dignities before they were entrusted with important offices. John is already in February 528, by a retrospective fiction of which the Byzantines were fond, an 'ex-quaestor of the imperial palace' (titular not a real quaestorship), consular and patrician.[48] Tribonian is a titular master. In April 531 John became in due course and in reality praetorian prefect of the east.[49] Like Tribonian he was Justinian's protégé, and was given a titular rank so that he could act,

---

[39] *RE* 1.12. 2419.

[40] Stein, *Deux questeurs* 366; Diehl 104; Browning 83. Holmes, 2. 442, creates the office of master of the *agentes in rebus* (viz. secret police) for Tribonian to hold! So also Kübler, *Act. cong. iurid. int. Roma* 1934, 1 (1935) 20.

[41] *C. Haec* 1 (13 Feb. 528 *virum illustrem comitem largitionum inter agentes et magistrum scrinii libellorum sacrarumque cognitionum*). The first rank is titular and the second active: Stein, *Deux questeurs* 366; contra Diehl 104.

[42] Below, nn. 121, 126.   [43] Above, n. 41.

[44] *C. Haec* 1 (13 Feb. 528 *Iohannem virum excellentissimum ex quaestore sacri nostri palatii consularem atque patricium*). One way of conferring honorary rank was to make the honorand, by a fiction, the ex-holder of an office which would confer that rank.

[45] Ibid. (*Basilidem virum excellentissimum ex praefecto praetorio Orientis et patricium.*) This time the past office is probably genuine.

[46] Ibid. (*Leontium virum sublimissimum magistrum militum ex praefecto praetorio consularem atque patricium*). He may be the law professor who taught at Beirut in 487 or 488 and was praetorian prefect under Anastasius: *C. Tanta Δέδωκεν* 9; Lydus 3.17; Collinet, 141–54 and 'La carrière de Léontius'; *Comptes-rendus de l'Académie des Inscriptions et Belles-Lettres* (1921) 77–84.

[47] On Phocas see below, nn. 65–6.   [48] Above, n. 44.

[49] *CJ* 6.27.5, 6.46.6, 6.30.20, 21 etc.

so to speak, as a minister without portfolio for a time before being slotted in to a suitable vacancy in the regular administration. John was however politically the weightier figure: an administrator and fiscal expert against an organiser, propagandist and scholar.[50] He was a patrician by 528, whereas Tribonian attained this dignity, if at all, after 534.[51] Tribonian is recorded with the rank of exconsul on 16 December 533, whereas John is a consular in 528. Tribonian, the scholar, is somewhat in the shadow of John, the ingenious and unpopular administrator.

That Tribonian owed his career to Justinian is clearly recorded in one of the Latin *Novels* (new laws, i.e. those after 534) which he composed for the emperor. Speaking in 537 he makes Justinian describe him as 'your sublimity, whom we have promoted, whom we have put in charge of our endeavours in the field of law, by whose effort and hard work all ambiguity and vagueness in the laws has turned into their present harmony and elegant brevity'.[52]

For a period of fifteen months in 528–9 Tribonian worked on the new code of imperial constitutions. According to his own account of the matter he 'gave proof of his ability' in the course of the work.[53] An attempt is made in a later chapter to identify, in part, his contribution.[54] The resulting *Codex Iustinianus* was promulgated on 7 April 529. Its compilation, in so short a period, was regarded as an outstanding achievement and left a deeper impression on the chroniclers than the codifications of 530–4.[55]

It was perhaps before the publication of the first *Codex* that Justinian began a purge of pagans and heretics in high office.[56] This comprised two steps. First he ordered an investigation into pagan practices by officials.[57] For such practices the penalty was death. Secondly he reinforced the laws against non-believers by enacting that no heretic or pagan might hold public office or succeed to an estate.[58] Three months was allowed for the offenders to embrace orthodox beliefs.[59] If they did so, they might remain in office,

[50] On the rivalry see Stein, *Deux questeurs* 365, summarised in *Studi bizantini e neoellenici* v (Roma 1939) 709.

[51] Below, nn. 156–8.   [52] *N.* 75. 2 (Nov.–Dec. 537).

[53] *C. Deo auctore* 3 (15 Dec. 530).   [54] Below, ch. 7.

[55] Cedrenus 1.646 (2nd year of Justinian = 528–9); Malalas 448B (Indiction 7, 528–9 or perhaps 6, 527–8); Marcellinus anno 531, *Patr. Lat.* 51.917.

[56] On Justinian's persecutions see Diehl 553f.; Bury II. 364f.; Stein, *Deux questeurs* 368; *N.* 37.6 (1 Aug. 535).

[57] *CJ* 1.11.9 (undated: officials and bishops to undertake investigation into pagan practices; bequests for the support of paganism void; previous legislation against pagans confirmed).

[58] *CJ* 11.11.10 (undated: death penalty for relapse; unbaptised debarred from public office or property holding unless they and their families accept the orthodox faith; no pagan to teach or receive public salary; death penalty for pagan sacrifices; those who become orthodox without their families forfeit their goods and public office on the ground of insincerity); cf. Theophanes 1.276; Malalas 449D 451; Cedrenus I. 642. Nothing in *CJ* 1.11.10.2 justifies the closure of the schools of Athens. Were they in fact closed? Alan Cameron *Proc. Camb. Philol. Soc.* (1969) argues not.

[59] Malalas 449D; Theophanes 1.276.

but any relapse was punishable by death.[60] If they failed to become orthodox their property was forfeit, at the end of the three-month period.[61]

The precise date of these events is difficult to determine, partly because the investigative and legislative measures were probably not undertaken at the same time. Malalas is as usual obscure, but seems to place the purge in Indiction 6 or 7,[62] between September 527 and August 529; Theophanes puts it in Indiction 8,[63] late 529. It is conceivable that both are in a sense right, viz. that the three-month time limit expired on 1 September 529. Considerations of style show that the orthodox officials had replaced the pagans and heretics by 17 September 529.[64] Clearly the investigations had begun earlier. In the purge, Thomas, a member of the First Law Commission, was removed from the quaestorship. As his memory was later revered,[65] he cannot have been put to death. Phocas, conceivably identical with the commissioner of that name,[66] was purged but also survived since he became praetorian prefect in 532.[67] Thomas was replaced as quaestor by Tribonian.[68] There was also a change in the praetorian prefecture, Demosthenes for Menas.[69]

These events brought Tribonian to the quaestorship and so gave him responsibility for drafting legislation and acting as the emperor's mouthpiece. The first set of laws which evince the new style was promulgated on 17 September 529. Two months later we find a constitution addressed to him as quaestor.[70]

Tribonian's first quaestorship lasted from about the beginning of

[60] *CJ* 1.11.10 pr.

[61] Theophanes 1.276. Malalas 449D adds that heretics were expelled from Roman territory.

[62] He mentions it after Justinian's codification (448B ἀνακωδίκευσις ἐγένετο τῶν παλαιῶν νόμων: the first use ever of the term codification), but before the return of Hermogenes, master of offices, from Persia (449E), which he places in Indiction 7, and before the consulship of Decius (450C = A.D. 529). As he has previously mentioned (430C) that Justinian's second consulship (A.D. 528) ended in Indiction 7 he may intend to assign the purge to Indiction 7, and the *Codex Iustinianus* undoubtedly belongs to that indiction year (*C. Summa*, 7 Apr. 529), as does the embassy of Hermogenes to the Persian king (Malalas 447A: summer of 529, Bury II. 81 n. 4).

[63] Theophanes I. 276 A.M. 6022, Indiction 8 (Sept.–Dec. 529).

[64] *CJ* 1.2.24 etc. (Demostheni pp.) below, ch. 3 nn. 551–65.

[65] N. 35 pr. (23 May 535) Malalas says of him, Phocas and others that they died (ἐτελεύτησαν), Theophanes that they were caught (συνελήφθησαν), and lost their property (above, n. 58). The penalty depended on the offence (above, nn. 57–8) but Theophanes must be right so far as Thomas and Phocas are concerned.

[66] The man who was purged in 529 (Malalas 449, Theophanes I. 276) was Phocas, son of Craterus, grandson of Salvius, who later became praetorian prefect in 532 (below, nn. 125f.). Lydus 3.72–6 praises his birth, nobility, generosity and asceticism. He says that P. began his career as a silentiary. I do not see why he should not be the *vir eminentissimus magister militum consularis atque patricius Phocas* of *C. Summa* 2 (7 April 529): both patricians. Bury who asserts that he is different (2.368 n. 1) seems to confuse the commissioner Phocas with Basilides, who, unlike Phocas was indeed praetorian prefect of Illyricum at the time of *C. Summa*.

[67] *Wars* 1.24.18.   [68] *CJ* 7.63.5 (17 Nov. 529).   [69] Above, n. 64.

[70] Above, n. 68.

September 529 to 14 January 532, when he was dismissed as a result of the Nika rioting.[71] In the meantime a radical programme of law reform and codification had been launched. Although this was in a sense a continuation of the programme already begun by the First Law Commission under John of Cappadocia, from another point of view it was an innovation. The preparation of an up-to-date book of imperial laws, the *Codex Iustinianus*, had been mainly a practical enterprise. The *Codex* was intended to serve as a handbook for officials, barristers, judges and to some extent laymen who wanted, in a succinct form, the most important legislative texts. It is true that the *Codex* contained, for the period before Constantine, much that was not legislation: more than two thousand imperial rescripts of a declaratory character which were included only because they, like the later legislation, were issued on imperial authority. Even with this qualification, the first commission was largely concerned with offering guidance in litigation, and its main aim purports to be the shortening of lawsuits.[72] The legislation of the first two years of Justinian's reign, in the quaestorship of Thomas, conforms to this general policy. A number of important reforms are undertaken, many of them designed to increase the predictability of legal decisions by improving the rules of evidence.[73]

With the replacement of Thomas by Tribonian a different spirit invaded the quaestor's office. The new quaestor was a scholar. With his advent something in the nature of an academic takeover occurred. The new laws breathe the atmosphere of the study. There are citations from classical jurists, Ulpian and the like.[74] The quaestorship took on a new role, that of solving the legal conundrums left unsettled by the old writers.[75]

The Second Law Commission, which was set up on 15 December 530 under Tribonian's chairmanship, reflects this new spirit. Its objects were primarily scholarly and academic.[76] The best of the past was to be collected, condensed and preserved. But pure scholarship was not the sole consideration. There was a need to revise the system of legal education so as to make it more relevant to modern conditions. This led to the project of producing two books of partly similar and partly differing nature. The *Digest* was to be a textbook of legal education and a repository of ancient learning. The *Institutes* was simply an up-to-date textbook. The first (*Digesta*, *Pandectae*) was planned as an anthology and compendium of private legal writings composed by jurists from Quintus Mucius in the Republic to Arcadius Charisius in the fourth century. In fifty books, it would provide the texts for the future law student, with the exception of the *Institutes*, which he would read in his first year. The latter was planned as an up-to-date version of the *Institutes* of Gaius, the second-century writer.[77]

[71] *Wars* 1. 24.17. [72] *C. Haec* pr. 3 (13 Feb. 528).
[73] Especially *CJ* 1.4.21–4.2.17–4. 20.18–4.21.17–4. 30.14, 15–5.15.3–10.22.5 (1 June 528).
[74] Below, ch. 3 n. 40. [75] Below, ch. 3 nn. 167–71.
[76] Wieacker, *Vom römischen Recht* (1961) 242r. and cf. 55 *ZSS* (1935) 282–305; 102 *Z. ges. Staatsw.* (1942) 462–75.
[77] *C. Deo auctore* 11 (15 Dec. 530), *C. Imperatoriam* 6 (21 Nov. 533).

If the main thrust of the Second Law Commission was to remake the system of legal education, there were a number of subsidiary objects which cannot be left out of account. The new law course was intended to be both more attractive to students and more efficient in preparing them for practice and for public responsibilities, for example as provincial governors and so as judges.[78] Indirectly this would help to preserve Latin culture in the east. An incentive was needed for a Greek-speaking student to take the trouble to learn Latin, and a better course meant a better incentive. With the improved syllabus one could expect an increase in the number of able Greek-speaking candidates who were willing to learn at least enough of the language to read the texts in the original: in contrast the lectures themselves were in Greek.[79] By this means yet another desirable aim could be achieved, that of raising the standard of entrants to the leading bars, especially that of the praetorian prefect of the east.

The *Digest* project was intended also to serve a more immediately practical end. The fifty-book volume, though not easy to refer to, would be a handbook for use by the barristers and judges who wished for fuller information on a point of law than was to be found in the inevitably summary texts of the *Codex Iustinianus*. To look at the matter from another point of view, the existence of such an anthology reduced the danger of surprise in lawsuits. Where previously a barrister might undermine his opponent by citing an obscure and hitherto unnoticed authority, the field of choice was now limited to the texts collected in the *Digest* or *Pandects*, which were considered literally to contain everything capable of being cited in court.[80]

Finally there were the ulterior objects of the enterprise: prestige, preservation and propaganda. These are best set out in the concluding words of *C. Deo Auctore*, the text which set up the Second Law Commission on 15 December 530:[81]

> in maximam et aeternam rei memoriam deique omnipotentis providentiae argumentum nostrique imperii vestrique ministeri gloriam.

The project was to preserve the treasures of the past (*aeterna rei memoria*),[82] to demonstrate, by the accomplishment of a seemingly impossible task, the omnipotence of God and minister to the glory both of Justinian and of Tribonian himself.

How Tribonian organised the work of the commission is set out in a later chapter.[83] He was an excellent organiser. He worked hard, taking a full share of the burden himself,[84] insisted on steady and regular progress[85] and

[78] *C. Imperatoriam* 7 (21 Nov. 533).

[79] Collinet, 212–14, shows that the substitution of Greek for Latin in the lectures at Beirut took place between 381 and 420.

[80] *C. Deo auctore* 5 (15 Dec. 530).   [81] *C. Deo auctore* 14 (15 Dec. 530).

[82] Diehl 251, 'conserver à la postérité' etc., a sharp intuition. Or one could take it as 'to the great and lasting memory of the achievement', the *res* being at the time a future thing, the envisaged compilation. *C. Omnem* 4 (16 Dec. 533) has *et maneat . . . Papiniani et per hoc in aeternum memoria*, perhaps a contemporary parallel.

[83] Below, ch. 4.   [84] *Commissioners* 246f.

[85] *Trail* 530.

was willing to delegate a great deal of responsibility to colleagues whom he trusted as competent lawyers.[86] By these means it was possible to accomplish in three years the completion of the *Digest* and *Institutes*, a task which, when it was first broached was said to be impossible, and later, it was alleged, could not be done in less than ten years.[87]

These comments on the time schedule are taken from *C. Tanta/Dedôken*, which promulgated the *Digest* on 16 December 533. *C. Tanta* at least was drafted by Tribonian.[88] They have a bearing on the question of who was responsible for the launching of the Second Law Commission and the *Digest-Institutes* project. The objection that the *Digest* would take ten years to complete was an argument against its being undertaken at all.

For the project, as it turned out, required the services of the quaestor, the master of petitions and imperial trials (Constantinus), four law professors out of eight in post in the eastern empire and eleven barristers from the praetorian prefect's court.[89] These men could not be spared from their normal duties for ten years. Tribonian met the objections, which no doubt sprang from others of Justinian's advisers, such as John, partly by the energy which enabled him to double the role of quaestor with that of chairman of the commission, partly by ingenious arrangements, described later,[90] which allowed Constantinus and one of the professors, Cratinus, to perform part of their ordinary function and which gave the barristers the opportunity of combining practice with part-time service on the commission.[91] From all this it can be deduced that with another quaestor Justinian would have had to be content with the code of imperial constitutions, perhaps revised from time to time as new laws were added and old ones repealed. Tribonian's personality and abilities were at least a sine qua non of the *Digest-Institutes* project. But so was Justinian's overweening ambition. Most emperors would not have wished to sponsor, evidently against the advice of at least some officials, such a far-ranging reform in the interests of scholarship and of a small group of academically-minded lawyers and bureaucrats. He, on the other hand, was determined to outdo Theodosius II, who had been forced to abandon a similar, though less ambitious project, in the 430s,[92] the more so as the Visigoths had by now granted their Roman subjects a code of laws,[93] based on the code of Theodosius and combining, though in an unscholarly way, imperial laws with private legal writings of authority.

Nostri imperii vestrique ministeri gloria[94] is crucial. The project required the

---

[86] Above, n. 84.

[87] *C. Tanta* Δέδωκεν 12 (16 Dec. 533). The Greek version is more explicit.

[88] Below, ch. 3 nn. 635–48.

[89] *C. Tanta* 9 = Tribonian, Constantinus, professors Theophilus (Constantinople), Dorotheus (Beirut), Anatolius (Beirut), Cratinus (Constantinople), barristers Stephanus, Menas, Prosdocius, Eutolmius, Timotheus, Leonides, Leontius, Plato, Iacobus, Contantinus, and Iohannes.

[90] Ch. 5 p. 169.   [91] Below, Appendix I and *Trail* 53of.

[92] *CTh* 1.1.5 (26 March 429).   [93] Lex Romana Visigothorum (506).

[94] *C. Deo auctore* 14 (15 Dec. 530).

combination of two able and ambitious men of contrasting abilities, Justinian to provide the political weight and Tribonian to execute an apparently over-ambitious undertaking. So is *dei omnipotentis providentiae argumentum*.[95] In a sense it is not too fanciful to see in the success of the Second Law Commission an encouragement for the invasion of Vandal North Africa, which was to come in 533 when the success of the scholarly enterprise was already assured. The desperate character of the *Digest* project is emphasised both before and after the event. In December 530 we are told that the project 'which no one (else) has dared to hope to achieve or to decide on, seemed to us a most difficult, indeed an impossible, task. But we stretched our hands to heaven and invoked eternal aid, and so placed this task too in our intentions, relying on God, who can by his mighty power grant ultimate success in quite desperate enterprises.'[96] By November 533 'we have by heaven's favour fulfilled a desperate task, walking as it were on the deep'[97] and again in December 533 it is said of the completion of the *Digest* that 'no one before our reign ever hoped or really believed that it was within the bounds of human possibility'.[98] This repeated emphasis leads to the inference that for Justinian the demonstration of God's omnipotence and favour to himself was not the least of what he sought from the timely completion of the *Digest*. If with God's help the impossible becomes possible in a legal, why not in a military, enterprise? It is not too much to think that Justinian was emboldened, when the Vandal crisis came in 533, to override the advice of John of Cappadocia and the military,[99] by the thought that he had by then the assurance that one impossible enterprise at least had come to fruition.[100]

Le goût de l'impossible. Since *Deo auctore* antedates, while North Africa postdates, the Nika rebellion, this taste was not the by-product of that miraculous catastrophe. The disposition to undertake something like the *Digest* project may well have been in Justinian's mind from the beginning of his reign if not before. The decision to carry it out came later; it can hardly antedate Tribonian's quaestorship. Pringsheim argued that, since we know from a papyrus[101] that the first *Codex Iustinianus* retained Valentinian's law of citations the *Digest* project could not have been in mind in 528–9.[102] Valentinian's enactment laid down the rules for deciding a point of law in controversy among the old writers when imperial constitutions did not

---

[95] Ib.   [96] *C. Deo auctore* 2 (15 Dec. 530).   [97] *C. Imperatoriam* 2 (21 Nov. 533).
[98] *C. Tanta* pr. (16 Dec. 533).   [99] *Wars* 3. 10. 2–21.
[100] The immediate occasion of the invasion was Gelimer's action in killing and confiscating the property of Roman subjects in the Vandal kingdom. But Justinian did not always react boldly, not for example at the time of Nika. Now he did. For the timing: the draft *Digest* was completed not later than the end of March 533 (below, ch. 5 n. 180) and the Roman forces set sail about the same time (*Wars* 3.12.1). 'Among those who witnessed their sailing perhaps most who were competent to judge believed they would never return': Bury II. 129.
[101] *P. Oxy.* 1814.
[102] F. Pringsheim, 'Die Entstehungszeit des Digestenplanes und die Rechtsschulen', *Atti del Cong. int. di dir. rom.*, Roma 1933:1 (1934) 449f. = *Ges. Abh.* 2 (1961) 41f.

cover the point.[103] If the *Digest* project was already envisaged these rules would shortly be out of date and so had no place in the *Codex*.

Pringsheim was both wrong and right. He was wrong in that, even had Justinian decided in 528 to proceed in due course to a compendium of the learned law contained in the writers, he would have been forced to retain the law of citations, or something similar, as an interim measure for deciding cases until the new compendium was ready. But he was right in another sense. The *Digest* project could not have been undertaken until Tribonian was quaestor. Thomas could not have directed it, and unless we suspect Justinian of a cynical manoeuvre, the masquerade of a purge in the summer of 529 in order to replace Thomas by Tribonian, Justinian could not have decided to proceed with it until Thomas left. After all, Thomas might have recanted and embraced orthodoxy.

When exactly was the decision taken? It may have been at any time between September 529 and August 530 when the series of constitutions known as the Fifty Decisions begin.[104] These are intended to solve controversies among the old jurists as a preliminary to putting together a compendium of their writings. My inclination is to favour a later rather than an earlier date, 530 rather than 529. Tribonian had to argue his case. There were obstacles: time, expense, precious manpower, hostility to Latin. The enterprise was 'in the beginning beyond all hope and later, when we had shown that the project was feasible, it was thought that it would not be finished compiling in ten years'.[105] The new quaestor argued, I believe, in advance of the project that it could be done in three.[106] By the middle of 530, at the latest, Justinian accepted his case.[107]

Though the details of Tribonian's chairmanship of the Second Law Commission are best dealt with later,[108] the general character of his contribution may be set out in his own words in *C. Tanta*, when the project was complete. In the description which he puts into Justinian's mouth, Tribonian is 'a man distinguished for his literary style and knowledge of the law, who shines in practical affairs and who has always made the execution of our instructions his first priority'.[109] The self-praise is not an overstatement, unless to those who, as a matter of taste, find his prose disagreeable.

Before the *Institutes* were published in November and the *Digest* in

---

[103] *CTh* 1.4.3 (7 Nov. 426).   [104] Ch. 5 nn. 24f.

[105] *C. Δέδωκεν* 12 (16 Dec. 533).

[106] Otherwise Justinian would not have authorised it. But there is a widespread view to the contrary, e.g. Holmes II. 722 'to their surprise the work advanced more rapidly than expected' etc. On the detailed time-table see ch. 5.

[107] Rubin sees a connection between the victory at Daras (June 530: Theophanes I. 277 A.M. 6022 Indiction 8) and the *Digest* project. This, if correct (and it is psychologically plausible) is another argument for a late date; cf. de Francisci, *Storia del diritto romano* 3.1 (1936–9) 257, not seeing the relation of the Fifty Decisions to the *Digest* project; F. Pringsheim, op. cit.; Soubie, *Recherches sur les origines des rubriques du Digeste* (1960), 20; P. Pescani, 'Il piano del digesto e la sua attuazione', 77 *BIDR* (1974) 229.

[108] Below, chs. 4–6.

[109] *C. Tanta* 9 (16 Dec. 533 *qui similiter eloquentiae et legitimae scientiae artibus decoratus et in ipsis rerum experimentis emicuit nihilque maius nec carius nostris unquam iussionibus duxit*).

December 533, Tribonian's political career suffered a temporary setback. Between 20 February and 30 May 530[110] Julian was dismissed from the praetorian prefecture and replaced by John of Cappadocia, whose ingenuity in raising new taxes and increasing the yield of old, not to mention his taste for administrative economy, aroused the resentment of the senatorial aristocracy and of others. According to Procopius, whose *Wars* and *Secret History* are as usual concordant in substance and this time in tone, Tribonian as quaestor 'was determined to enrich himself and was always ready to sell justice for gain. His general practice was to repeal some laws each day and propose others, selling both repeals and new laws to those who wanted them according to their needs.'[111]

It is always difficult with Procopius to fix the precise measure of truth in a given statement. This passage from the *Wars* was published openly in Justinian's lifetime and so cannot have been such as to cause the emperor grave offence. There is something in the accusations of bribery, and when Tribonian died, leaving a family, Justinian is said to have confiscated part of his property as a penalty.[112] Perhaps Tribonian shared the faults, as well as the virtues, of Lord Chancellor Bacon, whom in many ways he closely resembles.[113] A man of superior intellect may think himself above moral inhibitions. In his defence he might, like the Chancellor, urge that the repeals or innovations were laudable in their own right, apart from any pecuniary inducement. In any case, both Justinian and Tribonian looked at law empirically. It was not a texture of sacred dogma, like the Christian religion, but a series of expedients, like medicine.[114] If one does not cure, another can be tried. Highly intelligent people change their minds. From the details of his legislation one can infer that Tribonian sympathises with the man who pays a debt uncertain whether it is due,[115] or who pays money for a purpose which he later wishes not to pursue.[116] Indeed, he develops in several contexts the legal doctrine of *locus poenitentiae*.[117] One may infer that even without bribes the legislation of Tribonian's quaestorship would have charted a zigzag course.

The bribes augmented the aura of uncertainty and the resentment of

[110] *CJ* 2.58.2 etc. (20 Feb. 531 Iuliano pp.), 6.27.5 etc. (30 April 531 Iohanni pp.), Malalas 465B.

[111] *Wars* 1.24.16; cf. *SH* 20.16; Malalas 475B.   [112] *SH* 20.17.

[113] As Gibbon notes: ch. 44 nn. 72–4.

[114] References to legislation as remedial (with *remedium*, θεραπεύειν etc.): explicitly in *N.* 111 pr. (1 June 541) and cf. *CJ* 4.1.12.3 (30 Oct. 529), 7.63.5.1c (17 Nov. 529), 8.33.3 pr. (18 March 530), 5.70.7.4 (1 Sept. 530), 5.13.1.15a (1 Nov. 530), 5.16.27.1 (1 Dec. 530), 2.58.2.8a (20 Feb. 531), 7.17.2 pr. (1 Sept. 531), 6.23.30 (18 Oct. 531), 7.6.1.2, 2.40.5.1 (1 Nov. 531), 7.54.3.2 (27 Nov. 531), *C. Tanta* 18 (16 Dec. 533), 4.35.23.3 bis; 7.2.15.1a, 4; 5.3.20 (Iohanni pp.); 7.39.9 (Demostheni pp.), *N.* 3 pr. 3; 4.1 (16 March 535), 136.2 (1 April 535), 8 ep. (15 April 535), 23 pr. (3 Jan. 536), 39 pr. (17 April 536), 60 pr. (1 Dec. 537), 73 ep., 74 ep. (4 June 538), 89 ep. (1 Sept. 539), edict 9.5 (undated).

[115] *CJ* 4.5.11 (1 Oct. 530).

[116] *D.* 12.4.5 (Ulp. 2 disp.) has been interpolated along these lines.

[117] *Inst.* 3.23 pr.; Kaser, *Das römische Privatrecht* 2 (1959) 269 n. 51.

those affected by changes, for example, in the law of succession.[118] The great families felt resentment against the two upstarts, John and Tribonian, for upsetting tax exemptions and family settlements. In January 532 an opportunity came for this resentment to be given practical expression.

Before becoming emperor Justinian supported the fans of the Blue circus faction against the Greens and allowed them to dominate the streets in many towns of the empire.[119] After his accession he resolved on the impartial suppression of violence and so instructed his officials.[120] Eudaemon, prefect of the city of Constantinople, tried to put this into practice and sentenced seven members of both factions to death.[121] By a hangman's blunder one Green and one Blue survived and took refuge in the church of St Laurentius across the Horn. Eudaemon sent soldiers to guard them: it was Sunday 11 January.

The Greens at least were already in a state of unrest. They had, it seems, previously protested in the hippodrome against one Kalepodios.[122] Their exchanges with the official spokesman have been preserved. Now the Blues were also dissatisfied, and when on Tuesday the racing in the hippodrome of Byzantium began, the crowd, with both factions in concert, took the opportunity to ask for mercy. Justinian was present but foolishly failed to respond. It was now that he paid the penalty for his new-found impartiality, because the Blues, instead of directing their hostility towards the Greens, combined with them under the watchword Nika ('conquer'). Still unable to secure the pardon of the condemned men, they broke into the city

---

[118] Restrictions on rights of patrons *CJ* 6.4.3 (30 Oct. 529), 4 (1 Dec. 531); changes in formalities of wills *CJ* 6.23.27 (18 March 530), 28 (28 March 530), 29 (20 Feb. 531), 30 (18 Oct. 531); settlements and conditions 6.25.7 (22 July 530), 8 (29 July 531), 9 (29 July 531), 10 (29 July 531), 6.26.10 (29 July 531), 11 (29 July 531), 6.27.4 (17 Nov. 530), 5 (30 April 531), 6 (29 July 531); disinheritance 6.28.4 (1 Sept. 531), 6.29.3 (17 Nov. 530), 4 (17 Nov. 530); acceptance or rejection of an inheritance 6.30.19 (30 Oct. 530), 20 (30 April 531), 21 (30 April 531), 22 (27 Nov. 531); taking possession 6.33.3 (18 March 531); disqualifications for taking 6.35.11 (30 April 531); legacies 6.36.23 (17 Nov. 530), 24 (30 April 531), 25 (1 Nov. 531); interpretation 6.38.3 (20 Feb. 531), 4 (30 April 531); duties of widows 6.40.2 (20 Feb. 531), 3 (1 Nov. 531); fideicommissa 6.42.30 (30 Oct. 529), 31 (30 April 531), 32 (17 Nov. 531), 6.43.1 (17 Sept. 529), 2 (20 Feb. 531), 3 (1 Sept. 531), 6.46.6 (30 April 531), 6.49.7 (18 Oct. 530); mothers' rights of succession 6.57.5 (17 Sept. 529), 6 (1 Oct. 530); intestacy 6.58.12 (18 Oct. 530), 13 (1 Nov. 531), 14 (27 Nov. 531), 6.59.11 (17 Sept. 529). It was clearly impossible for a family with property to keep pace with the changes in the law and adjust its testamentary dispositions accordingly.

[119] *SH* 7.1–38. On the nature of these fan-clubs, see Alan Cameron, *Byz. Zeit.* 76 (1974) 74; *Circus Factions* (1976).

[120] P. Karlin-Hayter, 'Les Akta dia Kalapodion', *Byzantion* 43 (1973) 87, 103, denies this except for political offences.

[121] Bury II. 39–48 and Stein II. 449–56 contain clear accounts, for which the main sources are Malalas 473; Theophanes 1.181; Evagrius 4.13; *Chron. Pasch.* 620; Zonaras 2.271; Marcellinus anno 532 (=*Patr. Lat.* 51. 917f.); Victor Tonnensis anno 530; Zacharias Scholasticus 188; Cedrenus 1.674; *Wars* 1.24.

[122] The *Akta dia Kalapodion* is the record, preserved by the Green secretariat, of the demonstration: Theophanes 1.181–4; P. Maas, 'Metrische Akklamationen der Byzantiner', *Byzantium* 21 (1912) 28. According to Cameron, *Circus Factions* 318f. it was not connected with the Nika revolt.

prison, released the convicts and turned to arson. On Wednesday fourteen more races were due. The crowd now put forward political, not merely factional or humanitarian, demands. They demonstrated against Eudaemon, John of Cappadocia and Tribonian. The emperor was not at the hippodrome, but the demands were reported to him by Basilides and others. This time Justinian decided to yield. The three ministers, unpopular with different classes of the population for very different reasons, left office. The concession merely whetted the appetite of certain senators, who on the Thursday determined to rid themselves of Justinian in favour of a more pliable ruler. They tried to proclaim Probus, one of the nephews of Anastasius, but he was out of town.

For the next three days inconclusive street fighting took place between troops loyal to Justinian and the insurgents. On the Saturday the emperor blundered again. He feared treachery from the senators in the palace and especially from Hypatius and Pompeius, two other nephews of Anastasius. So he dismissed them all from the palace. On the Sunday Justinian tried to imitate Anastasius.[123] Descending to the hippodrome he promised on the gospels to grant an unconditional amnesty. The manoeuvre was a failure. Unlike Anastasius, respected even by his ideological enemies, Justinian had a well-deserved reputation for duplicity. Now the crowd discovered that Hypatius and Pompeius had left the palace. They fetched Hypatius and forced him to be proclaimed emperor. It was the turn of Hypatius to make a mistake. He went to the hippodrome and took his place in the imperial Kathisma, within striking distance of the palace. Justinian, inclined to escape by sea, was persuaded by Theodora to stay and fight. At last the emperor acted decisively. He sent Narses to distribute bribes to the Blues in order to win back part at least of his factional support. He sent two generals, Belisarius and Mundus, to intimidate and if necessary attack the demonstrators. Killing, it is said, 30,000 or more, they restored order.

Hypatius and Pompeius were executed on Monday 19 January. Eighteen or more senators were punished by confiscation of their property and/or banishment.[124]

John of Cappadocia was replaced by Phocas, perhaps the man who was a member of the First Law Commission,[125] a patrician whom Procopius calls 'a clever man, well-fitted to preside over the administration of justice'.[126] Phocas' unorthodoxy was not held against him in the emergency. But in 546 another purge instigated by John of Ephesus uncovered his persistent paganism, and he committed suicide rather than face the inquisition.[127]

---

123 On 7 Nov. 512 Anastasius appeared in the hippodrome and, offering to resign the throne, appeased the revolt of the orthodox against his monophysite proclivities. Marcellinus anno 512, *Chron. Pasch.* 1. 609–10 B.C., Evagrius iii 44 = *Patr. Gr.* 86.2. 2698–9.

124 *Wars* 1.24.56, 57.

125 *C. Haec* 1 (13 Apr. 528 *virum eminentissimum magistrum militum consularem atque patricium*), *C. Summa* (7 Apr. 529, same).

126 *Wars* 1.24.18; Lydus 3. 72f.

127 Malalas 449: *Chron. Pasch.* 621. Still 'glorious' on 6 April 539 (*N.* 82.1.1). In the end he was buried like a donkey, without cortège or prayer: Diehl 556.

Basilides, also a commissioner on the First Law Commission[128] became quaestor: 'well-known among the patricians for his sense of equity and of good reputation.'[129] Justinian had temporarily to replace the upstarts by patricians. The reshuffle did not last long. By 18 October 532 John is again praetorian prefect[130] and Tribonian is drafting the constitutions addressed to him, though not as quaestor.[131]

The Nika rebellion had only a slight impact on the progress of the Second Law Commission. Tribonian remained chairman and in that capacity composed the laws which the commission's work called forth, including the prefaces *Imperatoriam, Omnem* and *Tanta* which accompanied the promulgation of the *Institutes* and *Digest* in November and December 533.[132] Not one constitution can with certainty be ascribed to Basilides.[133] He was an insurance policy rather than a quaestor.

At the time of Nika the Commission was still excerpting the old authorities. Its disruptive effect can be seen in the work of Constantinus, chairman of the Papinian committee, who was at the same time master of petitions and imperial trials. As we shall find in a later chapter, Constantinus' rate of excerpting declined sharply in the five and a half months after Nika.[134] He was of course responsible for preparing for the emperor's court—the consistory—the cases against the eighteen senators whose property was ultimately confiscated and no doubt against others who in the outcome were luckier. This time-consuming and delicate labour was responsible for some deficiencies in the *Digest*, for example the fact that it contains few excerpts from certain books of Scaevola's *digesta*.[135]

The commission over which Tribonian presided, after excerpting the classical legal writings, preparing a draft of the *Digest* and revising that draft, turned to the preparation of a new first-year students' textbook, the *Institutes* of Justinian. For this purpose a sub-committee of three was sufficient, and the student primer was put together by Tribonian, Theophilus and Dorotheus.[136] The *Institutes* had been planned or at least envisaged as part of the project in 530.[137] The same is not true of the second edition of the *Codex*, which was called for because the number of reforming constitutions made necessary by the commission's work turned out far to exceed the 50 which the title 'Fifty Decisions' implied would suffice.[138] In the event there were over three times as many,[139] and the first *Codex Iustinianus* was no longer really serviceable.

---

[128] *C. Haec* 1 (13 Feb. 528), *C. Summa* 2 (7 April 529).
[129] *SH* 1.24.18; *Chron. Pasch.* 621D. A man the patricians liked.
[130] *CJ* 3.10.3 (18 Oct. 532) etc.   [131] Below, ch. 3 nn. 589–605.   [132] Ib.
[133] Below, ch. 3 n. 587 and ch. 8 n. 155.   [134] Below, ch. 5 n. 122.
[135] *Commissioners* 264–5.   [136] *C. Imperatoriam* 3 (21 Nov. 533).
[137] *C. Deo auctore* 11 (15 Dec. 530).   [138] *C. Cordi* 1 (16 Nov. 534).
[139] There are 154 Latin constitutions referable to the work of the commission between 1 Aug. 530 and 14 Jan. 532, 27 between then and 16 Nov. 534, 4 prefaces, 185 in all, omitting 11 undated constitutions of Justinian's reign drafted by Tribonian before 16 Nov. 534 (below, ch. 3 nn. 657–68). I have counted as separate constitutions those which are reproduced separately in *CJ*, even if originally joined together.

For this reason, after the *Digest* and *Institutes* were finished, another sub-committee of the commission,[140] consisting of Tribonian and Dorotheus with the help of three of the barristers who had worked on the *Digest*, were authorised to prepare a second edition of the *Codex*. Two of the barristers were the most junior of the original eleven (Constantinus and Iohannes), the third the second senior, Menas. The working method was to amend and fill in a copy of the first edition.[141] This was presented to Justinian, who ordered a new edition to be made from the amended text. It was promulgated on 16 November 534.[142]

The constitution which did this, drafted of course by Tribonian, describes him as 'the agent of our work in the sphere of law': *legitimi operis nostri minister*.[143] That described the situation of fact. Nominally, however, Tribonian was not yet quaestor for the second time. It is true that he had advanced some steps on the ladder of rehabilitation. On 21 November 533 he is described as *magister* and *ex quaestor*.[144] The magistracy may still be titular, *inter agentes*. But on 16 December of the same year he is *magister officiorum et ex quaestore sacri nostri palatii et ex consule*.[145] The reward for the successful completion of the 'impossible' *Digest* is therefore the post of master of offices, administrative head of the civil service, and an honorary exconsulship. His rank and office have not changed by 16 November 534.[146] But if E. Stein is right in dating *Novel* 23 to 3 January 535 rather than 536, Tribonian was again quaestor on that date.[147] He briefly combined the post with that of master of offices, but by 16 March 535 Hermogenes was restored to the mastership.[148] On grounds of style it is likely that Tribonian was responsible for the legislation of 1 January 535.[149] Hence the evidence of style fits the conclusions of E. Stein. Justinian, it seems, restored Tribonian to the quaestorship as he all along intended, as soon as the work of the Second Law Commission was finished.

The second quaestorship is evidenced by texts of 16 April[150] and 23 May 535.[151] Hermogenes died sometime before 18 March 536, by which date he

---

[140] *C. Cordi* 2 (16 Nov. 534).   [141] *C. Cordi* 4 (16 Nov. 534).

[142] Noticed by the *Chronicon Paschale* 633D (Justiniano IV et Paulinos conss = A.D. 534).

[143] *C. Cordi* 2 (16 Nov. 534).

[144] *C. Imperatoriam* 3 (21 Nov. 533). But on 17 Nov. 533 (*CJ* 1.3.53 etc.) Hermogenes was *magister officiorum*.

[145] *C. Tanta* pr. (16 Dec. 533).   [146] *C. Cordi* 2 (16 Nov. 534).

[147] Stein II. excursus K; *N.* 23 (*Triboniano illustri magistro officiorum et quaestori sacri palatii*).

[148] *N.* 2 (16 March 535). On Hermogenes, in turn Justinian's general, ambassador and trouble-shooter see *RE* 8.1 'Hermogenes' no. 20 (Benjamin); Procopius, *Wars* 1. 13.10.12f., 19f., 35; 1.14.1f., 20f., 44, 53; 1.16.10; 1.18.16; 1.21; 1.10.23; 1.22.16. Malalas 445, 447–9, 452, 461, 465–8, 471, 477; Theophanes *A.M.* 6021 (I. 274 528 A.D.) 6022 (I. 276 = 529 A.D.), *Chron. Pasch.* 621; Marcellinus ad. 533; *Zach. Rhet.* 9.7.17; *CJ* 1.3.53 (=9.13.1), 5.17.11, 7.24.1, 11.48.24; *N.* 138 (a rescript by Justinian to him about his private affairs); 10 (16 Apr. 535), and below, n. 152; Stein, *Deux questeurs* 369.

[149] Below, ch. 3 nn. 678–80.   [150] *N.* 17 (16 April 535).

[151] *N.* 35 (23 May 535).

is 'of glorious memory'[152] and Basilides, familiar face, goes to the offices.[153] Tribonian remains quaestor in November/December 537 when Justinian conferred on him a special mark of favour. He was given the right to hear civil and administrative appeals from Sicily on the emperor's behalf.[154] Tribonian here pays himself some vicarious compliments of notable warmth. By his effort and hard work all ambiguity and vagueness in the laws has been turned into their present harmony and elegant brevity.[155]

It is possible that as a reward for his services he was made a patrician. Though none of the texts mentions this, Diehl[156] reproduces a seal of Tribonian with on the obverse + *theo | tokeb | oethe* + (i.e. *theotoke, boêthe*, 'Mother of God, help me') and on the reverse + *tri | bou | pat*. The latter could be taken as *tribo. hupat* or *tribou. pat.*, 'Tribonian (ex) consul'[157] or 'Tribonian patrician'. The lettering, however, suggests the latter interpretation. If the seal is the quaestor's, as Diehl takes it, he achieved the patriciate in the latter part of his career, since otherwise it should be mentioned in the prefaces to the codification.[158]

During his second quaestorship Tribonian's position relative to John of Cappadocia seems to have been weaker than during his first. John had had less than a year as praetorian prefect before Nika, but he was restored to office before Tribonian.[159] The changed position after 535 is shown in two ways. One is that constitutions addressed to the praetorian prefect of the east are now always in Greek whereas before they were nearly always in Latin.[160] Lydus, a vehement supporter of the use of Latin in the central administration, and especially in legal texts, makes it clear that John favoured Greek.[161] From the point of view of administrative efficiency, which was John's forte, there was everything to be said for Greek. Lydus tells us, for example, that when Phocas was made praetorian prefect he, Lydus, had to find him a tutor so that he could learn Latin.[162] But the use of Greek, besides being contrary to tradition, undermined the status of the

---

[152] *N.* 22.46 pr. (18 March 536).

[153] *N.* 22 copy = *Corp. Iur. Civ.* 3.186 (18 March 536.).

[154] *N.* 75 = 104 (Nov./Dec. 537).

[155] Above, n. 52. In Tribonian's second quaestorship the office is mentioned chiefly in connection with its appellate jurisdiction, in *N.* 7.9 pr. (15 April 535), 24.4, 25.5.3, 26.5 pr., 27.2 (18 May 535), 28.8, 29.5 pr. (16 July 535), 20 (18 March 536), 30.10 (18 March 536), 50.1 (1 Sept. 537), 53.2 (1 Oct. 537), 114 (1 Nov. 541).

[156] Diehl, 103.

[157] Above, nn. 147–8 and *C. Tanta* 9; *C. Δέδωκεν* pr., 9; *C. Omnem* 2.

[158] The patrician status of John, Leontius, Phocas and Basilides is mentioned in *C. Haec* 1 (13 Feb. 528) and *C. Summa* 2 (7 April 529). The Second Law Commission contained no patricians.

[159] For John's second prefecture see *CJ* 3.10.3 (18 Oct. 532 Iohanni pp.) etc. For Tribonian's rehabilitation see above, nn. 140–5.

[160] Below, ch. 4 nn. 87–104.

[161] Lydus 3.68, referring particularly to John's encroachment, with the result that 'since that time everyone drafts documents about matters of which he is completely ignorant'.

[162] Lydus 3.73.

quaestor and the staff of the central offices (*scrinia*), whose expertise in Latin suddenly became less important.

Tribonian fought for Latin. Some details of the linguistic battle are considered later.[163]

E. Stein has drawn attention to some other aspects of the rivalry between the two.[164] A constitution of June 534, when Tribonian was master of offices and John praetorian prefect, requires imperial instructions (viz. in fiscal matters) addressed to the duke or *augustalis* (in Egypt) or to provincial governors to be registered and approved in the prefect's office, failing which they are void.[165] The measure was directed against the master of offices, who was normally responsible for the dispatch of these documents.

Another constitution addressed to John, which is undated but similar in purport,[166] forbids any minister except the praetorian prefect to issue summonses to *curiales* or *officiales* in the provinces to appear in Constantinople or another province, and thereby (given their tax liability) endanger the interests of the treasury. Exception is made only for a summons issued by the emperor (viz. via the master of offices) specifically requiring this and then only with approval of the praetorian prefect.[167]

Tribonian tried to protect his subordinates, especially those who had kept the records of the Second Law Commission, but had to be content with a compromise. The five men in question (Theodosius, Epictetus, Quirillus, Sabbatius and Perigene) from the office of records (*memoriales*) were supernumerary to the quaestor's establishment of assistants (*adiutores*).[168] There was clearly pressure from the praetorian prefect, interested in economy, to reduce the numbers attached to the quaestor to the twenty-six established posts. Although the text of 535, when Tribonian was quaestor,[169] puts a brave face on it, all that he was able to secure was that, if any of the established staff wished to resign their office and had no heir or son willing and capable of succeeding to it, the five should, on offering 100 *solidi*, have a prior right to fill the post.[170]

By a law of Theodosius II the records of appeals from the *iudices spectabiles* were kept by the staff of the office of letters (*epistulares*), a valuable prerogative.[171] When Justinian reformed the system of appeals,[172] Tribonian being quaestor and John praetorian prefect, they lost this function to the staff of the praetorian prefecture (*praetoriani*) and secured only a rather miserable consolation prize, the right to share with the praetorian officials the servicing of appeals from the *comes Orientis*.[173]

[163] Below, ch. 4 and *N.* 66.1.2 (1 May 538); Lydus 2.12, 3.68, *CSHB* 177–8.
[164] Stein, *Deux questeurs* 369–61.   [165] *N.* 152 (1 June 524).
[166] *N.* 151. The date may be earlier than 1 June 534 when *N.* 152 also addressed to John prescribed that imperial ordinances addressed to provincial governors should be invalid unless first registered with the praetorian prefect. It baldly asserts that a contrary practice would be absurd (ἄτοπος).
[167] *N.* 151.1 above.   [168] *N.* 35.8 (23 May 535).   [169] *N.* 35.4 (23 May 535).
[170] *N.* 35.8–10 (23 May 535).   [171] *CJ* 7.62.32.2 (Theo. et Val. Cyro pp.).
[172] *N.* 23 (3 Jan. 536 or 535).   [173] *N.* 20.7 (18 March 536).

All in all, John had the better of the administrative tussles.

Tribonian held the quaestorship until his death[174] but is not otherwise mentioned in the sources after 537. His career must be traced henceforth from the internal evidence of style or from undated references by the historians. The first leads to the conclusion that the last constitution composed by him is either, as E. Stein would prefer, *N.* 114 of 1 November 541 or, as I believe, *N.* 157 of 1 May 542. The evidence is set out in a later chapter.[175] It is appropriate here to advert rather to the evidence of Procopius.

There are two items in Procopius which may help to fix the date of Tribonian's death. In the *Secret History* he says that when Tribonian died he was succeeded by Junilus, who held the quaestorship for no less than seven years.[176] Junilus died and was succeeded by Constantinus, who amassed a large fortune in a short time and behaved in an intolerable way.[177]

An earlier generation of scholars, believing the *Secret History* to have been written in 558–9, placed Tribonian's death, though without giving reasons, in 545 or 546.[178] Haury showed that this was incorrect and concluded that the *Secret History* was composed in 550.[179] This has been generally accepted, but is not quite accurate. Procopius, drawing a distinction between reigning and governing, says that Justinian had already been *governing* for thirty-two years at the time of writing.[180] Haury showed that his government, as opposed to his reign, dates from Justin's accession.[181] Since Justin was elected on 9 July 518[182] the *Secret History* is being written after 8 July 550. But there is no reason why it should not have been composed in whole or in part in 551, since until 9 July 551 it remained true that Justinian's government had lasted thirty-two not thirty-three years. All that can be said against

---

[174] *Wars* 1.25.2; *SH* 20.17.   [175] Ch. 4 pp. 2–14.   [176] Chs 4, 9, 11, ch. 8 nn. 159f.
[177] Below, ch. 8 nn. 193f.

[178] 546: Krueger, *Geschichte der Quellen des römischen Rechts* (2nd ed. 1912) 367, 545; Rudorff, *Römische Rechtsgeschichte* 1. 296; Puchta, *Instit.* 1[10]. 388; Kroll, *CJC* 3. 776, 544–5; Diehl, 105.

[179] J. Haury, *Procopiana* 1 = *Jahresbericht des Königlich bayerischen Realgymnasiums zu Augsburg* (1890–1) 9f.

[180] Διοίκησις, βασίλεια: *SH* 24.29. The other references to 32 years having passed (*SH* 18.33, 23.1, 24.33) are to be interpreted in the same sense. Texts showing that in Procopius' opinion Justinian *governed* when Justin ruled include *Buildings* 1.3.3; *SH* 6.19, 12.29.

[181] Above, n. 180 and *SH* 6.26 (not yet ten days in power when he killed Amantius). Amantius was put to death at the beginning of Justin's reign since he had given money to Justin to distribute to his troops in order to secure the election of a puppet. Theocritus (Malalas 410; *Chron. Pasch.* anno 518; Marcellinus anno 519; *Zach. Schol.* 9.1; Cedrenus 1. 637–8). It is true that there are authorities who place the killing of Amantius in 519 (Victor Tonnensis ad 519 = *Patr. Lat.* 68. 941). But since Justin had double-crossed Amantius, a speedy dispatch was called for. Procopius, loc. cit., alleging that there was no reason for the killing, is hypocritical. Other writers dated Justinian's government from the murder of Vitalian (July 520): Bury II. 21: Zonaras *Epit. hist.* 14.5. 34.

[182] *Chron. Pasch.* 611B.

this is that Procopius does not mention the truce with Persia of 551,[183] nor Justinian's subsidy to Chosroes on that occasion,[184] nor the devastating earthquakes of that year.[185] But we do not know exactly when in 551 these events occurred, nor would Procopius, if he had already begun the book, necessarily retrace his steps to mention them.

This has some bearing on the date of Tribonian's death, which on Procopius' account should be situated at least seven years before 9 July 551, i.e. before 9 July 544. This can be accepted as a rough *terminus ad quem*, though the 'seven years' of Procopius looks, in light of the evidence of style, an exaggeration.[186] Some time must be allowed for Constantinus to amass his fortune.

The other passage of Procopius follows his account of the Nika rebellion. The historian points out that Tribonian and John were later both restored to their former offices. 'And Tribonian lived on in office for many years and received no unpleasant treatment from anyone. He died of a disease. For he was smooth and agreeable and by the superiority of his education was able to conceal his pathological love of money.'[187] John, however, in the tenth year of his office, was removed by an intrigue of Antonina, the wife of Belisarius, and Theodora.[188]

John became prefect for the first time not later than 30 April 531[189] and was dismissed on 14 January 532,[190] only to return not later than 18 October 532[191] and fall from power between 7 May and 1 June 541.[192] The minimum extent of the two periods taken together is 9 years and 227 days, so that Procopius is accurate in his calculations. The 'many years' which Procopius awards Tribonian might tempt one to think that he outlasted his senior contemporary by some years, but the historian is concerned to contrast rather their fate than their durability. Tribonian outlasted John by at most a year.

Interest resides in Procopius' account of Tribonian's death. The word which he uses, νόσος,[193] also serves in his narrative on 17 occasions for 'plague'.[194] The more precise λοιμός is used in nine texts.[195] The most serious outbreak of plague in his writings is the one brilliantly described in chapter 22 of book 2 of the *Wars*. He tells us that 'during these times'[196] the pestilence which broke out nearly annihilated the whole human race. The 'times' can be fixed from the previous chapter, which relates the third invasion of Roman territory by Chosroes, in the early spring of 542,[197] and

183 *Wars* 8.15.1–2. It seems to have been concluded in the autumn of 551: Bury ii. 117.
184 *Wars* 8.15.3–7.
185 *Wars* 8.25.16–23; Malalas 485D–E (Indiction 14 = Sept. 550–Aug. 551).
186 Below, ch. 4 n. 180.   187 *Wars* 1.25.2.   188 *Wars* 1.25.3–30.
189 *CJ* 6.27.5 etc.   190 *Wars* 1.24.17; above, nn. 110, 122, 125.
191 *CJ* 3.10.3 etc.   192 *N.* 109 (7 May 541); *N.* 111 (1 June 541 Theodoto pp.).
193 *Wars* 1.25.2; above, n. 187.
194 *Wars* 2.22.4, 5, 9, 10, 14, 18 bis, 19, 23, 33, 35, 37; 1.21.1, 16 bis; 2.24.8, 12 (always ἡ νόσος): on the plagues of the reign see Stein ii. 756–61.
195 *Wars* 2.22.1, 13, 23; 2.23.21; *SH* 4.1, 6.22, 18.44.   196 *Wars* 2. 22.1.
197 *Wars* 2. 20–1. Chosroes invaded in 540, 541, 542 and 544. In 542 he set out 'at

by the fact that, according to Procopius, Belisarius was recalled after Justinian recovered from the plague but before the campaign of 543.[198]

The plague, the historian says, started from Pelusium in the Nile delta and spread in two directions, westwards to Alexandria and the rest of Egypt, eastwards to Palestine. From there it spread over the whole world.[199] In the second year, in the middle of spring, it reached Byzantium, where the historian was staying.[200] There it remained for four months, being especially virulent for three.[201] Another account, by Malalas, makes the period two months.[202]

The question is whether the disease of which Tribonian died (νόσος) was the plague (ἡ νόσος)[203] and, if so, what year and season must be assigned. The timing fits at least approximately that derived from the style of the *Novels*.[204] But in what year did the plague reach Byzantium? Procopius says 'the second' which evidently means the second counting from its origin in Egypt. From the example of John's prefecture, lost in the 'tenth year',[205] we know that in this sort of calculation of time Procopius counts from day to day.

Procopius does not give the year and month of the original outbreak, but he does give an idea of the direction of movement and something can be constructed from mentions by the chronographers. To follow these one must bear in mind that the indiction (i.e. financial or tax) year ran from 1 September to 31 August in a cycle of fifteen years. The current indiction began on 1 September 537, so that Indiction 5 runs from 1 September 541 to 31 August 542 and so on.

According to Malalas, God, seeing the increase in sin, sent a plague in Indiction 5, causing destruction in all towns and country districts. It raged so long that there were not enough undertakers. God's compassion prevailed in Byzantium for two months.[206]

If Malalas has hit on the right year the plague came to Constantinople between May, the middle of spring,[207] and August, the end of the fifth indiction year, 542. The epidemic lasted either two months, as the bishop asserts, or four, with Procopius. Malalas, anything but a lucid chronographer, slightly complicates the story by introducing earlier in the same indiction year a woman who prophesies floods which will sweep all away within three days. It was indeed reported, he says, that many cities had been submerged. 'At that time also a θνῆσις of men occurred in Egypt and

---

the beginning of spring' for Commagene and Palestine (*Wars* 2.20.1, 2.20.17–18). Bury II. 104–106; Rubin 350; Cedrenus I. 652 (14th year of Justinian = 541–2).

[198] *Wars* 2.21.24; 2.24.9–16; *SH* 4. 3, 13.   [199] *Wars* 2.22.6.   [200] *Wars* 2.22.9.
[201] *Wars* 2.23.1.   [202] Malalas 482C.
[203] Clearly it need not be, for Justin also ἐτελεύτησε νόσῳ (*SH* 9.54) and in his case the cause of death was an ulcer in the foot (Malalas 424), said by Stein to be syphilitic: II. 273 n. 1.
[204] Ch. 4 nn. 105–6.
[205] Above, nn. 189–92.   [206] Malalas 482 BC.   [207] *Wars* 2.23.1.

Alexandria'.[208] Θνῆσις, death, is the same term as Malalas later uses for the plague,[209] so that Malalas might be referring to the earlier progress of the plague to the Nile delta, which Procopius also notices. In that case a possible interpretation is that the disease reached Alexandria in the earlier part of the fifth indiction year, viz. in the autumn of 541, and Byzantium in the later part. On another interpretation the bishop is referring to floods. As Procopius notices, the plague operated at all seasons of the year and always started from the coast and worked its way inland.[210] This is an indication that it was carried to regions distant from Pelusium by rats on board ship.[211]

Theophanes brings the plague to Byzantium in the fifth year of the indiction but in October, viz. October 541 (A.M. 6034).[212]

Evagrius, a more reliable historian, records that the plague struck Antioch in 542.[213] Marcellinus Comes[214] records it in Italy in Indiction 6 (September 542–August 543), evidently continuing an anti-clockwise circuit of the Mediterranean.

Something can also be gleaned from Edict 7, of 1 March 542, which on grounds of style can be assigned to Tribonian.[215] The subject is bankers' contracts. The preface says that as virtue shines in adversity, so imperial providence is shown in time of subjects' misfortune. 'Though we hope that no evil may ever befall the republic, if the instability of human affairs or the motions of the divine will press on human evils, an opportunity is provided for a display of imperial humanity and foresight. That this is at present the case,' the text continues, 'needs no emphasis. For no one has to be told what everyone has experienced, that mortal danger is spreading to all parts.'[216] The unforeseen events have caused special difficulties, so they allege, to bankers.

The reference is undoubtedly to the plague, which Tribonian with studied equivocation attributes to the instability of human affairs or to the motions of the divine will.[217]

In sum, the evidence of the sources is not completely consistent. There are four firm points in the story. The plague began in Egypt.[218] It reached Byzantium in the middle of spring, i.e. in May.[219] Procopius was there. It reached Antioch in 542, two years after Chosroes sacked the city.[220] In March 542 it was generally known that it was spreading everywhere.[221] Given these firm points we can reject Theophanes' date for its arrival in

[208] Malalas 481, 9–10.
[209] Malalas 482B,C, 489D (Indiction 6 = 557–8: θνῆσις = bubonic plague).
[210] *Wars* 2.22.3,9.   [211] *Wars* 2.22.9.
[212] Theophanes *A.M.* 6034, October Indiction 5.
[213] Evagrius 4.29 = *Patr. Graec.* 68(2) 2752C (two years after its capture by Chosroes in 540).
[214] Marcellinus ind. 6, post. cons. Bas. anno 2 (Jan.–Aug. 543 = *Patr. Lat.* 51. 945).
[215] Below, nn. 216 and 217 (διὰ τῆς *in rem*), epil. (τὰ τοίνυν παραστάντα ἡμῖν etc.; below, ch. 4. n. 40).
[216] Edict 7 praef. (1 March 542).   [217] Above, n. 216.   [218] *Wars* 2.22.6.
[219] *Wars* 2.22.9.   [220] Above, n. 213.   [221] Edict 7 (1 March 542); above, n. 216.

Byzantium, October 541,[222] accept Malalas, year 5 of the indiction, and plump for May 542.[223] It rages in the capital for two or three months and persists in a milder form for four. In 543 it strikes Italy.[224]

If this is right Tribonian could well have died in the epidemic of 542. He succumbed to 'a disease'.[225] The last composition in his style is dated 1 May 542.[226] Is it rash to conclude that the disease of which the quaestor died was the plague, and that he died in the summer of 542? Justinian himself was affected.[227] His death was awaited, more eagerly by some than others, but he recovered and punishment was meted out to the generals who had prematurely intrigued for the succession.[228]

If Tribonian was happy in the time, he was less so in the consequence, of his death. Justinian, says Procopius, confiscated part of his property, although he was survived by a son and many grandchildren.[229] This, it is implied, was retribution for his corrupt practices as quaestor.

The foregoing account of Tribonian's career rests overwhelmingly on two reliable sources, the *Corpus Juris* and Procopius. It seemed best not to complicate the story by introducing the two notices in the Suda until they could be controlled by something more substantial. The tenth-century lexicon mentions two Tribonians. The first is T 956:[230]

> Tribonianus son of Macedonianos, barrister in the court of the prefects. This Tribonian was a Hellene and atheist and opposed the Christian faith in every particular. He was a flatterer and trickster. He persuaded Justinian the emperor that he would not die but be taken up to heaven in the flesh. He was Justinian's quaestor. He possessed natural ability and was inferior to no contemporary in his educational attainments. He was keen always to sell justice for gain. It was his normal practice to repeal some laws and propose others each day, selling them to those who wanted, according to their need. He lived on for many years in office and died of a disease without suffering ill from anyone. For he was smooth and agreeable and able by the superiority of his education to hide his pathological love of gain.

Most of this we have met already in Procopius, from whom the Suda has copied. The story about Justinian being taken up to heaven is in the historian also.[231] He is illustrating how easy it was to take in the emperor, with his simpleminded religious beliefs and naive vanity. 'On one occasion, Tribonian, acting as assessor, said that he was simply terrified that one day he (Justinian) might disappear, taken up to heaven on account of his piety. Such praises or rather jokes Justinian interpreted according to the bent of his disposition.' No doubt Tribonian was given to flattering those whom it was in his interest to conciliate, but it should be noted that Procopius treats this remark as a joke, or a hidden jibe. Tribonian had a sense of humour. At least one text drafted by him can be regarded as verging on a parody of

---

[222] Above, n. 212.

[223] Above, n. 206. So E. Stein, 2. 841, relying mainly on Procopius.

[224] Above, n. 214.   [225] *Wars* 1.25.2.   [226] Below, ch. 4 pp. 126–34, and nn. 86f.

[227] *Wars* 2.23.20; *SH* 4.1.   [228] *SH* 4.2–12.

[229] *SH* 20.17: μοῖρα is perhaps to be taken as 'half'.

[230] Suidas, *Lexicon* τ 956.   [231] *SH* 13.12.

Justinian's prose.[232] Obviously such tactics would not have been possible had the emperor not been devoid of humour.

The Suda's opening sentences do not come from Procopius and their source can only be guessed. Tribonian was the son of Macedonianus and a barrister in the prefects' courts (viz. that of the praetorian prefect of the east). There is nothing to object to so far. What of the allegation that he was a Hellene, an atheist and an enemy of Christianity?

One must distinguish between non-Christian philosophical beliefs and pagan practices. Under the policy of 529 practices entailed the death penalty, beliefs, if not renounced in time, forfeiture of property.[233] Reversion to paganism was, however, a capital offence.[234] If Tribonian actually sacrificed to the ancestral gods he was running a grave risk and would have been denounced or detected rather than promoted in the purge.[235] Even pagan views could hardly have been advocated in the open. Justinian was not a cynic.[236] He would not have tolerated open dissent from however eminent an adjutant. It may, however, be argued that Tribonian dissembled.

There seems no certain way of detecting from a man's writings the character of his beliefs or the firmness of his convictions. Tribonian was writing propaganda for Justinian just as Claudian had for Stilicho.[237] In neither case need the writer share his master's views. Nevertheless Tribonian conveys a sense of genuine religious feeling.[238] It may be said that such feeling is compatible with paganism. Yet the theme of *divina humanitas*, which is explicit in *C. Tanta*[239] and implicit in the legislative programme of these years seems to me a specifically Christian one, though it may be Pauline, or even Nestorian, *divina humanitas*, not *humana divinitas*. Much the same goes for the insistence on equality, ἰσότης,[24] which has religious implications and in one passage of the *Novels* is related specifically to St Paul's brocard that in Christ there is neither male nor female, slave nor free.[241] Could a non-Christian have acted for so long and with such brilliance as the mouthpiece of a deeply committed Christian?

Diehl, a sensitive writer, thought that Tribonian was openly non-Christian and that Justinian tolerated this in the interests of the state.[242]

---

[232] N. 36.6 (1 Jan. 535), see ch. 3 n. 679; *Justinian* n. 194.   [233] *CJ* 1.5.18.

[234] *CJ* 1.11.10 (undated).

[235] Above, nn. 57–8; *CJ* 1.11.10.4 (death penalty); cf. von Ludewig, *Vita Iustiniani* (1731) 189.

[236] See however below, n. 242.

[237] Alan Cameron, *Claudian: Poetry and Propaganda at the Court of Honorius* (1970), esp. chs 2, 3, 9, 12.

[238] Ecclesiastical texts composed by Tribonian include *CJ* 1.2.21 (529), 22 (30 Oct. 529), 23 (18 March 530), 1.3.48 (23 Aug. 531), 49 (1 Sept. 531), 50 (1 Sept. 531), 51 (1 Nov. 531), 53 (17 Nov. 533), 54 (Iohanni pp.), 1.4.24 (17 Sept. 529), 27 (1 Sept. 530), 28 (1 Oct. 530), 31 (1 Oct. 531), 1.5.19 (Demostheni pp. 529), 21 (29 July 531), 22 (1 Sept. 531).

[239] *C. Tanta* pr. (16 Dec. 533)   [240] Below, ch. 4 n. 22, ch. 9 n. 22.

[241] N. 5.2 (17 March 535).

[242] Diehl 552; Bury 1.369 ('Tribonian...seems to have made no pretence at disguising his opinions'); Barker 72.

The 'paganism' of the time was, he says, really a philosophical *'opposition de salon'*.[243] But Justinian was far from tolerant. No one who was not an orthodox Christian was to hold any public office;[244] in particular, no such person was allowed to teach.[245] Justinian saw that Hellenism in education kept paganism alive. He determined to eradicate it. How could he have allowed an avowed non-Christian to prepare a new scheme of legal education for the youth of the empire? Then there is the matter of Tribonian's seal.[246] This, if it refers to our Tribonian, shows him invoking the protection of the Mother of God. Openly at least Tribonian conformed.

Still, there are difficulties. To the quaestor Marcus Aurelius is the most philosophical of emperors, the prince of philosophy.[247] Marcus was a pagan and an opponent of Christianity. But then so presumably were nearly all the classical lawyers. How did Justinian take the passages praising Marcus? How did Tribonian intend them? There are two possibilities. Either he was, as the Suda maintains, a secret pagan, or his classicism is a literary convention, not inconsistent with a humanistic form of Christianity. Unfortunately we do not know how reliable were the sources of gossip, apart from Procopius' *Secret History*, on which the lexicon drew.

Lawyers are seldom notable for their piety and one can generally assume at least a certain anti-clericalism in the legal profession, nourished in the sixth century by a silent competition for jurisdiction between the episcopal and civil courts. Support of a tenuous sort for the notion that Tribonian was not as deeply religious as Justinian may be drawn from the comparison of the texts of *C. Δέδωκεν* and *C. Tanta*. If, as argued earlier,[248] the Greek version is the earlier, it seems reasonable to suppose that Justinian saw the Greek draft before Tribonian made the Latin adaptation. The Latin version introduces religious themes more strongly than the Greek.[249] Perhaps this reflects Justinian's comments on the Greek draft.

Unlike the other quaestors of the age Tribonian had a deep and detailed grasp of the law of the pagan empire, with its ancillary institutions and history.[250] He loved and revered them, though he was prepared to sweep much of the ancient learning into the limbo of history when it seemed over-subtle or discriminatory.[251] Such a man, steeped in the non-Christian past, invited the reproach of paganism. Small wonder that it attached to him. He may, like Procopius, have been impatient of theological niceties;[252] in any case dogma was, in the terminology of the Elysée, a reserved topic.[253]

---

243 Ib.: 'c'était une opposition de salon, de gens du monde, et de beaux esprits d'université, sans grande portée pratique.' If so, the opposition was of the type which invites persecution.

244 *CJ* 1.5.18.5, 6 (undated).   245 Ib. 18.4; *CJ* 1.11.10.2 (undated); Malalas 451.

246 Above, nn. 156–8.   247 Below, ch. 3 nn. 56f.   248 Above, n. 21.

249 *C. Tanta* 1 (above, p. 12), 9 (*deo propitio*, not in Greek), 18 (*divinae res, humani iuris condicio*, not in Greek), 19 (*quo enim antiquitas digna divino non est visa iudicio*, not in Greek), 21 (*deo adnuente*, not in Greek).

250 Below, ch. 9 n. 37.   251 Below, ch. 9 nn. 88, 99.   252 *Wars* 5.3.6–10.

253 Justinian composed texts dealing with Christian dogma himself: *Justinian* 121–2.

One reference only to Christian antiquities is to be found in his work: the church of the Holy Resurrection has daily to re-enact Christ's miraculous feeding of the multitude, so great is the flock of pilgrims.[254] Not much can be made of this. To stand one's distance in talking of the church and its doings was a literary convention.[255] In sum, Tribonian thought himself to be and was the intellectual superior of the bishops and theologians of his day. They may have had their revenge in a lampoon which fell into the hands of the compiler of the Suda. One possibility is that Tribonian was a Christian of Jewish descent. Converts were not caught by the disabilities which prevented Jews holding office or acting as barristers in the fifth century.[256] Side had two synagogues.[257] A seven-branched candlestick in relief has been found in the excavations of the site.[258] The town has also an early Christian colony, which suffered under Diocletian. A synod of twenty-five bishops from Pamphylia and Lycaonia met there in 390.[259] A scholar of taste and intelligence, intellectually impatient and given to flattery and cupidity, might, according to notions current even in the ancient world,[260] be of Jewish origin or descent. That might explain the hostile notice in the Suda. It does not make Tribonian a pagan.[261]

We have not finished with the Suda, which contains a second Tribonian, as follows:[262]

> T 957. Tribonian from Side also a barrister in the prefect's court, a poly-math. He wrote: Commentary on the Canon of Ptolemy, in verse; Conjunction of the Cosmic and Harmonic Disposition of Stars at Birth; On the Presiding and Conducting Stars; On the Houses of the Planets, and why each in particular occupies its House; On the 24 units of metre and the 28 units of rhythm; Paraphrase of the Catalogue of the Homeric Ships; Macedonian Dialogue or Treatise on Happiness; Life of the Philosopher Theodotus in three books; prose Treatise on Consuls, dedi-cated to the emperor Justinian; Treatise on Kingship to the same; On the Changes of the Months (in verse).

254 N. 40 pr. (18 May 536). Unless one counts N. 103 pr. 1 (Christ as the culmination of the history of Palestine).

255 Thus Procopius continually talks about 'the Christians' as if he were not one himself, e.g. *Wars* 8.25.13, *SH* 27.12: see A. and A. Cameron, *Class. Quar.* 14 (1964) 317; Averil Cameron, *Historia* 15 (1966) 466.

256 J. Juster, *Les Juifs dans l'empire romain* (1914); J. Starr, *The Jews in the Byzantine Empire* (1939); E. Demougeot, 'La politique antijuive de Théodose II': *Akt. XI int. byz. kong.* (1958) 95; *C. Sirm.* 6 in fin.; *CJ* 1.4.15; 2.6.8 (468); 1.5.12.9 (527); N. 37.7 (1 Aug. 535).

257 W. Ruge, 'Pamphylien', in *RE* 18.3.354–407 at 388, 396; A. W. Von Buren, 'Inscriptions from Asia Minor', *JHS* 28 (1908), 180f., no. 29; M. Vincent, *JHS* (1909) 130; L. Robert, *Etudes Anat.* (1937) 412.2 and *Rev. de Phil.* 84 (1958) 36f.

258 A. M. Mansel, *Die Ruinen von Side* (Berlin 1963), 12–13.

259 Ibid. 12.

260 On the Jewish reputation for cupidity see Juster 2.312 n. 3. It has also been suggested that Procopius was Jewish, but this is refuted by F. Dahn, *Prokopius von Cäsarea* (1865) 193f.

261 Stein, *Deux questeurs* 367, also rejects the idea that Tribonian was a pagan.

262 *Suidae Lexicon* T 957.

It is a curious list. It proceeds from astronomy and music via belles lettres to philosophy and public affairs. The end of the list is not out of keeping with what we know of the quaestor. The beginning seems quite out of character. The fact that this Tribonian is said to come from Side in Pamphylia suggests some connection with the previous one.[263] So does the learning. Both were polymaths.[264] Opinions differ as to whether there were one or two Tribonians. Gibbon identified the two.[265] Kübler held that the astronomer and littérateur became interested in affairs of state and graduated to the law. The chronological work was of service in dating the constitutions in the *Codex Iustinianus*.[266] E. Stein however thought them different.[267]

The Suda says of the second that he was *also* a barrister in the praetorian prefect's court. There is nothing inherently improbable about two barristers from the same family practising before that court in the course of thirty-seven years. Furthermore the lexicon mentions, under the historian Agathias, who continued Procopius' history and was himself a barrister, that he 'flourished at the same time as Paul the Silentiary, Macedonius the prefect and Tribonian, in the time of Justinian'.[268] Agathias' dates are *c.* 532 to 582;[269] Paul the Silentiary died about 575.[270] Neither was a contemporary of the quaestor Tribonian, and the Tribonian mentioned alongside them must have flourished at the end of Justinian's reign. Since he is not further explained, he must, in that company, be the writer of the astronomical and musical works we have listed. It is of course conceivable that some items in the list might have been composed by the quaestor and mistakenly attributed to his eponym.

One more Tribonian, who may be non-existent, identical with the second, or possibly a third man of the same name from the epoch of Justinian, now falls to be mentioned.

Edict 9, another law on bankers' contracts, is addressed to 'Tribonian prefect of the city'.[271] The text has not preserved the date. It is tempting to identify the addressee with the second Tribonian. On the other hand a note in an anonymous Bodleian manuscript led Zachariae to propose as the correct reading 'to Tribonian the quaestor, copy to the prefect of the city'.[272] Tribonian was never prefect of the city, so far as we know; he could hardly have combined this post with the quaestorship. The text of Edict 9 has some, though no conclusive, marks of the quaestor's style.[273] On the whole it may be preferable to accept Zachariae's amendment and conclude that this constitution throws no light on the second Tribonian: but a third Tribonian, prefect of the city, is not to be excluded.

Though it would not be impossible to amalgamate the Suda's two men,

[263] Above, nn. 14–15.   [264] Above, nn. 24, 25, 230.

[265] Gibbon ch. 44 n. 733; W. G. Holmes 2.442 (noticing discrepancies).

[266] B. Kübler *RE* 2.12. 2421–2: *Atti del cong. int. di dir. rom.* 1. 24–7.

[267] Stein, *Deux questeurs* 376.   [268] *Suidae Lexicon*, ed. Adler, 1.15.7–8.

[269] Averil Cameron, *Agathias* ch. 1.   [270] *OCD* 792.

[271] Edict 9 (undated, reign of Justinian).

[272] Schoell-Kroll 3.772 line 6 n.; Cod. Bodl. 3399.

[273] Edict 9.1; cf. below, ch. 9 n. 22.

nothing forces us to this extreme step. The second could be a son or grandson of the quaestor, or some other member of a family of scholars.

Such are the ascertainable facts, in the present state of our resources, about the career and personality of Tribonian. If technicalities are disregarded, he was Justinian's minister for legislation and propaganda[274] for nearly twelve years, between September 529 and May 542. In these years the three volumes of the *Corpus Juris* and most of the surviving legislation of Justinian's reign were produced. He drafted about three-quarters of the surviving constitutions of Justinian's reign.[275] He planned and directed the work of the Second Law Commission which produced the *Digest*, the *Institutes* and the second *Codex Iustinianus*. He took an active part in the execution of the plan, doing more work himself, where we can form a judgment, than any of the other commissioners.

For an assessment of his character and achievement, however, it will be best to wait until we have studied his style and methods of organisation in more detail.

[274] Rubin 146–68 deals fully with the propagandistic aspect but fails to notice the role of the quaestor in this respect.

[275] The 240 constitutions, Latin and Greek, of Tribonian's first quaestorship as recorded in *CJ*, plus the 43 others in that compilation which can on grounds of style be attributed to him, together with *C. Omnem* and *Imperatoriam*, together make up 285 constitutions and amount to 12,525 lines of *CJ* length, out of a total of 411 constitutions and 17,235 lines for all Justinian's constitutions in *CJ* plus *Omnem* and *Imperatoriam*. Tribonian's compositions come to 69 per cent of the number of constitutions and 74 per cent of the lines they occupy. For the *Novels* only the dated constitutions can be counted, since I have made no attempt to assign the undated ones. Here the constitutions of Tribonian's second quaestorship come to 124 as printed in the Schoell-Kroll edition out of 155 and 20,894 lines out of 26,867, i.e. to 80 and 78 per cent respectively. These figures for lines differ from those given in the preface n. 1 since the length of line in *CJ*, Schoell-Kroll and Lenel, *Palingenesia*, differs.

CHAPTER THREE

His Latin Style

INTRODUCTION

It is a main purpose of this book to delineate the style of its central figure. The material from which this can be done consists in the first place of the constitutions drafted by Tribonian during his two quaestorships. The dates of these are known roughly but not precisely from other evidence, and one object of the inquiry into style is to make it possible to fix them more closely. A second object is in the long run more important. If the quaestor's norms of style can be accurately fixed we can then proceed to identify some of his interventions as a compiler of the *Institutes* and the *Digest*. We can move from the *Codex* to the other two volumes of the codification. Finally, the style is likely to be the best clue to the personality and outlook of the outstanding lawyer of the age.

One might suppose that four hundred years after the French humanists set about the historical investigation of Justinian's *Corpus Juris* there would be a copious literature about Tribonian's manner of writing: for the fact that he was the key figure in the execution of the codification has long been known and is indeed proclaimed in the sources for all to hear. It is a curiosity in the history of scholarship that this is not the case. Although the approximate dates of his quaestorships are not in doubt,[1] and although the quaestor's responsibility for the drafting of legislation is well established,[2] scholars have hesitated to draw the conclusion that Tribonian drafted the constitutions enacted during his periods of office, or at any rate to draw conclusions from that conclusion. Perhaps this is in part because of a suspicion that, as Procopius alleges,[3] Justinian did his own drafting, or at least intervened to a greater extent than previous emperors. Procopius is right, but when the matter is carefully investigated it turns out that the emperor himself is responsible for at most ten constitutions out of a total of over four hundred,[4] and most of these fall outside Tribonian's terms of office. Another discouragement may have been the fear that it would be impossible to disentangle the roles of the different commissioners in the work of the second commission. The fear has turned out exaggerated[5] and in any case a grasp of Tribonian's ways is a help in unfolding the details of the commission's methods.

Whatever the explanation, scholars have concentrated their efforts on an

---

[1] Above, ch. 2.
[2] *Not. Dig. Or.* xiii, *Occ.* x *sub dispositione viri illustris quaestoris, leges dictandae preces.*
[3] *SH* 14.1f.   [4] *Justinian* 116–21.   [5] Below, chs 5–7.

attempt to depict a 'Byzantine', 'Justinianic' or 'Tribonianic' style which is not in fact confined to the appropriate periods but spreads over Justinian's whole reign and sometimes the whole sixth century.[6] Very little use can therefore be made of previous investigations. We have to start from scratch.

We have also to start from Tribonian's Latin style, although in his second quaestorship he drafted mostly in Greek. This is because the Latin style is more important for the identification of Tribonian's part in the *Institutes* and *Digest*, which are composed almost entirely in Latin. There is also a technical reason. There is an excellent vocabularium for the *Codex Iustinianus*,[7] an adequate one for the *Institutes*[8] and a useful if imperfect one for the *Digest*.[9] A similar work for the Latin *Novels* is on the point of completion.[10] From these aids it is possible with patience to derive word counts and word frequencies[11] and to compare these for Tribonian's periods of office with similar counts for other periods and for the volumes of the codification as a whole. To be any use for purposes of identifying the author of texts a study of style must be comparative: how frequently does A use *iuramentum* in comparison with B, at what rate is *nullo permittimus modo* found in 529–31 in comparison with 518–29.

Although Mayr's concordance extends to the Greek constitutions,[12] in the *Codex Iustinianus* these form only 11 per cent of the volume of that work.[13] So far as the much bulkier Greek *Novels* are concerned a concordance is planned but is far from completion.[14] The result is that the depiction of Tribonian's Greek style is to a large extent guesswork, and insofar as it can be essayed at all a scholar must proceed by analogy with what has been learned about his Latin. Tribonian's Latin is therefore the object of this chapter. His Greek is briefly discussed in the next.

To identify the documents drafted by an author with the help of criteria of style two comparisons are necessary. The first is between the style of the document or set of documents in question and the norms of the language as

[6] E. Grupe, 'Zur Latinität Justinians', *ZSS* 14 (1893) 224, 15 (1894) 327; L. Chiazzese, *Confronti testuali* (1935) 506; cf. H. Erman, *Festschrift Koschaker* 1 (1939) 157, 163 (der Jurist Justinian!).

[7] R. von Mayr and M. San Nicolò, *Vocabularium Codicis Iustiniani* (2 vols Prague 1923, 1925).

[8] Ambrosino, *Vocabularium Institutionum Iustiniani Augusti* (Milan 1952).

[9] *Vocabularium Iurisprudentiae Romanae* (= *VIR* 1894–   ) which lacks part of the letter I; also K, L, M, part of P and Q.

[10] As part of *Legum Iustiniani Imperatoris Vocabularium*, being compiled under the auspices of the University of Florence.

[11] For the *Digest* the method is described in Honoré, 'Word frequencies and the study of Roman law', 30 *Cambridge Law Journal* (1972) 280.

[12] Vol. 2 was edited by M. San Nicolò (1925).

[13] As printed in the stereotype edition of the *Corpus Iuris* there are 147 Greek constitutions comprising 5842 lines (including inscriptions and subscriptions) and 4536 in Latin comprising 51,334 lines. The number of words per line averages about 5.85 but this result is arrived at by sampling and may contain a small error.

[14] Auspices as in n. 10 above.

a whole. 'Language' here means simply a reasonably large pool of material of which the document or documents to be studied form a segment. In the case of imperial constitutions the Latin texts of the *Codex Iustinianus* form a convenient pool of legal Latin. The second comparison is between the documents under study and the work of contemporaries from whom the supposed author must be distinguished. In the case of Tribonian the contemporaries are taken to be the quaestors of the period from Anastasius (491–) together with Justinian himself. The two comparisons are directed towards answering two questions: how does the language of the corpus under study relate to that of the linguistic continuum, e.g. legal Latin, and how does it relate to the peculiarities of writers of the same period. To be reliable, norms of style should be distinctive in both contexts. If the first alone were treated as sufficient we should be in danger of depicting not Tribonian's style but the legal Latin of the earlier sixth century. If the second alone were attended to we should be in danger of attaching importance to words which chance to appear in one corpus and not in another contemporary corpus, although in the larger framework of the language as a continuing whole this has no real significance, and hence of wrongly identifying the author of dubious or disputed documents.

It is naturally a help if the corpus of material to be studied is fairly extensive. In the present case it is. From 17 September 529[15] to 27 November 531 we have 222 Latin constitutions in the *CJ* amounting in Krueger's stereotype edition to 8381 lines of text.[16] In counting lines, inscriptions and subscriptions are included. Part lines are counted as wholes. The first comparison is with the Latin of the *CJ* as a whole, or rather with the bulk of it. For tactical reasons I count only the constitutions up to the end of the first quaestorship at this stage, and omit those which were enacted during the quaestorship of Basilides (January 532 to November 534) and also undated constitutions of Justinian which are presumptively later than April 529 (i.e. which are not addressed to Mena pp.). Thus 91 constitutions (42 of the quaestorship of Basilides and 49 of Justinian *sine die et consule*) are left on one side at the initial stage because one of the objects of the study is to determine which if any of them was composed by Tribonian. This leaves 48,520 lines of Latin up to January 532.[17] These 48,520 form the 'pool' against which the vocabulary and structure of the texts of the first quaestorship are assessed. It is adopted as a 'pool' partly for the reason already adumbrated. The search for traits of style is enormously helped by the fact that von Mayr's vocabularium[18] lists each inflection of a word separately: thus *quiescente* and *quiescentibus* (which turn out to be marks of Tribonian's style) are easily separated from the other parts of the verb *quiescere*, which are not. In contrast with the convenience of von Mayr the concordances to the *Theodosian*

---

[15] Although Tribonian is first mentioned as quaestor on 17 Nov. 529 (*CJ* 7.63.5 *Iustinianus* A. *Triboniano quaestori sacri palatii*) the effective change in the style of drafting occurs, as will be seen, on 17 Sept. 529; below, nn. 551–65.

[16] And 21 Greek laws amounting to 1636 lines.

[17] 57,176 lines of which 5842 are Greek.   [18] Above, n. 7.

Code[19] (*CTh*) and *Novels* (*CThN*)[20] do not afford the inquiring scholar this valuable assistance. Hence, though they form a corpus of legal Latin which is relevant to our inquiry, I have used them, as will be seen, only in a secondary capacity.

For certain purposes the constitutions in *CJ* from Constantine onwards form a more reliable 'pool' than is constituted by the Latin of the *CJ* as a whole. This is of course because the character of legal Latin (or at least the Latin of imperial constitutions) changed markedly in the age of Constantine. The constitutions from 306 to January 532 in *CJ* come to 30,048 lines of Latin. As has been mentioned, a subsidiary comparison is often possible with the constitutions of the *Theodosian Code* and Theodosian and post-Theodosian *Novels*. For these no line count is available, but a rough word count can be made by sampling, and compared with the similar estimate for the words in the *CJ*. From this it emerges that the *CTh*[21] and *CThN*[22] together comprise about 219,184 words, while the *CJ* up to January 532 comprises about 330,000.[23] An allowance for overlap must be made, since the *CJ* texts of the period from Constantine to Anthemius are largely drawn from *CTh* and *CThN*. Here only a guess is possible. I have assumed that three-quarters of the material in *CJ* in this period comes from *CTh* and *CThN*. If that is so then the effective contribution to the bulk of legal Latin forming the 'pool' made by *CTh* and *CThN* together comes to just under 41 per cent of the volume of the *CJ* material in Latin up to January 532.[24] If this is converted into equivalent *CJ* lines it amounts to about 19,836.[25]

The point of these calculations is to enable the reader to judge for himself

[19] O. Gradenwitz, *Heidelberger Index zum Theodosianus* (Berlin 1925).

[20] O. Gradenwitz, *Ergänzungband zum Heidelberger Index zum Theodosianus* (Berlin 1929).

[21] Gradenwitz *HIT* gives 2009 columns of average length (by sampling) 82.4 words and *EHIT* gives 111 similar columns for the inscriptions and subscriptions, which are included in this count. The word total should therefore be within a thousand or so of 174,688.

[22] By a similar calculation to that in n. 21 there are 540 columns amounting to 44,496 words, plus or minus a few hundreds.

[23] In the Krueger edition the *CJ* has 976 columns of text, and the columns average 397 words (by sampling) which gives 387,472 words in all to within a thousand or two. By *line counting* (including inscriptions and subscriptions) there are 57,176 lines in *CJ* of which the Latin constitutions up to January 532 comprise 48,743, i.e. 85 per cent. 85 per cent of 387,472 is about 330,000.

[24] From nn. 21 and 22 the total for *CTh* and *CThN* is close to 218,000–220,000 (219,184) but an allowance must be made for the overlap between *CJ* and *CTh/N* which is put at three-quarters of the 16,675 lines in *CJ* from Constantine to Anthemius. These 12,506 lines correspond roughly to 84,753 words, so that the effective contribution of *CTh/N* is taken to be 134,431 words, which is just over 40 per cent of 330,000 (above, n. 23).

[25] Converting words (including inscriptions and subscriptions) to lines of *CJ* (also including inscriptions and subscriptions) at the rate of 6.777 words to a line, a figure which is arrived at by dividing the estimated number of words in *CJ* (387,472) by the results of an actual line count including inscriptions etc., i.e. 57,176. The 'pool' comprised by *CJ* Latin up to January 532, *CTh* and *CThN* less estimated overlap therefore comprises about 68,579 lines or 464,431 words.

the plausibility of the claim that certain words and expressions are marks of Tribonian's style. They can be summarised for this purpose in the following way. Material of the first quaestorship (8381 lines of Latin) amounts to:

(i) 17.2 per cent of Latin in *CJ* up to January 532.
(ii) 27.6 per cent of Latin in *CJ* from 306 to January 532.
(iii) about 12.2 per cent of Latin in *CJ*, *CTh* and *CThN* up to January 532.
(iv) about 16.7 per cent of Latin in *CJ*, *CTh* and *CThN* from 306 to January 532.

Consequently a mark of style ought to occur considerably more frequently in the texts of the first quaestorship than these percentages would suggest. In practice it will be found that it is rarely if ever that a word or phrase is counted as mark of style unless at least half of the occurrences in *CJ* belong to the first quaestorship, and at least a third of the occurrences in *CJ*, *CTh* and *CThN* combined. A precise arithmetical rule is however to be avoided. Much depends on the total number of occurrences, the context and the type of expression.

The footnotes enable the reader to ascertain the number of instances in each category. They are set out in the following order: (a) instances of a word's occurrence between September 529 and January 532 listed chronologically; (b) instances, prefaced by 'cf.', of its occurrences after January 532 or in undated constitutions of Justinian other than those of Mena's prefecture, in the constitutions *Imperatoriam* and *Summa* which fall in this period but are not included in *CJ* and in the Latin *Novels* of Justinian; (c) instances, prefaced by 'but' and listed chronologically, in which the expression occurs in *CJ* texts before September 529; and (d), where this is ascertainable without great difficulty, the number of instances in which it occurs in the *CTh* and *CThN*. Here only a total is given, prefaced by *CTh/N*. The reader who wishes to follow up these texts can find them via Gradenwitz's indices.

The result is that from the footnotes the reader can discover the number of texts belonging to the first quaestorship (a), the remaining *CJ* texts up to January 532 (c), and (in many instances) the number of *CTh/N* texts (d). As to the (b) instances these will at a later stage be treated as evidence for Tribonian's authorship of the texts from which they are taken, except in the case of pope John II's letter to Justinian of 25 March 534, reproduced at *CJ* 1.1.8.

By way of illustration an example may be helpful. The footnote for *interpretor* runs as follows:

502. *CJ* 1.14.12.2, 3 (30 Oct. 529 bis), 7.40.1.1a, 1d (18 March 530 bis), 5.27.11.1 (18 March 530), 6.23.28 pr. (27 March 530), 6.2.21.1 (22 July 530), *C. Deo auctore* 4, 12 (15 Dec. 530), 6.28.3 (20 Feb. 531); cf. *C. Tanta* 21 (16 Dec. 533) but 9.23.1 (5 Sept. 212), 6.37.1 (Ant.), 12.51.1 (15 March 425), 1.14.2 (6 Nov. 426), *CTh/N* 5.

There are therefore ten instances of *interpretor* in the first quaestorship (a), four *CJ* instances before September 529 (d), five other *CTh* or *CThN* instances and one instance after January 532. Since ten out of fourteen *CJ* instances up to January 532 is well over a half, and ten out of nineteen instances up to that date in *CJ*, *CTh* and *CThN* combined is well over a third, there is a good case for counting this word as a mark of Tribonianic style.

When a list of marks of style has been drawn up on the basis indicated, it requires to be thinned out in order to take account of the second comparison. Here I am concerned to distinguish Tribonian's style from that of his contemporaries. For this purpose a rough but not arbitrary rule is adopted (and broken only once). Any expression which occurs more than once in the *CJ* in the period from Anastasius to praetorian prefecture of Menas (491 to April 529) is rejected as a mark of style.[26] (In practice I have been more stringent than this suggests and have often rejected expressions which otherwise qualified but which occurred once in the thirty-eight years preceding the first quaestorship.) For example *coartare* (in the metaphorical sense 'restrict') at first seems a promising expression. Eleven of the first nineteen texts with *coartare* are indeed from our period, two are Justinianic but later. Of the eight remaining, however, two are from constitutions of April 529 and the word is therefore rejected as a mark of Tribonian's style. In this way a fair number of traditional 'Justinianic' words are struck from the list, though of course other well-known expressions survive.

The reason why this somewhat stringent procedure is adopted is of course that we ultimately wish to disentangle the compositions and interventions of Tribonian in the *Corpus Iuris* from those of other contemporaries, including the other compilers of the codification. This requires us to focus on the idiosyncratic features of his style and not on those which are the common currency of the age.

In principle any expression which was found more than once in Justinian's own compositions is also eliminated. Only one such word—*deproperare*—was however found. On the other hand I have not expelled a suggested mark of style merely because it is found in the letter of pope John II to Justinian which appears as *CJ* 1.1.8. Indeed it is a matter of interest that, so far as one can judge from a short text, the pope's secretary writes more like Tribonian than any other of his contemporaries, and at a first reading one might mistake the hand for that of the quaestor.

[26] The period includes the tenures of at least four quaestors any of whom may have influenced or worked with Tribonian (i) 1 Jan. 492–1 Jan. 499 (ii) 18 Nov. 500–20 Nov. 506, 1 April 517–1 Dec. 517 (iii) Proclus 1 Dec. 518 (*CJ* 7.63.3) to 22 April 527 (*CJ* 5.3.19) (iv) Thomas 13 Feb. 528 (*C. Haec*) to 7 April 529 (*C. Summa*). These periods are of course always minima, since only the dates on which texts which have been preserved can be enacted can be taken into account in fixing the limits of tenures. Of these (iii) is Justin's quaestor Proclus on whom see *CJ* 12.19.13 (Iustinus), *N.* 35.1 (23 May 535), Lydus 3.20, *SH* 6.13, 9.41, *Wars* 1.11.11; (iv) is Thomas, fifth-ranking member of Justinian's First Law Commission (*C. Haec* 1, *C. Summa* 2) purged in 529 (ch. 2 n. 65) dead by 23 May 535 (*N.* 35 pr.); (ii) is probably Iohannes who is said to have had a long term of office and an inflated staff (*N.* 35 pr.; 23 May 535). There are only two surviving constitutions between 20 Nov. 506 and 1 April 517 and it is possible that the tenure stretched continuously for 17 years. The name of (i) is unknown. Styles are examined in ch. 8.

Those expressions which survive the two processes of comparison form a list of marks of style derived from the text of the first quaestorship. This list is then used to identify the author of other Latin constitutions of the period up to 542 in stages. Counting the initial operation, there are five stages in the process. (i) In the first, as explained, the characteristics of the constitutions of the first quaestorship are set out. A subsidiary purpose of this exercise is to establish that, although Tribonian's first quaestorship is attested in the prescript of a text only from 17 November 529,[27] he was in fact already in office two months earlier. (ii) Next, the Latin constitutions between Nika and the completion of the second edition of the *Codex* on 16 November 534 are analysed in order to segregate those composed by Tribonian (though he was not quaestor) from those composed by the quaestor Basilides or by Justinian himself. (iii) The four prefaces which belong to the work of the Second Law Commission (*Deo auctore*, *Omnem*, *Tanta* and *Cordi*) are scrutinised from the point of view of authorship. (iv) The same is done for the undated constitutions of Justinian in the *CJ*, other than those early texts which are addressed to Menas pp. and so are known to belong to the period before Tribonian's first quaestorship. (v) The same is done for the Latin *Novels* of the period 535 to 542. In the last four stages, which involve the identification of constitutions as Tribonianic or non-Tribonianic with the help of the initial list of marks of style, I have allowed myself a certain liberty to use arguments by analogy. In particular I have felt justified in so arguing from the use in the initial list of a present indicative verb expressing the majestic plural to a perfect indicative or a present participle of the same root (e.g. from *existimamus* to *existimavimus* and *existimantes*) and conversely from the participial to the indicative form. There are a few other examples, the merits of which the reader will be able to judge as he comes to them. In this way a list of marks of style is progressively built up. In the end over five hundred items enter the list, which can then be used to identify some of Tribonian's interventions in the *Institutes* and the *Digest*. Description and identification being the main purpose of this chapter, the critical assessment of Tribonian's style can be left until later.

THE MAIN FEATURES OF TRIBONIAN'S LATIN STYLE

The main points to be considered are (a) the sources he uses, (b) the image of the emperor he presents, (c) the concepts he prefers, (d) the aesthetic and rhetorical aspects of his vocabulary, (e) syntactical traits, (f) some expressions of frequent occurrence in his work and (g) a list of miscellaneous words which satisfy the criteria for marks of style. An alphabetical list of the expressions discussed is to be found in Appendix 2, with references to the part of the text where they occur.

(a) *Use of sources.* The enactments of 17 September 529, which make up 15 constitutions in *CJ*, and the similar number of 30 October 529 introduce the

[27] *CJ* 7.63.5.

reader to a trait which is uncommon in the practice either of the secretaries *a libellis* up to Diocletian or of the quaestors from Constantine onwards. This is the habit of citing the opinions of classical jurists. It is true that Ulpian, still alive, is mentioned in a text of 222;[28] secretary no. 12 of the reign of Gordian, has three citations,[29] one of Modestinus who was presumably then still living. A text of 250 cites Papinian.[30] In these cases the deceased jurists are given a sort of formal title: *vir consultissimus*: and Gordian's minister uses the same expression of the emperor Marcus;[31] respect due to learning. A rescript of 283 relies on Papinian, *vir prudentissimus*,[32] as does one of 293;[33] in 287 Paul receives the same compliment,[34] and in 290 Ulpian.[35] In 321 an enactment of Constantine brushes aside the notes of Paul and Ulpian to adopt Papinian's view.[36]

There is nothing more in the *Codex Theodosianus* apart from one mention of Scaevola by a late-fourth-century quaestor,[37] nothing in the Theodosian and post-Theodosian *Novels*.[38] The fifth-century renaissance in legal studies yields a single reference to Julian (i.e. Salvius Iulianus) in 473.[39] Nothing more between then and September 529. Then, after 14 scattered references in three centuries, we have 64 citations in just over two years. These are set out in the footnotes in chronological order.[40] The references to classical jurists then become more sporadic but continue until February 541,[41]

---

[28] *CJ* 8.37.4 (31 March 222 Ulpian).

[29] *CJ* 3.42.5 (12 Feb. 239 Modestinus), 5.4.6 (21 Aug. 239 Paul), 6.37.12 (11 July 240 Papinian).

[30] 7.32.3 (28 March 250 Papinian).

[31] *CJ* 7.2.6. (Gordianus, assignable to the same quaestor: Honoré, 'Private rescripts', (forthcoming) *ANRW* 2.14, at n.798).

[32] *CJ* 6.42.16 pr. (12 Nov. 283).   [33] *CJ* 5.71.14 (14 Nov. 293).

[34] *CJ* 9.22.11 (22 June 287).   [35] *CJ* 9.41.11 (27 Nov. 290).

[36] *CTh* 9.43.1 (14 Sept. 321).   [37] *CTh* 4.4.3 (396).

[38] O. Gradenwitz, *Ergänzungsband* 89–91.

[39] *CJ* 6.61.5.1 (1 June 473) again due to an important quaestor whose approximate dates of office are 468–74, name unknown: responsible inter alia for the well-known constitution of Leo on the form of stipulations (*CJ* 8.37.10, 1 Jan. 472).

[40] *CJ* 3.28.33.1 (17 Sept. 529 Paul), 6.30.19 pr. (30 Oct. 529 Paul), 6.42.30, 7.45.14 (both 30 Oct. 529 Pap.), 2.55.5.3 (27 March 530 Paul), 6.25.7.1 (22 July 530 Pap.), 7.7.1. 1, 1a (1 Aug. 530 Ulp., Paul, Marcellus bis, Julian bis, Marcianus, Africanus), 4.5.10.1, 2 (1 Aug. 530 Ulp., Marcellus, Celsus, Pap. bis, Julian bis), 5.70.7.1a (1 Sept. 530 Tertullian), 5.4.25.2 (1 Oct. 530 Ulp.). 3.33.15.1, 2 (1 Oct. 530 Julian bis), 6.29.3.1 (17 Nov. 530 Sabiniani), 6.2.22.3a (17 Nov. 530 Papinian bis), 2.18.24.1 (17 Nov. 530 Julian bis), *Deo auctore* 6, 10 (15 Dec. 530 Ulp., Pap. ter, Paul, Marcianus, Julian), 6.22.10.3 (20 Feb. 531 Celsus), 6.25.9.1 (29 July 531 Pap.), 6.26.10 pr. 1, (29 July 531 Sabinus bis), 6.26.11 pr. (29 July 531 Ulp. bis), 6.24.14 pr. (29 July 531 Ulp., Sabinus), 6.25.10 (29 July 531 Ulp., Pap. ter), 6.46.7 pr. (29 July 531 Ulp.), 8.47.10 pr., 1a, 1b (1 Sept. 531 Pap. bis, Paul, Marcianus bis), 3.28.36.2 (1 Sept. 531 Ulp., Modestinus), 6.28.4.3 (1 Sept. 531 Ulp.), 3.28.35.1 (1 Sept. 531 Pap.), 6.49.7.1b (18 Oct. 531 Ulp.), 3.34.14 pr. (18 Oct. 531 libri Sabiniani), 6.40.3.2 (1 Nov. 531 Ulp., libri Sabiniani), 6.58.14.1 (27 Nov. 531 Paul).

[41] *CJ* 7.32.12 pr. (531/532 libri Sabiniani), 7.2.15.1a, 5.4.28 pr. (both 531/2 Ulp.), 3.33.17 pr. (18 Oct. 532 libri Sabiniani), *C. Tanta* 18 (16 Dec. 533 Julian), *C. Imperatoriam* 6 (21 Nov. 533 Gaius), *C. Omnen* 1, 4, 5 (16 Dec. 533 Gaius, Pap. quinq., Paul

which brings the classicism of Justinian's reign to an end so far as this feature is concerned.

The new quaestor of 529 stamps the imperial laws with the imprint of the scholar and indeed of the esoteric. Whereas the rare earlier references to the classics evince a certain deference on the emperor's part, these are more ambivalent. Our quaestor adopts the language of the insider. Not 'Paulus' but 'Iulius Paulus';[42] not 'Africanus' but 'Sextus Caecilius';[43] not 'Ulpianus ad Sabinum' but 'libri Sabiniani'.[44] With this goes the assumption that he (or, if one prefers, Justinian) is intellectually on a level with, if not slightly above, the great men of the past. This applies particularly to the series of Fifty Decisions beginning in August 530, which commonly cite the varying opinions of the old writers before making a choice or elaborating a compromise between them;[45] but the assumption of superiority is not confined to the few months of that exercise. Of the authors cited Papinian, with 16 mentions, heads the list, followed by Ulpian with 13, Julian 9, Paul 7, Marcianus 4, Marcellus 3 and Celsus 2. Modestinus, Africanus and even Tertullian *de peculio castrensi*, hardly mainline reading, are not forgotten, and there are six mentions of Sabinus or commentaries on Sabinus. One might infer that in late 529 and early 530 the quaestor was working through the *quaestiones* of Paul and Papinian.[46] At any rate his sources are not confined to those mentioned in the law of citations[47] or included in the existing law syllabus.[48]

An expression which combines familiarity with contempt illustrates Tribonian's ambivalent attitude to the old writers: to him they are often *veteres*, which is short for *veteres iuris auctores*[49] or *veteres iuris conditores*.[50] Forty-two of the first 46 uses of this abbreviation belong to our period.[51] It

---

ter), *CJ* 6.51.1.9 (1 June 534 Ulp.), *C. Cordi* 3 (16 Nov. 534 Ulp., Sabinus), *N.* 4.1 (15 March 535 Pap.), 22.43 (17 March 536 Q Mucius Scaevola), 74 (4 June 538 Julian), 87 (18 May 539 Julian), 97 (17 Nov. 539 Ulp.), 108 pr. 2 and 108.1 (1 Feb. 541 Pap. bis).

42 E.g. *CJ* 3.28.33.1, 6.30.19 pr.; above, n. 40.   43 *CJ* 7.7.1.1a; above, n. 40.

44 *CJ* 3.33.17 pr., 6.40.3.2; above, n. 40. Cf. 'Massurius Sabinus' *CJ* 6.24.14 pr., 'Salvius Iulianus' *Deo auctore* 10, ibid.

45 Especially *CJ* 7.7.1, 4.5.10, 8.47.10; above, n. 40.

46 *CJ* 3.28.33.1, 6.30.19 pr., above, n. 40, refer expressly to Paul's *quaestiones* and 7.45.14, ibid. to Papinian's.

47 *CTh* 1.4.3 (6 Nov. 426 Papinian, Paul, Gaius, Ulpian, Modestinus, Scaevola, Sabinus, Julian, Marcellus).

48 *C. Omnem* 1, 4.5 (16 Dec. 533 Gaius, Paul, Papinian).

49 *CJ* 5.16.6.1 (5 Dec. 229), 5.17.3.3 (31 Aug. 290), 6.22.10.5 (20 Feb. 530), 7.7.1 pr., 1b (1 Aug. 530).

50 *CJ* 2.12.23 (4 Feb. 363), 9.1.19 (13 Aug. 374), 4.39.9 (1 Nov. 531), *Veteres iuris interpretatores C. Summa* 3 (13 April 529), 6.23.30 (18 Oct. 531).

51 *CJ* 2.55.4.5 (30 Oct. 529), 6.4.3 pr., 8.53.34.4a (30 Oct. 529 bis), 6.2.20 pr., 4.28.7 pr. (1 Aug. 530), 5.70.7.2 (1 Sept. 530), 5.4.25 pr., 7.4.14 pr., 3.33.16 pr. (1 Oct. 530), 6.49.7. 1b (22 Oct. 530), 6.29.3 pr., 6.37.23 pr., 6.2.22. 1d, 3, 4 (17 Nov. 530 ter), 4.18.2.1, 1d (20 Feb. 531 bis), 4.37.6, 6.30.20 pr., 6.30.21.1 pr. (bis) 6.35.11 pr., 6.27.5.1, 1c, 1d (ter), 6.46.6.1, 2.46.3.2 (30 April 531), 6.25.8 pr., 6.61.8.4, 6.24.14.1 (29 July 531), 2.41.2, 6.43.3 pr., 1a (bis), 7.47.1.2, 3.31.12.1 (1 Sept. 531), 4.11.1.1, 4.54.9 pr., 7.40.3

is found once, in the curious combination *veterum scita*, in the preceding tenure, and three times in earlier centuries.[52]

The flavour of the study pervades the following excerpt from a text reforming the law about the freeing by one owner of a slave owned in common with someone else:[53]

> Sed et alia constitutio Severi et Antonini principum reperta est ex qua generaliter necessitas imponebatur socio partem suam socio vendere, quatenus libertas servo imponatur, licet nihil lucri ex substantia socii morientis alii socio accedat, pretio videlicet arbitrio praetoris constituendo, secundum ea quae et Ulpianus libro sexto fideicommissorum et Paulus libro tertio fideicommissorum refert, ubi et hoc relatum est, quod Sextus Caecilius iuris antiqui conditor definivit socium per praetorem compelli suam partem vendere, quatenus liber servus efficiatur: quod et Marcellus apud Iulianum in eius digestis notat.

Even by way of preamble this resembles a learned treatise rather than a statute. The citations are multiplied in order to impress, not because the recipient of the constitution may want to verify the references.

A similar trait is the multiplication of technical remedies in the alternative: action *in rem* or *in personam*, *utilis* or direct, and so forth,[54] in a manner meaningful at this period only to an academic mind.

Parallel to the citation of classical jurists is the mention of emperors before Constantine, especially Marcus.[55] He first appears in a constitution of October 530.[56] In April 531 he is *prudentissimus princeps, princeps philosophiae, sanctissimus Marcus*,[57] whose enactments must be saved from even the appearance of imperfection.[58] Like the jurists, Marcus recurs from time to time until February 541,[59] and then vanishes. He is a talisman of intellectual

---

pr. (18 Oct. 531), 5.11.7 pr. (1 Nov. 531), 7.33.12 pr. (27 Nov. 531), 4.37.7 (531) cf. 6.35.12 pr., 7.72.10 pr., 8.37.15 pr. (18 Oct. 532), 5.3.20.9, 4.34.12 (531/2), *C. Tanta* 1, 6a, 8c, 11, 13, 20 (16 Dec. 533 sex), 6.51.1.2a, 5 (1 June 534 bis), *C. Cordi* 3 (16 Nov. 534) but 5.3.15 pr. (16 Oct. 319), 5.37.22.5a (15 March 326), 8.50.20.3 (11 Dec. 409), 1.2.19 (528), *CTh/N* 10 (but in several of these the *veteres* are not necessarily lawyers).

[52] Above, n. 51.   [53] *CJ* 7.7.1 (1 Aug. 530).

[54] *CJ* 5.13.1, 5a (1 Nov. 530 *per actionem in rem directam vel per utilem vel per condictionem*), 6.43.1.1 (*non solum personalem actionem sed etiam in rem ... et insuper utilem Servianam*).

[55] Commonly referred to up to Diocletian, then only from 530 onwards: *CJ* 6.26.2 (204), 4.57.2 (222), 4.57.3 (224), 6.54.7 (225), 5.62.5, 12.35.7, 7.1.3 (Alex.), 7.2.6 (Gord.), 5.62.17 (265), 9.41.11 (290), 2.36.3 pr., 5.17.5, 5.62.18.1 (294).

[56] *CJ* 5.4.25.2, 3 (1 Oct. 530 bis *quod d. Marci constitutioni deese videtur*).

[57] *CJ* 6.35.11 pr., 2, 3 (20 April 531).

[58] *Ne princeps philosophiae plenus aliquid videatur imperfectum sanxisse ... merito enim nobis sanctissimi Marci per omnia constitutionem replere placuit: nihil enim actum esse credimus dum aliquid addendum superest.*

[59] *CJ* 7.2.15 pr., 1a, 2 (531/2 ter), 5.17.12 (11 Aug. 534: Μάρκῳ τῷ φιλοσοφωτάτῳ τῶν αὐτοκρατόρων); *N.* 22.19 (18 March 536: ὁ φιλοσοφώτατος Μάρκος), 60.1 (1 Dec. 537 Μάρκος ὁ φιλοσοφώτατος τῶν αὐτοκρατόρων), 108 pr. 2 (1 Feb. 541: ὁ φιλόσοφος ἐν βασιλεῦσι Μάρκος). Not in *CTh/N*.

distinction and moral probity. No wonder Tribonian was later to be stigma-
tised the sworn enemy of the Christian religion.

In the autumn of 529 classical learning invades the quaestor's office.
Other quaestors had been content with general expressions: *veteres leges,
vetera iura, antiqui* or the like.[60] Even under Justinian this is true in the first
two[61] and the last twenty-three years of his reign.[62] The age beheld a handful
of men who were deeply concerned with the heritage of classical culture.
In law, or at any rate in legal administration, one alone stands out.

(b) *The emperor's image*. From the same date another change of tone is to
be noted. All quaestors speak in the emperor's name.[63] Tribonian took this
aspect of his office to heart. This shows in the great range of verbs which he
introduces to describe the disposition and activities of the emperor. Earlier
quaestors portray rather distant and conventional emperors who say
sancimus,[64] *permittimus,*[65] *vetamus*[66] and the like. The new quaestor hardly
ever departs from the majestic plural,[67] but he presents a vivid, even
intimate, imperial personality. New expressions found in the first quaestorship include *abominamur,*[68] *absolvimus,*[69] *adgredimur,*[70] *adspicimus,*[71] *amplec-
timur,*[72] *ampliavimus,*[73] *aperimus,*[74] *audivimus,*[75] *coartamus,*[76] *complectamur,*[77]
composuimus,[78] *(nullo modo) concedimus,*[79] *concludimus,*[80] *conscripsimus,*[81]

---

[60] *Ius vetus CJ* 11.33.2.2 (30 Jan. 314), 9.42.3.4 (14 Oct. 369), 8.57.1 pr. (1 April 320),
4.3.1.2 (5 March 394), 9.2.17.1 (6 Aug. 423), 12.20.4.2 (Leo), 9.35.11 (2 Nov. 478),
7.39.4 pr. (29 July 491). *Veteres leges CJ* 5.33.1.1 (30 Dec. 389), 11.69.1.1 (Zeno). *Antiquae
leges CJ* 1.14.8 (17 Oct. 446), 5.5.8 (1 Sept. 475; cf. *certis legum conditoribus placuit* ibid.).
Ius antiquum CJ 9.46.7 (25 Nov. 366), 5.37.24.1 (25 Feb. 396), 5.5.6.2 (10 Dec. 396),
7.62.31 (30 March 423), 6.18.1 (20 Feb. 428), 5.30.3 (1 July 472), 6.20.18 (21 July 502).
Antiqua iura CJ 4.35.22.3 (23 July 506).
[61] *CJ* 3.28.30.1 (1 June 528 *vetera iura*), 8.53.33.2 (1 June 528 *vetera iura*), 6.56.7 (1
June 528 *veteres leges*) 4.32.26.2 (11 Dec. 528 *veteres leges*), 1.2.19 (528 *veteres leges, vetera
iura*), 3.28.32 (1 April 529 *antiquae leges*), 8.37.12 (6 April 529 *veteres leges*), 3.22.6 (3 Aug.
528/9 *veteres leges*). In this quaestorship (Thomas) the plural is standard.
[62] N. 118 pr. (16 July 543 ἐν τοῖς παλαιοτέροις χρόνοις), 119 (20 Jan. 544 ἐν τοῖς παλαιοῖς
νόμοις).
[63] Cassidorus, *Varia* 6.5.   [64] *VCJ* 1.2719–81.   [65] *VCJ* 1.1799.   [66] *VCJ* 1.2537.
[67] Never in the first quaestorship but see Just. *Inst.* 2.3.30 (*secta temporum meorum non
patitur*, echoing *CJ* 10.11.2.1, 6 Sept. 238 *ne quid in persona tua quod est sectae temporum
meorum alienum adtemptetur*), N. 36.6 (1 Jan 535 *quae igitur pro securitate Africae mea sanxit
aeternitas, haec sublimitas tua . . . manifestare deproperet* and below, n. 130.
[68] *CJ* 1.2.21.1 (Demostheni pp. 529).   [69] *CJ* 8.53.36.1 (18 Oct. 531).
[70] *CJ* 3.28.33 pr. (17 Sept. 529 bis), 2.55.5.3, 3.1.14 pr. (27 March 530), 5.13.1 pr.
(1 Nov. 531).
[71] *CJ* 8.40.28.3 (18 Oct. 531).   [72] *CJ* 7.33.12 pr. (27 Nov. 531).
[73] *CJ* 8.39.4 pr. (1 Sept. 531).
[74] *CJ* 5.27.12.4 (1 Nov. 531); cf. *C. Tanta* 22 (16 Dec. 533), *C. Omnem* 2 (16 Dec. 533).
[75] *CJ* 8.33.3 pr. (18 March 530); cf. *C. Omnem* 7 (16 Dec. 533).
[76] *CJ* 7.63.5.2 (17 Nov. 529).   [77] *CJ* 5.70.7.4 (1 Sept. 530).
[78] *CJ* 5.13.1.2a (1 Nov. 531)0 cf. 17 intro. (16 April 535); cf. *C. Omnem* 4 (16 Dec.
533).
[79] *CJ* 4.1.11.2 (18 Sept. 529), 4.21.20.2 (18 March 530), 3.1.13.2c (27 March 530);
cf. 7.2.15.1b (531/2), 6.21.18 (18 Oct. 532), 6.23.31.3 (5 July 534).

consummavimus,[82] *curamus,*[83] *decoramus,*[84] *dedicamus,*[85] *deduximus,*[86] *delevimus,*[87] *derogamus,*[88] *diximus,*[89] *donamus,*[90] *donavimus,*[91] *emendamus,*[92] *enumeravimus,*[93] *exigimus,*[94] *existimamus,*[95] *expectamus,*[96] *expellimus,*[97] *fovemus,*[98] *illigamus,*[99] *inducimus,*[100] *induximus,*[101] *imponimus,*[102] *inspeximus,*[103] *interpretamur,*[104] *introducimus,*[105] *introduximus,*[106] *invenimus,*[107] *laudamus,*[108] *medemur,*[109]

[80] *CJ* 8.53.34.4a (30 Oct. 529), 5.27.11.4 (18 March 530) but 1.4.3.4 (25 Feb. 385).

[81] *CJ* 5.27.11 pr. (18 March 530); cf. *C. Tanta* 5 (16 Dec. 533).

[82] *CJ* 8.17.12.6 (27 Nov. 531).   [83] *CJ* 8.17.12.8 (27 Nov. 531).

[84] *C. Deo auctore* pr. (15 Dec. 530).

[85] *CJ* 6.57.5.1 (17 Sept. 529); cf. *N.* 9 epil. (14 April 535).

[86] *CJ* 6.28.4.8 (1 Sept. 531); cf. *C. Tanta* 7a, 9 (16 Dec. 533 bis).

[87] *CJ* 3.33.14.2 (1 Oct. 530).   [88] *CJ* 6.58.14.5 (27 Nov. 531).

[89] *CJ* 6.61.6.3a (30 Oct. 529), 11.48.20 pr. (30 Oct. 629), 3.38.12 pr., 3 (22 July 530 bis), 6.43.2.1 (20 Feb. 531), 6.61.8.1b (29 July 531), 8.47.10.3, 4 (1 Sept. 531 bis), 8.17.12.5 (27 Nov. 531); cf. *C. Omnem* 4 (16 Dec. 533) but 6.49.6.3 (1 Sept. 489), 1.1.8.25, 30 (pope John II bis, 6 June 534). *Supra d.* (3.38.12 pr., 11.48.20 pr.), *secundum quae d.* (6.43.2.1, 6.61.6.3a, 8.17.12.5) and *superius d.* (6.61.8.1b) are confined to the period Sept. 529–Nov. 531.

[90] *CJ* 6.42.30 (30 Oct. 529), 8.21.2.2 (1 Aug. 530), 5.13.1.13c (1 Nov. 531); cf. *N.* 35.8, 10 (23 April 535 bis).

[91] *CJ* 5.13.1.13c (1 Nov. 530), 8.17.12.4 (27 Nov. 531) but 1.14.2 (6 Nov. 426).

[92] *CJ* 7.62.39 pr. (27 March 530).

[93] *CJ* 10.32.67.6 (Demostheni pp. 529), 4.21.20.2 (18 March 530), 6.61.8.6c (29 July 531), 2.46.3.2 (30 Aug. 531), 5.13.1.9 (1 Nov. 531); cf. *C. Omnem* 5 (16 Dec. 533), 6.58.15.3a (15 Oct. 534), *N.* 35.7 (23 April 535) but 5.5.7.2 (4 April 454).

[94] *C. Deo auctore* pr. (15 Dec. 530) but 10.40.9 = 12.1.13 (10 Nov. 392) and *C. Imperatoriam* 2 (*ereximus*).

[95] *CJ* 3.28.34.1, 6.24.14.2 (both 29 July 531), 6.43.3.1b (1 Sept. 531); cf. *C. Omnem* pr. (16 Dec. 533).

[96] *CJ* 2.40.5 pr. (1 Nov. 531).   [97] *CJ* 4.38.15.2 (1 Aug. 530).

[98] *CJ* 8.17.12.8 (27 Nov. 531).   [99] *CJ* 6.61.8.6 (29 July 531), *CTh/N* 0.

[100] *CJ* 6.61.6.1c (30 Oct. 529), 6.25.7 pr. (22 July 530), 6.27.5.1b (30 April 531); cf. 6.51.1.9 (1 June 534).

[101] *CJ* 3.1.13.5 (27 March 530), 5.13.1.1c (1 Nov. 531) but 5.9.1.2 (18 Dec. 380).

[102] *CJ* 1.5.19.3 (Demostheni pp. 529), 3.1.13.2b (27 March 530), 1.2.23.4 (18 March 530), 5.70.7.3a, 4 (1 Sept. 530), 6.43.2.3 (20 Feb. 531), 5.37.28.2a (18 Oct. 532) but 9.9.29.1 (25 April 326).

[103] *CJ* 8.48.6 (1 Nov. 531).

[104] *CJ* 6.61.6.4 (30 Oct. 529), 8.21.2.2 (1 Aug. 530), 7.7.2.2 (17 Nov. 530).

[105] *CJ* 6.61.6 pr. (30 Oct. 529).

[106] *CJ* 5.70.7.1a (1 Sept. 530), 5.13.1.13b (1 Nov. 531) but 7.62.32.3 (Theo et Val).

[107] Seventeen texts: *CJ* 6.30.19 pr., 6.61.6 pr. (30 Oct. 529), 3.1.14.1 (27 March 530), 6.25.7.1b (22 July 530), 8.21.2.1 (1 Aug. 530), 3.33.15.1 (1 Oct. 530), 6.27.5.1b, 6.35.11 pr. (both 30 April 531), 6.26.11 pr. (29 July 531), 5.37.26.3 (23 Aug. 531), 8.39.4 pr. (1 Sept. 531), 8.47.10.1b (1 Sept. 531), 6.23.30, 7.40.3.1, 8.40.28.1 (all 18 Oct. 531), 6.40.3.2 (1 Nov. 531), 5.13.1.2a (1 Nov. 531), cf. 7.72.10 pr. (18 Oct. 532), 7.2.15.4 (531/2), 5.17.11.2b (17 Nov. 533), *C. Tanta* 7a (16 Dec. 533), *C. Omnem* 11 (16 Dec. 533), 1.1.8.31 (6 June 534, pope John II), 6.23.31 pr. (5 July 534), *C. Cordi* 3 (16 Nov. 534), *N.* 23 pr. (3 Jan. 536).

[108] *CJ* 6.29.3.1 (17 Nov. 530); cf. 1.1.8.37 (6 June 534, pope John II), *N.* 37.11 (1 Aug. 535).

[109] *CJ* 6.23.28.5 (27 March 530), 6.25.7 pr. (22 July 530).

novamus (=we innovate),[110] *opinamur,*[111] *posuimus,*[112] *praediximus,*[113] *promulgavimus,*[114] *putamus,*[115] *redegimus,*[116] *referimus,*[117] *reperimus,*[118] *repperimus,*[119] *reposuimus,*[120] *respeximus,*[121] *risimus,*[122] *sustentamus,*[123] *sustinuimus,*[124] *sustulimus,*[125] *veremur.*[126]

It will be noticed that many of these innovating verbs are used in the perfect. This has some significance: the quaestor presents his sovereign as a self-reflective person, who thinks of his activities in a temporal context. Another sign of this is the use of *tempora* (age, reign, days) with possessive adjectives: *tempora nostra,*[127] *vestra,*[128] *Anastasiana,*[129] even, with a conscious echo of the early third century, *tempora mea.*[130] Of course behind this we are conscious of Justinian's view of his historical role, but in the earlier part of the reign, in the quaestorship of Thomas, the picture is blurred: *tempora praeterita*[131] and *posteriora,*[132] not yet *nostra.* Tribonian is specially fond of *invenimus,*[133] which means 'it has come to our notice' and also 'we have found a solution'. The image, in modern terms, is that of a ruler who leaves no problem untackled.

[110] *CJ* 6.61.6.1b (30 Oct. 529), *CTh/N* o.   [111] *CJ* 7.7.2.2 (17 Nov. 530), *CTh/N* o.

[112] *CJ* 6.29.4.1 (17 Nov. 530), 2.58.2.4 (20 Feb. 531), 6.28.4.5, 7.17.2 pr. (1 Sept. 531); cf. 1.3.54.7 (Iohanni pp. 531–4), *C. Tanta* 23 (16 Dec. 533), *C. Omnem* 4 bis, 5 bis (16 Dec 533), *N.* 33 (15 June 533 bis) and *ponimus* (*C. Omnem* 8), above.

[113] *CJ* 10.32.67.4 (Demostheni pp. 529), 8.53.35.3 (18 March 530), 2.55.5 pr., 4.20.20 (27 March 530); cf. 1.3.53.5, 9.13.1.3 (17 Nov. 533), 6.51.1.5 (1 June 534 bis), *N.* 112.2.1 (9 Sept. 541).

[114] *CJ* 5.70.7.1b (1 Sept. 530), 6.22.11 pr. (29 July 531), 6.23.30 (18 Oct. 531), 6.40.3 pr. (1 Nov. 531); cf. *C. Tanta* 11 (16 Dec. 533), *C. Cordi* 1 (16 Nov. 534), *N.* 36 pr. (1 Jan. 535), but 12.23.11 (29 June 416).

[115] *CJ* 7.4.17.2 (17 Nov. 530), 6.30.22.13 (27 Nov. 531); cf. 7.71.8.1 (531/2) but 8.55.7.4 (20 Sept. 349), 7.65.5.1 (30 Jan. 378) and cf. *putavimus C. Tanta* 10 (16 Dec. 533), but 9.9.19 (5 Dec. 287).

[116] *C. Deo auctore* 9 (15 Dec. 530).   [117] *CJ* 8.17.12.9 (287 Nov. 531).

[118] *CJ* 7.5.1 (530).   [119] *C. Deo auctore* 1 (15 Dec. 530).

[120] *C. Deo auctore* 2 (15 Dec. 530); cf. *C. Tanta* 5 (16 Dec. 533 bis).

[121] *CJ* 8.21.2 pr. (1 Aug. 530), *C. Deo auctore* 3 (15 Dec. 530), 6.42.32.3 (27 Nov. 531), *CTh/N* o.

[122] *CJ* 1.14.12.2 (30 Oct. 529), *CTh/N* o.

[123] *C. Deo auctore* pr. (15 Dec. 530), *CTh/N* o.   [124] *CJ* 7.24.1 pr. (531–4).

[125] *CJ* 6.40.3 pr. (1 Nov. 531), 8.17.12.1 (27 Nov. 531), *CTh/N* o.

[126] *CJ* 2.58.2.4 (20 Feb. 531).

[127] *CJ* 6.57.5.1 (17 Sept. 529 *nostris temporibus indignum*), 4.18.2.1 (20 Feb. 531 *tam nostris t. quam iustis legibus contrarium*), 4.35.23.3 (531/2 *in tanta temporum nostrorum benivolentia*); cf. 6.21.18 (18 Oct. 532 *indignum nostris t.*), 7.24.1 pr. (531/2), 1.29.5 (Iustinianus Zetae *nostra felicia t.*), *C. Tanta* 6b (16 Dec. 533) but 1.3.30.3 (8 March 469), 9.19.6 (1 Dec. 526). *Nostri imperii tempora* (*C. Tanta* pr., 16 Dec. 533).

[128] *C. Tanta* 19 (16 Dec. 533 bis: you live in great times).

[129] *C. Deo auctore* 1 (15 Dec. 530 *Romuleis t.*); cf. 4.35.23.3 (531/2 *Anastasianis t.*), *N.* 11.1 (14 April 535 *Attilanis t.*).

[130] *CJ* 2.3.30.4 (1 Nov. 531 *secta temporum meorum*); cf. 7.24.1 pr. (531/4 *religio t. meorum*).

[131] *CJ* 4.30.14 pr. (1 June 528), 8.58.2 (1 June 528), *C. Summa* pr. (7 April 529).

[132] *CJ* 7.21.6.1 (8 June 260), *C. Summa* 1 (7 April 529).

[133] *C. Summa* 1 (7 April 529).

A closely related usage is that of the nominative plural participle to describe the emperor's doings according to the construction (*decidentes sancimus*, for example) which was common in the sixth century. Here some of the same, some different verbs are to be listed: *adgredientes*,[134] *adspicientes*,[135] *ampliantes*,[136] *compescentes*,[137] *concludentes*,[138] *corrigentes*,[139] *decidentes*,[140] *declinantes*,[141] *definientes*,[142] *expellentes*,[143] *existimantes*,[144] *gubernantes*,[145] *imponentes*,[146] *invenientes*,[147] *putantes*,[148] *reminiscentes*,[149] *respicientes*,[150] *respuentes*,[151] *separantes*,[152] *tollentes*,[153] *trahentes*.[154]

The use of *nosmet*[155] for *nos* is perhaps another index of the attempt to present the emperor as intimately concerned with his subject's affairs. By contrast the constitutions of our period are distinctly reserved so far as the use of personified imperial virtues (*mansuetudo nostra* etc.) is concerned. *Noster vigor*,[156] used once, is unusual. The relation of the emperor to the law is made intimate (*iura nostra*);[157] still more so his responsibility for the atmosphere of the reign, where, harking back to Alexander and Gordian, Tribonian uses the first person singular: *secta temporum meorum*.[158] Of the

[134] *CJ* 7.7.2.2 (17 Nov. 530); cf. *C. Tanta* 1 (16 Dec. 533).

[135] *CJ* 6.61.6.1a (30 Oct. 529).   [136] *CJ* 5.20.2 (1 Aug. 530).

[137] *CJ* 5.70.7.3a (1 Sept. 530).

[138] *CJ* 3.31.12.1 (1 Sept. 531), 5.13.1 pr. (1 Nov. 531), 5.27.12 pr. (1 Nov. 531); cf. *C. Tanta* 5, 7 (16 Dec. 533 bis).

[139] *CJ* 7.39.9.1 (Demostheni pp. 529), 6.23.28.6 (27 March 530), 8.41.8 pr. (22 July 530), 8.47.10 pr. (1 Sept. 531), 6.28.4.2 (1 Sept. 531), 8.47.11 (1 Nov. 531), 6.58.14.6, 7.54.3.2 (27 Nov. 531), cf. 6.31.6 pr. (18 Oct. 532), 6.51.1.1c, 4 (1 June 534 bis), Appx. 1.1 (7 April 540) but 5.9.9. (13 April 529), *CTh/N* 0.

[140] Ch. 5 nn. 26–7.   [141] *CJ* 6.2.22.3a, 6.29.3.1 (17 Nov. 530).

[142] *CJ* 11.48.20.3 (30 Oct. 529), 7.64.10 (Demostheni pp. 529).

[143] *CJ* 4.27.3 pr. (1 Nov. 531), 7.25.1 (530/1) and *expellens C. Imperatoriam* pr. (16 Nov. 533).

[144] *CJ* 6.26.10.1 (29 July 531); cf. 6.51.1.14a (1 June 534).

[145] *C. Deo auctore* pr. (15 Dec. 530).

[146] *CJ* 11.48.20 pr. (30 Oct. 529), 7.7.7 pr. (1 Aug. 530), 3.1.16 (20 Feb. 531); cf. 6.51.1.11b (1 June 534), *N.* 23 pr. (3 Jan. 536).

[147] *CJ* 7.63.5.4 (17 Nov. 529); cf. 4.35.23 pr. (531/2), *C. Omnem* 2 (16 Dec. 533), *C. Tanta* 17 (16 Dec. 533).

[148] *CJ* 8.10.13 (1 Sept. 531).

[149] *CJ* 8.17.12.4 (27 Nov. 531); cf. *C. Omnem* 4 (16 Dec. 533), *N.* 9.3 (14 April 535).

[150] *CJ* 4.38.15.2 (1 Aug. 530), 6.2.21.2 (1 Oct. 530), 8.17.12.2, 4 (27 Nov. 531 bis); cf. *C. Tanta* 1 (16 Dec. 533), 6.23.31 pr. (5 July 534) but 5.4.23 pr. (520–3), *CTh/N* 0.

[151] *C. Tanta* 6a (16 Dec. 533).   [152] *CJ* 2.52.7 pr. (1 Sept. 531).

[153] *CJ* 3.28.33.1 (17 Sept. 529), 6.40.2 pr. (20 Feb. 531), 8.47.11 (1 Nov. 531); cf. 4.34.12, 5.3.20.7.7.32. 12 pr. (531/2). In view of the use of *tollimus* in *CJ* 6.23.25 (11 Nov. 528), 7.17.1.1 (same) *tollentes* should perhaps be eliminated as a mark of Tribonian's style.

[154] *CJ* 6.51.1.11b (1 June 534).   [155] *CJ* 7.37.3.1c, 3 (27 Nov. 531).

[156] *CJ* 3.28.34.1 (29 July 531).

[157] *CJ* 7.15.3.2 (1 Nov. 531 *nec antiqua iura nec nostra*); cf. Nov. 114.1.1 (1 Nov. 541); cf. *C. Omnem* 2 (16 Dec. 533 *nostrum nomen merere*).

[158] *CJ* 2.3.30.4 (1 Nov. 531); cf. 7.24.1 pr. (*religio temporum meorum*). For *tempora mea* see *CJ* 4.7.2 (17 Nov. 215), 9.9.9 (26 Jan. 224), 10.11.2.1 (6 Sept. 238) and *meum saeculum*

imperial phrases which appear for the first time one may cite *imperialis maiestas*,[159] *principalis* and *divalis constitutio*,[160] *augusta maiestas*,[161] *augustum remedium*.[162] Other phrases serve to emphasise the Roman character of the empire: *Romana sanctio*[163] and *dicio*,[164] not to mention the phrase *antiqua Roma*[165] which is important as an indication of perspective. Perhaps as an affectation, Greek words (*Graeca vocabula*)[166] are spoken of in a rather distant way.

The quaestorship of September 529 is marked off from previous tenures by its assumption of a problem-solving role. Two linguistic signs of this are the use of *quaerebatur* and *dubitabatur* to introduce legal conundrums. While the first is used only from 1 October 530, when the *Digest* project was already in the course of preparation, the latter is found from the beginning of the tenure, though it becomes a refrain only when the series of Fifty Decisions gets under weigh in the autumn of 530. There is no precedent in *CJ* either for the 16 uses of the former[167] or the 40 of the latter,[168] nor for the partici-

---

CJ 9.8.1 (Alex.). The first person singular is found under certain fifth-century quaestors: *CJ* 11.24.1 (23 July 416), 1.30.1 (26 April 424), 1.30.2 (29 April 424), 1.2.8 (10 Oct. 424 = 10.16.12.3), 11.12.1.1, 2; 11.10.7 pr., 4 (Leo), 10.5.3 (Leo et Anth.). In the fourth century only 9.18.7 pr. (5 July 358) but for speech as opposed to writing one can add 12.46.1.1, 3 (Constantine 1 March 320).

[159] *CJ* 1.14.12 pr., 5 (30 Oct. 529 bis), 5.16.27.1 (1 Dec. 530), 3.1.16 (29 Feb. 531), 7.37.3.1b (27 Nov. 531); cf. 12.3.5.1 (531/4) and cf. *imperatoria maiestas* below, n. 769.
[160] *C. Deo auctore* 6 (15 Dec. 530), 6.38.4.1 (30 April 531); cf. *C. Tanta* 1, 10,14 (16 Dec. 533) but 2.3.19 (19 Nov. 290) and below, n. 458.
[161] *CJ* 2.46.3 pr. (30 Aug. 531); cf. 12.3.5 pr. (531/3) but 10.1.4 pr. (Dio. et Max. AA), 12.35.14 (19 March 400 itp.; cf. *CTh* 7.1.18).
[162] *CJ* 5.16.27.1 (27 Nov. 531); cf. *C. Tanta* 18 (16 Dec. 533), *CTh*/N o.
[163] *CJ C. Deo auctore* 2 (15 Dec. 530), *CTh*/N o.
[164] *CJ* 8.51.3.1 (17 Sept. 529); cf. *C. Imperatoriam* 1, N. 36 pr. (1 Jan. 535), N. 62 pr. (1 Jan. 537) but 5.5.2 (11 Dec. 285 *sub dicione Romani nominis*) *CTh*/N o and see n. 341.
[165] *CJ* 2.52.7 pr. (1 Sept. 531), *CTh*/N o and below, n. 340.
[166] *CJ* 2.55.4.6 (30 Oct. 529), 4.66.3 pr. (18 March 530), *C. Deo auctore* 8 (15 Dec. 530); cf. *C. Tanta* 2 (16 Dec. 533), but 1.54.3 (13 Sept. 239), perhaps the source; *CTh*/N o.
[167] *CJ* 6.2.21 pr. (1 Oct. 530), 6.2.22.1, 4.27.2 pr., 6.27.4 pr. (17 Nov. 530), 6.42.31 pr. (28 Feb. 531), 6.42.31 pr., 6.27.5.3, 6.30.20 pr., 6.37.24 pr., 6.46.6 pr. (30 April 531), 6.26.11 pr. (29 July 531 bis), 3.28.36.1 (1 Sept. 531), 4.1.13 pr. (18 Oct. 531), 5.14.11 pr., 5.27.12 pr. (1 Nov. 531); cf. 6.49.8, 3.34.14 pr. (18 Oct. 532), 5.4.28 pr. (531/2).
[168] Introducing a doubt, hence not in the negative form *minime dubitabatur* (*CJ* 6.20.19.1, 1 June 528), *CJ* 6.57.5 pr. (17 Sept. 529), 6.61.6.4 (30 Oct. 529), 4.66.3 pr. (18 March 530), 4.5.10 pr. (1 Aug. 530), 6.22.9 pr. (1 Sept. 530), 8.47.10.4 (1 Sept. 531), 8.56.4 (1 Sept. 531), 3.33.16 pr., 7.4.14 pr., 5.4.25.2, 5.4.26 pr., 6.57.6 pr. (all 1 Oct. 530), 2.18.24 pr. (17 Nov. 530), 7.4.16 pr. (17 Nov. 530), 6.21.22.4a (17 Nov. 530), 6.29.3 pr. (17 Nov. 530), 11.48.22.3 (20 Feb. 531), 8.40.27 (20 Feb. 531), 6.27.5 pr., 6.30.20.1 (30 April 531), 6.38.4 pr. (30 April 531), 6.25.10 pr., 6.26.10 pr., 6.46.7 pr. (29 July 531), 1.3.49 pr., 2.3.29 pr., 2.41.2, 3.28.36.1c, 3.28.37.1d, 8.10.13, 6.43.3 pr., 1a bis, (all 1 Sept. 531), 6.49.7.1b (18 Oct. 531), 3.33.17 pr. (18 Oct. 531), 4.54.9 pr. (18 Oct. 531), 5.11.7 pr. (1 Nov. 531), 2.3.30 pr., 8.37.14 pr., 6.37.25 pr., 6.58.13 (all 1 Nov. 531); cf. *C. Tanta* 10 (16 Dec. 533), 7.71.8 pr. (531/2).

pial form *dubitatus*,[169] which occurs six times; the categorical *non dubitatur* is found earlier,[170] but not the inquiring *dubitatur*.[171]

(c) *Preferred concepts.* From the point of view of ideas the most striking words are *natura* and *humanus*. Of the first 59 mentions of *natura* in *CJ*, 49 come from our period. If the 21 mentions in *CTh/N* are taken into account the proportion for the first quaestorship remains strikingly high.[172] In particular the texts of this period stress the nature of institutions (*sua natura*, all eight *CJ* texts, with one from *CTh/N*,[173] *sui natura*, all six texts),[174] though they also in a more standard use contrast the natural with the legal or artificial[175] and speak of *natura* as a creative or controlling force.[176]

So far as *humanus* is concerned the period has six of the first eight texts with *humanum est/esse*,[177] the first four with *humanius est*,[178] only two with *humanissimum est*,[179] and three of the first four with *inhumanum/e*.[180] We also find the first texts with *humanior sententia*.[181] The notion of *humanitas*

---

[169] *CJ* 1.14.12.2 (30 Oct. 529), 4.37.6, 6.27.5.3 (30 April 531), 2.46.3 pr. (30 Aug. 531), 3.28.37.1e (1 Sept. 531), 6.58.13 pr. (1 Nov. 531).

[170] *CJ* 6.28.1 pr. (26 June 204), 8.44.6 (8 March 222), 12.36.1 pr. (13 Nov. 223), 7.18.3 pr. (18 May 323). No instance in Sept. 529–Nov. 531.

[171] 6.23.28.6 (27 March 530), 6.38.4.1c (30 April 531), 3.1.18 (1 Nov. 531).

[172] *CJ* 6.43.1.1, 3.28.33.1 (17 Sept. 529), 8.53.34.3 (30 Oct. 529), 7.40.1.1 (18 March 530), 6.23.28.1, 5 (27 March 530 bis), 5.51.13 pr., 7.7.1.6a, 8.37.13.2 (1 Aug. 530), 3.33.13 pr., 3.33.15.2 (1 Oct. 530), 2.18.24.2 (17 Nov. 530), *C. Deo auctore* 1 (15 Dec. 530), 2.58.2.2a, 6.22.10 pr., 3 (bis), 6.40.2.1, 6.43.2.1, 2 (bis), 4.18.2 pr. (20 Feb. 531), 6.61.8.4, 6.26.11.1 (29 July 531), 8.47.10.1a bis, 1d bis, 1g, 4 (sex.), 2.55.6, 7.17.2.1, 6.28.4.1, 7.47.1.1 (bis, all 1 Sept. 531), 6.58.12.1, 2 (18 Oct. 531 bis), 5.11.7 pr., 5.13.1.1d, 2 bis, 2a, 5f, 6, 8, 9, 10, 15b (1 Nov. 531 dec.), 7.54.3 pr., 6.58.14 pr., 5 (bis all 27 Nov. 531); cf. *C. Tanta* 18 (16 Dec. 533), 4.35.23 pr. (531/2), 3.34.14.1 (18 Oct. 532), 6.51.1. 2a, 6, 6a, 9c bis, 11b (1 June 534 sex.), *C. Cordi* 4 (16 Nov. 534) but 5.18.6.3 (26 Oct. 290/293), 6.56.1 (23 March 291), 4.19.23 (25 Dec. 294,) 4.24.11 (28 Dec. 294), 3.28.28 pr. (6 Feb. 321), 5.16.24.1 (27 Feb. 321), 9.51.13.2c (14 Sept. 321), 9.18.6 (4 Dec. 357), 8.2.3 pr. (27 July 395 *lex naturae*), 5.4.23 pr. (520/523), *CTh/N* 21, *naturaliter CJ* 3.42.9, 4.26.12 (294), 5.12.30 (30 Oct. 529), 5.13.1.7 (1 Nov. 530), 6.22.10.2, 5 (bis), 6.43.2.1 (20 Feb. 531); cf. *C. Tanta* 13 (16 Dec. 533).

[173] *CJ* 3.28.33.1, 3.33.15.2, 5.13.1.8, 2.18.24.2, 5.11.7 pr., 8.47.10.1d, 3.34.14.1; above, n. 172; cf. 4.35.23 pr. (531/2), *CTh/N* 1.

[174] *CJ* 5.13.1.2a, 5f.; 6.51.1.6, 6a; 7.7.1.6a, 8.53.34.3; above, n. 172, *CTh/N* 0.

[175] *CJ* 8.47.10.4 (1 Sept. 530), 6.58.14.5 (17 Nov. 531), 6.61.8.4e (29 July 531).

[176] *CJ* 6.23.28.1 (27 March 530), 8.47.10.1a bis, 1d (1 Sept. 530 ter), 6.40.2.1, 6.22.10 pr., 3 (20 Feb. 531), 6.28.4.1, 7.47.1.1, 2.55.6 (1 Sept. 531), 6.58.12.1, 2 (18 Oct. 531 bis), 6.58.14 pr. (27 Nov. 531), cf. *CJ* 8.48.6 (1 Nov. 531).

[177] *CJ* 3.33.12.1 (1 Aug. 530), 6.37.23.2 (30 April 531), 8.39.4.1 (1 Sept. 531), 5.13.1.14a, 8.37.14 pr. (1 Nov. 531), 6.30.22.1 (27 Nov. 531); cf. 6.38.5.1 (18 Oct. 532) but 4.44.2 (28 Oct. 285), 1.14.8 pr. (17 Oct. 446), *CTh/N* 0.

[178] *CJ* 8.21.2.1 (1 Aug. 520), 3.33.15.2 (1 Oct. 530), 6.27.5.1b (30 April 531), 2.40.5.1 (1 Nov. 531); cf. 7.2.15.3 (531/2), *CTh/N* 0.

[179] *CJ* 5.35.3.2 (18 March 530), 3.33.12.1 (1 Aug. 530), *CTh/N* 0.

[180] *CJ* 6.40.2.2 (20 Feb. 530), 3.28.34 pr. (29 July 531 *inhumane*), 7.31.1 pr. (18 Oct. 531); cf. 11.48.23 pr. (531/4), *N.* 35.10 (23 April 535), Nov. 34 pr. (15 June 535), *CTh/N* 2 but 10.35.2.2 (2 March 443).

[181] *CJ* 3.33.13.1, 7.4.14.1 (1 Oct. 530), 7.7.2.3 (17 Nov. 531); cf. 7.71.8.1, 5 (531/2).

is naturally found in earlier constitutions,[182] but with Tribonian's quaestor-ship there comes a special emphasis on this notion (φιλανθρωπία) as a ground of decision. We also find the first three texts contrasting the human and divine.[183]

(d) *Aspects of Tribonian's vocabulary.* The new quaestor favours an ornate, majestic and sonorous form of composition. It is coloured by a cumulation of metaphors and instances; yet its basic structure is simple. Far removed from the excessive intricacy, the miasmic smog of the *Codex Theodosianus*, it is equally distant from the plain, unrhetorical Latin of most of the third-century secretaries *a libellis*. The tradition to which it stands closest is rather that of the more literary of the classical drafters of constitutions: the secretaries of 238–41, 254–8 and 290–1. Its stately power (not immune from descent into absurdity) emerges from the following constitution, which reforms and simplifies the formalities for the emancipation of children.[184]

> Cum inspeximus in emancipationibus vanam observationem custodiri et venditiones in liberas personas figuratas et circumductiones inextricabiles et iniuriosa rhapismata, quorum nullus rationabilis invenitur exitus, iubemus huiusmodi circuitu in posterum quiescente licentiam esse ei, qui emancipare vult vel ex lege Anastasiana hoc facere vel sine sacro rescripto intrare compententis iudicis tribunal vel eos adire magistratus, quibus hoc facere vel legibus vel ex longa consuetudine permissum est.

This long ponderous sentence makes its effect by the accumulation of detail. The contrast between the long outlandish words of the introductory clause (*circumductiones, rhapismata, circuitus*) and the relative brevity of those that follow is meant to present vividly to the reader the difference between the complexity of the old law and the straightforward character of Justin-ian's reform. The style is rhetorical in its selection of a vocabulary but not complex in syntax, nor does the author aim at the jigsaw effect (with adjec-tive, noun and participle widely separated) which was so popular in the fourth and fifth centuries and of which, indeed, Justin's quaestor Proclus is fond.

The text is of course meant to be read aloud. The second line has a sibilant effect (*iniuriosa rhapismata*) which is not untypical. Tribonian liked adjectives in *-osus*. Our period provides a number of examples: *com-pendiosus,*[185] *contentiosus,*[186] *dolosus,*[187] *explosus,*[188] *formidolosus,*[189] *lucrosus,*[190]

---

[182] E.g. in the quaestorship of Thomas: *CJ* 5.27.8 (1 June 528), 6.26.9 (11 Dec. 528).

[183] *CJ* 1.2.22 pr. (30 Oct. 529), 1.2.21 pr. (Demostheni pp. 529), *C. Deo auctore* 1 (15 Dec. 530); cf. *C. Tanta* 18 (16 Dec. 533), *CTh/N* 0.

[184] *CJ* 8.48.6 (1 Nov. 531).   [185] Below, n. 374.

[186] *CJ* 2.58.1 pr., 3.28.33 pr. (17 Sept. 529); cf. *N.* 35.5 (23 April 535), *CTh/N* 0.

[187] *CJ* 2.18.24.2 (17 Nov. 530); cf. 8.36.5.1 (18 Oct. 532), 7.32.12 pr. (531/2) but 5.18.6.1 (26 Oct. 290/3, *CTh/N* 0 and *dolose* 6.23.29.7 (20 Feb. 531), *N.* 36.4 (1 Jan. 535), *CTh/N* 0.

[188] *CJ* 7.15.1.3 (18 March 530), 6.42.31.1 (30 April 531), 6.38.4.1a (30 April 531), 6.25.8 (29 July 531); cf. *N.* 37.3 (1 Aug. 535) but 7.71.6 (1 May 386 itp *CTh* 4.20.3); on *explodere* in general see n. 425, below.

[189] *CJ* 6.30.22.1 (27 Nov. 531), *CTh/N* 0.   [190] *CJ* 6.30.22.1b (27 Nov. 531), *CTh/N* 0.

ludibriosus,[191] *odiosus*,[192] *periculosus*,[193] *ridiculosus*,[194] *spinosus*,[195] *studiosus*,[196] *tenebrosus*,[197] *verbosus*.[198] Other words which seem to be liked for their sibilance include *increbescere*,[199] *ingemiscere*,[200] *resuscitare*,[201] and *sciscitare*.[202] If to these we add *resonare*,[203] *consonantia*[204] and *discordia*,[205] the suspicion grows that Tribonian's sensuous language is as much or more oriented towards sound than sight. In a visually perceptive age and with a writer given to sensory metaphors, one can point to few distinctive expressions concerned with light: *sub umbra*[206] points rather to its exclusion. But of his appreciation of the aesthetic aspects of law and legislation there can be no doubt: *pulcher*[207] (only in the superlative), *eloquens*[208] and *bellus*[209] (only in the superlative); these adjectives and the abstract noun *pulchritudo*[210] are not found in *CJ* before this tenure.

He likes the grand manner: long, outlandish and compound words, extended rhythmic periods. To illustrate this I begin with some of the expressions of negative meaning prefixed by *in-*: *improbabilitas*,[211] *infeli-*

---

191 *CJ* 5.70.6.1 (1 Sept. 530), *CTh/N* 0.

192 *CJ* 7.40.3.3 (18 Oct. 531), 2.3.30.2 (1 Nov. 531); cf. 3.10.3 (18 Oct. 532), 9.13.1.3b (17 Nov. 533), *C. Tanta* 6a (16 Dec. 533) but 10.15.1.1 (10 Oct. 474), *CTh/N* 1.

193 *CJ* 3.1.14.3 (27 March 530), 2.3.30.2 (1 Nov. 531) but 9.25.1 (18 Dec. 293), 1.40.6 (9 Dec. 385), *CTh/N* 2.

194 *CJ* 1.14.12.5 (30 Oct. 529) and *ridiculus*; cf. 8.4.11 pr. (18 Oct. 532), *C. Omnem* 2 (16 Dec. 533), *ridere CJ* 1.14.12.2 (30 Oct. 529), 8.55.10.1 (18 March 530), *CTh/N* 0.

195 *C. Deo auctore* 9 (15 Dec. 530), *CTh/N* 0.

196 *CJ* 3.33.15.2 (1 Oct. 530), *C. Deo auctore* 1, 7, 11 (15 Dec. 530); cf. *C. Tanta* 1, 9 (16 Dec. 533), 1.3.54.11 (Iohanni pp. after 17 Nov. 533) but 11.26.1 (20 June 382), 1.3.26 (17 Sept. 459), *CTh/N* 2.

197 *CJ* 6.43 3.2 (1 Sept. 531 *tenebrosissimus*), *CTh/N* 1.

198 *CJ* 7.40.1.1c, 7.62.39.1a (27 March 530), *CTh/N* 0.

199 *CJ* 4.1.12 pr. (30 Oct. 529), 6.43.1.2 (17 Sept. 529), 6.2.22.1b (17 Nov. 530); cf. *C. Tanta* 6b (16 Dec. 533), *N.* 111.1 (1 June 541), *CTh/N* 0.

200 *CJ* 7.63.5.1c (17 Sept. 529), *CTh/N* 2.

201 *CJ* 3.1.13.2c, 7.62.39.1a (27 March 530), 5.37.25.1 (20 Feb. 531); cf. *C. Tanta* 23 (16 Dec. 533), *N.* 36 pr. (1 Jan. 535), *CTh/N* 0.

202 *CJ* 6.23.28.4 (27 March 530), *CTh/N* 0.

203 *CJ* 7.4.16 pr. (17 Nov. 530), *CTh/N* 0.

204 *CJ* 6.58.14 pr. (27 Nov. 531); cf. *C. Imperatoriam* 2, *C. Tanta* pr. (16 Dec. 533), *CTh/N* 0.

205 *C. Deo auctore* 1, 4 (15 Dec. 530 bis), 6.30.21.1 (30 April 531); cf. *C. Tanta* 15, 21 (16 Dec. 533) meaning 'inconsistency' and *concordia* (*C. Deo auctore* 8 (15 Dec. 530); cf. 6.51.1.11b (1 June 534) meaning 'consistency'. *CTh/N* 0.

206 *CJ* 1.51.14.2 (17 Sept. 529); cf. *N.* 11.1 (14 April 535) but 1.7.3.2 (11 May 391), *CTh/N* 1.

207 *C. Deo auctore* 5, 7 (15 Dec. 530); cf. *C. Imperatoriam* 7 (21 Nov. 533), *C. Omnem* 4 (*pulcherrimus Papinianus*), 7, 9 (16 Dec. 533), *C. Tanta* 5, 11, 17 (16 Dec. 533), *CTh/N* 0.

208 *CJ* 10.32.67.1 (Demostheni pp. 529); cf. *C. Cordi* 2 (16 Nov. 534), *CTh/N* 0.

209 *CJ* 6.35.11.2 (30 April 531); cf. 7.2.15.4 (531/2), *C. Omnem* 4 (16 Dec. 533), 6.58.15.1b (15 Oct. 534), *CTh/N* 0.

210 *CJ* 5.13.1.2a (1 Nov. 531); cf. *C. Omnem* 3 (16 Dec. 533), *C. Tanta* pr. (16 Dec. 533) but 9.47.17 (21 March 315), *CTh/N* 3.

211 *CJ* 7.47.1.1 (1 Sept. 531), *CTh/N* 0.

citas,[212] and the adjectives *inaestimatus,*[213] *inelegans,*[214] *inexorabilis,*[215] *in-extricabilis,*[216] *inhumanus,*[217] *inmutilatus,*[218] *inrationabilis,*[219] *inrecusabilis,*[220] *inrevocabilis,*[221] *inusitatus.*[222] There are several abstract nouns in -*tas*: apart from those with prefix -*in*: *malignitas,*[223] *novitas*[224] (=modern times), *posteritas*[225] (=later ages), *sanitas,*[226] *scrupulositas,*[227] *simplicitas,*[228] *sinceritas,*[229] *verbositas.*[230] Of collective nouns one may mention *advocatio*[231] and *vituperatio.*[232]

Appellatorius,[233] *ambulatorius*[234] and *adiutorium*[235] have a sound in common. *Laxamentum,*[236] *adsimulatio,*[237] *circumductio,*[238] *circumcludere,*[239]

---

[212] *CJ* 7.63.5.1c (17 Sept. 529 *luctuosis infelicitatibus*), *CTh/N* 0.

[213] *CJ* 5.12.30 pr. (30 Oct. 529), 5.13.1.15c (1 Nov. 531), *CTh/N* 0.

[214] *CJ* 7.54.3.1 (27 Nov. 531) and *ineleganter* 11.48.22.2 (20 Feb. 531); cf. 6.51.1.9 (1 June 534), *CTh/N* 0.

[215] *CJ* 7.63.5.4 (17 Sept. 529) but 10.71.4 (440/441), *CTh/N* 0.

[216] Below, n. 375.   [217] Above, n. 180.

[218] *CJ* 6.29.4.1 (17 Nov. 530), 5.37.26.5 (23 Aug. 531), 6.58.12.1 (18 Oct. 531), 4.54.9 pr. (18 Oct. 531), 6.50.18 pr., 5.13.1.16a (1 Nov. 531); cf. 5.3.20.7 (531/532), *N.* 37.12 (1 Aug. 535) but 8.5.1.1 (23 Oct. 326), *CTh/N* 0.

[219] *CJ* 5.9.10.5 (17 Sept. 529), 6.43.3.2a (1 Sept. 531), 7.37.3.1a (27 Nov. 531), *CTh/N* 0.

[220] *CJ* 3.1.13.8a (27 March 530), *CTh/N* 0.

[221] *CJ* 5.12.31.3, 8.33.3.3e (18 March 530), 5.11.7.3 (1 Nov. 531), *CTh/N* 0.

[222] *CJ* 3.1.14.1 (27 March 530), 4.18.2 (20 Feb. 531); cf. *C. Cordi* 3 (16 Nov. 534) but 3.32.12 (8 May 293), *CTh/N* 2.

[223] *CJ* 5.14.11.4 (1 Nov. 530), 4.27.2.1, 7.4.16.1 (17 Nov. 530), 7.6.1.11a (1 Nov. 531), 6.30.22.2b (27 Nov. 531); cf. 7.32.12 pr. (531/532) but 10.34.3.1 (Zeno), *CTh/N* 0.

[224] *CJ* 6.58.14.4 (27 Nov. 531); cf. *N.* 23.3 (3 Jan. 536 bis), but 10.32.23 (1 Nov. 362).

[225] *CJ* 6.43.1 pr. (17 Sept. 529), 5.59.4 (20 Feb. 531), 6.58.14.1 (27 Nov. 531), 4.37.6 (531); cf. *C. Tanta* 21 (16 Dec. 533), *N.* 111 pr. (1 June 541). *CTh/N* 1 meaning 'later developments'.

[226] *CJ* 6.23.28.1 (27 March 530), 5.70.6.1, 5.70.7.8 (1 Sept. 530), *CTh/N* 1.

[227] *CJ* 1.14.12.2 (30 Oct. 529), 7.40.1.1 (17 March 530), 8.37.13.1 (1 Aug. 530), 6.27.4.2 (17 Nov. 530) but 7.71.6 (1 May 386), *CTh/N* 0.

[228] *CJ* 5.51.13 pr. (1 Aug. 530), 2.41.2 (1 Sept. 531), 8.40.28 (531), 6.30.22.16 (27 Nov. 531); cf. 6.23.31 pr. (5 July 534) but 1.18.1 (25 April 212), 6.21.3 pr. (1 Nov. 213), 9.45.6 (Dio et Max AA et CC), *CTh/N* 0.

[229] *C. Deo auctore* 1 (15 Dec. 530) but 1.4.13 pr. (March/April 456).

[230] *C. Deo auctore* 12 (15 Dec. 530), *CJ* 5.13.1.5 (1 Nov. 531); cf. *C. Tanta* 21 (16 Dec. 533), 8.53.37 (Iohanni pp. after 18 Oct. 531).

[231] *CJ* 6.58.12 pr. (18 Oct. 531), 2.3.30 pr. (1 Nov. 531); cf. 2.7.29 pr. (531/4), *CTh/N* 0 = 'bar').

[232] *CJ* 6.33.3 pr. (18 March 530) and cf. *vituperare CJ* 4.65.35.3 (Iustinianus ad senatum), *C. Tanta* 13 (16 Dec. 533), both *CTh/N* 0.

[233] *CJ* 7.63.5.4 (17 Sept. 529); cf. *N.* 23.1 (1 Aug. 535), *CTh/N* 0.

[234] *CJ* 6.2.22.1b (17 Nov. 530), *CTh/N* 0.   [235] Below, n. 393.

[236] *CJ* 5.70.6 pr. (1 Sept. 530), 7.54.3.3 (27 Nov. 531), *CTh/N* 1.

[237] *CJ* 2.18.24.2 (17 Nov. 530) and *adsimulare: CJ* 1.51.14.2 (27 Sept. 529), 4.21.21 pr. (20 Feb. 530); cf. 4.35.23.2 (531/2) but 1.9.11 (29 May 408), *CTh/N* 1.

[238] *CJ* 8.48.6 (1 Nov. 531), *CTh/N* 1.

[239] *CJ* 1.2.23.2 (27 March 530); cf. 6.51.1.1b (1 June 534), *N.* 9.1 (14 April 535), *CTh/N* 0.

condicticius,[240] *conductionalis,*[241] *consentaneus,*[242] *copulativus,*[243] *corroborare,*[244] *deteriorare,*[245] *exaggerare,*[246] *expurgatio,*[247] *frequentare,*[248] *interemptio,*[249] *medicamen,*[250] *oppigneratio,*[251] *pigneratio,*[252] *ratiocinator,*[253] *redarguere,*[254] *supereminere,*[255] *tergiversari,*[256] and *vituperatio*[257] are portmanteau words. Among the more outlandish expressions we may count *aenigma,*[258] *antecellere,*[259] *antinomia,*[260] *circuitus,*[261] *emponema,*[262] *ludibrium,*[263] *praepeditus,*[264] *rhapisma,*[265] and *transcursio.*[266]

An impression of weight is lent by the quaestor's fondness for compound verbs and adverbs when the simple word would be usual or at least possible (e.g. *exoriri* for *oriri*). The compound of course often conveys a more emphatic meaning. Examples are: *coadunare,*[267] *collaudare,*[268] *commanere,*[269]

[240] *CJ* 1.3.45.6 (17 Oct. 530), *CTh/N* 0.
[241] *CJ* 11.48.22.2 (30 April 531), *CTh/N* 0.
[242] Six of the first nine texts: *CJ* 7.63.5.5 (17 Nov. 529), 6.2.21.4 (1 Oct. 530), 4.11.1 pr. (18 Oct. 531), 5.13.1.1a (1 Nov. 531), 7.6.1.8, 9 (1 Nov. 531 bis); cf. 8.37.15.1 (18 Oct. 532), *C. Tanta* 1, 5, 11 (16 Dec. 533 ter), 6.51.1.2, 3a (1 June 534) but 7.43.8 (29 Sept. 290), 12.35.13 pr. (1 Feb. 398), 1.22.5 (6 Nov. 426), *CTh/N* 5.
[243] *CJ* 6.38.4.1a (30 April 531) and *copulatio CJ* 5.4.26.1 (1 Oct. 530), 11.48.21 pr. (22 July 530), *CTh/N* 0.
[244] *CJ* 4.1.11.2 (17 Sept. 529), 10.32.67.4 (Demostheni pp. 529), 8.53.34.1b (30 Oct. 529), 6.35.11 pr. (30 Apr. 531); cf. *N*. 9.2 (14 April 535) but 7.36.1 (Gord.), *CTh/N* 0.
[245] *CJ* 3.33.15.2 (1 Oct. 531), *CTh/N* 1.   [246] *CJ* 8.53.34.3 (30 Oct. 529), *CTh/N* 2.
[247] *CJ* 5.4.23.5 (1 Oct. 530), *CTh/N* 0.
[248] *CJ* 6.4.3.2 (30 Oct. 529), 7.7.1.7 (1 Aug. 530), 6.40.2.2 (20 Feb. 531), 8.53.35 pr. (18 March 530); cf. 5.17.11.2b (17 Nov. 533), *C. Cordi* 4 (16 Nov. 534), 1.3.54.11 (Iohanni pp. after 17 Nov. 533), *N*. 11.2 (14 April 535), *N*. 23.1 (3 Jan. 536) but 9.24.2 (6 July 326), *CTh/N* 16.
[249] *CJ* 3.33.14.1, 3.33.15.2 (1 Oct. 530), 7.15.1.2a (18 March 530), *CTh/N* 0.
[250] *CJ* 6.23.28.1 (27 March 530), *CTh/N* 0.
[251] *CJ* 8.33.3.3 (18 March 530), *CTh/N* 0.
[252] *CJ* 1.2.21.2 (Demostheni pp. 529), *CTh/N* 0.
[253] *CJ* 6.37.23 pr. (17 Nov. 530), *CTh/N* 0.
[254] *CJ* 4.21.21 pr. (20 Feb. 531 bis), but 10.3.2 (28 Oct. 239), *CTh/N* 1.
[255] *CJ* 6.61.7.2 (18 March 530), *CTh/N* 0.
[256] *CJ* 6.30.22.13a (27 Nov. 531), *CTh/N* 1.
[257] Above, n. 232.
[258] *CJ* 1.14.12.4 (30 Oct. 529), *C. Deo auctore* 13 (15 Dec. 530), 7.25.1 (530/1), *CTh/N* 0.
[259] *CJ* 8.53.35.2 (18 March 530), 3.33.13.3 (1 Oct. 530); cf. 7.71.8.2 (531/2) but 1.28.3 (13 July 376), *CTh/N* 2.
[260] *C. Deo auctore* 8, 13 (15 Dec. 530 bis), *CTh/N* 0.
[261] Below, n. 411.
[262] *CJ* 4.66.2.1 (17 Sept. 529), 4.66.3 pr., 5 (17 March 530 bis), *CTh/N* 0.
[263] *CJ* 8.47.10 pr. (1 Sept. 530), 6.61.8.6a (29 July 531), 7.25.1 (530/1), *CTh/N* 2, meaning 'joke', 'laughing-stock'.
[264] *CJ* 3.28.34.1 (29 July 531), 3.28.36.2b (1 Sept. 531), *CTh/N* 1.
[265] *CJ* 8.48.6 (1 Nov. 531), *CTh/N* 0.   [266] *CJ* 6.23.27.3 (18 March 530), *CTh/N* 0.
[267] *CJ* 8.53.34.3 (30 Oct. 529), 6.23.28.6 (27 March 530), *C. Deo auctore* 2 (15 Dec. 530); cf. 7.71.8.2 (531/2), *C. Tanta* 6a (16 Dec. 533) but 1.51.7 (23 March 422), 1.1.4 (7 Feb. 452), *CTh/N* 1.
[268] *CJ* 3.1.14.1 (27 March 530) but 1.40.3 (1 Nov. 331), *CTh/N* 2.
[269] *CJ* 3.28.36.2a (1 Sept. 531), 8.37.14.2 (1 Nov. 531) but 12.40.5.2 (12 June 413), *CTh/N* 3.

conclamare,[270] *defraudare*,[271] *deperire*,[272] *deperdere*,[273] *erubescere*,[274] *exaudire*,[275] *exoriri*,[276] *illigare*,[277] *increbescere*,[278] *infigere*,[279] *ingemiscere*,[280] *innodatus*,[281] *perraro*,[282] *praefulgere*,[283] *praeparatio*,[284] *profluere* (met.),[285] *profundere*,[286] *redarguere*,[287] *reluctari*,[288] *reponere*.[289]

Comparative adverbs catalogue some of the qualities the minister admired: *apertius*,[290] *clarius*,[291] *latius*,[292] *pinguius*,[293] *plenius*,[294] *subtilius*.[295] Does this point to an expansive, even corpulent man? The list of distinctive adjectives and participles used adjectivally is in its own way equally revealing: *amarus*,[296] *amicalis*,[297] *anceps*,[298] *angustus*,[299] *confusus*,[300] *crassus*,[301]

[270] *CJ* 6.59.11 pr. (17 Sept. 529), *CTh/N* 0.   [271] Below, n. 424.

[272] *CJ* 7.63.5.3 (17 Sept. 529), 4.66.3.1 (18 March 530), 3.33.15.2 (1 Oct. 530), 6.38.4.1c (30 April 531); cf. 7.2.15.1a (531/2), 5.4.28.1 (531/2), 3.34.14 pr. (18 Oct. 532) N. 62.5 (23 March 538) but 5.37.22.3 (15 March 326), 5.35.2.2 (21 Jan. 390), 11.6.6 (19, Jan. 409), 1.5.8.12 (1 Aug. 455), *CTh/N* 5.

[273] *CJ* 4.21.21 pr., 2 (20 Feb. 531), 8.17.12 pr. (27 Nov. 531); cf. 3.34.14 pr. (18 Oct. 532), N. 62.5 (23 March 538), *CTh/N* 0.

[274] *CJ* 3.28.33.1 (17 Sept. 529), 6.23.28.2 (27 March 530), 6.2.22.4 (17 Nov. 530), 4.18.2.1a (20 Feb. 531); cf. 6.51.1.1b (1 June 534) but 1.54.6.6 (21 Aug. 399), *CTh/N* 2.

[275] *CJ* 6.22.10.3 (20 Feb. 531); cf. 6.35.12.1 (18 Oct. 532), *CTh/N* 0.

[276] Below, n. 386.

[277] *CJ* 1.2.21 pr. (Demostheni pp. 529), 2.55.4.2 (30 Oct. 529), 7.40.1.1b, 4.29.22.1 (18 March 530), 8.40.26.7 (27 March 530), 6.61.8.6 (29 July 531); cf. 11.48.23.1 (531/4), *CTh/N* 4.

[278] Above, n. 199.   [279] *CJ* 6.30.22.1a (27 Nov. 531), *CTh/N* 1.   [280] Above, n. 200.

[281] *CJ* 4.31.14.1 (1 Nov. 531); cf. *C. Tanta* 18 (16 Dec. 533), *CTh/N* 0.

[282] *C. Deo auctore* 9 (15 Dec. 530); cf. *C. Omnem* 1 (16 Dec. 533), *CJ* 6.51.1.3 (1 June 534), *CTh/N* 0.

[283] *C. Deo auctore* 2 (15 Dec. 530); cf. *C. Omnem* 4 bis (16 Dec. 533), *C. Tanta* 1 (16 Dec. 533), 1.1.8.2 (25 March 534, John 11) but 4.20.9 (25 Aug. 334); cf. *fulgor CJ* 5.4.28.2 (531/2), 7.24.1 pr. (531/4), *C. Tanta* 1 (16 Dec. 533), *CTh/N* 1.

[284] *CJ* 3.28.34.1 (29 July 531), 3.28.36.2b (1 Sept. 531), *CTh/N* 0.

[285] *CJ* 8.53.34.4 (30 Oct. 529), 6.23.27 pr. (18 March 530), *CTh/N* 2.

[286] *C. Deo auctore* 6 (15 Dec. 530) but 6.23.15.1 (1 Feb. 339), *CTh/N* 1.

[287] Above, n. 254.

[288] *CJ* 8.27.7 (238), 11.59.6.1 (383); 4.1.12.1a (30 Oct. 529), 2.58.2 pr. (20 Feb. 531).

[289] *CJ* 4.1.12.2a (30 Oct. 529), 6.23.28.6 (27 March 530), *C. Deo auctore* 2, 7 (15 Dec. 530 bis), 1.3.48.3 (23 Aug. 531); cf. *C. Tanta* 5 ter, 11 (16 Dec. 533) but 7.49.1 (19 Dec. 212).

[290] *CJ* 5.12.31.6 (18 March 530), 6.2.22.4b (17 Nov. 530), 5.37.28.3 (1 Oct. 531), 6.24.14 pr. (29 July 531); cf. *C. Tanta* 11 (16 Dec. 533), 6.51.1.9 (1 June 534), N. 112 pr. (9 Sept. 541) but 5.17.8.1 (9 Jan. 449 bis), *CTh/N* 0.

[291] *CJ* 2.3.30.4 (1 Nov. 531), *CTh/N* 0.

[292] *CJ* 6.25.7.1 (22 July 530), 2.40.5.1 (1 Nov. 531); cf. 6.51.1.10 (1 June 534) but 1.7.4.3 (7 April 426), *CTh/N* 0.

[293] *CJ* 4.1.12 pr. (30 Oct. 529), 6.25.7.1 (22 July 530), 7.71.7 (20 Feb. 531), *CTh/N* 0.

[294] *CJ* 2.55.5.3 (27 March 530), 5.13.1.1b, 6.58.13.2 (1 Nov. 531); cf. 4.65.35 pr. (Iustinianus ad senatum), but 5.34.13 (409), *CTh/N* 1.

[295] *CJ* 6.22.10.3 (20 Feb. 531); cf. N. 112. 3.1 (9 Sept. 541), *CTh/N* 0.

[296] *CJ* 8.21.2.2 (1 Aug. 530), *CTh/N* 1.

[297] *CJ* 1.2.22.1 (30 Oct. 529), 1.3.50.1 (1 Sept. 531); cf. *C. Tanta* 23 (16 Dec. 533), 6.58.15.5 (15 Dec. 534), N. 112 epil. (9 Sept. 541), *CTh/N* 0.

[298] *CJ* 4.5.10.1 (1 Aug. 530), *CTh/N* 1.

[299] *CJ* 7.47.1 pr. (1 Sept. 531), 7.31.1 pr. (18 Oct. 531), *CTh/N* 4.

effluens,[302] *effusus,*[303] *flebilis,*[304] *fretus,*[305] *gravidus,*[306] *incognitus (legibus),*[307] *incorporalis*[308] (in the phrase *incorporalia iura*), *infelix,*[309] *infinitus,*[310] *innocuus,*[311] *intestinus,*[312] *legitimus*[313] (*conversatio, finis, moderamen, causa*), *localis,*[314] *merus,*[315] *minuscula,*[316] *miser,*[317] *mollis,*[318] *opulentus,*[319] *perfectius,*[320] *placidus,*[321] *profusus,*[322] *prolixus (spatium* etc.),[323] *puerilis,*[324] *regalis,*[325]

---

[300] *CJ* 5.12.30 pr. (30 Oct. 529), *C. Deo auctore* 1, 5 (15 Dec. 530 bis); cf. *C. Imperatoriam* 2 (21 Nov. 533), *C. Omnem* 1 (16 Dec. 533), *C. Tanta* 1 (16 Dec. 533) but (all early) 2.3.7 (30 July 213), 6.42.3 (9 Dec. 215), 6.50.6 pr. (28 Dec. 223), 10.2.3 pr. (Dio etMax. AA), *CTh/N* 2.
[301] *CJ* 6.24.14.2 (29 July 531: *crassior*), *CTh/N* 1.

[302] *CJ* 7.63.5.4 (17 Sept. 529), 4.20.19.3 (18 March 530), 3.1.13.5 (27 March 530), *CTh/N* 0.
[303] *CJ* 6.27.5.1c (30 April 531), 5.11.7.5 (1 Nov. 531); cf. *N.* 36 pr. (1 Jan. 535), 35 pr. (23 April 535), *CTh/N* 4 and *effuse CJ* 7.40.1.1a (18 March 530), 2.46.3.1 (30 Aug. 531), *CTh/N* 0.
[304] *CJ* 7.71.7 (20 Feb. 531), 6.30.22.13a (27 Nov. 531), *CTh/N* 0.
[305] *CJ* 4.29.24.1 (1 Aug. 530), *C. Deo auctore* 2 (15 Dec. 530), 4.54.9.1 (18 Oct. 531); cf. *C. Cordi* 3 (16 Nov. 534) but 7.19.1 (223), 11.8.13 (23 Feb. 426), *CTh/N* 5.
[306] *CJ* 5.27.11.3 (18 March 530), *CTh/N* 1.
[307] *CJ* 6.2.21.5 (1 Oct. 530), 2.3.30.4 (1 Nov. 531) and 2.46.3.2 (30 Aug. 531 *veteribus non incognitum*).
[308] *CJ* 7.37.3.1d (27 Nov. 531), *CTh/N* 0.
[309] *CJ* 5.12.31 pr. (18 March 530); cf. 7.24.1 pr. (531/4), *CTh/N* 3.
[310] *CJ* 1.2.23.2 (18 March 530), *C. Deo auctore* 1 (15 Dec. 530), 3.1.16, 4.21.21.4 (20 Feb. 531), 7.47.1 pr. (1 Sept. 531); cf. *C. Tanta* 18, 21 (16 Dec. 533 bis), *N.* 36 pr. (1 Jan. 535), *CTh/N* 8.
[311] *CJ* 5.9.10.5 (17 Sept. 529), *CTh/N* 1.
[312] *CJ* 6.58.14.5 (27 Nov. 531); cf. *C. Tanta* pr. (16 Dec. 533), *N.* 36 pr. (1 Jan. 535), *CTh/N* 0.
[313] 'Of the law, of laws': *conversatio CJ* 1.5.21.2 (29 July 531), *moderamen* 3.28.36.1 (1 Sept. 531), *finis* (6.43.3.4); cf. *N.* 112.3.1 (9 Sept. 541) but 12.35.18.6 (1 Jan. 492) both *finem legitimum sortiri*), *causa CJ* 2.52.7.2 (1 Sept. 531) but 5.19.1 (3 Nov. 422 itp. cf. *CTh* 3.13.3) and *CJ* 9.9.34 (10 March 421 itp. cf. *CTh* 3.16.2).
[314] *CJ* 11.48.20.1 (30 Oct. 529), 8.10.13 (1 Sept. 531), *CTh/N* 0.
[315] *CJ* 1.14.12.4, 6.4.3.2 (30 Oct. 529); cf. 6.58.12.1 (18 Oct. 532), *Nov.* 62.1.2 (1 Jan. 537), but 6.6.3 (1 Nov. 223), 6.23.19 pr. (18 Feb. 413), *CTh/N* 2.
[316] *CJ* 3.28.33 pr. (17 Sept. 529), *CTh/N* 2.
[317] *CJ* 3.1.13.8 (27 March 530), 7.31.1 pr. (18 Oct. 531); cf. 4.65.35 pr. (Iustinianus ad sen.), *N.* 36.2 (1 Jan. 535) but 9.4.1.3 (30 June 320), 12.63.1.1 (2 Feb. 383).
[318] *CJ* 4.31.14.1 (1 Nov. 530) but 9.12.8.3 (6 March 390) and *mollire CJ* 4.29.25.1 (1 Nov. 531).
[319] *CJ* 8.53.34.4b (30 Oct. 529); cf. *C. Tanta* 17 (*opulentissimus*) but 5.5.7.1 (4 April 454), *CTh/N* 0.
[320] *CJ* 7.40.2 pr. (18 Oct. 531).
[321] *C. Deo auctore* 14 (15 Dec. 530, *deo placido*), *CTh/N* 1.
[322] *C. Deo auctore* 6 (15 Dec. 530), *CTh/N* 0.
[323] *CJ* 10.32.67.4 (Demostheni pp. 529 *p. tempus*), 11.48.20 pr. (30 Oct. 529 *p. spatium*); cf. 3.34.14 pr. (18 Oct. 532 *p. spatium*), *N.* 36 pr. (1 Jan. 535 *p. annositas*), 35 pr. (23 April 535 *p. tempus*), *CTh/N* 3.
[324] *CJ* 6.61.8.6 (29 July 531), *CTh/N* 0.
[325] *CJ* 1.51.14.3 (17 Sept. 529), 1.14.12.1 (30 Oct. 529), 7.37.3.1b (27 Nov. 531) = imperial but 12.63.1 pr. (2 Feb. 383), 5.27.3.2 (16 Dec. 443), *CTh/N* 1.

rudis,[326] *simplex*,[327] *stultus*,[328] *supinus*,[329] *testamentarius*,[330] *timidus*,[331] *tumidus*,[332] *vanus*,[333] *voluptuarius*.[334] We may add the gerundive *ferendus*[335] (tolerable) in rhetorical questions, also *fulciendus*.[336] There is a certain softness about this list of adjectives; it speaks also to the intellectual's contempt for the sluggish. *Minisculus*[337] ('tiny') is a baby word; it can be coupled with *cunabula*,[338] 'cradle'.

Superlative adjectives include *acutissimus*,[339] *apertissimus*,[340] *brevissimus*,[341] *difficillimus*,[342] *frequentissimus*,[343] *humanissimus*,[344] *longissimus*,[345] *manifestissimus*,[346] *perfectissimus*,[347] *subtilissimus*,[348] *tristissimus*,[349] besides the aesthetic

[326] CJ 8.53.35 pr. (18 March 530), *C. Deo auctore* 11 (15 Dec. 530), 6.30.22.14a (27 Nov. 531); cf. *C. Omnem* 9 (16 Dec. 533) *Inst.* 1.1.5 but 2.6.7. pr. (1 March 370), *CTh/N* 0.

[327] Meaning 'simple-minded': 5.51.13.1 (1 Aug. 530), *C. Deo auctore* 11 (15 Dec. 530), 6.40.3.1 (1 Nov. 531).

[328] CJ 5.51.13.1 (1 Aug. 530), 6.24.14.2 (29 July 531); cf. 8.37.15 pr. (18 Oct. 532), *Inst.* 4.75, *CTh/N* 0.

[329] CJ 6.27.5.1c (30 April 531), 6.24.14.2 (29 July 531), *CTh/N* 0.

[330] CJ 5.35.3.2 (27 March 530 *et testamentariae et legitimae*), 1.5.21.3 (29 July 531), 5.59.5 pr. bis, 2 (1 Sept. 531 *sive testamentarii sive per inquisitionem dati* etc. ter), 1.3.51 pr. (1 Nov. 531) but 6.59.8 (10 Oct. 294), 5.42.4 (13 Dec. 294), 9.31.1.1 (12 Jan. 378), 5.33.1.3 (30 Dec. 389), and 5.35.2.3 (21 Jan. 390 itp. cf. *CTh* 3.17.4).

[331] CJ 3.1.14.5 (27 March 530), *CTh/N* 0.

[332] CJ 1.14.12.1 (30 Oct. 529), *CTh/N* 0.

[333] CJ 1.14.12.2 (30 Oct. 529), 7.5.1 (530), 4.18.2.1d (20 Feb. 531), 7.17.2.2 (1 Sept. 531), 8.48.6 (bis), 7.61.5 (1 Nov. 531), 6.30.22.13a (27 Nov. 531); cf. *C. Tanta* 21 (16 Dec. 533) but 9.9.17 pr. (27 July 257), 1.11.2 (25 May 385), 12.57.9.1 (Arc. et Hon.), *CTh/N* 5.

[334] CJ 5.13.1.5f. (1 Nov. 531), *CTh/N* 0.

[335] CJ 5.30.5.1 (30 Oct. 529), 6.25.7 pr. (22 July 530), 6.61.8.6a (29 July 531), 1.3.48.2 (23 Aug. 531), 12.33.7.1 (1 Sept. 531), 4.54.9.1 (18 Oct. 531), 4.1.12.1a (18 Oct. 531), 6.58.14.2 (27 Nov. 531), cf. 6.51.1.4 (1 June 534).

[336] CJ 7.17.2 pr. (1 Sept. 531).   [337] CJ 3.28.33 pr. (17 Sept. 529).

[338] CJ 7.4.14.1 (1 Oct. 531), 7.25.1 (530/1); cf. *C. Imperatoriam* 3 (21 Nov. 553), *CTh/N* 0. *Cunabula iuris* is in D. 1.2.2.38 (*Pomp. 1 enchir.*), Claudian, *Stil.* 3.138.

[339] CJ 6.42.30 (30 Oct. 529); cf. *C. Omnem* 4 (16 Dec. 533), *CTh/N* 0.

[340] Below, n. 407.

[341] CJ 6.28.4.8 (1 Sept. 531); cf. *C. Omnem* 1 (16 Dec. 533), *C. Tanta* 13 (16 Dec. 533) and *brevior* CJ 8.53.34.4a (30 Oct. 529), *CTh/N* 0.

[342] CJ 4.29.23 pr. (1 Aug. 530), *C. Deo auctore* 2 (15 Dec. 530).

[343] CJ 11.48.20 pr. (30 Oct. 529), 6.29.4.1 (17 Nov. 530), *C. Deo auctore* 10 (15 Dec. 530); cf. 7.71.8.3 (531/2), *C. Cordi* 6 (16 Nov. 534).

[344] Above, n. 179.   [345] CJ 1.2.23.1, 2 (18 March 530 bis), 6.30.22.3 (27 Nov. 531).

[346] Fifteen texts out of first 22: CJ 6.33.3.4 (18 March 530), 3.1.13.4 (27 March 530), 8.47.10.1d (1 Sept. 530), 3.33.14.1 (1 Oct. 530), 6.2.22 pr. (bis), 6.37.23.1 (17 Nov. 530), 1.5.21.1, 6.24.14.2 (29 July 531), 6.28.3, 6.40.2 pr. (20 Feb. 531), 5.37.26 pr. (23 Aug. 531), 6.28.4.2 (1 Sept. 531), 5.13.1.3a, 8.37.14.2 (1 Nov. 531); cf. 6.58.15.1b (15 Oct. 534), N. 138 (before 15 April 535), 112 pr. (9 Sept. 541) but 5.60.1 (29 July 213), 2.44.1 (1 July 274), 5.30.2 (5 April 293), 5.12.20 (27 April 294), 4.13.3 (20 Feb. 294), 8.53.24 (5 Feb. 299), 8.55.9 (6 Nov. 426).

[347] Below, n. 405.

[348] CJ 6.23.28 pr. (27 March 530), 7.33.12.3a (27 Nov. 531); cf. *C. Tanta* 18 (16 Dec. 533), *CTh/N* 0.

[349] CJ 2.3.30.2 (1 Nov. 531); cf. N 34 pr. (15 June 535), *CTh/N* 1.

group previously mentioned.[350] Superlative adverbs include *apertissime*,[351] *frequentissime*,[352] *longissime*[353] and *perfectissime*.[354] The use of *puta*,[355] *verbi gratia*,[356] is didactic, almost professorial.

'Justinian's' love of metaphor and capacity for mixing them has not gone without comment.[357] There is no basis for the reproach so far as the emperor personally is concerned. His style can be ornate but is not specially figurative.[358] Nor is that of Thomas; quite the reverse, despite his use of *amputare* for to repeal.[359] Tribonian is very different. He revels in images and figures. It would be impracticable to document them, but the reader will note that a fairly high proportion of Tribonianic expressions are used in an unusual or at any rate not the literal sense, for example *via*[360] for 'method' not 'right of way'. Here is an example:[361]

> Sed cum prospeximus quod ad portandum tantae sapientiae molem non sunt idonei homines rudes et qui in primis legum vestibulis stantes intrare ad arcana eorum properant, et alia ad mediocrem emendationem(?) praeparandam esse censuimus, ut sub ea colorati et quasi primitiis omnium imbuti possint ad penetralia eorum intrare et formam legum pulcherrimam non coniventibus oculis accipere.

The initiation of students requires the preparation of an elementary textbook and an elaborate set of images.

(e) *Structure and grammar*. There is little to be said about these topics. The texts often follow something of the following pattern: description of the problem, the emperor's reasons (e.g. with a present participle), the action he takes, including the principle of the new law, and finally qualifications and exceptions (e.g. with a *nisi* clause or more often an ablative absolute such as *nullo praeiudicio generando*).[362] This pattern is like that of his predecessor Thomas, except that the introductory description tends to be more elaborate.

Tribonian's word order is fairly but not strikingly 'open': the verb precedes the object noun from time to time but not with much regularity. The rhythm is extended, not the clauses with four stresses favoured by Proculus,[363] but the five to six of an 'orchestral' style:[364]

> ut liceat vobis prima legum cunabula / non ab antiquis fabulis discere / sed ab imperiali splendore appetere / et tam aures quam animae vestrae / nihil

350 Above, nn. 207–10.   351 Below, n. 407.
352 *CJ* 7.6.1.9 (1 Nov. 531) but 11.75.5 (29 April 431).
353 *CJ* 2.58.2.6 (20 Feb. 531) but 9.24.1.5 (21 Nov. 321).
354 Below, n. 406.
355 The first seven texts: *CJ* 4.27.2 pr. (1 Nov. 530), 6.37.23 pr. (17 Nov. 530), 5.37.26.2 (23 Aug. 531), 3.28.36.1b, 5.59.5.1, 3.28.37.1e (1 Sept. 531), 4.37.6 (531); cf. 5.17.11.1a (17 Nov. 533), 6.51.1.9b (1 June 534).
356 *CJ* 6.38.4.1b (30 Apr. 531) but 12.8.2.3 (440/441), *CTh*/*N* 0.
357 E.g. Rubin.   358 *Justinian* 111–16.   359 Below, ch. 8 n. 98.
360 Below, n. 415.   361 *C. Tanta* 11 (16 Dec. 533).   362 Below, n. 422.
363 Below, ch. 8 nn. 33–9, 87–94.   364 *C. Imperatoriam* 3 (21 Nov. 533).

inutile nihilque perperam positum / sed quod in ipsis optinet argumentis accipiant.

Of purely grammatical or syntactical features there is little to be said. The Latin is orthodox for the period. Tribonian, it is true, sometimes uses the alternative perfect *praestavi* for *praestiti*.³⁶⁵ As will be seen he likes the imperfect *erat* for 'there was', 'it was', or for the conditional 'it would be'.³⁶⁶ In compound tenses he favours the pluperfect: 47 of the first 102 texts (*fuerat obligatus, depositae fuerant* etc.), or 46 per cent against the expected 17 belong to this period:³⁶⁷ also four of five texts with *fuerat/fuerant* and an adjective.³⁶⁸ Though it is not easy to document the matter, the quaestor is much given to putting rhetorical questions, sometimes in series. A constitution about the validity of imperial interpretations of the law elicits several:³⁶⁹

> quid enim maius, quid sanctius imperiali est maiestate? vel quis tantae superbiae fastidio tumidus est ut regalem sensum contemnat . . . ? Cur autem ex suggestionibus procerum . . . ad nos decurritur et quare ambiguitates iudicum quas ex legibus oriri evenit aures accipiunt nostrae, si non a nobis interpretatio mera procedit? vel quis legum aenigmata solvere et omnibus aperire idoneus esse videbitur nisi is, cui soli legis latorem esse concessum est?

(f) *Common idiosyncrasies.* It may be convenient to collect in this section a

³⁶⁵ *CJ* 2.58.1 (17 Sept. 529), 6.22.12 (1 Sept. 531), 4.1.13 pr. (18 Oct. 531); cf. 4.35.23 pr. (531/2) but 2.1.4 (11 March 212).

³⁶⁶ *CJ* 4.32.28 pr. (17 Sept. 529 bis: *differentia erat . . . hoc erat* (would be) *certe ponere*), 11.48.20.3a (30 Oct. 529), 4.20.20, 7.62.39.2 (27 March 530), 1.2.23.2 (18 March 530), 3.33.12.1 (1 Aug. 530), 5.13.1.11, 14a (1 Nov. 531 bis), 4.11.1 pr. (18 Oct. 531), 6.27.5.1 (30 April 531), 5.37.26 pr. (23 Aug. 531), 3.28.37.1e (1 Sept. 531), 7.31.1 pr. (18 Oct. 531); cf. 5.3.20.1 (531/2 *melius erat* = 'would be'), *C. Omnem* 1 (16 Dec. 533), *C. Tanta* pr., 13, 17 (16 Dec. 533 ter), 6.51.1.11g (1 June 534), *C. Cordi* 3 (16 Nov. 534 *promptum erat* = 'it would be obvious'), *N.* 11.3 (14 April 535) but 5.14.8 (9 Jan. 450), 12.35.18.1 (1 Jan. 492), 6.20.19.1 (1 June 528 *palam erat quod.*). The idiom is in Gaius *Inst.* 1.190 (*aequum erat* = 'it would be fair').

³⁶⁷ *CJ* 3.28.33 pr., 4.32.28 pr., 5.27.10 pr. (17 Sept. 529), 10.32.67.6 (Demostheni pp. 529 bis), 6.23.27.3, 7.40.1.2 (18 March 530), 2.55.5 pr., 6.23.28.5 (27 March 530), 8.37.13.1 (1 Aug. 530), 5.70.7.9, 11 (bis), 8.47.10 pr. (bis), 1f., 3 (1 Sept. 530 quat), 3.33.16 pr. (1 Oct. 530), 6.29.3 pr. (1 Nov. 530 bis), 6.2.22.1a ter, 3 (17 Nov. 530 quat.), *C. Deo auctore* 7 (15 Dec. 530), 4.18.2.1 (20 Feb. 531), 6.35.11.1 (30 April 531), 6.26.11 pr. (29 July 531), 5.37.26 pr. (23 Aug. 531), 2.46.3.2 (30 Aug. 531), 1.3.49 pr., 3.28.37.1a, 1e bis (ter), 5.59.5.1, 6.28.4.1, 4, 5, 8 bis (quinq.), 6.43.3.3a, 7.17.2.1 (1 Sept. 531), 4.1.13 pr., 7.31.1.2, 7.40.3.1 (18 Oct. 531), 7.6.1.8, 10 (1 Nov. 531 bis), 5.16.27 pr. (17 Nov. 531); cf. 4.35.23.3 (531/2), 4.34.12 (531/2), 6.31.6 pr. (18 Oct. 532), *C. Tanta* 10, 13 (16 Dec. 533), *C. Omnem* 4 bis (16 Dec. 533), 6.51.1.1b, 3 bis, 4, 8 (1 June 534 quinq.), 6.58.15.1b (15 Oct. 534), *C. Cordi* pr. (16 Nov. 534), *N.* 11.1, 2 (14 April 535), 112.3.1 (9 Sept. 541). In view of the large number of texts of this period the fact that two instances are found in the preceding 38 years (*CJ* 12.37.16.8.3, Anast.) is no bar to treating this as a mark of style.

³⁶⁸ *CJ* 6.28.4.8 (1 Sept. 531), 5.13.1.7a, 7.6.1.1a (1 Nov. 531), 8.17.12.1 (27 Nov. 531); cf. 6.58.15.2 (15 Oct. 534), *C. Tanta* 20a (16 Dec. 533), *Inst.* 1.5.3, 1.29.5 (Iustinianus Zetae mm.) but 2.52.5.2 (15 Oct. 312).

³⁶⁹ *CJ* 1.14.12 (30 Oct. 529).

number of words and expressions which occur between September 529 and November 531 with special frequency, i.e. at least six times, and are hardly or not at all found at other periods. The new quaestor likes to separate *nullo* from *modo* by a verb, as in *nullo concedimus modo*, which is found twelve times in this period and not at all before it.[370] *Iuramentum*, 'oath', instead of *iusiurandum* occurs 27 times in our period and neither before nor after.[371] *Absimilis*, with ten occurrences, is previously found only in a rescript of 293.[372] The first 12 texts with *variare* come at this time.[373] There are 8 instances of *compendiosus* and, in effect, only one precedent,[374] none for the eight instances of *inextricabilis*.[375] There are 17 texts with *exoriri* and three precedents, none within the previous century.[376] *Annalis* (*tempus/spatium/ remedium* etc.)[377] has 26 mentions, with two forerunners from the time of Zeno,[378] and one from April 529. It illustrates a habit of substituting

---

[370] *CJ* 10.32.67.6 (Demostheni pp. 529), 4.21.20.2, 6.23.27.3 (both 18 March 530)ʼ 6.23.28 pr. (27 March 530), 7.15.2 (1 Aug. 530), 3.33.15.2 (1 Oct. 530), 2.18.24.2 (17 Nov. 530), 6.30.21.3 (30 April 530), 6.22.11.1 (29 July 531 bis), 1.4.31.1 (1 Oct. 531), 7.40.2.1 (18 Oct. 531); cf. 7.2.15.1b (531/2), 7.32.12.2 (531/2), 6.38.5.1 (18 Oct. 532), C. Tanta 10,14, 23 (16 Dec. 533 ter), C. Omnem 9 (16 Dec. 533), 7.24.1 pr. (531/4), N. 36.4, 5 (1 Jan. 535 bis).

[371] *CJ* 2.58.1 pr., 4.1.11.2 (17 Sept. 529), 2.55.4.1, 2, 3, 5 (quat.), 4.1.12 pr., 1, 1a, 3, 4a bis, 4b, 4d, 5 (30 Oct. 529 non.), 4.21.20.3, 8.33.3.3b, 5a (bis), 5.35.3 pr. (18 March 530), 3.1.14.4, 5 (27 March 530), 2.58.2, 3a, 8 (20 Feb. 531 bis), 6.43.2 pr. (20 Feb. 531). 6.40.2 pr., 2 (20 Feb. 531 bis), 6.42.32 (27 Nov. 531), *CTh/N* o.

[372] *CJ* 4.28.7 pr., 1 (1 Aug. 530 bis), 4.27.2.2, 6.37.23.1d (both 17 Nov. 530), 4.18.2.1 (20 Feb. 531), 1.5.21.1 (29 July 531), 5.59.5 pr., 2.52.7.2, 8.56.4 (1 Sept. 531), 6.58.12.2 (18 Oct. 531) but 2.21.3 (18 April 293), *CTh/N* o.

[373] *CJ* 8.53.34.3a, 4, 4a (30 Oct. 529 ter), 5.27.11.4, 7.40.1.1a (both 18 March 530), 4.20.20 (27 March 530), 6.2.22.3a (17 Nov. 530 bis), 6.22.10.2, 5 (20 Feb. 531 bis), 6.38.4.1 (30 April 531), 3.1.18 (1 Nov. 531); cf. 1.1.8.5 (25 March 534, John 11), *CTh/N* o.

[374] *CJ* 6.61.6.4 (30 Oct. 529), 7.62.39.1a (27 March 530), 5.70.7.4 (1 Sept. 530), 3.33.13 pr. (1 Oct. 530), 7.17.2 (1 Sept. 531), 7.31.1.4, 3.34.13 (18 Oct. 531), 6.58.13.1 (1 Nov. 531); cf. C. Tanta 7 (16 Dec. 533) but 9.22.22.2 (25 March 320 itp. cf. *CTh* 9.19.2), 6.60.4 (1 Sept. 468), *CTh/N* 1.

[375] *CJ* 6.43.1 pr. (17 Sept. 529), 5.70.7.3, 4, 8 (1 Sept. 530 ter), 6.27.5.1e (30 April 531), 7.47.1.1 (1 Sept. 531), 8.48.6 (1 Nov. 531), 7.33.12.3b (27 Nov. 531), *CTh/N* o.

[376] *CJ* 4.21.19 pr. (17 Sept. 529), 6.33.3.2, 8.33.3.5a, 7.40.1 pr. (18 March 530), 4.38.15 pr., 7.7.1 pr. (1 Aug. 530), 5.70.7.3 (1 Sept. 530), 6.2.22.4, 6.29.4 pr. (17 Nov. 530), 6.27.5.1 (30 April 531), 6.30.21 pr. (30 April 531), 6.61.8 pr. (29 July 531), 1.3.49 pr., 3.31.12.1, 8.47.10 pr. (1 Sept. 531), 3.28.37 pr. (1 Sept. 531), 6.23.30 (18 Oct. 531); cf. C. Tanta 6, 7 (16 Dec. 533) but 3.22.5 (2 Aug. 294), 7.19.7 pr. (Constantinus), 3.21.2 (31 May 423), *CTh/N* 9.

[377] Not. e.g. *legatum CJ* 6.37.22 (11 Dec. 528).

[378] *CJ* 6.30.19.2, 3, 4 (30 Oct. 529 quat.), 7.63.5.1b, 2, 4 (17 Nov. 529 quat.), 7.40.1.1a, 1b (18 March 530), 3.1.13.8a (27 March 530 bis), 5.13.1.7b (1 Nov. 531), 4.18.2.1 (20 Feb. 531 bis), 6.33.3.3 (18 March 530), 6.61.8.4b (29 July 531 bis), 1.3.48.3 (23 Aug. 531), 3.28.36.2a, 3.31.12.2, 6.43.3.1b (all 1 Sept. 531), 7.31.1.1, 2; 3.34.13 (18 Oct. 531), 6.30.22.11, 13a (27 Nov. 531 bis); cf. 7.2.15.1a bis, 1b, 4, 4a (531/2 quinq.), 11.48.23 pr. (531/4), N. 112.3.1 (9 Sept. 541 ter) but 12.3.3.1, 12.7.2.2 (both Zeno), 1.20.2 (1 April 529), *CTh/N* o. The end of the last text (*quae a praetore constitutae annali tempore coartatae sunt*) looks itp. but such arguments must be rejected at the present stage of the inquiry.

temporal adjectives for nouns: other examples are *quadrimenstris*,[379] *semenstris*.[380] Outside the temporal sphere the adjectival forms of emperors' names afford a parallel, as in *constitutio/tempora* (not *lex*) *Anastasiana*,[381] or those of towns: *advocatio Caesariensis*.[382] *Trames*, used once each in the fourth and fifth centuries comes up eight times,[383] *recusatio*, twice foreshadowed, six.[384] *Quiescente/-ibus* in the ablative absolute construction meaning 'being repealed/abolished' as in '*edicto divi Hadriani penitus quiescente*' is used for the first eight times.[385] There are 15 mentions of *respuere* with none of the five precedents closer than the fourth century.[386] *Articulus* in a metaphorical sense ('structure') is found eight times and is unprecedented in *CJ*.[387] *Satis* in the sense of 'too' or 'quite . . . enough', qualifying a neuter adjective, as in '*satis absurdum est*', is used 20 times, with three old and one recent precedents.[388] *Interpretor* (apart from the form *interpretamur* already mentioned)

[379] *CJ* 7.54.3 pr., 3 (27 Nov. 531 bis), *CTh/N* 0.

[380] *CJ* 7.63.5.1, 1a (17 Nov. 529 bis = *semestris*), 3.1.13.2, 8.40.26.2 (27 March 530), *CTh/N* 0.

[381] Above, n. 127 and *CJ* 1.3.49.1 (1 Sept. 531 *Leoniana* c.), 6.30.22.15 (27 Nov. 531 *Gordiana* c.); cf. 4.35.23 pr. (531/2 *Anastasiana* c.), 5.3.20.7 (531/2 *Leoniana* c.), *CTh/N* 0 and *principalis constitutio*; above, n. 160.

[382] *CJ* 2.3.30 pr. (1 Nov. 531 *Caesariensis*); cf. 6.58.12 pr. (18 Oct. 531 *Caesariana*), cf. 8.4.11 pr. (18 Oct. 532 *Illyriciana advocatio*), 6.38.5 pr. (same), and 2.7.29 pr. (531/4 *Illyriciani advocati*), *CTh/N* 0.

[383] *CJ* 7.15.1.1a (18 March 530), 5.70.7.9 (1 Sept. 530), 2.58.2.12 (20 Feb. 531), 6.61.8.1 (29 July 531), 3.28.36.2 (1 Sept. 531), 3.31.12 pr. (1 Sept. 531), 5.13.1 pr., 7.6.1.12a (1 Nov. 531); cf. *C. Imperatoriam* pr. (21 Nov. 533), *C. Omnem* pr. (16 Dec. 533) but 1.5.2.1 (3 Aug. 379), 1.12.6.5 (28 Feb. 466), *CTh/N* 6.

[384] *CJ* 3.1.13.9 (27 March 530), 7.45.16 (17 Nov. 530 bis), 3.1.16 pr. (20 Feb. 531), 6.61.8.6b (29 July 531), 3.1.18 (1 Nov. 531); cf. 5.37.28.1, 2a, 2b (18 Oct. 532 ter) but 7.45.11 (Dio et Max. AA et CC), 12.57.3 (Val. et Val.) 2 Oct. 365 ?), *CTh/N* 2.

[385] *CJ* 11.48.20.3 (30 Oct. 529), 6.33.3 pr., 7.40.1.1b (18 March 530), 5.70.6 pr. (1 Sept. 530), 6.40.2 pr. (20 Feb. 531), 2.58.2.8a (20 Feb. 531), 6.46.6.1 (30 April 531), 8.48.6 (1 Nov. 531); cf. *C. Tanta* 19 (16 Dec. 533), *N.* 36.2 (1 Jan. 535).

[386] *CJ* 1.2.21 pr. (Demostheni pp. 529), 4.20.20 (27 March 530), 4.28.7 pr. (1 Aug. 530), 3.33.14.1 (1 Oct. 530), 6.27.4.2 (17 Nov. 530), 6.30.20 pr. (30 April 531), 1.5.21 pr. (29 July 531), 6.61.8.6a (bis), 6.25.10.1 (both 29 July 531), 1.3.48 (23 Aug. 531), 2.41.2 (1 Sept. 531), 6.58.12.1, 4.11.1 pr. (18 Oct. 531), 6.30.22.1b (27 Nov. 531); cf. 8.25.11.2, 7.2.15.2 (531/2), 6.51.1.10b, 11b (1 June 534), 1.1.8.2 (25 March 534, John 11), *N.* 36.2 (1 Jan. 535), 37.7 (1 Aug. 535) but 3.32.19 (25 Dec. 293), 6.31.3 (294), 3.36.25 (13 April 295), 7.62.21 (25 July 355), 10.60.1.1 (14 Sept. 385), *CTh/N* 9.

[387] *CJ* 6.61.6.1c (30 Oct. 529), 1.2.21.1 (Demostheni pp. 529), 4.28.7.1 (1 Aug. 530), 8.47.10.1d (1 Sept. 531), 5.13.1.1b, 6.58.13.2 (1 Nov. 531), 6.30.22.16 (27 Nov. 531), 8.17.12.6 (27 Nov. 531); cf. *C. Tanta* 3, 8 (16 Dec. 533 bis), 6.51.1.5, 10 (1 June 534 bis), *C. Cordi* 1 (16 Nov. 534), *N.* 62.1.3 (1 Jan. 537), *CTh/N* 2, also *articulatus CJ* 6.22.10.3, 6.23.29.2 (20 Feb. 531).

[388] *CJ* 4.1.11 pr., 6.57.5.1 (17 Sept. 529), 3.28.33.1 (17 Sept. 529), 5.12.31.6 (18 March 530), 5.27.11.3 (18 March 530), 4.28.7 pr. (1 Aug. 530), 4.29.24.1 (1 Aug. 530), 7.4.15, 3.33.16.1 (both 1 Oct. 530), 4.31.14.1 (1 Nov. 531), 4.18.2.1 (20 Feb. 531), 4.21.21.4 (20 Feb. 531), 6.40.2.2 (20 Feb. 531), 2.52.7 pr. (1 Sept. 531), 7.31.1 pr. (18 Oct. 531), 7.6.1.8 (1 Nov. 531 bis), 6.30.22.1, 5 (27 Nov. 531 bis), 11.48.22.4 (531); cf. 12.3.5.2 (531/4), 11.48.23 (531/4), 7.24.1 pr. (531/4), 1.3.54.2 (Iohanni pp. after 17 Nov. 533), *N.* 35.10 (23 April 535), 37.8 (1 Aug. 535), 23 pr. (3 Jan. 536) but 3.15.1 (4 Oct. 196), 5.37.22.3 (15 March 326), 11.66.5.1 (383–4), 4.32.26 pr. (11 Dec. 528 *s. supervacuum est*).

occurs 14 times with four distant antecedents.[389] Many writers use idio-syncratic expressions for dying and Tribonian is no exception. *Ab hac luce eximi*[390]/*decedere*[391] are exclusively his, though *ab hac luce subtrahi*,[392] found 13 times in our period, is offset by two recent uses, and cannot be accounted a reliable signpost.

In contrast some weight attaches to the occurrence in our period of the first seven uses of *adiutorium*,[393] *consequentia*,[394] *progenies*,[395] *supervenire*,[396] *trutinare*,[397] *quantuscumque*[398] and *nimia subtilitas*[399] (the latter a phrase of Gaius) in *CJ* and the first eight of *melioratio*,[400] six of seven for *protelare*,[401] with a distant fourth-century precedent, eight of nine for *vallare* (in a meta-phorical sense)[402] with a precursor of 472, seven of nine for *reclamare*,[403]

---

[389] Above, n. 104 and *CJ* 1.14.12.2, 3 (30 Oct. 529 bis), 7.40.1.1a, 1d (18 March 530 bis), 5.27.11.1 (18 March 530), 6.23.28 pr. (27 March 530), 6.25.7.1 (22 July 530), 6.2.21.1 (1 Oct. 530), *C. Deo auctore* 4, 12 (15 Dec. 530 bis), 6.38.3 (20 Feb. 531); cf. *C. Tanta* 21 (16 Dec. 533) but 9.23.1 (5 Sept. 212), 6.37.1 (Ant.), 12.15.1 (15 March 425), 1.14.2 (6 Nov. 426), *CTh/N* 5, and *interpres CJ* 1.14.12.5 (30 Oct. 529), 5.70.7.1a (1 Sept. 530), 6.2.22.1, 7.4.17 pr. (17 Nov. 530); cf. *C. Tanta* 9 (16 Dec. 533) but 1.13.2 (18 April 321).

[390] *CJ* 7.15.1.1a (18 March 530), 3.33.17.1 (18 Oct. 531), *CTh/N* 0.

[391] *CJ* 5.70.7.1b (1 Sept. 530); cf. *N.* 11.7 (14 April 535), *CTh/N* 0.

[392] *CJ* 6.59.11 pr. (17 Sept. 529), 4.1.12 pr. (30 Oct. 529), 5.27.11.1 (18 March 530), 4.20.20 (27 March 530), 8.40.26.5 (27 March 530), 3.33.12 pr. (1 Aug. 530), 6.49.7.1b (23 Oct. 530), 5.13.1.14 (1 Nov. 530), 7.4.16 pr. (17 Nov. 530), 6.29.3 pr. (17 Nov. 530), 6.30.20.1 (30 April 531), 6.35.11.2 (30 April 531), 7.17.2.1 (1 Sept. 531); cf. 6.51.1.2a (1 June 534) but 12.19.11 (Anast.), 10.35.3.1 (1 June 528).

[393] *CJ* 5.27.11.3 (18 March 530), *C. Deo auctore* pr. (15 Dec. 530), 11.48.22 pr., 7.71.7 (20 Feb. 531), 3.28.34 pr. (29 July 531), 6.28.4.4, 6.43.3.1a (1 Sept. 531); cf. *N.* 37.10 (1 Aug. 535), *CTh/N* 0.

[394] *CJ* 11.48.20 pr. (30 Oct. 529), 4.29.22 pr. (18 March 530), 6.23.28.2 (27 March 530), *C. Deo auctore* 8, 13 (15 Dec. 530 bis), 6.24.14.3 (29 July 531), 5.27.12.2 (1 Nov. 531); cf. *C. Tanta* 21, 22 (16 Dec. 533), *C. Omnem* 1, 2, 3 (16 Dec. 533 *per consequentias, per suam consequentiam*).

[395] *CJ* 5.27.10.1, 1.4.24, 8.51.3 pr. (17 Sept. 529), 11.48.21 pr. (22 July 530), 6.57.6.1 (1 Oct. 530), 5.11.7.2, 8.48.6 (1 Nov. 531); cf. 6.58.15 pr. (15 Oct. 534), *CTh/N* 6.

[396] *CJ* 8.41.8.1 (22 July 530), 6.22.10.1, 4 (20 Feb. 531 bis), 3.28.37.1f., 3.31.12.1 (1 Sept. 531), 5.13.1.3 (1 Nov. 531), 6.30.22.5 (27 Nov. 531); cf. 6.51.1.3, 11d (1 June 534 bis), *CTh/N* 0.

[397] *CJ* 5.27.10.3 (17 Sept. 529), 4.1.12.2c, 4c (30 Oct. 529 bis), 7.62.38 (Demostheni pp. 529), 4.21.20.3 (18 March 530), 3.1.14.2 (27 March 530), 3.1.18 (1 Nov. 531); cf. 7.71.8.3 (531/2), *N.* 62.1.2 (1 Jan. 537), *CTh/N* 0.

[398] *CJ* 8.53.35.4 (18 March 530), 8.40.26.2, 3.1.13.1 (27 March 530), 7.7.1.1b (1 Aug. 530), 6.30.20 pr. (30 April 531 bis), 7.54.3.2 (27 Nov. 531); cf. 11.48.23 pr. (531/4), 5.17.11.1a (17 Nov. 533), Nov. 34.1 (15 June 535), 23.4 (3 Jan. 536), *CTh/N* 1.

[399] *CJ* 5.12.31.6 (18 March 530), 3.33.13.2 (1 Oct. 530), 6.25.8.1 (29 July 530), 6.49.7 pr., 4.11.1.2 (18 Oct. 531), 6.42.32.1, 6.58.14.1 (27 Nov. 531), *CTh/N* 0.

[400] *CJ* 4.66.2.1 (17 Sept. 529), 4.66.3 pr., 1, 3 bis, 5 (18 March 530 quinq.), 2.18.24.2 (17 Nov. 530), 6.43.3.4 (1 Sept. 531), *CTh/N* 0.

[401] *CJ* 6.30.19 pr. (30 Oct. 529), 5.12.31.8 (18 March 530), 3.1.13.1, 8 (27 March 530 bis), 4.20.19.2 (18 March 530), 2.58.2.12 (20 Feb. 531); cf. 5.37.28.2b (18 Oct. 532) but 12.37.6 (4 April 377), *CTh/N* 3.

[402] *CJ* 2.55.4.3, 8.53.34.4 (30 Oct. 529), 6.33.3 pr. (18 March 530), 2.55.5 pr. (27 March 530), *C. Deo auctore* 5 (15 Dec. 530), 8.56.4 (1 Sept. 531), 5.13.1.2 (1 Nov. 531),

with two distant harbingers, all nine uses of *repletio*,[404] and the first nine of *perfectissimus*[405] and *perfectissime*[406] used otherwise than as a title of rank; 11 of the first 14 uses of *apertissimus*;[407] all 12 of *fugiens*[408] (referring to the defendant in an action), all six of *figura*,[409] all nine of the plural form *altercationes*,[410] all eight of *circuitus*[411] (often *inextricabiles*), the first six of *semovere*,[412] six of the first seven cases of *consummare*.[413] Of *melius*[414]

8.17.12.4 (27 Nov. 531), but 1.3.32.3 (4 April 472), *CTh/N* 1.

[403] *CJ* 5.9.10 pr. (17 Sept. 529), 8.53.35.4 (18 March 530), 8.40.26.4 (27 March 530), 3.33.16.2 (1 Oct. 530), 6.27.4.2 (17 Nov. 530), 6.61.8.1, 1b (29 July 531 bis) but 7.19.7 pr. (Constantinus), 10.10.5.1 (9 Oct. 435), *CTh/N* 2.

[404] *CJ* 6.33.3 pr. (18 March 530), *C. Deo auctore* 6, 9 (15 Dec. 530), 3.28.34.1 (29 July 531), 6.28.4.5, 3.28.36 pr., 1a, 1b, 2 (quat. both 1 Sept. 531), cf. 7.2.15.4 (531/2). So far as *replere* is concerned ten of the first twelve texts are from our period but two come from the preceding quaestorship of Thomas. *CJ* 4.1.12.6 (30 Oct. 529), 3.1.13.4, 8a (27 March 530 bis), 5.4.25.3 (1 Oct. 530), *C. Deo auctore* 7 (15 Dec. 530), 6.23.28.1 (1 March 531), 6.35.11.3 (30 April 531), 3.28.35.2, 3.28.36 pr. (1 Sept. 531), 6.50.18 pr. (1 Nov. 531); cf. *C. Tanta* 18 (16 Dec. 533), *C. Cordi* 3, 4 (16 Nov. 534 bis) but 3.28.31 (11 Dec. 528), 3.28.32 (1 April 529), *CTh/N* 0.

[405] *CJ* 6.23.27.1 (18 March 530), 8.53.35.5b (18 March 530), 5.70.6.1 (1 Sept. 530), 5.59.4 (20 Feb. 531), 6.42.32.1 (27 Nov. 531); cf. *C. Tanta* 13, 18 (16 Dec. 533 bis), 6.58.15.1a (15 Oct. 534).

[406] *CJ* 4.32.28 pr. (17 Sept. 529), 1.51.14 pr. (17 Sept. 529), 2.55.5.3 (27 March 530), 7.33.12.3b (27 Nov. 531).

[407] *CJ* 7.63.5.4 (17 Nov. 529), 4.32.28.1 (17 Sept. 529), 7.40.1.2 (18 March 530), 6.2.22.4, 6.37.23.1 (17 Nov. 530), 7.71.7, 3.1.16, 4.18.2.1 (20 Feb. 531), 6.30.21.2 (30 April 531), 3.28.34.1 (29 July 531), 6.58.13.3 (1 Nov. 531); cf. 3.34.14.1 (18 Oct. 532) but 10.11.5 (22 March 335), 4.19.25 (18 May 382), 4.30.13 (Iustinus). *Apertissime* also conforms to the criteria for marks of style: seven of the first nine texts: *CJ* 5.9.10 pr., 5.70.7.1a (1 Sept. 530), 7.62.39.1 (27 March 530), 6.38.4.1b (30 April 531), 6.61.8 pr. (29 July 531), 6.58.14.1, 6.30.22.1b (27 Nov. 531); cf. *C. Tanta* 18 (16 Dec. 533), 6.51.1.10, 10e, 11c (1 June 534 ter) but 10.34.3 (Zeno), 10.35.3.2 (1 June 528), *CTh/N* 0.

[408] *CJ* 7.39.9 pr. (Demostheni pp. 529), 2.55.5 pr., 1 (27 March 530 bis), 3.1.13.2, 2a bis 3, 9 (27 March 530 quinq.), 2.58.2 pr., 4 (20 Feb. 531 bis), 6.61.8.13, (29 July 531 bis).

[409] *CJ* 6.33.3 pr., 8.53.35.2 (18 March 530), 2.58.2.11 (20 Feb. 531), 5.13.1.7, 5.11.7.2, 7.6.1.10 (1 Nov. 531), *CTh/N* 0.

[410] *CJ* 7.40.1 pr. (18 March 530), 7.7.1.1b, 6.2.20.1, 8.37.13 pr. (1 Aug. 530), 3.33.14.1 (1 Oct. 530), 6.38.4.1 (30 April 531), 6.61.8 pr. (29 July 531), 7.40.3.1 (18 Oct. 531), 3.1.17 (1 Nov. 531); cf. 4.34.12 (531/532), *N.* 35.3 (23 April 535): also *altercare*: *CJ* 3.33.16 pr. (1 Oct. 530), 6.27.5.1a (30 April 531), 6.43.3.1 (1 Sept. 531) but 3.24.3 pr. (Zeno), *CTh/N* 0.

[411] *CJ* 6.43.1 pr. (17 Sept. 529), 2.55.4.7 (30 Oct. 529), 8.47.11 (27 Oct. 530), 7.47.1.1 (1 Sept. 530), 5.70.7.4, 8 (1 Sept. 531), 8.48.6 (1 Nov. 531), 6.30.22.1b (27 Nov. 531).

[412] *CJ* 1.51.14.1 (17 Sept. 529), 6.4.3 pr. (30 Oct. 529), *C. Deo auctore* 7 (15 Dec. 530), 7.31.1.1 (18 Oct. 531), 6.58.14 pr. (27 Nov. 531), 4.37.7. (531); cf. 7.71.8 pr. (531/2), *C. Omnem* 1 (16 Dec. 533), *C. Tanta* 17 (16 Dec. 533), *Inst.* 1.1.25, *CTh/N* 0.

[413] *CJ* 6.22.9.1 (1 Sept. 530), 8.17.12.6 (27 Nov. 530), *C. Deo auctore* 2 bis, 14 (15 Dec. 530 ter), 7.54.3.2 (27 Nov. 531); cf. *C. Tanta* 1, 9, 12 (16 Dec. 533 ter) but 6.23.21.5 (12 Sept. 439).

[414] *CJ* 7.4.14.1 (1 Oct. 530), 6.2.22.1d (17 Nov. 530), *C. Deo auctore* 6 (15 Dec. 530), 5.59.4 (20 Feb. 531), 6.27.5.3a, 6.38.4.1a (30 April 531), 6.61.8.5a (29 July 531), 6.43.3.3, 7.47.1 pr. (1 Sept. 531), 4.1.13.1 (18 Oct. 531), 2.40.5.1, 8.37.14.2 (1 Nov. 531), 11.48.22.1 (531); cf. 7.2.15.3, 5.4.28.4 (531/2), 5.3.20.1 (531/4), *C. Tanta* 10 (16 Dec. 533), *C. Cordi*

we find 13 of the first 17 texts, and of *via*[415] (used metaphorically) 13 of the first 22; of the others only two are later than Constantine. Of the first 50 mentions of *iterum*,[416] 39 come in our period and of the others only one is recent.

The catalogue of words and expressions used with exceptional frequency in the first quaestorship ends with some which to a greater or lesser extent illuminate the minister's thought. Two concern equality. Twenty-seven of 31 texts with *differentia* occur in this period,[417] nearly always in a context denying or obliterating differences (*quae enim differentia?*[418] *nulla erit differentia*,[419] *supervacua differentia*[420] etc.); there is one recent precedent of 520–3. Concern with equality is also demonstrated by the seven texts with

---

4 (16 Nov. 534), but 5.50.2.1 (5 Dec. 223), 3.38.3 (15 June 290), 3.27.1 pr. (1 July 391), 5.4.20.1 (408/9).

[415] *CJ* 5.12.30.1 (30 Oct. 529), 3.1.13.2b, 3, 4 (27 March 530 ter), 6.25.7 pr. (22 July 530), 6.37.23.1 (17 Nov. 530), *C. Deo auctore* 1 (15 Dec. 530), 4.21.21.4 (20 Feb. 531), 6.40.2.2 (20 Feb. 531), 3.31.12 pr. (1 Sept. 531), 7.6.1.12a (1 Nov. 531), 7.37.3.1d (27 Nov. 531), 6.30.22.1a (27 Nov. 531); cf. 1.1.8.29 (25 March 534 John 11), 6.51.1.1, 1a, 4 (1 June 534 ter), *C. Cordi* 3 (16 Nov. 534) but 4.65.10 (22 Feb. 239), 5.71.11 pr. (20 Nov. 290), 4.51.3 (17 Oct. 293), 8.43.2 (27 Dec. 293), 9.22.16 (6 Feb. 294), 7.16.31 (11 Nov. 294), 8.43.3 (27 Nov. 294), 1.2.14.8 (470), 12.5.4.5 (Leo), *CTh/N* 12.

[416] *CJ* 4.32.28.1 (17 Sept. 529), 5.27.10 pr., 4.1.11 pr., 2 (bis), 6.43.1.2, 8.51.3.2 (17 Sept. 529), 5.30.5.1, 4.1.12.4d, 6.61.6.3, 11.48.20 pr. (30 Oct. 529), 4.20.19.3, 8.53.35.2, 8.55.10.1 (18 March 530), 3.1.13.2c, 6.23.28.1, 3 (bis), 4.20.20, 7.62.39.1 (27 March 530), 3.38.12 pr. (22 July 530), 5.70.6 pr., 1 (bis, 1 Sept. 530), 6.2.21.4 (1 Oct. 530), 6.37.23.2 (17 Nov. 530), *C. Deo auctore* 9 (15 Dec. 530), 7.71.7 (20 Feb. 531), 4.18.2.1 (20 Feb. 531), 4.21.21 pr., 1, 4 (20 Feb. 531 ter), 6.37.24.1 (30 April 531), 6.61.8.6a (29 July 531), 8.47.10 pr., 1c (bis), 3.28.36.2 (1 Sept. 531), 7.6.1.3, 10 (bis), 8.37.14 pr. (1 Nov. 531); 5.16.27 pr., 6.58.14.1 (27 Nov. 531); cf. 8.10.14 pr. (18 Oct. 532), *C. Imperatoriam* 1 (21 Nov. 533), *C. Omnem* 4 (16 Dec. 533), *C. Tanta* pr., 7e (16 Dec. 533 bis), 2.7.29.1 (531/4), 1.1.8.3, 29 (25 March 534 John 11, bis), *N.* 11.2 (14 April 535), 35.2 (23 April 535), 111 pr. (1 June 541), 112.3.1 (9 Sept. 541 bis) but 7.9.3.1 (18 March 290/293), 7.16.27 pr. (30 March 294), 10.41.3.2 (Dio et Max. AA et CC), 9.4.1.3 (30 June 320), 1.2.1 (3 July 321), 1.19.5 (18 Sept. 365), 9.47.23.1 (18 April 414), 1.51.5 (11 Dec. 415), 11.19.1 pr. (27 Feb. 425), 11.54.1.2 (1 Sept. 468), 7.70.1 (1 June 528), *CTh/N* 34.

[417] *CJ* 4.32.28 pr. (17 Sept. 529), 2.55.4.6 (30 Oct. 529), 7.15.1.3 (18 March 530), 7.7.1.1b, 4.28.7.1, 7.15.2 (1 Aug. 530), 5.70.6 pr., 8.47.10.3 (1 Sept. 531), 4.27.3 pr., 4.31.14 pr. (1 Nov. 531), 11.48.21.1 (22 July 530), 2.52.7 pr. (bis) 6.28.4.1, 2,8 (ter) (1 Sept. 531), 3.34.13, 7.31, rubric, 1.5 (18 Oct. 531), 4.27.3 pr., 4.39.9, 6.58.13.3, 5.13.1 pr. (1 Nov. 531), 7.33.12.2, 7.37.3.1a, 6.58.14.1 (27 Nov. 531), 7.25.1 (530/1); cf. 4.30.16 (531/2), 7.71.8.6 (531/2), 4.34.12 (531/2), 5.3.20.1 (531/2), 6.51.1.1b (1 June 534), 6.58.15.2 (15 Oct. 534), 8.53.37 (Iohanni pp. after 18 Oct. 531) but 4.30.10 (Dio et. Max. AA et CC), 6.60.4 pr. (1 Sept. 468), 1.3.36 (28 March 484), 5.4.23.1b (520–3 *neque differentiam aliquam*), *CTh/N* 0.

[418] *CJ* 2.55.4.6 (*qualis?*), 4.32.28 pr., 7.37.3.1a, 11.48.21.1; cf. 4.30.16, above, n. 417.

[419] *CJ* 4.31.14 pr., 7.33.12.2, 7.7.1.1b, 4.28.7.1, 8.47.10.3, 7.25.1; cf. 7.71.8.1, 8.53.37. Also *sine ulla d.* (6.58.15.2), *d. expellentes* (4.27.3 pr.), *d. resecantes* (5.13.1 pr.), *explosa/explosis d.* (7.15.1.3, 3.34.13), *sublata, sublatis d.* (7.31, rubric, 7.31.1.5), *sub obtentu d.* (6.28.4.8), *non piam d.* (6.58.14.1), *non est d.* (7.15.2), *non per d.* (6.58.13.3), *d. locorum... absurdum* (2.52.7 pr.), *nihil est quod d. possit introducere* (4.39.9), all above, n. 417.

[420] *CJ* 2.52.7 pr.; cf. 4.34.12, above, n. 417.

an ablative absolute ending in *nullo discrimine* (*interposito*[421] etc.): one precedent of 366.

Terminal or savings clauses are often revealing. One pointing to preoccupation with the protection of individual rights is signalled by the phrase *nullo* (*praeiudicio*/*impedimento*) *generando* which appears seven times as a savings clause;[422] it occurs once before in 294. Another Tribonianic termination is *procul dubio observando*.[423]

Seventeen of 18 uses of *defraudare*[424] point to a vice which seems to figure prominently in Tribonian's thoughts. *Explodere* in a metaphorical sense (repeal) gives a clue to the prevailing spirit of reform; our period has eight of its 12 instances, with one modern example under Anastasius.[425] The optimism of the age rather than of the quaestor is hinted at by the 17 texts with *possibilis*, not counted as a mark of style in view of two recent precedents.[426]

(g) *Other marks of style*. To end what is inevitably something of a catalogue of characteristic words and turns of phrase, it seems best to abandon a narrative form, which would have tried the talent of a Holdsworth, and resort to an alphabetical list of cases not so far mentioned which satisfy the crtieria adopted.

They include:

[421] *CJ* 1.4.24, 5.27.10.3 (*nec ullo*), 8.51.3.1, 9.41.18 (17 Sept. 529), 7.62.38 (Demostheni pp. 529), 6.22.10.6 (20 Feb. 531), 6.58.14 pr. (27 Nov. 531) but 11.48.6 (366), *CTh*/*N* o.

[422] *CJ* 4.1.12.4d (30 Oct. 529), 11.48.20.3, 3a, 5 (30 Oct. 529 ter), 6.30.21.2 (30 April 531), 6.61.8.1 (29 July 531), 6.30.22.11 (27 Nov. 531); cf. 7.71.8.7 (531/2), 1.3.54.6 (Iohanni pp. after 17 Nov. 533), but 2.24.5 (8 Dec. 294), *CTh*/*N* o.

[423] *CJ* 3.1.13.9 (27 March 530), 3.38.12.3 (22 July 530), 5.51.13.2 (1 Aug. 530), 6.61.8.4d (29 July 531), 7.6.1.6 (1 Nov. 531), 6.58.14.7 (27 Nov. 531); cf. 11.48.24 pr. (17 Nov. 533), *CTh*/*N* o.

[424] *CJ* 5.9.10.6 (17 Sept. 529), 7.63.5.4 (17 Nov. 529), 1.5.19.3 (Demostheni pp. 529), 8.53.35.5c (18 March 530), 6.25.7 pr. (22 July 530), 2.58.2.4 (20 Feb. 531), 4.18.2.1 (20 Feb. 531), 6.38.4.1c (30 April 531), 6.25.8.1 (29 July 531), 6.27.6 (29 July 531), 8.47.10 pr., 1e (1 Sept. 531 bis), 3.28.36.2 (1 Sept. 531), 6.43.3.1b (1 Sept. 531), 7.6.1.5 (1 Nov. 531), 6.37.25.1 (1 Nov. 531), 8.17.12.8 (27 Nov. 531); cf. 11.48.23 pr. (531/4), *N*. 35.4 (23 April 535) but 12.57.14.1 (27 Dec. 471), *CTh*/*N* 2.

[425] 1.14.12.5 (30 Oct. 529), 7.15.1.3 (18 March 530), 8.37.13.1 (1 Aug. 530), 6.42.31 pr. (30 April 531), 6.38.4.1a (30 April 531), 8.56.4 (1 Sept. 531), 3.28.35.1 (1 Sept. 531), 3.34.13 (18 Oct. 531) but 3.31.7.1 (22 July 294), 3.40.1 (3 Sept. 362), 7.71.6 (1 May 386 itp. *CTh* 4.20.3), 7.39.5 (17 Nov. 500), *CTh*/*N* 3.

[426] It is something of a surprise that this word is not in *CTh* or in *CJ* until the sixth century. *CJ* 8.53.34.2a, 4a (30 Oct. 529 bis), 7.62.39.2, 3.1.14.4 (27 March 530), 8.37.13.1, 3.33.12 pr., 1 (1 Aug. 530 bis), 1.4.27.2, 5.70.7.6a, 7.47.1 pr. (1 Sept. 531), 7.4.14 pr. (1 Oct. 530), *C. Deo auctore* 4 (15 Dec. 530), 4.18.2.1, 4.21.21.2 (20 Feb. 531), 6.27.5.1 (30 April 531), 6.61.8.3 (29 July 531), 3.28.34.1 (29 July 531); cf. *C. Tanta* pr. (16 Dec. 533 bis), 7.2.15.1 (531/2) but 5.4.23 pr. (520–3), 4.20.18 (1 June 528). For the reverse side of the coin *impossibile est* is found in *CJ* 7.40.1 pr. (18 March 530), 4.38.15.2 (1 Aug. 530), 5.70.6.1 (1 Sept. 530), 6.2.21.5 (1 Oct. 530); cf. *C. Tanta* 13, 17 (16 Dec. 533) but 4.58.3.1 (17 April 286). *Impossibilis* is in *CTh* 11.13.3 (412).

(a) *abunde* (in the phrase *sat(is) abundeque*),[427] *acies*[428] in a metaphorical sense, *adsimulare*,[429] *advenire*[430] (met.), *ambulare*[431] (met.), *argumentari*,[432] *atqui*,[433] *attingere*,[434] *ab* or *de aula*.[435]

(b) *bene* (*prospicere* etc.).[436]

(c) *calores*,[437] *cautela* (in the phrase *cum debita* etc. *cautela*),[438] *cerebrum*,[439] *cominus*,[440] *communicatio*,[441] *compositor*,[442] *concessio*,[443] *concrescere*,[444] (*legum*) *conditor*,[445] *confinium*,[446] *coniectura*,[447] *coniunctum*,[448] *cor* (in the phrase *cordi . . . est*[449]), *corruptor*,[450] *convalere*.[451]

(d) *delere*[452] (met.), *deludere*,[453] *desperare*,[454] *dicere* (in the phrase *secundum*

[427] *CJ* 1.51.14 pr. (17 Sept. 529), 8.53.34.4a (30 Oct. 529), 4.21.20 pr. (18 March 530) 7.7.2.3 (17 Nov. 530); cf. 6.58.15.2 (15 Oct. 534), *N.* 37.3 (1 Aug. 535), *CTh/N* 1.

[428] *CJ* 5.70.7.3a (1 Sept. 530).

[429] *CJ* 1.51.14.2 (17 Sept. 529), 4.21.21 pr. (20 Feb. 531); cf. 4.35.23.2 (531/2) but 1.9.11 (29 May 408), *CTh/N* 2.

[430] *CJ* 6.23.28.1 (27 March 530), 5.70.6 pr. (1 Sept. 530), 11.48.22 pr. (20 Feb. 531), 2.3.30 pr. (1 Nov. 531); cf. *N.* 114.1.1 (1 Nov. 541), *CTh/N* 9.

[431] *CJ* 3.1.14.1 (27 March 530), 5.70.7.9 (1 Sept. 530), 7.6.1.12a (1 Nov. 531); cf. 5.3.20.6 (531/2), *C. Omnem* pr. bis (16 Dec. 533), *CTh/N* 0.

[432] *CJ* 6.24.14.2 (29 July 531), 5.37.26.4 (23 Aug. 531), *CTh/N* 0.

[433] *CJ* 5.12.31.2 (18 March 530), *CTh/N* 0.

[434] *CJ* 5.51.13.2 (1 Aug. 530), 5.70.7.1a (1 Sept. 530), 7.7.1.3, 2.18.24.1 (17 Nov. 530); cf. 8.4.11.1 (18 Oct. 532) but 5.14.4 (9 June 240), 1.9.4 (6May 368/370/373 itp. cf. *CTh* 7.8.2), 1.3.40 (19 Nov. 524 = 6.23.23), meaning 'affect'.

[435] *CJ* 2.55.4.7 (10 Oct. 529), 7.37.3.1c (27 Nov. 531); cf. *N.* 23.1 (3 Jan. 536), *CTh/N* 0

[436] In the phrase *bene prospicere* (*CJ* 6.58.14 pr. (27 Nov. 530); cf. *CJ* 7.37.3 pr. (Iustinianus Floro), *CTh/N* 0.

[437] *CJ* 6.61.8.9a (29 July 531), *CTh/N* 0.

[438] *CJ* 11.48.20.1 (*omni*), 8.33.3.4c (*competenti*), 5.37.25 pr. (*omni*); cf. *N.* 114 pr. (1 Nov. 541), *CTh/N* 0.

[439] *CJ* 6.22.10.3 (20 Feb. 531), *CTh/N* 0.

[440] *CJ* 1.14.12 pr. (30 Oct. 529) but 7.51.3 (30 March 423), *CTh/N* 1.

[441] *CJ* 8.33.3.4c (18 March 530); cf. 1.1.8.39 (25 March 534 John 11), *CTh/N* 0.

[442] *CJ* 6.28.4.3 (1 Sept. 531), *CTh/N* 0.

[443] *CJ* 6.4.3.2 (30 Oct. 529), 3.28.35 pr. (1 Sept. 531) but 5.72.2 (Aur.), 8.11.1 (27 July 338), *CTh/N* 3.

[444] *CJ* 5.4.28.2 (531/2).

[445] *CJ* 1.14.12.5 (30 Oct. 529), 7.40.2.2 (18 Oct. 531); cf. 6.37.26 pr. (18 Oct. 532), 9.9.35 pr. (18 Oct. 532), *C. Tanta* 18 (16 Dec. 533), *CTh/N* 3.

[446] *CJ* 5.70.6.1 (1 Sept. 530), 6.2.22.4 (17 Nov. 530), *C. Tanta* 5 (16 Dec. 533) but 2.52.6 pr. (19 July 327), *CTh/N* 2.

[447] *CJ* 3.1.13.2a (27 March 530), 4.38.15.2 (1 Aug. 530), 6.2.21.1, 2 (1 Oct. 530 bis); cf. *C. Tanta* 18 (16 Dec. 533), *N.* 111 pr. (1 June 541).

[448] *CJ* 6.37.23.2, 2a (17 Nov. 530); cf. 6.51.1.10a, 10c, 11, 11g (1 June 534 quat.), *CTh/N* 0.

[449] *CJ* 6.4.3.2 (30 Oct. 529), 1.2.23.2 (28 March 530), 3.1.16 (20 Feb. 531); cf. *C. Cordi* pr. (16 Nov. 534), *N.* 35.4 (23 April 535), 37.7 (1 Aug. 535) but 9.9.27 (1 June 295), *CTh/N* 4.

[450] *CJ* 6.2.20.1 (1 Aug. 530), *CTh/N* 1.

[451] *CJ* 8.53.34.3, 4b (30 Oct. 529 bis.).

[452] *CJ* 3.28.33.1 (17 Sept. 529), 5.12.30 pr. (30 Oct. 529), 3.33.14.2 (1 Oct. 530), 7.54.3 pr. (27 Nov. 531); cf. *N.* 36 pr. (1 Jan. 535), *CTh/N* 2.

quod dictum est[455]), *dictator*,[456] *die noctuque*,[457] *divalis (constitutio)*,[458] *documentum* (met.).[459]

(e) *elimare*,[460] *emendare*,[461] *enucleare*,[462] *experimentum*,[463] *explanare*,[464] *ex postfacto*,[465] *exsulere* (met.).[466]

(f) *fabula*,[467] *fenerator*,[468] *finis (certus)*,[469] *fortitudo*,[470] *frons* (met.),[471] *frenare*,[472] *furere*.[473]

(g) *gnaviter*.[474]

(h) *herilis*,[475] *huc atque illuc*.[476]

---

[453] *CJ* 1.51.14.3 (17 Sept. 529), 4.66.3.1 (18 March 530), 3.2.3.1 (27 March 530), 2.58.2.4 (20 Feb. 531) but 3.29.1 (19 Aug. 245), *CTh/N* 2.

[454] *CJ* 4.1.11 pr. (17 Sept. 529), 3.1.14.4 (27 March 530), 5.70.6.1 (1 Sept. 530), *C. Deo auctore* 2 (15 Dec. 530); cf. *C. Tanta* 18 (16 Dec. 533) but 11.48.2.1 (29 April 357), *CTh/N* 5.

[455] *CJ* 1.2.23.3 (18 March 530), *C. Deo auctore* 9 (15 Dec. 530), 7.47.1.2 (1 Sept. 531), 8.48.6 (1 Nov. 531), 6.30.22.7 (27 Nov. 531); cf. *C. Tanta* 22 (16 Dec. 533), 7.2.15.7 (531/2), 6.51.1.9e (1 June 534).

[456] *CJ* 7.62.39.1a (27 March 530), *CTh/N* 0 = 'author'.

[457] *CJ* 7.37.3.4 (28 Nov. 531); cf. *N.* 37 pr. (23 April 535).

[458] *CJ* 5.9.10 pr. (17 Sept. 529), 5.35.3.1 (18 March 530); cf. *C. Deo auctore* 9 (15 Dec. 530), *C. Cordi* 4 (16 Nov. 534) but 9.12.8.2 (7 March 390).

[459] *CJ* 8.33.3 pr. (18 March 530 *ipsis rerum documentis*), *C. Deo auctore* 3 (15 Dec. 530); cf. 6.23.31 pr. (1 June 534 *ipsis rerum documentis*) meaning 'proof'.

[460] *C. Deo auctore* 4 (15 Dec. 530); cf. *C. Tanta* 11 (16 Dec. 533), *C. Omnem* 2 (16 Dec. 533), *N.* 35.4 (23 April 535), *CTh/N* 2, and *elimatio C. Cordi* 3 (16 Nov. 534), *CTh/N* 0.

[461] Fourteen texts of which eight are from this period: *CJ* 3.28.3.1 (197), 2.1.3 (202), 7.44.2 pr. (371), 7.63.2 pr. (440), 1.14.9 (454), 7.39.7 pr. (1 Dec. 525), 4.1.12.1c (30 Oct. 529), 7.62.39 (27 March 530), 5.13.1.1c (1 Nov. 530), *C. Deo auctore* 1, 2, 6 (15 Dec. 520 ter), 3.28.36.1a (1 Sept. 531), 4.11.1 pr. (18 Oct. 531); cf. 6.37.26 pr. (18 Oct. 532), *C. Tanta* pr. 18 (16 Dec. 533 bis), 5.30.20 pr. (531–3), 6.51.1.1 (1 June 534), *C. Cordi* 1 (16 Nov. 534).

[462] *C. Deo auctore* 11 (15 Dec. 530), 6.28.4.3 (1 Sept. 531); cf. *C. Cordi* 1 (16 Nov. 534), *CTh/N* 0.

[463] *CJ* 7.6.1.1a (1 Nov. 531); cf. *C. Tanta* 9 (16 Dec. 533), *N.* 111 pr., 1 (1 June 541 bis) but 6.54.2 (Marcus), *CTh/N* 2.

[464] *CJ* 7.40.1 pr. (18 March 530), 7.62.39.1a (27 March 530), *C. Deo auctore* 13 (15 Dec. 530), 7.6.1.2 (1 Nov. 531); cf. *N.* 112 pr. (9 Sept. 541) but 9.42.2 pr. (26 Nov. 319), 6.36.8.1 (15 Feb. 424), *CTh/N* 3.

[465] *CJ* 6.30.21.2 (30 April 531).

[466] *CJ* 4.29.23 pr. (1 Aug. 530), *C. Deo auctore* 9 (15 Dec. 530), *CTh/N* 1.

[467] *CJ* 7.40.1.1d (18 March 530); cf. *C. Imperatoriam* 3, *CTh/N* 0.

[468] *CJ* 8.33.3.4c (18 March 530); cf. 7.71.8.3 (531/2), *Inst.* 4.12 pr., *CTh/N* 0.

[469] *CJ* 7.39.9 pr. (Demostheni pp. 529), 5.70.7.4 (1 Sept. 530), 5.11.7.2, 5.27.12 pr. (1 Nov. 531) but 7.45.7.9 (Dio et Max. AA et CC bis).

[470] *CJ* 5.13.1.1a (1 Nov. 531), *CTh/N* 2.

[471] *CJ* 4.34.11.2 (30 Oct. 529 *prima fronte*), *CTh/N* 2.

[472] *CJ* 5.27.12.3 (1 Nov. 531) but 10.35.2.1 (8 March 443), *CTh/N* 2.

[473] *CJ* 3.33.12.1 (1 Aug. 530) but 6.36.5 (30 Oct. 294), *CTh/N* 1.

[474] *CJ* 7.37.3.1 (27 Nov. 531); cf. 1.3.54.11 (Iohanni pp. after 17 Nov. 533), *CTh/N* 1.

[475] *CJ* 6.46.6 pr. (30 April 530), 4.27.2.2 (17 Nov. 530), *CTh/N* 1.

[476] *CJ* 6.43.2 pr. (20 Feb. 531); cf. *C. Tanta* 21 (16 Dec. 533); *CTh/N* 0.

(i) *iactare*,[477] *ictus*[478] (met.), *imposuimus*,[479] *inclinare*,[480] *indutiae* (met.),[481] *ineleganter*,[482] *infitiatio*,[483] *interitus* (met.),[484] *interventor*,[485] *introitus*,[486] *iracundia*.[487]

(l) *lascivia*,[488] *latitudo*,[489] *legislator*,[490] *lis* (in the phrase *litem suam facere*),[491] *locum habere*,[492] *locum vindicare*,[493] *lugere*.[494]

(m) *materia* (met.),[495] *mediare*,[496] *mercatio*,[497] *modus* (in the phrase *multis modis*),[498] *monstrum*.[499]

(n) *nodus*,[500] *nox* (in the phrase *noctu dieque*).[501]

(o) *(antiqua) observatio*,[502] *obviam ire*,[503] *ordinator*.[504]

---

[477] *CJ* 7.40.1.1c (18 March 530), 7.6.1.5, 5.11.7.5 (1 Nov. 531); cf. *C. Tanta* 21 (16 Dec. 533) but 9.30.2 (6 March 466), 1.40.14 (7 Aug. 471) = 12.57.14 pr., *CTh/N* 2.

[478] *CJ* 3.28.33 pr. (17 Sept. 529), *CTh/N* o.

[479] *C. Tanta* pr., 1 (16 Dec. 533 bis).

[480] *CJ* 6.61.8.1 (28 July 531) but 8.55.1.2 (17 June 249), *CTh/N* 2.

[481] *CJ* 4.1.12.4a (30 Oct. 529), 8.40.26.2 (27 March 530), 6.22.9 pr., 5.70.6 pr. (1 Sept. 530), 7.54.3.3 (27 Nov. 531); cf. 7.71.8 pr., 5 (531/2 bis) but 11.62.2.1 (Val. et Val.), 3.25.1.1 (20 Jan. 439), *CTh/N* 12.

[482] *CJ* 11.48.22.3 (20 Feb. 531); cf. 6.51.1.9 (1 June 534), *CTh/N* o.

[483] *CJ* 4.21.19 pr. (17 Sept. 529) but 4.5.4 (9 April 293), *CTh/N* o.

[484] *CJ* 3.34.13 (18 Oct. 531 = limitation of an action), *CTh/N* o.

[485] *CJ* 7.54.3.3 (27 Nov. 531), *CTh/N* o.

[486] *CJ* 3.1.13.2 (27 March 530), *CTh/N* 1.

[487] *CJ* 1.3.48.8 (23 Aug. 531), *CTh/N* 2.

[488] *CJ* 5.9.10.2 (17 Nov. 529), *CTh/N* o.

[489] *CJ* 4.11.1.2 (18 Oct. 531), *N.* 75.2 (Dec. 537), *CTh/N* o.

[490] Seven of the first eight texts: *CJ* 3.1.14 pr. (27 March 530), 1.14.12.4 (30 Oct. 529), 8.47.10.5 (1 Sept. 530), 4.5.11 pr. (1 Oct. 530), 4.18.2.1a (20 Feb. 531), 5.11.7.1 (1 Nov. 531), 6.30.22 pr. (27 Nov. 531); cf. *C. Tanta* 20, 20a (16 Dec. 533), Nov. 112 pr. (9 Sept. 541) but 1.14.5.1 (7 April 439), *CTh/N* o and see below, n. 682 (*legum lator*).

[491] *CJ* 2.3.29.2 (1 Sept. 531).

[492] In the infinitive preceded by the verb on which the infinitive depends, e.g. *censemus locum habere*: *CJ* 6.26.10 pr. (29 July 531), 8.10.13 (1 Sept. 531), 7.40.3.3 (18 Oct. 531), 8.14.7 (18 Oct. 531), 5.13.1.15 (1 Nov. 531); cf. 8.14.7 (18 Oct. 532), 4.30.16 (531/2), 7.2.15.1b (531/2) but 4.30.5 (Alex.).

[493] *C. Deo auctore* 8 (15 Dec. 530), 6.30.20.1 (30 April 531), 7.6.1.13 (1 Nov. 531); cf. *C. Tanta* 15 (16 Dec. 533), *C. Omnem* pr. (16 Dec. 533).

[494] *CJ* 6.59.11 (17 Nov. 529), 6.61.6.1a (30 Oct. 529), 7.39.9 (Demostheni pp. 529), 7.4.16.4 (17 Nov. 530), 8.17.12 pr. (27 Nov. 531), *CTh/N* o, meaning 'to be sorry that'.

[495] Seven of the first nine texts: *CJ* 3.1.13 pr. (27 March 530), *C. Deo auctore* 4, 5 (15 Dec. 530), 6.27.5.1 (30 April 531), 7.31.1.4 (18 Oct. 531), 4.11.1.2 (18 Oct. 531), 8.37.14 pr. (1 Nov. 531); cf. 6.51.1 pr., 1c (1 June 534) but 7.51.3 (30 March 423), 7.63.2 pr. (21 May 440).

[496] *CJ* 5.4.26.2 (1 Oct. 530 *deo mediante*), *CTh/N* o.

[497] *CJ* 7.6.1.4 (1 Nov. 531 bis), *CTh/N* o.

[498] *CJ* 7.6.1.1a (1 Nov. 531); cf. *Inst.* 1.5.1 bis.

[499] *CJ* 6.29.3.1 (17 Nov. 530), *CTh/N* o.   [500] *CJ* 4.29.23 pr. (530), *CTh/N* o.

[501] *CJ* 7.37.3.4 (27 Nov. 531 *n. dieque laborant* viz. Justinian and Theodora); cf. *N.* 37 pr. (1 Aug. 535).

[502] *CJ* 7.6.1.6 (1 Nov. 531), *CTh/N* o.

[503] *CJ* 2.55.4.7 (30 Oct. 529) but 12.35.16 (Leo).

[504] *CJ* 4.5.10.1 (1 Aug. 530), *CTh/N* o.

(p) *paulatim*,[505] *paulisper*,[506] *peculiare*,[507] *percontabamur*,[508] *perversio*,[509] *pluraliter*,[510] *ponimus*,[511] *positio*,[512] *praemature*,[513] *primordium*,[514] (*iuris*) *prudentia*.[515]

(q) *quapropter*.[516]

(r) *radix* (met.),[517] *recludere*,[518] *regimen*[519] (of persons), *regressus* (right of regress),[520] (*iuris*) *regula*,[521] (*antiqua, vetus, generalis*), *reminisci*,[522] *retia* (met.),[523] *retrorsus*.[524]

(s) *sapientia*,[525] *satura*,[526] *secta*[527] (*mea* etc.), *seorsum*,[528] *stimulus* (met.),[529] *stirpitus*[530] (*eruere*), *studiosissimus*,[531] *subigere*.[532]

[505] *CJ* 2.58.2.4 (20 Feb. 531); cf. 7.24.1.1 (531/4), 11.48.24.1 (Hermogeni mo., after 20 Feb. 531), *N*. 35.1 (23 April 535) but 4.44.8 (1 Dec. 293), *CTh/N* 4.

[506] *CJ* 6.23.28.2 (27 March 530) but 10.44.2 (Dio et Max. AA).

[507] *CJ* 7.15.1.3 (18 March 530), 5.16.27.1 (27 Nov. 531); cf. *C. Tanta* pr., 6a (16 Dec. 533 bis) in the phrase *peculiare est, fuit* etc.

[508] *C. Tanta* 1 (16 Dec. 533).

[509] *CJ* 7.47.1.1 (1 Sept. 531); cf. *C. Tanta* 21 (16 Dec. 533), *CTh/N* 0.

[510] *CJ* 7.4.14.1 (1 Oct. 530), *CTh/N* 0.   [511] *C. Omnen* 8 (16 Dec. 533).

[512] *CJ* 6.29.4.1 (17 Nov. 530), *CTh/N* 0.

[513] *CJ* 7.63.5.2 (17 Sept. 529), 6.33.3.2 (18 March 530) but 6.17.1 (21 Oct. 293), *CTh/N* 0.

[514] *CJ* 8.55.10.2 (18 March 530), 3.1.14.1 (27 March 530), 2.58.2 pr., 9 (20 Feb. 531); cf. *C. Imperatoriam* 3, *C. Tanta* 20 (16 Dec. 533), *C. Omnem* 3 (16 Dec. 533), *C. Cordi* pr. (16 Nov. 534) but 4.29.19 (15 Dec. 294), *CTh/N* 5.

[515] *CJ* 4.38.15 pr. (1 Aug. 530), 6.2.21.1, 3.33.15 pr. (1 Oct. 530), 4.18.2.1d (20 Feb. 531), *C. Deo auctore* 11 (15 Dec. 530); cf. *C. Tanta* 12 (16 Dec. 533), Nov. 112 pr. (9 Sept. 541) but 1.51.1 (14 July 286).

[516] Seven texts out of ten: 4.32.28.1, 5.27.10.3, 5.9.10.3 (17 Sept. 529), 7.6.1 pr., 6.58.13.2 (1 Nov. 531), 8.17.12.5 (27 Nov. 531) but 11.44.1 (1 Oct. 325), 5.8.1 pr. (1 Feb. 409), 3.13.7.1 (15 Feb. 502).

[517] *CJ* 3.28.35.3 (1 Sept. 531); cf. 5.4.28.4 (531/2), *CTh/N* 2.

[518] *CJ* 7.31.1 pr. (18 Oct. 531), 6.58.14.3 (27 Nov. 531); cf. 6.51.1 pr., 1a (1 June 534 bis).

[519] *CJ* 2.55.5 pr. (27 March 530) = 'authority over (persons)'.

[520] Seven texts out of nine: *CJ* 8.44.8 (6 Dec. 222), 6.20.3 (18 June 239), 6.30.19.4 (30 Oct. 529), 3.1.13.2c (27 March 530), 8.47.10.2 (1 Sept. 530), 4.29.23.1 (530), 7.17.2.1 (1 Sept. 530), 7.31.1 pr. (18 Oct. 531), 7.37.3.3 (27 Nov. 531).

[521] *Iuris regula*: *CJ* 6.2.20.1 (1 Aug. 530), 1.3.50 pr., 2.3.29.1 (1 Sept. 531); *CTh/N* 2; *generalis regula*: 6.2.21.1, 2, 4, 5 (1 Oct. 530 quat.); *vetus regula*: *CJ* 6.27.4.1 (17 Nov. 530), 6.38.4.2, 6.27.5.1d (30 April 531), 2.3.30.3 (1 Nov. 531) and 4.11.1 pr. (18 Oct. 531 *r. qua vetustas utebatur*) but 7.62.32.6 (Theo. et Val.); *antiqua regula*: 6.24.14.2 (29 July 531); cf. 7.32.12.2 (531/2), *CTh/N* 0.

[522] *CJ* 8.17.12.4 (27 Nov. 531), *CTh/N* 1.   [523] *CJ* 4.29.23 (1 Aug. 530), *CTh/N* 0.

[524] *CJ* 8.17.12.9 (27 Nov. 531), *CTh/N* 0.

[525] *CJ* 8.47.10 pr. (1 Sept. 530), 4.27.2 pr. (17 Nov. 530); cf. *C. Tanta* 11, 17 (16 Dec. 533), 1.1.8 pr. (25 March 534 John 11), *CTh/N* 1.

[526] *CJ* 7.6.1 pr. (1 Nov. 531); cf. *C. Omnem* 1 (16 Dec. 533), *CTh/N* 0.

[527] *CJ* 2. 3.30.4 (1 Nov. 531) imitating 9.8.2 (3 Feb. 224), 9.22.5 (30 Aug. 230), 10.11.2.1 (6 Sept. 238).

[528] *CJ* 3.28.36.2a (1 Sept. 531), *CTh/N* 0.

[529] *CJ* 5.70.6.1 (1 Sept. 530), 5.13.1.5c (1 Nov. 531), *CTh/N* 3.

[530] *CJ* 5.12.30.2 (30 Oct. 529) but 10.12.2 pr. (22 April 444), *CTh/N* 1.

[531] *C. Tanta* 1 (16 Dec. 533), *CTh/N* 0.

[532] *CJ* 6.42.30 (30 Oct. 529); cf. *N*. 11.2 (14 April 535) but 1.26.3 (2 May 389).

(t) *tangere* (met.),[533] (sed) *tantummodo*,[534] *tenor* (*constitutionis*),[535] *templum iustitiae*,[536] *tractatus*[537] (in the phrase *subtiliore* etc. *tractatu habito*), *tradere*[538] (meaning 'transform'), *transformare*,[539] *translabi*,[540] *transponere*.[541]

(v) *verisimile est*,[542] *vigilantia*,[543] (*suus*) *vigor*,[544] *volumen*,[545] *vovere*,[546] *vulnus*[547] and *vulnerare* (met.).[548]

About 96 per cent of the Latin constitutions between September 529 and November 531 contain one or more of the marks of style so far listed.[549] There are nine which do not.[550] For this various explanations are possible. A quaestor will not necessarily draft every text enacted during his period of office. He may be ill, absent or otherwise occupied. If the text is short it may be by the quaestor's hand yet contain none of his distinctive expressions. Occasionally the dating may lead us astray. Not least, the foregoing analysis is incomplete. Given unlimited time and patience it would be possible to add a good deal to it, and perhaps thereby to reduce the list of nine unplaced constitutions.

[533] *CJ* 2.55.5.3 (27 March 530), 5.59.5.2 (1 Sept. 531), *CTh/N* 2.
[534] *CJ* 6.61.6.2 (30 Oct. 529), 6.43.1.5 (17 Nov. 529), 4.21.20.2 (18 March 530), 8.53.36.3 (18 Oct. 531), *CTh/N* 0.
[535] *CJ* 7.7.2.3 (17 Nov. 530), 6.61.8.4d (29 July 531), 6.22.12 (1 Sept. 531); cf. 6.58.15.4 (15 Oct. 534 all *secundum constitutionis tenorem*) but 1.3.20.1 (15 Dec. 434), 12.3.4.1 (Zeno both *pro tenore constitutionis*).
[536] *C. Deo auctore* 5 (15 Dec. 530); cf. *C. Tanta* 20 (16 Dec. 533). The temple of justice was dedicated in 13 A.D.: Ovid, *Ep ex Ponto* 3.6.234; *Fasti Praenstini*, 8 Jan. 13 A.D.
[537] *CJ* 6.30.22.1b (27 Nov. 531 *ampliore t.h.*), 5.70.7.1a (1 Sept. 530 *in tali tractatu proposito*); cf. 6.51.1.10 (1 June 534 *cum subtiliore t.*), 6.58.15.1a (15 Oct. 534 *subtiliore, t.h.*) but 3.4.1.2 (20 May 440 *habito t.*), *CTh/N* 3 (none quite comparable).
[538] *C. Deo auctore* 1 (*viae dilucidae t.*), 7 (*ordini moderato t.*), 14 (*fini t.*), 5.11.7.2 (1 Nov. 531); cf. *C. Tanta* 1 (*certo moderamine t.*), 10 (*taciturnitati t.*), 18 (*modis et regulis t.*), 23 (*bella quietae perpetuae t.*). I may have missed some texts.
[539] *CJ* 2.58.2.11 (20 Feb. 531), 7.31.1.1 (18 Oct. 531); cf. *C. Tanta* 10, 21 (16 Dec. 533), *C. Cordi* 4 (16 Nov. 534), *N.* 11.5 (14 April 535), *CTh/N* 0.
[540] *CJ* 6.30.19.3 (30 Oct. 529), 7.37.3 pr. (27 Nov. 531), *CTh/N* 0.
[541] *CJ* 4.66.3.3 (18 March 530), 5.13.1.14a (1 Nov. 531), *CTh/N* 0.
[542] *CJ* 5.27.10.2 (17 Sept. 529), 2.55.4.7 (30 Oct. 529), 6.25.7.1 (22 July 530), 6.24.14.4 (29 July 531), 3.33.17.2 (18 Oct. 531), but 9.22.1 (7 March 212) 2.19.2 (26 June 226), 2.41.1 pr. (22 Sept. 232), *CTh/N* 0.
[543] *CJ* 7.31.1 pr. (18 Oct. 531); cf. *C. Tanta* pr. (16 Dec. 533), *CTh/N* 2.
[544] *CJ* 1.2.22 pr. (30 Oct. 529), 7.40.1.1b (18 March 530), 7.62.39.1 (27 March 530), 3.1.13.11 (27 March 530), 2.58.2.4 (20 Feb. 531); cf. 6.51.1.1 (1 June 534), *Inst.* 4.18.3.
[545] *CJ* 7.62.29.1a (27 March 530), 8.41.8 pr. (22 July 530), 5.4.24 (1 Aug. 530), *C. Deo auctore* 2 bis, 4, 7 (15 Dec. 530 quat.), 6.38.4.1 (30 April 531); cf. *C. Imperatorium* 2 (21 Nov. 533), *C. Omnem* 1, 2, 3 ter, 4, 7 (16 Dec. 533 sept.), *C. Tanta* 5 bis, 7e, 8, 12 bis, 14, 17 bis, 21, 22 (16 Dec. 533 undec.), *CTh/N* 3.
[546] *CJ* 3.38.12 pr. (22 July 530), *CTh/N* 0.
[547] *CJ* 6.58.14.5 (27 Nov. 531), *CTh/N* 0.   [548] *CJ* 2.40.5.1 (1 Nov. 531), *CTh/N* 2.
[549] Of 222 constitutions 213 contain such indications.
[550] *CJ* 7.45.13 (30 Oct. 529), 5.29.4 (18 Oct. 530), 2.44.4 (22 July 530), 1.4.28 (1 Oct. 530), 3.1.15 (20 Feb. 531), 1.5.22 (1 Sept. 531), 4.51.7 (18 Oct. 531), 4.18.3 (1 Nov. 531), 5.37.27 (1 Nov. 531).

In support of the view that Tribonian was responsible for the constitutions enacted from 17 September 529 onwards it may be noted that all 15 texts of that date have appropriate marks of style, as do 13 of 15 texts of 30 October 529, and all five texts addressed to Demosthenes praetorian prefect without date and allotted by Krueger to the year 529 (since the first constitutions of 530, dated 18 March, are addressed to a new praetorian prefect, Julianus). The indications of style in each text follow; for present purposes any mark which is found only in the period before 17 November 529 are disregarded.

(a) 17 September 529

CJ 1.4.24 (*progenies, nullo discrimine habito*).[551]

8.51.3 pr. (*progenies*), 1 (*nullo discrimine habito, Romana dicio*), 2 (*iterum*) = 1.4.24 in part.[552]

1.51.14 pr. (*sat abundeque, perfectissime*), 1 (*semovere*), 2 (*adsimulare, sub umbra*), 3 (*deludebat, regalis culminis*).[553]

2.58.1 pr. (*iuramentum, praestaverit, contentiosa instantia*).[554]

9.41.18 (*nullo discrimine interposito*).[555]

3.28.33 pr. (*minisculus, contentiosus, adgredimur, fuerat derelicta, legitimis ictibus*), 1 (*tollentes, erubescere, Iulius Paulus, adgredimur, suam naturam fallere, satis enim crudele videtur*).[556]

5.9.10 pr. (*apertissime, reclamare, divalis constitutio*), 2 (*lascivia*), 3 (*quapropter*), 5 (*innocuus, inrationabilis*), 6 (*defraudari*).[557]

4.1.11 pr. (*iterum, satis enim absurdum est, desperavit*), 2 (*corroborare, iuramentum, iterum*).[558]

4.21.19 pr. (*exorire, infitiationes*).[559]

4.32.28 pr. (*constitutum fuerat, perfectissime, fuerat concessum, quae differentia erat?, erat non rebus sed verbis leges ponere*), 1 (*quapropter, apertissimus, iterum*).[560]

4.66.2.1 (*emponemata, melioratio*).[561]

5.27.10 pr. (*iterum, fuerant nati*), 1 (*progenies, quomodo non est iniquissimum?*), 2 (*verisimile est*), 3 (*quapropter, trutinare, nec ullo habeatur discrimine*).[562]

6.57.5 pr. (*dubitabatur*), 1 (*satis iniuriosum, satis acerbum, dedicamus*).[563]

6.43.1 pr. (*quis admittet?, inextricabilis circuitus, posteritas, quis utatur ambagibus?*), 1 (*unam naturam imponere, personalem actionem, in rem, utilem Servianam*), 2 (*increbescere, iterum*), 5 (*tantummodo*).[564]

6.59.11 pr. (*conclamare, lugeat*).[565]

[551] Nn. 395, 421.   [552] Nn. 395, 164, 421, 416.

[553] Nn. 427, 406, 412, 429, 206, 325, 453.   [554] Nn. 371, 365, 186.

[555] N. 421.   [556] Nn. 316, 186, 70, 367, 478, 153, 274, 40, 70, 172–4, 388.

[557] Nn. 407, 403, 458, 488, 516, 311, 219, 424.

[558] Nn. 416, 455, 388, 244, 371, 416.   [559] Nn. 376, 483.

[560] Nn. 367, 406, 417, 418, 369, 366, 516, 407, 416.   [561] Nn. 262, 400.

[562] Nn. 416, 367, 395, 542, 369, 516, 397, 421.   [563] Nn. 168, 388, 85.

[564] Nn. 369, 375, 225, 411, 172–4, 54, 199, 416, 534.   [565] Nn. 270, 494.

(b) 30 October 529

CJ 1.2.22 pr. (*suus vigor, cur non faciamus discrimen inter res humanas et divinas?* *quare non conservetur?*), 1 (*amicalis*).[566]

    1.14.12 pr. (*imperialis maiestas, cominus*), 1 (*quid enim maius, quid sanctius?, regalis sensus*), 2 (*invenimus, interpretatus est, dubitatus, vana scrupulositas*), 3 (*interpretari*), 4 (*cur decurritur, quare accipiunt? merus, quis videbitur?, aenigmate, legis lator*), 5 (*explosus, ridiculosus*).[567]

    2.55.4.1 (*iuramentum*), 2 (*iuramentum, illigaverint*), 3 (*iuramentum, vallare*), 5 (*iuramentum, veteres*), 6 (*Graecis vocabulis, qualis enim differentia est?*), 7 (*ab aula, circuitus, cur non amputamus?, non est verisimile, obviam ire*).[568]

    4.1.12 pr. (*iuramenta* bis, *increbescere, pinguius*), 1 (*iuramentum*), 1a (*iuramentum, quis enim ferendus est?*), 2c (*trutinare*), 3 (*iuramentum*), 4a (*iuramentum, indutiae*), 4b (*iuramentum* bis), 4c (*trutinare*), 4d (*nullo impedimento generando, iuramentum, iterum*), 5 (*iuramentum*), 6 (*replere*).[569]

    5.12.30 pr. (*inaestimatus, deleta, confusa*), 1 (*via*), 2 (*stirpitus eruere*).[570]

    5.30.5.1 *cui* (*qui*) *enim ferendum est?, iterum, haec certe et nominum et rerum foeda confusio est*).[571]

    6.4.3 pr. (*semovere, veteres*), 2 (*concessio, merus, cordi est, frequentare*).[572]

    6.30.19 pr. (*Iulius Paulus, invenimus, protelare*), 2 (*annale tempus* bis), 3 (*annali tempore translapso*), 4 (*annale tempus*).[573]

    6.42.30 (*acutissimus, Papinianus, subegit, donamus*).[574]

    6.61.6 pr. (*invenimus, introducimus*), 1a (*lugere, adspicientes*), 1b (*novamus*), 1c (*legis articulus, inducimus*), 3 (*iterum*), 3a (*diximus*), 4 (*dubitabatur, compendiosus, interpretamur*).[575]

    7.45.13–14 (*Papinianus*).[576]

    8.53.34. 1b (*corroborare*), 3 (*coadunare, secundum sui naturam*), 3a (*veteres, variare, causa humanior*), 4 (*variabatur*), 4a (*veteres, sat abundeque, variare, concludimus*).[577]

    11.48. 20 pr. (*imponentes, prolixum tempus, frequentissima consequentia, diximus, iterum*), 1 (*localis, cum omni cautela*), 3 (*definientes, nullo praeiudicio generando* bis, *quiescentibus*), 3a (*moris erat, nullo praeiudicio generando*), 5 (*nullo praeiudicio generando*).[578]

There remain two texts. CJ 4.34.11.2 has the expression *prima fronte*,[579]

[566] Nn. 156, 369, 183, 297.

[567] Nn. 159, 440, 369, 325, 107, 169, 237, 389, 333, 333, 237, 389, 369, 315, 258, 490, 188, 194.

[568] Nn. 371, 371, 277, 382, 402, 371, 51, 166, 417, 435, 411, 369, 542, 503.

[569] Nn. 371, 199, 293, 371, 371, 335, 397, 371, 371, 481, 371, 397, 422, 371, 416, 371, 404.

[570] Nn. 213, 300, 452, 415, 530.

[571] Nn. 335, 416; cf. CJ 4.32.28 pr., above, n. 560.

[572] Nn. 412, 51, 443, 315, 449, 248.   [573] Nn. 40, 107, 401, 378, 540, 378, 378.

[574] Nn. 339, 40, 532, 90.

[575] Nn. 107, 105, 494, 135, 110, 387, 100, 416, 89, 168, 374, 104.   [576] N. 40.

[577] Nn. 267, 172–4, 51, 373; cf. *sententia humanior* nn. 181, 373, 51, 427, 373, 80.

[578] Nn. 146, 323, 416, 394, 89, 343, 438, 422, 385, 142, 422, 366, 422, 422.

[579] N. 471.

but this cannot count for present purposes since it is not found in texts between 17 November 529 and November 531. *CJ* 7.45.13 is an important text (*non exemplis sed legibus iudicandum est*) but lacks a distinctive mark of identification.

(c) Iustinianus Demostheni pp. undated

CJ 1.2.21 pr. (*iuris divini, humanis nexibus, respuere*), 1 (*iuris articulis, abominamur*), 2 (*pignoratio*).[580]

1.5.19. 3 (*imponimus, defraudare*).[581]

7.39.9 pr. (*fugientes, lugere, finis certus*), 1 (*corrigentes, praepeditus*).[582]

7.62.38 (*nullo discrimine habito, trutinare*).[583]

10.32.67. 4 (*prolixum tempus, corroborantes, praediximus*), 6 (*enumeravimus, concessum fuerat, nullo patimur modo*).[584]

It follows that Tribonian was quaestor at least as early as 17 September 529. Indeed it may be that the date of 7.63.5 (*Iustinianus Triboniano quaestori sacri palatii*) should be altered from 17 November to 17 September of that year. Since he must be allowed some time to draft the legislation of 17 September, his tenure of office should be dated not later than the beginning of September.

At this point when we pass from listing the marks of style of Tribonian's first quaestorship to using the list in order to identify other constitutions composed by him, it is appropriate to explain the method employed, though that is perhaps to some extent evident from the discussion of the constitutions of September and October 529 and those addressed to Demosthenes pp. without date.

The various constitutions of undetermined authorship are listed in groups, and against each a note is made of the items from the list of marks of style which are to be found in it. The conclusions to be drawn naturally depend on the length of the constitution, the number of items from the list found in it, and their relatively idiosyncratic nature. Clearly the fact that a text contains a single item from the list is by no means conclusive. On the other hand the fact that a number of constitutions from the same group—for example those enacted on the same day, or belonging (like the Prefaces) to the same general type—all or nearly all include some item from the list is significant. In these instances the evidence pointing to Tribonian as the author of one of the documents strengthens the case for regarding him as the author of the rest.

In the end the weight to be attached to the various items is a matter of scholarly judgment. The footnotes refer the reader to the earlier passages of this chapter where the relevant texts are listed and so enable him to make up his mind.

---

[580] Nn. 183, 386, 387, 68, 252.   [581] Nn. 102, 424.
[582] Nn. 408, 494, 469, 139, 264.   [583] Nn. 421, 397.
[584] Nn. 323, 244, 113, 370, 367, 122, 93.

DATED CONSTITUTIONS FROM JANUARY 532 TO NOVEMBER 534

On 14 January 532 Tribonian was dismissed from the quaestorship as a concession to the Nika rioters, who at the instigation of a senatorial faction hostile to Justinian demanded and obtained his dismissal along with that of John of Cappadocia.[585] John was soon restored to office.[586] Tribonian had to wait until the completion of the codification in November 534, but he remained chairman of the Second Law Commission and in that capacity continued to draft certain constitutions even when he was not quaestor. Other constitutions of the period between January 532 and November 534 were however drafted by Justinian himself, and yet others we may presume to be the work of Basilides, who had been the fourth senior member of the First Law Commission.[587] It is therefore necessary to consider the constitutions of this period individually and in groups according to their date.

Omitting Greek texts, the first group comprises nineteen constitutions concerned with the work of the *Digest* commission which were enacted on 18 October 532. These in effect bring the reforming work of the commission to a close so far as published texts are concerned; thereafter the commission introduced certain changes without special statutory authority, though the words of C. *Deo auctore* could on one view be interpreted as providing a general mandate to improve the law.[588]

Of the nineteen constitutions of 18 October 532 seventeen contain Tribonianic marks of style. In particular:

CJ 3.10.3 (*odiosus*)[589]
>3.34.14 pr. (*quaerebatur, libri Sabiniani, deperdere, deperire, prolixum spatium*), 1 (*sua natura, apertissimus*).[590]
>5.37.28. 1 (*recusatio*), 2a (*recusatio, imponimus*), 2b (*recusatio*), 3 (*apertius*).[591]
>6.21.18 (*tempora nostra, nullo modo concedimus*).[592]
>6.31.6. pr. (*cum fuerat ei permissum, corrigentes, antiquitas observabat*).[593]
>6.35.12. pr. (*veteres*), 1 (*exaudire*).[594]
>6.37.26. pr. (*legum conditores, emendare*).[595]
>6.38.5. pr. (*Illyriciana advocatio*), 1 (*humanum esse, nullo etenim modo*).[596]
>6.49.8. pr. (*quaerebatur*).[597]
>7.72.10. pr. (*invenimus, veteres, quid enim iustius est?*).[598]
>8.4.11. pr. (*Illyriciana advocatio, ridiculum est*).[599]
>8.10.14. pr. (*iterum*).[600]
>8.14.7 (*sancimus . . . locum habere, utraque Roma*).[601]

---

585 *Wars* 1.25.1; Malalas 475B.
586 The constitutions of 18 Oct. 542 are addressed to Iohannes pp.
587 C. *Haec* 1 (13 Feb. 528).   588 C. *Deo auctore* 7 (15 Dec. 530).
589 N. 192.   590 Nn. 167, 40, 273, 272, 323, 172-4, 407.
591 Nn. 384, 384, 102, 384, 290.   592 Nn. 127, 79.
593 Nn. 367, 139; cf. *antiqua observatio* 519.   594 Nn. 51, 275.
595 Nn. 445, 461.   596 Nn. 231, 382, 177, 370.   597 N. 167.
598 Nn. 107, 51, 369.   599 Nn. 231, 382; cf. *ridiculosus* n. 194.   600 N. 416.
601 Nn. 492; cf. *antiqua Roma* n. 165.

8.25.11.2 (*respuere*).[602]
8.36.5.1 (*dolosus*).[603]
8.37.15 pr. (*stultus, veteres*), 1 (*consentaneus*).[604]
9.9.35 pr. (*legum conditores*).[605]

This leaves two texts which contain no specific mark of Tribonian's style as illustrated earlier, but on the other hand contain nothing inconsistent with it.[606] The proportion containing such marks is high enough to justify the conclusion that this block of constitutions was drafted by the ex-quaestor.

The next constitution is an exchange of letters between John II and Justinian:[607] the latter wrote on 6 June 533 and the pope replied on 25 March 534. Justinian's letter was composed by the emperor himself.[608]

On 17 November 533 there are five texts, originally, it seems, forming a single constitution addressed to Hermogenes, master of offices. Even however if they are treated as five separate constitutions, they all contain Tribonianic marks of style:

1.3.53. 5 (*praediximus*).[609]
5.17.11. 1a (*puta, quantuscumque*), 2b (*invenimus, frequentare*).[610]
7.24.1 pr. (*satis impium, sustinuimus, infelix, fulgor, religio temporum meorum nullo patitur modo* = in part 11.48.24), 1 (*paulatim*).[611]
9.13.1. 3 (*praediximus*), 3b (*odiosus* = in large part 1.3.53).[612]
11.48.24. pr. (*illo procul dubio observando*), 1 (*paulatim*).[613]

The legislation is concerned with rape and divorce and does not arise directly out of the work of the law commission which, so far as the *Digest* was concerned, was at the time on the point of publication.[614] If nevertheless Tribonian's hand is patent, this must be considered an irregularity on Justinian's part. The emperor surreptitiously allowed his minister to fulfil the functions of the quaestorship though he was technically not in office.

On 16 December 533 *C. Tanta* enacted the *Digest*. This together with two other contemporary prefaces (*C. Omnem* and *Imperatoriam*) are considered in a separate section devoted to the Prefaces.

Next come two constitutions addressed to Belisarius on the reconquest of North Africa, CJ 1.27.1 and 2. The latter is dated 13 April 534 and the former must be nearly if not exactly contemporaneous. Both these were drafted by Justinian himself.[615]

On 1 June 534 there is a notable and optimistic constitution *de caducis tollendis* addressed to the senate of Constantinople. It has no fewer than 46 marks of Tribonian's style:

[602] N. 386.   [603] N. 187.
[604] Nn. 328, 51, 242.   [605] N. 445.   [606] CJ 6.20.21, 6.50.19.   [607] CJ 1.1.8.
[608] *Justinian* 116–17.   [609] N. 113.   [610] Nn. 355, 398, 107, 248.
[611] Nn. 388, 125, 309, 158, 127–30, 370, 505.   [612] Nn. 113, 192.
[613] Nn. 423, 505.   [614] On 16 Dec. 533.   [615] *Justinian* 117–19.

C. 6.51.1 pr. (*materia, recludere*), 1 (*emendare, suus vigor, multas invenientibus vias*), 1a (*vias recludentes*), 1b (*circumcludere, erubescere, scripti fuerant, sine differentia*),[616] 1c (*materia, corrigentes*), 2 (*consentaneus*), 2a (*in rerum natura, veteres*), 3 (*perraro, statutum fuerat, coniunctus fuerat, supervenire*),[617] 3a (*consentaneos*), 4 (*fuerat complexum, corrigentes, ferendus*), 5 (*praediximus, articulus, veteres*), 6 (*propter sui naturam*), 6a (*sui natura*),[618] 8 (*fuerat defectum*), 9 (*Ulpianus, inducimus, ineleganter, apertius*), 9b (*puta*), 9c (*facti natura, ipsa natura concedit, quid enim si?*), 9e (*secundum quod dictum est*), 10 (*latius, articulus, apertissime, cum subtiliore tractatu*),[619] 10a (*coniunctim*), 10b (*respuere*), 10c (*coniunctum*), 10e (*apertissime*), 11 (*coniunctim*), 11b (*unam naturam, imponentes, respuere*), 11c (*apertissime*), 11d (*supervenire, coniunctim*), 14a (*existimantes*).[620]

A constitution of 5 July 534 relaxing the formalities for will-making in areas of illiteracy is also by Tribonian's hand:

C. 6.23.31 pr. (*invenimus, quomodo possunt?, simplicitas* and cf. *dei humanitas*), 3 (*nullo modo concedimus*).[621]

On 15 October 534 there occurs an alteration to the law of intestate succession. Again the authorship is unmistakable:

C. 6.58.15 pr. (*progenies*), 1a (*subtiliore tractatu habito, perfectissimus*), 1b (*fuerat deminutus, manifestissimus, bellissimum*), 2 (*sine ulla differentia, si consanguinei fuerant, satis abundeque*), 3a (*enumeravimus*), 4 (*constitutionis tenor*), 5 (*amicalis*).[622]

With the exception of *C. Cordi* of 16 November 534, this brings to a close the list of dated constitutions drafted in Latin during the quaestorship of Basilides. If the texts of 17 November 533 are treated as five units, we have 30 such constitutions, of which 25 are shown to be by Tribonian's hand,[623] three by Justinian,[624] and two are unassigned.[625] There are also the four prefaces *Imperatoriam, Omnem, Tanta* and *Cordi* which have been left for future discussion.

It is to this discussion that I now turn.

---

[616] Nn. 495, 518, 461, 544, 415, 518, 415, 239, 274, 367, 417.

[617] Nn. 495, 139, 242, 172–4, 282, 367, 396.

[618] Nn. 242, 367, 139, 335, 113, 387, 51, 172–4.

[619] Nn. 367, 40, 100, 482, 290, 355, 172, 369, 455, 292, 387, 407, 537.

[620] Nn. 448, 386, 448, 407, 448, 172–4, 146, 386, 407, 396, 448, 144.

[621] Nn. 107, 369, 238; cf. *divina humanitas C. Tanta* pr. (16 Dec. 533), n. 79.

[622] Nn. 395, 537, 405, 367, 346, 209, 417, 427, 368, 93, 535, 297.

[623] Seventeen texts of 18 Oct. 532 (above, nn. 589–605), five of 17 Nov. 533 (above, nn. 609–13), one of 1 June 534 (nn. 616–20), one of 5 July 534 (n. 621) and one of 15 Oct. 534 (n. 622).

[624] *CJ* 1.1.8, 1.27.1.2 (534, 13 April 534).   [625] *CJ* 4.34.11, 7.45.13 (30 Oct. 529).

FIVE PREFACES

It has been assumed that *C. Deo auctore* of 15 December 530 which fell in Tribonian's first quaestorship was drafted by him. But since someone might take the view that the emperor himself was responsible for composing the prefaces as opposed to ordinary legislation, it is as well to demonstrate the truth of the assumption, omitting as before any marks of style which are found only in this constitution.

C. Deo auctore pr. (*gubernantes, adiutorium, decoramus, erigimus, sustentamus*), 1 (*studiosus, divinas et humanas res, repperimus, trames, Romuleis temporibus, confusus, infinitus, humana natura, viae dilucidae tradere, discordia, sinceritas*), 2 (*consummare, volumen, praefulgere, coadunare, Romana sanctio, volumen, difficillimus, resposumius, fretus, desperare, consummare*),[626] 3 (*respeximus, ingenii tui documenta*), 4 (*interpretor, elimare, materia, discordia, volumina*), 5 (*materia, pulcherrimo opere, templum iustitiae, confusus, vallare*), 6 (*melius, Aemilius Papinianus, repletio, principales constitutiones, fuerint profusae*),[627] 7 (*studiosus, semovere, repletio, quam pulcherrimus, ordini moderato tradere, volumen, quid possit antiquitas?, reponere, fuerant conscripta, veteres*), 8 (*antinomia, Graeco vocabulo, sibi vindicet locum, concordia, consequentia*), 9 (*secundum quod dictum est, exsulare, redegimus, iterum, divales constitutiones, repletio, spinosus, perraro*),[628] 10 (*frequentissimus, Salvii Iuliani*), 11 (*enucleare, rudis, studiosus, (iuris) prudentia*), 12 (*verbositas, interpretantes*), 13 (*compendiosa aenigmata, antinomiae, consequentia, explanari*), 14 (*placidus, fini tradere, consummatio*).[629]

There is nothing in *C. Deo auctore* to remind one of Justinian's own letters and constitutions. The next question is whether the four prefaces enacted during the quaestorship of Basilides were composed by him, by Justinian or by Tribonian. The first is *C. Imperatoriam* of 21 November 533 which enacted the new *Institutes*.

C. Imperatoriam pr. (*legitimus trames, expellens*), 1 (*utraque via, iterum, dicio Romana*), 2 (*confusus, ereximus, consonantia, volumina, desperatus,*) 3 (*cunabula, fabula, primordium*), 7 (*pulcherrimus*).[630]

The system of legal education was reformed by *C. Omnem* of 16 December 533, which also conforms to Tribonian's ways:

[626] Nn. 145, 393, 84, 94, 124, 196, 183, 119, 383, 129, 300, 310, 172, 415, 538, 205, 229, 413, 545, 283, 267, 163, 545, 342, 120, 305, 454.

[627] Nn. 121, 459, 389, 460, 495, 205, 545, 495, 207, 300, 402, 414, 40, 386, 404, 160, 286.

[628] Nn. 196, 412, 545, 369, 367, 260, 166, 493, 205, 394, 455, 466, 116, 416, 458, 404, 282, 195.

[629] Nn. 343, 40, 230, 389, 462, 326, 196, 515, 374, 258, 260, 394, 464, 538, 413, 321.

[630] N. 383; cf. *expellentes* nn. 143, 415, 416, 164; cf. *erigimus* nn. 94, 300, 204, 545, 454, 338, 467, 514, 207.

C. *Omnem* pr. (*quis cognoscit?, existimavimus, ambulare, sibi vindicare locum, tramites, ambulandum est*), 1 (*confusus, perraro, consequentia, satura, erat enorme, volumen* ter, *semovere, brevissimus, Pauliana responsa, inconsequentia*),[631] 2 (*invenientes, miserrimus, aperimus, elimatas, consequentia, ridiculus, rudis, volumen*), 3 (*consequentia, pulchritudo, volumen* ter, *primordium*),[632] 4 (*posuimus, composuimus, praefulgere* bis, *diximus, fuerant positae, acutissimus, posuimus, volumen, pulcherrimus, composita fuerant, iterum, bellissimus, primordia, reminiscentes*), 5 (*enumeravimus, Pauliana responsa, posuimus* bis),[633] 7 (*volumina, pulcherrimus, audivimus*), 8 (*ponimus*), 9 (*pulcherrimus, rudis, quis enim appellet?, nullo patimur modo, optimo ordini tradimus*), 11 (*viam aperire, invenimus*).[634]

C. *Tanta* of the same date enacted the *Digest*. The existence of a parallel but not identical Greek text, C. Δέδωκεν, has given rise to a controversy as to which was original and which the translation. It is relevant to ask whether Tribonian drafted C. *Tanta*. There is no room for doubt on this score:

C. *Tanta* pr. (*divina humanitas, iterum, vigilantia, pulchritudo, erat mirabile, Romana sanctio, nostri imperii tempora, intestinus, consonantia, peculiare fuit, respeximus, imposuimus, emendabat*),[635] 1 (*principales constitutiones, praefulgere, adgredientes, studiosissima opera, confusus, certo moderamini tradere, percontabamur, veteres, effusus, imposuimus, consummantes, natura, respicientes*),[636] 2 (*Graeco vocabulo*), 3 (*articulus*), 5 (*reponere, volumen, consentaneus, in confinio, reposuimus* bis, *concludentes, conscripsimus, pulcherrima iura*),[637] 6 (*exoriri, articulus*), 6a (*peculiare fuerat, coadunare, existimavimus, veteres, odiosus, respuentes*), 6b (*increbuit, nostris temporibus*),[638] 7 (*exoriri, compendiosus, concludentes*), 7a (*invenimus, deduximus*), 7c (*volumen*), 7e (*volumen, iterum*), 8 (*articulus, volumen*),[639] 8c (*veteres*), 9 (*studiosissimus, deduximus, consummare, interpres*), 10 (*taciturnitati tradere, nullo patiamur modo, rectissimis tradatur regulis, transformare, principalis constitutio, fuerat relata, putavimus, dubitabatur, in melius, decorum fuerat*),[640] 11 (*sapientia, rudis, pulcherrimus, veteres, elimatus, consentaneus, reponere, promulgavimus, apertius*),[641] 12 (*consummare, volumen* bis, *compendiosus, (iuris) prudentia*), 13 (*vituperare, brevissimus, fuerat permixta, impossibile erat, perfectissimus, veteres, expositae fuerant,*

[631] N. 369; cf. *existimamus* nn. 95, 431, 493, 383, 346, 300, 282, 394, 526, 366, 545, 412, 341, 40.

[632] Nn. 147, 317, 74, 460, 394; cf. 194, 326, 545, 394, 210, 545, 514.

[633] Nn. 112, 78, 283, 89, 367, 339, 112, 545, 207, 367, 416, 209, 514, 149, 93, 40, 112.

[634] Nn. 545, 207, 75, 511, 207, 326, 369, 370, 538, 415, 107.

[635] Cf. nn. 183, 416, 543, 210, 366, 163; cf. *tempora nostra* nn. 127, 312, 204, 507, 121, 479, 461.

[636] Nn. 160, 283, 531, 300, 538, 508, 51, 303, 479, 413, 172, 150, 242.

[637] Nn. 166, 387, 289, 545, 242, 446, 120, 138, 81, 207.

[638] Nn. 376, 387, 507, 367, 267; cf. *existimamus* nn. 95, 144, 51, 192, 386, 199, 127.

[639] Nn. 376, 374, 138, 107, 86, 545, 416, 545, 387, 545.

[640] Nn. 51, 196, 531, 86, 413, 389, 538, 370, 538, 539, 160, 367; cf. *putamus* nn. 115, 414, 367, 168.

[641] Nn. 525, 326, 207, 51, 460, 242, 289, 114, 290.

fuerat sparsum, erat incivile),[642] 14 (*principalibus constitutionibus, volumen, nullo concessimus modo*), 15 (*sibi locum vindicare, aliam naturam inducit, discordia*), 16 (*idoneum fuerat, quis adprehendere possit?*),[643] 17 (*fuerant positae, inpossibile erat, volumen* bis, *non dicimus, opulentissima brevitas, sapientia, fuerant incogniti, pulcherrimus, semovere, conditores, invenientes, respuere*),[644] 18 (*perfectissimus, divinae res | humani iuris, in infinitum, formas edere natura novas deproperat, non desperamus, innodatus, augustum remedium, emendare, regulis competentibus tradere, Iulianus, subtilissimus legum conditor, apertissimus, coniectura*),[645] 19 (*vestris temporibus* bis, *antiquioribus quiescentibus*), 20 (*veteres, primordium, manifestissimus, legislator*), 20a (*legislator, digni fuerant, quid amplius esse intellegatur?*),[646] 21 (*transformare, consequentia, iactare, verbositas, huc atque illuc, in infinitum, Romana sanctio, confusus, posteritas, quemadmodum admittatur vana discordia?, volumen, interpretari*),[647] 22 (*per consequentias, volumen, aperimus, secundum quod dictum est*), 23 (*posuimus, suus vigor, amicalis* bis, *resuscitare, nullo volumus modo, bella, perpetuae quieti tradere*).[648]

Over 160 marks of style have been listed. The last of the prefaces enacted during the quaestorship of Basilides is *C. Cordi* of 16 November 534, which introduces the second edition of the *Codex Iustinianus*:

C. Cordi pr. (*Cordi est, primordium, volumen, fuerant dispersae*), 1 (*promulgavimus, articulus, emendatus, enucleare*),[649] 2 (*eloquens*), 3 (*fretus, inusitatus, elimatio, via dilucida, satis validum, satis esse firmum, invenimus, Ulpianus, promptum erat*), 4 (*divales constitutiones, frequentari, varia rerum natura*).[650]

In the result all four Latin prefaces of the interregnum must be attributed to Tribonian. Nor is this a surprise. They all concern the work of the Second Law Commission. Conversely the two prefaces which relate to the first commission (*C. Haec* of 13 February 528 and *C. Summa* of 7 April 529) are by another hand. They are referred to in a later chapter.[651]

UNDATED CONSTITUTIONS TO NOVEMBER 534

The next group of constitutions consists of those which are of the reign of Justinian, were enacted before 16 November 534 since they appear in the revised *Codex*, but, as they are not addressed to the praetorian prefects

[642] Nn. 413, 545, 374, 796, 232, 341, 367, 366, 405, 51.
[643] Nn. 160, 545, 370, 493, 172, 205, 367, 369.
[644] Nn. 367, 366, 545; cf. *diximus* nn. 89, 319, 367, 207, 412, 445, 545, 147, 386.
[645] Nn. 405, 310, 183, 172, 454, 162, 461, 538, 40, 348, 445, 407, 447.
[646] Nn. 128, 385, 51, 514, 346, 490, 490, 368, 369.
[647] Nn. 539, 394, 477, 230, 476, 310, 163, 300, 369, 225, 333, 205, 545, 389.
[648] Nn. 394, 545, 74, 455, 112, 544, 297, 201, 370, 538.
[649] Nn. 449, 514, 367, 545, 367, 114, 387, 461, 462.
[650] Nn. 208, 305, 222, 460, 415, 388, 107, 40, 51, 458, 248, 172.
[651] Ch. 8 nn. 99, 118, 120, 122.

Menas (1 June 528–7 April 529),[652] Demosthenes (17 September 529–30 October 529)[653] or Iulianus (18 March 530 to 17 November 530),[654] cannot be definitely assigned to a period either within or outside Tribonian's first quaestorship.

Thirteen of these are addressed to John of Cappadocia praetorian prefect. The minimum extent of his two prefectures up to the end of 534 are set by the dates 30 April 531 to 17 January 532[655] and 18 October 532 onwards.[656] Eleven of the thirteen contain marks of Tribonian's authorship:

CJ 4.30.16 (*indubitati iuris est . . . locum habere, quae enim differentia est?*).[657]

4.34.12 (*differentiam tollentes, depositae fuerant, altercationes*).[658]

4.35.23 pr. (*praestavit, in sua natura remanere, invenientes, Anastasiana constitutio*).[659]

5.3.20 pr. (*emendare*), 1 (*quare non permittitur? quae differentia potest inveniri, melius erat?*), 3 (*quare non dabitur?*), 6 (*ambulare*), 7 (*Leoniana constitutio, exaequatio, inmutilatus, tollentes*) 9 (*veteres*).[660]

5.4.28 pr. (*Ulpianus, quaerebatur*), 2 (*superventus*), 4 (*melius est, radix*).[661]

7.2.15 pr. (*divus Marcus*), 1 (*quaerebatur*), 1a (*Ulpianus, Marcus, deperire, annale tempus*), 1b (*consultissimus princeps = Marcus*,[662] *sancimus, locum habere, nullo concedimus modo*), 2 (*respuere, divus Marcus*), 3 (*melius est, humanius est*), 4 (*invenimus, bellissimus, repletio*), 4a (*annale tempus*).[663]

7.32.12 pr. (*libri Sabiniani, tollentes, malignitas, dolose*), 2 (*antiqua regula, nullo fieri modo*).[664]

7.71.8 pr. (*semovere, dubitabatur, indutiae*), 1 (*putamus, humanior sententia*), 2 (*coadunare, antecellere*), 3 (*frequentissimus, fenerator, trutinare*), 5 *humanior sententia, indutiae*), 6 (*nulla quidem differentia*), 7 (*nullo praeiudicio generando*).[665]

8.53.37 (*quid opus est? verbositas, nulla differentia*).[666]

11.48.23 pr. (*satis inhumanum est, defraudari, quantuscumque*), 1 (*quaerebatur, illigare*).[667]

12.3.5 pr. (*augusta maiestas*), 1 (*quis enim patiatur?*), 2 (*satis certum est*).[668]

A more difficult law addressed to John between 17 Nov. 533 and 12

---

[652] *CJ* 1.4.21 etc. (1 June 528), *C. Summa* (7 April 529).

[653] *CJ* 1.4.24 (17 Sept. 529) etc., 1.2.22 (30 Oct. 529) etc.

[654] *CJ* 1.2.23 (18 March 530), 1.3.46 (17 Nov. 530).

[655] *CJ* 6.27.5 (30 April 531), *Wars* 1.24.17.   [656] *CJ* 3.10.3 (18 Oct. 532).

[657] Nn. 492, 369, 417, 418.   [658] Nn. 420, 417, 153, 367, 410.

[659] Nn. 365, 172–4, 147, 381.

[660] Nn. 461, 369, 417, 414, 366, 369, 431, 381, 218, 153.

[661] Nn. 40, 167; cf. *supervenire* nn. 396, 444, 283, 517.

[662] Nn. 55, 167, 40, 55, 378, 272, 55.

[663] Nn. 492, 370, 79, 386, 55, 414, 178, 107, 209, 404, 378.

[664] Nn. 40, 153, 187, 521, 370.

[665] Nn. 412, 481, 168, 115, 181, 259, 267, 468, 343, 397, 481, 181, 417, 422.

[666] Nn. 369, 230, 417.   [667] Nn. 388, 180, 424, 398, 167, 277.

[668] Nn. 161, 369, 388, 159.

Sept. 534 is *CJ* 1.3.54. It concerns married people one or both of whom opt for the religious life, and Christian slaves of Jews and Pagans. There are certain features which point to Tribonian:

C. 1.3.54.2 (*satis contrarium visum est*), 6 (*nullo impedimento generando*), 7 (*posuimus*), 11 (*frequentare, naviter et studiossissime*).[669]

But the early part of the statute has some phrases which remind one of Justinian's own compositions. In particular *cognitum etenim nobis est quod* is a vulgar construction found in the emperor's letters[670] but not otherwise in Tribonian's writing. The opening words of the constitution *Deo nobis auxilium praebente* call to mind Justinian's *deo auxiliante*,[671] but represent a smoother version of the emperor's phrase. This is a teasing constitution. I am inclined to think that Tribonian has worked over an imperial draft which was perhaps confined to the earlier part of the text and did not include the later passages dealing with the apparently unrelated topic of Christian slaves.

One constitution is addressed to Vigilantius, count of the domestics.[672] This was clearly not composed by Tribonian, and as it does not display the marks of Justinian's style either, it should presumably be assigned to Basilides: one of two constitutions which can perhaps be put to his account. It opens:

CJ 12.17.4 Lege pragmatica sine fine victura praefiniendum ac constituendum credidimus ut . . .

This type of reflexive opening in which the nature of the legislation is mentioned in the opening words is alien to Tribonian's practice, though it is found in Justin's quaestor Proclus.[673] The text contains *diem supremum claudere* for 'to die' which does not occur in Tribonian's drafts. The use of *indipiscor* is also not Tribonianic.[674]

More doubt surrounds *CJ* 1.29.5, addressed to Zeta, master of soldiers for Armenia. The structure is closer to Tribonian's than in the previous case, but this is not a strong argument, since the structure of Tribonian's compositions is by no means unusual for the period.

Cum propitia divinitate . . . sit delatum imperium . . . pertractantes perspeximus oportere . . . per hanc legem constituere. . .

---

[669] Nn. 388, 422, 112, 248, 474, 196.

[670] Justinian to Hormisdas (*Patr. Lat.* 63. 475D), Three Chapters Decree (*Patr. Lat.* 69.36A); cf. *CJ* 1.14.8.1 (17 Oct. 446).

[671] *CJ* 1.27.1.10, 12, 21; 1.27.2.7 (13 April 534) both of Justinian's composition: Justinian 117–19.

[672] *CJ* 12.17.4.

[673] *CJ* 7.63.4 (28 May 520), 6.22.8 (1 June 521), 2.7.26 (13 Feb. 524), 12.19.14 (Iustinus Matiano mo.).

[674] *VCJ* 1.1278.

The text contains no marks of his style, but is not inconsistent with it and must be left unassigned.

This leaves one final constitution of Justinian addressed to the senate. It forbids soldiers to lease land or houses.[675] The rhetorical effects (pr. *altius et plenius* 1 *ex militibus pagani, ex decoratis infames constituti*) might be Tribonian's and there are a few marks of his style:

CJ 4.65.35 pr. (*plenius, corrigentes*), 3 (*vituperare*).[676]

But the text is left unassigned.

THE LATIN NOVELS

The next stage is to analyse the Latin *Novels*[677] in order to see which of them can be attributed to Tribonian. There are sixteen certain or possible *Novels* in this category between the beginning of 535 and the end of 542; also three documents of 540–2 printed as Appendices to the *Corpus Iuris* stereotype edition. After this there is nothing in Latin until 552, when Tribonian was certainly dead. In what follows I have treated it as permissible to note marks of style which appear in the constitutions of Tribonian discussed in the previous pages which cannot be shown to have been drafted during his first quaestorship but which were enacted before the publication of the second edition of the *Codex* at the end of 534. The first *Novel* comes on 1 January 535.

N. 36 pr. (*infinitus, effusus, Romana dicio, promulgavimus, prolixa annositas, delere, resuscitare, intestinus*), 2 (*requisitione quiescente, miser*), 4 (*nullo concedimus modo, respuere, dolose*), 5 (*nullo patimur modo*).[678]

The epilogue to this constitution (s.6) could be regarded as verging on a parody of Justinian's own prose:[679]

Quae igitur pro securitate Africae mea sanxit aeternitas, haec sublimitas tua per edicta sua in omnem Africanum tractum proponenda manifestare cunctis civibus Africanis deproperet, ut omnes quod in transactis annis observari oporteat scientes hoc observare festinent.

Two more *Novels* were enacted on 14 April 535 and one on 16 April:

N. 9 pr. (*anterior Roma*), 1 (*circumcludebant, paulo*), 3 (*reminiscentes*), epil. (*dedicamus*).[680]

---

[675] *CJ* 4.65.35.   [676] Nn. 294, 139, 232.

[677] C. C. Triantaphyllides, 'Lexique des mots latins dans Théophile et les novelles de Justinien', *Etudes de philologie néogrecque*, ed. J. Psichari (Paris 1892), is some help.

[678] Nn. 310, 303, 164, 114, 323, 452, 201, 312, 385, 317, 370, 386, 187, 370.

[679] *Justinian* 117; above, n. 67.

[680] Cf. *antiqua Roma* nn. 165, 239, 149, 85 and ch. 7 n. 17.

N. 11 (1 *fuerat constituta, Attilanis temporibus, sub umbra*), 2 (*frequentare, iterum, subigere, nostra dicio, fuerat constituta*), 3 (*non erat utile*), 5 (*transformare*), 7 (*ab hac luce decedere*).[681]

N. 17: covering letter (*legum latores, deperditam, laudabiliter, composuimus*).[682]

In the body of *Novel* 17 the Greek text is however authentic.

Some time before 15 April 535 *Novel* 138 was addressed to Hermogenes, master of offices:

N. 138 (*manifestissima est constitutio*).[683]

This is in effect a rescript to Hermogenes concerning a debt owed by him personally (*nullum adversus te inquietudinem proponere concedatur*).[684]

April 23 of the same year brings another Latin *Novel*:

N. 35 pr. (*effusus, prolixum tempus*), 1 (*paulatim*), 2 (*iterum*), 3 (*altercationes*), 4 (*elimare, cordi nobis est, defraudari*), 5 (*contentiosus*), 7 (*enumeravimus*), 8 (*donamus*), 10 (*donamus, satis durum atque inhumanum est*).[685]

There are two Latin laws of 15 June 535:

N. 33 (*posuimus, nitens, destinavimus, posuimus*).[686]
N. 34 pr. (*inhumanus, tristissimus*), 1 (*quantuscumque*).[687]

On 1 August 535 there is a *Novel* on a topic dear to Justinian, the church of Africa. But he did not draft it:

N. 37 pr. (*noctu dieque festinamus*), 3 (*prolixitas temporis, explosus, sat abundeque*), 7 (*non respuimus, nobis cordi est*), 8 (*satis absurdum est*), 10 (*quis non confitetur?, adiutorium*), 11 (*laudamus*), 12 (*inmutilatus*).[688]

After a gap of six months we find a text addressed to Tribonian:

N. 23 (3 Jan. 536) pr. (*imponentes, invenimus, satis esse damnosum*), 1 (*appellatorius, frequentare, calores*), 2 (*imperatoria maiestas, quod enim vitium est?, quis tantae est auctoritatis?*), 3 (*novitas* bis), 4 (*quantuscumque*).[689]

---

[681] Nn. 367, 129, 206, 248, 416, 367, 532; cf. *Romana dicio* 164, 367, 366, 539, 391.
[682] Cf. *legislator* n. 490, *legum conditor* 445, 273, *C. Tanta* 9 (16 Dec. 533 both *gubernare laudabiliter*), 78.
[683] N. 346.   [684] N. 138.
[685] Nn. 303, 323, 505, 416, 410, 460, 449, 424, 186, 93, 90, 90, 388, 180.
[686] N. 112, *C. Cordi* 4 (16 Nov. 534), *CJ* 5.17.11.2a (17 Nov. 533), n. 112.
[687] Nn. 217, 349, 398.
[688] N. 457, *C. Tanta* 7e (16 Dec. 533; cf. *prolixum tempus* n. 323), 188, 427, 122, 386, 449, 388, 369, 393, 108, 218.
[689] Nn. 146, 107, 388, 233, 248, 437, *C. Imperatoriam* pr. (21 Nov. 533), 369, 224, 398.

A year later there is another Latin constitution:

N. 62 (1 January 537), pr. (*Romana dicio*), 1.2 (*trutinare, merus*), 1.3 (*articulus*), 2.2 (*connumeramus*).[690]

A *Novel* which is duplicated belongs to December 537:

N. 75 (=104), 1 (*anterior Roma*), 2 (*latitudo, pulchra brevitas*), 3 (*putavimus*).[691]

In March 538 there is a constitution to the governor of Mysia about the redemption of captives:

N. 65 (23 March 538) pr. (*inhibuimus*) 1.5 (*defraudare, deperire*).[692]

The style is consistent but we notice some signs of a falling off in power. No more Latin constitutions appear until 7 April 540:

Appendix 1 pr. (proposuimus), 1 (*corrigentes*).[693]

This constitution is regarded by E. Stein as a forgery:[694] it is left unassigned. After the fall of John of Cappadocia in May 541 Tribonian seems to have attempted to revert to drafting texts in Latin for the oriental prefecture. On 1 June we find a bilingual text:

N. 111 pr. (*coniectura, experimentum, iterum, sanitas*), 1 (*experimentum, protelatio*).[695]

This text gives an impression of renewed vigour. The next, of 9 September 541, does the same:

N. 112 pr. (*legislator, prudentia, apertius, explanare, manifestissimus*), 2.1 (*praediximus*), 3.1 (*fuit intimata, finem legitimum sortiatur, annale tempus, subtilius, annale tempus, iterum, annale spatium, iterum*), epil. (*amicalis*).[696]

On 6 October we have an instruction concerning the council of Byzacenum in North Africa:

Appendix 11: This text contains no marks of Tribonian's style. Its authorship cannot be determined.

The next to be considered is a *Novel* of 1 November 541:

[690] Nn. 164, 397, 315, 387; cf. *connumeravimus CJ* 9.13.1.1b (18 Nov. 533), *enumeravimus* n. 93 above.

[691] N. 680, *C. Cordi* 2 (16 Nov. 534), *C. Tanta* 11 (16 Dec. 533), nn. 489, 207; cf. *putamus* nn. 115, 148.

[692] Cf. *inhibentes CJ* 8.10.14.2 (18 Oct. 532), nn. 424, 272.

[693] *C. Cordi* pr. (16 Nov. 534), n. 139.   [694] *Bas-Empire* 2.413.

[695] Nn. 447, 463, 416, 226, 463; cf. *protelare* n. 401, *C. Cordi* 3 (16 Nov. 534).

[696] Nn. 490, 515, 290, 464, 346, 785, 113, 367, 313, 378, 295, 378, 416, 378, 416, 297.

N. 114 pr. (*cum competenti cautela*), 1.1 (*advenerit, iura nostra*).[697]

In its general tenor it is consistent with Tribonian's manner and the subject matter also speaks to his influence.

This is the last Latin constitution drafted by Tribonian which has survived. The next, of 29 October 542, also concerning the council of Byzacenum, is identifiably by Justinian himself.[698] A gap of ten years intervenes before the next Latin text.

The results of the inquiry can now be summarised. Between September 529 and October 542 we have 275 dated Latin constitutions and 16 undated texts which must fall somewhere within this period.[699] Of these 258 dated[700] and 13 undated[701] constitutions appear to have been drafted by Tribonian, the latest on 1 November 541.[702] Four dated constitutions are by the hand of the emperor himself.[703] One undated text is by a third hand,[704] probably Basilides. One is something of a Justinian-Tribonian hybrid.[705] Thirteen dated[706] and one undated text,[707] which contain no sufficient indices of authorship, are unassigned.

In retrospect we can now add to the list of Tribonian's marks of style a hundred and fifty or more which have emerged from our study of the constitutions dated from 532 onwards and of the undated texts which have been assigned to his authorship. It is necessary to do this, since the greater the length and precision of the list we assemble, the greater will be its utility for study of the history of other texts in the *Corpus Iuris* (*Digest, Institutes* and constitutions contained in the first edition of the *Codex*).

In particular we can add:

(a) *abdicatio*,[708] *abdicavimus*.[709] *acceptabilis*,[710] *acerbus*,[711] *accomodavimus*,[712] *adimplevimus*,[713] *adiudicavimus*,[714] *adpetimus*,[715] *agnaticius*,[716] *annositas*,[717]

---

[697] Nn. 438, 440, 157.

[698] *Appendix* 111 (*Iussio Iustiniani imperatoris pro privilegio concilii Byzaceni*) = *Corp. Iur. Civ.* 111 (Schoell/Kroll) 797; above, ch. 1 n. 268

[699] Dated: Sept. 529 to Nov. 531, 222; Oct. 532 to Nov. 534, 30; prefaces, 4; Jan. 535 to Oct. 542, 19 (16 Novels, 3 Appendices); undated: Iohanni pp. 13, Zetae mm. 1, Vigilantio cd. 1, ad senatum 1.

[700] Sept. 529 to Nov. 531, 213; Oct. 532 to Nov. 534, 25; prefaces, 4; Jan. 535 to Oct. 542, 16.

[701] Iohanni pp. 11, Zetae mm., 1, ad senatum 1.   [702] N. 114.

[703] *CJ* 1.1.8. 7–24 (6 June 533), 1.27.2.1, 2 (13 April 534), *Appendix* 111 (29 Oct. 542).

[704] *CJ* 12.17.4 (Vigilantio cd.).

[705] *CJ* 1.3.54 (between 17 Nov. 533 and 12 Sept. 534).

[706] Sept. 529 to Nov. 531, 9 (above, n. 550), Oct. 532 to Nov. 534, 2 (above, n. 625), *Appendix* 1, 11 (above, p. 119).

[707] *CJ* 5.4.27 (Iohanni pp.).

[708] *CJ* 6.31.6.2 (18 Oct. 532) = renunciation of an inheritance not the Greek institution in *CJ* 8.46.6 (15 Nov. 288 = ἀποκήρυξις of children), *CTh*/*N* o.

[709] N. 65 pr. 2 (23 March 538).   [710] N. 37.7 (1 Aug. 535), *CTh*/*N* o.

[711] *CJ* 4.35.23.3 (531/2), 9.13.1.1a (27 Nov. 533), *CTh*/*N* 1.

[712] *C. Imperatoriam* 6 (21 Nov. 533)   [713] *C. Imperatoriam* 2 (21Nov. 533).

[714] *C. Tanta* 6a (16 Dec. 533).   [715] N. 114 pr. (1 Nov. 541).

[716] *CJ* 6.58.15.4 (15 Oct. 534), *CTh*/*N* o.   [717] N. 36 pr. (1 Jan. 535), *CTh*/*N* 3.

anterior Roma,[718] *appellamus*,[719] *aptissimus*,[720] *avidus*,[721] *avidissime*.[722]

(c) *carius*,[723] *cessamus*,[724] *cicatrix* (met.),[725] *clare*,[726] *commentator*,[727] *completus*,[728] *concinnitas*,[729] *conculcatio*,[730] *congregatio*,[731] *connumeramus*,[732] *connumeravimus*,[733] *conrivare*,[734] *constringimus*.[735]

(d) *dedecus*,[736] *deficientia*,[737] *destinavimus*,[738] *desuetus*,[739] *detestabilis*,[740] *didicimus*,[741] *direximus*,[742] *discordare*,[743] *discrevimus*,[744] *disiungere*[745] / *disiunctim*,[746] *dissonans*,[747] *distinguimus*,[748] *ditissimus*,[749] *dupliciter*.[750]

(e) *effulgere*,[751] *elementa*[752] (pedagogic), *emicere*,[753] *ereximus*,[754] *eruditissimus*,[755] *exaequatio*,[756] *excerpsimus*,[757] *exiguitas*,[758] *existimavimus*,[759] *exornare*.[760]

(f) *ferocitas*,[761] *flagrare*,[762] *florescere*,[763] *formosus*,[764] *fulgor*.[765]

(g) *Gaius noster*,[766] *glomerare*,[767] *gradatim*.[768]

[718] N. 9 pr. (14 April 535), 75.1 (Dec. 531), *CTh/N* o.
[719] *CJ* 4.65.35.1 (Iustinianus ad senatum).   [720] *C. Tanta* 11 (16 Dec. 533).
[721] *C. Cordi* pr. (16 Nov. 534), *CTh/N* 2.   [722] *C. Cordi* pr. (16 Nov. 534), *CTh/N* o.
[723] *C. Tanta* 9 (16 Dec. 533), *CTh/N* o.   [724] N. 114 pr. (1 Nov. 541).
[725] N. 111 pr. (1 June 541), *CTh/N* o.   [726] *C. Omnem* 2 (16 Dec. 533), *CTh/N* o.
[727] *C. Tanta* 20a, 21 (16 Dec. 533 bis.), *CTh/N* o.
[728] N. 36.5 (1 Jan. 535), *CTh/N* o.   [729] N. 36.4 (1 Jan. 535), *CTh/N* o.
[730] *CJ* 3.34.14.1 (18 Oct. 532), *CTh/N* o.
[731] *C. Tanta* 4 (16 Dec. 533), *C. Cordi* 3, 4 (16 Nov. 534 bis) = 'collection of material', *CTh/N* o.
[732] N. 62.2.2 (1 Jan. 537), *CTh/N* o.   [733] *CJ* 9.13.1.1b (17 Nov. 533), *CTh/N* o.
[734] *C. Omnem* 2 (16 Dec. 533), *CTh/N* o.   [735] N. 62.1.3 (1 Jan. 537).
[736] *CJ* 9.13.1.3b (17 Nov. 533), 7.24.1 pr. (531/4), *C. Tanta* 21 (16 Dec. 533), *CTh/N* 5.
[737] N. 35.8 (23 May 535), *CTh/N* o.
[738] *CJ* 5.17.11.2a (17 Nov. 533), N. 33 (15 June 535).
[739] *C. Omnem* 1 (16 Dec. 533), *CTh/N* o.
[740] *CJ* 1.3.53.2 = 9.13.1.1c (17 Nov. 533) but 8.50.7 (3 Feb. 291), *CTh/N* o.
[741] *CJ* 4.35.23.1 (531/2).   [742] N. 33 (15 May 535).
[743] N. 111 pr. (1 June 541), *CTh/N* o.
[744] N. 112.1 (11 Sept. 541), *CTh/N* o.
[745] *CJ* 6.51.1.10d, 10e (1 June 534 bis), *CTh/N* o.
[746] *CJ* 6.51.1.10a, 10c, 10d, 11b, 11g (1 June 534), *CTh/N* o.
[747] *C. Tanta* 19 (16 Dec. 533), *CTh/N* o.   [748] N. 111 pr. (1 June 541).
[749] *C. Omnem* 2 (16 Dec. 533).   [750] *CJ* 8.10.14.1 (18 Oct. 532), *CTh/N* o.
[751] N. 62 pr. pr. (1 Jan. 537), *CTh/N* o.
[752] *C. Omnem* pr. (16 Dec. 533), *C. Tanta* 11, 23 (16 Dec. 533 bis), *CTh/N* o.
[753] *C. Tanta* 9 (16 Dec. 533), *CTh/N* o.   [754] *C. Imperatoriam* 1 (21 Nov. 533).
[755] *C. Tanta* 17 (16 Dec. 533).   [756] *CJ* 5.3.20.7 (531/2), *CTh/N* o.
[757] *C. Omnem* 3 (16 Dec. 533), *CTh/N* o.
[758] *C. Tanta* 16 (16 Dec. 533) but 11.3.2.3 (3 Aug. 375), *CTh/N* 2.
[759] *C. Omnem* pr. (16 Dec. 533), *C. Tanta* 6a (16 Dec. 533).
[760] N. 37.9 (1 Aug. 535), *CTh/N* 1.   [761] *CJ* 7.24.1 pr. (531/4), *CTh/N* 1.
[762] *CJ* 1.3.53.1 = 9.13.1.1 (17 Nov. 533), *CTh/N* o.
[763] N. 37.9 (1 Aug. 535), *CTh/N* 1.   [764] *C. Cordi* 3 (16 Nov. 534), *CTh/N* o.
[765] *CJ* 5.4.28.2 (531/2), 7.24.1 pr. (531/4), *C. Tanta* 1 (16 Dec. 533), *CTh/N* 3.
[766] *C. Imperatoriam* 6 (21 Nov. 533), *C. Omnem* 1 (16 Dec. 533); cf. *Inst.* 4.18.5, *CTh/N* o.
[767] *C. Tanta* 7e (16 Dec. 533), *CTh/N* o.
[768] *C.* 7.2.15.4a (531/2), 6.38.5.1 (18 Oct. 532) but 12.20.5 (*Arc., Hon. et Theo.*), *CTh/N* 3.

(i) *imperatoria maiestas,*[769] *imperialiter,*[770] *infinitas,*[771] *inhibentes,*[772] *inhibuimus,*[773] *innumerosus,*[774] *inscientia,*[775] *inumbrare,*[776] *inutilitas,*[777] *invius,*[778] *irrite.*[779]

(l) *laetificari,*[780] *laudabiliter,*[781] *legitimum opus,*[782] *legitima scientia,*[783] *legitima veritas,*[784] *ab hac luce recedere,*[785] *luculentus,*[786] *luxuriosus.*[787]

(m) *imperatoria maiestas,*[788] *moderate,*[789] *molimentum.*[790]

(n) *nitens,*[791] *nutrix*[792] (met.).

(o) *obductus,*[793] *in occulto,*[794] *opulentissimus,*[795] *orbs Romana.*[796]

(p) *parcere*[797] (met.), *particulatim,*[798] *pedisequus,*[799] *perlegere,*[800] *perpensius,*[801] *pertractare,*[802] *placabilis,*[803] *potestativus,*[804] *praecellere,*[805] *praefecimus,*[806] *praeoccupare,*[807] *praeposuimus,*[808] *primitiae,*[809] (*legum*) *professores,*[810] *prolixitas*[811] (*temporis*), *proposuimus,*[812] *protelatio,*[813] *proveximus,*[814] (*legum*) *prudentes,*[815] *putavimus.*[816]

---

[769] C. *Imperatoriam* pr. (16 Dec. 533), N. 23.2 (3 Jan. 536), 62 pr. (1 Jan. 537) CTh/N 0.

[770] CJ 6.51.1.14a (1 June 534).

[771] C. *Tanta* 12 (16 Dec. 533), CTh/N 0.   [772] CJ 8.10.14.2 (18 Oct. 532).

[773] N. 65 pr. (23 March 538).   [774] C. *Imperatoriam* 1 (21 Nov. 533), CTh/N 0.

[775] C. *Tanta* 17 (16 Dec. 533), CTh/N 1.

[776] C. *Tanta* 6b (16 Dec. 533), CTh/N 0.

[777] CJ 3.34.14.1 (18 Oct. 532), CTh/N 0.

[778] C. *Omnem* 1 (21 Nov. 533), CTh/N 0.   [779] N. 62.2.5 (1 Jan. 537).

[780] C. *Omnem* 4 (21 Nov. 533), CTh/N 0.

[781] C. *Tanta* 9 (16 Dec. 533); cf. N. 17 introd. (16 April 535), CTh/N 0.

[782] C. *Cordi* 2 (16 Nov. 534), N. 75.2 (Dec. 537).

[783] C. *Tanta* 9 (16 Dec. 533).

[784] C. *Tanta* 12 (16 Dec. 533); cf. 10 (*legum veritas*).

[785] N. 112. 1 (11 Sept. 541) and *ab humano consortio recedere,* ibid.

[786] C. *Imperatoriam* 1 (21 Nov. 533).   [787] CJ 5.17.11.2 (17 Nov. 533), CTh/N 0.

[788] Above, n. 443.   [789] C. *Tanta* 21 (16 Dec. 533), CTh/N 0.

[790] N. 62.1.1 (11 Sept. 541).   [791] C. *Cordi* 4 (16 Nov. 534), N. 33 (15 June 535).

[792] C. *Omnem* 7 (16 Dec. 533), CTh/N 1.

[793] C. *Cordi* 3 (16 Nov. 534), N. 111.1 (1 June 541), CTh/N 0.

[794] CJ 6.51.1.11g (1 June 534).   [795] C. *Tanta* 17 (16 Dec. 533), CTh/N 0.

[796] CJ 6.51.1 pr. (1 June 534), 6.23.31.1 (5 July 534), but 4.42.1 (Constantinus).

[797] C. *Tanta* 10 (16 Dec. 533), 6.51.1.14a (1 June 534), CTh/N 1.

[798] C. 4.35.23.1 (531/2), C. *Tanta* 13 (16 Dec. 533), CTh/N 1.

[799] C. *Tanta* 5 (16 Dec. 533), CTh/N 0.

[800] C. *Omnem* 1 (16 Dec. 533 bis), 5.17.11.2b (17 Nov. 533), C. *Tanta* 17 (16 Dec. 533), CTh/N 0.

[801] N. 62.2 (1 Jan. 537), CTh/N 0.

[802] CJ 6.21.18 (18 Oct. 532), 1.29.5 (Iustinianus Zetae mm.) but 12.37.5 (8 April 370/3), CTh/N 2.

[803] N. 65.1.5 (23 March 538), CTh/N 0.   [804] CJ 6.51.1.7 (1 June 534), CTh/N 0.

[805] CJ 6.58.15.2 (15 Oct. 534), CTh/N 1.   [806] N. 75 pr. (Dec. 537).

[807] CJ 6.51.1.10e (1 June 534), CTh/N 1.

[808] C. *Tanta* 11 (16 Dec. 533), N. 75.2 (Dec. 537).

[809] C. *Tanta* 11 (16 Dec. 533), CTh/N 0.   [810] C. *Tanta* 22 (16 Dec. 533).

[811] C. *Tanta* 7e (16 Dec. 533), N. 37.3 (1 Aug. 535), CTh/N 1.

[812] C. *Cordi* pr. (16 Nov. 534), Appx. 1 pr. (7.4.540).

[813] N. 111.1 (1 June 541), CTh/N 0.   [814] N. 75.2 (Dec. 537).

[815] CJ 8.25.11.1 (18 Oct. 532).   [816] N. 75.3 (Dec. 537).

(q) *quotidie.*[817]

(r) *rectissimus,*[818] *regulariter,*[819] *repellimus,*[820] *respondentes,*[821] *retegere,*[822] *retraximus,*[823] *ridiculus.*[824]

(s) *sagacitas,*[825] *sanctio imperialis,*[826] *sceleratissimus,*[827] *scripsimus,*[828] *sitire,*[829] *sparsim,*[830] *stagnus*[831] (met.), *subicimus,*[832] *superventus,*[833] *supponimus.*[834]

(t) *tempestivus,*[835] *tener,*[836] *transveximus,*[837] *turbosus.*[838]

(u) *umbilicus*[839] (met.).

(v) *venustus,*[840] *versabatur,*[841] *vilissimus,*[842] *visio.*[843]

---

[817] *CJ* 7.71.8 pr. (531/2), *CTh/N* o.   [818] *C. Tanta* 10 (16 Dec. 533).

[819] *C. Tanta* 8c (16 Dec. 533) but 6.42.14.1 (19 Aug. 255), *CTh/N* o.

[820] *CJ* 6.51.1.11b (1 June 534).   [821] *CJ* 6.38.5 pr. (18 Oct. 532) = 'answering'.

[822] *C. Cordi* 3 (16 Nov. 534), *CTh/N* o.   [823] *N.* 112.1 (11 Sept. 541).

[824] *CJ* 8.4.11 pr. (18 Oct. 532), *CTh/N* 2.

[825] *N.* 62.2 (1 June 538), *CTh/N* 2.

[826] *C. Tanta* 18 (16 Dec. 533), 6.23.31.1 (5 July 534), *CTh/N* o.

[827] *N.* 37.5 (1 Aug. 535), *CTh/N* o.   [828] *C. Omnem* 8 (16 Dec. 533).

[829] *C. Omnem* 1 (16 Dec. 533), *CTh/N* o.

[830] *C. Omnem* 4 (16 Dec. 533), *CTh/N* o.

[831] *C. Omnem* 2 (16 Dec. 533), *CTh/N* o.

[832] *CJ* 9.13.1.3a = 1.3.53.5 (17 Nov. 533), *CTh/N* o.

[833] *CJ* 5.4.28.2 (531/2), *CTh/N* o.   [834] *CJ* 6.58.15.4 (15 Oct. 534), *CTh/N* o.

[835] *C. Omnem* pr., *C Tanta* 21 (16 Dec. 533), *CTh/N* 2.

[836] *CJ* 6.21.18 (18 Oct. 532), *CTh/N* o.

[837] *CJ* 6.58.15.4 (15 Oct. 534), *CTh/N* o.

[838] *C. Omnem* 2 (16 Dec. 533), *CTh/N* o.

[839] *C. Tanta* 5 (16 Dec. 533), *CTh/N* o.   [840] *CJ* 7.2.15.5 (531/2), *CTh/N* o.

[841] *CJ* 6.51.1.1b (1 June 534).   [842] *C. Tanta* 12 (16 Dec. 533) = cheap.

[843] *C. Tanta* 13 (16 Dec. 533), *CTh/N* 1.

CHAPTER FOUR

His Greek Novels

During Tribonian's first quaestorship laws were written mainly in Latin;[1] the same is true of the term of office of Basilides.[2] But from 535 onwards, during Tribonian's second term, the proportions are reversed. Most laws are now in Greek, a few are drafted in Latin and some have been transmitted to us in both languages, probably only a fraction of those actually dispatched in this way.[3]

It is not practicable (for me at least) to fix the norms of Tribonian's Greek style in the absence of a concordance to the *Novels*, since the lacuna makes the calculations of word frequencies impossible. What is feasible with the tools available is the delimiting of the borderline between Tribonian and the succeeding quaestor Junilus. This is done with the help of certain features of style which can be counted without a concordance. To a limited extent analogies with Tribonian's Latin style are of value: mainly as regards the use of sources. In the upshot it is possible to reach, if not an incontrovertible, at least a plausible conclusion about the date at which Tribonian ceased to be quaestor. But it is not possible in general to identify undated constitutions or those of the quaestorship of Basilides as being (or not being) the work of Tribonian. This would require the determination of Tribonian's norms of Greek style not just in relation to Junilus but in relation to the norms of Greek legal writing, or Greek legal writing of the age, in general.

Since the substantial aim of this study is to fix the date of Tribonian's departure, it may be wise to recall the evidence independently available about his second term of office. Tribonian is mentioned as quaestor (for the second time) in a series of *Novels* running from 16 April 535 to November/December 537. From the scrutiny of the Latin *Novels*[4] we found signs that he composed a series of constitutions running from 1 January 535 to 1 November 541. Procopius implies that Tribonian died before 9 July 544. The historian is, he claims, writing the *Secret History* after thirty-two years of

---

[1] In the period 17 Sept. 529 to 14 Jan. 532 there were 222 Latin and 21 Greek constitutions preserved in *CJ*.

[2] Counting constitutions in *CJ* plus the prefaces *Omnem, Imperatoriam* and Δέδωκεν there are 35 Latin and 12 Greek laws in this period.

[3] From 535 to 541 there are 115 Greek and 21 Latin constitutions of which four are counted twice (*N.* 111 and 112, bilingual; *N.* 32 (Greek) = *N.* 34 (Latin); *N.* 7, composite of a Latin and a Greek constitution). On the *Novels* see Wenger §84, literature at n. 1.

[4] Above, ch. 3 nn. 677–98.

Justinian's reign,[5] in which he includes that of Justin, who acceeded to the throne on 9 July 518. Hence the year of composition runs from 9 July 550 to 8 July 551: the date usually assigned is 550.[6] At the time of writing Constantinus is quaestor and has rapidly amassed a fortune in that office.[7] Before him Junilus held the post for no less than seven years.[8] Tribonian preceded Junilus.[9] So Tribonian left office not later than 8 July 544. Putting this together suggests that it would be valuable to look for points of style in the Greek *Novels* which vanish in 541, 542 or 543.

Analogies from Tribonian's Latin suggest that he remained quaestor until at least the early part of 541. Classical jurists are cited in *Novels* 22.43 (18 March 535),[10] 4.1 (15 June 535),[11] 74 pr. (4 June 538), 87 pr. (18 May 539),[12] 97.6.1 (17 November 539)[13] and 108 pr. 2 and 1 (1 February 541).[14] Marcus Aurelius is mentioned in *N.* 22.19 (18 March 535), 60.1 pr. (1 December 537) and 108 pr. 2 (1 February 541), Antoninus Pius in *N.* 78.5 (18 January 539), Alexander Severus in *N.* 22.37, 38 (18 March 536). The *lex Aquilia* is mentioned in *N.* 18.8 (1 March 536), the *XII Tables* in 22.2 pr. (18 March 536), the *lex Cincia* in 22.43 and 162.1 pr., the *lex Iunia* and the *SC Largianum* in *N.* 78 pr. (18 January 539), the *lex Iulia miscella* in 162.1 pr. (9 June 539), the 'Trebellian dogma' in *N.* 1.1.1 (1 January 535). No references to classical jurists, emperors, laws and doctrines by name occur thereafter. Thus *N.* 119.2 (20 January 544) which repeals part of the *lex Aelia Sentia* does not mention it by name though it does refer to it expressly.[15] In sum, name-dropping is out.

There is therefore a prima facie case for supposing that Tribonian was in office on 1 February, and perhaps on 1 November 541. It seems reasonable to focus the search in the first instance on the year 542. There are four indications in particular that this was a transitional year: the character of the prefaces, the form of the epilogues, the use in the Greek *Novels* of Latin letters to express fines, and the words used to express Justinian's normative attitudes.

As will be seen from the table later in the chapter the prefaces of 535 to 541 are relatively long. They run on an average to 20 or more half-lines as printed in the double column Schoell-Kroll edition.

From 543 to 546 they are shorter, then from 548 to 555 they again lengthen. Not only are the prefaces of the 535–41 period long, they are marked by certain features which disappear in 543–8. The text often explains the circumstances giving rise to the legislation in a sentence which

---

[5] *SH* 18.33; 23.1; 24.29, 33.   [6] Haury, *Procopiana* (1890) 9f.; above, ch. 2 n. 179.

[7] *SH* 20.20. If Constantinus had left office by the time of writing Procopius does not mention his successor. Since his point is that Justinian kept making bad appointments to important offices the likelihood is that Constantinus was still quaestor; but the point is not crucial. On grounds of style the quaestorship of Constantinus could be extended to 553 or 555 and he was undoubtedly quaestor at the time of the Fifth Council of Constantinople (below, ch. 8 n. 206).

[8] *SH* 20.19.   [9] *SH* 20.17.   [10] Quintus Mucius Scaevola.   [11] Papinian.

[12] Both Julian.   [13] Ulpian.   [14] Papinian bis.

[15] σχολάζοντος τοῦ νόμου τοῦ πρώην κωλύοντος.

runs 'we have learned of such-and-such a problem': ἴσμεν,[16] ἠκούσαμεν[17] or the like.[18] They are frankly propagandistic; the emperor's industry and dedication are repeatedly emphasised,[19] and subjects are told of their luck in living under such a solicitous ruler.[20] In particular the emperor's humanity[21] (φιλανθρωπία) and leaning towards equality[22] (ἰσότης) is stressed. The historical background[23] to the legislation is on several occasions set out and the writer speaks of 'lovers of ancient learning in all its forms'.[24]

The author is conscious of the need not simply to justify the content of the new laws but to explain why recourse to new legislation is desirable. Hence not only is the occasion which gave rise to the legislation—often a case heard by Justinian in his judicial capacity[25] or a petition[26]—set out, but the policy of generalising from particular circumstances is defended.[27] In addition the variety of human affairs (ποικιλία), their unpredictable character, the sports which nature continually produces[28] all serve to explain why new laws are constantly being enacted. The tone is self-conscious. Laws are like medicines; if one fails, try another.[29] Anonymous critics are upbraided for not seeing that each new, unforeseen mischief demands a remedy.[30]

None of these features is to be found in the prefaces of the period 543–6. Here there are even some constitutions which have no preface.[31] In others the introduction is brief and jejune.[32] Much of the legislation is simply consolidation[33] and the vivid picture of the emperor's motives presented in 535–41 is missing. Even given the gloomy political climate of the 540s one might expect something more articulate and inspiring.

In this respect, as in others, the year 542 is transitional. There are five Greek constitutions:

[16] See below, n. 72.   [17] N. 106 pr. (7 Sept. 540), 108 pr. (1 Feb. 541).

[18] N. 19 pr. (Ἦλθεν εἰς ἡμᾶς).   [19] Justinian's constant labours: above, ch. 1 n. 230.

[20] E.g. N. 45 epil. (1 Sept. 537).   [21] Ch. 8 n. 20.   [22] Ch. 9 n. 22.

[23] N. 24 pr. (18 May 535 praetors), 25 pr. (18 May 535 Lycaonia), 26 pr. (18 May 535 the Thracian character), 29 pr. (16 July 535 Paphlagonia), 15 pr. (13 Aug. 535 *defensores civitatis*), 13 pr. (15 Oct. 535 *praefectus vigilum*), 38 pr. (15 Feb. 536 municipalities and decurions), 30 pr. (18 March 536 Cappadocia), 103 (1 July 536 Palestine), 47 pr. (31 Aug. 537 Roman monarchy), 105 pr. (28 Dec. 537 the consulship), 89 pr. (1 Sept. 539 rights of illegitimate children).

[24] N. 30 pr. (18 March 536).

[25] N. 2 pr. (16 March 535), 44 pr. (17 Aug. 537), 61 (1 Dec. 537), 66 (1 May 538), 88 (1 Sept. 539), 91 (1 Oct. 539).

[26] N. 101 (1 Aug. 539), 93 (11 Oct. 539).   [27] Ch. 1 n. 263.   [28] Ch. 1 n. 262.

[29] Ch. 1 n. 308.   [30] Ch. 1 n. 299; cf. Procopius *SH* 6.21; 11.1.–2.

[31] N. 119 (20 Jan. 544), 132 (4 April 544), 128 (6 June 545).

[32] N. 125 (8 lines: since many judges after a long trial refer the decision to us, we enact the following to prevent undue delay), 120 (9 May 544, 5 lines: we consolidate the laws concerning leaseholds), 124 (15 June 544, 4 lines: we enact the present law to prevent judicial corruption), 130 (1 March 545, 5 lines: it is important for the army not to do damage in transit through the provinces), 131 (18 March 545, 4 lines: we make the present law about church canons etc.—no reason stated), 123 (1 May 546, 8 lines: we consolidate certain laws about the church, bishops and clerics).

[33] N. 120, 123 (above, n. 32).

N. 115 (1 Feb. 542) preface 18 lines. ἦλθεν εἰς γνῶσιν τῆς ἡμετέρας γαληνότητος . . .[34]

Edict 7 (1 March 542) preface 22 lines. Virtue shines in adversity, imperial virtue in the adversity of subjects. If the instability of human affairs[35] or the actions of the deity press on human misfortunes an opportunity is presented for the display of imperial foresight and φιλανθρωπία.[36] That this is the present position everyone knows; there is no need to relate what everyone has experienced [viz. the plague], the college of bankers has approached us with a request . . .

N. 116 (9 April 542) preface 17 lines. Next to God the safety of the state depends on the army. Some try to attract soldiers and allies into private employment. This we have decided to forbid. We endure much labour[37] over their (soldiers') training and preparation, so that they may be efficient.

N. 157 (1 May 542) preface 12 lines. We have been told (ἐμάθομεν) of doings unworthy of our times in Mesopotamia and Osroene. *Coloni* from different estates marry, then the owners try to separate them or their children. The problem can only be solved by our providence (πρόνοια).

N. 117 (18 Dec. 542) preface 3 lines. We think it necessary to make a general law about various matters which have come to our notice.

A second criterion for fixing the end of Tribonian's second questorship comes from the epilogues to the *Novels*. Since these are not preserved in the *CJ* their history effectively starts from 535. The forms are clearly conventional, but they vary somewhat. In 535 to 541 a typical epilogue runs:[38]

τὰ τοίνυν παραστάντα ἡμῖν καὶ διὰ τοῦδε τοῦ θείου δηλούμενα νόμου ἡ σὴ
ὑπεροχὴ ἔργῳ καὶ πέρατι παραδοῦναι σπευσάτω

The first and last phrases, in particular, are much used. Of 115 Greek constitutions (counting as enumerated in the Schoell-Kroll edition)[39] 71 have[40]

---

[34] Cf. *N*. 19 pr., n. 18 above.   [35] τὸ τῶν ἀνθρωπίνων πραγμάτων εὐμετάβλητον.
[36] Cf. n. 21 above.   [37] Cf. n. 19 above.   [38] *N*. 110 (26 April 541).
[39] For other purposes one might count differently, for as Stein shows (op. cit. 374) *N*. 8 consists of four constitutions with four addressees and *N*. 17 of two.
[40] (Always in the epilogue) *N*. 2 (16 March 535), 10 (15 April 535), 121 (15 May 535), 12 (16 April 535), 32 (15 June 535), Edict 3 (23 July 535), Nov. 15 (13 Aug. 535), 16 (13 Aug. 535), Edict 12 (18 Aug. 535), *N*. 38 (15 Feb. 536), 18 (1 March 536), 19 (17 March 536), 20 (18 March 536), 21 (18 March 536), 22 (18 March 536), 31 (18 March 536), 39 (17 April 536), 40 (18 May 536), 103 (1 July 536), 42 (6 Aug. 536), 46 (18 Aug. 536), 139 (535–6), 154 (535–6), Edict 4 (535–6), 43 (17 May 537), 44 (17 Aug. 537), 48 (18 Aug. 537), 49 (18 Aug. 537), 47 (31 Aug. 537), 50 (1 Sept. 537), 51 (1 Sept. 537), 54 (1 Sept. 537), 53 (1 Oct. 537), 55 (18 Oct. 537), 57 (18 Oct. 537), 59 (3 Nov. 537), 61 (1 Dec. 537), 63 (9 March 538), 66 (1 May 538), 68 (25 May 538), 70 (1 June 538), 71 (1 June 538), 72 (1 June 538), 74 (4 June 538), 76 (15 Oct. 538), 80 (10 March 539 τὰ τοίνυν τῷ ἡμετέρῳ παραστάντα κράτει), 133 (16 March 539), 81 (18 March 539), 82 (8 April 539), 83 (18 May 539), 84 (18 May 539), 87 (18 May 539), 85 (26 May

τὰ παραστάντα ἡμῖν
τὰ ἡμῖν παραστάντα
τὰ τοίνυν παραστάντα ἡμῖν
τοίνυν τὰ παραστάντα ἡμῖν
τὰ παραστάντα τοίνυν ἡμῖν

i.e. 'what we have thus provided'. Of 13 *Novels* between 543 and 546 on the other hand, only one has this formula,[41] but of seven between 548 and 553 five have this or yet another variant.[42] The pattern points to three quaestorships falling approximately within the three times spans. Of the five Greek *Novels* of 542:

N. 115 (1 February 542) Ἅπαντα δὲ ταῦτα κρατεῖν θεσπίζομεν
Edict 7 (1 March 542) τὰ τοίνυν παραστάντα ἡμῖν
N. 116 (9 April 542) τὰ τοίνυν παραστάντα ἡμῖν
N. 157 (1 May 542) τὰ τοίνυν παραστάντα ἡμῖν
N. 117 (18 December 542) Ἅπερ τοίνυν ἡ ἡμετέρα διετύπωσε γαληνότης

The change apparently comes between May and December 542. Common too are phrases with ἔργον/ἔργῳ καὶ πέρατι such as:

ἔργῳ καὶ πέρατι παραδοῦναι σπευσάτω/σπευσάτωσαν
καὶ ἔργῳ καὶ πέρατι παραδοῦναι φροντισάτω

or the related εἰς ἔργον ἀγαγεῖν σπουδασάτω, i.e. 'put into effect at once'. Here there are 36 epilogues out of 115 with such expressions between 535 and 541,[43] then none between 543 and 553, followed by a single text in 555.[44] Of the *Novels* of 542:

---

539), 101 (1 Aug. 539), 88 (1 Sept. 539), 89 (1 Sept. 539), 90 (1 Oct. 539), 91 (1 Oct. 539), 92 (10 Oct. 539), 95 (1 Nov. 539), 96 (1 Nov. 539), 97 (18 Nov. 539), 98 (16 Dec. 539), 99 (20 Dec. 539), 100 (20 Dec. 539), 106 (7 Sept. 540), 107 (1 Feb. 541), 110 (26 April 541), 109 (7 May 541), 113 (22 Nov. 541), 153 (12 Dec. 541).

41 N. 130 (1 March 545).
42 Edict 8 (17 Sept. 548), N. 129 (16 June 551), 146 (8 Feb. 553), 147 (15 April 553), 149 (1 June 555).
43 (Always in the epilogue except where indicated) N. 2 (16 March 535), 5 (17 March 535 εἰς ἔργον ἄγεσθαι παρασκευάζειν), 7 (15 April 535), 10 (15 Apr. 535), 121 (15 April 535), 12 (16 May 535), 24.6.1 (18 May 535 αὐτὸς δὲ εἰς ἔργον ἄξεις), 32 (15 June 535), Edict 8 (23 July 535 παραφυλάξαι καὶ πέρατι παραδοῦναι σπευσάτω), N. 16 (13 Aug. 535), Edict 3 (18 Aug. 535), 38 (15 Feb. 536 καὶ φυλάττειν καὶ ἔργῳ παραδιδόναι σπευδέτω), 103 (1 July 536), 139 (535-6), 154 (535-6), Edict 4 (535-6), N. 44 (17 Aug. 537), 50 (1 Sept. 537), 53 (1 Oct. 537 κρατεῖν καὶ πέρατι παραδιδόναι σπευδέτω), 56 (3 Nov. 537), 63 (9 March 538), 80 (10 March 539 εἰς ἔργον ἀγαγεῖν σπουδασάτω), 133 (16 March 539), 85 (25 June 539), 88 (1 Sept. 539), 90 (1 Oct. 539), 91 (1 Oct. 539), 92 (10 Oct. 539), 95 (1 Nov. 539), 96 (1 Nov. 539), 98 (16 Dec. 539), 99 (15 Dec. 539), 100 (20 Dec. 539), 110 (26 April 541), 109 (7 May 541), 153 (12 Dec. 541).
44 N. 159 (1 June 555 καὶ ἔργῳ καὶ πέρατι παραδοθῆναι καὶ παραφυλαχθῆναι προστάξάτω).

N. 115 (1 February 542) εἰς τὴν ἀπάντων γνῶσιν ἐλθεῖν παρασκευασάτω
Edict 7 (1 March 542) βέβαια φυλαξάτω
N. 116 (9 April 542) πᾶσι δῆλα καταστῆσαι σπευσάτω
N. 157 (1 May 542) εἰς ἔργον ἀχθῆναι καὶ παραφυλαχθῆναι προνοησάτω
N. 117 (18 December 542) πᾶσι κατάδηλα γενέσθαι σπουδασάτω

The indications are less clear, but the last use of the formula for thirteen years occurs in May 542.

The epilogues provide converse evidence that Tribonian was not quaestor in December 542. *Novels* 117 (18 December 542), 118 (16 July 543), 120 (9 May 544) and 131 (18 March 545) introduce a new theme. The promulgation of the constitution in the provinces is to take place without imposing expense on the provincials.[45] Van der Wal draws attention to the changing instructions to the addresses, especially the praetorian prefect, concerning publication of the law in the provinces.[46] Indeed *Novels* 120 and 131 forbid the prefect to publish them himself and announce that the emperor will see to the matter free of charge. Other *Novels* of 544–6 order the prefect to publish the law in Constantinople, no mention being made of other places. But from *Novel* 127 of 1 September 548 the old formula is reintroduced. Though Van der Wal does not attempt an interpretation, we can explain the changes by postulating a new quaestor in December 542 and another in September 548. After Tribonian's departure an economy drive is in force. There is a hint that the formula ἔργῳ καὶ πέρατι παραδοῦναι σπευσάτω was in his time taken as an excuse for wasting money on publicity. But from 548 we have a quaestor who stands firmly in the Tribonianic tradition.

A third point concerns the use of Latin in Greek constitutions. In the sixth century it was not uncommon to put technical terms into Latin[47] or into a Latin root with a Greek termination.[48] Alternatively they might be transliterated, naturally with a Greek termination.[49] Nothing turns on this so far as Tribonian's habits of composition are concerned. He follows the normal pattern.[50] But the *Novels* of 535–41 use Latin in two other contexts which are less usual. Latin is used for the amount of fines and occasionally, apart from this, for the number of things (lamps, officials) being discussed. It is also used, with a Greek article, for the names of actions (i.e. the technical designation of legal claims), proceedings, laws etc.

[45] *N.* 117 epil. (18 Dec. 542), 118 epil. (16 July 543), 120 epil. (9 May 544), 131 epil. (18 March 545), 125 epil. authenticum (13 Dec. 543).

[46] Van der Wal, *Manuale Novellarum Justiniani* (1966), 13 n. 4.

[47] E.g. *ad responsum N.* 25.1 (18 May 535), 26.2.1 (18 May 535), *litigator N.* 124.2 bis (15 June 544).

[48] E.g. *exheredatovs, exheredationos* (*N.* 1.1.4, 1 Jan. 535), *agnatos* (*N.* 118.2, 16 July 543).

[49] E.g. ῥεφερενδαρίων (*N.* 113 pr., 27 Nov. 541).

[50] Generally in the mixed form, Latin root and Greek termination: *N.* 12.1 (10 Oct. 535 *incestov, damnatov*), 13.3 (15 Oct. 535 *consistorianῶν*: 13.1 has *praetoras plebis, praetores* and *praetores plebis*), 31.2 (18 March 536 *commonitoriων* but also *commonitoria*), 102.2 (27 May 536 *spectabilios*), 110 pr. (26 Apr. 541 *traiecticιων*). The transcription by Schoell–Kroll is not entirely reliable: van der Wal, *Manuale* 11 n. 3.

So far as fines are concerned there are 26 *Novels* between 535 and 541, of which 19 give the fine in Latin,[51] for example:[52]

τῷ τε εὐδοξοτάτῳ κοαίστορι ποινὴν ἐπικεῖσθαι *quinquaginta librarum auri*

Of the remaining seven, three have a mixture of Latin and Greek,[53] a Latin number with a Greek unit of currency, as in:[54]

ποινὴν *quinque* χρυσίου λίτρας ζημιωθήσεται

In four *Novels* the amount or amounts are in Greek. One of these, prescribing a penalty for a husband who unilaterally divorces his wife without good cause, was perhaps not thought of as a fine.[55] For the other three[56] there is no obvious explanation.

In 544–6 there are four *Novels* prescribing fines, each time in Greek.[57] In 553 there is a text setting out a fine in Latin,[58] in 556 one in Greek.[59] The chronological pattern is therefore like that for the prefaces[60] and epilogues.[61] In the crucial year 542 we have three texts:

N. 116.1 (9 April 542) ἀνὰ *decem librarum auri* ποινὴν εἰσπραχθήσονται
N. 157 epil. (1 May 542) *trium librarum auri* ποινῆς ἐπικειμένης
N. 117.11,13 ter (18 December 542) δέκα χρυσίου λιτρῶν ποινήν (and three similar fines entirely in Greek

The pattern is now familiar, and suggests a change of style between May and December 542.

Apart from fines, Latin numbers appear occasionally, not regularly, for salaries, periods of time, factories and the like. There are 14 *Novels* between

---

51 N. 7.9 pr. (15 April 535), 136 ep. (1 April 535), 8.13 (15 April 535), 15.6.1 (13 Aug. 535), 14.1 (1 Dec. 535), 38 ep. (15 Feb. 536), Ed. 4.3 (535–6), N. 51.1 (1 Sept. 537), 56.1 (3 Nov. 537), 58 (3 Nov. 537), 60.1.1 (1 Dec. 537), 105.2.2 (28 Dec. 537), 64.2 (19 Jan. 538), 63.1 (9 March 538), 69.4.3 (1 June 538), 79.3 (10 March 539), 113.1.1 (22 Nov. 541), 116.1 (9 April 542), 157 ep. (1 May 542).

52 N. 7.9. pr. (15 April 535).

53 N. 10.1 (15 April 535), 30.6.1 (18 March 536), 102.3 (27 May 536).

54 N. 102.3 (27 May 536).

55 N. 22.18 (3 Jan. 536 but note that ζημιόω is used: ἑκατὸν λίτρας ζημιωθήσεται . . . μὴ πλέον τῶν ἑκατὸν τοῦ χρυσίου ζημιούσθω λιτρῶν.

56 N. 85.3.1 (25 June 539 ter), 153 ep. (12 Dec. 541), 112.2 (10 Sept. 541). The first is addressed to Basilides mo., the second to Elias pp. for Illyricum. Perhaps the identity of the addressee has some elusive significance in these cases. The third is a bilingual text, in which Latin is used in the Latin and Greek in the Greek version: not really an exception.

57 N. 122 ep. (23 March 544); 128.1 (quat.), 12 (bis), 19 (bis), 20, 21 (6 June 545), 123.8, 27, 43 (1 May 546), 126.3 (546).

58 N. 145.1 (8 Feb. 553).   59 N. 134.1, 9 pr. bis (1 May 556).

60 Table below, p. 135.   61 Above, nn. 40–5.

535 and 539 with this quirk,[62] and one each in 548[63] and 553.[64] The year 542 has one example:

N. 116.1 (9 April 542) εἰ μὴ ἐντὸς *triginta dierum* προθεσμίας

Once more, the style of 548–53 resembles that of 535–41, and that of the first half of 542 is like that of 535–41.

It is not easy to say when this habit of putting Latin numbers in Greek constitutions started or what the reason for it is. A text of Anastasius[65] and one of Justin[66] give fines in Greek. A Greek edict which is dated between 531 and 535 gives the amount of repayment (*simplum, duplum*) in Latin.[67] It can be argued that the amount of a fine, at least, is so important an operative part of the text that it needs to be emphasised by a change of script. But the oddity may just be a personal idiosyncrasy.

As mentioned, the constitutions of 535–41 use a combination of Greek and Latin in another context, this time academic. The names of legal claims (*actio*, ἀγωγή), securities, statutes and the like are introduced and put in the form:[68]

καὶ μὴν καὶ τὴν *iniuriarum* . . . κινεῖν

which means 'and also bring the action for insult'. The owner's action *in rem* to recover his property (*vindicatio*) becomes:[69]

ἡ *in rem* ἡ περὶ δεσποτείας

There are eleven *Novels* between 535 and 541 in which a phrase of this type occurs.[70] The last instance in the *Novels*, is:

[62] N. 8 Notitia 49 (15 April 535 a sliding fine), Edict 1.1 (17 April 535 salaries), N. 12.3 (15 May 535 years), 28.4.1 (16 July 535 *officiales*), 13.3.1 (13 Oct. 535 salary), 38.6 (15 Feb. 536 indiction), 30.2,6,11 (18 March 536 salaries, taxes), 31.1.2 ter (18 March 536 salaries), 102.2 bis (27 May 536 salaries), 103.1 (1 July 536 salary), 43.1 (17 May 537 factories), 59.5 ter (3 Nov. 537 salaries), 82.9 (8 April 539 salary), 80.8 ter (10 March 539 salaries).
[63] Edict 8.3.2, 4 (17 Sept. 548 *vicariani*, torches).
[64] N. 147.2 (15 April 553 *sedecim* πρόσθεν *annis*).
[65] N. 168 (512).   [66] N. 166 ep. (edict of Demosthenes pp. 521–3).
[67] Edict 2.1 pr. (531–5 *duplum, simplum* = sliding fines).
[68] N. 71.1 (1 June 538).   [69] N. 91.1 (1 Oct. 539).
[70] N. 1.2.1, 2 quat. (1 Jan. 535 ἐκ τοῦ *Falcidiov*, παρακατασχεῖν *Falcidiov* = *lex, portio Falcidia*), 18.2 (1 March 536 περὶ τῆς de *inofficioso* κειμένων νόμων = *querela de inofficioso testamento*), 22.41, 43 (3 Jan. 536 τὴν *legatorum servandorum causa* καλουμένην = *cautionem*, ὁ γὰρ καλούμενος *Iulios miscellas* παλαιὸς νόμος), 39 pr. (17 April 536 *fideicommissov persecutiones, in rem missiones*, τῆς ῥηθείσης *in rem missionos* κύκλοι), 46.2 (18 Aug. 536 τὸ *pro soluto* σχῆμα = *titulo*), 61.1.1 (1 Dec. 537 οἵπερ καὶ αὐτὴν τὴν *in rem* δεδώκασι = *actionem*), 63.1 (9 March 538 ἡ *vi bonorum raptorum* = *actio*), 71 (1 June 538 above, n. 68), 162.1 (9 June 539 διὰ τῆς *ex stipulato*, διὰ τοῦ *ex lege condicticiov*), 91.1 (1 Oct. 539 above, n. 69), 108.2 (1 Feb. 541 *in rem* αὐτοῖς χαρισάμενοι καὶ τὴν τοῦ *fideicommissov persecutiona*).

Edict 7.7 (1 March 542 διὰ τῆς *in rem* ἢ δι' ἄλλης νομίμου ἀγωγῆς).

The style of 535–41 is once again continued in the first half of 542.

Another test which points to the year 542 as a year of transition involves studying the normative verbs which most commonly express the emperor's attitudes. The accuracy of this study cannot be guaranteed in the absence of a concordance and I have refrained from giving text references; but the general picture which emerges is unlikely to be false. In most tenures the stock verb is θεσπίζομεν. In 535–41 however βουλόμεθα runs it close with 143 mentions to 167 in all against 87 for δίδομεν and 56 for ᾠήθημεν. The latter expression is found only once after 541. Between December 542 and 546 κελεύομεν is overwhelmingly commoner than the other normative verbs. Συγχωροῦμεν and παρακελευόμεθα are also relatively frequent. In 548 to 555 none of the listed expressions is common, but θεσπίζομεν heads the field. In 556 κελεύομεν returns as the favourite and so continues.

The changing proportions in which the eight leading normative verbs are found are striking enough to be worth setting out in the form of a table, which appears on p. 133. The total material in each year is now counted in lines.[71] This is the result of a count, in which the unit is a single column line in the Schoell–Kroll edition of the *Novels*. Prescripts are omitted but subscriptions included, in view of the format of the edition.

Taken *grosso modo* the picture is clear enough. The proportions of θεσπίζομεν and βουλόμεθα remain fairly even to the end of 541. From 543, indeed from December 542, κελεύομεν overtakes both. The year 542 is once again transitional:

N. 115 (1 Feb. 542, 494 lines θεσπίζομεν 15, συνείδομεν 7, κελεύομεν 6, βουλόμεθα 4, παρακελευόμεθα 2, δίδομεν 2)

Edict 7 (1 March 542), 248 lines θεσπίζομεν 3, συνείδομεν 2, βουλόμεθα 1, παρακελευόμεθα 1)

N. 116 (9 Apr. 542, 59 lines συνείδομεν 1, συγχωροῦμεν 1)

N. 157 (1 May 542, 21 lines θεσπίζομεν 1)

N. 117 (18 Dec. 542, 540 lines κελεύομεν 19, συνείδομεν 8, θεσπίζομεν 7. βουλόμεθα 5, συγχωροῦμεν 5, παρακελευόμεθα 3).

---

[71] The dating follows the Schoell–Kroll edition of the *Novels* but omitting Edict 4 and *Novels* 154, 139, which they assign to 535–6, 77 which they put in 535, and Edict 13 which they assign to the period 1 Sept. 538 to 31 Aug. 539, besides those which they date simply as before or after a certain terminus. Of these one should probably assign to Tribonian Edict 4 (1 ᾠήθημεν 2 τὰς *decem librarum auri*, βουλόμεθα bis 3 κρατεῖν βουλόμεθα, ποινὴν *viginti librarum auri*, epil. τὰ τοίνυν παραστάντα ἡμῖν . . . ἔργῳ καὶ πέρατι παραδοῦναι σπευσάτω), N. 154 (pr. τοὺς ῥωμαϊκοὺς . . . νόμους, Justinian's incredulity 1 ἠβουλόμεθα, βουλόμεθα ter, ep. τὰ τοίνυν παραστάντα ἡμῖν . . . ἔργῳ καὶ πέρατι παραδοῦναι σπευσάτω), and Edict 13 (pr. τὰ σμικρότατα—cf. N. 15 ep. (13 Aug. 535); 63.1 (9 March 538); 67.2 (1 May 538); 69.1 (1 June 538); 73.8.2 (4 June 538)–13.1 βουλόμεθα bis, καθάπερ εἴρηται below, n. 83, 3 βουλόμεθα 4 *quinque librarum auri* λήψονται, *mille solidos*, βουλόμεθα 5 καθάπερ ἔμπροσθεν εἴρηται 7 βουλόμεθα 8 βουλόμεθα 9 βουλόμεθα 11 καθάπερ εἴρηται 15 ᾠήθημεν 16 βουλόμεθα 18 βουλόμεθα, ᾠήθημεν 19 βουλόμεθα 24 ἴσμεν 25 καθάπερ εἰπόντες ἔφθημεν 26 βουλόμεθα 28 βουλόμεθα); cf. ch.1 n. 245.

Year	Lines of Greek const.	θεσπί-ξομεν	βουλό-μεθα	δίδ-ομεν	ᾠήθ-ημεν	συνείδ-ομεν	κελεύ-ομεν	συγχωροῦ-μεν	παρακελ-ευόμεθα
535	7021	47	34	28	24	7	1	10	1
536	4060	24	27	18	8	1	2	8	0
537	2419	26	21	7	4	5	0	2	0
538	1577	12	12	3	6	0	0	0	0
539	4072	43	39	25	13	6	14	10	1
540	93	1	0	0	0	0	0	0	0
541	764	14	10	6	1	1	7	3	1
542 (to May)	843	19	5	2	0	10	6	1	1
542 (from Dec.)	540	7	5	0	0	8	19	5	3
543	251	3	5	0	0	2	7	1	1
544	866	11	4	4	0	6	32	7	4
545	792	11	2	1	0	1	42	2	2
546	1103	10	0	4	0	1	34	15	2
548	247	5	1	0	0	2	6	0	0
551	122	1	0	2	0	0	1	0	0
553	325	4	1	2	0	0	0	0	0
555	272	1	0	0	1	0	0	0	0
556	620	2	6	4	0	1	36	3	0
558	90	1	0	1	0	0	5	0	0
559	144	1	0	0	0	0	0	0	0
565	94	1	0	0	0	0	4	0	0
	26315	244	172	107	57	51	216	67	16

The figures can be used to argue in favour of Stein's thesis that Tribonian leaves the scene at or towards the end of 541. The proportion of uses of βουλόμεθα to θεσπίζομεν falls in the first half of 542. On the other hand the proportion of κελεύομεν has not yet risen beyond its frequency in 539 and 541. Scrutiny of the eight commonest normative verbs does not in fact yield a clear indication. If however some other verbs used in the majestic plural are taken into account, the balance is tilted in favour of classing the texts of the first half of 542 with those of 535–41. Edict 7 of 1 March 542 has both ἴσμεν and οἰόμεθα. Of the dated texts ἴσμεν occurs 41 times in 535–41[72] and apart from this text, once each in 553[73] and 559.[74] Οἰόμεθα occurs otherwise

[72] N. 4 pr. (16 March 535), 3 pr. (16 March 535), 6.8 (16 March 535), 7.3.1 (15 April 535), 17.8.1 (16 April 535), 13 pr. (15 Oct. 535 ter), 18.3 (1 March 536), 22.14 (18 March 536 bis), 39 pr. (17 April 536), 102.3 (27 May 536), 42 pr. (6 Aug. 536), 44.2 (17 Aug. 537), 48 pr. (18 Aug. 537), 49 pr. (18 Aug. 537 bis), 52 pr. (18 Aug. 537), 50 pr. (1 Sept. 537), 51 pr. (1 Sept. 537), 53.2 (1 Oct. 537), 56 pr. (3 Nov. 537), 68 pr. (25 May 538), 69.3 (1 June 538), 70 pr. (1 June 538), 73 pr, 6 (4 June 538 bis), 74 pr. 2 and 74.4 (4 June 538 bis), 90.5, 9 (1 Oct. 539 bis), 94.2 (9 Oct. 539), 95 pr. (1 Nov. 539), 97.3, 6 pr., 6.1 (17 Nov. 539 ter), 99 pr. (20 Dec. 539), 100.2 (20 Dec. 539), 107.3 (1 Feb. 541), 108 pr. 2 (1 Feb. 541), 110 pr. (26 April 541).
[73] N. 156.1.   [74] N. 141.1 (15 March 559).

only four times, twice in 536[75] and twice in 538.[76] Ἐμάθομεν is found in *Novel* 157 of 1 May 542. There is a previous occurrence in 536[77] and a subsequent one in 553.[78] In addition μανθάνομεν is found once in 535[79] and μεμαθήκαμεν six times between 535 and 539.[80] *Novel* 115 of 1 February 542 twice has καθάπερ εἴρηται[81] which is found three times apart from this text, twice in 539[82] and once in 541.[83] The texts of 535–9 abound in similar phrases, especially καθάπερ εἰπόντες ἔφθημεν, which is met 37 times.[84] In later years such phrases are rare and other forms are preferred, with καθὼς instead of καθάπερ.[85]

The evidence of style therefore points to the conclusion that Tribonian left office between 1 May 542 (*Novel* 157) and 18 December 542 (*Novel* 117). At this point, however, the arguments of E. Stein come into play.[86] He places the end of the quaestorship shortly after 1 November 541 (*Novel* 114). His argument is based on the language in which the constitutions are drafted. He relies on the changing balance between Latin and Greek constitutions.

Up to the end of 534, during Tribonian's first quaestorship and that of Basilides, Latin is the normal language of legislation. From 535 Greek takes its place.

According to Stein the change in the language of laws which dates from 535 is to be interpreted as a victory of John of Cappadocia over Tribonian.[87] The change essentially concerned texts addressed to the praetorian prefect of the east, which form the bulk of constitutions preserved in the *Novels*. After 535 only one of these is in Latin until John's dismissal in 541.[88]

---

[75] N. 18.10 (1 March 536), 30.1 (18 March 536).   [76] N. 73.3 (4 June 538 bis).

[77] N. 38.5 (15 Feb. 536).   [78] N. 146 pr. (8 Feb. 553).

[79] N. 17.13 (16 April 535).

[80] N. 7.8 (15 April 535), 28 pr. (16 July 535), 15.1 (13 Aug. 535), 13.1, 4 (15 Oct. 535), Edict 3 (23 July 535).

[81] N. 115.3.13, 4.9 (1 Feb. 542).   [82] N. 81.1 (13 March 539), 97.3 (17 Nov. 539).

[83] N. 112.3.2 (10 Sept. 541); also Edict 13.1, 5, 11.

[84] N. 1.1.2, 2.2 bis (1 Jan. 535 ter), 5.2.1., 9.1 (17 March 535 bis), 6.1.7. 10, 6.2 (16 March 535 ter), 7.5.2 (16 April 535), 8.2, 8, 13 (15 April 535 ter), 10 pr. (15 April 535), 24.4 (18 May 535), 28.5 (16 July 535), 15.5 (13 Aug. 535), 38 pr. 3, 6 (15 Feb. 536 bis), 20.3 (18 March 536), 21.2 (18 March 536), 22.22, 48.1 (18 March 536 bis), 30.7 (18 March 536), 103.3.2 (1 July 536), 42.1.1 (6 Aug. 536), 49.1 (18 Aug. 537), 61.2 (1 Dec. 537), 66.1.2 (1 May 538), 74.1 (4 June 538), 133.5 (16 March 539), 82.7, 10 (8 April 539 bis), 101.3 (1 Aug. 539), 89.9 pr. (1 Sept. 539 bis), 102.2 (10 Oct. 539 bis), 105.2.1, 4 (1 Nov. 539 bis). Cf. 89.3 (1 Sept. 539 καθάπερ προειπόντες ἔφθημεν), 7 pr., 1 (15 April 535 bis), 39 pr. (17 April 536, all ὅπερ εἰπόντες ἔφθημεν), 12.3 (16 May 535 καθὰ φθάσαντες εἴπομεν).

[85] N. 119 pr. (20 Jan. 544), 124.3 (15 June 544 both καθὼς εἴρηται), 134.12 (1 May 556 καθὼς προείπομεν). But καθάπερ εἰρήκαμεν is found in N. 123.17 (1 May 546) as well as in 88.2 pr. (1 Sept. 539) and 115.3.12 (1 Feb. 542).

[86] *Deux questeurs* 365.   [87] On their rivalry see above, ch. 2 nn. 159–73.

[88] Between 535 and 541 there are 69 constitutions addressed to Iohannes pp. Or. and four to Theodotus pp. Or. Of these only N. 62 (1 Jan. 537) is in Latin. N. 143 (21 May 563 Areobindo), though tentatively assigned by Kroll (*CJC* III, 707) to Areobindus pp. (ten years previously) need not be addressed to a pp., as Stein, *Deux questeurs* 373, shows.

Certain of the indications can conveniently be summarised in a table:

Year	Number of Greek consts.	Prefaces: half-lines	Average per const.	Epilogue: (1) παραστάντα	(2) ἔργῳ etc.	Latin fines
535	28	890	32	10	11	6
536	15	590	39	12	2	3
537	19	432	23	13	4	5
538	12	281	23	8	1	3
539	26	555	21	21	12	1
540	1	63	63	1	0	0
541	8	163	20	5	3	1
542 (to May)	4	69	17	3	1	2
542 (from Dec.)	1	3	3	0	0	0
543	2	23	11	0	0	0
544	6	60	10	0	0	0
545	3	9	3	1	0	0
546	2	17	8	0	0	0
548	2	32	16	1	0	0
551	1	28	28	1	0	0
553	3	70	23	2	0	1
555	1	155	155	1	1	0
556	1	7	7	0	0	0
558	1	21	21	0	0	0
559	2	21	10	0	0	0
565	1	19	19	0	0	0
	139	3508	25.2	79	35	22

The Latin constitutions of this period are addressed to Africa,[89] Italy[90] or the Balkans.[91] For Illyria some are in Latin,[92] others in Greek,[93] and the same is true of texts addressed to the *quaestor Iustinianus exercitus* who administered a mixed area.[94] The principle adopted was that the language of the area addressed determined the language of the constitution. Where the intended audience was simply an official the language seems to depend on his predilection. Four *Novels* to Tribonian are all in Latin,[95] as is one to

[89] *N.* 36 (1 Jan. 535), 37 (1 Aug. 535 both to Salomon pp. Africae).

[90] *N.* 9 (14 April 535 to pope John II).

[91] *N.* 11 (14 April 535 to Catellianus archbishop of Prima Iustiniana), *N.* 34 (15 June 535 to Agerochius governor of Haemimontus), 65 (23 March 538 to the governor of Mysia).

[92] *N.* 33 (15 June 535), *App.* 1 (7 April 540 Dominico pp. [Ill.]). The original text of *N.* 165 also to Dominico pp., is lost.

[93] *N.* 153 (12 Dec. 541 ʹΗλία ἐπ ʹΙλλ), 162 (9 June 539 Δομνίκῳ ἐπ).

[94] Moesia 11 and Scythia: Nov. 41 (18 May 536, Latin), 50 (1 Sept. 537, Greek).

[95] *N.* 23 (3 Jan. 536), 35 (23 May 535), 17 (covering letter 16 April 535), 75 (= 104) Dec. 537).

Hermogenes mo. answering a petition made by him in his private capacity.[96]

The one exception to the practice set out is *Novel* 62 (1 January 537) which is addressed to John and deals with the careers and seniority of senators. It may have been the quaestor's role as legal adviser to the senate[97] or the historical background of this constitution[98] which accounts for its Latinity.

The series of Greek *Novels* addressed to John as praetorian prefect continues until *N*. 109 (7 May 541). *N*. 111 (1 June 541) is addressed to Theodotus pp. or, in Latin. Between these dates John fell from office, disgraced through an intrigue, it seems, of Antonina and Theodora.[99] Stein interprets the reversion to Latin as reflecting Tribonian's renewed influence after John's departure.[100] The series of *Novels* which went to the praetorian prefecture in 541 and 542 are best tabulated:

> *N*. 110 (26 April 541) Iohanni pp. Or. Greek
> *N*. 109 (7 May 541) Iohanni pp. Or. Greek
> *N*. 111 (1 June 541) Theodoto pp. Or. Latin
> *N*. 112 (10 September 541) Theodoto pp. Or. bilingual
> *N*. 114 (1 November 541) Theodoto pp. Or. Latin
> *N*. 113 (22 November 541) Theodoto pp. Or. Greek
> *N*. 115 (1 February 542) Theodoto pp. Or. Greek
> *N*. 116 (9 April 542) Theodoto pp. Or. Greek
> *N*. 117 (18 December 542) Theodoto pp. Or. Greek

It is to be observed that *Novel* 114 reinforces the position of the quaestor by requiring imperial ordinances (*sacrae iussiones*) to have the *subscriptio* or *adnotatio* of the quaestor.[101] Any governor or official who acts on an ordinance without this confirmation is subjected to a fine.

Stein takes the substance of this as a sign that Tribonian was still in office on 1 November 541. The change of language in *Novel* 113, however, points to his departure before 22 November of that year.

From internal evidence of style, as we have seen, *Novels* 111, 112 and 114 should go to Tribonian's account.[102] So far there is no dispute. Nor is there anything to rebut the inference that *Novel* 117 is by another hand.[103] It is the intervening texts which are in dispute. For Stein the language points to Tribonian's successor. But the character of the prefaces and epilogues and the use of Latin for fines resembles earlier rather than later Greek con-

---

[96] *N*. 138 (Hermogeni mo. before the death of Hermogenes who is 'of blessed memory' in *N*. 22.46 pr., 18 March 536).

[97] Stein, *Deux questeurs* 374; Cassiodorus, *Varia* 5.6 (*a te senatus quaerit iuris auxilium*).

[98] The preface discusses the historical role of the senate and the transition to imperial rule.

[99] *Wars* 1.25.13f.   [100] Op. cit. 374.

[101] A parallel to the requirements on *N*. 151 and 152 in favour of the praetorian prefect.

[102] Above, ch. 3 nn. 695, 696, 697.

[103] In particular, the three-line preface to this long constitution is too jejune for Tribonian: the fine is in Greek and the predominant normative verb is κελεύομεν.

stitutions and points to Tribonian as the author.[104] One cannot escape the difficulty by imagining that Tribonian's successor for a time used drafts prepared by him, since on Stein's view these drafts would have been in Latin.

Although Stein's interpretation of the return of Latin in June 541 is acceptable, it does not follow that Tribonian was able to maintain his reactionary programme (as it would seem to many) for long. For a few months John's unpopularity would commend the reversal of his policy. Then the inconvenience of the old practice would become clear and Justinian, who himself wrote on church matters in Greek, may have intervened to prescribe the common tongue as the language of laws for the east.

The likelihood is, then, that most of the Greek constitutions between 1 January 535 and 1 May 542 are to be attributed to Tribonian, and that he left office (by death, Procopius implies[105]) between that date and 18 December 542.[106]

In the absence of a proper concordance to the *Novels* it has not been possible to establish the authorship of the individual constitutions with the rigour that is in principle desirable. Such indications as are available at this stage can be traced from the Table of Texts at the end of the book. Although all the Greek constitutions in the appropriate period contain at least some mark which is consistent with Tribonian's authorship, it remains possible that some of these laws are by another hand.

Noailles argued that only general laws, not pragmatic sanctions or rescripts, were composed by the quaestor.[107] Since no fewer than ten of the constitutions in the pertinent period are described in the text as pragmatic sactions[108] this, if true, would be important. But there is no discernible difference of style between what purport to be general laws and pragmatic sanctions.[109] The practice seems to have been for the quaestor to compose

---

[104] See table above, p. 135.   [105] *Wars* 1.25.2.   [106] Ch. 2 nn. 193–228.

[107] *Novelles* 10f.

[108] N. 136 ep. (1 April 535), 121 ep. (15 April 535), Ed. 12 ep. (18 Aug. 535), N. 103 ep. (1 July 536), 43.1.1, ep. (17 May 537), 59 ep. (3 Nov. 537), 64.2 (19 Jan. 538), 162 ep. (9 June 539), Ed. 7.4, ep. (1 March 542), 157 ep. (1 May 542). The constitutions are called πραγματικὸς νόμος or πραγματικὸς τύπος. A general law is just a νόμος (N. 43.1.1, 17 May 537) or κοινὸς νόμος (162 epil . . . 9 June 539).

[109] N. 136 epil. (τὰ τοίνυν παραστάντα ἡμῖν above, n. 40, ποινῆς *librarum auri decem* above, n. 52), 121 epil. (τὰ παραστάντα ἡμῖν, ἔργῳ καὶ πέρατι παραδοῦναι σπευσάτω above, n. 43), Edict 12 (1 ᾠήθημεν, epil.τὰ παραστάντα ἡμῖν), N. 103 (pr. pr. history of Palestine, pr. 1 origin of Christianity 1 ἄχρι *decem librarum auri, viginti duas libras auri* αὐτῷ δίδομεν above, n. 62, 3.2 καθάπερ εἰπόντες ἔφθημεν above, n. 84, βουλόμεθα epil. τὰ τοίνυν παραστάντα ἡμῖν, ἔργῳ καὶ πέρατι παραδοῦναι σπευσάτω), 43 (pr. βουλόμεθα, ᾠήθημεν 1 *mille centum ἐργαστήρια*, epil. τὰ παραστάντα ἡμῖν), 59 (pr. ᾠήθημεν 2 τουτέστι *per singulum mensem quadringentos solidos* etc., κατὰ *sex menses* 3 μετὰ τόκου τοῦ *tertiae partis* 5 ἄχρι *tremessis solidi, dimidiam partem solidi* λαμβάνειν, τῶν ἀκολούθων . . . *quattuor siliquas* κομιζομένων 6 *duodecim solidorum* ποσότητα etc. 7 ποινὴν . . . *quinquaginta librarum auri*, καθάπερ εἰπόντες ἔφθημεν, βουλόμεθα epil. τὰ παραστάντα ἡμῖν), 64 (1 βουλόμεθα, ter, διότι πανταχόθεν ἡμῖν ἰσότητος μέλει 2 ποινήν, *quinque librarum auri*), 162 (1 pr. τοῦ *Cinciou* νόμου τοῦ παλαιοῦ 1 διὰ τῆς *ex stipulato*, διὰ τοῦ *ex lege condicticiou* 1.2 βουλόμεθα, 1), Edict 7 (pr. φιλανθρωπία, bis 2 βουλόμεθα, 3 τῆς τῶν ἡμετέρων

pragmatic sanctions. Later we find an example of a pragmatic sanction composed in Latin by Justinian himself.[110] This is not to minimise the difference between general laws and sanctions. Pragmatic sanctions are frequently declared void if contary to the general law.[111] To meet this possible objection, one pragmatic sanction is expressly declared equivalent to a proper law.[112] Whatever their status, the quaestor at least sometimes composed them, since one *Novel* penalises a quaestor who composes one inconsistent with the general law.[113]

Rescripts are another matter, if by 'rescript' is meant an imperial instruction, *sanctio, iussio* or the like (in Greek often κέλευσις[114]). These indulgences, concessions and privileges granted by the emperor had a baneful influence on the ordinary course of justice.[115] In one *Novel* Justinian promises to obey the law of the land and to refrain from making concessions by way of rescript.[116] Illegal rescripts are to be disregarded.

Such 'rescripts' are not to be confused with laws issued in answer to a petition from judges or officials who want a point of law cleared up.[117] These may be termed rescripts, but there is no reason why they should not be composed by the quaestor. Imperial instructions are another matter. Composed by the emperor or some member of his immediate entourage, they understandably did not find their way into the various collections of *Novels* save by chance. In the period of Tribonian's second quaestorship the only exception seems to be a Latin document of 541.[118]

χρόνων δικαιοσύνης ἀλλότριον; cf. ch. 3, n. 127, epil. τὰ τοίνυν παραστάντα ἡμῖν), N. 157 (pr. ἐμάθομεν above, nn. 77–8, epil. τὰ τοίνυν παραστάντα ἡμῖν, εἰς ἔργον ἀχθῆναι καὶ παραφυλαχθῆναι προνοησάτω, *trium librarum auri* ποινῆς ἐπικειμένης,).

[110] *Appendix* II (29 Oct. 542), *Justinian* 120–1.

[111] Edit 12 (18 Aug. 535, distinguishing between the validity of pragmatic sanctions and *commonitoria* or letters), N. 38.6 (15 Feb. 536 ἐκ τῆς θείας αὐλῆς), 69.4.2 (1 June 538), 113 (22 Nov. 541 invalidating imperial interference in litigation), 116.1 (9 Apr. 542). Distinguish the invalidation of pragmatic sanctions emanating from the quaestor's office: N. 7.9, 10 (15 April 535), 152.1 (1 June 534).

[112] N. 43.1.1 (17 May 537).   [113] N. 7.9 (15 April 535).

[114] *Iussiones* (N. 114. 1 pr. 1 Nov. 541), θεῖοι τύποι ἢ θεῖαι κελεύσεις (N. 113 pr. 22 Nov. 541), μήτε πραγματικὸν τύπον μήτε ἑτέραν ἀντιγραφὴν μήτε θείαν ἡμῶν τινα ἔγγραφον ἢ ἄγραφον κέλευσιν ἢ κατάθεσιν. (N. 113.1).

[115] Above, n. 111.   [116] N. 59.7.   [117] N. 112 pr. (11 Sept. 541).

[118] *Appendix* II (6 Oct. 541).

CHAPTER FIVE

Temple of Justice: the Digest

This chapter deals with Tribonian's role in the composition of the *Digest*, his major achievement.* That the writings of lawyers of authority such as Gaius, Papinian and Ulpian might be condensed and combined in a comprehensive and exclusive form—what we should now call a code—was not a new idea in the sixth century. Three hundred years earlier there had been a fashion for condensing or excerpting material from well-known writers. Examples are the *Sententiae* of Paul,[1] the *Regularum Liber Singularis* of Ulpian[2] and the *Iuris Epitomae* of Hermogenianus.[3] In the fourth century there developed a related form of legal literature in which excerpts from different writers and from imperial constitutions were combined in titles or subject-headings in order to present a panoramic view of different branches of the law. The *Vatican Fragments*[4] and the *Collatio Legum Mosaicarum et Romanarum*[5] are the leading examples of this technique. In the next century Theodosius II, in design at least, took the movement towards codification a stage further. He intended that his first commission of A.D. 429, after collecting the constitutions from Constantine onwards in a single volume, hould combine under appropriate headings the three imperial codes (the Gregorianus, Hermogenianus and the new Theodosianus) with the private writings of the jurists.[6] The resulting code would be free from error and obscurity and would serve as a guide for all who wished to know what to avoid and what to do.

The second stage of the Theodosian project had however to be aban-

---

* Parts of it have appeared in 87 *ZSS* (1970) 246, 88 *LQR* (1972) 31, 530, 89 *ZSS* (1972) 351, 90 *ZSS* (1973), 262 and 48 *Tulane LR* (1974) 869. I am grateful to these publications and to Dr Alan Rodger, for permission to use the material. See Wenger s. 81; Wieacker *ZSS* 91 (1972) 293f.; Kunkel, *Introduction to Roman Legal and Constitutional History*, tr. J. M. Kelly (2nd ed. 1973) 170–1; Verrey, *Leges geminatae a deux auteurs et compilation du Digeste* (Lausanne 1973).

[1] Generally regarded as a late third-century compilation, declared authentic by *CTh* 1.4.2 (327/328); F. Schulz, *Roman Legal Science* (1946) 176–9.

[2] Perhaps third- or early fourth-century: Schulz, *Science* 180–1.

[3] Between about A.D. 300 and 320 with a preference for 300–5: D. Liebs, *Hermogenians Iuris Epitomae* (1964) 19–22.

[4] The original collection was completed shortly after 318; Schulz, *Science* 311.

[5] The original collection may have been as early as the beginning of the fourth century (Schulz, *Science* 313–14). Theological material and a constitution of 390 (Coll. 5.3) was added later.

[6] *CTh* 1.1.5 (26 March 429). F. Ebrard, 'Das Theodosische Projekt eines "Predigesto"', *Studi Alternario* 1 (1953) 581, denies this.

doned.[7] When Justinian returns to the codification of private legal writings he does so in a less ambitious form. Excerpts from the jurists are to be collected in a single volume of 50 books, which is however to be *separate* from the code of imperial constitutions. Tribonian and his helpers are told to read and condense the old writers of authority in such a way that there is, so far as possible, no overlap and no inconsistency in the resulting antho-logy.[8] The excerpts are to be combined in an aesthetically satisfying form in fifty books, arranged in titles according to the classifications of the code of constitutions and of the praetor's edict in such a way that the resulting volume contains the whole of the law.[9] No author is to be preferred auto-matically to the rest. The commission is to choose the juster view irrespective of author.[10] The chosen excerpts are to be endowed with Justinian's authority.[11] The commissioners are given power to correct, shorten, com-plete and amend the text of the old writers.[12] Thereafter no one may argue that the amended text is incorrect.[13] Obsolete laws are to be rejected and only those accepted in court practice or by the custom of Constantinople included.[14] The future volume is to have the name *Digest* or *Pandects*.[15] No commentaries on or interpretations of it are to be allowed.[16]

The constitution *Deo auctore* setting up the commission to prepare the *Digest* is dated 15 December 530. It is a question how long before that date the decision to proceed with it was taken. Pringsheim argued[17] that the decision was reached about September 530, the series of Fifty Decisions, settling certain disputes among the old writers, having begun to be issued on 1 August 530. This presupposes that the Fifty Decisions was an inde-pendent project in the course of which it became clear that the larger under-taking was both desirable and possible. In favour of Pringsheim's view is the problem-solving role which Tribonian adopted from his appointment in September 529 onwards.[18] The Fifty Decisions, on this view, is no more than the formalisation of an existing practice. But the choice of a fixed number of problems to be solved and their designation by a special term, *decisio*,[19] could be interpreted differently. It might be taken to show that Tribonian was concerned to refute an objection to the *Digest* project, namely that there were innumerable points of conflict among the old jurists, and that many years would be needed to resolve them. By listing the main undecided points and disposing of them month by month, the ground would be cleared for the larger scheme.

In this connection it is relevant that the progress of the commission's work is best understood on the assumption that the actual excerpting began on 15 December 530 and that all the preparatory work had been

---

[7] Appointment of the second Theodosian commission: *CTh* 1.1.6 (20 Dec. 435).

[8] *C. Deo auctore* 4 (15 Dec. 530).   [9] *C. Deo auctore* 5.   [10] *C. Deo auctore* 5.

[11] *C. Deo auctore* 6.   [12] *C. Deo auctore* 7.   [13] *C. Deo auctore* 7.

[14] *C. Deo auctore* 10; cf. *C. Tanta* 11 (16 Dec. 533).   [15] *C. Deo auctore* 12.

[16] *C. Deo auctore* 12.

[17] F. Pringsheim, 'Die Entstehungzeit des Digestenplanes', *Atti cong. Int.* (1933) Roma 1.449f.; above, ch. 1 nn. 161–3.

[18] Ch. 3 nn. 167–71.   [19] Below, nn. 26–32.

done previously.[20] This means that Tribonian's team had been selected, the necessary books collected, the various editions collated, and the Beirut professors had arrived in Constantinople by that date.[21] *Deo auctore* was issued only when all was ready. In that way the time apparently taken by the commission on its labours could be cut by several months. This in turn helped to meet the objection that the project would take an inordinate time.

If this is right it seems likely that when in the summer of 530 Justinian agreed to the Fifty Decisions he either agreed at the same time to the *Digest* project, treating the Fifty as a preliminary, or agreed to the larger enterprise conditionally on the Fifty Decisions proving a practicable enterprise. The fact that in the event far more than fifty legal problems had to be solved in the course of the commission's work did not in the end prejudice Justinian's assent to the scheme. As will be seen, the series of Fifty was not completed until 30 April 531, months after the *Digest* commission had started excerpting, and the need for additions to the list of fifty became evident as early as October 530.

The credit for the *Digest* conception must be shared between the emperor and his quaestor. Justinian had a good knowledge of the legislation and history of the previous century and he was determined to outdo Theodosius II. He must have known of the abortive plan of 429. There is no reason why he should not have entertained the idea of proceeding step by step with the codification of Roman law as soon as the resources were available. The question in his mind was not whether in principle the law of the jurists should be codified but whether such a code was practicable. Certain conditions had to be met. There must be an adequate supply of academic expertise. This the Theodosian commission lacked, but in the past century the law schools had flourished and their talent was now available. The codification must be carried out with all deliberate speed. Since it would require the services of eminent ministers, professors and barristers a prolonged period of service on the commission would interrupt the ordinary course of law, administration and teaching. It is clear that objections were made to the project on the ground of the time it would take. 'When the undertaking was first envisaged hopes did not extend even to finishing it in ten years,'[22] says *C. Tanta*, while the Greek version insists that when first mooted the *Digest* was thought a hopeless undertaking, and later, when Justinian had shown it to be practicable, ten years seemed too little for its completion.[23] Justinian was in a hurry and would not have launched the *Digest* without a detailed timetable. Hence the key to its inception was Tribonian, who had proved his organising ability on Justinian's first commission and was able to demonstrate precisely how the work could be terminated in three years without undue disruption of the central government, the faculties or the praetorian prefect's court.

The rest of this chapter is mainly concerned to elucidate Tribonian's

[20] Trail 88 *LQR* (1972) 537-9; 'Work in progress', 88 *LQR* (1972) 51-2.
[21] *Background* 871-4.   [22] *C. Tanta* 12 (16 Dec. 533).
[23] *C. Δέδωκεν* 12 (16 Dec. 533); *Progress* 36-7.

programme and to show how he executed it on time. I shall deal in turn with
(a) the Fifty Decisions, (b) other preparations, (c) the excerpting of the
ancient jurists' works, (d) the distribution of the excerpts into titles, (e) the
editing of the books and titles in the form of a first draft, and (f) the final
draft of the *Digest*.

It may be convenient to summarise the conclusions before embarking on
the story. The preparations were in the main completed by 15 December
530, when C. *Deo auctore* announced the project, though the series of Fifty
Decisions was not terminated until 30 April 531 and some books by ancient
writers (mainly the Appendix) turned up later. The excerpting began on
15 December 530 and ended about 9 July 531. It was done by three committees (traditionally called the Sabinian, edictal and Papinian committees)
working in parallel on a list of books assigned to each of them. Each committee possessed two senior commissioners, a chairman and a junior
member, supplemented as occasion required by one or more barristers.
Within each committee the excerpting was divided between the two commissioners, each assisted by a team of barristers when necessary. The time-
table was based on the assumption that the Sabinian and edictal committees would excerpt a book a day, the Papinian committee five books a
week. The committee chairmen assigned the excerpts to the appropriate
title headings. When the excerpting was finished the assembled excerpts,
classified by titles and committees, were united in the form of a first draft of
the *Digest*. This work was done by the three committees also, the Sabinian
committee being entrusted with the drafting of books 1, 4, 7 etc., the
Papinian committee with books 2, 5, 8, the edictal committee with books 3,
6, 9, etc. Each committee had to present a draft book twice a month, so that
in all six books were completed each month and the whole draft (in effect of
48 books, books 30 to 32 being a single unit) occupied eight months and was
completed in the course of March 533. The final revision then took place
and Justinian scrutinised the text, presumably in the late spring of 533.
Thereafter he authorised the promulgation of the *Digest* and enough copies
were made for its use as announced by C. *Tanta/Δέδωκεν* on 16 December
533, three years from the start of the excerpting.

THE FIFTY DECISIONS

The Fifty Decisions, which are to be distinguished from 'other numerous
constitutions incident to the execution of the proposed work' (viz. the
Digest)[24] were issued between 1 August 530 and 30 April 531. The most
recent thorough study of them is by Schindler,[25] who lists 34 of the 50 as
having been incorporated in the *Codex Repetitae Praelectionis*. His selection

---

[24] *C. Cordi* 1 (16 Nov. 534).

[25] *Justinians Haltung zur Klassik* (Köln/Graz 1966), summarised at 336; earlier discussions by di Marzo, *Le quinquaginta decisiones di Giustiniano* (1899/1900); de Francisci,
BIDR 22 (1910) 155f., 23 (1911) 39, 186f.; Wenger 580 (11).

is however based on considerations of substance: were the questions regarded or presented as cases in which the old jurists were at loggerheads? His list, like those of previous scholars, ends with constitutions of 17 November 530, since the Fifty Decisions were intended as a prelude to the composition of the *Digest* and were meant to be settled before the larger work could proceed. But if linguistic considerations are taken as a guide a slightly different picture emerges. The verb *decidere* is used of Justinian's legislative activity not merely from 1 August to 17 November 530 but in certain constitutions of 30 April 531. It is nowhere so used in *CJ* outside these temporal limits, either by Tribonian or by other quaestors. It therefore seems reasonable to identify the Decisions with the texts in which *decidere* appears, even though this means prolonging the period in which Justinian enacted the Fifty Decisions beyond 17 November 530 and indeed beyond 15 December 530 when *C. Deo auctore* set up the *Digest* commission. It may be that not all the fifty controverted points of law could be thoroughly investigated before the commission was set on foot, or that Justinian was not satisfied with the solutions proposed to some of them at the consistory at which they were first debated. If a few (we can identify three) were left over for the first half of 531 this would not prevent the commission from starting work. It was enough that Tribonian had demonstrated that the disputes between the ancient jurists were neither so numerous nor so complex that they could not be satisfactorily solved in time for the commission to take the new solutions into account. This it need not do in the earliest stages of its work. In any case the commission had to reconcile itself to digesting changes in the law as it went along. Even before 15 December 530 controverted points of law not listed among the original fifty had obtruded themselves. These points were settled by constitutions which overlap chronologically with the Fifty Decisions but are distinguishable from them by the absence of *decidere* in the text.

On the view here taken, then, in order to qualify as a *decisio* the text of the constitution must contain a part of *decidere* such as *(nos) decidentes*,[26] *(nobis) decidentibus*,[27] *decidendum est*,[28] *decidimus*,[29] *decidendam esse censemus*[30] or a self-referential phrase such as *ludibrium per hanc decisionem expellentes*.[31]

These marks of identification can be used to count *decisiones*. Thus in *CJ* 6.2.22 we find *nobis decidentibus* twice, at 1d and 3a and *decidimus* at 4. The constitution as incorporated in the *CJ* therefore includes three *decisiones*, not one.

This is made explicit at 6.2. 22.4, where Tribonian specifically refers to a

[26] *CJ* 3.33.12 pr., 4.28.7 pr., 4.29.24 pr., 4.38.15.1, 5.51.13 pr., 7.7.1.1b, 8.21.2 pr., 8.37.13 pr. (1 Aug. 530), 5.70.6.1 (1 Sept. 530), 3.33.12 pr., 3.33.14.1, 3.33.16.1, 4.5.11.1, 5.4.25.3, 5.4.26.1, 6.57.6.1, 7.4.14 pr. (1 Oct. 530), 2.18.24.1, 6.37.23.2a (17 Nov. 530).
[27] *CJ* 4.5.10.2, 6.2.20.1 (1 Aug. 530), 3.33.15.2 (1 Oct. 530), 6.2.22.1d, 3a (bis), 6.27.4.2, 6.29.4.1 (17 Nov. 530).
[28] *CJ* 6.22.9 pr. (1 Sept. 530).   [29] *CJ* 6.2.22.4, 6.29.3 pr. (17 Nov. 530).
[30] *CJ* 6.30.20.2 (30 April 531), 6.30.21.1 (30 April 531).
[31] *CJ* 7.25.1 (Iuliano pp. 530).

third doubt (*dubitatio*) having arisen in the same area and asks why Justinian should not also resolve that.[32] According to Tribonian's method the appropriate word (*decidentes* etc.) is used once and once only for each *decisio*. On this basis we can say that 34 *decisiones* (not the same 34 as Schindler's) have survived in *CJ*. These include all ten constitutions of 1 August 530.[33] *CJ* records four constitutions of 1 September,[34] but these reduce to two *decisiones* since 5.70.7 is part of the same constitution which appears at 5.70.6 and does not purport to be a separate *decisio*.[35] The twelve constitutions of 1 October 530 comprise nine *decisiones*.[36] Two more are parts of these nine.[37] The tenth text is *CJ* 6.2.21, which from the point of view of substance could be a *decisio*, but purports to be declaratory of the existing law.[38] This shows that two months after the series of *decisiones* began a new controversy, not on the original list, had emerged and been studied sufficiently for a conclusion to be reached. From the twelve constitutions of 17 November 530 as recorded in *CJ* we can derive eight *decisiones*,[39] three of which are contained in *CJ* 6.2.22.[40] On the other hand four texts of this date have no appropriate expression[41] and must be classed rather with the other constitutions pertaining to the commission's work. By late November 530, therefore, the proportion of new controversies to those listed in the original fifty has increased, as one would expect. In *CJ* 4.27.2, 7.4.16, 7.4.17 and 7.7.2, then, the appropriate words are missing, though in point of substance and chronology these texts are not distinguishable from others of 17 November 530 which do contain these identifying words. It may be noted that whereas 7.4.14 is a *decisio*[42] and 7.4.15 a fragment of one,[43] 7.4.16 and 17

---

[32] *CJ* 6.2.22.4 (17 Nov. 530 *cum autem in confinio earum dubitationum tertia exorta est, quare non et eam decidimus,*).

[33] *CJ* 3.33.12, 4.5.10, 4.28.7, 4.29.24, 4.38.15, 5.51.13, 6.2.20, 7.7.1, 8.21.2, 8.37.13. This leaves out *CJ* 7.15.2, which according to Krueger is part of 7.7.1 (*CJC* 2.509). *CJ* 5.20.2 (*ampliantes sancimus*) is dated 23 July 530. Krueger's suggestion that the date should be amended to 1 Aug. is therefore probably wrong. *CJ* 4.29.23 (Iuliano pp. *resolventes . . . sancimus*) is not dated and Krueger is again probably wrong in his tentative assignment of it to 1 Aug. 530.

[34] *CJ* 1.4.27, 5.70.6, 5.70.7, 6.22.9.

[35] According to Krueger (*CJC* 2.509) all originally a single constitution, but there are two decisions at 5.70.6.1 (*decidentes sancimus*) and 6.2.20.1 (*nobis decidentibus*; cf. *Inst.* 4.1.8 *per nostram decisionem sanximus*).

[36] *CJ* 3.33.13, 3.33.14, 3.33.15, 3.33.16, 4.5.11, 5.4.25, 5.4.26, 6.57.6, 7.4.14.

[37] *CJ* 1.4.28 and 7.4.15, again according to Krueger.

[38] *CJ* 6.2.21.2 (1 Oct. 530 *quam interpretationem prisca quidem iura per coniecturam introducebant: nos autem altius et verius ad eam respicientes generalem regulam sic ab initio esse prolatam accipimus*).

[39] *CJ* 2.18.24, 6.2.22 ter, 6.27.4, 6.29.3, 6.29.4, 6.37.23.

[40] *CJ* 6.2.22.1d, 3a, 4 (17 Nov. 530 *nobis decidentibus, nobis haec decidentibus, quare non decidimus?*).

[41] *CJ* 4.27.2.1 (*nobis verior eorum sententia videtur*), 7.4.16.1 (*nos autem heredis malignitatem coercentes sancimus*), 7.4.17.1, 2 (*miramur, censemus ilico ad libertatem eripi servum*), 7.7.2.2 (*opinamur, interpretamur*).

[42] *CJ* 7.4.14 pr. (1 Oct. 530 *vetus iurgium decidentes*).

[43] *CJ* 6.57.6–7.4.14–7.4.15 (Krueger 2.509).

are not.[44] Again, whereas *CJ* 7.7.1[45] is a *decisio*, 7.7.2 is not.[46] The difference is however purely formal.

The eight or nine constitutions of 30 April 531 comprise three *decisiones*[47] and at least three texts which are not *decisiones* though they purport to settle ancient controversies.[48]

In some cases the shortening of the text may have led to the excision of *decidentes* or some other appropriate word. This is undoubtedly true of *CJ* 7.5.1 (530) reforming the law as to the status of freedmen, which *Institutes* 1.5.3 shows to have been a *decisio*.[49] *CJ* 7.25.1 (Iuliano pp. undated) should, following Di Marzo[50] but contrary to Schindler,[51] be accounted a *decisio* since it runs *antiquae subtilitatis ludibrium per hanc decisionem expellentes*— a formula which though not found elsewhere clearly implies that a *decisio* is being rendered. On the other hand Schindler on the grounds of date[52] rejects *CJ* 5.11.7,[53] 5.14.11[54] and 5.16.27.[55] The linguistic evidence confirms this view, since none of these texts contains a decisory expression. In the result 34 *decisiones*[56] can be identified, of which 33 demonstrably contain a decisory expression. The remainder, if incorporated in *CJ*, escape detection.

The system of linguistic identification by the use of *decidere* or *decisio* is typical of Tribonian's methods. Its use lends weight to the view that the Fifty Decisions were promulgated in a separate volume,[57] which was of course intended to have effect only until the *Digest* project was completed. There is nothing to show precisely when it was published, but the sooner the better from the point of view of government and legal practice. Clearly Tribonian underestimated, whether deliberately or not is difficult to say, the number of ancient controversies which needed resolution in order that the *Digest* project could proceed. Reforming constitutions, some of them dealing with ancient controversies, continued during 531 and, after an interlude caused by the Nika riots, in October 532. Schindler counts 42 of

---

[44] Above, n. 17.   [45] *CJ* 7.7.1.1b (1 Aug. 530 *generaliter sancimus*).
[46] Above, n. 40.

[47] *CJ* 6.30.20.2 (*dubitationem decidendam esse censemus*), 6.30.21.1 (*discordiam decidendam esse censemus*), 6.27.5.1a (*nobis autem alius modus huiusmodi decisionis inventus est*). Krueger, *Geschichte der Quellen und Literatur des römsichen Rechts* (1912) 369, argues for *CJ* 8.48.10 (1 Sept. 531) on the basis of *Turiner Institutionenglosse* n. 241. There is no linguistic support for this identification.

[48] *CJ* 6.35.11, 6.38.4, 6.37.24 (joined by Krueger to 6.42.31) and possibly 4.37.6 (Iohanni pp.). *CJ* 6.46.6 is joined by Krueger to 6.27.5.

[49] *Inst.* 1.5.3 (*dediticios per constitutionem expulimus, quam promulgavimus inter nostras decisiones*) referring to *CJ* 7.5 (*de dediticia libertate tollenda*).

[50] S. di Marzo, *Le quinquaginta decisiones di Giustiniano* (1899) 60.

[51] *Justinians Haltung* 336 n. 1.   [52] Ibid.

[53] *CJ* 5.11.7 (Iohanni pp. 1 Nov. 530 Haloander, 1 Nov. 531 Krueger: *utramque dubitationem certo fini tradentes sancimus*).

[54] *CJ* 5.14.11 (Iohanni pp. 1 Nov. 530, 1 Nov. 531 scr. *sancimus itaque*).

[55] *CJ* 5.16.27 (Iohanni pp. 1 Dec. 530, 27 Nov. 531 scr. *firmam esse censemus*).

[56] All those noted above, nn. 10, 12, 13, 16, 24 and *CJ* 7.25.1. The number happens to be the same as that given by Schindler.

[57] *Inst.* 1.5.3.

these as incidental to the task of the commission,[58] but while it was necessary for his purposes to make such a classification there is no need for us to
do so. Tribonian, with the concurrence of the emperor, continued to regard
it as his task to solve legal conundrums left unsettled by past lawyers. He
introduces the problems with *quaerebatur*,[59] *dubitabatur*[60] or the like but does
not use *decidentes* or similar expressions in presenting the solutions.

A note on the use of *decisio* in *CJ* may be helpful. The word does not
appear until Justinian's reign. In the quaestorship of Thomas it applies to
the decision of lawsuits, *decisio litium*,[61] and the desire for a speedier end to
litigation is said to be the chief reason for the codification of the imperial
constitutions.[62] Under Tribonian's aegis *decisio* means either this[63] or,
apart from one text where it has the general meaning 'resolution of a
controversy',[64] one of the Fifty Decisions.[65] The need for the rapid resolution of doubts and conflicts is a leading theme of Justinian's administration.
He was as impatient of prolonged controversy in law as in religion. The
methodical application of the term *decisio* to the settling of a limited number
of controveries among the ancient jurists is however Tribonianic.

OTHER PREPARATIONS

Apart from the settlement of disputed points of law, ancient law treatises
had to be collected, members of the commission appointed and assembled,
the time-table and method of work settled and the necessary working
documents prepared.

The books to be read and excerpted included all those classical works
which were regarded as authoritative according to the norms of the law of
citations, viz. the complete works of Papinian, Paul, Ulpian, Modestinus,
and Gaius and the authors cited by them, together with any other writings of
repute.[66] A priori no preference was to be given to one over another.[67] It
seems that many of the non-standard works came from Tribonian's private
library,[68] but others came from less accessible sources, presumably private
libraries outside Constantinople, and formed the nucleus of what was to be

---

[58] *Justinians Haltung* 336 n. 2.   [59] Ch. 3 n. 167.   [60] Ch. 3 n. 168.

[61] *C. Haec* 3 (13 Feb. 528); 7.64.10 pr. (6 April 529).   [62] *C. Haec* 3 (13 Feb. 528).

[63] *CJ* 1.14.12.4 (30 Oct. 529), 8.10.14.2 (18 Oct. 532).

[64] *C. Tanta* 1 (16 Dec. 530 *quia omnes disputationes et decisiones in se habent legitimas*—of
the *Digest*).

[65] *CJ* 3.33.13.4 (1 Oct. 530 *quam decisionem locum habere censemus*—the present constitution), 6.2.22.4b (17 Nov. 530 *ex praesente autem lege et anterioribus nostris decisionibus*),
6.27.5.1a (30 April 531 ? *nobis autem alius modus huiusmodi decisionis inventus est*), 6.27.6 (29
July 531 *decisione nostra quam fecimus* = 6.27.5), 6.51.1.10b (*secundum quod et in divinis
nostri numinis decisionibus statutum est* = 6.30.20). *C. Cordi* 1, 5 (16 Nov. 534 *tam quinquaginta decisiones fecimus quam alias ad commodum propositi operis pertinentes plurimas constitutiones promulgavimus . . . vel ex decisionibus nostris vel ex aliis constitutionibus quas antea fecimus*).

[66] *C. Deo. auctore* 4 (above, n. 8).

[67] *C. Deo auctore* 6. In particular, the views of Papinian were not to be automatically
preferred.

[68] *C. Tanta* 17 (16 Dec. 533).

called by modern scholars the Appendix.[69] This consists of writings received by the commission after 15 December 530, the official starting date for its work. The list of works belonging to the Appendix which was drawn up by Bluhme and Krueger is valuable but cannot be accepted *au pied de la lettre* because of possible transfers to or from the lists of works initially assigned to each committee.[70] We may say that it amounted to about a hundred books.

The total of books which we can identify as having been read by the commission comes to 1528,[71] a book being a conventional unit of composition, the notional length of a papyrus roll—a variable measure, but on the average about 1500 lines or 10,000 words. Tribonian puts the total at nearly two thousand books,[72] which is either an exaggeration or takes account of the preliminary work of reading different editions or versions of certain texts in order to select the best, and of reading and rejecting certain texts which contained nothing of interest or authority.

The extent to which the *Digest* was Tribonian's child is brought out by the fact that, in contrast with Theodosius' two commissions and Justinian's first, the quaestor was given a free choice as to the membership of the new commission.[73] Of this he took advantage. The composition of the commission was different from that of the previous bodies. Theodosius' commissions were entirely official,[74] his second had but one academic lawyer.[75] Justinian's first commission had one professor, Theophilus, and two barristers practising before the court of the praetorian prefect of the east, who at that time was Menas (not himself a commissioner).[76] By contrast the Tribonian commission consisted of six senior commissioners and eleven barristers.[77] Of the six, four were law professors, two from Constantinople[78] and two from Beirut,[79] the most celebrated centre of legal erudition. The balance was therefore quite different: predominantly professorial and practising. This was because the aims of the new commission were related to legal education and practice and required members who could read the Latin texts without difficulty. The *Digest* was meant to form the basis of a new law syllabus, intellectually superior and more attractive to students

---

[69] *Corp. Iur. Civ.* (Krueger-Mommsen) 2.931; Schulz, *Science* 320.

[70] *Trail* 535.   [71] *Commissioners* 251–3, 314.

[72] *C. Tanta* 1 (16 Dec. 533).   [73] *C. Deo auctore* 3 (15 Dec. 530).

[74] Seven officials or ex-officials and one barrister, Apelles: *CTh* 1.1.5 (26 March 429).

[75] Fourteen officials or ex-officials, one law teacher, Erotius, and one member, Neoterius, whose status cannot be determined: *CTh* 1.1.6.2 (20 Dec. 435).

[76] *C. Haec* 1 (13 Feb. 528 six officials or ex-officials: Iohannes, Leontius, Phocas, Basilides, Thomas, Constantinus; one 'awaiting portfolio': Tribonian; one professor: Theophilus; two barristers: Dioscorus and Praesentinus).

[77] *C. Tanta* 9 (16 Dec. 533 two officials: Tribonianus, Constantinus; four professors: Theophilus, Dorotheus, Anatolius, Cratinus; eleven barristers: Stephanus, Mena, Prosdocius, Eutolmius, Timotheus, Leonides, Leontius, Plato, Iacobus, Constantinus, Iohannes). See P. de Francisci, 'Dietro le quinte della compilazione Guistineanea', *Mélanges Meylan* (1963) 111; B. Kübler, 'Die Gehilfen Justinians bei der Kodification', *Acta cong. int. iur. Romae* 1 (1935) 17.

[78] Theophilus, Cratinus.   [79] Dorotheus, Anatolius.

than the old one, and also to provide a handbook for use at the bar, particularly before the higher courts. The necessary linguistic and technical qualifications for such an enterprise were to be found among those who had studied law at the leading schools. Since 460 these included all those practising before the court of the praetorian prefect of the east.[80] This accounts for the eleven barristers. They could read or help read the texts and give advice as to which rules of law were important in the daily life of the courts.[81] But they had no rank other than that of advocate, and their function was subordinate to that of the ranking commissioners. They were assistants.

The six illustrious commissioners could alone settle, subject to the overriding authority of Tribonian and Justinian, the detailed wording of the authentic *Digest* text. Three of the six had been on the first commission, three were new. The old hands were Tribonian himself, Constantine,[82] master of petitions and imperial trials, and Theophilus, professor of law in Constantinople and responsible for legal studies in that city, whom we may without too great anachronism call the dean of the metropolitan law faculty.[83] The new faces included Cratinus, a junior colleague of Theophilus, and two teachers of distinguished repute from Beirut, Dorotheus[84] (who in the event became Tribonian's chief collaborator) and Anatolius,[85] whose father and grandfather had both been professors of law, and who was expert in the interpretation of texts. In this way half the strength of the two law faculties was consumed, there being eight professors in all,[86] and the two leading law ministers were saddled with extra burdens, as were the eleven barristers practising before the leading court. This made the detailed time-table important.

Though *Deo auctore* does not lay down a time schedule, it seems clear that Justinian would not have authorised the project unless Tribonian had agreed to work to a fixed programme and to complete the work in three years. Leading lawyers could be spared no longer. Even as it was, arrangements were made to ensure that the operations of government, practice at the bar, and legal education were disrupted no more than need be.[87] Tribonian was a man of consuming energy, comparable with Justinian himself. He simply cumulated his work on the commission with his normal duties as quaestor until he lost the latter post in January 532. Constantinus

---

[80] *CJ* 2.7.11.2 (1 Feb. 460).   [81] *C. Deo auctore* 10 (15 Dec. 533); above, n. 14.

[82] *C. Haec* 1 (13 Feb. 528), *C. Summa* 1 (6 April 529), *C. Tanta* 9 (16 Dec. 533); Stein, *Deux questeurs* n. 24; *Progress* n. 34.

[83] *C. Tanta* 9 (16 Dec. 533 *in hac splendidissima civitate laudabiliter optimam legum gubernationem extendentem*); *RE* 2.5.2138. The argument of Alan Cameron, 'The end of the ancient universities', *Cahiers d'histoire mondiale* 10 (1966–7) 635 against the existence of faculty organisation is overstated; cf. *C. Omnem* 10 (16 Dec. 533).

[84] *RE* 5.1572.   [85] *RE* 1.2073.

[86] *C. Omnem* inscription (16 Dec. 533) lists Theophilus, Dorotheus, Theodorus, Isodorus, Anatolius, Thalelaeus, Cratinus, Salaminus.

[87] *CTh* 1.1.6.3 (20 Dec. 435) provided for substitutes to be chosen by the emperor in case of ill health or public business. But substitutes have to learn routine from scratch.

was given a reduced stint during the first eighteen months: five-sevenths of the number of books allotted to the main body of senior commissioners.[88] The same applied to Cratinus, who continued some of his lectures to students in Constantinople.[89] The Beirut professors could not of course perform their academic duties, in view of the distance between Constantinople and Beirut. As to the barristers, their work was arranged so that their practice could continue, and account was taken of the judicial holiday period.[90]

For the excerpting to begin, two working documents were needed. The first was a list of the ancient works to be read by each of the three committees into which Tribonian divided the commission. The list of books was to be read and excerpted in a given order and at a given pace, namely one book per day for the Sabinian and edictal committees and five books a week for the Papinian committee.[91] The books to be read were further divided into groups and the excerpts were to be handed in group by group on or before the appropriate day.[92] Thus the Papinian committee had to begin by reading a group of works consisting of the *quaestiones, responsa* and *definitiones* of Papinian, amounting to 58 books, for which the allowance was seven-fifths of 58, viz. 81 days. Counting 15 December 530 as the first day, the excerpts from these works were therefore due on 5 March 531.[93]

The first working document therefore corresponds largely to the *Ordo Librorum Iuris Veteris in compilandis digestis Observatus* which, on the basis of Bluhme's reconstruction of the committees, and subject to Krueger's amendments, is printed in the stereotype editions of the *Digest* as Additamenta 1.[94] This may be called the Bluhme-Krueger Ordo (or BK Ordo). The actual working document differed in that the works were, as will be explained, assembled in groups to be read successively in accordance with a time-table which was perhaps also incorporated in the working document.[95]

The second working document was a list of titles or subject-headings into which the fragments excerpted were to be distributed. This list, as instructed by *Deo auctore*,[96] followed the classifications of the *Codex Iustinianus* and of the perpetual edict, whichever appeared most appropriate. It was needed because the assignment into titles was done group by group as the work of reading proceeded. The final version of the *Digest* contains 432 titles.[97] It may be guessed that the initial list was of about the same length, but naturally modification was sometimes called for, whether by way of addition, deletion or amalgamation, as the excerpting went on.[98]

---

[88] *Trail* 532. [89] Ibid. 533. [90] Ibid. 537–41. [91] Ibid. 531f.
[92] *Commissioners* 285–313. [93] *Trail* 537.
[94] *Corp. Iur. Civ.* (Krueger-Mommsen) 1. 874–8.
[95] This is reconstructed in *Trail* 538–41.
[96] *C. Deo auctore* 5 (16 Dec. 530 above, n. 9).
[97] *Distribution* 354. This is to count books 30, 31 and 32 as separate titles. Since books 31 and 32 are continuations of the title *de legatis et fideicommissis* it can be argued that the total is really 430.
[98] A. Soubie, *Recherches sur les Origines des rubriques du Digeste* (1960).

C. Deo auctore says that the members of the commission have been 'introduced into our palace'[99] and *C. Tanta* that they 'came together'.[100] Perhaps a large room in Justinian's palace was assigned to Tribonian and his helpers. Files or boxes were needed for each title, so that as the excerpting progressed each committee was able to put its contributions separately into the appropriate container in the order in which they had been read and excerpted. The precise physical mechanism employed is not known.[101]

THE EXCERPTING

In a study published in 1820 the young Bluhme discovered that the works from which the *Digest* is compiled were read in four 'masses'.[102] The evidence on which he relied is derived from the inscriptions to the texts. These give the author, work and book from which each text is taken, for instance 'Iulianus libro decimo digestorum'. The sequence in which the inscriptions follow one another is found to be regular as regards 83.6 per cent of the texts; in other words only one text in six fails to conform to a regular order.[103] This regularity is not however an overall regularity but rather a regular sequence of inscriptions within four groups of works which we may christen A, E, P and S.[104] As between the groups the sequence varies from title to title, and not all groups are represented in every title. Thus the order may be SEPA, EPS, SPAE, ES, SEP etc. It is as if the titles were hands of cards in which, so far as five cards out of every six were concerned, the player, when he looked at his cards, found that they were arranged in suits and, within each suit, in numerical order, but that in some hands hearts came first, in others spades and so on. Bluhme interpreted the 'suits' as masses and, within each suit, the numerical order as the order in which the commissioners were to read the works assigned to them. He then postulated that each mass was assigned to a different committee, except that the fourth mass, the so-called post-Papinian mass or Appendix, went to the Papinian committee. His reason for this exception is sound: the fourth mass seldom comes in any position other than immediately after the Papinian

---

99 *C. Deo auctore* 3 (15 Dec. 530).

100 *C. Tanta* 9 (16 Dec. 533) *et cum omnes in unum convenerunt gubernatione Triboniani viri excelsi ut tantum opus nobis auctoribus possint conficere, deo propitio in praedictos quinquaginta libros opus comsummatum est*). The Latin text here takes on a miraculous character which is absent from the Greek: *C. Δέδωκεν* 9.

101 Whatever it was, it was such that the texts remained in order while in the container but could be scattered when taken out of it. *Editing* 265 n. 11.

102 F. Bluhme, 'Die Ordnung der Fragments in den Pandektentiteln', 4 *ZGR* (1820) 257f. = 6 Labeo (1960) 50f. The background is given in V. Savigny, *Briefwechsel mit Friedrich Bluhme 1820–60* (ed. Strauch 1962) nos. 1–4. Precedents for the compiler's methods: F. Schulz, *Atti cong. int. dir. Rom-Roma* II (1935) 11.

103 Of a possible 8695 displaceable texts 1419 are displaced: *Editing* 263. The displaced texts are analysed according to book, title and category at 284–304.

104 The editio maior of the *Digest* by Mommsen and the stereotype Krueger-Mommsen edition of the *Corpus Iuris* record the sequence of masses for each title and use these letters. There are a few mistakes: *Editing* 285f., footnotes.

mass. Bluhme named the committees the Sabinian, edictal and Papinian committees after the initial works in the three main groups. These names, together with his explanation of the fourth mass as an appendix of works discovered after the excerpting had begun,[105] have been generally accepted.

Bluhme's work has resisted all attempts at critical demolition.[106] It contains the essential clues to the organisation both of the excerpting and of the assembly of the excerpts into titles. The study of the five-sixths of the texts which come in a regular sequence forms the evidence on which we can elucidate the process of excerpting. The remaining one-sixth of the texts provides the basis for a study of the editorial process.

Our understanding of Tribonian's method remained virtually in the state in which Bluhme left it for a century and a half. In the summer of 1969, however, I was prompted by certain questions put by Alan Rodger to pursue the investigation where Bluhme left it off. With the help of Lenel's *Palingenesia* I counted the number of lines excerpted from each work and book in the BK Ordo, whose accuracy I provisionally assumed. From the resulting count the rate of excerpting per book could be fixed, and I hoped that the rhythm of excerpting by the different committees would emerge from this. It did, but the information threw no light on the internal organisation of the committees.[107] Progress with this was made only when the figures for certain works read concurrently by the commissioners were analysed from the point of view of the use of sources.

Bluhme noticed that certain works (for instance Ulpian and Paul on the edict and Gaius on the provincial edict) were excerpted concurrently, not successively. The evidence for this is that appropriate extracts from Paul and Gaius are woven into, not appended to, the relevant parts of Ulpian's work, sometimes in the form of a chain of texts, sometimes not. Bluhme further established the sections or slices of edictal commentary into which the committee split the three main edictal works for purposes of excerpting:

[105] Bluhme, 4 *ZGR* (1820) 257, 317–18.

[106] Notably by F. Hofmann, 'Die Compilation der Digesten Justinians', *Kritische Studien* (1900), rebutted by Th. Mommsen, *ZSS* 22 (1901) 1; P. Krueger, ibid. 11; P. Jörs, *RE* 5 (1905) 496; G. Longo, *BIDR* 19 (1907) 132; P. Bonfante, *Storia del dir. rom.* (1909) 607, 620. H. Peter, Mommsen versus Hofmann, *Mélanges Meylan* (1963) 253, is psychologically interesting but does not shake the refutation. Most recently P. Pescani, *Il piano del Digesto* (c. 2 n. 107) 241–67 tries to show that the recension of *leges geminae* would not vary in the way they do if Bluhme's committees had excerpted the texts. But the variations were introduced at the editorial not the excerpting stage (below, n. 153) and each book was edited separately (n. 168f.). So *leges geminae* may be expected to appear in slightly different versions in different books. When they appear twice in the same title (*D.* 23.3.80, 83; 24.3. 24.4, 62; 42.1.6 pr., 18; 17.2.52.4, 61) the explanation is that a secretarial mistake has occurred. The editors have wished to shift a text from one position in the title to another and the secretaries have left in both versions. See Honoré, 'Labeo's *posteriora* and the *Digest* commission', *Daube Noster*, ed. Watson (1974), 172.

[107] The rhythm of excerpting indirectly throws light on the pattern in which the titles were later edited: below, pp. 183–4. Bluhme did not think the work was subdivided within the committees (*ZGR* 257, 339). Wieacker argues for single-handed excerpting of the works like the edictal commentaries which concern the same subject-matter: *ZSS* 89 (1972) n. 131.

these sections are set out in the BK Ordo. Thus, Ulpian ed. books 1–6 together with Paul ed. books 1–5, Gaius ed. prov. book 1 and Callistratus ed. mon. book 1 init. forms the first section of edictal commentary; Ulpian ed. book 7, Paul ed. book 6–7 and Gaius ed. prov. book 2 from the second section, and so on. The edictal committee's first assignment was divided into fourteen sections of edictal commentary taken from the earlier books on the edict; their second assignment was a further twenty-five such slices taken from the latest books on the edict. If the number of lines excerpted per book is studied section by section it emerges that the balance of sources differs between the even- and odd-numbered sections. In particular the odd-numbered sections of edictal commentary excerpted by the edictal committee give considerably more weight to Paul's commentary relatively to Ulpian's than the even-numbered sections. The following table will make the matter clear. It analyses the excerpts made by the compilers from the early part of the various edictal commentaries.

(a) Odd-numbered sections (7)

Total	$38\frac{1}{2}$ books	7050 lines	182.3 lines/book
Ulpian	$15\frac{1}{2}$,,	4487 ,,	289.5 ,,
Paul	$17\frac{1}{2}$,,	1893 ,,	108.2 ,,
Gaius	$4\frac{1}{6}$,,	602 ,,	144.5 ,,
Paul/Ulpian	%	42.2 ,,	37.4 ,,
Gaius/Ulpian	%	13.4 ,,	49.9 ,,
Gaius/Paul	%	31.8 ,,	133.5 ,,

(b) Even-numbered sections (7)

Total	$25\frac{1}{12}$ books	5472 lines	218.2 lines/book
Ulpian	$9\frac{1}{2}$,,	3872 ,,	407.6 ,,
Paul ed.	$9\frac{1}{2}$,,	1052 ,,	110.7 ,,
Gaius	$4\frac{1}{3}$,,	523 ,,	120.6 ,,
Paul/Ulpian	%	27.2 ,,	27.2 ,,
Gaius/Ulpian	%	13.5 ,,	29.6 ,,
Gaius/Paul	%	49.6 ,,	108.9 ,,

The next 21 sections of edictal commentary excerpted by the edictal committee yield a similar source analysis:

(a) Odd-numbered sections (11)

Total	$38\frac{1}{2}$ books	4702 lines	123.5 books/line
Ulpian	$15\frac{1}{2}$,,	3442 ,,	222.0 ,,
Paul	$16\frac{1}{2}$,,	1071 ,,	64.9 ,,
Gaius	$6\frac{1}{12}$,,	165 ,,	27.1 ,,
Paul/Ulpian	%	31.1 ,,	29.2 ,,
Gaius/Ulpian	%	4.8 ,,	12.2 ,,
Gaius/Paul	%	15.4 ,,	41.8 ,,

(b) Even-numbered sections (10)

Total	$25\frac{2}{3}$ books	4383 lines	170.7 lines/book	
Ulpian	$10\frac{1}{2}$,,	3708 ,,	353.1	,,
Paul	$10\frac{1}{2}$,,	580 ,,	55.2	,,
Gaius	$4\frac{2}{3}$,,	95 ,,	20.3	,,
Paul/Ulpian	%	15.6 ,,	15.6	,,
Gaius/Ulpian	%	2.6 ,,	5.7	,,
Gaius/Paul	%	16.4 ,,	36.8	,,

The most significant test of the selection of sources by the compilers consists of the percentage which the number of lines per book taken from one author forms of the number of lines per book taken from another. The figures for both lines and lines per book are given under Paul/Ulpian etc. They show that the preference for Paul against Ulpian is higher in the odd-than in the even-numbered sections (37.4 against 27.2 and 29.2 against 15.5). Such a consistent preference as between the two major authors represented in the *Digest* suggests that the excerpting of the edictal commentaries by the edictal committee was carried on by two different teams or sub-committees, one of which had a greater relative inclination towards Paul's contributions than the other.

Once this hypothesis was formed it proved possible to test it in a much simpler way. If we turn from the works excerpted jointly by the commissioners to those excerpted separately, it is detectable from the lists established by Bluhme and Krueger that successive works often fall into *groups* made up of two *lots* each consisting of an equal number of books. A *group* here means a set of works numbered successively in the BK Ordo. For purposes of identification the whole BK Ordo has been divided into groups numbered from I to XLIII, as set out in Appendix 1. A lot is a subdivision of a group allotted to a particular commissioner or team as his or their task. A simple example is:

Group III   10. Ulp. 10 disputationes
             11. Ulp. 10 omnium tribunalium
Group IV   12. Ulp. 6 opinionum
             13. Ulp. 6 de censibus

Here the ordinals 10, 11 etc. are those of the relevant works in the BK Ordo. They come from the list of works assigned to the Sabinian committee. It is easy to see how, on the supposal that the committee excerpted in two subcommittees, the first was responsible for the ten books of Ulpian's *disputationes*, the second for the ten books of Ulpian on *omnia tribunalia*, the first again for the six books of Ulpian's *opiniones*,[108] the second for his six books *de censibus*. Each of these works forms, in our terminology, a lot.

It soon became clear that the whole BK Ordo was susceptible of analysis into groups of works and that each group could be subdivided into lots,

[108] Not in fact written by Ulpian: Schulz, *Science* 182.

which, in the case of works excerpted separately, consist of an exactly equal number of books. The examples so far given are simple. Other groups have a more complex structure; otherwise the phenomenon would long ago have been noticed. For example, the first work in a group may consist of a given number of books, and this work may be followed by two or more works which together make up the same number of books as the first.

Here is an example from the Papinian committee:

XXXV 216. Venuleius   19 stip.
      217. Neratius   3 resp.
      218. Paul   4 Nerat.
      219. Tryphoninus disp. 1–12

There can be no doubt that this is intended as a group, because it ends in the middle of the 21 books of Tryphoninus. The break occurs in the middle of family law, between *de iure dotium* and *de tutelis*. So it is not the subject-matter which dictated a pause at book 12 of his *disputationes*. The reason can only be that with the twelfth book a group of 38 books had been constituted which fell into two lots of 19.

The pattern can be a little more complicated when a variant is introduced. Instead of the first work containing a number of books equal to all the remainder, the first two works do so. For example, the last group of the appendix is as follows:

XLIII 269. Pomp. 20 epist.
       270. Pomp. 5 SCC.
       271. Scae. 1 qu. pub. tract.
       272. Val. 7 act.
       273. Venul. 10 act.
       274. Venul. 6 interd.
       275. Fur. Anth. 1 ed.

The first two works by Pomponius comprise 25 books, the remainder together make up 25. There is some attempt here to group according to authorship. There is another example of this pattern in group xxv.

In another pattern the group is made up of works which together amount to a given number of books followed by a work containing that given number of books. An example is the group which ends the Sabinian list. This group begins at the works *de officiis* (88f.).

XVII 88. Ulp. 1 off. cur. reip.
      89. Ulp. 1 off. cons.
      90. Paul 2 off. proc.
      91. Venul. 4 off. proc.
      92. Sat. 1 poen. pag.
      93. Maec. 1 leg. Rhod.
      94. Iav. 10 post. Lab.

The grouping pays some attention to subject-matter, since all the undigested Sabinian works on *officia* are put together. But two odd *libri singulares* are thrown in to make up the number of ten and so balance the ten-book work of Iavolenus.

Tribonian did not hesitate to depart from the criterion of subject-matter in order to form a numerically correct grouping. Thus Ulpian 10 *off. proc.* is not placed with 90 and 91 where, on grounds of subject, it ought to find a place, but is at 47 where it completes a group.

XI   43. Paul 7 reg.
      44. Marci. reg. lib. 5
      45. Pomp. 1 reg.
      46. Ulp. 1 reg.
      47. Ulp. 10 off. proc.

As will be shown, 43 must be the beginning of a group, because of the break which occurs at 42 Marcian 4 *reg.* Hence the reason for putting Ulpian's treatise on the proconsul in, so to speak, the wrong place is to balance the ten books of *regulae* beginning with Paul.

A simple example from the Papinian committee is:

XXXIX 245. Gai. 3 manum.
      246. Gai. 3 verb. obl.
      247. Gai. 6 leg. XII tab.

Here is an example from the edictal mass. After a short group of works *de re militari* (171–2) we come to:

XXIX 173. Tert. 1 cast. pec.
      174. Mod. 4 poen.
      175. Lic. Ruf. 13 reg.
      176. Call. ed. mon. 3–4
      177. Papirius Iust. 20 const.

Here a group of twenty miscellaneous works, including a bit of a larger work by Callistratus, is balanced by a twenty-book treatise of Papirius Iustus. The fact that the first two books of Callistratus *ed. mon.* were included in the first group digested by the edictal commission (95–100), while the last half of his work comes nearly at the end, is an argument for the view that the grouping was arranged by the edictal commissioners at the outset, not left to be made up while the work was in progress.

The Sabinian committee too adopted this pattern:

XII   48. Paul 1 SC Sil.
      49. Paul 1 port. lib. damn.
      50. Paul 2 leg. Iul.

51. Paul 1 conc. form.
52. Macer 2 pub. iud.
53. Venul. 3 iud. pub.
54. Paul 1 pub. iud.
55. Marci. 2 pub. iud.
56. Maec. 14 pub. iud.

The group ends with the last of the works on *publica iudicia*. The basis of groupings is partly the subject-matter, but in order to balance the 14 books of Maecianus some minor works of Paul are introduced. In the list above, one such work is missing and must be supplied from the list in the index Florentinus in order to make up the full lot of 14 books.

In another variant the work whose number of books together equals the other is placed in the middle, in a 'sandwich' position. In this case the order in which the excerpts were submitted to the commission is different from the order in which they were assigned to the commissioners and, of course, very likely different again from the order, inaccessible to us, in which they were actually read. To explain this one must postulate a committee chairman, responsible for the first lot in each group, and a second commissioner, responsible for the second. In the normal way the two commissioners finish their task more or less simultaneously. The second lot of texts excerpted is handed to the chairman who files them and distributes them into titles after his own lot. But sometimes the second commissioner finishes earlier and hands his extracts to his senior colleague, who puts them between the excerpts from the earlier and later parts of his own assignment. Such a sandwich arrangement only occurs when the whole of the junior colleague's lot is intercalated in this way; and this shows that the junior could not submit an incomplete fraction of his lot, while on the other hand the chairman might, if he wished, divide his own lot into two parts for the purpose of submitting extracts to the director.

Such a sandwich arrangement is of course only possible if the chairman has been allotted more than one work to digest. Here is an example from the appendix:

XLI   263. Paul 6 sent. imp.
         264. Q. Mucius 1 horon.
         265. Labeo 10 post. Iav. epit.
         266. Proc. 3 post. Lab.

Here the chairman is responsible for 263, 264 and 266. His colleague finishes 265 after the chairman has finished 264 but before he finishes 266. Hence it is possible to insert Labeo's work, which from the point of view of assignment is item 266, at 265.

Group XXII presents an intricate example of a sandwich not easy to unravel at first glance. The edictal committee has adopted the following order:

XXIII	141. Mod. 1 diff. dot.	5 lines
	142. (Mod. 6 exc.	628 lines
	143. (Ulp. 1 off. pr. tut.	19 lines
	144. (Ulp. 1 exc.	8 lines
	146. Mod. 19 resp.	839 lines
	147. Mod. 1 enuc. cas.	34 lines
	148. Mod. 1 praescr.	29 lines
	149. Mod. 12 pand.	385 lines

This is a group of 42 books. The first commissioner had to read 141–4 and 149, of which 142–4 were digested jointly. The second commissioner was assigned 146–8. But the latter finished his 21 books before his colleague had reached the end of Mod. 12 *pand.* So his contribution was inserted in the middle.

The number of lines excerpted from each work has been inserted in order to show why the sandwich situation arose. The first commissioner took 1045 lines from the works entrusted to him, the second 902. The former took 385 lines from his last work, the *pandectae* of Modestinus. Consequently, he was unlikely to have finished the *pandectae* before his junior colleague, but would probably come to the end of the other work entrusted to him. We see not merely why a sandwich is possible but where exactly the filling must come.

The following group XXIV is also a sandwich.

The fact that works appear in the list away from the place which subject-matter would suggest is a valuable clue to the composition of a group. Thus, why does Paul 2 *de iure fisci* appear at 133 when it ought to be grouped with Callistratus 4 *de iure fisci* (158) if subject-matter were the criterion? To see the answer we must analyse the list from 124, the beginning of a group of works *ad Plautium*.

XX	124. Paul ad Plaut. 1–14
	125. Iav. ad Plaut. 1
	126. Pomp. ad Plaut. 1
	127. Iav. ad Plaut. 2
	128. Pomp. ad Plaut. 2–3
	129. Paul ad Plaut. 15–18
	130. Iav. ad Plaut. 3–5
	131. Pomp. ad Plaut. 4–7
	132. Paul 4 ad Vitellium
	133. Paul 2 de iure fisci.

This is a little more complicated, but the clue is that at 127 to 131 the works *ad Plautium* were digested in a different order from 124 to 126. If we label the edictal commissioners C and D, C undertook 124 to 126, a total of 16 books. D was assigned 127 to 131, a total of 14 books. So D was two books short. D was therefore given *ad Vitellium* (132), but this would have left him in turn two in excess of C. This is the explanation of the displacement of Paul 2 *de iure* Lsci. It was brought in at 133 to be added to C's quota and so to fill up the proper number of books, 36 in all, of which 18 were assigned to each commissioner. After 133 the list goes on to a new group, viz. the *digesta* of Celsus and Marcellus. Paul's *de iure fisci* is therefore introduced not because it has any real connection with the surrounding works but simply as ballast.

The existence of breaks in the process of digesting which are, from the point of view of subject-matter, arbitrary is a help in detecting the composition and limits of the different groups. This is because these apparently arbitrary breaks generally end one group and mark the beginning of the next. An example from the *disputationes* of Tryphoninus has been mentioned already.[109] After the break at Tryph. 12 *disp.* there are nine books of his left and these are made into a group as follows:

XXXVI   220. Paul 3 man.
         221. Tryph. disp. 13–21
         222. Paul 3 decr.
         223. Gai. 3 reg.

The remaining nine books of Tryphoninus are balanced by three works containing three books each. This group illustrates the 'sandwich' form.

An interesting and complicated example of an apparently arbitrary break comes in the *epistulae* of Proculus. Thus we find:

         155. Proc. epist. 1–6
         156. Pomp. 15 var. lect.
         157. Proc. epist. 7–11

For the reasons mentioned 155 must be the end of a group. No considerations of subject-matter could dictate a break between the sixth and seventh books of Proculus' *epistulae*. So we read on from 156:

XXV   156. Pomp. 15 var. lect.
         157. Proc. epist. 7–11
         158. Call. 4 iur. fisc.
         159. Paul 2 cens.
         160. Call. 6 cogn.
         161. Tertull. 8 quaest.

After that we come to a different group of books *ad legem Iuliam et Papiam* which was digested jointly. Our group consists of 40 books, of which 156 and 157 make up 20, while 158 to 161 make up another lot of 20. We have incidentally confirmed that the compilers had available exactly eleven books of the *epistulae* of Proculus, not eight as stated by the Florentine index, or some larger number than the eleven attested in the inscriptions.[110]

[109] Above, p. 17.   [110] *Pal.* 2.159 n. 2.

It remains to show the composition of the group preceding the one just studied, viz. the group ending at 155. The work preceding 155 Proc. *epist*. 1–6 is Pomponius 39 *ad Q. Mucium*. We must therefore look for a lot which balances the 39 books of Pomponius. Reading Krüger's list backwards we find that 149 Mod. 12 *pand*. must be excluded and so the proper point at which to start is 150:

XXIV 150. Mod. 1 de heuremat.
      151. Mod. 1 de inoff. test.
      152. Iav. 15 ex Cass.
      153. Iav. 14 epist.
      154. Pomp. 39 ad Q. Mucium
      155. Proc. epist. 1–6

The group so formed appears unsatisfactory, since there are only 31 books in the works listed at 150 to 153, which, together with the six books of Proculus' epistles, make up 37 instead of the 39 required to balance Pomp. 39 *ad Q. Mucium*. This cannot be right, because if the group had been so composed the commissioners would have interrupted the digesting of Proculus after the eighth book, not the sixth. Nor would it be an adequate explanation that the commissioners did not bother about the difference between 37 and 39 books, that Commissioner D of the edictal committee did not mind doing two extra books. The matter was governed by a directive rather than by personal preference.

The explanation is that the two *libri singulares* of Modestinus listed in the Florentine index but of which no extracts appear in the *Digest* ought to be brought in at this point. Quite apart from the theory here advocated the proper place for these two *libri singulares* is next to 151 Mod. 1 *de inoff. test*., to which they are cognate in point of length, authorship and subject-matter. The sequence should run:

      151. Mod. 1 de inoff. test.
      151a. Mod. 1 de legatis et fideicommissis.
      151b. Mod. 1 de testamentis.

Once this independently justifiable insertion is made there is a group of 78 books from 150 to 155 divided into two lots of 39 books each. The second commissioner's contribution of extracts from Pomp. 39 *ad Q. Mucium* has been inserted in the sandwich position presumably because he finished the whole of his work after his senior colleague had completed 153 but before the latter had finished 155.

The *regulae* of Marcianus also provide an example of a work which was digested in apparently arbitrary sections. It was handled by the Sabinian committee together with the *regulae* of Neratius, Paul, Ulpian and Scaevola at 36 to 44. But whereas the latter works were each digested as a whole, with no break, the *regulae* of Maecianus were taken in three parts, viz. 40

lib. 1–2, 42 lib. 3–4, and 44 lib. 5. These breaks cannot be explained on the basis of subject-matter since otherwise the *regulae* of Neratius etc. would necessarily have been divided in a corresponding way. Instead, the divisions are made in order to mark the end of a group:

IX	36.	Nerat. 15 reg.
	37.	Ulp. 7 reg.
	38.	Scae. 4 reg.
	39.	Paul 1 reg.
	40.	Marci. reg. 1–2
X	41.	Ulp. 2 resp.
	42.	Marci. reg. 3–4
XI	43.	Paul 7 reg.
	44.	Marci. reg. 5
	45.	Pomp. 1 reg.
	46.	Ulp. 1 reg.
	47.	Ulp. 10 off. proc.

We have already studied group XI. Group IX appears defective since the works listed at 37 to 40 amount to only 14 against the 15 books by Neratius. Again, it will not do to say that the commissioners did not mind about the difference of one book. The explanation is rather that there is a book missing at or about 39, viz. Gaius 1 *reg.* which, under Krüger's scheme, stands at 224 in the Papinian mass. As Krüger notes, the proper location cannot be determined from the only surviving fragment (*D.* 1.7.21) and we are therefore free to put it at an equally or more appropriate point, next to Paul 1 *reg.* If we read:

39.	Paul 1 reg.
39a.	Gai. 1 reg.
40.	Marci. reg. 1–2

group IX consists of 30 books, 15 by Neratius and 15 by other authors. Group X provides another good example of a work listed out of its proper context. Ulp. 2 *resp.* has no connection from the point of view of subject-matter with the series of *regulae* into which it is inserted. Its place there is due solely to the need to balance two books of Marcianus. When these two were disposed of there was a residue of ten books of *regulae*, including the final book of Marcianus, to balance the ten books of Ulpian on the proconsul.

The examples we have examined from the *disputationes* of Tryphoninus, the *epistulae* of Proculus and *regulae* of Marcianus show that each of the three committees employed the device of splitting a work to be digested at a point determined not for any reason of subject-matter but in order to make up an appropriate even number of books, under the influence, perhaps, of the division of the works into codices.

It is too much to expect that the groupings will always appear on the face of Krüger's list. Sometimes we must take account of other factors, in particular the rate of excerpting, as it appears from the Palingenesia. This is important when we come to consider certain important works which, as they stand in Krüger's list, do not seem to fall into any group.

The *quaestiones* of Papinian was the first work entrusted to the Papinian committee and it, together with Papinian's other works, was treated separately, not in conjunction with the corresponding works of Paul and Scaevola. Thus we have at the start of the Papinian mass:

XXXI   180. Pap. 37 quaest.
        181. Pap. 19 resp.
        182. Pap. 2 def.

At first sight these works do not fall into two equal lots, but when we look at the detailed statistics for the *quaestiones* of Papinian we find that they do.

The total number of lines taken from the *quaestiones* is 3333, giving an average of 90.1 lines for each of the 37 books. But a radical change in the volume of material taken occurs at the end of book 29. Thus:

Papinian: *quaestiones*
Books 20–9   227, 44, 37, 107, 6, 15, 55, 273, 237, 162 lines
Books 30–7   14, 23, 25, 8, 2, 22, 70, 38 lines

Notice that the ten books up to book 29 are well up to the average for the work as a whole. There are in fact 1163 lines of extract averaging 116.3 lines per book, and the last three books up to book 29 are all above the average. After book 29 a dramatic change takes place. The number of lines per book falls to 25.25 per book (202 lines for 8 books).

This is rather surprising, since the *quaestiones* was the first work to be digested by the Papinian committee. *C. Omnem* s.4 stresses the importance of reading the *quaestiones* as well as the *responsa* of Papinian. Why was there such a hurry? The puzzle increases when we look at the figures for the *responsa* and *definitiones*:

31. Pap. 19 resp.   3050 lines   av. 160.5
32. Pap. 2 def.   220 lines   av. 110.0

Immediately after the rush to finish the *quaestiones*, there was apparently plenty of time to make copious extracts from the *responsa* and *definitiones*.

The solution is that Papinian's works 180 to 182 form a group of 58 books divided for numerical reasons into two lots of 29 books each. The first 29 books of the *quaestiones* were allotted to E. F was assigned the last 8 books, together with Papinian's *responsa* and *definitiones*. E worked in a steady and orderly way. F, perhaps because the last 8 books of the *quaestiones* were bound in the same codex as some of the previous volumes, so that E had possession of these books to begin with, started on the *responsa* and *definitiones*. When E had finished his 29 books F had still to read his 8 books of *quaestiones*. Hence he did this part of his work in a great hurry.

The statistics set out on the previous page repay study. They display a pattern which the commissioners often repeated. When they were approaching the end of an assignment, and were pressed for time, there would come a point at which the rate of extraction per book dropped to a minimum. For E this point occurs at books 24–5, and for F at books 33–4. Then, in the very last book or books the rate picks up again, since the commissioner now knows that he is going to reach the end in time. This pick-up point occurred for E at books 27–9 and for F at books 36–7. The phenomenon is of course relative. F's pick-up effort still leaves him at a very low rate in comparison with E. But the phenomenon should be recognised because it can be used to determine the place at which a group or lot ends.

A still more striking example of a 'collapse' in the rate of extracting is to be found in the *digesta* of Iulianus. The 90 books of this work yielded in all 4425 lines, average 49.2 lines per book. But the first 62 books gave 4102 lines in all, average 66.16, while the last 28 provided only 323 lines at an average of 11.54. To appreciate the point fully it is necessary to set out the figures book by book beginning at book 50:

Iulianus: *digesta*
Books 50–62   9, 49, 146, 45, 103, 38, 66, 49, 15, 28, 74, 97, 97 lines
Books 63–90   3, 45, 22, 0, 0, 0, 21, 27, 0, 0, 7, 0, 0, 0, 4, 45, 0, 8, 5, 14, 5, 16, 2, 67, 3, 5, 3, 11 lines

The last 13 books from 50 to 62 were digested in a perfectly orderly way and produced 816 lines at an average of 62.76 per book. As in the case of the *quaestiones* of Papinian, the last three books yielded rather more material than the average. But after book 62 a most dramatic collapse takes place, and scant justice is done to the last 28 books of the great jurist whose works the commissioners themselves placed at the head of the index Florentinus.

The *digesta* of Iulianus belong to a group stretching from 14 to 20 which is followed by a group of institutional works which were extracted jointly. Thus:

v	14. Iulianus 90 dig.	4429 lines
	15. Alfenus Varus 7 epit.	389 lines
	16. Paul 8 epit. Alfeni	442 lines
	17. Iulianus 1 ambig.	90 lines
	18. Iulianus 4 Urs. Feroc.	351 lines
	19. Iulianus 6 Minic.	256 lines
	20. Africanus 9 quaest.	1902 lines

The total number of books in this group is 125, and it was split 62 and 63. One can perhaps regard this group as a very minor exception to the principle of equal division of labour, since the second Sabinian commissioner B had one more book to read than A. A's assignment was the first 62 books of Iulianus' *digesta*. B's consisted of the last 28 books, plus the other works down to and including Africanus. B began with the other works, perhaps because the division into codices was such that A initially possessed the whole of the *digesta*. From these he made copious extracts amounting to 3430 lines from 35 books, average 98.0 lines per book. By this time A had completed his 62 books, from which he took 4106 lines, average 66.2 lines per book. B was 28 books in arrear, and was compelled to skim over the last 28 books of the *digesta* at lightning speed, copying a few lines here and there.

In the appendix too there is a group the composition of which can only be understood from a survey of the number of lines taken from each book. Between the end of group XL and the beginning of group XLII there intervene 48 books, 40 books of Scaevola's *digesta* and 8 of Paul's epitome of Labeo's *pithanon*. How are these 48 books grouped? One possible division would be between Scae. 24 and 25 *dig*. But this is not how the commissioners have arranged the work. They have made two breaks in Scaevola's *digesta*, at the end of books 13 and 29. The figures for lines taken from each book are:

Scaevola: *digesta*
- (i) bks 1–13: 69, 49, 10, 48, 142, 43, 118, 9, 32, 30, 52, 0, 6
- (ii) bks 14–29: 74, 176, 260, 197, 260, 118, 227, 276, 359, 59, 111, 70, 47, 86, 121, 58
- (iii) bks 30–40: 4, 26, 11, 33, 9, 0, 0, 0, 0, 0, 0

From the first 13 books 608 lines were taken at an average of 46.8 per book. From the next 16, 2499 lines were taken, average 156.2. The next eleven yield only 83 lines, average 7.5. Such a strange pattern could hardly arise if one person was responsible for the whole 40 books, or even for the first 29. Instead, the commissioner who undertook the first 13 books also did the last eleven, very hastily. His colleague read the middle part in a conscientious way and made copious extracts from them. A break is made at books 13–14 for reasons of subject-matter. At book 14 the treatment of legacies and *fideicommissa* begins. These continue into the early part of book 23. But the style does not change radically until book 29 is finished (*de stipulationibus*). The break at book 29 marks the end of the junior commissioner's quota. The reason for the 'collapse' in the last eleven books may partly be preoccupation of the chairman with editorial and official business, partly the division of the *digesta* into codices, which may have meant that the chairman did not have these books available to him while his colleague was reading books 14–29.

The group is composed as follows:

XLII	267. sect. (i)	Scaevola 40 dig. bks 1–13
	sect. (ii)	bks 14–29
	sect. (iii)	bks 30–40
	268. sect. (iv)	Labeo 8 Paul. epit.

Each commissioner handled 24 books, E sections (i) and (iii), F sections (ii) and (iv). This is the first time we have met the pattern of alternate sections. Another example of work in alternate sections occurs in group xxxiv.

This group could at first sight have been digested simply by assigning to one commissioner Paul *sent.* (5 books) and Gaius *cas.* (1 book), to the other Hermogenianus *iur. epit.* (6 books). Instead the commissioners divided these works into six sections, no doubt because there was enough repetition or similarity of content to make this convenient and to justify a system of joint digesting. The division was as follows:

xxxiv	205–6	sect. (i)	Paul sent. 1 init.	$1\frac{1}{2}$ bks
			Hermo iur. epit. 1	
	207–8	sect. (ii)	Paul sent. 1 fin., 2	$2\frac{1}{2}$ bks
			Hermo. iur. epit. 2	
	209–10	sect. (iii)	Paul sent. 3	2 bks
			Hermo. iur. epit. 3	
	211–12	sect. (iv)	Paul sent. 4	2 bks
			Hermo. iur. epit. 4	
	213–14	sect. (v)	Paul sent. 5	3 bks
			Herm. iur. epit. 5–6	
	215	sect. (vi)	Gaius 1 cas.	1 bk

This is unbalanced, since sections (i), (iii) and (v) come to $6\frac{1}{2}$ books, sections (ii), (iv) and (vi) to $5\frac{1}{2}$. One might argue that by way of exception an imbalance was admitted in this particular group, but the more likely solution is that a *liber singularis* from which no extracts have survived formed part of section (vi). In that case each commissioner read $6\frac{1}{2}$ books. The best candidate for the missing position is Scaevola 1 *de quaestione familiae*, since most of the other works of this jurist were assigned to the Papinian committee.

The foregoing examples justify the conclusion that the compilers often followed the suggested method of dividing the material into groups which were subdivided into equal lots, and went to great trouble to ensure an exact equality. Indeed it seems that they followed the mechanical principle rigorously whenever works excerpted one by one were being read. The details of the suggested division into groups and lots are set out in Appendix 1.

COMPOSITION OF THE COMMITTEES

The next problem concerns the interpretation of these phenomena so far as the membership and composition of the different committees is concerned. There were three committees and six senior commissioners, consisting of two law ministers and four professors, plus eleven practising barristers.[111] The system adopted by Tribonian of reading and excerpting in three committees, each subdivided into two, requires that two senior commissioners should be assigned to each committee. Since Tribonian was one of the six

[111] Above, n. 77.

he must have been a member of one of the committees,[112] and it is not difficult to allot him his proper slot as the senior commissioner (i.e. chairman) of the Sabinian committee, which excerpted the greatest volume of texts, and which may be regarded as historically senior in that it read the commentaries on Sabinus which dealt with the *ius civile*, as opposed to the praetorian innovations contained in the edict.

Before the allocation of the senior commissioners to the three committees is dealt with, however, it is desirable to say something of the role of the barristers. This role can be explained, so far as the excerpting is concerned, on the assumption that they were not permanently assigned to a given committee but allotted to one or the other from time to time as circumstances required. Their aid was essential whenever a group of works was read jointly. Joint reading was desirable in those cases where a substantial overlap was to be expected between two or more works, of which an obvious example is constituted by the three leading commentaries on the edict. Here Ulpian, Paul and Gaius all naturally followed in the main the order in which Julian had codified the edict. It was therefore both possible and profitable to arrange for their treatises to be read simultaneously. But for this the senior commissioners needed the help of the barristers. While the senior lawyer, as chairman of the sub-committee, read Ulpian, the most modern and comprehensive text, two barristers were also present to peruse the corresponding portions of Paul and Gaius and to draw attention to any divergences from the main text. If the senior commissioner considered that a fragment of Paul or Gaius not in Ulpian should be included, he so instructed. Hence the excerpts from the edictal commentaries acquired the well-known interwoven pattern with which students of the *Digest* are familiar.

If this explanation is adopted, it is possible to understand why eleven barristers were allotted to the commission. This was the maximum number required to service the three committees at any one time—or perhaps it would be more correct to say that ten was, so far as can be judged, the maximum, and the eleventh was a spare. But it was only during certain periods that the full strength of the bar was called on: in particular between December 530 and May 531 and again between the latter part of June and the middle of August 531. At other periods, when the committees were mainly engaged in reading works separately, the barristers could attend to their practice. After the middle of August 531 the number called on at any one time never exceeded four, and was generally less.[113] Even in the months when they were all on duty this did not entail permanent, daily attendance in the palace. The reading sessions were naturally fixed so as to enable practice to continue. It is this that explains the at first sight surprising configuration of the successive sections of works excerpted jointly, for example,

---

[112] *C. Deo auctore* 3 (15 Dec. 530) does not confine Tribonian to a supervisory role (*ita tamen ut tui vigilantissimi animi gubernatione res omnis celebretur*) but superimposes it on him. Contra Pescani 233; cf. Bluhme 276; Bonfante, *Storia del diritto romano* 2 (1923) 51.

[113] Details in *Trail* 537–9.

edictal commentary. As has been mentioned, Bluhme identified these. Assuming the correctness of his work, the length of the successive sections is surprisingly uneven. Thus if we study the 14 sections which make up the early part of the edictal commentaries (group XVIII) we find that number of books excerpted in each section is:

$$12\tfrac{1}{2},\ 4,\ 5\tfrac{1}{2},\ 7\tfrac{1}{2},\ 7\tfrac{1}{3},\ 3,\ 3\tfrac{2}{3},\ 2\tfrac{1}{3},\ 2\tfrac{1}{3},\ 2\tfrac{1}{2},\ 4\tfrac{5}{6},\ 2\tfrac{1}{2},\ 2\tfrac{1}{2},\ 3\tfrac{1}{4}$$

The odd-numbered sections come in all to $38\tfrac{2}{3}$ books, the even-numbered to $25\tfrac{1}{12}$. Why are the sections so irregular, and why did Tribonian not insist on each commissioner reading an equal number of books, as in the case of works excerpted separately?

The explanation is the need for speed. In works such as the edictal commentaries the two teams worked on a leap-frogging system. The first began with book 1 of Ulpian's edictal commentary and the corresponding parts of the other authors, the second started at book 7. But for some reason, for example that the barristers servicing the first team were more readily available than those servicing the second, when the first team had reached book 6 the second was just coming to the end of book 7. Hence the first team begins again at book 8 while the second moves on to the latter part of book 10. There is no interruption in the progress of the committee's work except that caused by the non-availability of the barristers at certain times. In this way neither the progress of the commission nor the proceedings of the prefect's court was unduly interrupted.

The assignment of senior commissioners to the three committees is the next topic to be considered. If each committee had two such commissioners, the senior of whom may be called the chairman, it seems *a priori* likely that the three most senior of all (Tribonian, Constantinus and Theophilus), who had been on Justinian's first codifying commission, would be the three chairmen, with the three newcomers (Dorotheus, Anatolius and Cratinus) filling the junior post on each committee.

Tribonian and Constantinus were the two non-professorial senior members. It is possible to test the idea that they chaired two of the committees in the following way. The distribution of the texts excerpted by the chairmen and junior members of each committee can be studied, and the proportion of texts assigned to a given topic treated as a measure of the commissioner's interest in the topic. Certain branches of the law which notoriously did not interest Roman legal writers or, presumably, professors must have concerned officials. These include criminal law, evidence and public law. Suppose we test the proportion of texts which the various commissioners assigned to these topics. First, letters are assigned to the six as follows:

Sabinian committee: chairman A, second member B
edictal committee: chairman C, second member D
Papinian committee: chairman E, second member F

We then get the following results:[114]

   (i) So far as criminal law is concerned, A is clearly first and E, some way behind, is equal second with B.[115]

  (ii) So far as public law is concerned (including appeals, military, fiscal and local government law), E comes first, A second.[116]

 (iii) Book 2 titles 3–6 of the *Digest* deal with the law of evidence. Here E comes first and A second.[117]

Conversely there are certain titles of the *Digest* of peculiarly academic concern. Thus the last two titles of all deal with the meaning of words and the rules of ancient law. Here A and E come last.[118] The same is true of the number of twin texts (*leges geminatae*) excerpted by the various commissioners. A and E come last:[119] they respected the prohibition in *C. Deo auctore* against repetition more strictly than the others.

The chairman of the Sabinian (A) and Papinian (E) committees therefore display interests in the selection of texts which point to their being officials rather than professors. If Tribonian is A, chairman of the Sabinian committee, Constantinus should be E. There is independent evidence to support this hypothesis. Constantinus was *magister scrinii libellorum et sacrarum cognitionum*.[120] He was hence responsible for the preparation of cases for hearing in the consistory before Justinian himself. In January 532 the Nika riots broke out. On 18 January Belisarius and Mundus massacred the people in the hippodrome. On 19 Hypatius and Pompeius were executed. In the aftermath many dissident senators were rooted out. In some instances their property was confiscated initially, but later returned in part.[121] Complex issues must have occupied the attention of the imperial consistory for some months from January 532. It would not be surprising if Constantinus could give less attention than usual to the work of the commission during this period.

Such a disturbing effect is visible in the excerpting effort of E, chairman

---

[114] *Progress* 47–52.

[115] Figures for *D.* 48 (number of texts followed in brackets by percentage which the number of texts allotted by the commissioner bears to the total number of texts excerpted by him): A 152 (6.2), B 69 (3.9), C 36 (1.8), D 43 (2.6), E 36 (3.9), F 37 (3.4).

[116] Appeals are included because Justinian was particularly concerned to reorganise the appeal system which had become clogged (Jones 1. 482). Figures for *D.* 49 to 50.15: A 103 (4.2), B 42 (2.4), C 53 (2.6), D 65 (3.9), E 49 (5.3), F 44 (4.0).

[117] Figures for *D.* 22.3–6: A 26 (1.1), B 4 (0.2), C 8 (0.4), D 12 (0.7), E 13 (1.4), F 6 (0.6).

[118] Figures for *D.* 50.16 (*de verborum significatione*): A 38 (1.5), B 31 (1.7), C 97 (4.7), D 70 (4.2), E 15 (1.6), F 22 (2.0); for *D* 50.17 (*de diversis regulis iuris antiqui*): A 44 (1.8), B 32 (1.8), C 79 (3.9), D 56 (3.4), E 16 (1.7), F 16 (1.5). For the two titles combined A 82 (3.3), B 63 (3.6), C 126 (7.6), D 126 (7.6), E 31 (3.3), F 38 (3.5).

[119] *Leges geminatae*: A 6 (0.2), B 9 (0.5), C 25 (1.2), D 20 (1.2), E 0 (0.0), F 4 (0.4).

[120] *C. Haec* s. 1, *Summa* s. 2. Duties in *Not. Dig. Or.* xix: *magister libellorum cognitiones et preces tractat.* Jones, I. 504.

[121] *Wars* 1.24.56–8.

of the Papinian committee. If we study the pace of excerpting of the two
Papinian commissioners group by group, we find that while they were reading the main Papinian mass, the first 291 books, the chairman and his junior
colleague kept pace with one another, E in fact averaging 77 lines a book
to F's 69. When they came to read the Appendix of 118 books, F's rate of
extracting did not change significantly. He averaged 61 lines a book, but
E's rate dropped dramatically to 18 lines a book, less than a quarter of his
previous effort.[122]

Nothing similar occurs in the proceedings of the other two committees
and it is natural to think that the call of official business accounts for the
falling off in E's rate of work.

This strengthens the provisional identification of E, chairman of the
Papinian committee, as Constantinus. But it raises a further problem about
the staffing of the committees. Why was the second senior commissioner
put in charge of the committee which excerpted a smaller number of books
than the other two. Ought Constantinus not to have been made chairman
of the edictal committee?

The answer depends on a study of the number of books allotted to each
committee. The basis of calculation is the BK list. Some amendments are
necessary.

For 15 Alfenus Varus 40 *dig.* we should read Alfenus Varus 7 *dig. ab
anonymo epit.* since the larger work, though recorded in the Florentine index,
was not available to the compilers. For reasons explained, 224[123] Gai 1 *reg.*
should be transferred from the Papinian to the Sabinian mass and placed
with the Sabinian committee's groups of *regulae*, probably next to 39 Paul
1 *reg.* With these amendments the Sabinian committee has a total of 536
books.

In the edictal committee's list 145 Mod. 4 *de praescriptionibus* should be
eliminated for the reasons given by Lenel.[124] When this is done the total for
that committee is 571 books. At first sight this does not support the thesis of
equal distribution, but as Bluhme showed,[125] $13\frac{1}{2}$ books of edictal commentary (112–23) initially given to the Sabinian committee were later transferred
to the edictal committee. When the $13\frac{1}{2}$ books are returned to the Sabinian
committee the latter has an initial total of $549\frac{1}{2}$, the edictal committee of
$557\frac{1}{2}$. But even these figures do not perfectly represent the initial distribution by Tribonian, because they do not take account of works from which
no extracts have survived.

Some of the works mentioned in the Florentine index were not available
to the compilers, for example the *digesta* of Alfenus Varus.[126] But the *libri
singulares* were. Thus, the edictal list should be supplemented by two *libri
singulares* of Modestinus, *de testamentis* and *de legatis* which on grounds
explained[127] come next to 151 Mod. 1 *de inofficioso testamento*. There are
also two points at which the Sabinian list needs to be supplemented. One

[122] *Commissioners* 314.　　　[123] Above, p. 160.
[124] *Pal.* 1. 723 n. 1.　　　[125] Bluhme, 283f.
[126] Also Sabinus 3 *de iure civili*, Ulpian 10 *pandectarum.*　　　[127] Above, p. 159.

is the region 48 to 51 where the four *libri singulares* of Paul need to have added to them for numerical reasons one other *liber singularis*, perhaps out of the *libri singulares* of Paul mentioned in the index but not so far allocated.[128] Again at 82–4, which consists of three *libri singulares* of Paul, there is one book missing, which could be supplied in the same way.[129]

If these additions are made, there would be $551\frac{1}{2}$ books initially allocated to the Sabinian committee and $559\frac{1}{2}$ to the edictal committee. There remain nine unallocated *libri singulares*. One of these (probably Scaevola *de quaestione familiae*) should go between 215 and 216 in the Papinian mass,[130] leaving eight books. Let us allot these to the Sabinian committee. Then the Sabinian and edictal committees each start with $559\frac{1}{2}$ books. It may seem incredible that the division could have been so precise, but Tribonian displayed equal exactitude in dividing up the work within each committee.

The Papinian committee was given a smaller number of books, which comes, after the transfer of Gai 1 *reg.* to the Sabinian committee, to 291 books. To these must be added the 118 books of the Appendix, making 409 in all. The Papinian committee actually read 10 more books (*Iavolenus ex posterioribus Labeonis*) which had been allocated to the Sabinian committee. The circumstances surrounding this transfer are complex,[131] but for present purposes can be disregarded, since the transfer was unofficial. It did not affect the time-table of the two committees. They were required to excerpt at the same pace as if it had not taken place.

The Papinian committee's assignment may therefore be taken as 409 books against 573 for the edictal committee as finally adjusted. The fraction 409/573 is very close to 5/7; 409 is 5/7 of 572.6. This suggests that the rate of excerpting required by these two committees was in the proportion of 7 to 5. While it would be somewhat misleading to say that the Papinian committee worked a five-day week, its stint seems to have been fixed by Tribonian on the basis that Constantinus would require extra time for his official duties as *magister libellorum et sacrarum cognitionum*. This explains why the second senior commissioner headed the committee which excerpted less than the other two.

Given that two committee chairmanships have been identified, the remaining posts present less difficulty. The third chairmanship, that of the edictal committee, should go to the third senior commissioner, Theophilus (C). The second Papinian commissioner (F) must be Cratinus. He, like his chairman, was given a reduced assignment. This is explicable only if he was partly absorbed by official duties, which must in his case be professorial. But since the two professors from Beirut could not be instructed to lecture in the law school of Constantinople, and since Theophilus was chairman of the committee with the largest assignment, this leaves only Cratinus, a junior professor from the capital city. To minimise the disruption of law teaching it was reasonable to ask him to continue his lectures, or part

---

[128] Below, Appendix 1, p. 267. [129] Below, Appendix 1, p. 266. [130] Below, p. 280.
[131] Explanation in Honoré, 'Labeo's *posteriora* and the *Digest* commission', *Daube Noster*, ed. A. Watson (1974), 161.

of them, concurrently with his work in the commission. It is in fact possible to infer the subject-matter of his courses. From his selection of texts, we can deduce that he was specially interested in two first-year and one second- or third-year course. His favourite subjects are husband and wife, legacies (including trusts), and the part of the edictal course *de rebus* which dealt with special contracts. In the books on husband and wife his contribution is second to Tribonian;[132] on legacies and trusts he comes first,[133] on special contracts second to B, the junior Sabinian commissioner.[134] An interesting feature of F's interests is their consistency. Thus, while not primarily a criminal, tort or property lawyer, he does insert texts in the titles on adultery,[135] pillaging the estate of a deceased person,[136] and the division of an inheritance,[137] which fit in with his interest in husband and wife and legacies. It seems fair to assume that his interests are built round the two first-year courses on matrimonial property and legacies, and the second- or third-year edictal course *de rebus*, in which special contracts formed an important element. There remain the second positions on the Sabinian and edictal committee to be filled by Dorotheus and Anatolius from Beirut. The Sabinian position (B) should go to Dorotheus, both on the ground that he, as the senior of the two, should be Tribonian's colleague and because the close association of Tribonian and Dorotheus is shown by their remaining colleagues on the sub-committees which drafted the *Institutes*[138] and the second edition of the *Codex Iustinianus*.[139] Anatolius must therefore have been the colleague of Theophilus on the edictal committee. Each committee therefore had a mixed composition, either an official with a professor or two professors from different law schools:

	Sabinian	*edictal*	*Papinian*
chairman	Tribonian	Theophilus	Constantinus
second member	Dorotheus	Anatolius	Cratinus

THE TIME-TABLE

The last organisational detail which we must elucidate is the time-table for excerpting. As was noted, the decline in Constantinus' activity as a commissioner coincides with the transition from the excerpting of the main

---

[132] Figures for *D*. 25–6: A 327 (9.6), B 47 (2.6), C 50 (2.4), D 48 (2.9), E 24 (2.6), F 58 (5.3). For the proprietary aspects of marriage alone (*D*. 23.2–5, 24.1 and 24.3): A 184 (7.5), B 39 (2.2), C 31 (1.5), D 20 (1.2), E 21 (2.3), F 46 (4.2).

[133] *D*. 30–6 (legacies and *fideicommissa*): A 177 (7.2), B 288 (16.2), C 121 (5.9), D 157 (9.5), D 160 (17.3), F 262 (23.9).

[134] Figures for *D*. 16.3–19 (*bonae fidei iudicia*, mostly contracts); A 135 (5.5), B 183 (10.3), C 66 (3.2), D 41 (2.5), E 30 (3.2), F 62 (5.7).

[135] *D*. 48.5: A 35 (1.4), B 8 (0.5), C 0 (0.0), D 2 (0.1), E 2 (0.2), F 7 (0.6).

[136] *D*. 47.19 (*expilatae hereditatis*): A 1, B 2, C 0, D 0, E 0, F 3.

[137] *D*. 10.2 (*familiae erciscundae*): A 7 (0.3), B 7 (0.4), C 28 (1.4), D 1 (0.1), E 5 (0.5), F 9 (0.8). 27 of C's 28 texts come from the section of edictal commentary which was assigned to him.

[138] *C. Imperatoriam* 3 (21 Nov. 533).   [139] *C. Cordi* 2 (16 Nov. 534).

Papinian mass to the Appendix.[140] This decline we associated with the aftermath of the Nika rebellion.

As a ranging shot, let us suppose that on the very day after the Nika rebellion ended Constantinus began preparing the cases against those implicated, and that precisely on that day the Papinian committee began to read that part of its assignment known as the Appendix in which the chairman's relatively meagre contribution is from the beginning so striking. The rebellion ended on 19 January 532.[141] Assuming that the Papinian committee was required to read the same number of books per day or per week as previously (and only so can one explain why its chairman should have been pressed for time) then a simple calculation shows that the committee should have finished all the books it had to read on 30 June 532: if the 291 books of the main Papinian mass were read in the 401 days available up to 19 January 532, the 118 books of the Appendix were read in the next 162 days, and that takes one to the last day of June. If so, the total time spent in excerpting was 564 days.

This is of course only a ranging shot. It would be a coincidence if the end of the rebellion precisely coincided with the day prescribed for the Papinian committee to start on the Appendix. We can however obtain a more precise time schedule in the following way. The number of books read by the other two committees, the Sabinian and edictal committees, was originally equal. But in the course of the commission's work certain books were transferred from the Sabinian committee, whose chairman was also the commission chairman, to the edictal committee, with the result that the latter in the end read rather more books. The number read by the edictal committee, so far as can be ascertained, was 573.[142] Now 573 is too close to 564 for a mere coincidence. The number of books and the number of days allotted for reading them must in the case of the edictal committee have been the same (573 books in 573 days), and our ranging shot has produced a result which is nine days too short. It was a necessary feature of the commission's work that the committees must all finish on the same day, because the next stage, that of assembling the excerpted fragments into titles and books, could only begin when everything had been read and every fragment copied out. It therefore follows that Tribonian arranged for all the committees to finish work about 9 July 532, nine days later than we earlier, as a result of the ranging shot, supposed, and 573 days after the work began.

The edictal committee was required, then, to read a book a day. This does not mean that the commissioners had to work on Sundays and feast days. Each committee had two commissioners: they divided the work between

---

[140] Above, nn. 120–2.

[141] Malalas 474 places the outbreak of rioting on 13 Jan. 532 and the massacre in the hippodrome on Sunday 18 Jan. *Chronicon Paschale* puts the massacre on 18 Jan., the executions of Hypatius and Pompeius on 19 Jan. Procopius, *Wars* 1.24.19, 22 puts the massacre on the sixth day of the insurrection. In effect all agree, and Monday 19 Jan. may be taken to mark the end of the rebellion.

[142] Above, p. 169.

them. Nor did they have to hand in their excerpts at the end of each day or week. The work was so organised that they had to excerpt a group of books, varying from two to over a hundred, in a corresponding number of days. For example, 70 days were allotted for the edictal committee to read the *digesta* of Celsus and Marcellus: in the event the chairman of the committee read 36 of these books and his colleague 34.[143] Clearly they could work in spurts if they wished, and in the case of works read jointly, with the assistance of the barristers attached to the commission, much will have depended on when the barristers were free.

If the edictal committee's assignment was one book per day, so was the Sabinian's committee, though the latter slipped behind somewhat and ended by reading 37 books fewer than its sister committee, 536 as against 573.[144] What of the Papinian committee? Since it had to read 5/7 of the number of books assigned to the edictal committee we may assume that it had to read at 5/7 of the edictal's committee's pace, viz. five books a week instead of seven, divided as before between the two commissioners or their teams. At this pace the transition from the main Papinian mass to the Appendix came on 25 January 532, not on 19 January. That is close enough to the date of the Nika rebellion to be plausible.

In the outcome we are able without undue speculation to work out the timetable of the excerpting stage, the composition of the committees and the books for which each commissioner was responsible, not to mention the number of barristers required for each group of works. These results are possible because of two factors: the accuracy of Bluhme's work and the simple methods of Tribonian. While the results probably need some amendment in detail there is no reason why the suggested dates for the excerpting of each group should be as much as a week wrong. The rough, and methodically incorrect[145] researches of Longo,[146] de Francisci[147] and Hugo Krueger[148] into the time-table of excerpting can therefore be jettisoned, as can any suggestion that the commissioners relied on a

[143] Below, Appendix 1, p. 273.   [144] Above, n. 125.

[145] These authors attempted to correlate chronologically the excerpting of texts with the issue of constitutions on points which may be supposed to have required solution because they were raised by the text excerpted. Such a method is incapable of yielding sound results because (i) the interval between the discovery that there was a problem needing solution and the relevant imperial constitution might be anything from a few weeks to many months, depending on the amount of discussion and research required, the availability of Justinian, and his attitude to the solution first proposed (ii) *C. Deo auctore* 9 instructs the compilers not to repeat in the *Digest* what is in the (first) code, and the same would *mutatis mutandis* apply, presumably, to reforming constitutions. Since this somewhat obscure instruction fell to be interpreted by six excerpting commissioners, who may not have adopted an identical interpretation, nothing can be deduced from the failure of a *Digest* text to reflect a solution proposed in a reforming constitution of 530–2. Hugo Krueger noticed the first but not the second flaw in the method.

[146] Longo, 19 *BIDR* (1907) 145.

[147] P. de Francisci, 22 *BIDR* (1910) 155; 23 (1911) 39, 186; 27 (1914) 5; 30 (1921) 154.

[148] H. Krueger, *Die Herstellung der Digesten Justinians und die Gang der Exzerption* (1922).

predigest or on partial compilations made by their predecessors.[149] There was no need for them to do so. The time available was ample, provided they made a sustained effort. One book, about 10,000 words or 30 modern pages, is no great reading task for two commissioners between them in a day. Suppose that Byzantium abounded in predigests, there was no need to call on them. Tribonian would have thought it highly unscholarly, as well as unnecessary, to do so.[150]

THE DISTRIBUTION OF THE EXCERPTS INTO TITLES[151]

The choice of excerpts fell to the six senior commissioners working individually. If Theophilus omitted a passage from Ulpian book 3 on the edict, no one else on the commission could recover it. That passage was lost to posterity. The distribution of the texts into titles may however reasonably be regarded as a function of the committee chairmen. Once the excerpting of a group of works was complete the contribution of each committee had to be assembled, marked for its appropriate heading and placed each in the receptacle for that title heading. Alternatively it may be supposed that the marking of excerpts for titles was a continuous process. Each commissioner as he authorised an excerpt gave it a mark from the list of available titles which was one of the commission's working documents. The first possibility, however, that the chairmen did this task group by group, is slightly preferable, since it would ensure greater uniformity and efficiency, while interrupting the work of excerpting less.

The pattern of distribution of texts gives evidence of the varying interests of the different commissioners.[152]

THE EDITING OF THE DIGEST TITLES: FIRST DRAFT[153]

The compilation of titles and books from the individual fragments excerpted by the commissioners in their three committees formed the penultimate stage of the commission's work. This stage has been very little studied. Bluhme seems to have assumed,[154] as have most later scholars who thought about the matter, that the editorial stage, as we may call it,[155] consisted of

---

[149] G. Diósdi, 'Das Gespenst der Prädigesten', *Labeo* 17 (1971) 187, showed that ample time was available without recourse to the hypothesis of a predigest: cf. O. Lenel, 34 *ZSS* (1903) 384, 388; ch. 9 nn. 64f.

[150] Unscholarly not to read much more widely in the sources than was required by the old law syllabus: *C. Omnem* 1 (16 Dec. 533). Instruction to commissioners to read the old books: *C. Deo auctore* 4 (15 Dec. 530: *legere et elimare*). They actually did so: *C. Tanta* 1 (16 Dec. 533 *quae necesse esset omnia et legere et perscrutari*).

[151] *Distribution* 351.   [152] E.g. above, nn. 115–19. Details in *Distribution* 355–62.

[153] *Editing* 262.   [154] *Bluhme* 257.

[155] The use of this phrase does not imply that all the editing of individual texts, including interpolations, was done at this second stage. Clearly the excerpters had to make routine changes like *traditio* for *mancipatio* and to shorten the texts and edit them in a suitable literary form. As regards other changes, it remains an open question how far the changes were made at the first and how far at the second stage.

joint sessions of the whole commission. There is no direct evidence of this, and a priori it seems most unlikely. To have compiled the 432 titles of the *Digest* from the 9950 texts which had been excerpted in plenary session would have been to adopt the most time-consuming possible method. Speed was a consideration pressing in the opposite direction, towards a system of delegation such as had been adopted for the excerpting stage. Besides, there was already a committee organisation, which could be retained at the editorial stage if delegation was thought advisable. What we should expect is that Tribonian, having used the committees for excerpting, would retain them as teams for combining the fragments into books and titles. The question remained, however, whether the editorial process could be studied. For some time it defied numerical investigation, but in the summer of 1971 the appropriate technique was discovered. At least one criterion of editorial intervention is in fact available. This consists of deviations from the expected order of the fragments as established by Bluhme and Krueger. When a text is out of order—and the count shows that 1416 fragments of a possible 8695[156] are displaced—this must in general be due to the activity of the commissioners at the time they put the texts together in draft titles. There are a few exceptions, when it seems that the texts have been displaced as a result of a mechanical accident,[157] but not many. It is true that a scholar who studies the displaced texts is often tempted to think that the position in which they appear in the title in question is arbitrary. But it is in general dangerous to attribute displacement to accident. The compilers, or some of them, were influenced by what seems to a modern, systematic mind, a rather loose association of ideas.[158] In this they did not differ from Julian in his codification of the perpetual edict or Ulpian in his edictal commentary. What seems to us a far-fetched association of texts is not on that account alone to be rejected as unintentional. Secondly, we must make proper allowance for texts, or parts of texts, which have dropped out of the final version of the *Digest*. These excisions may lead to awkward transitions from one text to the next, yet it may be that originally the sequence read smoothly. For these reasons the assumption underlying the present study is that all the displacements of texts from the Bluhme-Krueger order are due to the activity of the commissioners at the time when they drafted the 432 *Digest* titles.[159]

If we start from this assumption, the main clues to the editorial activity of

[156] Since one text in every title is undisplaceable, the number of fragments in all the *Digest* titles is 8695 plus 432, the number of titles, viz. 9127. The difference between 9127 and 9950 (the number of texts excerpted) is accounted for by the fact that two or more texts excerpted from different sources were frequently combined in a *Digest* fragment. The number of *texts* distributed into titles is therefore 823 greater than the number of fragments appearing in the final work.

[157] *D.* 29.2.58–65; below, n. 165.

[158] E.g. *D.* 21.2.42 (pregnant slave), 43 (pregnant cow).

[159] The assumption is false, since some changes were made at the second editorial stage when a final draft was made. But it is assumed that the last minute changes were relatively few, and can for a statistical study be disregarded.

the compilers are two. First, we can study types of shift. Secondly, we can count the displacements and from the figures so arrived at estimate the degree of editorial activity in the different titles and books of the *Digest*. But before either of these is possible it is necessary to be clear what the order of the texts was as they came to the compilers. Here again there are two questions to be answered: whether the BK Ordo is correct and in what physical form the fragments were excerpted and distributed into titles.

In general I assume that the BK Ordo is correct, with some minor amendments mentioned above.[160] In addition, two further amendments to the Bluhme-Krueger table must be made. (i) The texts from Iavolenus 10 *post. Lab.* and from Labeo 10 *post. Iav. epit.*, must be grouped together in such a way that the texts from book 1 and the first third of book 2 of these works belong to the Sabinian mass, while the texts from the second two-thirds of book 2 and all the remaining books belong to the Appendix.[161] It involves a number of changes in the asterisking of *Digest* texts by Krueger, the general effect of which is to reduce appreciably the number of texts to be treated as displaced. (ii) Contrary to the BK notation the works on *fideicommissa* which run from nos. 194 to 199 in their Ordo were read jointly and not separately as they indicate. Otherwise a number of texts would have to be regarded as displaced where there is really no reason to suspect this and where Krueger does not insert asterisks.[162] (iii) A third point is that Paulus *sententiae* and Hermogenianus *iuris epit.* (Bluhme-Krueger nos. 205 to 214) must be assumed to have been read jointly in sections.[163]

These alterations serve to establish a canon of correct order, viz. the amended BK Ordo, which is what we mean by the BK Ordo from now on. Any text which departs from it is treated as a displaced text.

The second preliminary point concerns the physical form in which the fragments were excerpted. As we shall see, the way in which fragments were shifted strongly suggests that the excerpts were on separate pieces of papyrus or parchment, *schedae*,[164] stacked on top of one another so that each mass for a given title consisted of a pile of fragments. In each pile the first

---

[160] Above, pp. 156, 160, 164.   [161] Watson, *Daube Noster* 161.

[162] D. 32.1.1–3, 5–18; 34.5.5–7; 35.1.86–91; 36.1.65–75; 50.17.93–6 taken together show that either Valens *fid.* 1–4, Ulp. *fid.* 1–4, Maec. *fid.* 1–8, Gai. 2 *fid.*, Paul *fid.* 1–2 and Pomp. *fid.* 1–2 were read jointly or that the editors transposed a large number of texts without apparent reason. *Commissioners* 270 should be amended *pro tanto*.

[163] *Commissioners* 266, 308. See D. 39.5.33–4, 39.4.9–11, 29.2.94–6, 50.5.10–12, 50.16.222–3.

[164] The evidence for this is: (i) the 1421 displacements which we are concerned to study; these are with few exceptions displacements of individual texts, not blocks, and such displacements would have been greatly facilitated and much time saved, if the texts could be moved about one by one: (ii) the arrangement in D. 29.3.58–65 (n. 165 below) is explicable only if it was mechanically possible for the individual texts to be scattered and replaced in the wrong order. This does not exclude the possibility that when works such as the edictal commentaries were read together long chains of texts from more than one work were written out at the excerpting stage as a single unit on a long strip or roll. What the secretaries needed was stocks of paper or parchment of different sizes and lengths. N. Lewis, *Papyrus in Classical Antiquity* (1974) 36–9, 56–7.

text came at the bottom, the second next from the bottom and so on, until the last text to be added to the pile came at the top. The fragments were therefore, when the excerpting stage ended, in the reverse of the BK Ordo. It perhaps helps to visualise them as in boxes or files. The Byzantine administration had a filing system, of which we know little, and must therefore have had a method of keeping papers in files. Suppose there to have been a box, *kista*, for each title and, within it, a file for each of the four masses. The editorial process begins by the removal of these files, usually one by one. They are then turned upside down so that they are in the BK Ordo.[165] The editor then goes through them, and in doing so may displace some of them.

To study how this was done it is best to analyse *D*. 35.1 (*de conditionibus et demonstrationibus*) a long title which has been methodically edited. It is easier to see the structure of long than short titles. In *D*. 35.1 the masses come in the order SEPA (Sabinian, edictal, Papinian, Appendix) and each of the masses finishes with a coda of displaced texts, thus:

S	main mass	2–40
	coda	41–42
E	main mass	43–64
	coda	65–69
P	main mass	70–98
	coda	99–104
A	main mass	108–112
	coda	113

The coda consists of texts displaced from the BK order but which preserve that order *inter se*. Thus:

35.1	41 Ulp. 34 ed	= BK 4–9 (iii)
	42 Afr. 2 quaest.	= BK 20
35.1	65 Paul 62 ed.	= BK 95–100 (vi)
	66 Mod. 10 resp.	= BK 146
	67 Iav. 11 epist.	= BK 153
	68 Iav. 2 Cass.	= BK 152
	69 Gai. 3 leg. Iul. et Pap.	= BK 162–67 (v)
35.1	99 Pap. 18 qu.	= BK 180
	100 Pap. 7 resp.	= BK 181

---

[165] The evidence that the piles were turned upside down is (i) the fact that they appear in the *Digest* in the order in which they were read, not in the reverse order, and (ii) the fact that in *D*. 29.2.58–65 the texts belonging to the end of the Sabinian mass have been shuffled in a way which could not be accounted for by considerations of subject-matter, but rather points to a mechanical accident. Such an accident could have occurred only when the bottom texts of the mass were at the top of the pile, since it is possible accidentally to scatter the top but not the bottom texts of a pile. The likelihood is that when the Sabinian pile was removed from its file the top texts were knocked on to the floor and replaced in the wrong order. The reconstituted pile was turned upside down, and the editor proceeded to edit it in the order which we now have in *D*. 29.2.

101 Pap. 8 resp.	= BK 181
102 Pap. 9 resp.	= BK 181
103 Paul 14 qu.	= BK 182–84 (iv)
104 Paul 14 resp.	= BK 188

There is a slight exception at 35.1.67, 68 where the order of two neighbouring works by Iavolenus is reversed, but something is slightly wrong here because the second text, 68, is inscribed 'Iavolenus' instead of 'Idem'. If we disregard this minor exception,[166] the effect is similar to that produced when a player has a pile of cards, and goes through them one by one, discarding two or three which he places successively at the bottom of the pile. The cards at the bottom are not of course in the original order but they remain in the same relation to one another as they were originally.

The editor of *D.* 35.1, then, has gone through each mass in turn, discarding certain texts which he put at the bottom of the pile so as to form what we shall call a mass coda. This process is only possible if the fragments, before editing, were on separate pieces of parchment or papyrus.

THE TYPES AND NUMBER OF DISPLACEMENTS

In order to use the number of displaced texts as an index of editorial activity it is necessary to form a conception of the different types of displacement and of the principles for individuating displacements. The issues involved are however technical and appear out of place in a biography of Tribonian. Let us therefore assume them solved[167] and ask how we can then proceed to unravel the organisation of the *Digest* commission's editorial work.

THE ORGANISATION OF THE EDITORIAL WORK

I have so far invariably spoken of the 'editor' of a title as if the work was undertaken by a single commissioner in every case. It now remains to ask whether this assumption is correct and whether we can unravel the organisation of the editorial work. Clearly if the editorial work was undertaken in joint session of the whole commission we should expect a considerable evenness of editorial activity from title to title and from book to book. If, on the other hand, the editing was done by committees or by individual commissioners, we should expect some indication of the identity of the editing committee or commissioner to emerge from a comparison of the displacements from title to title or book to book.

For various reasons the book is more likely to have been the editorial unit than the title. Titles in the *Digest* are of very uneven length. Many titles have a single text only; *D.* 50.16 has 246 texts. A distribution by which each

[166] Such a mistake might occur when a text was inserted, not quite in the right place, after the first draft of the title had been made. This might in turn point to a secretarial error in overlooking the text when the first draft was written out.

[167] Types of displacement: *Editing* 266–70; individuation ibid. 271–3.

committee or commissioner undertook to edit the same number of titles
would have been a haphazard one. The existence of amalgamated titles
such as *D.* 1.3[168] is rather against the notion that the title was the editorial
unit, since, if that had been the case, the number of titles should have been
fixed at the outset, not changed as the work of editing proceeded.

The length of books, on the other hand, though not uniform, is much
more even, and the variation in the length of the books of the *Digest* is
probably not greater than the variation in the length of the *libri* written by
the classical authors, which were taken as units for purposes of reading and
excerpting. Further, the fact that *libri* were the units at the earlier stage is
some argument for the view that they were also units at the editorial stage.
Such a system would fit in with Tribonian's ideas of organisation.

Another argument in favour of the view that the book was the editorial
unit is that the number of books in the *Digest*, 50, is easily adapted to the
committee structure which was the basis of the excerpting. There were
three committees, and it would be natural to assign 16 units to each.

Books 30 to 32 form a single title, in which the order of masses SEPA
covers the materials from the beginning of book 30 to 32.103. It must be
regarded as single editorial unit. If this is done, the 50 books of the *Digest*
become 48 editorial units and these can be divided into three lots of 16.
This system is simple, fair to the commissioners and consistent with the
organisation at the excerpting stage.

If we turn now to the figures for displacements in individual books of the
Digest, we find that a clear pattern emerges. The basic criterion employed is
the frequency of displacements, which is measured by the number of displacements in a given book for each 100 texts that could have been displaced.
The number of displaced texts is calculated in the way described. The
number of displaceable texts is always one less than the total number of texts
in a title, and the total of displaceable texts for a book is found by finding the
sum of the displaceable texts for each title in it.

The percentage of displacements varies from 33.3 in book 1 to 4.7 in
book 50 of the *Digest*. In general it follows a downward trend, so that if the
books are grouped in twelves we get the following figures:

Books	
1–12	20.56
13–24	18.58
25–38	18.06
39–50	11.09

This shows that the editors in general made progressively fewer displacements as the work proceeded, since they were pressed for time. This is what
we would expect in any operation done to a time limit, and it is what we
found in our study of the rate of excerpting.

---

[168] *D.* 1.3 (*de legibus senatusconsultis et longa consuetudine*) is an amalgam of a title on
laws and SCC with one on custom. In such fused titles the masses appear twice.

But within the overall downward trend as the work progressed there are important variations. In particular a pattern emerges within each group of three books. Suppose we begin by dividing the *Digest* into 16 groups of three books: 1 to 3, 4 to 7, 10 to 12 etc.; including as one group 28 to 32 and ending with a sixteenth consisting of books 48 to 50. Within the groups the following pattern is noticeable. In general the rate of displacement in the first book of the group is higher than in the second, and the second is higher than the third. Suppose, then, that we analyse the displacements in a different way, by series. The first series consists of all the 16 books which form the first book of a group, viz. books 1, 4, 7, 10, 13, 16, 19, 22, 25, 28, 33, 36, 39, 42, 45, 48. The second series consists of books 2, 5, 8 . . . 49, and the third series of books 3, 6, 9 . . . 50. For the three series of 16 books the respective rates of displacement are as follows:

first series	(books 1, 4, 7 . . . 48)	20.61
second series	(books 2, 5, 8 . . . 49)	15.74
third series	(books 3, 6, 9 . . . 50)	13.17

The first series comes out higher than the other two in 12 groups out of 16, a strikingly high proportion. To be more specific, it comes highest in books 1–9 and in books 19–44 and 48–50. But in books 10–18 the first series comes only second or third in rate of displacement. Indeed, in the figures for those nine books as a whole it comes last:

first series books	10, 13, 16	15.5
second series books	11, 14, 17	19.4
third series books	12, 15, 18	17.2

The displacements in the books belonging to the first series are therefore consistently higher except in these books, and in books 45 to 47. So far as the second and third series are concerned, these show in general a lower rate of displacement than the first series, and *inter se* the second tends to be higher than the third. But this is not consistently the case. In the earlier books 1–15 the third series scores higher than the second in four groups out of five, and only slightly lower in the fifth. But in the later books 16–50 the second scores higher than the third in eight groups out of eleven.

How are the three series to be interpreted? Two possible views spring to mind. One is that an editorial team (whether a committee or an individual commissioner) was given the task of editing a group of three books, e.g. books 1, 2 and 3. Thus the first group of three books might be allotted to one committee, the second group to another and so on. This interpretation would be consistent with the general reduction in editorial activity towards the end of the *Digest* and with the general tendency within each group of three books for the activity of the editors to decline. The explanation would be that when they came to edit books 3, 6, 9 etc. the editors, whoever they were and whichever committee they belonged to, would tend to hurry in order to complete their editorial task by a given deadline. It is not so easy, however, to reconcile this interpretation with the anomalies we have drawn attention to, viz. the fact that the rate of displacement in the third series (3, 6, 9 etc.) begins by being greater than that in the second series (2, 5, 8 etc.) but later becomes less, and the fact that there is an anomalous decline in the rate of displacements of the first series in books 10, 13 and 16.

The alternative explanation is that the assignment of editorial tasks was by series, viz. that one committee[169] was assigned the books in the first series, 1, 3, 6 etc., another the books in the second series 2, 5, 8, and so forth. This is the view which I believe to be correct. There are in effect a number of arguments in its favour.

The first is that it is administratively a better arrangement. It means that Tribonian can set a date for the completion of each group of three books, after which the drafts of the whole group can be handed over to the secretaries for copying, rather than wait for the completion of three groups amounting to nine books, as would be necessary if each committee was assigned a block of three books. The book by book arrangement would enable Tribonian to keep a watchful eye on the progress of the editorial task more easily than if he had to wait for the longer period. In practice, this would mean that a deadline was set twice a month instead of once every six weeks.[170]

A second argument is that it is possible to match the pattern of excerpting to the pattern of editing if we suppose that the series 1, 4, 7 etc., 2, 5, 8 etc. and 3, 6, 9 etc. corresponded to committee assignments. Specifically it makes sense to correlate them in the following way:

first series	(books 1, 4, 7 etc.)	Sabinian committee
second series	(books 2, 5, 8 etc.)	Papinian committee
third series	(books 3, 6, 9 etc.)	edictal committee

It may occasion some surprise that the Papinian committee should appear as the second rather than the third committee. But the modern arrangement in the order Sabinian-edictal-Papinian, as in the Bluhme-Krueger *Ordo librorum* is not based on anything in the *Digest* itself. Since the chairman of the Papinian committee was the second senior commissioner, Constantinus,[171] it is natural that this committee should figure in second place.

Granted that this arrangement is not ruled out, the evidence for its correctness is as follows. The Sabinian committee was the most active

---

[169] I have not found acceptable evidence of a subdivision between the commissioners at this stage, nor of a separate role for the advocates. It would seem reasonable for the two senior commissioners (assisted perhaps by some of the advocates) to work jointly at this stage of the work in order to assure that each text was scrutinised, in addition to the original excerpter, by at least one and, if the excerpting committee was different from the editing committee, two further experts. The time allowed—a fortnight per book per committee—seems adequate for this method to be pursued.

[170] For the time scale see below, p. 185.   [171] Above, pp. 167–8.

committee so far as excerpting was concerned. In particular it excerpted at
the rate of 90.81 lines per book, compared with 65.93 for the edictal committee and 63.87 for the Papinian committee.[172] It would be natural for the
most active excerpters to be the most active editors and we have seen that the
rate of displacement for the first series exceeds that for the other two by
much the same proportion as the Sabinian committee's rate of excerpting
exceeded that of the other two committees:

	Rate of excerpting (lines per book)		Rate of displacement (texts per 100)
Sabinian committee	90.81	first series	20.61
Papinian committee	63.87	second series	15.74
edictal committee	65.93	third series	13.17

The Sabinian committee might therefore plausibly be regarded as the
editorial authority for the first series. Of the other two committees it seems
at first sight that the edictal committee, which excerpted slightly more lines
per book than the Papinian committee, would be treated as editors of the
second series, the Papinian committee of the third. But this is a misleading
picture. The rate of excerpting for the Papinian committee is unduly low,
because in the later stages of the work, when the Appendix was being read,
the chairman of the committee, Constantinus, was preoccupied with the
aftermath of the Nika riots.[173] If we look instead at the figures for the rate of
excerpting in the main Papinian mass, and adjust this on the assumption that
unless so preoccupied Constantinus' rate of excerpting would have declined
in the Appendix in the same proportion as that of his colleague Cratinus,[174]
we find that the adjusted overall rate for the Papinian committee, 70.57,
slightly exceeds that for the edictal committee, 65.93. Another factor to be
taken into account is that the figure for displacements in the third series is
unnaturally depressed by the last two titles of the *Digest*, which have 455
displaceable texts and only 14 displacements. If we disregard these rather
special titles, which alone account for the fact that the number of texts
belonging to the third series is over 300 greater than that belonging to the
other two, we obtain the following comparison:

---

[172] *Commissioners* 314. A small adjustment is required to take account of the transfer
of texts inscribed *Iavolenus ex posterioribus Labeonis* from the Sabinian to the Papinian
committee (above, n. 131). Since the committees were excerpting a different number of
books per week (above, p. 169) the number of lines per book forms the best basis of
comparison between them.

[173] Above, pp. 167–8.

[174] If in the Appendix Constantinus had excerpted at a rate which in relation to his
previous excerpting bore the same relation as his colleague F's to the latter's previous
excerpting (viz. that he had excerpted at a rate of 67.77 lines per book) then the overall
rate of excerpting for the Papinian committee would have been 70.57.

1 Lines per book excerpted	2 Displacements per 100	3 Ratio of 1 to 2
Sabinian committee 90.81	first series 20.61	4.41
Papinian committee 70.57 (adjusted)	second series 15.74	4.48
edictal committee 65.93	third series (adjusted) 14.88	4.43

From this it appears that, if there is an analogy between rate of excerpting and rate of displacement, the Papinian committee better fits the second and the edictal committee the third series. The same holds good if the analogy is taken to be between the rate of excerpting and the average number of displacements per book:

	1 Rate of excerpting (lines per book)	2 Average displacements per book	3 Ratio of 1 to 2
Sabinian committee	90.81	first series 35.25	2.58
Papinian committee (adjusted)	70.57	second series 27.69	2.55
edictal committee	65.93	third series 25.87	2.55

A further argument can be drawn from the different work-styles of the committees. If the rates of excerpting of the different committees are compared as the work progressed, the following contrast emerges. The Sabinian committee excerpts at a relatively even, though slowly falling, rate throughout. The Papinian committee also excerpts at a relatively even rate, but with some peaks and troughs. The edictal committee, however, excerpts at a rate which declines steadily from beginning to end.

If we look for analogues of these work-styles in the displacement of texts at the editorial stage, we will conclude that the editors of the second series work more like the Papinian committee and the editors of the third series more like the edictal committee. This is brought out if the editorial work is divided into quarters, each consisting of three groups. The figures are as follows (displacements per 100 texts):

Books	First series	Second series	Third series
1–12	25.20	15.76	19.82
13–24	21.01	19.81	15.20
25–38	20.67	19.25	14.99
39–50	16.41	10.30	10.73 (adjusted)

It will be noted that the rate of displacement in the third series steadily declines, while that in the second series undulates. Furthermore, the rate in the third series starts above that in the second, but subsequently falls below it. The analogy with the rate of excerpting of the edictal and Papinian committees respectively can be seen at a glance from the tables published in Appendix I.[175] It can be assumed that work-style is a characteristic which is likely to be displayed in a consistent way by a particular person. This is confirmed by a study of the style of working of the editors within each book. Most books consist of two or several titles, and by studying the rate of displacement title by title, we can see how the different editors tackled their task. Their work usually displays one of the following patterns:

(i) The early title or titles of the book show a high rate of displacement but this tails off in the later or last titles. This may be called the 'trochaic form'.

(ii) The early title or titles show a relatively low rate of displacement but the later or last titles display a higher rate, so that the effect is that of a strong finish. This may be called the 'iambic form'.

(iii) The first and last titles show a high rate of displacement but the middle title or titles displays less. This is the sagging or 'dip' form.

(iv) The first and last titles show a low rate of displacement but the middle titles display a higher rate. This constitutes the 'hummock' form.

In my judgment[176] the following conclusions can be drawn:

(a) The trochaic effect is found in ten books (4, 6, 21, 24, 28, 30–2, 34, 35, 44, 50) of which seven come from the third series, one from the second and two from the first. This form is therefore characteristic of the third series.

(b) The iambic effect is found in twelve books (9, 10, 13, 16, 17, 18, 19, 22, 33, 36, 42, 45) nine of which come from the first series, one from the second and two from the third. This form is therefore characteristic of the first series.

(c) The sagging or 'dip' effect is found in four books (8, 11, 26, 43) all of which come from the second series.

(d) The 'hummock' effect is found in four books (5, 38, 46, 49) three of which come from the second series and one from the third. Hence the hummock and hump effects are characteristic of the second series.

These results are valuable since they show that there are editorial styles characteristic of each of the three series. This naturally serves to confirm the notion that the series correspond to different editors or editorial teams. Furthermore the stylistic forms we have noticed within books fit in with the 'shape' of the editing as a whole. The Sabinian committee, if it is responsible for the editing of the first series of books, tends to finish strongly in the 'iambic' form. This is what we should expect from a study both of its rate of excerpting and of the figures in Table 2 for the books in the first series as a whole. Similarly the edictal committee, if correctly identified as the editor

---

[175] Below, pp. 278, 286.

[176] To form a judgment it is necessary to look at the table in *Editing* 285–302.

of the books in the third series, displays that tailing-off characteristic, in the 'trochaic form', which we have already noticed in the work of excerpting done by that committee and in the table of displacements for the third series which can be studied book by book in Table 2. Finally the same is true of the Papinian committee if it really is the editor of the second series. Both in its excerpting work and in the displacement for the second series in Table 2 we can notice a basic evenness which is broken by humps or hummocks, in short by undulations which seem characteristic of the working style of this committee.

These and other arguments[177] seem to justify the conclusion that for editorial purposes Tribonian assigned the books to the committees according to the following scheme:

Sabinian committee: books, 1, 4, 7, 10, 13, 16, 19, 22, 25, 28, 33, 36, 39, 42, 45, 48.

Papinian committee: books 2, 5, 8, 11, 14, 17, 20, 23, 26, 29, 34, 37, 40, 43, 46, 49.

edictal committee: books 3, 6, 9, 12, 15, 18, 21, 24, 27, 30-2, 35, 38, 41, 44, 47, 50.

Once this assignment is arrived at, its appropriateness is obvious. *C. Omnem* s.4 explains with laborious self-congratulation the device by which the third-year law students were enabled to retain the name Papinianistae. It was arranged by a beautiful device (*bellissima machinatio*) that the introductory texts in the titles of book 20, on mortgages, should be selected from his works. One of the results of the theory I propose is that book 20 is assigned to the Papinian committee, as was, when one comes to think of it, inevitable in the circumstances.

It is further appropriate in that, of the 23 titles in which the Appendix is separated from or precedes the Papinian mass, 13 turn out to have been edited by the Papinian committee.

It is possible to add a suggestion to explain the anomaly that in books 10, 13 and 16 the Sabinian committee did not display its normal pre-eminence in editorial activity. Although Tribonian had been dismissed from office as a result of the Nika riots in January 532 he remained chairman of the *Digest* commission, and there is little reason to doubt that he played a significant part in the discussions which preceded and the actual drafting of the imperial constitutions which the proceedings of the *Digest* rendered necessary.[178] In fact there was only one such group of constitutions after January 532, viz. the 19 constitutions addressed to John the Cappadocian on 18 October 532. Perhaps the preparation of these constitutions absorbed a large part of Tribonian's time during September and the early part of October 532, so that the editorial activity of the Sabinian committee

[177] For an argument based on the changing proportions of different types of displacement, see *Editing* 281–2.

[178] On Tribonian's authorship of these constitutions, see ch. 3 nn. 589–605.

suffered. This is reflected in the figures for displacements in books 10, 13, and 16 of the *Digest*.

If we assume that editing of the sixth group of books ended about 18 October 532, viz. that the Sabinian committee finished book 16 about then, and was then free to resume its normal energetic vein, this gives us a time scale for the editorial work. The work of excerpting finished about 9 July 532.[179] If the editing started in the middle of July and the sixth editorial group, consisting of books 16 to 18, was completed on 18 October 532, it is possible to calculate the average time needed to edit a group of three books, namely $16\frac{1}{6}$ days. At this speed the whole *Digest* was drafted by 29 March 533.

This however is only a ranging shot. A more likely arrangement is that each committee had to hand in a draft of two books a month, one each 15 or $15\frac{1}{2}$ rather than $16\frac{1}{6}$ days. Such an arrangement would be simple and therefore Tribonianic. It fits the work methods of Tribonian and Justinian, who arranged for legislative sessions to be held twice monthly if necessary, always on the days preceding and if necessary including the kalends of the following month or on those following the ides of the current month, or both.[180] A comparable arrangement would have been suitable for the delivery by the committees of their draft books. If this is correct the first draft of the *Digest* was finished in the middle, rather than at the end, of March 533.

THE FINAL DRAFT OF THE DIGEST

Common sense suggests that the first draft must have been revised, and certain changes in the law seem to have been introduced into the text at this late stage, for example the provision that the ownership of goods sold should pass to the buyer on delivery if the seller gave him credit.[181] These may be recognised by the circumstance that corresponding changes have not been made in other texts where they should have been, if a uniform version of the law was to be presented. Such last-minute changes seem to have been relatively few, and it is not easy to disentangle them from changes (if any) made at the instance of Justinian when he read the final draft. It is possible that the final draft was composed after a joint session of all six

---

[179] Above, p. 171.

[180] The dates of the constitutions in Tribonian's first quaestorship (*Corp. Iur. Civ.* ed. Krueger-Mommsen 11. 508-9) all fall on the kalends or days preceding the kalends of a month, and within that spectrum all between 18th and 11th days preceding, or between 5th day preceding and the kalends themselves. The only exceptions are Greek constitutions which are not concerned with the commission's work (*CJ* 1.4.25-3.43.1 ten days before the kalends, 1.4.26-3.2.4, 5-3.10.2-7.45.15-10.30.4-12.40.12-12.63.2 eight days before the kalends). This intermediate period was evidently used, if necessary, for Greek constitutions, while the early part of each month was kept free for the commission's work.

[181] Because the rule appears only in *D.* 18.1.19 (Pomp. 31 *QM*), in a text the displacement of which seems arbitrary, and in *Inst.* 2.1.41. Bluhme, 257, 263 omits this final recension.

senior commissioners, though the actual drafting would of course be done by Tribonian. Such a scheme would have been logical and consistent with the earlier organisation. This, as is obvious, relies on the maximum of delegation to the individual senior commissioners consistent with a reasonable attempt to secure uniformity in the final product. At the excerpting stage the working unit was a single commissioner with or without barrister assistants. Naturally this led to a rather uneven texture in the excerpts.[182] At the second stage when the first drafts of the various books and titles were composed the unit was, so far as we can judge, the committee consisting of two senior commissioners: the role, if any, of the advocates at this juncture is obscure. If then at the third stage, that of the final draft, the commission sat in joint session of all six, the overall design would exhibit a neat progression from the scrutiny of each text by a single commissioner to two and then to six. It might be hoped that in this way, despite decentralisation in the interests of speed, major inconsistences would be avoided. It cannot be pretended that Tribonian's aim, if such it was, was fully realised, since even expert lawyers with good memories find it difficult to remember the content of texts over a volume of material which runs to some 800,000 words and the perusal of which must have taken several weeks. Uniformity was to some extent sacrificed to speed. Tribonian may have overestimated the capacity of the human mind, as he assuredly did when framing the new law syllabus.

When complete, the final draft was presented to Justinian, who may be presumed to have read at least parts of it. Copies had then to be made before publication date on 16 December 533, and during the months required for this the _Institutes_ were drafted. Justinian's part in the actual execution of the project has not so far been discussed. It is described in the following terms: 'Our majesty too has at all times investigated and scrutinised what was being composed and if any doubts or uncertainties were found has invoked the heavenly spirit and altered or rendered the law in proper form.'[183] This suggests two forms of supervision. First, regular or even daily visits to the room in the palace where the commission worked, like the emperor's daily excursions to the building site of Hagia Sophia. Secondly, the bimonthly sessions at which doubtful points of law were solved by the issue of imperial constitutions.[184]

When every reservation is made, the chairmanship of the _Digest_ commission constitutes one of the most brilliant feats of organisation in the history of civil administration. Whether anyone else could have replaced Tribonian in A.D. 530 we cannot know, though the constitutions composed by preceding and succeeding quaestors give no evidence of a comparable intellectual drive. The future of European legal culture hung perhaps by a single human thread.

[182] And accounts for a puzzling feature of the _Digest_ long noted by scholars: Kunkel, _Introduction to Roman Legal and Constitutional History_ (2nd ed. 1973) 170-1.

[183] _C. Tanta_ pr. (16 Dec. 533).   [184] Above, n. 180.

CHAPTER SIX

Cradle of Laws: the Institutes

According to *C. Imperatoriam*[1] when the labour of preparing the *Digest* was completed Justinian gave a special mandate to Tribonian, chairman of the *Digest* commission, Theophilus, dean of the law school of Constantinople, and Dorotheus, the senior professor at Beirut, to prepare a new students' textbook, the *Institutes*. The need for such an elementary work for first-year students was recognised in December 530 in *C. Deo auctore*,[2] where it is said that after the completion of the *Digest* everything is to be governed by the two codices (i.e. the first *Codex* and the *Digest*) 'and anything else which may be promulgated to replace the elementary works, so that the raw intelligence of the student, nourished by a simple diet, may proceed more easily to advanced legal studies'.[3] Certainly the new law course would have failed at the outset had the students been plunged at the start into the rebarbative complexities of the *Digest*.

The execution of the plan can hardly have begun before mid-April 533, since the first draft of the *Digest* was not finished until mid-March at the earliest,[4] and it had then to be revised before presentation to the emperor, which may well not have taken place until late in May.

The preface to the *Institutes* (*C. Imperatoriam*), which was promulgated on 21 November 533, gives a retrospective but plausible account of the conception. Apart for the need to temper the wind to the shorn lamb there were two principal considerations. One was to attract good students by presenting an up-to-date version of the law such as the aspiring barristers would later meet in practice.[5] Hence the commissioners were to eliminate the obsolete and include references to imperial legislation altering or modernising the law. *C. Imperatoriam* is addressed to prospective students—*cupidae legum iuventuti*—and some features of the *Institutes*, for instance the inclusion of references to Homer, Virgil, Xenophon, Apelles, often, it is true in excerpts from the old writers,[6] are to be understood as a tacit plea to the young to put legal studies on the same intellectual and cultural level as history, literature or philosophy. The caviar of intellectual snobbery is accompanied by the

---

[1] *C. Imperatoriam* 3 (21 Nov. 533). On the *Institutes* see Wenger, *Quellen* §82.
[2] *C. Deo auctore* 11 (16 Dec. 533).   [3] Ibid.   [4] Above, ch. 5 nn. 178f.
[5] *C. Imperatoriam* 3 (21 Nov. 533).
[6] E.g. *Inst.* 1.2.2 (Virgil, Homer, Draco, Solon, the Athenians), 1.2.10 (Athenians and Lacedemonians), 2.1.34 (Apelles, Parrhasius), 2.7.1 (Homer, Piraeus, Telemachus), 2.15.4 (Parthenius), 3.23.2 (Homer, the Achaeans), 1.11.12 (Cato), 4.3.1 (Homer, *Odyssey*), 4.18.5 (Xenophon).

carrot of appointments to come. The law student who has completed the new course satisfactorily can look forward to an executive post in the government.[7]

An important element in the preparation of the *Institutes* was the desire to disseminate propaganda in favour of Justinian and to a lesser extent of Tribonian himself. The grandest exposition of this object is to be found at the end of *Deo auctore* in connection with the projected compilation of the *Digest*,[8] but *C. Imperatoriam* hints at a similar aim in a passage which defies logic. 'The elementary work,' it says, 'contains a brief account of the earlier law and of that which, later shrouded in obsolescence, has been illuminated by imperial reform.'[9] In the text of the *Institutes* the overwhelming though not exclusive emphasis is on the reforms of Justinian himself and his uncle.[10] As to Tribonian, there are three passages which stress the quaestor's responsibility for proposing changes adopted by Justinian.[11]

The *Institutes* assume the need for law reform. Their picture is of a law which changes with the times. Both in the past and especially, granted the able assistance of Tribonian, in the present the source of reform is the emperor. The student who under the old dispensation did not study imperial constitutions until the fifth year, and who even under the new will not return to them until then, must grasp from the outset the primacy of imperial legislation and among legislators the primacy of Justinian. It is a serious mistake to suppose that Justinian either was or presented himself as a conservative. Lawyers are indeed conservative, and Roman lawyers, like English, thought of legislation as a gloss on the common law, which in Rome was the law elaborated by the jurists. The syllabus, which comprised four years study of the jurists followed by one of imperial constitutions,[12] simply reflected their instinctive point of view, which the reforming team was determined to alter. Henceforth the student was to focus from the start

---

[7] *C. Imperatoriam* 7 (21 Nov. 533).   [8] *C. Deo auctore* 14 (15 Dec. 530).

[9] *C. Imperatoriam* 5 (21 Nov. 533).

[10] According to my count the *Institutes* refer to Justinian's reforming zeal (*nostra constitutio* and the like) in 87 passages, Anastasius has one reform (*Inst.* 3.5.1), Augustus as a reformer is mentioned in four (2.12 pr., 2.23.1, 2.23.12, 2.25 pr. but Justinian is determined to outdo him: *nuper et nos eundem principem superare contendentes . . . constitutionem fecimus*: 2.23.12), Claudius has one reform (*Inst.* 3.3.1), Gordian one (2.16.9), Hadrian four (*Inst.* 2.1.39, 2.19.6, 2.12 pr., 3.20.4), Justin two (*Inst.* 2.7.3, 2.12.4), Leo two (3.15.1, 3.19.14), Marcus three (2.6.14, 3.11 pr., 4.6.30), Nerva one (2.12 pr.), Pius one (1.8.2), Severus alone one (2.9.5), Severus and Antoninus two (1.26.3, 1.26.9), Trajan two (2.12 pr., 3.7.4), Zeno six (2.6.14, 3.24.3, 4.4.10, 4.13.10, 4.6.33e, 4.6.34). This makes 31 in all, just a third of the references to Justinian's reforms. I have not counted references which imply a declaratory decision (e.g. *idque d. Severus rescripsit*). Even if all the references to the enactment of constitutions by previous emperors are totalled (there are 65) they do not match the references to Justinian as legislator.

[11] *Inst.* 1.5.3 (two), 2.8.2, 2.23.12.

[12] *C. Omnem* 1, 5 (16 Dec. 533) makes it plain that in the fourth year of the old syllabus the students were reading the *responsa* of Paul on which no lectures were given. Under the new they are to read ten books of the *Digest* in the fourth year and in the fifth the codex of constitutions.

on the realities. The law is what the emperor lays down, not what Ulpian thought. If it can be shown that Ulpian favoured the new solution, so much the better, but its authority does not derive from him.

The method of composition is referred to, though not in detail, in *C. Imperatoriam*. From this we gather that all three commissioners took part in the work.[13] They excerpted all the classical elementary works but paid special attention to the *Institutes* and *Res Cottidianae* of Gaius, who is here first called *Gaius noster*.[14] Certain other commentaries were also taken into account.[15] Taken together, these materials make up the 'brief account of the earlier law'.[16] This was supplemented by reference to later, and especially Justinianic, developments.

How was the work organised? What parts did the three commissioners respectively play? The argument of the present chapter is a simple one, though it does not seem to have been advanced previously. Tribonian entrusted the law professors with the task of reading the old institutional books and preparing from them (and principally from the *Institutes* of Gaius) a draft. He modernised the text and inserted references to Justinian's legislation himself.

The older commentators assumed that the three commissioners worked jointly.[17] Then, in 1868, Huschke advanced the view[18] that the four books of the *Institutes* were allotted to the two professors in pairs, so that one undertook the drafting of books 1 and 2, the other of books 3 and 4. Tribonian confined himself to supervising the work of the law professors. Huschke thought that Dorotheus was responsible for the first two and Theophilus for the last two books, apart from 4.18, on criminal law, which Dorotheus wrote.

It is proposed to leave until later Huschke's arguments, which were largely based on alleged differences of style between the earlier and later books. One point must at once be made in his favour. From our knowledge of Tribonian's methods in the compilation of the *Digest* it is clear that he favoured a division of labour by books and not by subject matter, and, where considerations of speed permitted, the allocation of an equal number of books to each commissioner.[19] Since four books cannot be divided into three equal lots, there is much to be said a priori for the notion that he allotted two books to each professor. Indeed this feature of Huschke's theory has been widely accepted[20] (not for the reason given), though some scholars have proposed that the break should come at the end of the passages

---

[13] *C. Imperatoriam* 6 (21 Nov. 533).

[14] *C. Imperatoriam* 6 and again in *C. Omnem* 1 (16 Dec. 533).

[15] E.g. the *Institutiones* of Marcianus, Florentinus, Ulpian and Paul. Reconstructions by Ferrini, *Opere* 2, 307f.; Zocco-Rosa, *Ann. Ist. Stor. del Diritto Romano di Catania* 9, 10 (1901–11) 180f.

[16] Above, n. 9.   [17] E.g. Heineccius, *Recitationes*, prooemium 75.

[18] *Imp. Iustiniani Institutionum* IV, ed. P. E. Huschke (1868) praef.

[19] Ch. 5 nn. 17f.

[20] Grupe, *De Iustiniani Institutionum Compositione*: Katz-Dobrz, *RE* 9. 1573; Albertario, *Intro. allo. studio del dir. giustineaneo* (1935) 32; Wenger 600f.

dealing with succession,[21] viz. at book 3 title 12, instead of at the beginning of book 3. Nor has there been agreement about the identity of the professor responsible for each part. These are, however, relatively minor points. The real difficulty if Huschke's view is accepted is to explain Tribonian's role.

This role is crucial to an assessment of Huschke's idea. Unless the contributions of the chairman can be separately distinguished, there is no way either of disentangling the contributions of Theophilus and Dorotheus, or of deciding how important it is to do so. The question is not whether there is a contrast of style between the first and the last books, but whether such a contrast emerges once the passages attributable to Tribonian are excised. For Tribonian cannot be confined to a supervisory role. Those who think he could misconceive his image of himself. He was not a politician standing in need of expert assistance from professional lawyers. He was the greatest lawyer of the age; learned, practical, skilled in drafting.[22] As such he had played a full part in the work of the *Digest*, excerpting and editing with as much, indeed rather more, energy than any other commissioner.[23] Besides, though he was not actually quaestor when the *Institutes* were composed, he possessed outstanding talent as a propagandist. Would he be likely to allow Dorotheus or Theophilus to expound the merits of recent changes in the law enacted by Justinian and as often as not drafted by Tribonian himself?

It is indeed easy, building on Huschke, to construct a plausible hypothesis about the division of labour between the three. Suppose that Tribonian instructed the professors to revise the text of Gaius' *Institutes*, taking account of the other institutional works of Ulpian, Paul, Florentinus, Marcianus and the like, besides the *Res Cottidianae* of Gaius, but not to deal with post-classical developments unless already incorporated by interpolation in the texts. The professors were then to present their drafts to Tribonian, who would modernise the text and in particular contrast the darkness of the ancient complexities with the manifest humanity and simplicity of Justinian's own solutions.

The hypothesis accords with the political and psychological setting, and with the help of the set of norms of style developed in Chapter 3 it can be tested.

The procedure will be to examine all the passages in the *Institutes* in which Justinian is referred to, i.e. which contain *nos, nostra constitutio* or the like, or a verb such as *sancimus* governed by the majestic plural. What proportion of these passages contains marks of Tribonian's style? If the proportion is found to be high, that will be evidence of the truth of the hypothesis. We will then be able to ask whether there are any other passages in the *Institutes* which contain similar marks of style. Once the Tribonianic layer has been peeled off we shall then be a position to attack the Huschke theory directly and ask whether what remains displays evidence of the sort he suggests.

There appear to be 102 passages referring to Justinian in the *Institutes*.

---

[21] Buonamici, *Arch. Giur.* 58 (1897) 139; Ambrosino, *Atti. Verona* 1.133; Sangiorgi, *Ann. Palermo* 27.181, on which see J. A. C. Thomas, *The Institutes of Justinian* (1975) ix.
[22] C. *Tanta* 9 (16 Dec. 533).   [23] Ch. 5 n. 112.

They vary from a word or two to 50 or 60 lines. These are listed and the presence or absence of the appropriate marks of style noted. Two preliminary difficulties must be mentioned. One is to demarcate the passages in which the references to Justinian occur. Where are they to be taken to begin and end? Here the investigator must simply use his sense of style and coherence. In practice there are certain standard introductions, for example:

> quod nostra constitutio. . . .
> nostra autem constitutio. . . .
> sed haec quidem antea, nos autem. . . .

The last of these foreshadows the words of *C. Imperatoriam* about the contrast of the old law and the new imperial law.[24] These and similar expressions can often serve as a guide, but clearly the identification of the relevant passages is not just a mechanical operation. The second difficulty is that norms of style are relative, and not all the expressions listed in Chapter 3 can properly be used to mark off Tribonian's style from that of Theophilus and Dorotheus. In particular, ways of speaking, such as the use of *veteres* for classical lawyers, and other in-group or technical expressions which may be assumed to be common to academic lawyers though not to quaestors as a group, should not be used in the present context. On the other hand one can draw comfort from the evidence of the paraphrase of Theophilus, albeit drafted in Greek. From this it is plain that Theophilus wrote in a straightforward, indeed literal, manner and it is hardly likely that his Latin was greatly more rhetorical than his Greek. He makes no attempt to reproduce in his lectures the colourful language of the *Institutes*, and this would be hard to explain had he drafted the passages in question himself. It is true that we cannot say the same of Dorotheus, since the evidence from the Basilica does not permit a steady view of his style of composition. Here a different form of reassurance may be hoped for. If much the same contrast between the sobriety of the passages derived from the classical authors, but on our hypothesis concatenated by the professors, and the exuberance of the modernising parts is noted in both halves of the *Institutes*, this will be consistent with the notion that the writings of Dorotheus and Theophilus resembled each other more than either did Tribonian.

The passages are set out book by book. First the passage in question is demarcated by book, title, section and if necessary line. Then, in brackets, follow the opening words of the passage and the phrases, with line numbers, which show that the passage refers to Justinian, together with the expressions, if any, which point to Tribonian's authorship.

The latter are accompanied by references to the relevant footnotes in Chapter 3. Thus, for example, *Inst.* 3.2.7.6–18 (6–7 *quod iterum praetores corrigentes*[162] 9–10 *agnationis iure recluso*[163] 10 *sed nos . . . perfectissimo iure*[164] 11 *nostra constitutione* 14 *cum satis absurdum erat*[165] 15–16 *agnatis esse reclusum*)[166]

---

[24] *C. Imperatoriam* 5 (21 Nov. 533).

162. *N*. 416, 139.
163. *N*. 518.
164. *N*. 405.
165. *N*. 388.
166. *N*. 518'

means that a passage referring to Justinian is identified as running from line 6 to line 18 of *Inst*. 3.2.7, as is shown by the use of the phrases '*sed nos*' in line 7 and '*nostra constitutione*' in line 11. This passage contains the Tribonianic marks of style '*iterum*,' '*corrigentes*', '*secludere*', '*perfectissimus*', and '*satis . . . est*', for which the references are to be found in footnotes 416, 139, 518, 405 and 388 of Chapter 3 respectively.

BOOK I

Inst. 1.1.2   (1 *incipientibus nobis*   5 *rudis*[25]   10 *perducamus*   11 *leniore via*[26]

1.5.1   (1 *multis modis*[27]   5 *aliis multis modis*[28]   7 *nostris constitutionibus*)

1.5.3   (1 *antea tripertita fuerat*[29]   8 *non frequentabatur*[30]   9 *nostra pietas* 12 *cunabula*[31]   17 *promulgavimus*[32] *inter nostras decisiones*   18 *Triboniano viro excelso*   19 *altercationes*[33]   21 *eiusdem quaestoris*   23–25 *nullo discrimine habito*[34]   26 *donavimus*[35]   26–27 *multis modis*[36])

1.6.2   (2–3 *nostra constitutione*   6 *non est verisimile*[37])

1.6.7.7–23   (7–8 *quod non erat ferendum*[38]   10 *quare nos*   16 *nos mediam viam eligentes*[39]   20 *tetigerit*[40]   21 *cur non etiam?*[41])

1.7.1.2–7   (2–4 *quam tollendam esse censemus*   4 *satis fuerat inhumanum*[42])

1.10 pr.   10–14   (10 *variabatur*[43]   10–11 *nostra processit decisio*)

1.10.13.3–11   (3 *qualis est*   4 *naturalis fuerat . . .*[44]   6–7 *interdictum fuerat*[45]   8 *ex nostra constitutione*   11 *nostra constitutio*)

1.11.2   (1–2 *hodie ex nostra constitutione*   14 *legitimo modo*[46])

1.12.4.4–11   (4–5 *sed ex constitutione nostra*   7 *quis enim patiatur?*[47])

1.12.6.2–17   (2–3 *sed antea quidem*   3 *antiqua observatio*[48]   6 *nostra autem providentia*   6–7 *in melius reformavit*[49]   7–8 *fictione explosa*[50] 8 *recta via*[51])

1.12.8   (2–3 *secundum nostras constitutiones*   10 *diximus*[52])

1.22 pr.   2–14   (2 *pubertatem autem veteres*   4 *nostra autem maiestas*   5 *castitati temporum nostrorum*[53]   11 *disposuimus*)

1.25.13.2–9   (2–3 *minores autem excusabantur*   4 *a nostra autem constitutione*   6 *qua constitutione*   7–8 *cum erat incivile*[54])

Fourteen passages in book I therefore contain at least one mark of Tribonian's style. Five do not:

1.8.2   (*nostro imperio*) . . . (*causa legibus cognita*)

1.10.11   (1 *sunt et aliae personae*   4–5 *enumerari permisimus*)

[25] Ch. 3 (henceforth understood) n. 326.
[26] N. 415.   [27] N. 498.   [28] N. 498.   [29] N. 368.   [30] N. 248.
[31] N. 338.   [32] N. 114.   [33] N. 410.   [34] N. 421.   [35] N. 91.
[36] N. 498.   [37] N. 542.   [38] N. 366.   [39] N. 415.   [40] N. 533.
[41] N. 369.   [42] N. 368, 388.   [43] N. 373.   [44] N. 368.   [45] N. 368.
[46] N. 313.   [47] N. 369.   [48] N. 502.   [49] N. 414.   [50] N. 188.
[51] N. 415.   [52] N. 89.   [53] Nn. 127–30.   [54] N. 366.

1.11.12 (1–2 *apud Catonem bene scriptum refert antiquitas*[55] 3 *unde et nos eruditi* 3–4 *in nostra constitutione* 6 *constituimus*)

1.9.13–16 (13–14 *ita tamen vocantur* 14–15 *quod nostra constitutio*)

1.20.5 (1 *nos autem per constitutionem* 3–4 *disposumius*)

BOOK II

Inst. 2.1.34.3–6 (4 *nobis videtur melius esse*[56] 5 *ridiculus*[57] 6 *vilissimae tabulae*[58])

2.1.40.4–10 (*et ideo* 10 *ex nostra constitutione nulla differentia est*[59])

2.6.1 (1 *constitutum fuerat*[60] ... *nobis melior sententia resedit* 10 *defraudentur*[61] 12 *promulgavimus*[62])

2.6.14.4–17 (4 *constitutio autem divae memoriae Zenonis* 5 *bene prospexit*[63] 12 *nostra autem divina constitutio* 13 *promulgavimus*[64] 16 *Zenonianae constitutioni*[65])

2.7.1.6–14 (6 *hae mortis causa donationes* 8 *ambiguum fuerat*[66] 11–12 *a nobis constitutum est* 13–14 *nostra formavit constitutio*)

2.7.2–4 (2.2 *appellamus*[67] 7 *nostra constitutio* 9 *perfectum robur*[68] 2.13 *contra constitutio* 18 *invenimus*[69] 19 *ex nostris constitutionibus* 20 *posumius*[70] 23 *per nostram constitutionem* 24 *praestavimus*[71] 27 *in nostra constitutione* 3.1 *est et aliud genus* 3 *penitus erat incognitum*[72] 10 *divus Iustinus pater noster* 11 *fuerat permissum*[73] 17–18 *nos plenissimo fini tradere cupientes*[74] 4.1 *erat olim et aliud modus* 6 *defraudari*[75] 10 *invenimus viam*[76] 13–14 *legislatores*[77] 15 *manifestissimum est*[78] 18 *definivimus*[79])

2.8 pr. 6–15 (6 *quod nos corrigentes*[80] *deduximus*[81] 8 *Italicae fuerant*[82] 11 *imposuimus*)

2.8.1.7–13 (7 *sed ne creditores* 9 *nostra constitutione* 11 *cuius tenore*[83] 12–13 *satis abundeque provisum est*[84])

2.8.2.13–30 (13 *sed etiam hoc* 15–16 *Triboniani viri eminentissimi* 17 *promulgavimus*[85] 22–23 *disposuimus* 29–30 *non secundum nostram dispositionem*)

2.9.1.2–2 (15.1.2 *olim quidem* 8–9 *quod nobis inhumanum visum est*[86] 10 *pepercimus*[87] 12–13 *secudum antiquam observationem*[88] 13–14 *quae enim invidia est?*[89] 2.1 *hocque a nobis dispositum est* 6 *inhumanum quid accidebat*[90] 10–11 *statuimus*)

2.10.1–4 (1 *sed ut nihil penitus ignoretur* 2.1–2 *sed praedicta quidem* ... *postea vero* 3.1 *paulatim*[91] 3 *in unam consonantiam*[92] 4.1–2 *sed his omnibus ex nostra constitutione* 2 *propter testamentorum sinceritatem*[93] 5 *secundum illius constitutionis tenorem*[94])

2.10.10–11 (10.1 *sed neque heres* 7 *conturbatum fuerat*[95] 9 *coadunati fuerant*[96] 10–11 *coniuncti fuerant*[97] 13–14 *nos corrigentes*[98] 21 *nostro*

---

[55] But the reference to Cato could be taken as a Tribonianic mark. [56] N. 414.
[57] N. 824. [58] N. 842. [59] N. 417. [60] N. 367. [61] N. 424.
[62] N. 114. [63] N. 436. [64] N. 114. [65] N. 381. [66] N. 368.
[67] N. 719. [68] Cf. n. 320. [69] N. 107. [70] N. 112. [71] N. 365.
[72] N. 366. [73] N. 367. [74] N. 538. [75] N. 424. [76] Nn. 107, 415.
[77] N. 490. [78] N. 346. [79] Cf. n. 142. [80] N. 139. [81] N. 86.
[82] N. 368. [83] N. 535. [84] N. 427. [85] N. 114. [86] N. 217.
[87] N. 797. [88] N. 502. [89] N. 369. [90] N. 217. [91] N. 505. [92] N. 204.
[93] N. 229. [94] N. 535. [95] N. 367. [96] N. 367. [97] N. 367. [98] N. 139.

codici inseri permisimus   11.1 *legatariis autem*   4–5 *in quadam nostra
constitutione*   7 *licentiam damus*)

2.11.6   (1 *sciendum tamen est*   2–3 *principales constitutiones*[99]   5–6 *quod
nostra constitutio latius extendens*[100]   8 *cuius constitutionis tenore per-
specto*[101])

2.13.5   (1–2 *sed haec vetustas introducebat; nostra vero constitutio*   16
induximus[102]   17 *constitutioni nostrae*)

2.14 pr. 3–10   (3 *olim quidem*   5.5–6 *hodie vero ex nostra constitutione*
7 *induximus*[103]   9 *Massurium Sabinum*[104])

2.16.1   (1–2 *qua ratione excitati constitutionem in nostro posuimus codice*[105]
2–3 *qua prospectum est*)

2.18.3   (1–2 *sed haec ita accipienda sunt*   3 *quod nostra constitutio*   4–5
quantacumque pars[106]   6 *querela quiescente*[107])

2.19.6.4–17   (4–5 *sed hoc divus quidem Hadrianus*   6 *divus autem Gordianus*
7–8 *sed nostra benevolentia*   8 *imperio nostro*   9 *praestavit*[108]   10 *cuius
(constitutionis) tenorem*[109]   15 *nostrae constitutionis*)

2.20.2–3   (2.1–2 *sed olim quidem erant genera quattuor*[110]   8–9 *nostra autem
constitutio*   11 *una sit natura*[111]   15–16 *cuius constitutionis modum ex
ipsius tenore*[112]   16 *perfectissime*[113]   3.1–3 *sed non . . . existimavimus*[114]
invenimus[115]   6 *pinguiorem naturam*[116]   8 *nulla sit inter ea differentia*[117]
9 *ex natura fideicommissorum*[118]   10–11 *fideicommissi natura*[119]   11 *in
primis legum cunabulis*[120]   15–16 *natura utriusque iuris*[121]   17 *subtiliori-
bus auribus*)

2.20.23.5–17   (5 *sed ex constitutione nostra*   8 *diligentiore tractatu habito*[122]
9 *in nostra constitutione*   17 *praecellat*[123])

2.20.34.6–13   (6–7 *sed quia incivile esse putavimus*[124]   8 *vituperandum
fuerat visum*[125]   9–10 *per nostram constitutionem*)

2.20.35.5–9   (5–6 *sed simili modo et hoc correximus*[126])

2.20.36.23–31   (23–24 *at huiusmodi scrupulositas nobis non placuit*[127]
31 *secta temporum meorum non patitur*[128])

2.23.7   (1 *sed quia stipulationes*   4 *homo excelsi ingenii Papinianus*[129]
5–6 *nobis magis simplicitas placet*[130]   7 *differentiis*[131]   8 *exploso
senatusconsulto Pegasiano*[132]   9 *supervenit*[133]   15 *ex nostra auctoritate*
21/2 *praecipuum fuerat*[134]   26 *transponimus*[135])

2.23.12   (1–2 *et quia prima fideicommissorum cunabula*[136]   3 *divus Augustus*   4 *nuper et nos eundem principem superare contendentes* (!)   4–5
Tribonianus vir excelsus   22 *depereat*[137])

These 25 passages from book II contain at least one mark of Tribonian's style. A further ten have no such mark:

2.4.3.4   (*quae omnia statuit nostra constitutio*)

[99] N. 160.   [100] N. 292.   [101] N. 535.
[102] N. 101.   [103] N. 101.   [104] Nn. 40f.   [105] N. 112.   [106] N. 398.
[107] N. 385.   [108] N. 365.   [109] N. 535.   [110] N. 366.   [111] Nn. 172–4.
[112] N. 535.   [113] N. 406.   [114] Cf. *existimamus* nn. 95, 759.   [115] N. 107.
[116] Nn. 172–4; cf. 293.   [117] N. 417.   [118] Nn. 172–4.   [119] Nn. 172–4.
[120] N. 338.   [121] Nn. 172–4.   [122] N. 537.   [123] N. 805.   [124] N. 816.
[125] Nn. 232, 367.   [126] Cf. n. 139.   [127] N. 237.   [128] Nn. 158, 527, 130.
[129] Nn. 40f.   [130] N. 238.   [131] N. 417.   [132] N. 188.   [133] N. 396.
[134] N. 368.   [135] N. 541.   [136] N. 338.   [137] N. 272.

2.5.5.3–7 (3–4 *quam habitationem habentibus* 5 *nostra decisio*[138] 5–6 *permisimus*)

2.6.12.5–7 (5–6 *quod nostra constitutio*)

2.11 pr. 7–17 (7–8 *quod nostra constitutio* 17 *exposuimus*)

2.12 pr. 27–30 (27–28 *exceptis videlicet his quae ex constitutionibus... nostris propter diversas causas*)

2.12.3.5–10 (5 *saepe autem etiam litterati* 7 *unde nostra constitutio* 8–9 *secundum normam eius*)

2.12.4 (1 *caecus autem* 2–3 *lex divi Iustini patris mei* 3 *introduxit*)

2.18.2.2–3 (2.2 *secundum nostrae constitutionis divisionem*)

2.18.6.4–7 (4 *vel si donata fuerit* 5–6 *nostra constitutio mentionem fecit*)

2.20.27 (1 *sed nec huiusmodi species* 3 *in nostro codice constitutio posita est* 4 *medevimus* 6 *ex ipsius constitutionis lectione* 7 *nec per nostram constitutionem*)

BOOK III

Inst. 3.1.2a (1 *quibus connumerari necesse est* 3–4 *secundum divalium constitutionum tenorem*[139] 5–6 *nostrae amplexae sunt constitutiones* 16 *censuimus*)

3.1.14–16 (14.1–2 *sed ea omnia antiquitati placuerunt* 3 *a nostra constitutione* 4 *posuimus*[140] 5 *invenimus*[141] 10 *corrigentes*[142] *scripsimus*[143] 11 *definivimus*[144] 26–27 *nostra autem constitutione* 30 *servavimus* 32–33 *ex praefatae constitutionis tenore*[145] 15.1 *item vetustas* 10 *contra naturam*[146] 15–16 *naturae suffragio muniuntur*[147] 17 *diximus*[148] 16.1–2 *sed nos* 6 *a nostro codice segregavimus* 7 *concessimus* 7–8 *nostra autem constitutione* 13–14 *quam constitutionem nostram secundum sui vigorem*[149] 19 *iubemus* 20–21 *progenies*[150])

3.2.3a–4 (3a.1 *et haec quidem* 2 *simplicitatem*[151] 9 *differentiam*[152] 11 *paulatim*[153] 12 *corrigentes*[154] ... *adimplentes*[155] 3b.1 *nos vero* 3 *laudamus*[156] 4 *invenimus*[157] 4–7 *quare etenim dabatur?*[158] 12–13 *nostra constitutione* 4.1–2 *hoc etiam addendum nostrae constitutioni existimavimus*[159] 4–5 *definivimus*[160] 15 *semoti*[161])

3.2.7.6–18 (6–7 *quod iterum praetores corrigentes*[162] 9–10 *agnationis iure recluso*[163] 10 *sed nos ... perfectissimo iure*[164] 11 *nostra constitutione* 14 *cum satis absurdum erat*[165] 15–16 *agnatis esse reclusum*[166])

3.3.4–6 (4.1 *sed nos constitutione* 2 *nostro nomine decorato posuimus*[167] 3 *existimavimus respicientes ad naturam*[168] 8 *defraudabatur*[169] 9–10 *quid enim peccavit*[170] ? 5.1 *sed cum antea* 7 *nobis visum est recta et simplici via*[171] 12 *praeposuimus*[172] 6.1–2 *sed quamadmodum nos prospeximus*)

3.6.10.4–26 (4–5 *sed nostra constitutione* 6 *usque ad nostra tempora satis obscurum*[173] *atque nube plenum et undique confusum fuerat*[174] 20 *vocavimus*)

[138] Ch. 5 nn. 63–5, but too technical. [139] Nn. 458, 535. [140] N. 112.
[141] N. 107. [142] N. 139. [143] N. 828. [144] Cf. n. 142. [145] N. 535.
[146] Nn. 172–4. [147] Nn. 172–4. [148] N. 89. [149] N. 156. [150] N. 395.
[151] N. 238. [152] N. 417. [153] N. 505. [154] N. 139. [155] Cf. n. 713.
[156] N. 108. [157] N. 107. [158] N. 369. [159] Nn. 95, 144, 759.
[160] Cf. n. 142. [161] N. 412. [162] Nn. 416, 139. [163] N. 518. [164] N. 405.
[165] N. 388. [166] N. 518. [167] N. 112. [168] Nn. 759, 150, 172–4.
[169] N. 424. [170] N. 369. [171] N. 415. [172] N. 808. [173] Nn. 127–30.
[174] Nn. 388, 300, 368.

3.7.3–4 (3.1 *sed nostra constitutio* 3 *compendioso tractatu habito composuimus*[175] 7 *interpretati sumus*[176] 11 *ius quod erat*[177] 16 *deduximus*[178] 16–17 *patronis cum sua progenie semotis*[179] 24 *ex nostra constitutione* 27 *ex constitutione nostra* 32–33 *multis aliis casibus a nobis in praefata constitutione congregatis* 45 *fecimus* 4.1 *sed haec hodie* 4–5 *nullae erant*[180] 10 *cautum fuerat*[181] 13 *supervenit*[182] 17 *sed nostra constitutione* 20 *deleri*[183] 22–23 *ipsas vias*[184] 24 *transposuimus*[185])

3.9 pr. 9–11 (9–10 *sed et hic a nostra constitutione* 10–11 *iure civili non incognitus*[186])

3.9.4–8 (4.1 *sed eas quidem induxit* 2–3 *nobis autem nihil incuriosum praetermissum est sed nostris constitutionibus omnia corrigentes*[187] 5.1 *quae autem* 2 *posita fuerat*[188] 3 *compendioso sermone*[189] 5 *nostra constitutio* 6.1–2 *cumque antea* 4–5 *per constitutionem nostram* 7–8 *posuimus*[190] 9 *coartavimus*[191] 9–10 *ut sit aliqua differentia*[192] 12–13 *scrupulositate et inextracabili errore*[193] 7.1 *aliam vero* 4 *posita fuerat*[194] 5 *posuimus*[195] 9 *suo vigore*[196])

3.10.1.7–2.11 (1.7 *usus etenim* 9 *nostra prohibuit constitutio* 2.1–2 *nunc autem nos* 3 *coartavimus*[197] 10 *ex nostra constitutione*)

3.12 (pr. 1 *erant olim aliae* 4 *fuerat introducta*[198] 6 *posteritas*[199] 11 *perfectius*[200] 1.1–3 *erat adquisitio*[201] 5–6 *nostris temporibus*[202] 6 *existimantes*[203] 6–7 *a nostra civitate deleri*[204] 7 *nostris digestis*)

3.19.12.3–15 (1 *sed cum . . . 1–2 materiam contentiosis hominibus*[205] 6–7 *ideo nostra constitutio* 8–9 *scripsimus*[206] 12 *manifestissimis*[207])

3.19.13.8–13 (9 *sed cum* 10 *placuit nobis* 11 *iuris articulum*[208])

3.19.14.4–8 (4 *sed cum Leo* 6 *nobis placuit* 7 *perfectum robur*[209])

3.21.9–15 (9 *multum autem tempus* 10 *ex principalibus constitutionibus*[210] 12 *defraudari*[211] 12–13 *per constitutionem nostram*)

3.23.1.5–19 (5–6 *inter veteres satis abundeque hoc dubitabatur*[212] 6–7 *sed nostra decisio* 17 *nobis placuit*)

3.23.2.23–29 (23 *sed Proculi sententia* 27 *argumentatur*[213] 28–29 *et in nostris digestis latius significatur*[214])

3.27.7.6–16 (6 *quod veteres quidem* 8 *fuerant legata*[215] 8–9 *nostra autem constitutio* 9 *unam naturam*[216] 12 *sed tantummodo*[217])

3.28.3.6–9 (6 *sed si* 7 *antea dubitabatur*[218] 7–8 *post nostram decisionem*)

3.29.3a (1 *sed cum hoc quidem* 3–4 *item fuerat*[219] 6–7 *ideo nostra processit constitutio . . . apertissime*[220] 12–13 *secundum nostrae constitutionis definitiones* 14 *apertius*[221])

Hence 20 passages relating to Justinian in book III contain at least one mark of Tribonian's style. There are also six which do not:

[175] Nn. 537, 78. [176] N. 389. [177] N. 366.
[178] N. 86. [179] Nn. 395, 412. [180] N. 366. [181] N. 367. [182] N. 396.
[183] N. 452. [184] N. 415. [185] N. 541. [186] N. 307. [187] N. 139.
[188] N. 367. [189] N. 374. [190] N. 112. [191] Cf. n. 76. [192] N. 417.
[193] Nn. 237, 375. [194] N. 367. [195] N. 112. [196] N. 156. [197] Cf. n. 76.
[198] N. 367. [199] N. 225. [200] Cf. n. 320. [201] N. 366. [202] N. 127.
[203] N. 144. [204] N. 452. [205] N. 186. [206] N. 828. [207] N. 346.
[208] N. 387. [209] Cf. n. 320. [210] N. 160. [211] N. 424. [212] N. 168.
[213] N. 432. [214] N. 292. [215] N. 367. [216] Nn. 172–4. [217] N. 534.
[218] N. 168. [219] N. 367. [220] N. 407. [221] N. 290.

3.2.8.4–8   (4 *quod ex nostra constitutione*)

3.5 pr. 3–5   (3 *quo numero sunt*   5 *nostra erexit constitutio*[222])

3.10.3.5   (5 *per competentes   nostros magistratus*)

3.11.7   (1–2 *sed cum perspeximus*   2–3 *lata est a nobis plenissima constitutio*   5–6 *ex ipsa lectione constitutionis*)

3.23 pr. 5–24   (5 *sed haec quidem*   7–8 *nihil a nobis innovatum est*)

3.28 pr. 6–14   (6 *ut tamen*   10 *nostra discrevit constitutio*[223]   14 *secundum
novellae nostrae constitutionis divisionem*)

BOOK IV

Inst. 4.1.8.10–25   (10 *et cum nobis*   12 *altercationes*[224]   14–15 *nos huiusmodi
calliditati obviam euntes per nostram decisionem*[225])

4.1.16.6–28   (6 *sed nostra providentia*   7 *in decisionibus nostris*   19–20
commodata fuit   30–31 *manifestissimum est*[226])

4.6.8.4–7   (4 *sed ex nostra constitutione*   5 *plenius*[227]   7 *a nostris legibus
recedere*)

4.6.28.8–29.12   (28.8 *quamvis enim incertum erat*[228]   10 *nostra tamen
constitutio*   29.1 *fuerat antea*[229]   3 *invenientes*[230]   7–8 *naturam bonae
fidei iudicii*[231]   12 *induximus*[232])

4.6.30.8–15   (8 *sed nostra constitutio*   9 *latius*[233]   13 *satis impium esse
credidimus*[234]   15 *defraudetur*[235])

4.6.33e   (1 *sed haec quidem antea*   2 *lex Zenoniana et nostra*   8 *sicut supra
diximus*[236])

4.8.7   (1–2 *sed veteres quidem*   4 *asperitatem respuendam*[237]   5–6 *quis
enim patitur?*[238]   11 *legum commentatores invenimus*[239])

4.11.2–7   (2.1 *sed haec hodie*   5.3–4 *nulla differentia introducenda*[240]   6
secundum veterem regulam   6.1 *apertius et perfectissime*[241]   2–3 *in ipsis
rerum documentis*[242]   7.2–3 *in omnibus nostris provinciis*   5 *omnium
nostrarum civitatum*)

4.13.2.7–9   (7 *cuius tempora nos*   9 *constitutione nostra coartavimus*[243])

4.13.10.14–25   (14 *hodie autem*   17 *Zenonianae constitutioni*[244]   18 *legislator*[245]   19 *indutias*[246]   20 *natura actionis*[247])

4.13.11.7–12   (7 *eas vero exceptiones*   10 *frequentari nullo perspeximus
modo*[248]   12 *proteletur*[249])

4.16.1.13–22   (13–14 *ex nostra constitutione*   16 *haec autem omnia*   19
invenimus[250])

4.18.5.4–20   (4 *telum autem . . . Gaius noster*[251]   11 *invenire possumus* 12
appellamus[252]   13–14 *admonet nos Xenophon*   18 *odiosis*[253])

4.18.8   (1 *item lex Iulia*   2 *exoritur*[254]   9–10 *secundum nostrae constitutionis definitionem*   11 *apertius*[255])

4.18.12   (1 *sed exposuimus*   2–3 *quasi per indicem tetigisse*[256])

---

222 Cf. n. 754 but this is weaker.   223 Cf. n. 744 but this is weaker.
224 N. 410.   225 N. 503, ch. 5 nn. 31, 63–5.   226 N. 346.   227 N. 294.
228 N. 366.   229 N. 367.   230 N. 147.   231 Nn. 172–4.   232 N. 101.
233 N. 292.   234 N. 388.   235 N. 424.   236 N. 89.   237 N. 386.
238 N. 369.   239 Nn. 727, 107.   240 N. 417.   241 Nn. 290, 406.
242 N. 459.   243 Cf. n. 76.   244 N. 381.   245 N. 490.   246 N. 481.
247 Nn. 172–4.   248 Nn. 248, 370.   249 N. 401.   250 N. 107.   251 N. 766.
252 Cf. *invenimus* nn. 107, 719.   253 N. 192.   254 N. 276.   255 N. 290.
256 N. 533.

These fifteen passages from book IV contain at least one mark of Tribonian's style. A further six do not:

4.6.24.9–11   (9 *quod nostra constitutio*   9–10 *quae in nostro codice fulget*
   10–11 *ex lege condicticiam*[257])

4.6.25.5–8   (5–6 *item ex lege condicticia a nostra constitutione oritur*[258]
   7–8 *contra nostrae constitutionis normam*)

4.6.26.7–12   (7 *sed illa*   8–9 *infitiatione duplicatur*[259]   10 *magistratuum*
   nostrorum)

4.6.35.2–4   (2–4 *sed in eodem iudicio cognita veritate errorem suum corrigere*
   ei permittimus)

4.16 pr. 3   (*quod et nobis studio est*)

4.16.1.1–5   (1 *ecce enim*   2 *ex nostra constitutione*)

For the four books of the *Institutes* together there are 74 passages referring to Justinian which contain marks of Tribonian's style, against 27 which do not. The latter include some very short passages of no more than a few words.

Subject to Huschke's arguments, to which I return, the natural conclusion would be that Tribonian is the author of all the passages in question, not merely of the majority. For it would be difficult to conceive of a rational division of labour between him and the professors which would result in such a division of the texts.

What else can prima facie be put to Tribonian's account? First, there are nine places in the *Institutes*[260] which state that fuller information on the point is to be found in the *Digest*. Except as publicity for the *Digest* these are rather pointless. The texts do not give the *Digest* reference and the student would be hard put to it to look up the relevant passages: presumably practitioners went by the rubrics. They are analogous to other *Institutes* texts which say that the student can consult the wording of the relevant constitutions if he wishes. Eight of the nine references to the *Digest* use *latior* or *latius* in this connection.[261] A typical example is *sicut in latioribus digestorum libris opportunius apparebit*.[262] Four of these eight sentences occur in passages which have already been assigned to Tribonian[263] and it seems right to assign the other four to him also, especially as *latius* (though not *latior*) is a mark of his style.[264] The ninth passage is one of those considered above which refers to Justinian but was found not to contain any mark of Tribonian's style.[265] Since this last passage is the only one which occurs in the first two books of the *Institutes*, it could be argued that most of the references to the *Digest* were inserted by the professor responsible for the draft of the last two books. If that is so Theophilus cannot have drafted the last two books, because in his *Paraphrase* he fails to reproduce one of the references, namely the famous *unus casus* in which the possessor of property

257 N. 240 but too technical.   258 Above, n. 257.   259 N. 483 but too technical.
260 *Inst.* 1.10.11, 3.12.1, 3.23.2, 4.6.2, 4.6.5, 4.6.37, 4.13.6, 4.14.3, 4.18.1–2.
261 All except *Inst.* 1.10.11.   262 *Inst.* 4.6.2.
263 *Inst.* 3.12.1, 3.23.2, 4.14.3, 4.18.12.   264 Ch. 3 n. 292.
265 *Inst.* 1.10.11, above, p. 192.

is the plaintiff in an action 'as is more aptly explained in the more volumin-ous books of the *Digest*'.[266] Scholars have never been able to identify this case, if indeed it exists. Theophilus was equally at a loss and he passes it over in silence. So he cannot be the author of the reference to the *Digest*. If there was no other evidence, Dorotheus might be, but since, as we saw, four of the eight passages in the last two books contain marks of Tribonian's style, the ex-quaestor is likely to be responsible for the rest also. Incidentally the fact that Theophilus does not refer to the *unus casus* is not a conclusive argu-ment against Huschke's hypothesis that he drafted the last two books, in one of which the *unus casus* occurs. He may have been unable without embarrass-ment to ask Tribonian to elucidate the passage in question.

The policy of contrasting the old law with the new led to the insertion of several 'historical' passages apart from those already cited, some of which contain marks of Tribonian's style:

> *Inst.* 2.13 pr. 9–16 (9 *sed non ita* 10–11 *fuerat antiquitati observatum*[267] 11–12 *non fuerant heredes scripti*[268] 16 *necesse erat*[269])
>
> 3.3 pr. 1–4 (1 *lex duodecim tabularum* 2 *progeniem*[270] 4 *expellebat*)
>
> 3.9.2.11–14 (11 *nam angustissimis finibus*[271] 13 *praetor* 16 *dilatavit*)
>
> 3.15 pr. 10–15 (10–11 *sed haec sollemnia verba olim quidem in usu fuerunt* 11 *postea autem Leoniana constitutio*[272])
>
> 3.24.3.12–23 (12 *sed talis contractus . . . inter veteres dubitabatur*[273] 14 *lex Zenoniana* 16 *propriam statuit naturam*[274] 17 *inclinantem*[275] 18 *fulciendam*[276])
>
> 4.1.4.16–24 (16 *sed hae actiones* 20 *ex consequentia*[277] 22 *manifestissi-mum est*[278])
>
> 4.2.1.7–18 (7 *sed ne dum talia excogitentur inveniatur via*[279] 9 *melius divalibus constitutionibus*[280])
>
> 4.4.10.6–11 (6–7 *hoc videlicet observando* 7 *Zenoniana constitutio*[281] *secundum eius tenorem*[282]
>
> 4.11 pr. 1–2 (1–2 *alius antiquitati placuit, alium novitas amplexa est*[283])
>
> 4.15.4a.5–6 (5–6 *quorum vis et potestas plurimam inter se differentiam apud veteres habebat*[284])

In contrast with these ten historical passages which contain at least one mark of style there are two which do not:

> 3.5.1.4–13 (4–5 *exceptis solis tantummodo* 6 *lex Anastasiana* 12 *anteponit*)
>
> 4.15.4a.13–17 (13–14 *hodie tamen aliter observatur*)

Once more the Tribonianic passages so predominate that the natural inference is that all the passages which contrast the old state of the law with the new, and explain the stages of its evolution, are his.

[266] *Inst.* 4.6.2. [267] Ch. 3 n. 368. [268] N. 367. [269] N. 366. [270] N. 395. [271] N. 299. [272] N. 381. [273] N. 168. [274] Nn. 172–4. [275] N. 480. [276] N. 336. [277] N. 394. [278] N. 346. [279] N. 415. [280] Nn. 414, 458. [281] N. 381. [282] N. 535. [283] N. 224. [284] N. 417.

Nor is this necessarily the end of Tribonian's contributions. Huschke argued[285] that the author of the first two books (in his opinion Dorotheus) was also the compiler of the last title of the *Institutes*, 4.18, on criminal law (*de publicis iudiciis*). He pointed out that 4.17 on the office of judge (*de officio iudicis*) is introduced as if it were the last title: *superest ut de officio iudicis dispiciamus*,[286] 'it remains to examine the duties of a judge'. This makes it look as if 4.18 is an addendum to a draft which originally stopped at 4.17. But as 4.6 also begins with *superest* the argument is not strong. He also pointed out that 1.2.12 says that the whole law pertains to persons, things and actions, which would exclude criminal law, since 4.18 pr. tells us that criminal proceedings are not conducted by action and that they have nothing in common with other proceedings. It seems as if 1.1.4, which introduces the distinction between private and public law, and has been taken from Ulpian,[287] was added at the end of the first draft of title 1.1 in order to link up with 4.18. Indeed 1.1.4 does not follow naturally on what precedes:

> 1.1.3 Iuris praecepta sunt haec: honeste vivere, alterum non laedere, suum cuique tribuere. 4 Huius studii duae sunt positiones, publicum et privatum

As we have seen[288] at least three passages in 4.18 have marks of Tribonian's style and it is reasonable to attribute the composition of this title to him. But this does not mean that in composing it he did not use classical material on criminal law. Just as he took 1.1.4 from Ulpian so he may well have used, for instance, Marcianus on criminal trials. Tribonian's interest in criminal law, relatively to the other commissioners, is shown by the number of texts he allotted to book 48 of the *Digest*.[289] Hence he was the natural author of such a chapter, once it was decided to include it.

There are certain other passages which contain Tribonian's marks:

> *Inst.* 2.10.13.6–14.6 (14.1–2 *sed haec quidem*   2–3 *si quis autem*   5–6 *perfectissimum*[290] *testamentum*)
> 3.8.3.3–6 (4–5 *Claudianis temporibus*[291])
> 3.9.12 (1–2 *bene anteriores principes providerunt*[292])
> 4.6.40.5–6 (5 *inhumanum enim erat*[293])
> 4.7.5.4–5 (4–5 *stultissimus*[294] ... *facillime*)
> 4.18.3.3 (1 *lex Iulia maiestatis*   3 *suum vigorem*[295])
> 4.12 pr. 3–6 (3–4 *antiquitus competere* ... *certos fines*[296])
>   and perhaps
> 2.13.7.11–13 (11–12 *sed aliud adminiculum*   12 *paulo post*[297]   13 *manifestum fiat*)

A careful reader will not be in any doubt about the existence of two layers

---

285 Huschke, praef. vii.   286 *Inst.* 4.17.1.
287 *D.* 1.1.1.2 (Ulp. 1 *inst.*).   288 Above, nn. 251–6.   289 Ch. 5 n. 110.
290 N. 405.   291 N. 381.   292 Cf. *bene prospicere* n. 436.   293 Nn. 366, 217.
294 N. 328.   295 N. 544.   296 N. 469.   297 Ch. 7 nn. 15–19.

of text in the *Institutes*. Thus in 2.19.6 we are told that Hadrian allowed a person over 25 to change his mind about the acceptance of an inheritance:

> Sciendum tamen est divum Hadrianum etiam maiori viginti quinque annis veniam dedisse, cum post aditam hereditatem grande aes alienum quod aditae hereditatis tempore latebat, emersisset.

> Sed hoc divus quidem Hadrianus speciali beneficio cuidam praestitit: divus autem Gordianus postea in militibus tantummodo hoc extendit.

If one author had drafted both passages at the same time he would not have mentioned Hadrian twice. Apart from such repetitions there are many places where the addition comes at the end of a section or title.[298]

At first sight Huschke's work seems as secure as that of Bluhme on the *Digest* masses. On a closer investigation doubts emerge. First of all, Huschke begins with a serious mistake. He thinks that Tribonian's responsibility for the administration of the commission's work (*totius operis gubernatio*)[299] implies that he did not participate in the detailed work. As we saw in connection with the *Digest* this inference *ex contrario* is wrong. Perhaps it is aided by a confusion between the conditions under which a minister worked in the ancient world and the modern. Nowadays a minister of justice would hardly be expected to draft legislation himself and, even if himself a lawyer, would rely largely on advice from other legal experts. This was not the situation of a Roman quaestor. He was chosen for his knowledge of the law but also for his literary capacity. He was the emperor's speech-writer and it would not have been tolerable for him to allow someone else to speak on the emperor's behalf. This is why a priori there is a strong case against supposing that either of the professors was allowed to draft the passages of the *Institutes* which deal with Justinian's legislation.

Huschke, starting from the assumption that the professors composed the Justinianic passages, goes on to note a difference of tone between these passages in the first two and last two books. The latter, apart from texts where a contorted constitution is copied verbatim, are quieter. Thus he contrasts the passages which say that one of Justinian's constitutions can be consulted in the complete version:

> *Inst.* 2.11.6   *cuius constitutionis tenore perspecto licentia est nihil eorum quae ad praefatum ius pertinent ignorare*
> 2.20.2   *cuius constitutionis perpensum modum ex ipsius tenore perfectissime accipere possibile est*
> 2.20.27   *quod evidenter ex ipsius constitutionis lectione clarescit*
> 3.1.14   *quae specialiter et singillatim ex praefatae constitutionis tenore possunt colligi*
> 3.5.1   *quam facile est ex ipsius constitutionis verbis colligere*
> 3.7.3   *sicut ex ea constitutione intellegendum est*
> 3.11.7   *quas ex ipsa constitutionis lectione potest quis cognoscere*

[298] E.g. *Inst.* 1.5.3, 1.6.7.7, 1.7, 1.10.13.3, 1.11.12, 2.6.14.4, 2.7.2.–4.
[299] *C. Deo auctore* 3 (15 Dec. 530), *C. Tanta* 9, 11 (16 Dec. 533).

3.29.3   *secundum nostrae constitutionis definitiones quas licet ex ipsius lectione*
apertius cognoscere

4.4.10   *Zenoniana constitutio . . . secundum eius tenorem qui ex ipsa mani-*
festius apparet

4.18.8   *secundum nostrae constitutionis definitionem ex qua haec apertius*
possibile est scire

According to Huschke the last text and first three are in one style, the remaining six in another. Every reader can judge for himself, but to me the style is consistent throughout: always *ex constitutione*, or *ex constitutionis tenore/lectione/verbis*. It is is true that nothing as elaborate as the first two texts occurs thereafter. But the descent, if it may be so described, does not coincide with the end of book II, and may be more naturally accounted for on the view that the author of all the passages is the same but that his first efforts were rather more ornate than his later ones.

Huschke's next point is that the laudation of Justinian in the first two books is more excessive than in the later ones. He cites:

Inst. 1.10.11   *quas in libris digestorum seu pandectarum ex veteri iure collectarum*
enumerari permisimus

1.11.11   *illius adoptionis quae per sacrum oraculum fit*

2.6.14   *sacratissimum aerarium . . . nostra autem divina constitutio*

2.19.6   *nostra benevolentia . . . hoc praestavit beneficium et constitutionem tam*
aequissimum quam nobilem scripsit

2.20.2   *nostra constitutio quam cum magna lucubratione fecimus*

2.20.36   *huiusmodi enim testamentorum dispositiones valere secta temporum*
meorum non patitur

2.23.12   *et nos eundem principem* [*Augustus*] *superare contendentes constitu-*
tionem fecimus per quam disposuimus

The reference to *sacrum oraculum* in the second passage need not be ascribed to Tribonian. Apart from this the complacency of the passages cited does not seem much different from that of the following texts which Huschke does not cite:

Inst. 3.1.14   *solito more corrigentes*

3.1.16   *inseri concessimus*

3.3.5   *nobis visum est recta et simplici via*

3.6.10   *quod ius usque ad nostra tempora satis obscurum atque nube plenum*
et undique confusum fuerat . . .

3.7.3   *constitutio quam pro omnium notione Graeca lingua compendiosa*
tractatu habito composuimus

3.9.4   *nobis tamen nihil incuriosum praetermissum est sed nostris constitu-*
tionibus omnia corrigentes

3.11.7   *sed cum multas divisiones eiusmodi constitutioni deese perspeximus*
lata est a nobis plenissima constitutio

3.12   *non inseri concessimus*

4.1.6   *sed nostra providentia etiam hoc emendavit*

4.1.8 *nos huiusmodi calliditati obviam euntes per nostram decisionem sanximus*

The reader will, I think, notice a fundamental similarity of attitude throughout, which extends to the use of words of permission where one would expect a command (*enumerari permisimus = mandavimus, non inseri concessimus = inseri non concessimus, inseri concessimus = mandavimus*). Nevertheless one can see why Huschke reaches the conclusion he does. The drafter's enthusiasm is at its height in the early books. Yet taken as a whole the passages are simply variations on a theme, the excellence of Justinian's rule. In book II we have his all night sessions (*lucubratio*), his nobility, the tone of the régime (*secta temporum meorum*), and his superiority to his predecessors. In book III we have the obscurity of the previous law from which he has rescued his subjects, his condescension in using Greek so that freedmen can follow, his policy of leaving no stone unturned. If the themes are not identical they are not meant to be. Justinian's merits have many facets.

Huschke draws attention to the condescending tone adopted towards students in certain passages:

Inst. 1.1.2 *alioquin si statim ab initio rudem adhuc et informum animum studiosi multitudine ac varietate rerum oneraverimus . . .*

2.20.3 *operae pretium esse duximus interim separatim prius de legatis et postea de fideicommissis tractare, ut natura utriusque iuris cognita facile possint permixtionem eorum eruditi suptilioribus auribus accipere*

4.18.12 *haec exposuimus ut vobis possibile sit summo digito et quasi per indicem ea tetigisse. alioquin diligentior eorum scientia vobis ex latioribus digestorum sive pandectarum libris deo propitio adventura est*

The absence of similar passages in book III and the earlier titles of book IV is hardly significant. The problems of students fell to be mentioned at the beginning and end of the *Institutes*, and otherwise only in connection with a mode of exposition (treating legacies and fideicommissa separately) which was at variance with the new legislation providing for their assimilation.

Huschke's next point concerns what he regards as provincial solecisms in the first two books, namely *medevimus*,[300] *praestavit*,[301] *hactenus iuris habet*,[302] *perinde ac si*[303] and *libertati impedire*.[304] Of these *praestavi* is Tribonianic and has already been discussed.[305] *Perinde ac si* does not occur in any Tribonianic passages.[306] It is found in third-century rescripts.[307] The *medevimus* passage

[300] *Inst.* 2.20.27.   [301] *Inst.* 2.1.25, 2.19.6; cf. 2.7.2 (*praestavimus*).
[302] *Inst.* 2.5.2.
[303] *Inst.* 2.1.44, 2.9.3, 2.14.7 bis, 2.14.9, 2.17.3, 2.23.9, 3.1.9, 3.1.10, 3.7.2, 3.11.1, 3.15.4, 3.19.23, 4.3.15.
[304] *Inst.* 1.7 bis.   [305] Ch. 3 n. 365 and above, n. 301.
[306] None of the passages cited in n. 303 above is Tribonianic. *Inst.* 2.17.3 comes from a constitution of Severus and Antoninus.
[307] *CJ* 6.27.2 (169), 3.38.1 (193), 3.38.3.1 (197), 6.46.2 pr. (205), 9.23.1 (212 *atque si*), 4.6.1 (215), 2.9.1 (227), 8.5.1 pr. (326).

has no specific marks of the quaestor but could well pass as his.[308] He else-where uses *medemur* of the emperor's legislation,[309] so the use of *mederi* is not implausible, though *medevimus* is a hapax. But the reading may be incorrect.[310] *Hactenus iuris*[311] occurs in a passage without marks of Tribonian's style and may be assumed to come from a classical jurist. *Impedire* with the dative, though rare, is classical.[312]

The argument from solecism therefore amounts to very little, except to point to Tribonian as the author of certain passages in book IV which we have seen ought prima facie to be assigned to him.

Huschke next passes to three passages in book II which ascribe to Tribonian the credit for proposing certain of Justinian's legislative re-forms.[313] His explanation is that the provincial Dorotheus, flattered to be summoned to Constantinople to take part in the work of the commission, tried to curry favour with Tribonian by thus inserting these passages, and was rewarded by being retained for the work of compiling the second edition of the *Codex Iustinianus*.

The references occur however in texts which contain marks of Tribonian's style and are rather to be ascribed to the ex-quaestor himself. Both Justinian and Tribonian indulge in a sort of vicarious self-praise. There is no reason to suppose that Tribonian was modest and by the mores of the time it was in order to present the head of state with a draft laudatory of the drafter. Cassiodorus, whose position in Ostrogothic Italy was not dissimilar to that of Tribonian in Byzantium, does just this.

In his *Varia* he reports a speech of King Athalaric of the Ostrogoths to the Roman senate on the occasion of his own elevation to the praetorian prefecture in 533.[314] This speech, drafted by Cassiodorus in his capacity as Athalaric's secretary,[315] contains the most flattering account of every aspect of the honorand's character and achievements. 'If you consider his (Cassiodorus) merits we owe him everything we are giving him. For how can one sufficiently commend a man who has repeatedly filled the ears of the mighty with his brilliant compositions? He has performed the offices en-trusted to him with exemplary gravity and has striven to make the age one which redounds to the prince's credit.' Tribonian is reserved in com-parison.

The reason why these references do not occur in the second half of the *Institutes* is perhaps that they could not decently be multiplied indefinitely, even in the conditions of the sixth century, and Tribonian made the best use of the earliest opportunities which came his way: or just that he had less time to devote to the last two books. The notion that the object of the codification was to glorify Tribonian as well as Justinian was not new. It

---

[308] Above, p. 10.   [309] Ch. 3 n. 109.   [310] P. has *medebimur*.
[311] C. Ferrini, 'Sulle fonti delle Istituzioni', *Opere* I (1929) 307.
[312] Varro, *Ling. Lat.* 9.20.
[313] *Inst.* 1.5.3, 2.8.2, 2.23.12 and cf. 1.5.3 line 20 (*idem quaestor*).
[314] *Varia* 9.25 (*Mon. Germ. Hist. Auct. Ant.* 12.291–3).
[315] A. Momigliano, *Proc. Brit. Acad.* (1955) 207, 217.

appears in *C. Deo auctore* where the *Digest* is to be compiled, inter alia, to 'the glory of our reign and of your (Tribonian's) tenure of office'.[316]

But Huschke is right to point out that in the second half of the *Institutes* there are two passages in which the proposal for change (*suggestio*) is made by *humanitas* not by Tribonian.[317]

So far none of Huschke's points is compelling. At most he has discerned a change of mood, not of style, between the earlier and the later books. If we suppose the modernisation of the text to have been undertaken book by book we might well expect that considerations of speed, space and the need to avoid undue repetition would account for a slight change of tone or mood, no more in effect than a reduction in the rhetorical profusion of some of the earlier passages. Other arguments of Huschke are however weightier. A number of passages contain references to earlier or later parts of the text, but always within the half in which the reference occurs.

> *Inst.* 1.22.6   *secundum ea quae inferius proponemus* (=1.26)
>   2.1 pr.   *superiore libro de iure personarum exposuimus* (=book I)
>   2.1.11   *sicut diximus appellatur ius gentium* (cf. *D* 41.1.1 pr.)
>   2.16.9   *quod ius quale sit suo loco trademus* (=2.23)
>   2.17.4   *quod quibus modis accidit primo libro rettulimus* (=1.16)

Of these the first, fourth and fifth are copied from Gaius' *Institutes* and none of the others occur in passages with Tribonianic marks.

One can add the following texts:

> *Inst.* 2.11 pr.   *quam proxime exposuimus* (=2.10)
>   2.13.7   *quod paulo post vobis manifestum fiat* (=2.18)

The first of these occurs in a passage referring to a constitution of Justinian, but, as it happens, lacking specific marks of Tribonian's style. In the last two books Huschke cites:

> *Inst.* 3.6.11   *ut supra quoque tradidimus* (=3.6.1)
>   3.9 pr.   *sicut supra dictum est* (=3.1.9ff.)
>   3.27.6   *magis ut supra diximus ex distractu* (=3.14.1)
>   3.28.3 fin.   *ut supra dictum est* (=3.17.3)
>   4.13.2   *secundum quod iam superioribus libris scriptum est* (=3.21)
>   4.15.6   *ex sacris constitutionibus ut supra diximus* (=4.2.1)
>   4.17.4   *sicut iam dictum est* (=4.6.20)
>   3.1.15.17   *de quibus supra diximus* (=3.1.15 init.)
>   3.19.13   *ut iam dictum est* (=3.15.1)
>   4.1. pr.   *cum expositum sit superiore libro* (=book 3)
>   4.6.23   *secundum quae supra diximus* (=4.6.19)
>   4.6.33e   *sicut supra diximus* (=4.6.24)
>   4.11.5   *ut iam dictum est* (=4.11.1)
>   4.12.1   *quos supra diximus* (=4.12 pr.)

---

[316] *C. Deo auctore* 14 (15 Dec. 530).   [317] *Inst.* 3.2.7, 3.6.10.

There are fourteen references back in the second half against four references back and three forward in the first half. I have omitted references to constitutions and SCC just cited (*praefata constitutio, supra dicta senatusconsulta* etc., which are found in both halves). Six of the fourteen occur in passages which have marks of Tribonian's style, namely 3.1.15, 3.9 pr., 3.19.13, 4.6.33e, 4.11.5 and 4.13.2. A seventh (3.28.3) comes from a text which is in part Tribonianic (*licet antea dubitabatur*) but it is not certain that the reference to 3.17.3 was not in the original text. The remaining seven passages in the second half do not contain marks of his style and were presumably part of the original draft before it was modernised. One can summarise the position as follows. References forward occur only in the earlier books, as one would expect, and these belong to the original draft. References back in the original draft are much commoner in the later than the earlier books. References back in the modernising parts are relatively few and are confined to the later books: again this is to be expected. Huschke is right in saying that (with the quasi-exception of 4.13.2 *superioribus libris*, though Book III is really meant) they do not range out their respective halves of the work. They do in some degree support his view that the original draft was done in two halves, and that Theophilus was responsible for the second, since the paraphrase of Theophilus is liberally sprinkled with references to what the lecturer has said previously. Though one must be wary in arguing from Greek to Latin and from oral to written style this habit is one which might well survive the change of language and medium.

Even so, as Huschke realises, the argument is far from conclusive. One has also to take account of:

> *Inst.* 3.1.2   *ut et supra diximus* (=2.19.2, probably from Gaius 3.2)
>   3.2.1   *sunt autem agnati ut primo quoque libro tradidimus* (=1.15.1)
>   4.8.5   *quod casibus quibusdam effici primo libro tradidimus* (=1.3.4, 1.16.1, taken from Gaius 4.77)
>   4.10.2   *tutores quemadmodum constituuntur primo libro expositum est* (=1.14f. from Gaius 4.85 *primo commentario rettulimus*)
>   4.15.5   *secundo libro exposuimus* (=2.9.4 from Gaius 4.153 *secundo commentario rettulimus*)

Only the second presents a difficulty for Huschke and his argument is that though not copied directly from Gaius the reference is to something which the compiler of book III knew must have been dealt with earlier. He may be right and in any event none of the passages listed have marks of Tribonian's authorship. It is different with the texts cited for the next argument, viz. that repetitions occur of the sort which suggest that the compiler of the second half did not know about (or had forgotten) what was said in the first half.

Inst. 3.1.2a refers to *CJ* 5.27.10, 11 on the legitimation of children by subsequent marriage or presentation but this has been dealt with already at 1.10.13. Huschke argues that the second passage almost contradicts the first, but though the last sentence of 1.10.13 is certainly slipshod (and incidentally misleads Theophilus) this is an exaggeration.

Nevertheless the problem of the repetitions remains, and there are further examples:

Inst. 3.1.14   refers to *CJ* 8.47.10 though 1.11.2 has independently done so before
    3.9 pr.   refers to *CJ* 6.48.1 despite the earlier account of it at 2.20.27
    3.9.5   refers to *CJ* 8.48.6 despite the previous account at 1.12.6
    3.27.7   refers to *CJ* 1.3.54.7 (? 6.43.1) though 2.20.2 gives an account of *CJ* 6.43.1
    3.28 pr.   refers to *CJ* 6.61.6 despite the earlier account at 2.9.1
    3.7.4   cites *CJ* 7.6.1, referring to the *lex Iunia*, despite 1.5.3 which refers to the same constitution and to the *lex Iunia Norbana*. Here again both passages occur in texts which have marks of Tribonian's style.

In all these instances the later account does not mention the earlier, nor the earlier the later. So it is natural to assume with Huschke that they were drafted by different persons. Yet in the case of *CJ* 8.47.10, reforming the law of adoption, of *CJ* 6.48.1 on the institution of uncertain persons as heirs etc., of *CJ* 8.48.6 on the emancipation of children, of *CJ* 6.43.1 on the assimilation of legacies and *fideicommissa* and of *CJ* 7.6.1 on the abolition of the status of Latins both the earlier and the later text show marks of Tribonian's style. The only doubt concerns *CJ* 6.61.6 on the division of property between children and parents. Here the later reference may not be Tribonianic.

Huschke's argument is clearly a strong one and has perhaps been decisive in securing acceptance of his views. Nevertheless the introduction of a new editor from book 3 onwards is not the only possible interpretation of the facts. The old editor might have repeated, with some variation, earlier references to recent legislation, and he might have done this intentionally, as part of the programme of emphasising the importance of legislation as a source of law and of Justinian's legislation in particular. Nor would one necessarily expect him to refer on the second occasion to the earlier passages. As we saw above, the modernising editor of the *Institutes* (as opposed to those who prepared the original draft) does not often use this technique.

Huschke has two final arguments. One is that in the last books the exact words of a constitution are more often cited than in the earlier.

This occurs in particular in:

Inst. 3.1.2a.7–15   citing *CJ* 5.27.11 (18 March 530)
    3.2.3d.13–18   citing *CJ* 6.58.14 (27 Nov. 531)
    4.1.8.16–25   citing *CJ* 6.2.20 (1 Aug. 530)
    4.1.16.7–38   citing *CJ* 6.2.22.1, 2 (17 Nov. 530)
    4.18.6.3–15   citing *CJ* 9.17.1 (16 Nov. 318–9)

The first four constitutions were drafted by Tribonian as quaestor. It is something of a mystery why these verbal excerpts from constitutions should only be found in the last two books of the *Institutes*. In general the modernising passages paraphrase the imperial constitutions, adding the historical background and the reasons for their enactment. In particular the marks of Tribonian's style which the modernising passages consistently display are not to be accounted for on the hypothesis that they contain citations or part citations from constitutions drafted by him as quaestor. In the passages listed above, for example, there is only one such mark, viz. *manifestissimum est* in *CJ* 6.2.22.2 = *Inst.* 4.1.16. 30–31.

In 4.18.6 the law of Constantine is reproduced for the sake of the horrifying details of the punishment for parricide. The remaining texts come near the beginning of their respective books. A possible reason for this is that the editor, completing the draft book by book, begins by making an attempt where possible to reproduce the exact text of the constitutions cited (and drafted by himself) but soon comes to the conclusion that this would take up too much space or time. So he reverts to his normal policy of paraphrasing the enactments. While this 'verbatim' policy is adopted only for the beginning of books III and IV, something comparable is found in book I. Here the first opportunity is taken (at 1.5.3) of praising Tribonian for the proposal to abolish the status of Latins. In book II the earlier part of the text did not present an excuse for either of these techniques.

Finally Huschke draws attention to the use of adjectives formed from the names of emperors (*lex Anastasiana* etc.) in the last two books. But as he notes there is a contrary instance at 2.6.14 (*Zenoniana constitutio*).

In the end one must admit that, if some of Huschke's arguments are mistaken, others are weighty, and in particular the argument from repeated references to imperial constitutions in the two halves of the work. But it is questionable whether these arguments can prevail against the evidence that the modernising passages were composed in a uniform style throughout. By way of collecting some of this evidence I now list the marks of Tribonian's style which are to be found in modernising passages in both halves of the *Institutes*:

appellamus	*Inst.* 2.7.2.2, 4.18.5.12*
altercationes	1.5.3.32, 4.1.8.12
bene (*prospicere etc.*)	2.6.14.5, 3.9.12.1–2
corrigentes	2.8 pr. 6, 2.10.10.13–14, 3.1.14.10, 3.2.3a.12, 3.2.7.1–2, 3.9.4.3 and cf. 1.5.3.22, 2.20.35.5–6
(*correximus*)	
deduximus	2.8 pr. 6, 3.7.3.16
defraudare	2.6.1.10, 2.7.4.6, 3.3.4.8, 3.21.12, 4.6.30.15
definivimus	2.7.4.18, 3.1.14.11, 3.2.4.4–5
differentia	1.12.8.10, 2.1.40.10, 2.20.3.8, 2.23.7.7, 3.2.3a.9, 3.9.5.9–10, 4.11.5.3–4
erat	(it was, there was, etc.) 1.6.7.8, 1.25.13.8, 2.7.3.3, 2.7.4.1, 2.20.2.1–2, 3.7.3.11, 3.7.4.4–5, 3.12 pr. 1, 3.12.1.1–3, 4.6.28.8
existimavimus	2.20.3.3, 3.2.4.1–2, 3.3.4.3 cf. 3.12.1.6 (*existimantes*)
finis	(met) 2.7.3.17, 3.9.2.11, 4.12 pr. 3–4

frequentare	1.5.3.8, 4.13.11.10
fuerat	(with adjective or participle) 1.5.3.1, 1.7.1.4, 1.10.13.3, 2.6.1.1, 2.7.1.8, 2.7.2.11, 2.8 pr. 8, 2.10.10.7, 9, 10–11, 2.20.34.8, 2.23.7.21–2, 3.6.10.6, 3.7.4.10, 3.9.5.2, 3.9.7.4, 3.12 pr. 4, 3.27.7.8, 3.29.3a.3–4, 4.6.29.1
induximus	2.13.5.16, 2.14 pr. 7, 4.6.29.12
inhumanus	1.7.1.4, 2.9.1.8–9, 2.9.2.6, 4.6.40.5
invenimus	2.7.2.18, 2.7.4.10, 2.20.3.3, 3.1.14.5, 3.2.3d.4, 4.8.7.11, 4.16.1.19 cf. 4.6.29.3 (*invenientes*)
latius	2.11.6.6, 3.23.2.28–9, 4.6.30.9
legislator	2.7.4.13, 4.13.10.18
manifestissimus	2.7.4.15, 3.9.12.12, 4.1.16.30–1,** 4.1.4.22
melius	1.12.6.6, 2.1.34.4, 4.2.1.9
natura	2.20.2.11, 2.20.3.6, 9, 10–11, 15–16, 3.1.15.10, 15–16, 3.3.4.3, 3.24.3.16, 3.27.7.9, 4.6.29.7–8, 4.13.10.20
perfectus-ior-issimus	2.7.2.9, 2.10.13.5–6, 2.20.2.16, 3.2.7.10, 3.12 pr. 11, 3.19.14.7, 4.11.6.1
posuimus	2.7.2.20, 3.1.14.14, 3.3.4.2, 3.9.5.4–5, 3.9.7.5
satis abundeque	2.8.1.12, 3.23.1.5–6
satis . . . est (erat)	1.7.1.4, 3.2.7.14, 3.6.10.6, 4.6.30.13
tangere	(met.) 1.6.7.20, 4.18.12.2–3*
tempora nostra	1.22 pr. 5, 3.6.10.6, 3.12 pr. 5–6 cf. 2.20.36.31 (*tempora mea*)
tenor constitutionis	2.8.1.11, 2.10.4.5, 2.11.6.8, 2.19.6.10, 2.20.2.15–16, 3.1.2a.3–4, 3.1.14.32–3, 4.4.10.6–7
tractatu (habito) etc.	2.20.23.8, 3.7.3.3
via	(met.) 1.6.7.16, 1.12.6.8, 2.7.4.10, 3.3.5.7, 3.7.4.22–3, 4.2.1.7
rhetorical questions	1.6.7.21, 1.12.4.7, 2.9.1.13–14, 3.2.3b.4–7, 3.3.4.9–10, 4.8.7.5–6
antiquities	see above, n. 6
double name for jurists	2.14 pr. 9, 4.3.1.9
Leoniana etc. (*constitutio, tempora*)	2.6.14.16, 3.8.3.4–5, 3.15 pr. 11, 4.4.10.7, 4.13.10.17

Some of these turns of phrase, though Tribonianic in the context of the *CJ*, may have been common to him, Dorotheus and Theophilus, but of others this is rather implausible. Huschke rightly notes that Theophilus in his paraphrase tones down the more fulsome references to Justinian in the first two books. But the same is true of the later books: thus at 3.9.4 *sed nostris constitutionibus omnia corrigentes* is not reproduced in the paraphrase. And how could Theophilus, with his flat-footed prose, have written at 3.6.10 *quod ius usque ad nostra tempora satis obscurum atque nube plenum et undique confusum fuerat*?

Quite apart from the marks of style noted above, there is a general uniformity throughout the *Institutes* in the way in which the old law is contrasted with the new. For example:

Inst. 1.5.3.1 (*antea fuerat*), 4.6.29.1 (*fuerat antea*)
    1.12.6.2–3, 3.15.1.10 (*antea quidem*)
    2.10.14.1, 2.13.5.1, 2.18.3.1, 3.7.4.6, 3.15.1.10, 3.23 pr. 5, 4.6.33e.1,
        4.11.2.1, 4.18.12.1 (*sed haec . . .*)
    1.25.13.3–4, 2.9.1.2, 2.10.1.2, 2.14 pr. 3, 2.20.2.1, 3.15.1.10–11,
        (*olim quidem*)
    2.7.4.1 (*erat olim*), 3.12 pr. 1 (*erant olim*)
    1.11.2.1 (*sed hodie*), 2.14 pr. 5 (*hodie vero*), 4.11.2.1 (*sed haec hodie*),
        4.13.10.4 (*hodie autem*, 4.15.13.14 (*hodie tamen*)
    1.12.6.6 (*nostra autem providentia*), 4.1.16.6 (*sed nostra providentia*)

Indeed the uniformity of editorial style is pervasive. Nevertheless there
remain the differences, at least of tone, which Huschke noted. They appear
to show that the modernisation of the text was undertaken book by book
and that there was an interval between the editing of the first two and the
last two books. But to go further and suppose that the professors could
have drafted the passages referring to Justinian and his laws is to misread
the evidence of style and to postulate a violation of constitutional propri-
eties. These passages fell within Tribonian's province and they came from
Tribonian's pen.

That said, tribute must be paid to Huschke's acuteness. He may well
have been right about the allocation of the initial drafting. As already noted
the number of references back in the basic text points to Theophilus as the
drafter of the last rather than the first books. Huschke added that there are
places in the Paraphrase where Theophilus seems to treat the text of the
first part as if alien to himself.

Inst. 2.1.36.6   *eadem fere et de colono dicuntur*

Theophilus reproduces this but comments that *fere* is superfluous, which
seems to show that he did not draft this non-Tribonianic passage.

1.23.1   *item inviti adulescentes curatores non accipiunt praeterquam in litem;
curator enim et ad certam causam dari potest.*

The expression is defective, because minors can be compelled to have a
curator for purposes other than litigation, and Theophilus caters for this
by saying that a minor can be compelled to accept a curator only for a
definite lawsuit, since a curator can be appointed for such a *definite* suit,
adding characteristically 'as stated above'.

2.3.1   *item praediorum urbanorum servitutes sunt haec: ut vicinus onera vicini
sustineat.*

Theophilus mistakenly takes 'supporting a neighbour's burden' as a
general description of urban servitudes rather than as an instance of them:
this sounds absurd, but all servitudes are 'burdens' on land or buildings in
favour of neighbouring land or buildings.

2.20.25 deals with the need for certainty in appointing a legatee or fideicommissary. *En passant* the text says that certainty is also required for the appointment of a tutor. Theophilus omits this point; an implied criticism of the drafting.

These instances, all taken from texts without marks of Tribonian's style, seem inconsistent with the view that Theophilus was responsible for the initial draft of the first two books. On the other hand, as Huschke fails to notice, Theophilus misunderstands Tribonianic passages in *both* halves of the work, for example:

2.6 pr.   *putantibus antiquioribus dominis sufficere ad inquirendas res suas praefata tempora*

which Theophilus takes to mean 'the old owners thought they had enough time' etc., whereas it should be read 'the old lawyers considered that the periods mentioned were sufficient for owners etc.'. Against this:

4.6.2.18   *sane uno casu qui possidet nibilo minus actoris partes optinet sicut in latioribus digestorum libris opportunius apparebit.*

This famous and elusive case eludes Theophilus as it does the modern scholar. He does not mention it. But the passage, with its reference to the *Digest*, should, as we have seen, be accounted Tribonianic. Huschke's argument can therefore be strengthened. Theophilus misunderstands Tribonianic passages in both halves alike, but the basic text only in the first two books.

Hence Huschke is probably right about the division of labour between the professors. But if the professors were responsible only for the basic draft the division of labour between them, though naturally of interest, is not as crucial as it once seemed. If one looks at the matter realistically the joint authors of this most famous and widely-read of all students' lawbooks were Gaius and Tribonian. At many points the reader will best understand the text if he bears in mind that Tribonian admired and did his best to copy Gaius' principle of setting the law in its historical context and of stating it in as simple and systematic a form as he could.

CHAPTER SEVEN

Imperial Constitutions: the Codex

To determine the precise extent of Tribonian's contribution to the two codices of imperial laws of 7 April 529 and 16 November 534 respectively is more difficult than in the case of the *Digest* and the *Institutes*. We shall have to be content with a plausible but not demonstrable hypothesis.

The first edition was prepared by the commission under John of Cappadocia which was set up on 13 February 528 to codify the imperial laws found in the three earlier codes (Gregorianus, Hermogenianus and Theodosianus) and the new laws (*Novels*) of Theodosius II and his successors, up to Anthemius, together with later legislation including that of the first part of Justinian's own reign.[1] The code it produced was enacted by *C. Summa* on 7 April 529. The second edition was prepared by a committee under Tribonian as part of the work of the Second Law Commission under his chairmanship. The date on which this committee was constituted is not known[2] but its revised code (*Codex repetitae praelectionis*) was enacted by *C. Cordi* on 16 November 534.

The trouble stems from the fact that we do not possess the first edition of the *Codex Iustinianus*. There is therefore no direct way of studying the editorial work done by the committee which prepared the second edition. Instead we have to compare the text of the *Codex Theodosianus*, which has been preserved, with that of Justinian's second edition. This constitutes a comparison at three removes. In particular, any passage which bears the mark of Tribonian in the final version may, if it is genuinely his, have been introduced by him (i) as a member of the First Law Commission under John of Cappadocia at the time when that commission excerpted the earlier codices and novels, (ii) as a member of the first commission at the later stage when it actually compiled the first *Codex Iustinianus*, (iii) as chairman of Justinian's Second Law Commission at the time when he helped to prepare the second edition of the *Codex Iustinianus*. Because the texts underwent these three processes one must reckon with the possibility that even if a correct method of investigation is pursued no clear pattern may emerge.

There is another difficulty in our investigation. So far we have used the marks of Tribonian's style to identify documents composed either wholly

---

[1] *C. Haec quae necessario* (13 Feb. 528). On the first code see Wenger §80 (1).

[2] There are no constitutions setting up the committees which composed the *Institutes* and the *Codex Repetitae Praelectionis*, because these committees were sub-committees of the commission created by *C. Deo auctore* under Tribonian's chairmanship. An informal instruction or authorisation by Justinian was therefore sufficient.

or, in the case of the *Institutes*, in substantial part by him. These contain numerous traces of his intervention. His fingerprints, if present, appear all over the page. The work of the law commission in collecting the imperial laws contained in the codes of Gregorius and Hermogenianus, the Theodosian *Code* and the post-Theodosian *Novels* was, in contrast, mainly editorial. Changes of substance were made, but were comparatively rare. Many of the old constitutions were left unchanged or simply shortened. Over the whole range of texts in the *CJ* derived from the Theodosian *Code* there are hardly a dozen which contain marks of Tribonian's style. It is no use trying to identify one by one those texts which stand in a homographic relation to his known corpus of work. Instead we have to rely on the weaker relation of consistency of style in order to elucidate the editorial processes and the part of Tribonian in them.

Nevertheless the first step is to set out those texts which do contain Tribonian's marks of style and to see how they are distributed in the *CTh* and the *CJ* respectively. Where the editorial contribution is an addition to the Theodosian text I use the indication 'add.' and when it replaces an expression in the Theodosian text I use 'for'. The latter are sometimes the more interesting texts since they show what expressions the editor avoided and not only those he preferred.

The texts containing marks of Tribonian's style are now set out, the original *CTh* constitution being mentioned first, then the interpolation and its locus in the *CJ*:

CTh 2.26.5 add. *decernimus locum habere*[3] (*CJ* 3.39.6)
    3.5.2.1   add. *per condictionem aut per utilem in rem actionem*[4] (*CJ* 5.3.15.1)
    3.13.3   add. *sine causa legitima*[5] (*CJ* 5.19.1)
    3.17.4   *tutor testamentarius vel legitimus*[6] for *tutor legitimus* (*CJ* 5.35.2.3)
    3.16.2   add. *sine ulla legitima causea*[7] (*CJ* 9.9.34)
    4.20.3   add. *scrupulositate priorum legum explosa*[8] (*CJ* 7.71.6)
    7.1.17 pr.   *poenas consentaneas*[9] for *viginti libras auri* (*CJ* 12.35.13)
    7.1.17.1   add. *sub quorum regimine*[10] (*CJ* 12.35.13.1)
    7.1.18   add. *augusta maiestas*[11] (*CJ* 12.35.14)
    7.8.2   *attingere*[12] for *adtinere* (*CJ* 1.9.4)
    9.19.2   *compendioso spatio*[13] for *anni spatio* (*CJ* 9.22.22.2)
    12.1.152   add. *minime curialibus nexibus illigatus*[14] (*CJ* 2.7.3)

There are three borderline interpolations:

(i) *CTh* 3.1.4 *paulo vilioris pretii nomine* for *pretii nomine vilioris* (*CJ* 4.44.5).

There is a good case for calling *paulo* Tribonianic. Both *paulatim*[15] and *paulisper*[16] are marks of his style. *Paulo* occurs in four *CJ* texts, one of which

---

[3] Ch. 3 (henceforth understood) n. 492.   [4] N. 54.   [5] N. 313.   [6] N. 330.
[7] N. 313.   [8] N. 237, 188.   [9] N. 242.   [10] N. 519.   [11] N. 161.
[12] N. 434.   [13] N. 374.
[14] N. 277. But this text points equally to Thomas (below, n. 177).
[15] N. 505.   [16] N. 506.

is Tribonian's,[17] one is of the fourth century,[18] one is the present interpolation and one, relating to the institution of a grossly inadequate price (*laesio enormis*), is universally regarded as interpolated.[19] Though normally such arguments are to be eschewed in an inquiry such as the present, the argument from a text known to be interpolated to another text, ostensibly of Diocletian, making the same point in similar words is a peculiarly strong one. If it is right, one of the only two genuine texts with *paulo* is Tribonian's, and this would warrant the inclusion of the word as a mark of style.

(ii) *CTh* 12.7.2 add. *quotiens orta fuerit dubitatio* (*CJ* 10.73.2[20]). If this interpolation is left out of account one of the only two closely parallel texts is from Tribonian,[21] but as Thomas has *multa dubitatio orta est*[22] the case for calling this a mark of style is not strong.

(iii) *CTh* 16.2.31 *competentem vindictam tali excessui imponere non morentur* for *deposcant ut rei talium criminum non evadant* (*CJ* 1.3.10).[23]

Leaving this text on one side there are seven *CJ* texts with *non morentur*,[24] of which three are from Tribonian, and the others are not later than the early fourth century. There is therefore a fairly strong though not overwhelming case for attributing this interpolation to Tribonian. The results are inconclusive, since there are too few texts and too many ways in which they could have been interpolated. But of the twelve interpolations which prima facie suggest Tribonian's hand four occur in texts derived from book 3 and four from book 7 of the *CTh*. One of the three borderline texts is also derived from book 3. This suggests two themes for investigation: one, that many of the interpolations were introduced by John's commission at the excerpting stage; two, that the excerpting was done book by book, with a given commissioner being made responsible for each book to be excerpted. If both these are found to be plausible there would be a case for concluding that books 3 and 7 were assigned to Tribonian to excerpt.

On the first point it will be noted that the interpolation *sine causa legitima* occurs twice in texts derived from *CTh* book 3 and no other, but that these texts appear in different books of the *CJ* (5 and 9 respectively).[25] There are other instances of the same phenomenon. The unusual phrase *frustratoria dilatio* is twice interpolated in texts derived from *CTh* book 11 and no other, but the resulting texts appear in books 1 and 7 of the *CJ* respectively.[26] *Penitus arceantur* is interpolated in two texts deriving from book 2 *CTh* and

[17] *CJ* 8.37.13.2 (1 Aug. 530).

[18] *CJ* 11.62.2 (Constantine).   [19] *CJ* 4.44.8 (1 Dec. 293 *paulo minori pretio*).

[20] 23 April 363.

[21] *CJ* 8.53.36.2 (18 Oct. 531 *si aliqua dubitatio orta fuerit*) but 5.49.1.1 (7 Feb. 223).

[22] *CJ* 6.20.19.2 (1 June 528).   [23] 26 April 398.

[24] *CJ* 3.1.13.2b (27 March 530), *C. Deo auctore* 6 (15 Dec. 530); cf. *C. Tanta* 11 (16 Dec. 533) but *CJ* 3.31.6 (22 June 224), 12.61.1 (8 Nov. 314/5), 1.35.1 (1 Oct. 320), 11.61.3.1 (5 Sept. 415).

[25] Above, nn. 5, 7.

[26] *CTh* 11.30.1–*CJ* 7.61.1 (30 Dec. 312/13) and *CTh* 11.36.20–*CJ* 1.4.2 (8 July 369).

no other, but these appear respectively in books 2 and 3 of the *CJ*.[27] What this shows is that at least some of the more idiosyncratic interpolations were introduced at the excerpting stage. It also shows that the same commissioners excerpted a number of consecutive titles of the *CTh*, viz. 2.10 to 2.19, 3.13 to 3.16 and 11.30 to 11.36. This falls far short, however, of demonstrating that the same commissioner was responsible for excerpting a whole book. It is to the latter problem that attention is now directed.

On the second point one must bear in mind the numbers and composition of John's commission. This was set up on 13 February 528 and consisted of eight senior members and two barristers practising before the court of the praetorian prefect of the east.[28] The senior members in order of precedence were John himself, Leontius, Phocas, Basilides, Thomas, Tribonian, Constantinus and Theophilus, the two barristers Dioscurus and Praesentinus.[29] The Theodosian code consisted of 16 books. If Tribonian had been its chairman he would undoubtedly have made each senior commissioner responsible for excerpting two books, and he would probably have done this by a system of rotation so that one commissioner had to excerpt books 1 and 9, the next books 2 and 10 and so forth. Under such a system, if the strict order of seniority is followed, Tribonian would undertake books 6 and 14, since he is the sixth senior commissioner.

But Tribonian was not chairman of the First Law Commission. Though according to his own account he gave proof of his organising abilities during the course of its work[30] it is by no means clear that it was organised *mutatis mutandis* in the same way as the second commission. In fact the list of marks of style points, as noted, to books 3 and 7 as the most likely objects of Tribonian's editorial attention. But little weight can attach to this distribution unless it is supported by further evidence. This evidence might take the following form: it might be shown that the first commission's editorial work is consistent with John having adopted the book as the excerpting unit for the *CTh*. Such a chain of argument has its weaknesses, since it relies on the 'consistency' and not the 'homographic' relation. But it is, perhaps, better than nothing.

The first question is therefore whether John's commission adopted the book as the excerpting unit for the *CTh*.

The Mommsen edition of the *CTh*[31] enables this to be studied fairly easily. Mommsen sets out the editorial changes alongside the text of the *CTh*. It is simply a question of going through these in order to detect stretches in which the editing is, if not idiosyncratic, at least consistent. How far do these correspond to books of the *CTh*? It must be admitted that this procedure will be fruitful only if most of the interpolations were introduced by John's commission at the excerpting stage. As we have seen, there is some evidence for this conclusion, but if it is false the result will

---

[27] *CTh* 2.10.3–*CJ* 2.6.5 (30 March 325) and *CTh* 2.19.1–*CJ* 3.28.27 (13 April 319).
[28] *C. Haec* (13 Feb. 528).   [29] *C. Haec* 1 (13 Feb. 528).   [30] *C. Deo auctore* 3.
[31] *Theodosiani libri XVI cum constitutionibus Sirmondianis*, ed. Th. Mommsen (Berlin 1895) vol. I. II.

simply be that the investigation will not reveal a consistent editorial style for any considerable stretch of the *CTh*. The proof of the pudding's absence is that it cannot be eaten.

For the present investigation I use, besides 'add.' and 'for' the notation 'inc.' to mark the passages where the editor has decided to begin the *CJ* constitution or sentence from the words in question rather than with the words which begin it in the *CTh*. This can be significant as a matter of style. For example Justinian's quaestor Thomas likes to begin constitutions with *Eos qui, ii qui* etc.[32] One would therefore expect him to favour these beginnings when he is deciding at what point of the Theodosian text to start the *CJ* constitution. Mommsen uses '*inc.*' for the same phenomenon, and *redit* for the point where the *CJ* editor returns, after a break, to the *CTh* text.

Of the 16 books of the *CTh* three present no evidence of having been edited in a consistent fashion, three present evidence which stretches over less than half the constitutions excerpted from the book, one contains evidence of a tenuous character of editorial consistency over the bulk of the book and nine contain evidence of the same sort of a more substantial character. We find what we are looking for in roughly half the books of the *CTh*.

In texts originating in books 13, 14 and 15 it is impossible (for me at any rate) to detect an editorial style. In those from books 1, 3 and 10 the evidence stretches over less than half the book. In the book 1 texts (by which I mean those in the *CJ* derived from book 1 of the *CTh*: this elliptical manner of speaking will henceforth be taken for granted) the marks of consistency run from tit. 5.13 to 14.1, comprising 44 constitutions out of 142 (31 per cent). The editor cuts down the Theodosian text in such a way as to begin with a noun, or a phrase comprising a preposition and a noun, which denotes the subject-matter of the constitution. At two points he introduces *censemus* into the text.

> *CTh* 1.5.13 inc. *Palatinos qui*[33]   6.7 inc. *apparitores*[34]   9.1 inc. *Privilegiis*[35] 10.7 inc. *Palatinis*[36]   11.1 inc. *ad Palatinorum curam*[37]   11.2 inc. *ordinariorum iudicum*[38]   12.5 add. *censemus*[39]   12.7 inc. *in proconsulari provincia*[40] 14.1 inc. *omnia tributa* add. *censemus*.[41]

In book 3 we note the use of *ac* as a connective, of the phrase *sine causa legitima* and of *huiusmodi*. These features run from title 6.1 to 16.2, covering 22 constitutions out of 63 (35 per cent).

> *CTh* 3.6.1 *nepotes ac propinquos* for *nepotes propinquos*[42]   7.1 *huiusmodi* for *huius*[43]   8.2 *possidendi tantum ac fruendi* for *possidendi tantum*[44]   11.1 add.

---

[32] Ch. 8 nn. 107–8.   [33] *CJ* 11.74.2 (27 Nov. 400).   [34] *CJ* 12.58.1 (13 July 376).
[35] *CJ* 1.31.1 (1 Nov. 359).   [36] *CJ* 1.32.1 (27 Feb. 401).
[37] *CJ* 1.33.2 (23 Dec. 397).   [38] *CJ* 11.74.1 (24 May 398).
[39] *CJ* 1.12.5 (25 March 396).   [40] *CJ* 12.55.3 (28 Sept. 399).
[41] *CJ* 1.37.1 (17 Feb. 386).   [42] *CJ* 5.2.1 (17 June 380).
[43] *CJ* 5.4.18 (16 July 371).   [44] *CJ* 5.9.3 (17 Dec. 382).

huiusmodi ambitu[45]   13.3 add. *sine causa legitima*[46]   16.2 add. *sine legitima causa.*[47]

In book 10 the evidence stretches from title 10.30 to 21.3, 61 constitutions out of 144 (42 per cent). The editor favours the construction *ii qui* etc. and shows sensitiveness to the question of whether women are to be included in the scope of a law.

CTh 10.10.30   inc. *eorum patrimonia qui*[48]   19.15 *metellarii sive metellariae* for *metellarii/qui quaeve* for *qui* etc.[49]   20.1 *dignitatis cuiuscumque* for *dignitates*[50]   20.13 *cuiuscumque officii* for *eiusdem officii*[51]   21.2 *nemo vir* for *nemo* add. *nisi ii tantummodo quibus*[52]   21.3 *vestimenta virilia* for *vestimenta.*[53]

In one more book the proportion of text covered is great enough but the indications of consistent style are too thin. In book 5, the only indication is the use of the inverted conditional.

CTh 5.1.8   *mater si matrimonium contraxerit* for *mater teneatur ut, si non mutarit, conquirat*[54]   10.1 add. *liceat, modo si*[55]   18.1 *mulier si constitit* for *quod si constitit.*[56]

The evidence of consistent editorial intervention is better in the other nine books, viz. 2, 4, 6, 7, 8, 9, 11, 12 and 16.

Book 2 is one of the three in which the connective *sin autem* is found; *ita tamen ut* is also favoured. In the early part of the book the editor adopts a termination in which the last word of the sentence is an object noun or subject of the copula, the penultimate a verb and the antepenultimate qualifies the noun, as in *aliquam sustineant molestiam*. He likes *quaestio* (for *actio* etc.), *penitus arceri* and *si/nisi maluerit*. The marks stretch from tit. 1.7 to 26.1, i.e. over 78 constitutions out of 100.

CTh 2.1.7   add. *sin autem*, final *mariti sequantur condicionem*[57]   8.26 add. *ita tamen ut*, final *aliquam sustineant molestiam*[58]   9.2 add. *si hoc maluerit*[59]   10.3 add. *penitus arceantur*[60]   12.4 *sin autem* for *procurator*[61]   16.2 add. *ita tamen ut*[62]   17.1 *ita tamen ut* for *ita ut*[63]   19.1 *penitus arceantur* for *arceantur*[64] add. *quaestionem movere possunt*   19.2 *sin autem* for *tamen si*, add. *nisi maluerint*[65]   26.1 *ne huiusmodi quaestio terminetur* for *ne possit controversia* etc.[66]

[45] *CJ* 5.7.1 (17 June 380).
[46] *CJ* 5.19.1 (3 Nov. 422).
[47] *CJ* 9.9.34 (10 March 421).
[48] *CJ* 10.1.10 (8 July 421).
[49] *CJ* 11.7.7 (11 July 424).
[50] *CJ* 11.8.1 (21 July 317).
[51] *CJ* 11.8.10 (27 June 406).
[52] *CJ* 11.9.2 (30 March 382).
[53] *CJ* 11.9.4 (16 Jan. 424).
[54] *CJ* 6.56.5 (7 Nov. 426).
[55] *CJ* 4.43.2 (18 Aug. 329).
[56] *CJ* 11.48.16 (26 June 419).
[57] *CJ* 10.40.9 = 12.1.13 (10 Nov. 392).
[58] *CJ* 1.19.13 (26 July 409).
[59] *CJ* 2.4.40 (3 June 381).
[60] *CJ* 2.6.5 (30 March 325).
[61] *CJ* 1.12.21 (27 June 393).
[62] *CJ* 2.52.5 (25 July 315).
[63] *CJ* 2.44.2 (9 April 321).
[64] *CJ* 3.28.27 (13 April 319).
[65] *CJ* 3.28.28 (6 Feb. 321).
[66] *CJ* 3.39.3 (22 Feb. 330).

In book 4, one may note the insertion of *vero*, a liking for the prepositions *circa* and *per*, the inverted conditional construction and the use of *constitutus* for 'being in a certain position'.

These marks run from tit. 3.1 to 22.3 and cover 90 per cent of the texts, 72 out of 90.

> *CTh* 4.3.1　*heres constitutus* for *heres locatus*[67]　6.6 add. *quidquid vero*[68]　10.1 *manumissus ingratus circa patronum* for *libertis ingratis*[69]　10.2 *liberti si accusatores* for *quod si delatores*[70]　10.3 *libertinae condicionis homines si* for *l.c.h. permittimus* etc.[71]　13.9 add. *circa vectigal*[72]　14.1 *post hanc vero definitionem* for *postque hanc definitionem*, add. *per executorem, per longum tempus*[73]　21.1 add. *per interdictum quorum bonorum*[74]　22.3 add. *possessionum constitutarum, dominus constitutus, sin vero*.[75]

In book 6 we find the insertion of *etiam* and *etiam si*, a liking for beginning with *si quis* and *is* or *hic qui*, the use of *nec non, id est* and of the jussive subjunctive of *habere* and *ag-* or *cognoscere*. These signs extend from tit. 4.16 to 35.13, 171 constitutions out of 209 or 82 per cent.

> *CTh* 6.4.16　add. *etiam*[76]　5.2 inc. *si quis*[77]　12.1 inc. *eos qui*[78]　17.1 inc. *hos qui*[79]　23.1 add. *habeant, nec non*[80]　23.2 *etiam si* for *vel his*[81] etc.　24.9 *id est*[82]　26.8 *id est*[83]　26.14 *id est*[84]　28.4 inc. *etiamsi* red. *etiam*[85]　31.1 *cognoscant* for *cognoscerent*[86]　32.2 inc. *si quis*[87]　35.3 *memoriales etiam* for *aut scriniis memoriae* etc., add. *agnoscant, nec non etiam censualibus* for *censualibus*, add. *circa privilegia, habeant*[88]　35.13 *si quis* for *hoc autem*, *sustineat* for *censeatur*.[89]

In book 7, notably ornate, we note the use of *gratia* as a preposition, *scilicet* in a codal ablative absolute, the jussive subjunctive *audeat/audeant*, the inverted perfect passive subjunctive *fuerint convicti* etc., and a fondness for *hoc* (=what we have been talking about) especially *hoc facere*, and for *id est*. This gives an editorial unit running from title 1.13 to 20.2, 133 constitutions out of 174 (76 per cent).

> *CTh* 7.1.13　add. *hoc ipsum faciat* (pollutes a river)[90]　1.15 *fuerint reperti* vice *repertus fuerit*[91]　1.17 pr. *nemo audeat* vice *si qui repertus fuerit* add. *fuerint convicti . . . hoc facere vetamus*[92]　1.18 add. *nisi hoc publicae utilitatis*

[67] *CJ* 6.17.2 (28 Sept. 393).
[68] *CJ* 5.27.2 (13 Nov. 405).
[69] *CJ* 6.7.2 (27 July 332?).
[70] *CJ* 9.1.21 (6 Aug. 423).
[71] *CJ* 6.7.4 (30 March 426).
[72] *CJ* 4.61.9 (381–6).
[73] *CJ* 7.39.3 (14 Nov. 424).
[74] *CJ* 8.2.3 (27 July 395).
[75] *CJ* 8.4.7 (14 June 389?).
[76] *CJ* 1.39.1 (30 Dec. 359).
[77] *CJ* 12.8.1 (21 May 384).
[78] *CJ* 12.10.1 (25 Sept. 399).
[79] *CJ* 12.14.1 (21 March 413).
[80] *CJ* 12.16.1 (31 Oct. 415).
[81] *CJ* 12.16.3 (24 March 432).
[82] *CJ* 12.17.2 (18 Dec. 416).
[83] *CJ* 12.19.3 (15 Feb. 396).
[84] *CJ* 12.19.4 (15 Oct. 407).
[85] *CJ* 12.21.1 (8 Sept. 387).
[86] *CJ* 12.24.1 (19 June 365/8/70/73).
[87] *CJ* 12.25.1 (8 Feb. 416).
[88] *CJ* 12.28.2 (27 April 352).
[89] *CJ* 12.28.4 (6 July 386).
[90] *CJ* 12.35.12 (27 May 391).
[91] *CJ* 12.35.13 (1 Feb. 398).
[92] *CJ* 12.35.13 (1 Feb. 398).

gratia[93]   4.12 *nihil penitus accipere audeant*[94]   4.26 add. *id est exactoribus*[95]
4.35 *publica utilitate* vice *publica auctoritate*[96]   8.8 add. *absente scilicet comitatu*[97]
9.2 add. *salagmi gratia, id est*[98]   13.11 add. codal *mancipio scilicet reddendo*[99]
20.2 add. *sed etiam civili id est corporali sive personali.*[100]

Book 8 presents an example of a thorough editor. He consistently
deflates the Theodosian balloon but at the same time composes in a mod-
erately rhetorical vein. The text can be linked via the use of the connectives
sed nec and *quod si*, of the preposition *per*, of *concedere* and *coercere/coercitio*, the
codal ablative absolutes *poena (non) defutura* and *(dominio etc.) pertinente*, of
jussive subjunctives with *audere* and *habere facultatem* and with beginnings in
nemo and *nullus*. The editor tends to prefer plural to singular. These cover
186 constitutions out of 205 (91 per cent).

CTh 8.1.16   *poena coercendo* for *poena proposita*[101]   4.2 *neque audeant* for
sciant[102]   4.15   *non promittimus* for *nos promittimus*—audacious![103]   4.28 *sed
nec* for *neque*[104]   5.2 *poena non defutura*[105]   5.3 *nec alia via nisi per quam . . .
proficiscendi per eum*[106]   5.22 *indignatio exercenda* for *ultio exserenda*[107]   5.25
per publicum cursum[108]   5.35 *poena minime defutura*[109]   5.40 *cum neque
concessum sit* for *cum id tantum sit reservandum*[110]   5.41 *coercitione* for *poena*[111]
5.51 *publici cursus exhibitio debet committi* for *distribui*[112]   5.57 *facultas
concessa est* for *facultate concessa*[113]   5.58 inc. *nemo audeat* for *si quis subtraxerit,
per sollicitationem vel per receptionem* for *sollicitatione vel receptione*[114]   7.7
nullus audeat for *ne ullus audeat*[115]   7.17 *dare* for *navare*[116]   7.18 *sine augustis
adfatibus*[117]   7.19 *decesserint* for *haec fugerint*[118]   7.20 *contempserint* for
praesumpserint add. *nemo admittatur nisi*[119]   7.21 *quod si* for *quin si*[120]   8.6
impleant for *compleant*[121]   8.7 *provincias* for *provinciam*[122]   8.9 *si* for *sin* add.
per vices officiorum, continuare for *iterare*[123]   12.2 add. *ut per eum adquiratur*[124]
13.1 *nupserint* for *innupserit*[125]   13.6 *donationes* for *donationem*[126]   18.1 add.
dumtaxat habeant facultatem dominio pertinente per se vel per procuratorem[127]
18.5 *quaerere* for *conquirere*[128]   18.7 *usufructu dumtaxat pertinente.*[129]

[93] *CJ* 12.35.14 (19 March 400).
[95] *CJ* 12.37.11 (31 March 401).
[97] *CJ* 12.40.4 (22 Jan. 400).
[99] *CJ* 12.43.2 (15 May 382).
[101] *CJ* 1.51.6 (24 Oct. 417).
[103] *CJ* 12.57.6 (12 June 385).
[105] *CJ* 12.50.1 (14 May 316).
[107] *CJ* 12.50.3 (18 Feb. 365).
[109] *CJ* 12.50.8 (20 April 378).
[111] *CJ* 12.50.10 (20 Sept. 382).
[113] *CJ* 12.50.16 (24 Feb. 397).
[115] *CJ* 12.57.2 (27 May 358).
[117] *CJ* 12.59.2 (14 July 386).
[119] *CJ* 12.59.5 (25 July 415).
[121] *CJ* 12.60.1 (15 June 395).
[123] *CJ* 12.60.3 (22 Sept. 416).
[125] *CJ* 8.55.7 (20 Sept. 349).
[127] *CJ* 6.60.1 (18 July 319).
[129] *CJ* 6.60.2 (15 Oct. 395).

[94] *CJ* 12.37.3 (26 Nov. 364).
[96] *CJ* 12.37.15 (14 Feb. 423).
[98] *CJ* 12.41.1 (11 Oct. 340/61).
[100] *CJ* 12.46.1 (10 April 318).
[102] *CJ* 12.57.1 (10 May 315).
[104] *CJ* 12.57.12 (18 May 423).
[106] *CJ* 12.50.2 (15 Feb. 326).
[108] *CJ* 12.50.5 (25 March 365).
[110] *CJ* 12.50.9 (23 July 382).
[112] *CJ* 12.50.14 (30 July 392).
[114] *CJ* 12.50.17 (18 Feb. 398).
[116] *CJ* 12.49.5 (10 Dec. 385).
[118] *CJ* 10.32.48 (21 Dec. 397).
[120] *CJ* 12.49.7 = 12.59.6 (22 June 426).
[122] *CJ* 12.60.2 (14 July 395).
[124] *CJ* 8.53.26 (20 April 316).
[126] *CJ* 8.55.9 (7 Nov. 426).
[128] *CJ* 6.30.15 (6 April 349).

Book 9[130] is one of those where *sin autem* and *sin vero* are added, also *id est* and *non tamen*, *tantum, vero, huiusmodi* and *eiusmodi*, together with explicit references to criminal statutes such as the *lex Iulia peculatus*. Initial *quando* is favoured. These cover 94 per cent of the texts, 214 out of 222.

CTh 9.1.1   *huiusmodi honorem* for *honorem, non inlustris sed tantum clarissima* for *clarissimae*[131]   2.3 add. *non minus tamen*[132]   3.5 *eiusmodi* for *eius*[133]   7.7 add. *id est*[134]   16.11 add. *id est*[135]   25.2 *attemptare tantum* for *vel attemptare*[136]   26.3 add. *ad instar legis Iuliae ambitus*[137]   28.1 add. *lege Iulia peculatus*[138]   34.7 add. *huiusmodi delicti. sin vero, huiusmodi autem libellus*[139]   37.1 *sin autem* for *sin aliquid*[140]   37.2 *sin autem(bis)*[141]   37.4 *quando autem* for *abolitionem, post hoc vero tempus* for *post hoc tempus*[142]   42.1 add. *sin autem, id est, non tamen*[143]   42.24 *quando quis* for *sentiat latro, sin autem* for *sin*, add. *si vero*.[144]

In book 11 *autem* is inserted five times and *sin autem* twice. *Frustratoria dilatio* appears twice. The editor inserts the pronoun *is* in the interests of clarity and is moved by a concern for completeness, often adding cases not mentioned in the original text, at times one might think unnecessarily. He seems to prefer the singular to the plural.

CTh 11.1.14   *Ii penes quos* for *penes quos*[145]   1.25 *si non is intulerit* for *si non intulerit*[146]   8.1 add. *autem, amovenda atque prohibenda* for *amovenda*[147]   8.2 add. *vel aliis exactoribus*[148]   8.3 *iniurias seu laesiones* for *iniurias*[149]   9.2 *sin autem* for *cum si* and add. *aliamve rem*[150]   16.6 *extraordinariis et sordidis muneribus et susceptionibus et temonariis oneribus* for *extraordinariis et temonariis oneribus*[151]   16.11 add. *autem*[152]   30.1 *quotiens autem* for *si*, add. *sine aliqua frustratoria dilatione*[153]   30.2 add. *si fideiussoris idonei copiam non habeant* (correct, but one would expect the plural)[154]   30.6 add. *autem*[155]   30.30 add. several officials to the list[156]   35.1 add. *sin autem negotium* for *negotia*[157]   36.4 add. *autem*[158]   36.20 *frustratoria dilatio*[159]   36.26 *is cuius de ea re notio erit* for *cuius de ea re notio erit*[160]   37.1 *cum de possessione et eius momento* for *cum de possessione et momento*.[161]

[130] Studied by Bonini, *Ricerche di diritto Giustineaneo* (1968) 99.

[131] *CJ* 3.24.1 (4 Dec. 316/17).	[132] *CJ* 9.3.2 (30 Dec. 380).
[133] *CJ* 9.4.4 (29 June 371).	[134] *CJ* 9.9.32 (7 Dec. 392).
[135] *CJ* 9.18.9 (16 Aug. 389).	[136] *CJ* 1.3.5 (19 Feb. 364).
[137] *CJ* 9.26.1 (30 May 403).	[138] *CJ* 9.28.1 (10 Sept. 392).
[139] *CJ* 9.36.2 (16 Feb. 365/8/70/73).	[140] *CJ* 9.42.2 (26 Nov. 319).
[141] *CJ* 9.42.3 (14 Oct. 369).	[142] *CJ* 9.42.3 (14 Oct. 369).
[143] *CJ* 5.16.24 (27 Feb. 321).	[144] *CJ* 9.49.10 (23 Jan. 426).
[145] *CJ* 11.48.4 (1 May 366).	[146] *CJ* 10.16.10 (21 Dec. 395).
[147] *CJ* 10.20.1 (6 March 397).	[148] *CJ* 10.20.1 (14 March 400).
[149] *CJ* 1.55.9 (21 Jan. 409).	[150] *CJ* 4.46.3 (12 Dec. 337).
[151] *CJ* 12.23.1 (7 May 346).	[152] *CJ* 10.48.8 (19 March 365).
[153] *CJ* 7.61.1 (10 Feb. 319).	[154] *CJ* 7.62.12 (3 Nov. 314).
[155] *CJ* 1.21.1 (13 Aug. 316).	[156] *CJ* 7.67.2 (18 Dec. 362).
[157] *CJ* 7.66.6 (19 May 321).	[158] *CJ* 9.9.29 (29 Aug. 339).
[159] *CJ* 1.4.2 = 7.65.4 (8 July 369).	[160] *CJ* 7.65.6 (5 April 379).
[161] *CJ* 7.69.1 (18 Nov. 386).	

The marks covers 279 texts out of 306 (91 per cent).

In book 12 the connecting links are rather slender. We may note *condicio* for 'status', the use of *minime* for 'not', *compellere* and initial *quotiens/cumque*. They cover albeit sparsely 184 texts out of 273, 67 per cent.

CTh 12.1.51 *condicio* for *dignitas*[162]   1.152 add. *minime curialibus nexibus illigatus*[163]   3.1 add. *cuiuscumque sit condicionis*[164]   5.3 *compellat* for *impellat*[165] 6.2 *compellatur* for *incurrat*[166]   6.13 inc. *quotienscumque*[167]   7.2 add. *quotiens orta fuerit dubitatio.*[168]

The last book is 16, which has received a plain treatment. The *non . . . sed* construction is interpolated, also *ipse* and the phrase *ultimum supplicium*. These enclose in a rather thin web the texts from tit. 2.45 to 10.24, 149 out of 201 or 74 per cent.

CTh 16.2.45   *non solum iuris Italici sed etiam ipsius Romae veteris* for *Romae veteris*[169]   5.65 add. *et ultimo supplicio tradendis*[170]   6.6 *ultimo supplicio* for *statuti prioris supplicio*[171]   8.22 *non a senioribus sed ab ordinariis* for *a rectoribus provinciae*[172]   9.2 add. *ipso servo donando*[173]   10.24 add. *non ipsi talia vindicent sed.*[174]

In what has been set out I have necessarily written as if the hypothesis that each book was edited by a single commissioner in a uniform style were true. But the evidence leaves the matter open. There is considerable variation in the editing of the Theodosian texts. Some editors make few changes, some a fair number. Of the latter some concentrate on form, others on substance. Some interpolate in a plain style, others in an ornate rhetoric, others write elegantly. It is difficult to say whether these alterations of tone and method coincide with the beginning and end of books of the code. One can only say of the evidence that it does not rule out this method of editing. On the other hand one notices in places a certain unevenness, which might be due to the fact that the hypothesis is wrong, or simply to the effect of interpolations introduced at the compiling stage either by John's or Tribonian's commission.

So far no conclusion seems possible. There was however a second member of John's commission, Thomas, whose style is familiar from the constitutions he drafted during the period of the commission's labours.[175] If the same procedure is followed with him as with Tribonian, we get a list of only two homographic texts:

[162] *CJ* 10.32.22 (28 Aug. 362).
[163] *CJ* 2.7.3 (3 Aug. 396).
[164] *CJ* 10.34.1 (24 Nov. 386).
[165] *CJ* 10.32.52 (17 March 397).
[166] *CJ* 10.72.1 (19 July 325).
[167] *CJ* 10.72.5 (8 Jan. 367).
[168] *CJ* 10.73.2 (23 April 363).
[169] *CJ* 11.21.1 (14 July 421).
[170] *CJ* 1.5.5 (30 May 428).
[171] *CJ* 1.6.2 (21 March 413).
[172] *CJ* 1.9.15 (20 Oct. 415).
[173] *CJ* 1.10.1 (13 Aug. 339).
[174] *CJ* 1.11.6 (8 June 423).
[175] For the analysis of his style see below, ch. 8 nn. 93f.

CTh 4.22.3   *sin vero* for *illi vero* (*CJ* 8.4.7).[176]
CTh 12.6.30   add. *scire autem volumus* (*CJ* 10.72.13.1).[177]
CTh 9.34.7   add. *sin vero* (*CJ* 9.36.1)

One of the texts comes from book 12 and we can add a second:[178]

CTh 12.1.6   *ideoque praecipimus* for *praecipimus itaque* (*CJ* 5.5.3).

Not only is *ideoque praecipimus* evidenced for Thomas alone[179] but, more significant, *itaque* is not, though the *CJ* has 186 instances of this conjunction.[180] This makes a strong case for the view that Thomas excerpted book 12, which begins with the important tile *de decurionibus*. The other book, if any, allotted to him escapes detection.

In the end the evidence, fragmentary as it is, that Thomas edited book 12 adds something to the similar evidence that Tribonian edited books 3 and 7. It suggests the adoption by John of a method similar to but not as rigorous as that of Tribonian as chairman of the second commission. According to this two books of the *CTh* would be assigned to each commissioner to excerpt, but not in strict order of seniority nor in a fixed rotation. Indeed the choice might depend on the individual preferences of the commissioners, or their convenience. For the reasons given such a pattern can be discerned but dimly, and it is overlaid by the interpolations, not numerous so much as confusing, introduced at the compiling stage when the two commissions actually drafted the codices.

At the moment it seems impossible to carry the matter further. We cannot recognise the styles of the commissioners other than Tribonian and Thomas. We cannot say how the actual compilation of either the first or the second *Codex* was distributed among the lawyers who did the work.[181] Some of the problems involved may indeed be insoluble.

[176] Too numerous to set out in full. Those for Thomas are *CJ* 3.28.30.1, 4.20.18.1, 5.27.9.3, 6.56.7 pr., 2 (all 1 June 528), 5.16.25.1, 2; 6.26.9.1, 7.17.1.2, 7.39.8.1, 1a (11 Dec. 528 bis), 1.2.19 (Menae pp. 528), 7.62.37.1, 12.33.6 pr. (6 April 529 bis), *C. Summa* 4 (7 April 529).

[177] Only *CJ* 12.40.3 (400), 11.14.2.1 (404), 7.17.1.3 (11 Dec. 528), apart from the present text (=*CJ* 10.72.13.1 itp.).

[178] Another text from book 12 (*CTh* 12.1.152 = *CJ* 2.7.3) could be added, were it not that besides a mark of Thomas (*curialibus nexibus*) it contains a mark of Tribonian (*inligatus,* see ch. 3 nn. 96, 288; above, n. 14). *CJ* 10.32.64.2 (Zeno), 10.35.3.2 (1 June 528), 2.7.3 (396 itp.).

[179] *CJ* 5.74.3.1 (6 April 529), 5.5.3.1 (319 itp.); cf. 12.9.1.1 (444 *ideoque . . . praecipimus.*

[180] *VCJ* 1. 1383-4.

[181] So far as the second edition of *CJ* is concerned a guess is possible. Three of the four *CTh* texts with homographic marks of Tribonian's style (other than those from books 3 and 7 of *CTh*) are located in odd-numbered books of *CJ* (above, nn. 3, 8, 9 and cf. 23-4). This is consistent with Tribonian's having reedited the odd-numbered books of *CJ* (1, 3, 5, 7, 9, 11) leaving Dorotheus to reedit the even-numbered ones. If this guess were confirmed (and it is difficult to see how it could be) it would show that there was nothing in Tribonian's religious outlook to prevent his re-editing the religious and ecclesiastical material in book 1.

CHAPTER EIGHT

Six Other Quaestors

In the present chapter an attempt is made to show that five or six quaestors of the sixth century composed laws in styles which differ from that of Tribonian and from one another. The names of all or nearly all of them are known and in some cases we can supplement what the texts tell us from outside sources. It is important to the theme of this book to show that the depiction of Tribonian's style in accordance with certain numerically controlled procedures is not an isolated *tour de force* but merely an illustration of the fact that given a reasonable amount of relatively homogeneous material it should at all periods of late Roman history be possible to disentangle the laws composed by successive officials.

The sixth-century tenures of the quaestorship have been numbered consecutively, since it is not possible to put a name to all of them with certainty. The numbering begins somewhat arbitrarily at 61. A study of third-century rescripts[1] revealed 20 tenures of the secretaryship *a libellis* between 193 and 295. If 20 periods of office are allowed for the composers of constitutions in each of the fourth and fifth centuries, the sixth begins at no. 61.

NO. 61. 17 NOVEMBER 500 (CJ 2.4.43) TO 20 NOVEMBER 506 (CJ 2.7.23)

This tenure is made up of only seven Latin constitutions[2] but as these amount to 233 lines in *CJ* the evidence is not too slender for the identification of a period of office. An idiom which marks this tenure is *sine quadam* for *sine ulla*, which occurs in seven *CJ* texts in all, of which three are of our period and three others are undated constitutions of Anastasius.[3] *Compelli* with the object infinitive preceding, as in *iurare compelli*, occurs in 24 texts,

---

[1] Honoré, 'Private rescripts and their authors 193–280', *Aufsteig und Niedergang der römsichen Welt*, ed. Temporini 2.14. (R. Guilland, *Byzantion* 41 (1971) 90–1 confuses active with titular office and so lists three spurious quaestors for the sixth century: Dorotheus, John, Rufinus).

[2] *CJ* 2.4.43–2.7.21–7.39.5 (17 Nov. 500), 3.13.7 (15 Feb. 502), 6.20.18–6.58.11–8.48.5 (21 July 502), 2.7.22 (1 Jan. 505), 1.4.19–1.55.11 (19 April 505), 4.35.22 (23 July 506), 2.7.23 (20 Nov. 506). The Greek constitutions of the period are mostly undated and in the form of summaries from the Basilica.

[3] *CJ* 4.38.6 (Dio et Max. AA et CC), 3.13.7.1 (15 Feb. 502 *sine quadam fori praescriptione*), 4.35.22.3 (23 July 506 *sine quadam imminutione*), 2.7.23.2 (20 Nov. 506 *sine quadam suffragii solutione*); cf. 7.39.6.1 (Anast. Leontio pp. *sine quadam legitima interpellatione*), 12.19.11 (Anast. Eusebio mag. off. *sine quadam imminutione*), 12.37.17 pr. (Anast, Arcadio pp. *sine quadam mora*).

of which three are of this period and four others are undated texts of Anastasius.[4]

The author likes the emphatic *per*, as in *periniquum et temerarium*.[5] Perhaps his most obtrusive characteristic is a fondness for verbal doublets of the type *connumerati sunt vel fuerint*.[6] *Sunt vel fuerint* is found three times,[7] but we also have *motis et movendis*,[8] and *celebrandas vel iam celebratas*,[9] *deposuerunt vel deposuerint*,[10] and *factae seu faciendae*.[11] Besides these doublets where the change of tense carries with it an alternative sense there are others of a pleonastic sort: *gradum et officium*,[12] *munimine ac tuitione*,[13] *motis et pendentibus*.[14] Even apart from these traits, the constant desire of the quaestor to balance one word by another produces a style which is easy to recognise and tends to flatulence, a trait which we shall find to be in character.

The limits of the tenure prima facie run from 17 November 500[15] (*motis et pendentibus seu movendis . . . celebrandas vel iam celebratas . . .*) to 20 November 506 (*sine quadam suffragii solutione, agnito debito vel agnita causa*).[16] But some earlier and later texts, and some undated constitutions of Anastasius, appear to conform to the same style:

(a) *CJ* 12.16.5.1 (Anast. Polycarpo pp. [viz. 497–9][17] *adquisita sunt vel fuerint, sibimet vindicare vel auferre, fructum vel lucrum, datum est vel fuerit, curam seu provisionem, decorati sunt vel fuerint*).

It is possible therefore that the tenure may have begun somewhat before 17 November 500, but unlikely that it antedated 1 January 499, since a constitution of that date is too concise to be by the same author.[18]

After November 506 there are no more Latin constitutions until 517, when we have:

(b) *CJ* 4.29.21 (1 April 517 *pro uno contractu vel certis contractibus seu pro una vel certis personis, firmum illibatumque custodiri, usae sunt vel fuerint, accommodaverunt vel accomodaverint, consenserunt vel consenserint*).

[4] *CJ* 5.53.2 (212), 5.65.2 (239), 8.42.16 (293), 5.56.4 pr., 4.32.24, 4.10.12 (294), 3.36.25 (295), 4.35.19 (Dio. et Max. AA et CC), 1.37.1 (386), 10.71.4 (440–1), 12.23.12 pr. (Theo et Val.), 8.4.10.1 (481), 12.21.8 (484), 3.13.7.1 (15 Feb. 502), 6.20.18 (21 July 502), 2.7.22.6 (1 Jan. 505), 2.7.24.6 (1 Dec. 517 = 2.7.22.6), 7.39.5 (Anast. ad Thomam pp. III), 7.39.6.1 (Anast. Leontio pp.), 12.19.12.3–12.20.6 (Anast. Celeri mag. off., bis), 2.58.1 pr. (17 Sept. 529), 8.53.35.5e (18 Mar. 530), 4.20.19.2 (21 Mar. 530).

[5] *CJ* 3.13.7 pr. (20 Feb. 502; cf. 12.20.6.1 Anast. Celeri mo. *cum perabsurdum perque temerarium sit*). [6] *CJ* 3.13.7.1 (15 Feb. 502).

[7] Above, n. 6 and 2.7.22.6 (1 Jan. 505), 4.35.22.3 (23 July 506); cf. 4.29.21 (1 April 517), 12.37.17 pr. (Anast. Arcadio pp. bis), 7.51.6 (Anast. Stephano mag. mil.).

[8] *CJ* 2.4.43 (17 Nov. 500). [9] *CJ* 2.4.43 (17 Nov. 500).

[10] *CJ* 2.7.22.6 (1 Jan. 505). [11] *CJ* 4.35.22.3 (23 July 506).

[12] *CJ* 2.7.21 (17 Nov. 500). [13] *CJ* 4.35.22.2 (23 July 506).

[14] *CJ* 2.4.43 (17 Nov. 500). [15] *CJ* 2.4.43–2.7.21–7.39.5. [16] *CJ* 2.7.23.

[17] Polycarp pp. is attested in *CJ* 5.30.4 (1 April 498). The next pp. Or. whose date is attested is Constantinus (*CJ* 3.13.7, 15 Feb. 502), unless Arcadius is to be intercalated: Stein II. 782. On the style see above, n. 6.

[18] *CJ* 5.62.25 (1 Jan. 499).

(c) *CJ* 5.27.6 (1 April 517 *progenitos seu procreandos, quaestionis seu altercationis, astuta subtilique legum vel constitutionum occasione, legis beneficio et iuvamine*).

These texts conform to the style of those between 500 and 506. More doubt surrounds *CJ* 2.7.24 (1 December 517) which repeats verbatim 2.7.22 (1 January 505). This could be the act of an old man disinclined to think out a new formula, or of a successor slavishly copying his predecessor. It is not impossible that the tenure of no. 61 stretched from 500 or a little before up to 517. Justinian's *Novel* 35 of 23 December 535 mentions a long tenure of the quaestorship by Iohannes, during whose office the number of assistants provided by the *scrinia* increased beyond measure.[19] It is clear from this text that Iohannes was a predecessor of Proclus, who, as we shall see, held office under Justin. It is tempting to think that he was his immediate predecessor. In that case he is to be identified with no. 61 and the tenure of no. 61 probably stretched over the first seventeen years of the century, in which case it would be longer than any other of which we have a record. But the absence of Latin texts between 506 and 517 makes it impossible to be sure, and hence six years is all that can be securely attributed to him.

Of the 15 undated constitutions of Anastasius nine may fairly be attributed to no. 61:

CJ 7.39.7 (Idem = Anast. Leontio pp. pr.[20] *minime vel minus quam oportuerat, requiri seu profligari, sensui propositoque 1 sine quadam legitima interpellatione, dependere compelli*).[21]

7.51.6 (Anast. Stephano mag. mil. *munitus est vel postea meruerit, praestitis vel postea praebendis, praetermissum sit vel fuerit*).[22]

11.43.11 (Anast. Sergio pp. [viz. c. 517] *intimatis vel intimandis, violaverint vel violare concesserint*).[23]

12.19.11 (Anast. Eusebio mag. off. *pro solacio vel suffragio, hereditas vel successio, sibique petere ac vindicare, retractanda seu violanda, sine quadam imminutione*).[24]

---

[19] *N.* 35 pr. (23 Dec. 535). The prolix style and innumerable assistants are of a piece.

[20] Lydus 3.17. If Lydus means that Leontius was praetorian prefect when Coades (Kavadh) invaded the empire and Apion the patrician was in charge of the army finances the prefecture falls about 503 (*Wars* 1.8.5) and in any case between 15 Feb. 502 and 1 Jan. 505, on each of which Constantinus was in office (*CJ* 2.7.22, 4.35.22). If, however, the prefecture belongs to the period when Anastasius was incensed with Apion, the year is 510 (Marcellinus anno 510 n. 2). The latter year would give some slight support to the hypothesis of a continuous tenure. Bury I. 471 takes another view of the Lydus passage. On Leontius see Collinet 141–54; Stein II. 782.

[21] Above, nn. 3, 4, 12f.   [22] Above, nn. 6, 9, 12f.

[23] Cf. above, n. 9. The formula *violaverint seu/vel violare concesserint* is found in *CJ* only in four undated texts of Anastasius, the present and *CJ* 12.20.6.4, 12.37.17.3, 12.50.23.2, below, n. 24, 25, 26. Sergius pp. is mentioned in the inscription of *CJ* 5.27.6 (1 April 517), 2.7.24 (1 Dec. 517).

[24] Above, n. 3; cf. 12. Eusebius mo. is attested for 1 March 492 (*CJ* 1.30.3) and 31 Dec. 497 (*CJ* 2.7.20). If my identification is right his tenure extended or was renewed at least into 499.

12.19.12–12.20.6 (Anast. Celeri mag. off. 12.1 *exigere seu profligare,
agnoscere seu dependere,* 3 *offerre compelli, deposuerunt vel deposuerint* 4 *pro
sumptibus et expensis* 6 *deposuerunt seu deposuerint, commodis atque auxilio
potituris* | pr. *offerre compelli* 1 *intacta inviolataque, cum perabsurdum
perque temerarium sit* 2 *sortitis vel sortituris,* 4 *violaverint seu violare
concesserint*).[25]

12.37.17 (Idem = Anast. Arcadio pp. pr. *deputari vel etiam deputatos esse,
damnum seu dispendium, deputati sunt vel fuerint, deputati sunt vel fuerint,
perveniunt seu pervenerunt, sine quadam mora,* 2 *prout nobis placuit* 3 *violaverint seu violare concesserint*).[26]

12.50.23.2 (Anast. Armenio pp. *violaverint seu violare concesserint*).[27]

12.54.5 (Anast. magistris militum *pulsari et conveniri*).[28]

12.16.5 has been dealt with previously.[29]

Six undated constitutions of Anastasius are not attributed to no. 61.[30]

NO. 62. 1 DECEMBER 518 (CJ 7.63.3) TO
22 APRIL 527 (CJ 1.31.5)

Eleven constitutions can be attributed in the first instance to the next
quaestor.[31] These amount to 423 lines in *CJ*, 0.8 per cent of the Latin in *CJ*
and 1.3 per cent of the Latin from Constantine onwards.[32]

The new quaestor composes in an elegant and rhythmical style, marked
in particular by phrases in which a noun is separated from its adjective by
two (or, counting a short preposition sometimes three) intervening words,
as in:

interdicenda quoque cunctis licentia[33]
datas iure emphyteutico res[34]
debitorem sibi esse mortuum[35]
in huiusmodi deprehensus fuerit flagitio[36]

[25] Above, nn. 4, 5, 10, 23; cf. 12.   [26] Above, nn. 3, 6, 23; cf. 9, 12.
[27] Above, n. 23.   [28] Cf. above, n. 12.   [29] Above, n. 17.

[30] *CJ* 10.32.66 (Anast. Polycarpo pp. 1 *intactum illibatumque*) but the text is rhetoric-
ally more accomplished than those of no. 61, whose tenure may be supposed to have
started *during* the praetorian prefecture of Polycarp; 12.1.18 (Eusebio mag. off. cf.
12.19.11: the same applies to Eusebius); 12.5.5 (Eusebio mag. off. notably concise),
12.10.2 (Eusebio mag. off. *quin etiam*), 12.37.16 (Longino mag. eq. et ped. 1 *sine ullo dolo
vel fraude* 1a *hoc videlicet observando* 1b *nec ulla machinatione* 5 *hoc etiam adiciendo* 6 *hoc videlicet
ante omnia curando*—this is a long rhetorical text but without verbal redundancies);
12.49.12 (Spartiatio pp. Ill.). Some of these texts can positively be attributed to the
last quaestor of the fifth century, but his style falls outside the scope of the present study.

[31] *CJ* 7.63.3 (1 Dec. 518), 5.27.7 (9 Nov. 519), 2.7.25 (1 Dec. 519), 7.63.4 (28 May
520), 6.22.8 (1 June 521), 2.7.26 (13 Feb. 524), 1.3.40–6.23.23 (19 Nov. 524), 2.7.27 (20
Nov. 524), 12.33.5 (25 Dec. 524), 7.39.7 (1 Dec. 525), 9.19.6 (1 Dec. 526).

[32] All Latin in *CJ* 51,344 lines, Latin from Constantine 32,894.

[33] *CJ* 2.7.26.1 (13 Feb. 524).

[34] *CJ* 7.39.7.7 (1 Dec. 525; cf. ibid. pr. *nullis expirare lustrorum cursibus* 1 *prisca
constitutionum sanxit iustitia*).

[35] *CJ* 9.19.6 (1 Dec. 526).   [36] *CJ* 9.19.6 (1 Dec. 526).

suae condant moderamina voluntatis[37]

or is enveloped by adjectives so as to form a group of four words, as in:

statutis inserendos praesentalibus domesticis[38]

and the like. A variant in which nouns and adjectives alternate is illustrated by his delicate description of the ingenuity of Anastasius in reducing the budget:

parca posterioris subtilitas principis.[39]

He is fond of the repetition of a negative:

Nemo arbitretur . . . neque per oblationem precum neque per sacrum rescriptum . . . neque sub praetextu quodam altero[40]
nec impetratum nec pronuntiatum omnino nec insertum[41]

This is sometimes combined with the asyndeton construction:

nulla de cetero venia defendet, nullum sublevabit novum adminiculum . . . non ante lata sanctio . . . non adrogationum vel adoptionum praetextus . . . non astutiae . . . cum nimis indignum, nimis sit impium . . . .[42]

Another example of a repetitive asyndeton, this time not a negative expression, is to be found in:

ne locum quidem ullum relinquat insidiis tot oculis spectata, tot insinuata sensibus, tot insuper in tuto locata manibus.[43]

The reader soon acquires an ear for the author's grouping of words and stresses.

The plural *astutiae* is found in *CJ* only in this tenure; there is one previous text with *astutia.*[44] *Prout dictum est*[45] is confined to no. 62. *Inrepere* is a favourite word.[46] Hapax from this tenure are *eversio,*[47] *exercitare*[48] and *opprobrium.*[49] Of three uses of *iniustus* two belong to this period and the

---

[37] *CJ* 6.22.8 pr. (1 June 521).   [38] *CJ* 2.7.25.3 (1 Dec. 519).
[39] *CJ* 2.7.25 pr. (1 Dec. 519).   [40] *CJ* 7.63.3 (1 Dec. 518).
[41] *CJ* 12.33.5.1a (25 Dec. 524).
[42] *CJ* 5.27.7.3 (9 Nov. 519); cf. ibid 1 (*non incesta non nefaria*).
[43] *CJ* 6.22.8.2 (1 June 524).
[44] *CJ* 7.63.3 (1 Dec. 518 *ne praepediatur per astutias*), 5.27.7.3 (9 Nov. 519 *non astutiae*), 2.7.26 pr. (21 Aug. 524 *qualibet rursus ambitione vel astutia*) but 1.49.1.2 (11 Oct. 479).
[45] *CJ* 6.22.8.1b (1 June 521), cf. 5.4.23.8 (Justinus Demostheni pp.).
[46] Six *CJ* texts: 1.3.4.2 (361), 9.26.1.1 (400), 1.9.18.2 (439), 12.19.10.1 (Leo), 5.27.7.1 (9 Nov. 519), 1.3.40 = 6.23.23 (19 Nov. 524).
[47] *CJ* 6.23.23 (19 Nov. 524).   [48] *CJ* 7.63.4.1 (1 Dec. 518).
[49] *CJ* 1.3.40 = 6.23.23 (19 Nov. 524).

third to the praetorian prefecture of Demosthenes under Justin, which in effect falls within it.[50] Two of six instances of *incongruus*,[51] and one of five with *congruus* governing the dative come from this tenure; two of the remaining five belong to undated constitutions of Justin.[52] Of eight texts with *nimis* (*grave* etc.) *est* two come from our period and a third from an undated text of Justin.[53]

Of six texts with *sublevare* one belongs to our period and one, of Justin, to the praetorian prefecture of Demosthenes.[54] Of nine instances of *adfectare* two are dated to this tenure, a third addressed by Justin to Proculus.[55] *De cetero*, common in the early sixth century, is here alone found in the combination *de cetero volumus*:[56] *de cetero cessante* is confined to the next tenure.[57] Of the gerund and gerundive *indulgendum/us* two cases are dated to our period, one to 527 and one is addressed to Proclus.[58] The fifth is Tribonian's.

These features can be used to peg out a tenure which runs from 1 December 518 (*neque . . . neque . . . neque, astutiae, indulgendum*, elegant ending)[59] at least to 1 December 526 (*cum sit iniustum*).[60] The last dated text before 1 December 518 is a constitution of 1 December 517, which, as already mentioned, is a copy of an earlier composition by no. 61. It is likely that our quaestor was appointed by Justin, who became emperor on 10 July 518.

Of the three Latin constitutions of the joint reign of Justin and Justinian in the summer of 527 two appear to be in the style of no. 62 one in that of his successor, though the indications are not conclusive:

CJ 1.31.5.1 (22 April 527 *de cetero uolumus*).[61]
 5.3.19 (Iustinus Archelao pp., pr. *tanto donationem ante nuptias addita-*

[50] CJ 5.27.7.3 (9 Nov. 519), 9.19.6 (1 Dec. 526), 5.4.23.1 (Iustinus Demostheni pp.). CJ 6.22.8 (1 June 521) is addressed to Demosthenes pp. Archelaus was pp. by 19 Nov. 524 (CJ 1.3.40–6.23.23); Stein II. 783.

[51] CJ 3.13.1 pr. (214), 1.51.1 (286), 12.46.2 (328), 1.14.9 (454), 6.23.23 (19 Nov. 524 bis).

[52] CJ 5.74.1 (290), 6.22.8.1a (1 June 521), 12.19.13.2 (Iustinus Proculo qsp.), 12.19.14 pr. (Idem Tatiano mag. off.).

[53] CJ 4.16.4, 4.20.7 (293), 8.41.5 (294), 5.27.7.3 (9 Nov. 519 bis), 4.30.13 (Iustinus Theodoto pu), 4.1.12.3 (30 Oct. 529).

[54] CJ 10.32.14 (313), 12.57.6.1 (385), 11.58.7.2 (417), 10.16.12.3 = 1.2.8 (424), 5.27.7.3 (9 Nov. 519), 5.4.23 pr. (Iustinus Demostheni pp.).

[55] CJ 1.1.2.2 (381), 5.35.2.2 (390), 5.5.4.1 (Val. Theo. et Arc.), 11.28.1.1 (412), 10.32.55 = 12.57.12.1 (436), 12.57.14.1 (471), 5.27.7.3 (9 Nov. 519), 12.33.5.1 (25 Dec. 524), 12.19.13.1 (Iustinus Proculo qsp.).

[56] CJ 1.31.5.1 (22 April 527), 5.4.23.1b (Demostheni pp.).

[57] CJ 7.3.1 (1 June 528), 12.19.15.4 (Iust. et Iust. Tatiano mag. off. below, n. 61).

[58] CJ 7.63.3 (1 Dec. 518 *rescriptum indulgendum*), 12.33.5.2 (25 Dec. 524 *indulgendam licentiam*), 12.19.13 pr. (Iustinus Proculo qsp. *licentiam indulgendo*), 5.3.19 pr. (Iust. et Iust. Archelao pp. *indulgendum est namque*), 4.27.2.1 (17 Nov. 530 *neque enim indulgendum est*).

[59] CJ 7.63.3 (above, n. 40, 44): *ne, quod per angustias contingit temporum, tardus appellationis fautor suo dispendio refutetur.* [60] CJ 9.19.6; above, n. 50. [61] Above, n. 56.

mento, indulgendum est, 3 *pacta de amborum deminutionibus ineunda, exceptis videlicet his casibus, in hoc enim secundo matrimonio).*[62]

But

CJ 12.19.15 (Iust. et Iust. Tatiano mag. off. 4 *de cetero cessante, connumerare,* 5 *illo videlicet observando).*[63]

A feature which inclines me to extend this tenure to the joint reign of uncle and nephew is in the use of 1.31.5.2 of two turns of phrase which point more to no. 62 than to his successor: *ad haec* ('what is more')[64] and the final *ut* clause expressing the purpose of the legislation.[65] This, or a parallel *ne* clause is found in a number of texts securely or plausibly taken to be composed by him.[66]

Of the five undated Latin constitutions of Justin four can be put to the account of our quaestor:

CJ 4.30.13 (Iustinus Theodoto pu *nimis enim indignum esse iudicamus*)[67]
    5.4.23 (Iust. Demostheni pp. 1 *cum iniustum sit, scaenicis quidem sese ludis,* 1a *nulla praecedente inhonesta vita,* 1b *omni macula penitus direpta, de cetero volumus,* 2 *liberos ex tali matrimonio procreandos, alios ex priore matrimonio legitimos,* 4 *tale merentibus ab imperatore beneficium, aliam etiam omnem maculam,* 5a *dotalia inter eos etiam instrumenta,* 7 *matrimonia inter impares honestate contrahenda,* 8 *praeteritas etiam huiusmodi coniunctiones*)[68]
    12.19.13 (Iustinus Proculo qsp 1 *legitimusque iam resideat numerus* 2 *nec non iustitiae congruum, ordinandis videlicet isdem adiutoribus, adiutor quidem habeatur superior).*[69]
    12.19.14 (Idem = Iustinus Tatiano mag. off. pr. *integritati congruum ordinem* 1 *sacrae memoriae, sacrarum etiam epistularum).*[70]

There is a doubt concerning *CJ* 7.62.34 (Iustinus or Iustinianus Demostheni pp.). From its position in the title this should belong to Justin's reign and the tenure of no. 62. Though it has no distinctive marks of his style, it is at least not inconsistent with it.[71]

---

[62] Above, nn. 33f., 58.   [63] Below, nn. 101, 111; above, n. 57.

[64] *CJ* 1.31.5.2 (22 April 527); cf. 12.19.14.2 (Idem—Iustinus Tatiano mag. off.). Other uses of the phrase, though not in the final section of a constitution: 2.7.25.2 (1 Dec. 519).

[65] *Ut semper notitia eorundem scholarium certa sit neque publico damnum aliquod infligatur.*

[66] Final *ut CJ* 5.27.7.3 (9 Nov. 519), 6.22.8.2 (1 June 521 *ut . . . sed ne*), 12.19.13.2 (Iustinus Proculo qsp.), 4.30.13 (Iustinus Theodoto pu.), 5.4.23.8 (Iustinus Demostheni pp.), final *ne* 7.63.3 (1 Dec. 518), 12.19.14.2 (Iustinus Tatiano mag. off.), 5.3.19.3 (Iust. et Iust. Archelao pp.). It is hardly possible to document this for the whole of *CJ*.

[67] Above, n. 53.   [68] Above, nn. 33f., 50, 56.   [69] Above, nn. 33f., 52.

[70] Above, n. 52; cf. 43.

[71] *Nulli danda licentia,* cf. *CJ* 7.39.7.7 (1 Dec. 525); *dum* with indicative, cf. 2.7.25.2 (1 Dec. 519), 2.7.27 (21 Aug. 524).

No. 62 is undoubtedly Proclus (to adopt the Greek form for convenience) to whom *CJ* 12.19.13 is addressed.[72] In *CJ* 12.19.15 (Iustinus et
Iustinianus AA) he is described as *excelsae memoriae* and *magnificae memoriae*:
so he did not outlive Justin.[73] Esteem for his memory was not an empty
phrase. In the *Wars* Procopius deals with the proposal made by Cabades,
the Persian king, that Justin should adopt his son Chosroes.[74] Proclus, as
Justin's quaestor, is credited with having dissuaded Justin and Justinian
from this rash step. Procopius calls him a just man and unbribable.[75] He
attributes to the quaestor a dislike of innovation in general.[76] In particular
he was hostile to the proposal to adopt Chosroes. This, Proclus is made to
argue, is plainly aimed at securing the Roman empire for Chosroes, so
handing over the state to foreigners and blocking Justinian's own
ambitions. Hence, it is said, Proclus persuaded Justin to send envoys to
Cabades to tell him that the adoption (already, it seems, agreed) must take
place in the barbarian manner.[77] The implication was that it would be like
the 'adoption' of Theodoric by Zeno or that of Eutharic by Justin, about
A.D. 525. This was to place the Persian on a level with barbarians and
Chosroes was deeply offended.[78] In due course he avenged the insult by
invading the eastern provinces of the empire four times and sacking
Antioch.

Proclus figures in two passages of the *Secret History*. In Justin's reign,
it is said, the emperor's incompetence and illiteracy forced him to rely on
the judgment of his quaestor who conducted the government according to
his own discretion.[79] The second incident is much to Proclus', the quaestor's, credit. During his uncle's reign Justinian fell ill, and in his absence
Justin was told of the thuggery and mob rule which, with his nephew's
encouragement, the Blue faction indulged.[80] Theodotus, prefect of the
city,[81] tracked down and punished some of the malefactors. Then Justinian
recovered and tried to have Theodotus put to death as a sorcerer, relying
on false evidence obtained by torture. Everyone else stood aside but
Proclus pointed out that there was no real case against him. Theodotus
was saved, but exiled to Jerusalem.[82]

Proclus was a just man. It is by no means frivolous to make the point
that the marks of his style, which include the word *iniustus*,[83] confirm what
Procopius and Lydus say.[84] But the project to adopt Chosroes exposed the
limitations of a conservative lawyer in politics. Cabades was interested in
securing Roman help for the claim of Chosroes to the Persian, not the
Roman, throne. It was folly to insult him; and Justinian, along with his

[72] Imp. Iustinus A. Proculo *quaestori sacri palatii.*
[73] The text is about the vexed question of the number of assistants in the *scrinia.*
Proclus tried to contain the numbers, but to allow substitution for good cause, such as
illness: cf. *N.* 35.1 (23 May 535).
[74] *Wars* 1.11.   [75] *Wars* 1.11.11.   [76] *Wars* 1.11.13.   [77] *Wars* 1.11.22.
[78] *Wars* 1.11.30.   [79] *SH* 6.13.   [80] *SH* 9.35f.   [81] *SH* 9.37–8.
[82] *SH* 9.41–2.
[83] Above, n. 50; cf. *CJ* 12.19.13 (Iustinus Proculo qsp. *iustitiae congruum*).
[84] *Wars* 1.11.11; Lydus 3.20.

subjects, paid for it later.[85] Proclus was a powerful and respected figure under Justin and, had Justinian died before his uncle, would have been a contender, despite his flaws, for the throne. But it was he who died first.

It is convenient here to deal with the question whether the Latin correspondence of Justin and his empress Euphemia with pope Hormisdas was composed by Proclus.[86] No one can suppose the aged Justin capable of writing the seven letters attributed to him in 518–21, or Euphemia's single contribution. The style is also too elegant for Justinian, and the rhythms are, for what it is worth, not those of other quaestors of the early sixth century. Proclus is the obvious candidate for their authorship, but one cannot go further than to assert that their style is consistent with his. They do not contain enough unequivocal marks of his authorship to dispel doubt. Nevertheless:

Patr. Lat. 63.427 (7 Sept. 518 428A *litteras tuae sanctitati offerendas . . . nostras etiam epistolares paginas . . . nostrum pervenire disponat comitatum*).[87]

63.448 (22 April prob. 519 448D *nullis variantes ambiguitatibus, nullis divisi discordibus . . . sanctissimum patrum concilio congruentem . . . omnes concurrunt, omnes accelerant* 449A *scita patrum sanctissima, leges probatissimas* 449B *destinanda ubique principalia praecepta . . . pro remuneranda pace, pro conciliando*)[88]

63.479 (19 Jan. 520 480A *colligendis concordia sacratissimis ecclesiis* B *responsum pietatis vestrae referendum . . .resecari tandem dubitationes incongruae*)[89]

63.486 (7 July 520C *colligendas abunandasque venerabilies ecclesias . . . sincero et integro possint animo* D *transactis in plenum et elaboratis omnibus . . . nihil altercationis superesset alterius* 487A *clementiore quodam indigeant moderamine . . . vestro iam tantum pendet arbitrio . . . prima rei commovit exordia*)[90]

63.499 (31 Aug. 520B *de hac dimitteremus regis civitate . . .* C *pristinae voluerit reddere sanitati*)[91]

63.501 (13 Sept. 520 received 30 Nov. 530C *prono libentique suscipientes adfectu* D *tum Ponticae, tum Asianae, praecipue Orientales* 502B *propagandam quo possumus ordine coniunctionem . . . concessis exiguis et remissis, maiora et omni ratione quaerenda corrigi . . . non Acacii, non utriusque Petri, non Dioscuri vel Timothei . . . delibertata iam et prospecta diffinitio* C *priora vestrae sedis constituta . . . memorias mortuorum indicat contemnendas . . . indignum habeatur et incongruum . . . omnibus non solum defunctis . . . nomen tantum reticeatur Acacii* D *adunandas ubique venerabiles ecclesias*)[92]

63.521 (1 May 521 522D *religiosis alienae sunt episcopis* 523A *prout memoravimus*).[93]

---

[85] He invaded Roman territory four times (*Wars* 8.7.2; *SH* 18.23, 23.7) and captured Antioch in June 540 (*Wars* 2.8.1).
[86] Above, ch. 1.   [87] Above, nn. 33f.   [88] Above, nn. 33f., 42, 43, 52.
[89] Above, nn. 33f., 51.   [90] Above, nn. 33f.   [91] Above, nn. 33f.
[92] Above, nn. 33f., 41, 43, 51.   [93] Above, nn. 33f.; cf. 45.

Euphemia's letter to Agapetus is printed at:

63.487 (*c.* 520 *grato iucundoque suscepimus animo* ... *vitae quoque commendat integritas* ... *studiosa rectae fidei sollertia.*[94]

The rhythms are those of Proclus but the wide-ranging vocabulary is not in the nature of things really distinctive.

NO. 63. 13 FEBRUARY 528 (C. HAEC) TO 7 APRIL 529 (C. SUMMA)

The next tenure of the quaestorship covers 68 Latin constitutions and runs to 1633 lines in *CJ*, which comes to 3.2 per cent of the Latin in *CJ* and 5 per cent of the Latin from Constantine onwards.[95] As a numerical guide I have adopted the rule that to count as a mark of his style at least 15 per cent of the occurrences of an expression must occur in this period and that they must amount to at least four-fifths of the number of such occurrences in the constitutions of Tribonian's first quaestorship,[96] i.e. that the rate frequency in this tenure must be four times that in the next, the number of lines in the latter being five times as great.[97]

No. 63's laws lack the rhythms of his predecessor and the metaphorical luxury of his successor. Apart from the use of *amputare* for to repeal[98] the language is notably literal. The structure is like Tribonian's but the sentences are more complex. A constitution often begins with an elaborate participial phrase,[99] followed by the operative rule (often with *sancimus*)[100] and finally the gerundival ablative absolute, of which *illo videlicet observando* is a characteristic example.[101] His sentences are often long, and several exceed a hundred words.[102] In consequence they have to be bound together by recapitulatory phrases or 'additive' adverbs. An example of the

---

[94] Above, nn. 33f. For *integritas* cf. *CJ* 12.19.14 pr. (Iustinus Tatiano mo. above, n. 68). There are seven other *CJ* texts with *integritas*: *CJ* 9.51.13.2c (321), 10.26.1.2 (364), 11.26.1 (382 but this is bodily integrity), 1.3.30.2, 3 (8 March 469 bis), 1.3.33 (4 April 472), 1.5.10.3 (Leo? 466–72).   [95] Respectively 1633/51,334 and 1633/32,894.

[96] 17 Sept. 529–14 Jan. 532.   [97] 8381/1633=5.1.

[98] *CJ* 9.47.13 (Dio et Max. AA) 2.57.1 (342), 3.39.6 (392), 8.2.3.1 (395), 7.62.28 (396), 11.48.11 (Arc. et Hon.), 6.30.17 (407), 11.28.2 (436), 7.63.2 pr. (440), 6.60.4 pr. (1 Sept. 468), 12.50.22 pr. (Leo), 7.39.4 pr. (30 July 491), 5.4.23.7a (520–3), 9.19.6 (1 Dec. 526), C. Haec pr. (13 Feb. 528), 3.28.30 pr., 4.30.14.1, 5.27.9 pr., 6.20.19 pr., 3 (bis), 6.41.1 pr., 8.13.27 pr., 8.53.33 pr., 8.58.2 (1 June 528), 6.23.26, 8.37.11 (11 Dec. 528), 7.62.37.3, 8.37.12 (6 April 529), 7.63.5.4 (17 Sept. 529), 2.55.4.7 (30 Oct. 529), 8.33.3 pr. (18 March 530), 5.59.5 pr. (1 Sept. 531); cf. 4.35.23.1 (531/2), 3.10.3, 5.37.28.4, 6.35.12.1, 7.72.10 pr. (18 Oct. 532). This word is a good indicator of periods of law reform.

[99] E.g. *corrigentes* (*CJ* 5.9.9, 1 April 529).   [100] Ibid.

[101] *CJ* 11.43.7 (Theo. et Val.), 12.19, 15.5 (Iust. et Iust. Tatiano mo), 4.30.14.3 (1 June 528), 5.27.9.2, 5 (1 June 528 bis), 6.30.22.10 (27 Nov. 531).

[102] *CJ* 6.20.20.3 (6 April 529, 153 words), 4.21.17 pr., 5.27.9 pr. (1 June 528, both 123 words), 4.30.14.2 (1 June 528, 120 words), 3.28.30 pr. (1 June 528, 109 words), 6.20.19.2 (1 June 528, 107 words), 5.9.9 (1 April 529, 100 words) and especially the prefaces C. Haec (13 Feb. 528 s. 1, 112 words, s. 2, 168 words), C. Summa (7 April 529 pr., 116 words, s. 1, 160 words, s. 2, 150 words, s. 3, 113 words).

former is the recapitulatory conditional *si unus accepit . . ., si quid huiusmodi accidit*[103] and the recapitulatory demonstratives *haec quae necessario corrigenda esse multis retro principibus visa sunt, interea tamen nullus eorum hoc ad effectum ducere ausus est.*[104] The use of additives gives a structure such as *tollendis constitutionibus . . . similibus etiam . . . multis insuper aliis*,[105] which permits the almost indefinite prolongation of a sentence. Another aspect of his elaborate structures is the 'German' habit of using participles or gerundives as adjectives or in adjectival phrases, for example *ad hoc maximum et ad ipsius rei publicae sustentationem respiciens opus.*[106]

No. 63 is fond of three openings in particular; *eos qui, super* and *ille*.

CJ has 29 openings with *eos qui/quorum* etc. of which three are from our tenure[107] and two are addressed to Mena pp.[108] Of eleven beginning *super* (*instrumentis* etc.) four belong to this period, one to the next tenure.[109] Of eight constitutions which begin with *ille* or an inflexion of *ille* four belong to this period, including all three with *illam*.[110] Of gerundive forms no. 63 has all five texts with *connumerandus*[111] and three of eight with *computandus*.[112] Among negative adverbs he has two of four instances of *indistincte*,[113] one of four *indubitate*,[114] one of three *indiscrete*.[115] Certain, not all, uses of *locum habere* qualify for the list, in particular *locum habebit*[116] and *locum habere*

---

[103] *CJ* 6.20.20.3 (6 April 529).

[104] *C. Haec* pr. (13 Feb. 529); cf. *C. Summa* 1 (7 April 529 *cum sit necessarium multitudinem constitutionum . . . caliginem earum extirpare*) 4 (*si quae vero pragmaticae sanctiones... eas, si quidem...*).

[105] *C. Summa* 1 (7 April 529); cf. 4.30.14.1 (1 June 528 *instrumento . . . securitatibusque . . . illis etiam securitatibus*), 6.20.19.2 (1 June 528 *nepotibus resistentibus, sed etiam illis adserentibus*) etc.

[106] *C. Haec* 1 (13 Feb. 528); cf. ibid. 3 (*studentes certas et indubitatas et in unum codicem collectas esse de cetero constitutiones ut ex eo tantummodo nostro felici nomine nuncupando codice . . .*), *C. Summa* pr. (7 April 529 *multiplicibus et omnem providentiam continentibus modis*), 1 (*ad hoc commune praestandum beneficium*), 5 (*pro innato sibi circa rem publicam nostrasque dispositiones explendas studio*).

[107] *CJ* 9.2.1 (222), 4.2.3 (239), 2.44.1 (274), 6.34.2 (285), 4.20.5 (286), 6.2.14 (293), 8.17.9, 7.53.9 (294), 7.62.6 (Dio et Max. AA et CC), 10.52.6 (321–4), 10.32.22 (362), 9.39.1 (374), 11.41.3 (381), 10.48.11 (382), 11.43.3 (389), 1.54.6 (399), 11.70.4 (Arc. et Hon.), 12.12.2 (413), 12.21.5 (440/1), 1.7.6 (455), 11.10.6 (Leo et Anth.), 1.29.3 (Zeno), 12.54.5 (Anast.), 4.32.26 (11 Dec. 528), 7.54.2, 2.44.3 (6 April 529), 10.44.4, 12.34.1 (Iustinianus Menae pp.). [108] *CJ* 10.44.4, 12.34.1, above, n. 107.

[109] *CJ* 8.44.16, 9.41.9 (290), 7.61.2 (368), 11.63.4 (384–9), 11.6.6 (409), 10.1.9 (420), 4.2.17, 7.33.11, 8.13.27 (1 June 528), 12.33.6 (6 April 529), 4.38.15 (1 Aug. 530).

[110] *Illam CJ* 6.20.19, 8.53.33, 8.58.2 (all 1 June 528); *illud* 2.21.1 (223), 10.48.9 (368–70), 1.2.19 (Menae pp. 528), 3.38.12 (22 July 530), 6.37.26 (18 Oct. 530).

[111] *CJ* 4.30.14.2 (1 June 528), 9.44.3 (1 April 529), 5.74.3.1, 7.54.2, 12.33.6.1 (6 April 529).

[112] *CJ* 3.31.1.2 (170), 7.63.1 (320), 11.62.14 (491), 5.15.3 (1 June 528), 5.17.10, 7.39.8.1a (11 Dec. 528), 3.38.12 pr. (22 July 530).

[113] *CJ* 7.3.1 (1 June 528), 5.9.9.1 (6 April 529), 6.31.6 pr. (18 Oct. 532), 7.2.15.5 (531/2).

[114] *CJ* 2.4.12 (259), 9.41.7 (286), 6.23.25 (11 Dec. 528), 5.70.7 pr. (1 Sept. 530).

[115] *CJ* 9.41.5 (224), 7.39.8.1 (11 Dec. 528), 1.3.48.3 (23 Aug. 531).

[116] Seven texts of which three are from this tenure: *CJ* 5.12.1.2 (201), 3.13.1.1 (214)

followed by the governing verb (e.g. *locum habere sancimus*).[117] The latter construction occurs ten times each in this tenure and the next, out of 27 texts in all. Of five texts with *adicientes* (of the emperor) three are from no. 63.[118] A miscellaneous list of expressions satisfy the numerical tests: *planus*,[119] *brevis*,[120] *excessus*,[121] *sustentatio*,[122] *suppositio*,[123] *opitulari*[124] and *opitulatio*.[125] *Commiscere*,[126] *pubescere*[127] and *hicdem*[128] occur here only, once. We have three of four texts with *non licebit*:[129] indeed *licebit* in general— six texts out of 31, against six for Tribonian's first period, satisfies the tests.[130] Finally the connective *sin vero* occurs in 16 texts of this tenure out of 86 for *CJ* as a whole and 19 for Tribonians's first quaestorship.[131]

Though we have plenty of material composed by no. 63, he remains a colourless figure. The old writers, never cited by name, are swallowed up

---

2.3.26 (294), 6.30.18.3 (426 *habebunt*), 5.27.8.2 (1 June 528 *habebunt*), 5.27.9.1 (1 June 528), 6.20.20.1 (6 April 529).

[117] Twenty-seven texts of which ten come from this tenure and ten from the next: *CJ* 6.50.2 (197), 6.35.1.2 (204), 6.12.2 (224), 6.21.6 pr. (225), 6.1.1 (286), 6.50.12 (290), 7.62.6.1 (Dio. et Max. AA et CC), 1.4.21.2, 3.28.30.1, 4.2.17, 4.21.17.1, 4.30.14.6, 5.27.9.6, 6.20.19.2, 8.53.33.2 (1 June 528), 3.28.31, 4.32.26.5 (11 Dec. 528), 5.12.31.1 (18 March 530), 6.25.7.3 (22 July 530), 4.38.15.3 (1 Aug. 530), 3.33.13.4 (1 Oct. 530), 5.13.1.16d (1 Nov. 530), 6.42.31.2 (20 Feb. 531), 6.38.4.2 (30 April 531), 1.3.48.7 (23 Aug. 531), 1.5.22 (1 Sept. 531), 4.18.3 (1 Nov. 531), cf. 5.17.11.2a (17 Nov. 533), 9.13.1.6 (17 Nov. 533), 6.51.1.14 (1 June 534).

[118] *CJ* 1.16.1 (384), 1.12.6.8 (466), *C. Haec* 2 (13 Feb. 528), 4.21.17.2 (1 June 528 *illud etiam adicientes*), 1.53.1.3 (11 Dec. 528 same), cf. 6.35.12 pr. (18 Oct. 532).

[119] *CJ* 6.20.20 pr. (6 April 529 *plana sanctione*).

[120] As a positive adjective three texts out of seven: *CJ* 5.17.3.1 (290), 6.42.22 (293), 9.47.23.1 (414), *C. Haec* 2 (13 Feb. 528), 4.30.14.1 (1 June 528), *C. Summa* pr. (7 April 529), 6.23.28.3 (27 March 530). Surprising!

[121] *CJ* 2.12.23 (363), 1.3.10.2 (398 itp.), 4.30.14.2 (1 June 528), 9.44.3 (1 April 529), 5.60.3, 7.62.37.3 (6 April 529). The last four texts refer to lapse of time.

[122] Three texts of five: *CJ* 1.3.34 pr. (472), *C. Haec* 1 (13 Feb. 528), 5.12.29 (11 Dec. 528), *C. Summa* pr. (7 April 529), 1.3.48.6 (23 Aug. 531), cf. 1.17.2.12 (16 Dec. 533).

[123] Two texts out of three: *CJ* 5.74.3 pr., 1 (6 April 529 bis), 8.56.4 pr. (1 Sept. 530).

[124] Two of ten texts, one for Tribonian: *CJ* 5.62.16 (244), 5.18.6.1 (290/3), 9.41.13 (293), 7.35.6 (294), 2.9.3 (294), 9.36.2 (365), 3.6.3 (414), 2.50.8, 7.35.8 (6 April 529), 5.27.11.3 (18 March 530).

[125] Two texts out of three: *CJ* 8.35.12 (363), 10.44.4 (1 June 528), 5.16.26 (6 April 529).

[126] *CJ* 6.20.19.3 (1 June 528).   [127] *CJ* 5.60.3 (6 April 529).

[128] *CJ* 8.53.33.2 (1 June 528).

[129] *CJ* 3.11.5 (322), 3.28.30 pr., 4.20.17 (1 June 528), 7.70.1 (1 June 528).

[130] Above, n. 129 and 9.2.9.2 (289), 6.60.1.2 (319), 6.21.15.1 (334), 2.6.6.3 (368), 6.36.8.2 (424), 6.30.18 pr. (426), 12.60.5 (429 bis), 5.9.5.6 (439), 5.17.8.3 (449), 11.32.3 pr. (469), 5.14.9.1 (468), 1.3.31, 5.9.6.11 (472), 3.24.3.1 (485/6), 5.17.9 (497), 4.30.14.4 (1 June 528), 7.39.8.2, 3 (11 Dec. 528 bis), 8.53.34.2b (30 Oct. 529), 4.1.12.2c (30 Oct. 529), 7.6.1.2 (1 Nov. 531), 2.3.30.3 (1 Nov. 531), cf. 5.3.20.5, 8 (531/2 bis), 7.2.15.7 (531/2), 5.17.11.1 (17 Nov. 533).

[131] The texts are too numerous to set out in full (see *Voc. Cod. Iust.* 1. 2268–9). Those for the present tenure are: *CJ* 3.28.30.1, 4.20.18.1, 5.27.9.3, 6.56.7 pr., 2 (1 June 528), 5.16.25.1, 2; 6.29.9.1, 7.17.1.2, 7.39.8.1, 1a (all 11 Dec. 528), 1.2.19 (Menae pp. 528), 7.62.37.1, 12.33.6 pr. bis (6 April 529), *C. Summa* 4 (7 April 529).

in *veteres/antiquae leges*,[132] 'the old law'. Little is said of the motives for legislation. There are occasional mentions of *humanitas*.[133] *Iustum est*,[134] in contrast with the *iniustum est* of Proclus,[135] is prominent. Important reforms in the law of evidence, documentary proof, the family and succession took place.[136] Their spirit is restrained and technical. The law is tidied up and modernised. To read the constitutions of the early part of Justinian's reign is salutary for those who would attribute to 'Justinian' an antiquarian outlook, fondness for metaphors or an explicit philosophy of legislation.

It is true, but probably not important, that the tenure began in the joint reign of Justin and Justinian. Though *C. Haec* is the first *dated* text attributable to no. 63, *CJ* 12.19.15 (*Justinus et Iustinianus Tatiano mag. off.*) is his by both negative and positive texts. It is not the work of Proclus, who is already dead.[137] The final paragraph begins *illo videlicet observando*,[138] which points forward, as does the phrase *de cetero cessante*.[139]

The last constitutions of the tenure are those of 6 April and *C. Summa*, which promulgated the first *Codex Iustinianus*, probably on 7 April: all addressed to Mena pp. The next texts of are 17 September 529. They are composed by Tribonian and addressed to Demosthenes pp. This suggests that the change of praetorian prefect and quaestor was part of a single operation in the summer of 529, connected with the campaign against paganism. Supporting this conclusion is the fact that Justinian's undated constitutions to Demosthenes are all in Tribonian's manner, while those to Mena are in that of no. 63:

CJ 3.22.6 (Iustinianus Menae pp. ? 30 July 528 or 529 *veteres leges*,)[140]
CJ 12.34.1 (Iustinianus Menae pp. pr. initial *eos qui*).[141]

The date of replacement cannot be more exactly settled.

No. 63 is Thomas, quaestor at the time of *C. Haec*[142] and *C. Summa*.[143] He was the fifth senior of eight (or, if barristers are counted, ten) members of the First Law Commission.[144] In that capacity, as we saw earlier, he

---

132 *Veteres leges*: *CJ* 5.33.1.1 (389), 11.69.1.1 (Zeno), 6.56.7 (1 June 528 bis), 4.32.26.2 (11 Dec. 528), 8.37.12 (6 April 529); cf. 3.22.6 (Iustinianus Menae pp.) *antiquae leges*: 1.14.8 (446), 5.5.8 (475), 3.28.32 (1 April 529).

133 *CJ* 5.27.8 (1 June 528) and 6.26.9 (11 Dec. 528) both begin *Humanitatis intuitu*.

134 Three texts out of nine: *CJ* 5.25.1 (Pius), 2.1.6 (223), 1.9.9 (396), 1.3.20.1 (434), 12.23.14 (Theo. et Val. *iustum videtur*), 4.30.14.1 (1 June 528), 7.17.1, 8.16.9 (11 Dec. 528), 8.37.13 (1 Nov. 531), cf. 4.35.23.3 (531/2 *iustum fuerat*), 8.36.5.1 (18 Oct. 532).

135 Above, n. 60.

136 On proof *CJ* 1.4.21–4.2.17–4.20.18–4.21.17–4.30.14, 15–5.15.3–10.22.5; on succession *CJ* 3.28.30–6.23.24–6.41.1; on the status of children *CJ* 5.27.8, 9–10.35.3–10.44.4; on family inheritance 6.55.12–6.56.7–8.58.2 (all 1 June 528).

137 *CJ* 12.19.15.2 (Iust. et Iust.).   138 Above, n. 101.   139 Above, n. 57.

140 Above, n. 132.   141 Above, nn. 107–8.   142 *C. Haec* 1 (13 Feb. 528).

143 *C. Summa* 2 (7 April 529). Attributed by *Nuovissimo Digesto Italiano* '*Summa*' and Pescani, *Il Plano del Digesto* 229, to Tribonian; but see nn. 102, 105, 106, 120, 122, 131.

144 Iohannes (of Cappadocia), Leontius, Phocas, Basilides, Thomas, Tribonian, Constantinus, Theophilus (Dioscurus, Praesentinus).

probably excerpted book 12 of the *Codex Theodosianus*.[145] Though his term of office began when Justin was alive the latter was then so decrepit that he must be counted as Justinian's appointee. An important but perhaps not a dominant figure in the first phase of Justinian's programme of law reform and codification, he lasted until the publication of the first *Codex* on 7 April 529, then fell from grace. Justinian launched a summer purge and Thomas was said to be a pagan.[146] Nothing in the constitutions of the preceding 15 months tells for or against this. Whatever the truth, he was dismissed. He can hardly have suffered death for his beliefs, but neither did he survive long, since in December 535 Tribonian refers to his 'glorious memory'.[147] That *Novel*, it will be recalled, is about the establishment of assistants (*adiutores*) on the quaestor's staff. Proclus suggested that the number should be reduced to the agreed 26 by not filling vacancies, but that certain senior assistants from the three *scrinia* (*memoriales*, *epistolares* and *libellenses*) should have the right to subrogate others to fill their places.[148] The constitution embodying this compromise was however issued after Proclus' death,[149] and was probably drafted by Thomas. Later, 'owing to the complaints of certain *memoriales* the right was abolished and no substitution allowed'.[150] The amending constitution, which may have fallen in the quaestorship of Thomas, has not survived.

NO. 64. 17 SEPTEMBER 529 (CJ 1.4.24 ETC.) TO 14 JANUARY 532

This quaestorship was Tribonian's first.[151]

NO. 65. C. 15 JANUARY 532—NOT LATER THAN DECEMBER 534

Tribonian was succeeded by Basilides,[152] who had served on John's commission in 528–9 as the fourth senior member. In *C. Haec* he is ex-praetorian prefect of the east and a patrician.[153] In *C. Summa* he is presently praetorian prefect for Illyricum.[154]

One might suppose that it would be possible to fix his style, since like Thomas and Tribonian he was both quaestor and a member of John's commission. My efforts at least to do this have been unsuccessful. Only two constitutions in *CJ* are plausibly assignable to Basilides.[155] That is not enough, and no correlation with the editing of any book of the Theodosian code can be discerned. All that can be said is that Basilides quotes the ancient jurists verbatim instead of, like Tribonian, reporting their views.

---

[145] Ch. 7 nn. 176–80.   [146] Ch. 2 nn. 56–9.   [147] *N.* 35 pr. (23 May 535).
[148] *N.* 35.2 (23 May 353).   [149] *CJ* 12.19.15.2; above, n. 73.
[150] *N.* 35.3 (23 May 535).   [151] Ch. 3 nn. 15–584.   [152] *Wars* 1.24.18.
[153] *C. Haec* 1 (13 Feb. 528).   [154] *C. Summa* 2 (7 April 529).

[155] *CJ* 12.17.4 (Iustinianus Vigilantio cd.) above, ch. 3 n. 672; 9.8.6 (no inscription) see F. de Marini Avonzo, *Due giuristi severiani per un imperatore sconosciuto, Materiali per une Storia della Cultura) Giuridica,* 4 ed. G. Tarello (Bologna 1974) 13.

Procopius, speaking of his appointment to succeed Tribonian at the time of Nika, says he was a patrician known for his sense of fairness, and a man of good repute.[156] There is no way of telling when he left the quaestorship. But on 16 November 534 Tribonian is described as a master, ex-quaestor and ex-consul,[157] not as currently quaestor. Basilides may therefore have retained the title to the end of 534. Apparently Justinian left him little scope to display his talents, if any, as a draftsman of constitutions.

NO. 66. I JANUARY 535 (N. I) TO I MAY 542 (N. 157)

This was Tribonian's second quaestorship.[158]

NO. 67. 18 DECEMBER 542 (N. 117) TO I MAY 546 (N. 126)

We have 14 constitutions by the next quaestor, all in Greek, so that from now on the identification of quaestors and their tenures becomes more speculative. Some features of his tenure have been elicited in an earlier chapter.[159] His prefaces are jejune.[160] Composing in a period of setbacks and gloom, he lacks Tribonian's capacity for presenting government policy in a favourable light. His literary bent, if it can be so called, is for compilation.[161] He does not favour Tribonian's form of epilogue but instead takes the opportunity of urging economy in the promulgation of the text.[162] He uses Greek script for the amount of fines.[163]

Procopius gives us his name, Junilus,[164] and a hostile notice of his character and ability. When Tribonian died Justinian 'appointed Junilus, a Libyan by origin, to the office (of quaestor), a man who had not even heard of the law, since he was not a barrister. He knew Latin but as far as Greek is concerned he had never been taught, nor could he speak with a Greek accent. Indeed he often made an effort to pronounce a Greek word, only to incur the ridicule of his assistants. He was intent on making money by improper means and made no attempt to conceal his trafficking in imperial documents. He did not hesitate to extend his palm to anyone he met for a single gold stater. For no less than seven years the state was thus made a laughing-stock.'[165]

The historian's exaggeration is so palpable that one suspects private enmity. Nevertheless there is, as usual, something in what he says. The Greek *Novels* of the tenure lack distinction. Junilus was no propagandist. The endless repetition of the operative κελεύομεν[166] is tedious. Though one may to some extent discount the practising lawyer's complaint that a man

---

[156] *Wars* 1.24.18. [157] *C. Cordi* 2 (16 Nov. 534). [158] Ch. 3 nn. 678–97, ch. 4.
[159] Ch. 4 nn. 32f. [160] Ch. 4 n. 33. [161] Ch. 4 n. 34. [162] Ch. 4 n. 45.
[163] Ch. 4 nn. 57f. [164] Iounilos: *SH* 20.17. [165] Ibid.
[166] There are 135 instances of this in the 3588 lines of his constitutions as printed. Next comes thespizomen (34 times), sunchoroumen (28 times), suneidomen (18 times), boulometha (13 times) and parakeleuometha (10 times).

who has not been at the bar should not be made minister of justice, Junilus may have owed the appointment more to his theological interests than to his juridical expertise.

For it seems that the quaestor Junilus is the same man as the amateur theologian Junilus, author of the *Instituta regularia divinae legis*.[167] It is clear from Procopius that his name was Iunilus or Iunillus not Iunilius.[168] In a letter of recommendation, admittedly addressed to Junilus, the deacon Fulgentius Ferrandus of Carthage praises his character highly.[169]

Junilus is often called Afer or Africanus in view of his 'African' or 'Libyan' origin. The letter from Fulgentius Ferrandus creates the impression that Iunilus was not personally known to him and so not a member of the church of Carthage. From the preface to the *Instituta* it seems that Iunilus first came to know bishop Primasius of Hadrumetum in Constantinople, so he was presumably not from Hadrumetum either.[170]

The *Instituta* were composed about 542. E. Stein, who considered that Junilus succeeded Tribonian about November 541, therefore concluded that they were composed during his quaestorship. The chronology is a little complicated.

The work presents in dialogue form the catechetical teaching of Paul of Nisibis, a professor of Nestorian tendencies.[171] A work of this bent would not have been acceptable after Justinian's condemnation of the Three Chapters in 543/4,[172] which committed him to a firm anti-Nestorian policy. Paul visited Constantinople in 527 and Junilus implies that his adaptation is being made some time later.[173] Junilus also tells us in the preface to the *Instituta* that he was encouraged to undertake it by the advice of Primasius, a bishop who had come to Constantinople with other bishops 'in the interests of their province'.[174] Primasius came to the capital in 550 in connection with the Three Chapter controversy, but this cannot be the visit referred to. The 'interests of the province' must be connected rather with the provincial synod of Byzacenum. Two pragmatic sanctions on this subject were issued on 6 October 541 and 29 October 542, the first of

---

[167] Stein, op. cit. 378f.; H. Kihn, *Theodor von Mopsuestia und Junilus Africanus als Exegeten* (1880 Freiburg-i-Br.).

[168] Procopius calls him Iounilos (*SH* 20.17, 20) and Ferrandus Iunillus (A. Reifferscheid, *Anecdota Casinensia, Beigabe zum Verzeichnisse der Vorlesungen der Universitat Breslau: Index scholarum in Univ. litt. Vratislavensi per hiemem 1871–2* = Kihn, op. cit. 323–3) though Kihn, loc. cit. and Migne, Patr. Lat. 68.15 calls him Iunilius.

[169] *Nihil igitur mirum videbitur si misericors animus et lingua gratiosa sic odorem notitiae tuae per plurima loca diffundit . . . sed obsecro te . . . ut litterarum praesentium portitores talem te in suis negotiis experiantur qualem vera praedicat fama* (Kihn, op. cit. 233).

[170] Patr. Lat. 68.15B.   [171] *Inst. reg. div. leg. praef.* (=Patr. Lat. 68.15C).

[172] Justinian's edict against Origen which provided a good opportunity for a Nestorian point of view to be expressed, was published in Jerusalem in Feb. 543 and so can be dated Dec. 542 or Jan. 543. A few months later Justinian condemned the Three Chapters. Stein, *Deux questeurs* 380.

[173] Paul's visit: Stein, *Deux questeurs* 380; G. Mercati, *Studi e testi* 5 (1901) 184, 182f.

[174] *Inst. reg. div. leg. praef.* = Patr. Lat. 68.15B (*ad Constantinopolin peregrinae provinciae coegisset utilitas*).

uncertain authorship,[175] the second composed by Justinian himself.[176] The first mentions that the bishops Restitutus and Heraclius had paid a visit to Contantinople and that they 'advanced not merely ecclesiastical business but the interests of the whole province.'[177] Though Primasius is not mentioned, it was probably either on this occasion or with the 542 delegation that he came on a first visit. The Instituta therefore can hardly antedate the last months of 541. But nor can they be much later than 543, since Justinian's condemnation of the Three Chapters was issued a few months after his treatise (in the form of an edict) against Origen, which was published in Jerusalem in February 543.

Since on grounds of style I take 18 December 542 as the *terminus ante quem* for the start of Junilus' quaestorship, it follows that the theological work may have preceded the government office. Indeed Junilus could have written it in the hope of attracting Justinian's attention and securing preferment. Ferrandus calls Junilus *merito illustris*,[178] but this throws little light on the dates of his quaestorship, since he may have been *illustris* in virtue of another office before becoming quaestor and, in any case, we cannot date exactly the letter of Ferrandus.[179]

On internal evidence one would incline to allot Junilus a tenure of $3\frac{1}{2}$ years, from December 542 to May 546. Procopius says he held the reins for no less than seven.[180] We have no constitutions dated between 1 May 546 and 1 September 548, a gap of over two years. Nor is there any certainty about the tenure of the office between May and December 542. Junilus may have held office for just over six years, and in each of seven successive years. Even this would not save Procopius. But the historian's notice is virtually a diatribe and perfect accuracy is not to be expected.

The *Instituta regularia* is a dry work of classification,[181] but the dedication is at least livelier than the prefaces to the *Novels* of the period and supports the notion that Junilus' Latin was better than his Greek. The *Instituta* suggest indeed that Latin was his first official language,[182] and he cites according to the Itala which was clung to in Africa. He compares his two-book introduction to the widow's mite in a passage whose false humility is unattractive.[183] Procopius may not wholly misrepresent his character. There is no good reason to suppose he was a bishop.[184] He is more likely

---

[175] Ch. 3 p. 119.   [176] Ch. 1 n. 261; *Justinian* 121.   [177] Ibid.

[178] Fulgentius Ferrandus epist. (Kihn op. cit. 232): *Domino merito illustri praestantissimo atque in Christo carissimo filio sanctae matris ecclesiae catholicae Iunillo Ferrandus diaconus in Domino salutem.*

[179] Kihn op. cit. 323–3 proposes a date about 547 on the basis of Victor Tonnensis (=*Patr. Lat.* 68. 958), but this only tells us that Ferrandus, deacon of the church of Carthage, *'clarus habetur'* in 547.

[180] *SH* 20.19.   [181] Ed. J. P. Migne, *Patrologia Latina* 68 (1866) 15.

[182] *Inst. reg. div. leg.* c. 12 *essentiam quam latine et substantiam nuncupamus.*

[183] *Patr. Lat.* 68. 16c *Mihi nihil amplius duobus suppetit his minutis* (Luc. xxi 2) *et ipsis ab alio commodatis. Verum enimvero multum mihi de evangelico examinatore pollicetur, quia licet alii ex pretiosissimis pretiosa, ex plurimis valent plura largiri, ego tamen quia totum dedi plus obtuli.*

[184] Fulgentius Ferrandus addresses him as explained above, n. 170. Had he been a

to have been a laymen interested in church matters, like Justinian himself and like Socrates and Sozomenus under Theodosius II. Writing to Primasius he claims to be a student of, not an expert in, theology.[185] Of course he had a legal training. On this point Procopius does not even expect to be believed. Many 'churchmen', such as Minucius Felix, Tertullian, John Chrysostom, Theodore of Mopsuestia, Aurelius Prudentius Clemens, Paulinus of Nola, Ambrose and Sulpicius Severus were trained lawyers. The legalistic classifications of the *Instituta* are paralleled by subdivisions in the *Novels* he drafted.[186]

Novel 127 of 1 September 548 is by another hand. The preface reverts to the Tribonianic theme that the emperor may properly amend his own laws. In c. 1 he is 'justly correcting' the law of intestate succession. In c. 2 the law of antenuptial donations is 'worthy of correction' since 'in the light of experience' registration above a certain amount has been shown to be advisable. In c. 3 women who do not proceed to a second marriage are said to deserve better treatment than those who do. In c. 4 the penalties imposed on men divorcing without good cause are made the same as for women, since for equal wrongs equal penalties should be imposed.[187] The whole text is more raisonné than its predecessors. Edict 8 of 17 September 548 adopts Latin for the number of *vicariani*[188] and of lamps.[189] The preface points out that 'experience has shown'[190] that the civil magistrates of the Pontic diocese are inadequate for the maintenance of order and hence the vicariate of Pontus must be reconstituted. The epilogue makes use of a παραστάντα formula.[191] In general the constitutions of September 548 feel closer to Tribonian's style than to that of Junilus. Despite Procopius Junilus must be taken to have died not later than August 548. His successor was Constantinus.[192]

NO. 68. 1 SEPTEMBER 548 (NOVEMBER 127) TO 1 JUNE 555 (NOVEMBER 159)

The tenure of no. 68 comprises only eight surviving constitutions.[193] As these stretch over seven years it may be questioned whether the scaffolding is strong enough to support the weight put on it. With some hesitation I have decided that it is.

---

bishop *domino beatissimo et sancto patri* or the like would have been appropriate. To rescue his bishopric by locating it after Ferrandus' letter (? *c.* 547), is an act of desperation.

[185] *Inst. reg. div. leg. praef*: (=*Patr. Lat.* 68.15B) *scis ipse, venerabilis pater Primasi, quia vitae meae et propositi conscius, sicut divinae legis me studiosum habere non denego, ita doctorem dicere non praesumo.*

[186] *N.* 108 pr. (1 Feb. 541).

[187] Μηδεμίαν εἶναι διαφοράν = *nulla differentia*, above, ch. 3 n. 417.

[188] Edict 8.3.2 (17 Sept. 548).   [189] Edict 8.3.4 (17 Sept. 548).

[190] Edict 8 pr. (17 Sept. 548).   [191] Edict 8 epil. (17 Sept. 548).   [192] *SH* 20.20.

[193] *N.* 127 (1 Sept. 548), Edict 8 (17 Sept. 548), *N.* 129 (15 June 551), 145 (8 Feb. 553), 146 (8 Feb. 553), 147 (15 April 553), appx. 7 (13 Aug. 554), 159 (1 June 555). Appx. 6 (6 Sept. 552) is the work of Justinian. Above, ch. 1 n. 268.

The present quaestor resembles Tribonian and differs from Junilus in certain habits. He expresses fines in Latin letters[194] and occasionally uses Latin for the numbers of other things.[195] His prefaces are full and reasoned.[196] He does not call in the epilogues for economy in promulgating the text.[197] References to φιλανθρωπία recur.[198] The emperor is once again represented as learning of and disposing of problems as they arise.[199] The commonest operative verb is θεσπίζομεν.[200]

The start of the tenure has been discussed previously.[201] The last text of the tenure is taken, not without hesitation, to be a constitution of 1 June 555, which has an elaborate preface.[202] A text of 1 May 556 reverts to a plainer sort of preface and to expressing a fine in Greek script.[203]

Our quaestor's name is Constantinus. Procopius says that on the death of Junilus he succeeded to the office. 'Though not unacquainted with legal studies he was young and had as yet no experience of fighting cases in court. He was the most thievish and boastful of men. Justinian liked him very much and he became one of his closest friends, whom the emperor never hesitated to make use of to steal or to decide cases at law. Hence Constantinus made a great deal of money in a short time and assumed an extraordinarily boastful manner, treading the air and looking down on all mankind. Anyone who was willing to spend a large sum of money deposited it with one of his confidants and in that way succeeded in carrying out what he had in mind. But the man was quite impossible to meet or talk to, unless he was racing to the emperor or away from him, not walking, but in a great hurry, so as not to be troubled by persons approaching him on unprofitable business.'[204]

Once again the *parti pris* is evident. Procopius has the practising barrister's attitude to an appointee who has little court experience. Did he think that he himself, a barrister with an elegant literary style, would have been a better choice?

Procopius is writing between 1 July 550 and 30 June 551[205] and, since he mentions no later quaestor, one may assume that Constantinus was then

---

[194] N. 145 (8 Feb. 553 c. 1).

[195] Edict 8 (17 Sept. 548 c. 3.2), N. 147. 2 (15 April 553).

[196] Ch. 4 p. 135, table.

[197] Above, n. 162. Epilogues often use δῆλον ποιεῖν, γένεσθαι etc.: N. 127 (1 Sept. 548), Edict 8 (17 Sept. 548), N. 127 (1 Sept. 548), 129 (15 June 551), 145 (8 Feb. 553).

[198] N. 129 pr. (15 June 551), 147 pr. (17 April 553), 159 pr. (1 June 555).

[199] N. 127 pr. (1 Sept. 548 οὐκ ὀκνοῦμεν . . . μεμνήμεθα) ed. 8 pr. (17 Sept. 548 ἐξ αὐτῶν ἔγνωμεν τῶν πραγμάτων), N. 129 pr. (15 June 551 μεμνήμεθα), 146 pr. (8 Feb. 553 μαθόντες . . . ἐμάθομεν . . . μαθόντες), 147 pr. (17 April 553 πᾶσαν . . . ἐπινοοῦμεν ὁδόν), 145 pr. (8 Feb. 553 εὑρίσκοντες, μαθόντες . . . προσῆλθον ἡμῖν οἱ οἰκοῦντες), Appx. 7 (1 *meminimus* 13 *cognovimus* 20 *comperimus* 26 *cognovimus*).

[200] Which occurs ten times against four for κελεύομεν, two each for βουλόμεθα, συνείδομεν, ποιοῦμεν, ποιούμεθα, νομίζομεν, ἀποδίδομεν and μεμνήμεθα. Since this tenure comes to 1326 lines as printed in the Schoell-Kroll edition of *CJ*, the frequency of κελεύομεν is only three per 1000 lines against 38 in the tenure of Junilus (above, n. 166).

[201] Above, nn. 181–92. [202] Setting out the details of a will and codicil.

[203] N. 134 (1 May 556). [204] *SH* 20.20–3. [205] Above, ch. 2 nn. 178–80.

in office. Constantinus is recorded as quaestor on 8 May 553, at the second session of the Fifth Council of Constantinople, where he was Justinian's spokesman in presenting to the fathers the emperor's version of his negotiations with pope Vigilius.[206]

In 562–3 Malalas records a quaestor Constantinus who was concerned with the investigation of a plot.[207] This may or may not be our quaestor. In any case one should not postulate a continuous tenure from 548 to 562.

The name Constantinus was common. Our quaestor is not the commissioner Constantinus, master of petitions and sacred trials, who served both under John of Cappadocia and Tribonian and who was chairman of the Papinian committee.[208] That Constantinus was already senior in 530. Nor is he the Constantinus who was the tenth senior of eleven barristers from the praetorian prefect's court helping Tribonian's commission,[209] and later the second senior of three barristers helping to prepare the second edition of the *Codex Iustinianus*.[210] That Constantinus was clearly a junior barrister in 530 but could not be called young or inexperienced in 548. The quaestor is a third lawyer of that name, perhaps related to the others, perhaps not. Though not a member of Tribonian's commission he makes strenuous efforts to imitate the great man's style. For this reason among others I would attribute to him the composition of the pragmatic sanction *Pro petitione Vigilii*.[211]

[206] J. D. Mansi, *Sacrorum Conciliorum Nova et Amplissima Collectio* (Florence 1759–98) ix, 197–8.

[207] Malalas, 494E.

[208] *C. Haec* 1 (13 Feb. 528), *C. Tanta* 9 (16 Dec. 533); above, ch. 5 n. 82.

[209] *C. Tanta* 9 (16 Dec. 533).　　　[210] *C. Cordi* 2 (16 Nov. 534).

[211] *N.* 199 and (Tribonianic marks of style) Appx. 7 (13 Aug. 554, 5 *nostris temporibus, poena quiescente,* 6 *sancimus locum habere,* 14 *inrationabili modo,* 15 *nullo praeiudicio generando* 17 *iterum* 20 *ambulare* = 'circulate', of coins 27 *aperimus licentiam*).

CHAPTER NINE

The Last Jurist

Lawyers made an important contribution to the efflorescence of the sixth century. Some, like Agathias,[1] quietly proceeded from the study of rhetoric to the law school and thence to the bar, in which they gradually rose in seniority and eminence. Agathias was bored by his practice, lacked political ambition and took refuge in history,[2] but for all that he is visibly a lawyer-historian. Still more is this true of the ambitious Procopius,[3] who graduated to the political branch of the profession by becoming assessor to Belisarius, and later, perhaps after delays and disappointments, prefect of the city. Even if his legal background were not attested it could be deduced from the fact that he complains that Constantinus was appointed quaestor since, though learned in the law, he had not practised at the bar[4]—a complaint that only a barrister or ex-barrister would make. His bent was practical, and his best qualities as a historian show not in his understanding of events, which is often defective, but in his handling of evidence, which is outstandingly good.[5]

Tribonian was a lawyer more akin to Procopius than Agathias, oriented as he was towards a public career.[6] He must be assumed to have followed the standard cursus—rhetoric, law school, the bar of the praetorian prefect. Whether from there he did a stage as assessor, or whether some incident directly attracted Justinian's attention to his merits, remains uncertain. His temperament was more theoretical than that of his contemporary from Caesarea, and his mind was inflamed by contact with the texts of the law. The cool lucidity of the classical writers, their powers of analysis and invention, their sobriety and discipline, opened to him, as they did to St Gregory Thaumaturgus,[7] a new, daunting yet dazzling world in which one could combine true philosophy[8] with practical service to the state and citizen. He was swept along, and the passion which in Procopius flowed in dark channels issued for Tribonian in a powerful dedication to the temple of justice[9] and the science of law.[10]

[1] Averil Cameron, *Agathias* (1970) 3, 140–1.
[2] Agathias, *Hist.* 3.1 = *CSHB* 138.   [3] Ch. 3 n. 41.   [4] *SH* 20.20.
[5] Averil Cameron, *Agathias* 130–1.   [6] Ch. 2 nn. 37f.
[7] *Panegyric ad Originem* 1.7 (*Patr. Graec.* 3.85).
[8] *D.* 1.1.1.1 (Ulpian 1 inst. *veram nisi fallor philosophiam non simulatam affectantes*—lawyers). Ulpian means that the lawyer is not a sophist or orator: he gives his true opinion.
[9] *C. Deo auctore* 5 (15 Dec. 530), *C. Tanta* 20 (16 Dec. 533).
[10] *C. Tanta* 9 (16 Dec. 533 *legitima scientia*).

In his own eyes the quaestor 'was distinguished alike in the arts of eloquence and legal learning and one who had proved brilliant in practical affairs'.[11] In a sense this description epitomises a career which proceeds from rhetoric to law and then to the public arena. From another point of view, however, Tribonian is stressing that the compilation of the *Digest* required just this combination of talents: the capacity to compose constitutions in a style commensurate with the magnificence of the venture, a detailed acquaintance with the legal sources of every age and type, the diplomacy and practical good sense necessary to the success of a delicate enterprise. How far was Tribonian justified in thinking that he was specially suited to the task?

His style does not please everyone. Those who come to Justinian's legislation straight from the classical legal writers find it intolerably magniloquent, convoluted and rhetorical. But, valid as such a judgment may be *sub specie aeternitatis*, this is not the fairest way to judge Tribonian's prose. It should be looked at rather in the light of the Theodosian code, the post-Theodosian *Novels* and the legislation of the late fifth and early sixth centuries. From this point of view the picture is rather different. The century from 460 onwards was an age among lawyers of return to the classics, and this movement left its mark on legislative style. A study of the editing of the Theodosian code by Justinian's commissioners shows that they simplified the Theodosian rhetoric, substituted correct technical terms for circumlocutions and reduced the jigsaw puzzle aspect of Latin composition which made such a strong appeal to the rhetoricians. Instead of a concern to tease the reader and challenge him to match adjective and noun, participle and verb, the new style aimed at clarity and, in relative terms, simplicity. Tribonian was part of this movement, an enthusiast (strange as it may seem) for these linguistic and conceptual virtues. 'Confused' and 'complicated' are favourite terms of abuse.[12] Even in comparison with his predecessor Thomas[13] his constructions are notably straightforward; the same cannot always be said of his handling of concepts.

What marks off Tribonian from his contemporaries is the tone of self-conscious splendour and grandiloquence he imparts to Justinian's legislation. This can be absurd, as when the Pisidians are told that the use of the historic term 'praetor' is likely to deter the bandits who infest that area,[14] or merely irritating, as when law students are, by the use of the term *cunabula*, implicitly compared to babies.[15] But it is again important to realise that the sonorous splendour of Justinian's language as represented by Tribonian has a political purpose which could not, perhaps, in the circumstances of the age, be secured in any other way. To incite the Romaioi to pay the taxes,[16] fight the wars and in general make the sacrifices

---

[11] *C. Tanta* 9 (16 Dec. 533); ch. 2 n. 109.
[12] N. 35; ch. 3 n. 213; *N.* 1.1.1 (1 Jan. 535); 31 pr. (18 March 536), 64.2 (1 Sept. 537).
[13] Ch. 8 n. 99.   [14] N. 24.1 (18 May 535).   [15] Ch. 3 n. 338.
[16] N. 8.10.2 (17 May 535).

needed to carry out an ambitious programme it was essential to make them conscious of the greatness of the age in which they were living. This consciousness, centred in the emperor, had to suffuse ever-widening circles. One of the prime instruments for its diffusion was the law. To write in a plain or flat tone would have been to fail, to reject the spirit of Justinian's policy. Both Thomas and Junilus must, from this point of view, be accounted failures.[17]

The need to explain Justinian's conceptions of policy, to act as a propagandist, account for a certain repetitive quality in Tribonian's compositions. The emperor's solicitude for his subjects, the long hours he spends to enhance their welfare, is a frequent theme.[18] The case for an active, legislative policy is constantly reiterated.[19] Certain concepts recur in text after text: humanity conceived as a prime imperial virtue,[20] liberty as an ideal of external and internal policy,[21] equality and the avoidance of undesirable forms of discrimination,[22] nature as a guide to the ideal society.[23] None of these themes is new. They have roots in Stoic philosophy and in the ideology of the principate. In the hands of Justinian and Tribonian, however, they are given a more radical emphasis which is traceable to the influence of Christianity. It is true that radical-seeming impatience is often directed at obsolete distinctions, for instance that between the different classes of freedmen.[24] Here Tribonian's evident delight in consigning to the scrapheap a tangle of obsolete scrupulosity is largely an intellectual pleasure.[25] Yet not all Justinian's reforms can be so easily dismissed, in particular not those which favour equality in the relations of husband and wife.[26] Here we find a determined assault on contemporary prejudice, foreshadowed, it is true, by Gaius.[27] There was a dark side to Justinian's radicalism; the cruel mutilations which he, it seems, intensified if he did not introduce into civilian criminal law,[28] the drastic penalties against pagans and heretics which he, far more than his

[17] Ch. 8 nn. 98f., 159f.　　[18] Ch. 1 nn. 228f.　　[19] Ch. 1 nn. 298f.

[20] Ch. 3 nn. 177f. and *CJ* 5.16.27.1 (1 Dec. 530); *N.* 2.3 pr., 4.3, 6.2 (16 March 535), 24.2 (18 May 535), 32.1 = 34.1 (15 June 535), 18.5, 8 (1 March 536), 22.8, 13 (18 March 536), 30.11 pr. (18 March 536), 49 pr. (18 Aug. 537), 53.3.6 (1 Oct. 537); 81 pr. (18 March 539), 89 pr. (1 Sept. 539), 115.5.1 (1 Feb. 542).

[21] Ch. 1 n. 170; cf. *CJ* 7.7.2.3 (17 Nov. 530), 7.6.1.1b (1 Nov. 531), 7.15.2 (1 Aug. 530).

[22] Ch. 3 nn. 417, 421; *N.* 2.5 (18 March 535), edict 8 (17 April 535) and oath, 29.3 (16 July 535), 18.4.1 (1 March 536), 21.1 (18 March 536), 46 pr. (18 Aug. 537), 52.2 (18 Aug. 537), 64.1 (19 Jan. 538), 74.1 (5 June 538 no difference between legitimate and illegitimate children in a state of nature), 92 pr. (10 Oct. 539); 97 pr. (17 Nov. 539).

[23] Ch. 3 n. 172–4; C. Castello, 'Il pensiero Giustineaneo sull' origine degli *status hominum*', *Studi Albertario* 11 (1953) 197; W. A. Bonner, 'Origen and the tradition of natural law concepts', *Dumbarton Oaks Papers* 8 (1954) 49.

[24] *CJ* 7.6.1 (1 Nov. 531), *Inst.* 1.5.3, 1.7.

[25] Ch. 3 n. 237 (*scrupulositas*), 399 (*nimia subtilitas*), 258 (*aenigma*), 410 (*altercationes*), 261 (*circuitus*), 374 (*compendiosus*), 216 (*inextricabilis*), 281 (*innodatus*), 230 (*verbositas*), 198 (*verbosus*), 195 (*spinosus*).

[26] Ch. 1 nn. 89f., 98.　　[27] Gaius, *Institutes* 1. 190.　　[28] Ch. 1 nn. 136, 139.

predecessors, made an everyday reality.[29] Not much of this clouds Tribonian's compositions. He may be credited with a cheerful, expansive optimism.[30] Stupidity[31] and sloth[32] he despised, especially when they led to intellectual vices such as inaccurate terminology[33] or mere verbalism.[34] The law has no place for mystery.[35] Reading Tribonian, we are conscious of a strenuous but axiomatic superiority.

Scholarship, especially legal scholarship, *legitima scientia*, is his idol. The lover of ancient learning in all its forms[36] had, for the period, an excellent grasp of antiquities.[37] To identify his reading would require far more investigation than I have been able to undertake. So far as law is concerned, Tribonian's range extended to every genre and period of literature, to the extent that these survived in the sixth century. Before the *Digest* commission began to collect and read the classics we find him citing an obscure work such as Tertullian's *de castrensi peculio*.[38] His vocabulary is garnered from classical and post-classical, private and imperial writings. Yet one influence is fundamental. The writer who is thrice called '*Gaius noster*'[39] in texts composed by the quaestor is his inspirer and his model.

The second-century author Gaius stood apart from his contemporaries in at least four respects. First, he was notably interested in classification, that is in the systemisation of the law insofar as it involved division into genera and species: with this went a desire to simplify and generalise.[40] The Gaian classifications, the extent of whose originality is disputed, still form the basis of most expositions of European private law. In displaying an interest in this topic Tribonian was merely responding to his Greek intellectual environment and to the preoccupations of the Beirut law school.[41]

A second feature of Gaius' work is its historical orientation. In a passage which seems to derive from Aristotle he emphasises that, the beginning being the principal part of each thing, we best understand a thing by studying its beginnings.[42] Hence a lawyer should learn how law has evolved, what obtained previously and how it has come to be altered. Allied to this view of the importance of history, is a third motif: the desire to subject law to rational criticism and, if it proves defective, to say so.[43]

[29] Ch. 1 nn. 135, 140, ch. 2 nn. 56–69.

[30] Ch. 3 n. 290 (*apertius*), 291 (*clarius*), 292 (*latius*), 293 (*pinguius*), 294 (*plenius*).

[31] Ch. 3 n. 328 (*stultus*), 329 (*supinus*), 824 (*ridiculus*), 194 (*ridiculosus*), 191 (*ludibriosus*) 263 (*ludibrium*).

[32] Ch. 3 n. 329 (*supinus*), C. Omenm 1 (16 Dec. 533).   [33] N. 13 pr. (15 Oct. 535).

[34] *CJ* 4.32.28 pr. (17 Sept. 529), 8.41.8.1 (22 July 530), 6.43.2.3 (20 Feb. 531), 7.25.1 (531/2), 8.53.37 (Iohanni pp.), N. 97 pr. (17 Nov. 539).

[35] *Inst.* 3.6.10, 3.2.3a, 2.23.7.   [36] N. 30 pr. (18 March 536); ch. 4 n. 24.

[37] E.g. prefaces to *Novels* 24–30, 103; ch. 4 n. 23.

[38] *CJ* 5.70.7.12 (1 Sept. 530), ch. 3 n. 31.

[39] Ch. 3 n. 766, meaning in my view, 'our teacher Gaius'; Honoré, *Gaius* (1962) 129.

[40] Honoré, *Gaius* 97f.   [41] Jolowicz and Nicholas 476–7 (properly cautious).

[42] *D.* 1.2.2.1 (Gaius 1 leg. XII tab.); Aristotle, *Problemata* 1.10.13; Alexander of Aphrodisias, *De anima liber cum mantissa* (*Suppl. Arist.* ed. Bruns, Berlin 1887, 2.10.19).

[43] D. Nörr, *Rechtskritik in der römischen Antike* (1974) 92–8.

Tribonian too sees law in a historical perspective, as subject to flux. Hence legislation is an empirical branch of reason.[44] The codification rests on the dual Gaian view of history as a key to understanding and a repository of the obsolete—a theme to which we shall return.

A fourth feature of Gaius' work, which was a novelty in his own day, is its 'modern' attitude to imperial constitutions, which are freely cited without any sense that the emperor's contribution to the law is an excrescence on lawyer's law.[45] Tribonian likewise firmly echoes and accentuates the themes of Gaius and Ulpian in regard to the emperor's unlimited legal authority. No sooner is he appointed quaestor than he thunders off about the validity of imperial judgments and imperial interpretations.[46] The whole of Roman law is reduced by the codes to a series of imperial enactments in which Justinian has made everything his own,[47] and Tribonian even adopts the disingenuous argument that it is more creditable skilfully to amend than to compose a law in the first instance.[48]

Despite my critics, I remain convinced that the features of Gaius' writing noted above are to be accounted for by his composing in a Greek, provincial ambience, in which a more theoretical and abstract, more imperial and historical, more critical and rational Rechtsanschauung is to be expected than in a Roman or metropolitan environment.[49] If St Gregory thinks of Roman laws as eminently Hellenic[50] it is because he is seeing them through the eyes of those who like Gaius have moulded Roman law to a Hellenic frame. This has nothing to do with a supposed influence of Greek institutions on the substance of Roman law. It is an intellectual phenomenon, of the type to which Fergus Millar has pertinently drawn attention in other spheres.[51] Differences of style must not be allowed to obscure the fact that, whatever the character of the detail, the general notions underlying the codification, the ideology of exposition and critical assessment, are thoroughly Gaian.

Tribonian's scholarly standing has often been attacked. In the sixteenth century Hotoman's *Antitribonianus*[52] struck at his bad Latin and preference for 'foreign' jurists of the empire over those of the republic—whose works were not in fact available to the commission. He was also assailed for changing the classical texts, and a search was instituted for *emblemata Triboniani*.[53] He was also assailed from the opposite direction, and blamed for not modernising Roman law enough.[54]

---

44 For the reflection of this in the *Novels* see ch. 1 nn. 298–309.

45 D. Liebs, *Gaius und Pomponius: Gaio nel suo tempo* (1966) 68.

46 *CJ* 1.14.12 (30 Oct. 529).

47 *C. Deo auctore* 6, 7 (15 Dec. 530), *C. Tanta* 10, 20a (16 Dec. 533).

48 *C. Deo auctore* 6.   49 Honoré, *Gaius* 70f.

50 *Panegyric ad Originem* 1.7 (*Patr. Gr.* 3.85).

51 F. Millar, *A Study of Cassius Dio* (1964) 174f.; 59 *JRS* (1969) 12f.

52 Hotomannus, *Antitribonianus* (1567, new eds. 1603, 1616) = *Variorum Opuscula* 7 (1771) 192.

53 Literature in L. Chiazzese, *Confronti testuali* (1935) 5–37, especially J. J. Wissembach, (1607–1650) *Emblemata Triboniani* = *Variorum opuscula ad cultiorem iurisprudentiam*

Although the violent passions which Tribonian aroused in the renaissance have subsided, they have left an aftermath of depreciation which stands in the way of a sober assessment of his scholarly achievement. When the charges which rest on mistakes are left on one side there remains a substantial indictment to face. How can a scholar justify altering texts and attributing his alterations to the original? Can it be a reputable procedure to make Ulpian say what Justinian has enacted three hundred years later?

Interpolation was not an innovation of Justinian's age. The second commission of Theodosius II, which succeeded in compiling the Theodosian code, was instructed that 'so that the work may be short and clear, we give those who are to undertake the task the power of eliminating superfluous, adding necessary, changing ambiguous and amending incongruous words'.[55] The constitutions of so great a figure as Constantine I, as they appear in the code of Theodosius, are not therefore exactly what Constantine enacted. Nevertheless they are attributed to that emperor and assigned to the date on which he made them.

There is nothing extraordinary about this, provided a certain attitude to the law is current. The Supreme Court of Judicature Act 1925 remains just that even when it has been amended by the Supreme Court of Judicature (Amendment) Act 1959. To make the position quite clear, the words 'as amended' would nowadays often be added. But the concept of an enactment with a life history and a variable content is familiar to lawyers. Such a statute is designated by the original date and title but its contents change.

The attitude to the law which makes such ways of speaking possible is partly conceptual and partly ideological. Laws and rules are entities which are created, change and die, and this is connected with the belief that law, unlike religion, is not a direct reflection of immutable values nor simply a deposit of custom but that, while taking account of both, it embodies those formulae and expedients which at any given moment seem appropriate to secure the peace of the community and its well-being. To innovate in matters of Christian doctrine is by definition heresy,[56] but to innovate in law is the policy of a prudent legislator, who, like a physician, adapts his remedies to the patient and the disease.[57]

It is in the context of this legislative theory that the practice of interpolating texts must be viewed. Justinian's first commission, which like the Theodosian was concerned exclusively with imperial constitutions, had

---

adsequendam pertinentia 9 (1771). Tribonian was defended by many eighteenth-century writers, such as J. Wybo, *Tribonianus ab emblematibus Wissembachii liberatus* (1729) and Van Bynkershoek, praef. to *Novae observationes iuris Romani* (1733). Gothofredus assailed him with the words '*Deus bone, quot Triboniani facinora ... quot vulnera*' praef. to *Commentarius ad Cod. Theodos. iv.*

[54] F. Balduinus, on whom see H. E. Troje, 'Peccatum Triboniani', *SDHI* 36 (1970) 341.

[55] *CTh* 1.1.6 (20 Dec. 435).   [56] *CJ* 1.1.6.3 (15 March 533).   [57] Ch. 1 nn. 298f.

a remit similar to the Theodosian. The commissioners were told that 'we have given special permission for prefaces which are superfluous to the substance of the law, similar and contradictory passages, unless relevant to classification, and those which have become obsolete to be cut away ... and for [the commissioners] to compose laws from the three codes ... adding to and subtracting from them, indeed altering them when convenience requires it.[58] The authority given to the second commission for the *Digest* and *Institutes* is similar,[59] but Tribonian, the author of the formulation, adds a legal justification. In his eyes the powers of the Roman people were conferred by the 'royal law' on the emperor and by the emperor in turn on the lawyers like Ulpian whose treatises were then regarded as authoritative.[60] There was no fundamental distinction between imperial constitutions and authoritative private writings. Both were subject to the power of later emperors to repeal or amend.

According to this view the classical writings were a form of delegated legislation which could be amended by a subsequent legislative act on the emperor's part, just as Parliament, having given a minister power to make regulations, may later amend them. To attribute such an amended text of Ulpian to a certain book of Ulpian's commentary on the edict is no different in principle from the attribution of one of Constantine's laws, as amended, to Constantine. Still, one is conscious, not only for the time, of a strain in Tribonian's stridently autocratic view of the Roman constitution. Ulpian's writings were not regarded as authoritative because of a power conferred on him—if any such power was conferred—by Severus and Caracalla. He was respected for his learning and sense of justice, and what he said in commenting on the praetor's edict was valued because it displayed those qualities. Any recognition of his merits by the emperor was a consequence, not a cause of his status as a lawyer.

As Tribonian looks at the matter, he is himself on a level with Ulpian. He too has a delegated power from the emperor, set out in *Deo auctore*, to change the old classical texts and so, to that extent, to make law. Why then attribute the revised texts to Ulpian and his colleagues? One answer, given in *C. Tanta*, is respect for antiquity.[61] This is less hypocritical than it seems if we accept that, whatever the changes made by the compilers, they thought of themselves as retouching, perhaps embellishing, the originals rather than composing new laws—*accessio*, in the terminology of modern Romanists, rather than *specificatio*.

However one may seek to justify interpolations, there is little doubt that Tribonian, like the lawyers of Theodosius, was conscious of a conflict between the scholarly and practical aspects of his enterprise. The Theodosian commissioners were allowed to include in their code, for academic purposes only, obsolete laws.[62] Justinian's had no such licence. If nothing but currently valid law was to be admitted, the choice lay between

---

[58] *C. Haec* 2 (13 Feb. 528).
[59] *C. Deo auctore* 7 (15 Dec. 530).   [60] *C. Deo auctore* 7 (15 Dec. 530).
[61] *C. Tanta* 10 (16 Dec. 533).   [62] *CTh* 1.1.5 (26 March 429).

anonymous texts and falsification. Falsification was the lesser evil. Anonymity would have undermined the whole dialectic of legal education. So the pill had to be swallowed, and it was henceforth forbidden to compare, at least for citation in court, the revised version of Ulpian and his fellows with the original.[63] Ancient learning had to compromise, or be swept away.

Tribonian's academic instincts were, it seems to me, overridden by his sense of practical possibilities. Threatened with a world in which the Latin classics would be consigned to the scrap-heap, he tried to preserve as much of the classics as circumstances allowed. Had he not done so nothing but a few manuals would have survived. The alleged Roman preeminence in law would have seemed inexplicable. Who can say that Tribonian was wrong?

Some modern critics have until recently gone even further than their Renaissance predecessors in attacking Tribonian's reputation. They have accused him of making use in the compilation of the *Digest* of previous collections of material, sometimes described by the term 'predigest',[64] sometimes called a 'partial compilation'.[65] According to these scholars, the statements in the prefaces that the commission read, scrutinised and digested the ancient works[66] from which excerpts appear in the *Digest* are untrue. They used, at least so far as the best-known writings were concerned, existing collections of excerpts.

Except to those to whom a conspiratorial view of human affairs comes naturally, these theories are highly implausible. The alleged fraud would have been easily detected. As Schulz remarks, lawyers not on the commission would at once exclaim, 'This is only our dear old pre-Digest.'[67] But supposing that it had been possible to perpetrate such a fraud, it was contrary to the ethos of the enterprise to do so. For intellectual merit is the essence of what is claimed for the *Digest*, and lack of it what is imputed to the compilations until then used in legal education.[68] The truth in my view is quite different. The compilers refrained from exploiting whatever collections of material may have existed and rigorously insisted on going

---

[63] *C. Deo auctore* 7 (15 Dec. 530), *C. Tanta* 19 (16 Dec. 533).

[64] Ehrenzweig, 'Die Compilation der Digesten Iustinians', *Grünhut's Zeitschrift* 28 (1901); H. Peters, 'Die oströmischen Digestenkommentaren und die Entstehung der Digesten', *Berichte der sächsschen Gesellschaft d. Wiss., phil.-hist.* Kl 65 (1913) 3f.; =*Labeo* 16 (1970) 183, 335; comments by T. Kipp, *Geschichte der Quellen des römischen Rechts* (1919) 159 n. 14; Lenel *ZSS* 34 (1913) 373; Mitteis *ZSS* 34 (1913) 402; Rotondi, *Scritti* 187; Buckland, *Textbook* 40.

[65] Collinet, *La Genèse du digeste, du code et des institutes de Justinien* (1952) 56f.; Wieacker, *Vom römischen Recht* (1961) 242, 278; Arangio-Ruiz, *Precedenti scolastici del Digesto, Conf. per il XIV Centenario delle Pandette* (1932) 287; 'La compilazione Giustineanea e i suoi commentatori bizantini', *Scritti Ferrini* (1946) 81–117; Volterra, *Giustiniano I e le scuole di diritto, Gregorianum* 48 (1967); Guarino, *RIDA* 34 (1957) 269; *Atti Acc. Napoli* 79 (1968) 527.

[66] *C. Deo auctore* 4 (15 Dec. 530), *C. Omnem* 1 (16 Dec. 533), *C. Tanta* 1, 20 (16 Dec. 533), *C. Imperatoriam* 2 (16 Nov. 533), *N.* 35.4 (23 May 535).

[67] Schulz 321; cf. E. Volterra, *Gregorianum* 48 (1967) 77, 90; Robleda, *Ius privatum Romanum* (1960) 256.

[68] *C. Omnem* 1, 2 (16 Dec. 533).

back to the original sources. That they had ample time to do so was shown by Diósdi,[69] and, in greater detail, by the studies which form the basis of Chapter 5. According to my count, there are no more than nine texts in the whole *Digest* whose position cannot be accounted for either on the basis of Bluhme's hypothesis about the order of reading and excerpting or on editorial considerations which do not require the editors to have used any extrinsic collection of material.[70] If any extrinsic material was employed, its role was negligible.

The problem of interpolation and pre-existing compilations naturally leads to that of Tribonian's attitude to classical antiquity in general. To Riccobono it seemed that the law evolved by gradual stages from the classical period to the sixth century without any serious decline in juristic culture in the fourth and fifth.[71] From this point of view the historical elements in the codification were largely decorative or pedagogic. Pringsheim in contrast saw the law of 'Justinian' as the product of an archaising revival in which the old was often preferred to the more recent, irrespective of its practical utility in sixth-century conditions.[72] Justinian's law was not applied in practice and with him it died[73] or at least slept until the eleventh-century revival in Bologna. Schulz answered that Justinian was a classicist, not an archaist:[74] the past to which he looked was the classical age of the principate, not the Twelve Tables or even the Republic, and he looked to it as a model but in no spirit of slavish imitation.

Schindler's careful analysis leads him to emphasise the ambiguous character of 'Justinian's' relation to the classical age.[75] He often adopts classical or classicising solutions to legal problems but almost equally often criticises classical law and alters it out of considerations of equity, simplicity, distaste for forms and the like. So the classicising tendency was influenced and corrected by practical considerations.

How do these controversies stand in the light of the distinct roles which can now be attributed to Tribonian and Justinian? One thing is clear. Whatever archaising or classicising tendency the legal texts may evince is to be put to the account of the quaestor not the emperor.[76] References to named classical jurists,[77] to the emperors of the pagan empire,[78] to the

[69] G. Diósdi, 'Das Gespenst der Prädigesten', *Labeo* 17 (1971) 187f.; cf. Chiazzese, *Confronti testuali* 543–4; Schulz, *Roman Legal Science* 322.

[70] *Editing* 284, 304.

[71] *La verità sulle pretese tendenze arcaiche di Giustiniano: Conf. per il XIV centenario delle Pandette* (1931) 235.

[72] 'Die archaistische Tendenz Justinians', *Studi Bonfante* 1 (1929) 551 = *Abhandlungen* 2.9.

[73] Pringsheim, *Ges. Abh.* 2.40.

[74] *Geschichte der romischen Rechtswissenschaft* (1961) 353 = *History of Roman Legal Science* (1946) 343.

[75] *Justinians Haltung* 343; cf. Archi, *Giustiniano legislatore* (1970) 151f.

[76] *Justinian* n. 297. Justinian's culture is exaggerated by G. Ostrogorsky, *History of the Byzantine State* (1968) 69–70; Jones 1.270; Rubin 1.89; E. Grupe, *Kaiser Iustinian* (1923) 50 n. 3.

[77] Ch. 3 n. 40.   [78] Ch. 3 nn. 55f.

institutions and history of the ancient world before Constantine[79] proliferate in the quaestorship of Tribonian and are missing outside it. Under Thomas, Junilus and Constantinus nothing but the most general references to the 'old law'[80] are to be found. Justinian took a keen interest in law and in precedents for his innovations, but there is no evidence that he was a lawyer or classical scholar any more than he was an engineer or mathematician. Had he been closely acquainted with classical antiquity this would have emerged in his choice of quaestors other than Tribonian or the adding of classicising touches to their compositions. Justinian's mind was moulded by Christian and bureaucratic, not classical, influences.[81]

Tribonian is different.[82] He loved antiquity, and indulged his tastes to much the same extent as Gaius. Like him[83] he includes in the *Digest* much that is only of scholarly interest—the inscriptions to the texts, the historical parts of the *Institutes*[84]—not to mention the disputes between classical lawyers which help to sharpen the student's wits but cannot be said to represent current law.

Like his predecessor Tribonian is impatient with irrational or oversubtle rules. Nörr in an excellent study of the criticism of the law in the ancient world has pointed out how exceptional is the readiness of Gaius to turn a critical vision on the law.[85] He conjectures that this may be due to the fact that the critical passages in more orthodox jurists have not survived. But Tribonian would have welcomed such passages had they existed and used them to justify Justinian's innovations. Gaius brings an intelligence formed in the Greek tradition of inquiry to the systematisation and rationalisation of Roman law. Any such programme must reveal deficiencies in the existing rules, which escape those whose point of view is more traditional and casuistic. By the sixth century a critical attitude to ancient forms was widespread. Thomas uses terms like *scrupulosus*[86] and *supervacuus*[87] to describe objectionable legal complexities. Tribonian simply widens the vocabulary and intensifies the invective.[88] One may infer that Justinian was impatient of legal niceties for which no good reason could be adduced, and that Tribonian absorbed the rational outlook of Gaius,

---

[79] Above, n. 34 and *N.* 38 pr. (15 Feb. 535), 6.6 (16 March 535), 41 (18 May 536), 47 pr. (31 Sept. 537), 105 pr. (28 Dec. 537), 89 pr. (1 Sept. 539).

[80] Ch. 3 nn. 60–1.

[81] *Justinian* 121f.; E. Volterra, *Gregorianum* 48 (1967) 77f.; C. Capizzi, *Riv. Stud. Biz. e Neoellen.* NS1 (1964) 143 n. 1.

[82] Above, n. 33.   [83] *D.* 1.2.2.1 (1 leg. XII tab.); above, n. 40.

[84] E.g. *Inst.* 1.2.2; 1.2.10; 1.5.3; 1.11.11; 2.7.4; 2.10.1; (*sed ut nihil antiquitatis penitus ignoretur*); 2.23.4; 2.25 pr.; 3.3 pr.; 3.12.1; 3.15.1; 3.23.2; 4.1.4; 4.4.7; 4.4.33d; 4.11 pr.–1; 4.18.6; Schulz, 284.

[85] Above, n. 43.

[86] *CJ* 6.30.17 (17 March 407), 8.37.11 (11 Dec. 528) and in Tribonian.

[87] *CJ* 5.7.1.11 pr. (20 Nov. 290), 10.55.3.1 (Dio. et Max. AA), 11.6.2 (5 June 372), *C. Haec* 2 (13 Feb. 528), 6.41.1 pr. (1 June 528), 4.32.26 pr. (13 Dec. 528), 7.64.10.1 (6 April 529) and frequently in Tribonian.

[88] Above, n. 25.

whose criticism of the tutelage of women, for example, foreshadows the concern of Justinian and Tribonian with sexual equality.[89]

One can detect in Gaius a mild historical optimism, or at any rate a favourable assessment of the age in which he was living.[90] For Tribonian one can be more definite. After the classical age there came a decline; but the present epoch has surpassed anything achieved in the past.[91] Here Tribonian faithfully reflects Justinian's view of the neglect of which emperors, particularly in the past century, had been guilty.[92] Apart from this political use of history it served for Tribonian a pedagogic aim and furnished an occasion for the display of learning. One can therefore speak with Riccobono[93] of some elements in his work as purely decorative, though the gratuitous erudition is also meant to convince the intellectual Greek student that his decision to learn the law is consistent with cultivation of the arts and literature.[94]

None of the attitudes to the past so far delineated can properly be called classicising or archaising. Nor can the fact that, as Schindler points out,[95] Tribonian uses classical precedents to rebut the charge of innovation. Conscious of the criticism which his novelties aroused,[96] Justinian was glad to draw arguments from antiquity for the course he charted.[97] But this use of history, though more than merely decorative, hardly counts as a classicising or archaising tendency. Neither description, indeed, fits Justinian. Tribonian, on the other hand, may be termed a classiciser insofar as he reacts against the doctrines of the eastern law schools and rejoices in the revival of classical institutions. These doctrines, as Schindler has shown,[98] enter but little into the decision of legal controversies in Justinian's legislation, either in the Fifty Decisions or in the other constitutions passed in connection with the *Digest*. Tribonian preferred to go to the classical sources. He would out-classicise the law schools of Beirut and Constantinople, for reasons which are clearly expressed in *C. Omnem*. The law school syllabus and the method of instruction were intellectually disreputable. Not enough authors were read and much of what was read was obsolete and useless.[99] A deeper and more selective study of the classics was likely, he thought, to acquaint the student and lawyer with the best thinking, the most rational and humane solutions. But this implies no rigid preference for a classical rather than a modern answer to legal

---

[89] Ch. 1 n. 98.   [90] E.g. *Inst.* 1.53; 4.30.

[91] *C. Imperatoriam* 5 (21 Nov. 533); *C. Omnem* 11 (16 Dec. 533); *C. Tanta* 19 (16 Dec. 533), N. 17 intro. (16 Apr. 535); cf. ch. 1 nn. 133–4.

[92] Ch. 1 n. 223; N. 80.10 pr. (10 March 539).   [93] Above, n. 60.

[94] *Background* 880.   [95] *Justinians Haltung* 12f.

[96] Ch. 1 n. 299 in effect answering the sort of criticism to be found in Procopius (ch. 1 nn. 130–1).

[97] As in *Inst.* 2.1.41; N. 80. 10 pr. (10 March 539) and less specifically N. 119. 3 (20 Jan. 544).

[98] Schindler, *Justinians Haltung* 25f.; Volterra, 'Giustiniano e le scuole di diritto', *Gregorianum* 48 (1967) 77; P. Collinet, *Byzantion* 3 (1927) 1–15.

[99] *C. Omnem* 1 (16 Dec. 533).

problems, still less for the view of one particular author, such as Papinian. Tribonian's classicism in no way excludes the abandonment of classical solutions when they are unjust, inconvenient or incompatible with Christian ideals. It is of a piece with the empirical approach to legislation as an art similar to medicine.[100] A doctor might study Galen and often adopt his recommendations not because of any wish to return to the conditions of medical practice in the second century but because he believes that they are often the best he can reach.

It is by no means evident that the law professors shared this empirical attitude. Their interest lay not primarily in reform but in the preservation of the old texts or at least of those on which they were accustomed to lecture. If anyone on the commission clung blindly to the past for its own sake it was the professors: and it is generally agreed that the edictal committee, staffed by two professors, was more conservative than the Sabinian committee, headed by Tribonian.[101]

Tribonian and his emperor formed a working partnership. The quaestor owed his career to the emperor, and no doubt admired the drive which marked them both.[102] Justinian was happy to bask in the admiration which Tribonian's sonorous periods and learned disquisitions evoked. The quaestor was adept at surrounding Christian welfare legislation with a conservative aura, at marrying the Christian present to the pagan past.

Schindler and others have noted a change in 'Justinian's' view of the past when we turn from the *Digest* and *Institutes* to the *Novels*.[103] There is nothing surprising about this. Though Tribonian composed three-quarters of Justinian's *Novels* he was not addressing his mind when he did so to the problems of legal education. Hence innovatory tendencies have a clearer run, and the use of the classical in the *Novels* is mainly to provide precedents and pretexts.

The *Digest*, Tribonian's greatest achievement, found little echo in practice.[104] It does not claim to be intended primarily for that purpose. Whereas the *Codex* was meant to shorten lawsuits, the *Digest* is dedicated to the past, to God and to glory. Its practical purpose was mainly educational. Even for this it was too unwieldy and, above all, linguistically unmanageable. Yet it ultimately came into its own both in east and west and its anthological qualities, apparently so unsuited to a work which purports to be legislative, then proved its strongest feature. In the long run it was just as well that its architect was a scholar.

Tribonian's third claim was to be thought a successful man of affairs, one who shone in the practical business of government. This claim is justified so far as powers of organisation and diplomatic finesse are con-

---

[100] Ch. 1 n. 308.   [101] Ch. 5 nn. 111–39.

[102] *C. Tanta* pr. (16 Dec. 533).

[103] Schindler 333–4; van der Wal, *Labeo* 10 (1964) 220f. Contra Crifò, *Rapporti tutelari nelle Novelle Giustineanee* (1965) 165f.

[104] It is first cited by Paul the Deacon (*c.* 720–800), *Historia Romana = Patr. Lat.* 95; Rotondi, *Riv. ital. sc. giur.* 60 (1918) 239–68 = *Scr. giur.* 1. 340–69.

cerned. The *Digest* project called for the sort of engineering skill which Romans displayed in road construction and military fortification.[105] This Tribonian possessed. His pleasant manner kept him, as Procopius notes,[106] from paying the penalty of his corrupt ways; it too was an essential quality if the enterprise was to be carried through in a short time without treading too sharply on the toes of the praetorian prefecture, the imperial consistory, the law faculties and the bar.

But there were serious defects to set against these virtues. Tribonian's compositions have grandeur and the solutions they contain are often ingenious, but all too often they lack clarity and have not been thoroughly thought through.[107] He, like the builders of Hagia Sophia, worked in haste. In both cases Justinian must take part of the blame,[108] but even so the laws of this period consist at times more of guidelines, hints and sketches of possible legislative schemes than of mature conclusions. The frequent changes in important branches of property law, such as intestate succession and marriage settlements, cannot be justified. These are areas in which predictability is indispensable. Nor was the quaestor a good administrator. The desire to make the law plain and accessible to all is not matched by a proper assessment of how this might be done. John of Cappadocia had the sense to see that Greek must replace Latin as the legislative language of the eastern parts.[109] Tribonian made no more than half-hearted concessions to this view. Nor, despite the codification, was it easy for lawyers and citizens to ascertain the law. The *Novels* enacted after 535 were not collected in a single volume and we owe what we know of them to private enterprise. The virtues of the rule of law vanish in an age of kaleidoscopic change. For this reason the merits of the codification were more evident to later centuries, when time had passed for the mass of material to be analysed and digested in a real rather than a nominal sense, than to contemporaries.

Despite these shortcomings, and the financial corruption which, since Procopius mentions it in both the *Wars* and the *Secret History*, can hardly be denied,[110] Tribonian is a major figure in the cultural history of Europe and the greatest of all in the transmission of its legal heritage. Without the *Corpus Iuris* Europe would indeed have been different. The Theodosian code and the barbarian laws could not have formed the basis of university education in law. There would have been lawyers, no doubt, but not a learned legal profession nor a common conceptual framework of legal and administrative ideas, such as underlies the EEC. Without Tribonian, Justinian would perhaps not even have embarked on the *Digest* project, let alone have carried it through to a successful conclusion. After the 530s not much time remained. In 551 Beirut and its law school, with many of its

---

[105] Above, ch. 5.   [106] Ch. 2 n. 187.

[107] Noted, but attributed to Justinian, by van der Wal, *Labeo* 10 (1964) 220–3.

[108] Justinian and Hagia Sopha: R. Mainstone, *Transactions of the Newcomen Society* 28 (1965–6) 23f.; G. Sheja, *Istanbuler Mitteilungen* 12 (1962) 44f.

[109] Ch. 2 nn. 163–73.   [110] Ch. 2 n. 111.

lawyers, perished in a devastating earthquake.[111] Nothing could have saved Roman law after that.

In the eyes of contemporaries, Tribonian, as the most learned man of the age,[112] was entitled to a share in its splendours. In retrospect his achievement is as significant in its way as those of Anthemius, Procopius, Belisarius or Narses. None of the heroes was free from flaw, and they all owed much to Justinian, whether for stimulation or alienation. In each case the credit for achievement must be shared between an energetic and persistent political leader on the one hand and a gifted specialist on the other.

Law was Tribonian's specialism. He cannot as a lawyer match Ulpian, with whom in some ways he has much in common, any more than Procopius can match Ammianus. In the spectrum which ranges from lawyers who are keenest to do justice in the instant case to those whose main solicitude is legal certainty Tribonian lies close to the first extreme. He lacked, and Justinian did little to correct, the fine control which Ulpian, himself a devotee of *aequitas*, brings to the solution of legal disputes. Nevertheless, Tribonian, second to Ulpian in point of the volume of his legal compositions,[113] is closer to him in mind and quality than is generally recognised. The Tyrian Ulpian had the same learning and love of citation and he displayed the same unquenchable energy. He worked, as I hope to show in a later study, with the same methodical discipline. Both have been called mere compilers. In both cases the criticism is a half-truth. They built on their predecessors, but added to the material they found a cosmopolitan spirit, of Stoic or Judaeo-Christian inspiration, which they skilfully adapted to the demands of a practical discipline. Tribonian's inspirer Gaius shares with both of his successors the intellectual world of those who whatever their ancestry sought to apply Greek form to Roman matter. Men of their outlook transformed a Roman into a Romano-Greek empire. At the vanishing point of this empire and its culture stands Tribonian. The last Roman jurist, his was the hand which preserved and renewed Rome's lawyers and its laws.[114]

[111] Collinet 54–8; Agathias, *Hist.* 2.15: *CSHB* 96; *Patr.Gr.* 88. 1360.
[112] Ch. 2 nn. 24–5.　　　[113] Preface, n. 1.
[114] Wieacker, *Vom römischen Recht* (1961) 285 'nicht Erneuerung sondern Restauration' is too one-sided.

APPENDIX ONE

The Excerpting of Ancient Works for the Digest

This table is an amended version of that set out in 87 ZSS 285f., which in turn was based on Krueger's *Ordo librorum iuris veteris in compilandis digestis observatus.* His numbering of the works (1, 2, 3 etc.) has been retained. The large Roman numerals represent the groups into which the compilers divided the works they had to read. At the end of each group the estimated dates at which it was read and the maximum number of barristers needed to assist in the reading are recorded. The small Roman numerals (i, ii, iii) represent the sections into which the compilers in certain cases divided the groups. Whereas a group is divided between two commissioners, a section is assigned to a single commissioner. The six commissioners are denoted by the capital letters A, B, C, D, E and F. The key to their identity is given at the end of the table. The figures which follow the various works listed represent the number of lines taken from the work in question as actually or notionally printed in Lenel's *Palingenesia.* The averages express the number of such lines per book taken by the compilers from the work or works in question.

Sabinian mass.

I	1–3	Ulp. 51 Sab.	10,131	av. 198.6	
		Pomp. 36 Sab.[1)	2768	av. 76.9	
		Paul 16 Sab.	2228	av. 139.2	
	Total	103 books	15,127	av. 146.9 (9 sections)	
A	1–3	(i) Ulp. Sab. 1–14	1965	20 bks. 2535	
		Pomp. Sab. 1–4	356	av. 126.7	
		Paul Sab. 1–2	214		
		(iii) Ulp. Sab. 26–29	1096	9 bks. 1689	
		Pomp. Sab. 8–11	359	av. 187.7	
		Paul Sab. 5	234		
		(v) Ulp. Sab. 31–40 in.	1634	15½ bks. 2288	
		Pomp. Sab. 14–17	354	av. 147.6	
		Paul Sab. 7–8	300		
		(vii) Ulp. Sab. 44–50	1135	14 bks. 1545	
		Pomp. Sab. 23–27	201	av. 110.4	
		Paul Sab. 11–12	209		
		(ix) Pomp. Sab. 30–36	532	9 bks. 840	
		Paul Sab. 14–16	308	av. 93.3	

[1] *Pomp. Sab.* 28 not assigned.

Total	68½ bks.	8897	av. 129.9 (5 sections)
	Ulpian 34½ bks.	5830	av. 169.0
	Pomponius 24 bks.	1802	av. 75.1
	Paul 10 bks.	1265	av. 126.5

B 1–3

(ii)	Ulp. Sab. 15–25	3093	⎫ 16 bks. 3998
	Pomp. Sab. 5–7	510	⎬ av. 249.9
	Paul Sab. 3–4	395	⎭
(iv)	Ulp. Sab. 30	231	⎫ 4 bks. 504
	Pomp. Sab. 12–13	86	⎬ av. 126.0
	Paul Sab. 6	187	⎭
(vi)	Ulp. Sab. 40 fin–54	932	⎫ 10½ bks. 1542
	Pomp. Sab. 18–22	301	⎬ av. 146.9
	Paul Sab. 9–10	309	⎭
(viii)	Ulp. Sab. 51	45	⎫ 3 bks. 186
	Pomp. Sab. 29	69	⎬ av. 62.0
	Paul Sab. 13	72	⎭

Total	33½ bks.	6230	av. 186.0 (4 sections)
	Ulpian 16½ bks.	4301	av. 260.7
	Pomponius 11 bks.	966	av. 87.8
	Paul 6 bks.	963	av. 160.5

(15 Dec. 530–5 April 531: 4 barristers)

II 4–9

Ulp. ed. 26–52 in.	10,383	av. 391.8 (26½ bks.)
Paul ed. 28–48 in.	1919	av. 93.6 (20½ bks.)
Paul brev. 6–8[2])	36	av. 12.0
Gai. ed. prov. 9–18	1074	av. 107.4
Gai. ed. urb. 2 test.)	209	av. 41.8 (5 bks.)
3 leg.)		

Total	65 bks.	13,621	av. 209.6 (8 sections)

A 4–9

(i)	Ulp. ed. 26–30	3061	⎫ 11½ bks. 3721
	Paul ed. 28–31	397	⎬ av. 323.6
	Gai. ed. prov. 9–10 in.	246	⎬
	Paul brev. 6	17	⎭
(iii)	Ulp. ed. 33–34	669	⎫ 7 bks. 1043
	Paul ed. 35–37	294	⎬ av. 149.0
	Gai. ed. prov. 11	75	⎬
	Paul brev. 7	5	⎭
(v)	Ulp. ed. 37–38	578	⎫ 5½ bks. 759
	Paul ed. 39–40	92	⎬ av. 138.0
	Gai. ed. prov. 13–14 in.	89	⎭
(vii)	Ulp. ed. 46–50	1061	⎫ 12½ bks. 1316
	Paul ed. 43 fin.–46	83	⎬ av. 105.3
	Gai. ed. prov. 16–17	132	⎬
	Gai. ed. urb. 2 test.	40	⎭

Total	36½ bks.	6839	av. 187.4 (4 sections)
	Ulpian 14 bks.	5369	av. 383.5

[2] A has Gai. ed. prov. before Paul brev. (sects. i, iii); B has Paul brev. first (sect. iv).

	Paul ed. 12½ bks.	866	av. 69.3	
	Paul brev. 2 bks.	22	av. 11.0	
	Gaius ed. prov. 6 bks.	542	av. 90.3	
	Gaius ed. urb. 2 bks.	40	av. 20.0	

B 4–9 (ii)
Ulp. ed. 31–32 — 1405 ⎫
Paul ed. 32–34 — 703 ⎬ 5½ bks. 2318
Gai. ed. 10 fin. — 210 ⎭ av. 421.5

(iv)
Ulp. ed. 35–36 — 1269 ⎫
Paul ed. 38 — 55 ⎪ 5 bks. 1404
Paul brev. 8 — 14 ⎬ av. 280.8
Gai. ed. prov. 12 — 66 ⎭

(vi)
Ulp. ed. 39–45 — 2067 ⎫
Paul ed. 41–43 in. — 271 ⎬ 11 bks. 2442
Gai. ed. prov. 14 fin–15 — 104 ⎭ av. 220.0

(viii)
Ulp. ed. 51–52 in. — 273 ⎫
Paul ed. 47–48 in. — 24 ⎬ 7 bks. 618
Gai. ed. prov. 18 — 152 ⎪ av. 88.3
Gai. ed. urb. leg. 1–3 — 169 ⎭

Total	28½ bks.	6782	av. 238.0 (4 sections)
	Ulpian 12½ bks.	5014	av. 401.1
	Paul ed. 8 bks.	1053	av. 131.6
	Paul brev. 1 bk.	14	av. 14.0
	Gai. ed. prov. 4 bks.	532	av. 133.0
	Gai. ed. urb. 3 bks.	169	av. 56.3

(5 April–14 June 531: 6 barristers)

III	10–11	Ulp. 10 disp.	1928	av. 192.8
		Ulp. 10 omn. trib.	506	av. 50.6
	Total	20 bks.	2434	av. 121.7
	A 10	Ulp. 10 disp.	1928	
	Total	10 bks.	1928	av. 192.8
		Ulpian 10 bks.	1928	av. 192.8
	B 11	Ulp. 10 omn. trib.	506	
	Total	10 bks.	506	av. 50.6
		Ulpian 10 bks.	506	av. 50.6

(14 June–6 July 531: no barristers)

IV	12–13	Ulp. 6 op.	645	av. 107.5
		Ulp. 6 cens.	96	av. 16.0
	Total	12 bks.	741	av. 61.7
	A 12	Ulp. 6 op.	645	
	Total	6 bks.	645	av. 107.5
		Ulpian 6 bks.	645	av. 107.5

B 13	Ulp. 6 cens.	96		
Total	6 bks.	96	av.	16.0
	Ulpian 6 bks.	96	av.	16.0

(6 July–19 July 531: no barristers)

V 14–20	Iulianus 90 dig.	4429	av.	49.2
	Alf. Var. 7 dig. epit.	389	av.	55.6
	Paul 8 epit. Alf. dig.	442	av.	55.2
	Iulianus 1 ambig.	90	av.	90.0
	Iulianus 4 Urs. Feroc.	351	av.	87.7
	Iulianus 6 Minic.	256	av.	42.7
	Africanus 9 quaest.	1902	av.	211.3
Total	125 bks.	7859	av.	62.9
A 14	Iul. dig. 1–62	4106		
Total	62 bks.	4106	av.	66.2
	Iulianus 62 bks.	4106	av.	66.2
B 14	Iul. dig. 63–90	323		
15	Alf. Var. 7 dig. epit.	389		
16	Paul 8 epit. Alf. dig.	442		
17	Iul. 1 ambig.	90		
18	Iul. 4 Urs. Feroc.	351		
19	Iul. 6 Minic.	256		
20	Africanus 9 quaest.	1902		
Total	63 bks.	3753	av.	59.6
	Iulianus 42 bks.	1020	av.	24.3
	Alf. Var. 7 bks.	389	av.	55.6
	Paul 8 bks.	442	av.	55.2
	Africanus 9 bks.	1902	av.	211.3

(19 July–2 Dec. 531: no barristers)

VI 21–7	Flor. 12 inst.[3])	282	av.	23.5
	Marcian. 16 inst.	1287	av.	80.4
	Ulp. 2 inst.	120	av.	60.0
	Gai. 4 inst.[3])	180	av.	45.0
	Gai. 7 aur.[3])	533	av.	76.1
	Call. 3 inst.[3])	27	av.	9.0
	Paul 2 inst.	24	av.	12.0
Total	46 bks.	2453	av.	53.3 (7 sections)

[3] Florentinus inst. 12, Gaius inst. 4, Gaius aur. 4–7, and Callistratus inst. 1 not assigned.

A 21–7   (i) Flor. inst. 1–5

A 21–7	(i)	Flor. inst. 1–5	14
		Marci. inst. 1–2	170
		Ulp. inst. 1	93
		Gai. inst. 1	72
		Gai. aur. 1	20
		Paul inst. 1	4
	(iii)	Marci. inst. 4–9	576
		Flor. inst. 10–11	132
		Ulp. inst. 2	27
	(v)	Gai. inst. 3	11
		Gai. aur. 3	79
		Paul inst. 2	20
	(vii)	Marci. inst. 10–16	416

(i) 11 bks. 373 av. 33.9
(iii) 9 bks. 735 av. 81.7
(v) 3 bks. 110 av. 36.7
(vii) 7 bks. 416 av. 59.4

Total	30 bks.	1634	av. 54.5 (4 sections)
	Florentinus 7 bks.	146	av. 20.9
	Marcianus 15 bks.	1162	av. 77.5
	Ulpian 2 bks.	120	av. 60.0
	Gaius 4 bks.	182	av. 45.5
	Paul 2 bks.	24	av. 12.0

B 21–7	(ii)	Flor. inst. 6	21
		Marci. inst. 3	125
		Gai. inst. 2	97
		Gai. aur. 2	434
		Call. inst. 2	20
	(iv)	Flor. inst. 7–9	115
	(vi)	Call. inst. 3	7

(ii) 5 bks. 697 av. 139.4
(iv) 3 bks. 115 av. 38.3
(vi) 3 bks. 7 av. 2.3

Total	9 bks.	819	av. 91.0 (3 sections)
	Florentinus 4 bks.	136	av. 34.0
	Marcianus 1 bk.	125	av. 125.0
	Gaius 2 bks.	531	av. 265.5
	Callistratus 2 bks.	27	av. 13.5

(2 Dec. 531–21 Jan. 532: 9 barristers)

VII 28–31	Ulp. 5 adult.	471	av. 94.0
	Pap. 2 adult.	145	av. 72.5
	Pap. 1 adult.	89	av. 89.0
	Paul 3 adult.	85	av. 28.3
Total	11 bks.	790	av. 71.8 (2 sections)

A 28–31	(i) Ulp. adult. 1–3	325	
	Pap. adult. 1–2	145	8 bks. 598
	Pap. 1 adult.	89	av. 74.7
	Paul adult. 1–2	39	

Total	8 bks.	598	av. 74.7
	Ulpian 3 bks.	325	av. 108.3
	Papinian 3 bks.	234	av. 78.0
	Paul 2 bks.	39	av. 19.5

B 28–31 (ii) Ulp. adult. 4–5   146 }   3 bks. 192
            Paul adult. 3   46 }   av. 64.0

Total	3 bks.	192	av.	64.0
	Ulpian 2 bks.	146	av.	73.0
	Paul 1 bk.	46	av.	46.0

(21 Jan.–2 Feb. 532: 4 barristers)

VIII 32–5 Ulp. 1 spons.   7   av.   7.0
           Paul 1 dot. rep.   5   av.   5.0
           Paul 1 ads. lib.   18   av.   18.0
           Paul 1 iur. pat.   13   av.   13.0

Total	4 bks.[4])	43	av.	10.7

A 32 Ulp. 1 spons.
  33   Paul 1 dot. rep.

Total	2 bks.	12	av.	6.0
	Ulpian 1 bk.	7	av.	7.0
	Paul 1 bk.	5	av.	5.0

B 34 Paul 1 adsign. lib.
  35   Paul 1 iur. patr.

Total	2 bks.	31	av.	15.5
	Paul 2 bks.	31	av.	15.5

(2 Feb.–6 Feb. 532: no barristers)

IX 36–40 Neratius 15 reg.   33   av.   2.2
           Ulp. 7 reg.   107   av.   15.3
           Scae. 4 reg.   90   av.   22.5
           Paul 1 reg.   28   av.   28.0
           Gaius 1 reg.   2   av.   2.0
           Marci. reg. 1–2   109   av.   54.5

Total	30 bks.	369	av.	12.3

A 36 Neratius 15 reg.

Total	15 bks.	33	av.	2.2
	Neratius 15 bks.	33	av.	2.2

B 37 Ulpian 7 reg.
  38   Scaevola 4 reg.
  39   Paul 1 reg.
  39a   Gaius 1 reg.
  40   Marcianus reg. 1–2

Total	15 bks.	336	av.	15.5
	Ulpian 7 bks.	107	av.	15.3
	Scaevola 4 bks.	90	av.	22.5

[4] See however note below, p. 267.

	Paul 1 bk.	28	av.	28.0	
	Gaius 1 bk.	2	av.	2.0	
	Marcianus 2 bks.	109	av.	54.5	

(6 Feb.–10 March 532: no barristers)

X	41–2	Ulp. 2 resp.	141	av.	70.5
		Marci. reg. 3–4	278	av.	139.0
	Total	4 bks.	419	av.	104.7
	A 41	Ulp. 2 resp.			
	Total	2 bks.	141	av.	70.5
		Ulpian 2 bks.	141	av.	70.5
	B 42	Marci. reg. 3–4			
	Total	2 bks.	278	av.	139.0
		Marcianus 2 bks.	278	av.	139.0

(10 March–14 March 532: no barristers)

XI	43–7	Paul 7 reg.	76	av.	10.9
		Marci. reg. 5	76	av.	76.0
		Pomp. 1 reg.	50	av.	50.0
		Ulp. 1 reg.	18	av.	18.0
		Ulp. 10 off. proc.	1211	av.	121.1
	Total	20 bks.	1431	av.	71.5
	A 43	Paul 7 reg.			
	44	Marci. reg. 5			
	45	Pomp. 1 reg.			
	46	Ulp. 1 reg.			
	Total	10 bks.	220	av.	22.0
		Paul 7 bks.	76	av.	10.9
		Marcianus 1 bk.	76	av.	76.0
		Pomponius 1 bk.	50	av.	50.0
		Ulpian 1 bk.	18	av.	18.0
	B 47	Ulp. 10 off. proc.			
	Total	10 bks.	1211	av.	121.1
		Ulpian 10 bks.	1211	av.	121.1

(14 March–5 April 532: no barristers)

XII	48–56	Paul 1 SC Sil.	13	av.	13.0
		Paul 1 port. lib. dam.	53	av.	53.0
		Paul 2 leg. Iul.	12	av.	6.0
		Paul 1 conc. form.	8	av.	8.0
		Macer 2 iud. pub.	306	av.	153.0

		Venul. 3 iud. pub.	71	av. 23.7
		Paul 1 pub. iud.	44	av. 44.0
		Marci. 2 pub. iud.	217	av. 108.5
		Maec. 14 pub. iud.	19	av. 1.4
	Total	28(27)[5] bks.	743	av. 26.5
A 48		Paul 1 SC Sil.		
49		Paul 1 port. lib. damn.		
50		Paul 2 leg. Iul.		
51		Paul 1 conc. form.		
52		Macer 2 pub. iud.		
53		Venul. 3 iud. pub.		
54		Paul 1 pub. iud.		
55		Marci. 2 pub. iud.		
	Total	14 (13) bks.	724	av. 51.7
		Paul 7 bks.	130	av. 18.6
		Macer 2 bks.	306	av. 153.0
		Venuleius 3 bks.	71	av. 23.7
		Marcianus 2 bks.	217	av. 108.5
B 56		Maec. 14 pub. iud.		
	Total	14 bks.	19	av. 1.4
		Maecianus 14 bks.	19	av. 1.4

(5 April–5 May 532: no barristers)

XIII	57–63	(Marci. 1 form. hypoth.	428	av. 428.0
		(Gaius 1 form. hypoth.	96	av. 96.0
		Marc. 1 resp.	252	av. 252.0
		Neratius 7 membr.	411	av. 58.7
		Macer 2 off. prae.	60	av. 30.0
		Arc. Charis. 1 test.	59	av. 59.0
		Marci. 1 delat.	240	av. 240.0
	Total	14 bks.	1546	av. 110.4
A 57–8		(Marci. 1 form. hypoth.		
		(Gaius 1 form. hypoth.		
59		Marc. 1 resp.		
61		Macer 2 off. prae.		
62		Arc. Charis. 1 test.		
63		Marci. 1 delat.		
	Total	7 bks.	1135	av. 162.1
		Marcianus 2 bks.	668	av. 334.0
		Gaius 1 bk.	96	av. 96.0
		Marcellus 1 bk.	252	av. 252.0
		Macer 2 bks.	60	av. 30.0
		Arc. Charis. 1 bk.	59	av. 59.0

[5] One of Paul's *libri singulares* listed in the *Index Florentinus* is to be inserted between 48 and 52.

B 60   Neratius 7 membr.

Total	7 bks.	411	av. 58.7
	Neratius 7 bks.	411	av. 58.7

(5 May–20 May 532: 1 barrister)

XIV 64–6

	Ulp. 4 appell.	276	av. 69.0
	Macer 2 appell.	218	av. 109.0
	Marcianus 2 appell.	37	av. 18.5
Total	8 bks.	531	av. 66.4 (2 sections)

A 64–6

	(i) Ulp. appell. 1–2	198	
	Macer appell. 1	87	
	Marci. appell. 1	23	
Total	4 bks.	308	av. 77.0 (1 section)
	Ulpian 2 bks.	198	av. 99.0
	Macer 1 bk.	87	av. 87.0
	Marcianus 1 bk.	23	av. 23.0

B 64–6

	(ii) Ulp. appell. 3–4	78	
	Macer appell. 2	131	
	Marci. appell. 2	14	
Total	4 bks.	233	av. 55.7 (1 section)
	Ulpian 2 bks.	78	av. 39.0
	Macer 1 bk.	131	av. 131.0
	Marcianus 1 bk.	14	av. 14.0

(20 May–29 May 532: 4 barristers)

XV 67–81

	Paul 1 appell.	12	av. 12.0
	Rut. 1 leg. Falc.	4	av. 4.0
	Paul 1 leg. Fuf.	17	av. 17.0
	Paul 3 leg. Ael.	79	av. 26.3
	Ulp. 4 leg. Ael.	37	av. 9.2
	Paul 1 lib. dand.	20	av. 20.0
	Paul 1 lib. caus.	4	av. 4.0
	Paul 1 sec. tab.	36	av. 36.0
	Paul 1 iur. cod.	53	av. 53.0
	Paul 1 cent. iud.	34	av. 34.0
	Paul 1 adult.	3	av. 3.0
	Paul 1 SCC	5	av. 5.0
	Paul 1 SC Vell.	7	av. 7.0
	Paul 1 inter. fem.	12	av. 12.0
	Paul 1 or. Ant.	57	av. 57.0
Total	20 bks.	380	av. 19.0

A 67   Paul 1 appel.

68   Paul 1 leg. Falc.

	69	Paul 1 leg. Fuf.			
	70	Paul 3 leg. Ael.			
	71	Ulp. 4 leg. Ael.			

Total	10 bks.	149	av.	14.9
	Paul 6 bks.	112	av.	18.7
	Ulpian 4 bks.	37	av.	9.2

B 72	Paul 1 lib. dand.
73	Paul 1 lib. caus.
74	Paul 1 sec. tab.
75	Paul 1 iur. cod.
76	Paul 1 cent. iud.
77	Paul 1 adult.
78	Paul 1 SCC
79	Paul 1 SC Vell.
80	Paul 1 inter. fem.
81	Paul 1 or. Ant.

Total	10 bks.	231	av.	23.1
	Paul 10 bks.	231	av.	23.1

(29 May–19 June 532: no barristers)

XVI 82–7	Paul 1 exc. tut.	11	av.	11.0
	Paul 1 or. Sev.	27	av.	27.0
	Paul 1 var. lect.	8	av.	8.0
	Ulp. 1 pand.	7	av.	7.0
	Macer 2 re. mil.	96	av.	48.0
	Paul 1 poen. mil.	21	av.	21.0

Total	8(7) bks.[6]	170	av.	21.2

A 82	Paul 1 exc. tut.
83	Paul 1 or. Sev.
84	Paul 1 var. lect.
85	Ulp. 1 pand.

Total	4 bks.	53	av.	13.2
	Paul 3 bks.	46	av.	15.3
	Ulpian 1 bk.	7	av.	7.0

B 86	Macer 2 re. mil.
87	Paul 1 poen. mil.

Total	4(3) bks.[6]	117	av.	29.2
	Paul 2 bks.	21	av.	10.5
	Macer 2 bks.	96	av.	48.0

(19 June–28 June 532: no barristers)

[6] A *liber singularis* of Paul from the Florentine index should be inserted here. See note below, p. 267.

XVII	88–94	Ulp. 1 off. cur. reip.	67	av.	67.0	
		Ulp. 1 off. cons.	3	av.	3.0	
		Paul 2 off. proc.	15	av.	7.5	
		Ven. 4 off. proc.	39	av.	9.7	
		Sat. 1 poen. pag.	50	av.	50.0	
		Maec. 1 leg. Rhod.	8	av.	8.0	
		Iav. 10 post. Lab.	525[7])	av.	52.5	
	Total	20 bks.	707	av.	35.3	
	A 88	Ulp. 1 off. cur. reip.				
	89	Ulp. 1 off. cons.				
	90	Paul 2 off. proc.				
	91	Ven. 4 off. proc.				
	92	Sat. 1 poen. pag.				
	93	Maec. 1 leg. Rhod.				
	Total	10 bks.	182	av.	18.2	
		Ulpian 2 bks.	70	av.	35.0	
		Paul 2 bks.	15	av.	7.5	
		Venuleius 4 bks.	39	av.	9.7	
		Saturninus 1 bk.	50	av.	50.0	
		Maecianus 1 bk.	8	av.	8.0	
	B 94	Iav. 10 post. Lab.				
	Total	10 bks.	525	av.	52.5	
		Iavolenus 10 bks.	525	av.	52.5	

(28 June 532–9 July 532: no barristers)

Note. The following ten books listed in the Florentine index belong to the Sabinian mass:

Paul 1 off. pr. tut.	0	
Paul 1 extr. crim.	0	
Paul 1 form. hyp.	0	
Paul 1 leg. mun.	0	
Paul 1 leg. Vell.	0	(? XV)
Paul 1 iur. patr. ex leg. Iul.	0	(? VIII)
Paul 1 act.	0	(? XV)
Paul 1 don. int. cir. et ux.	0	(? VIII)
Paul 1 leg.	0	(? XV)
Paul 1 legit. hered.	0	(? XV)

One of these must be assigned to group XII, one to group XVI. The remaining eight cannot be assigned to a group with certainty. We have allotted four books

[7] Counting the texts with the inscription 'Iavolenus' rather than 'Labeo'. These texts were assigned to the Sabinian committee but in fact read by the Papinian commissioner F, and inserted partly in the Sabinian, partly in the Papinian mass (Honoré, 'Labeo's *posteriora* and the *Digest* commission', *Daube Noster*, ed. Watson 161f.). Since Tribonian did not adjust the timetable to take account of these changes I have left the excerpts in the Sabinian mass, assigned to B. If these books are subtracted and the group reassigned (e.g. A to read 88, 89, 90 and 93, B 91 and 92) the figures for the Sabinian mass must be modified as shown in note 8.

to each commissioner, but reconstructions are possible which would entail a different distribution.

Summary of Sabinian mass

Group	Books	Total lines	Average	Books	A Total lines	Average	Books	B Total lines	Average
I	103	15,127	146.9	68½	8897	129.9	33½	6230	186.0
II	65	13,621	209.6	36½	6839	187.4	28½	6782	238.0
III	20	2434	121.7	10	1928	192.8	10	506	50.6
IV	12	741	61.7	6	645	107.5	6	96	16.0
V	125	7859	62.9	62	4106	66.2	63	3753	59.6
VI	46	2453	53.3	30	1634	54.5	9	819	91.0
VII	11	790	71.8	8	598	74.7	3	192	64.0
VIII	4	43	10.7	2	12	6.0	2	31	15.5
IX	30	369	12.3	15	33	2.2	15	336	15.5
X	4	419	104.7	2	141	70.5	2	278	139.0
XI	20	1431	71.5	10	220	22.0	10	1211	121.1
XII	28(27)	743	26.5	14(13)	724	51.7	14	19	1.4
XIII	14	1546	110.4	7	1135	162.1	7	411	58.7
XIV	8	531	66.4	4	308	77.0	4	223	55.7
XV	20	380	19.0	10	149	14.9	10	231	23.1
XVI	8(7)	170	21.2	4	53	13.2	4(3)	117	29.2
XVII	20	707	35.3	10	182	18.2	10	525	52.5
Totals[8]	546[9]	49,364	90.41	303[10]	27,604	91.10	235[10]	21,760	92.60

Edictal mass

XVIII	95–100	Ulp. ed. 1–25	8359	av. 334.3
		Paul ed. 1–27	2945	av. 109.1
		Gai. ed. prov. 1–8, 19 in.[11]	1124	av. 132.2 (8½ bks.)
		Paul brev. 1–5[12]	2	av. 0.4
		Gai. ed. urb. praed. no. 49	4	av. 16.0 (¼ bk.)
		Call. ed. mon. 1–2	88	av. 44.0
	Total	67¾ bks.	12,522	av. 184.8

(14 sections)

C	95–100	(i)	Ulp. ed. 1–6	1398	12½ bks. 2074
			Paul ed. 1–5	501	av. 165.9
			Gai. ed. prov. 1	162	
			Call. ed. mon. 1 in.	13	
		(iii)	Ulp. ed. 8–10 in.	624	5½ bks. 988
			Paul ed. 8–9[13]	245	av. 179.6
			Gai. ed. prov. 3	119	

[8] If changes are made in accordance with note 7 above the figures are: 536 48,839 91.12 298 27,515 92.33 230 21,323 92.71.

[9] Includes 8 books not assigned to groups (see note, above) and 8 books not assigned to commissioners (see groups I, VI).

[10] Includes 4 books not assigned to groups (see note, above).

[11] There are no texts from Gaius ed. prov. 5 in section (vi) nor from ed. prov. 7 in section (x) nor from ed. prov. 8 in section (xiii).

[12] Paul brev. 1–2, 4–5 are not assigned.

[13] Paul ed. 8–10 (Krüger) but this does not fit Ulp. ed. and Gai. ed. prov.

(v)	Ulp. ed. 13–14	816	}
	Paul ed. 12 fin.–16	304	7⅓ bks. 1196
	Gai. ed. prov. 5 in.	44	av. 163.2
	Call. ed. mon. 2 in.	32	
(vii)	Ulp. ed. 16 fin.–17	538	
	Paul ed. 19 init., 21	335	3⅔ bks. 1057
	Gai. ed. prov. 7 in.	179	av. 288.0
	Call. ed. mon. 2 fin.	5	
(ix)	Ulp. ed. 19	377	2⅓ bks. 698
	Paul ed. 23	237	av. 299.6
	Gai. ed. prov. 7 fin.	84	
(xi)	Ulp. ed. 21 fin.–22	419	
	Paul ed. 25 in., 17–18 in.	212	4⅚ bks. 663
	Gai. prov. 8 in., 5 fin.	14	av. 137.3
	Call. ed. mon. 2 med.	18	
(xiii)	Ulp. ed. 24	315	2½ bks. 374
	Paul ed. 25 fin., 26	59	av. 149.6

Total	38⅔ bks.	7050	av. 182.3 (7 sections)
	Ulpian 15½ bks.	4487	av. 289.5
	Paul ed. 17½ bks.	1893	av. 108.2
	Gaius ed. prov. 4⅙ bks.	602	av. 144.5
	Callistratus ed. mon. 1½ bks.	68	av. 45.3

D 95–100	(ii) Ulp. ed. 7	72	
	Paul ed. 6–7	89	4 bks. 175
	Gai. ed. prov. 2	14	av. 43.7
	(iv) Ulp. ed. 10 fin.–12	1429	
	Paul ed. 10–12 in.	319	
	Gai. ed. prov. 4	173	7½ bks. 1943
	Paul brev. 3	2	av. 259.1
	Call. ed. mon. 1 fin.	20	
	(vi) Ulp. ed. 15–16 in.	804	3 bks. 1081
	Paul ed. 20	195	av. 360.3
	Gai. ed. prov. 6 fin.	82	
	(viii) Ulp. ed. 18	660	2⅓ bks. 915
	Paul ed. 22	186	av. 392.7
	Gai. ed. prov. 7 med.	69	
	(x) Ulp. ed. 20–21 in.	112	2½ bks. 153
	Paul ed. 24	41	av. 61.2
	(xii) Ulp. ed. 23	402	2½ bks. 632
	Paul ed. 18 fin., 19 fin.	177	av. 252.8
	Gai. ed. prov. 6 init.	53	
	(xiv) Ulp. ed. 25	393	
	Paul ed. 27	45	3¼ bks. 573
	Gai. ed. prov. 8 fin., 19 fin.	131	av. 176.3
	Gai. ed. urb. praed. no. 49	4	

Total	25 1/12 bks.	5472	av. 218.2 (7 sections)
	Ulpian 9½ bks.	3872	av. 407.6
	Paul 9½ bks.	1052	av. 110.7

Gaius ed. prov. 4⅓ bks.	522	av. 120.6
Paul brev. 1 bk.	2	av. 2.0
Gaius ed. urb. ¼ bk.	4	av. 16.0
Callistratus ed. mon. ½ bk.	20	av. 40.0

(15 Dec. 530–20 Feb. 531: 6 barristers)

XIX 101–23	Ulp. ⎰ ed. 56–81	7150	av. 275.0 (26 bks.)
	⎨ 2 ed. cur.	853	av. 426.5
	⎱ ed. 52 fin.–55	1106	av. 316.0 (3½ bks.)
	Total	9109	av. 289.2 (31½ bks.)
	Paul ⎰ ed. 53–78	1642	av. 63.2
	⎨ 2 ed. cur.	164	av. 82.0
	⎱ ed. 48 fin.–52	439	av. 97.6 (4½ bks.)
	Total	2245	av. 69.1 (32½ bks.)
	Paul brev. 16[14])	9	av. 9.0
	Gai. ⎰ ed. prov. 21 fin.–30[14])	244	av. 25.7 (9½ bks.)
	⎨ 2 ed. cur.	76	av. 38.0
	⎱ ed. prov. 19 fin.–21 in.	19	av. 9.5
	Total	339	av. 25.1 (13½ bks.)
	Gai. ed. urb. 6–8, 9 no. 46–48, 10[14])	138	av. 29.1 (4¾ bks.)
	Pap. 1 astunomikos	24	av. 24.0
Total 84¼ bks.		11,864	av. 140.4
			(25 sections)

C 101– 23	(i) Ulp. ed. 56	424 ⎫	
	Paul ed. 53–54[14]	559 ⎬	3¾ bks. 1019
	Gai. ed. prov. 21 fin.	34 ⎪	av. 271.7
	Gai. ed. urb. 9 no. 48	2 ⎭	
	(iii) Ulp. ed. 58–59	281 ⎫	
	Paul ed. 56–57 in.	33 ⎬	4½ bks. 328
	Gai. ed. prov. 22 fin.	10 ⎪	av. 72.9
	Gai. ed. urb. 10 no. 50	4 ⎭	
	(v) Ulp. ed. 61	158 ⎫	
	Paul ed. 58	31 ⎬	2⅓ bks. 204
	Gai. ed. prov. 23 med.	15 ⎭	av. 87.6
	(vii) Ulp. ed. 63	117 ⎫	
	Paul ed. 60	55 ⎬	3 bks. 183
	Paul brev. 16 fin.	5 ⎪	av. 61.0
	Gai. ed. prov. 24 in.	6 ⎭	
	(ix) Ulp. ed. 66	125 ⎫	
	Paul ed. 62	61 ⎬	3 bks. 200
	Gai. ed. prov. 24 fin.	7 ⎪	av. 66.7
	Gai. ed. urb. 10 no. 51–52	7 ⎭	

[14] No texts from Gai. ed. prov. 25 in sections (x) and (xi). In section (i) add Paul ed. 53 and Gai. ed. urb. 9 no. 48. No text from Paul brev. 16 in section (ix).

(xi)	Ulp. ed. 68	666 ⎫	3 bks. 700
	Paul ed. 64	10 ⎬	av. 233.3
	Pap. 1 astun.	24 ⎭	
(xiii)	Ulp. ed. 70–71 in.	694 ⎫	3½ bks. 723
	Paul ed. 65 fin.–66	26 ⎬	av. 206.6
	Gai. ed. prov. 25 fin.	3 ⎭	
(xv)	Ulp. ed. 72–73	348 ⎫	3½ bks. 390
	Paul ed. 68	25 ⎬	av. 111.4
	Gai. ed. prov. 26 fin.	17 ⎭	
(xvii)	Ulp. ed. 75	148 ⎫	2 bks. 182
	Paul ed. 70	34 ⎭	av. 91.0
(xix)	Ulp. ed. 77–78	214 ⎫	5½ bks. 446
	Paul ed. 72–74	212 ⎬	av. 81.1
	Gai. ed. prov. 27 in.	20 ⎭	
(xxi)	Ulp. ed. 80–81	267 ⎫	5 bks. 327
	Paul ed. 77–78	20 ⎬	av. 65.4
	Gai. ed. prov. 28	40 ⎭	
(111– (xxiii)	Ulp. ed. 54–55 in.	207 ⎫	6½ bks. 394
15)	Paul ed. 50–51	92 ⎬	av. 60.6
	Gai. ed. prov. 20	3 ⎪	
	Gai. ed. urb. 7–8	92 ⎭	
(120–3) (xxv)	Ulp. ed. 52 fin.–53	844 ⎫	
	Paul ed. 48 fin.–49	334 ⎬	4½ bks. 1211
	Gai. ed. prov. 19 fin.	10 ⎪	av. 269.1
	Gai. ed. urb. 6	23 ⎭	

Total	50 1/12 bks.	6307	av. 125.9
			(13 sections)
	Ulpian 18½ bks.	4493	av. 242.9
	Paul ed. 19½ bks.	1492	av. 76.5
	Paul brev. ½ bk.	5	av. 10.0
	Gai. ed. prov. 6⅓ bks.	165	av. 26.1
	Gai. ed. urb. 4¼ bks.	128	av. 30.1
	Pap. astun. 1 bk.	24	av. 24.0

D 101–	(ii)	Ulp. ed. 57	517 ⎫	2½ bks. 591
23		Paul ed. 55	63 ⎬	av. 236.4
		Gai. ed. prov. 22 in.	11 ⎭	
	(iv)	Ulp. ed. 60	239 ⎫	1⅚ bks. 306
		Paul ed. 57 fin.	57 ⎬	av. 167.2
		Gai. ed. prov. 23 in.	10 ⎭	
	(vi)	Up. ed. 62	158 ⎫	
		Paul ed. 59	77 ⎬	2⅚ bks. 253
		Paul brev. 16 in.	4 ⎪	av. 89.4
		Gai. ed. prov. 23 fin.	14 ⎭	
	(viii)	Ulp. ed. 64–65	211 ⎫	3 bks. 213
		Paul ed. 61	2 ⎭	av. 71.0
	(x)	Ulp. ed. 67	141 ⎫	2 bks. 202
		Paul ed. 63	61 ⎭	av. 101.0
	(xiv)	Ulp. ed. 71 fin.	865 ⎫	2 bks. 896
		Paul ed. 67	25 ⎬	av. 448.0
		Gai. ed. prov. 26 in.	6 ⎭	

	(xvi)	Ulp. ed. 74	168	3 bks. 229
		Paul ed. 69	55	av. 76.3
		Gai. ed. prov. 29	6	
	(xviii)	Ulp. ed. 76	483	3 bks. 603
		Paul ed. 71	89	av. 201.0
		Gai. ed. prov. 30	31	
	(xx)	Ulp. ed. 79	467	3½ bks. 602
		Paul ed. 75–76	125	av. 172.0
		Gai. ed. prov. 27 fin.	10	
(108–	(xxii)	Ulp. 2 ed. cur.	853	6 bks. 1093
10)		Paul 2 ed. cur.	164	av. 182.2
		Gai. 2 ed. cur.	76	
(116–	(xxiv)	Ulp. ed. 55 fin.	55	2½ bks. 81
19)		Paul 52 ed.	13	av. 32.4
		Gai. ed. prov. 21 in.	3	
		Gai. ed. urb. 9 no. 46–7	10	

Total	34⅙ bks.	5557	av. 162.6
			(12 sections)
Ulpian ed. 13 bks.		4616	av. 355.1
Paul ed. 15 bks.		753	av. 57.9
Paul brev. ½ bk.		4	av. 8.0
Gai. ed. prov. 7⅙ bks.		174	av. 24.3
Gai. ed. urb. ½ bk.		10	av. 20.0

(20 Feb.–15 May 531: 6 barristers)

XX	124–33	Paul 18 Plaut.	1653	av. 91.8
		Iav. 5 Plaut.	109	av. 21.8
		Pomp. 7 Plaut.	266	av. 38.0
		Paul 4 Vitell.	315	av. 78.7
		Paul 2 iur. fisc.	71	av. 35.5

Total	36 bks.	2414	av. 67.1 (5 sections)

C 124	(i)	Paul Plaut. 1–14	1143	16 bks. 1201
125		Iav. Plaut. 1	36	av. 75.1
126		Pomp. Plaut. 1	22	
133	(v)	Paul 2 iur. fisc.	71	2 bks. 71 av. 35.5

Total	18 bks.	1272	av. 70.7 (2 sections)
Paul 16 bks.		1214	av. 75.9
Iavolenus 1 bk.		36	av. 36.0
Pomponius 1 bk.		22	av. 22.0

D 127	(ii)	Iav. Plaut. 2	53	7 bks. 614
128		Pomp. Plaut. 2–3	51	av. 87.7
129		Paul Plaut. 15–18	510	
130	(iii)	Iav. Plaut. 3–5	20	7 bks. 213
131		Pomp. Plaut. 4–7	193	av. 30.4
132	(iv)	Paul 4 Vitell.	315	4 bks. 315 av. 78.7

Total	18 bks.		1142	av. 63.4
				(3[15]) sections)
	Paul 8 bks.		825	av. 103.1
	Iavolenus 4 bks.		73	av. 18.2
	Pomponius 6 bks.		244	av. 48.8

(15 May–20 June 531: 4 barristers)

XVI	134–5	Celsus 39 dig.		1056	av. 27.1
		Marcellus 31 dig.		1056	av. 34.1
	Total	70 bks.		2112	av. 30.2 (11 sections)
	C 134–5	(i) Cels. dig. 1–4	86 ⎱	7 bks. 162	
		Marc. dig. 1–3	76 ⎰	av. 23.1	
		(iii) Cels. dig. 6–8	133 ⎱	5 bks. 158	
		Marc. dig. 5–6	25 ⎰	av. 31.6	
		(v) Cels. dig. 13–16	112 ⎱	8 bks. 260	
		Marc. dig. 9–12	148 ⎰	av. 32.5	
		(vii) Cels. dig. 22	16 ⎱	2 bks. 65	
		Marc. dig. 16	49 ⎰	av. 32.5	
		(ix) Cels. dig. 24–27	131 ⎱	8 bks. 300	
		Marc. dig. 18–21	169 ⎰	av. 37.5	
		(xi) Cels. dig. 36–39	89 ⎱	6 bks. 103	
		Marc. dig. 30–31	14 ⎰	av. 17.2	
	Total	36 bks.		1048	av. 29.1 (6 sections)
		Celsus 20 bks.		567	av. 28.3
		Marcellus 16 bks.		481	av. 30.1
	D 134–5	(ii) Cels. dig.[16])	71 ⎱	2 bks. 108	
		Marc. dig. 4	37 ⎰	av. 54.0	
		(iv) Cels. dig. 9–12	92 ⎱	6 bks. 240	
		Marc. dig. 7–8	148 ⎰	av. 40.0	
		(vi) Cels. dig. 17–21)	203 ⎱	8 bks. 375	
		Marc. dig. 13–15	172 ⎰	av. 41.9	
		(viii) Cels. dig. 23	42 ⎱	2 bks. 65	
		Marc. dig. 17	23 ⎰	av. 32.5	
		(x) Cels. dig. 28–35	81 ⎱	16 bks. 276	
		Marc. dig. 22–29	195 ⎰	av. 17.2	
	Total	34 bks.		1064	av. 31.3 (5 sections)
		Celsus 19 bks.		489	av. 25.7
		Marcellus 15 bks.		575	av. 38.3

(20 June–29 Aug. 531: 2 barristers)

[15] This group is of mixed or irregular composition. Though it is divided into sections, the commissioners did not read alternate sections but composed the group as a 'sandwich'. This was permissible because the works were not read jointly.

[16] Krüger has Celsus dig. 6 in section (ii) but none of the texts in this book appear to correspond to Marcellus dig. 4. He omits Marcellus dig. 6 from (iii) but see texts in Lenel, *Pal.* 1.598–601 corresponding to Celsus dig. 6–8.

XXII	136–40	Ulp. 3 off. cons.	409	av. 136.3
		Mod. 9 diff.	231	av. 25.7
		Mod. 1 manum.	44	av. 44.0
		Mod. 10 reg.	414	av. 41.4
		Mod. 1 rit. nupt.	5	av. 5.0
	Total	24 bks.	1103	av. 46.0
	C 136	Ulp. 3 off. cons.		
	137	Mod. 9 diff.		
	Total	12 bks.	640	av. 53.3
		Ulpian 3 bks.	409	av. 136.3
		Modestinus 9 bks.	231	av. 25.7
	D 138	Mod. 1 manum.		
	139	Mod. 10 reg.		
	140	Mod. 1 rit. nupt.		
	Total	12 bks.	463	av. 38.6
		Modestinus 12 bks.	463	av. 38.6

(29 Aug.–22 Sept. 531: no barristers)

XXIII	141–4[17])	Mod. 1 diff. dot.	5	av. 5.0	
	146–9	⎰ Mod. 6 exc.	628	av. 104.7	⎱ 8 bks. 655
		⎨ Ulp. 1 off. pr. tut.	19	av. 19.0	⎬ av. 81.9
		⎱ Ulp. 1 exc.	8	av. 8.0	⎰
		Mod. 19 resp.	839	av. 44.2	
		Mod. 1 enuc. cas.	34	av. 34.0	
		Mod. 1 praes.	29	av. 29.0	
		Mod. 12 pand.	385	av. 32.1	
	Total	42 bks.	1947	av. 46.4	
	C 141	Mod. 1 diff. dot.			
	142–	⎰ Mod. 6 exc.			
	144	⎨ Ulp. 1 off. prae. tut.			
		⎱ Ulp. 1 exc.			
	149	Mod. 12 pand.			
	Total	21 bks.	1045	av. 49.8	
		Modestinus 19 bks.	1018	av. 53.6	
		Ulpian 2 bks.	27	av. 13.5	
	D 146	Mod. 19 resp.			
	147	Mod. 1 enuc. cas.			
	148	Mod. 1 praescr.			
	Total	21 bks.	902	av. 43.0	
		Modestinus 21 bks.	902	av. 43.0	

(22 Sept.–3 Nov. 531: 2 barristers)

[17] 145 Mod. 4 praescr. omitted. Above, p. 168.

XXIV	150–5	Mod. 1 heurem.	95	av.	95.0
		Mod. 1 inoff. test.	5	av.	5.0
		Mod. 1 test.	0	av.	0.0
		Mod. 1 leg.et fid.	0	av.	0.0
		Iav. 15 Cass.	373	av.	24.9
		Iav. 14 epist.	674	av.	48.1
		Pomp. 39 Q. Muc.	1001	av.	25.7
		Proc. epist. 1–6	267	av.	44.5
	Total	78 bks.	2415	av.	31.0
	C 150	Mod. 1 heurem.			
	151	Mod. 1 inoff. test.			
	151a	Mod. 1 test.			
	151b	Mod. 1 leg.et fid.			
	152	Iav. 15 Cass.			
	153	Iav. 14 epist.			
	155	Proc. epist. 1–6			
	Total	39(37) bks.	1414	av.	36.3
		Modestinus 4 bks.	100	av.	25.0
		Iavolenus 29 bks.	1047	av.	36.1
		Proculus 6 bks.	267	av.	44.5
	D 154	Pomp. 39 Q. Muc.			
	Total	39 bks.	1001	av.	25.7
		Pomponius 39 bks.	1001	av.	25.7

(3 Nov. 531–20 Jan. 532: no barristers)

XXV	156–61	Pomp. 15 var. lect.	93	av.	6.2
		Proc. epist. 7–11	139	av.	27.8
		Call. 4 iur. fisc.	169	av.	42.2
		Paul 2 cens.	22	av.	11.0
		Call. 6 cogn.	720	av.	120.0
		Tert. 8 qu.	15	av.	1.9
	Total	40 bks.	1158	av.	28.9
	C 156	Pomp. 15 var. lect.			
	157	Proc. epist. 7–11			
	Total	20 bks.	232	av.	11.6
		Pomponius 15 bks.	93	av.	6.2
		Proculus 5 bks.	139	av.	27.8
	D 158	Call. 4 iur. fis.			
	159	Paul 2 cens.			
	160	Call. 6 cogn.			
	161	Tert. 8 quaest.			
	Total	20 bks.	926	av.	46.3
		Callistratus 10 bks.	889	av.	88.9

Paul 2 bks.		22	av. 11.0
Tertullianus 8 bks.		15	av. 1.9

(20 Jan.–29 Feb. 533: no barristers)

XXVI	162–7	Ulp. 20 leg. Iul. et Pap.	572	av. 28.6
		Paul 10 leg. Iul. et Pap.	481	av. 48.1
		Clem. 20 leg. Iul. et Pap.	243	av. 12.1
		Gai. 15 leg. Iul. et Pap.	166	av. 11.1
		Maur. 6 leg. Iul. et Pap.	37	av. 6.2
		Marc. 6 leg. Iul. et Pap.	40	av. 6.7
	Total	77 bks.	1539	av. 20.0 (6 sections)

C 162–7 (i) Ulp. leg. Iul. et Pap. 1   99 ⎱ 2 bks. 132
            Paul leg. Iul. et Pap. 1   33 ⎰ av. 66.0
        (iii) Gai. leg. Iul. et Pap. 1–2 14   2 bks. 14 av. 7.0
        (v) Clem. leg. Iul. et
            Pap. 1–20   243 ⎫
            Gai. leg. Iul. et Pap. 13–15 152 ⎬ 35 bks. 342
            Maur. leg. Iul. et Pap. 2–3 37 ⎭ av. 12.3

	Total	39 bks.	578	av. 14.8 (3 sections)
		Ulpian 1 bk.	99	av. 99.0
		Paul 1 bk.	33	av. 33.0
		Gaius 15 bks.	166	av. 11.1
		Clemens 20 bks.	243	av. 12.1
		Mauricianus 2 bks.	37	av. 18.5

D 162–7 (ii) Ulp. leg. Iul. et Pap. 2–5 165 ⎱ 8 bks. 395
             Paul leg. Iul. et Pap. 2–5 230 ⎰ av. 49.4
        (iv) Ulp. leg. Iul. et
             Pap. 6–15   247 ⎫
             Paul leg. Iul. et   ⎬ 15 bks. 465
             Pap. 6–10   218 ⎭ av. 31.0
        (vi) Marc. leg. Iul. et
             Pap. 1–3   40 ⎫ 8 bks. 101
             Ulp. leg. Iul. et   ⎬ av. 12.6
             Pap. 16–20   61 ⎭

	Total	31 bks.	961	av. 31.0 (3 sections)
		Ulpian 19 bks.	473	av. 24.9
		Paul 9 bks.	448	av. 49.8
		Marcellus 3 bks.	40	av. 13.3
		Mauricianus leg. Iul. et Pap.	1,	4–6 and Marcellus leg.
		Iul. et Pap. 4–6 unassigned.		

(29 Feb.–16 May 532: 4 barristers)

XXVII	168–70	Macer 2 leg. vic.	49	av. 24.5
		Gai. 1 leg. Glit.	5	av. 5.0
		Paul 1 leg. Cinc.	3	av. 3.0

Total	4 bks.	57	av.	14.2
C 168	Macer 2 leg. vic.			
Total	2 bks.	49	av.	24.5
	Macer 2 bks.	49	av.	24.5
D 169	Gai. 1 leg. Glit.			
170	Paul 1 leg. Cinc.			
Total	2 bks.	8	av.	4.0
	Gaius 1 bk.	5	av.	5.0
	Paul 1 bk.	3	av.	3.0

(16 May–20 May 532: no barristers)

XXVIII	171–2	Arr. Menan. 4 re. mil.	147	av.	36.7
		Tarr. Pater. 4 re. mil.	19	av.	4.7
	Total	8 bks.	166	av.	20.7
	C 171	Arr. Menan. 4 re. mil.			
	Total	4 bks.	147	av.	36.7
		Menander 4 bks.	147	av.	36.7
	D 172	Tarr. Pat. 4 re. mil.			
	Total	4 bks.	19	av.	4.7
		Tarruntenus 4 bks.	19	av.	4.7

(20 May 532–28 May 532: no barristers)

XXIX	173–7	Tert. 1 cast. pec.	43	av.	43.0
		Mod. 4 poen.	164	av.	41.0
		Lic. Ruf. 13 reg.	72	av.	5.5
		Call. ed. mon. 3–4	34	av.	17.0
		Pap. Iust. 20 const.	161	av.	8.0
	Total	40 bks.	474	av.	11.8
	C 173	Tert. 1 cast. pec.			
	174	Mod. 4 poen.			
	175	Lic. Ruf. 13 reg.			
	176	Call. ed. mon. 3–4			
	Total	20 bks.	313	av.	15.6
		Tertullianus 1 bk.	43	av.	43.0
		Modestinus 4 bks.	164	av.	41.0
		Rufinus 13 bks.	72	av.	5.5
		Callistratus 2 bks.	34	av.	17.0
	D 177	Pap. Iust. 20 const.			
	Total	20 bks.	161	av.	8.0
		Papirius 20 bks.	161	av.	8.0

(28 May–7 July 532: no barristers)

XXX	178–9	Ael. Gall. 1 verb. sign.	2	av.	2.0
		Iul. Aqu. 1 resp.	6	av.	6.0
	Total	2 bks.	8	av.	4.0
	C 178	Ael. Gall. 1 verb. sig.			
	Total	1 bk.	2	av.	2.0
		Aelius Gallus 1 bk.	2	av.	2.0
	D 179	Iul. Aquila 1 resp.			
	Total	1 bk.	6	av.	6.0
		Aquila 1 bk.	6	av.	6.0

(7–9 July 532: no barristers)

Summary of Edictal mass

Group	Books	Total lines	Average	Books	C Total lines	Average	Books	D Total lines	Average
XVIII	67¾	12,522	184.8	38¾	7050	182.3	25¹²⁄₁₂	5472	218.2
XIX	84¼	11,864	140.4	50¹⁄₁₂	6307	125.9	34⅙	5557	162.6
XX	36	2414	67.1	18	1272	70.7	18	1142	63.4
XXI	70	2112	30.2	36	1048	29.1	34	1064	31.3
XXII	24	1103	46.0	12	640	53.3	12	463	38.6
XXIII	42	1947	46.4	21	1045	49.8	21	902	43.0
XXIV	78	2415	31.0	39	1414	36.3	39	1001	25.7
XXV	40	1158	28.9	20	232	11.6	20	926	46.3
XXVI	77	1539	20.0	39	578	14.8	31	961	31.0
XXVII	4	57	14.2	2	49	24.5	2	8	4.0
XXVIII	8	166	20.7	4	147	36.7	4	19	4.7
XXIX	40	474	11.8	20	313	15.6	20	161	8.0
XXX	2	8	4.0	1	2	2.0	1	6	6.0
	573[18]	37,779	65.93	300¾	20,097	66.82	261¼	17,682	67.68

Papinian mass

XXXI	180–2	Pap. 37 qu.	3333	av.	90.1
		Pap. 19 resp.	3050	av.	160.5
		Pap. 2 def.	220	av.	110.0
	Total	58 Pap.	6603	av.	113.8
	E 180	Pap. quaest. 1–29	3131	av.	108.0
	Total	29 bks.	3131	av.	108.0
	F 180	Pap. quaest. 30–37	202	av.	25.2
	181	Pap. 19 resp.	3050	av.	160.5
	182	Pap. 2 def.	220	av.	110.0
	Total	29 bks.	3742	av.	119.7

(15 Dec. 530–5 March 531: no barristers)

[18] Includes eleven unassigned books: see group XVIII (4 books), XVI (7 books).

XXXII 183–4   Paul 26 quaest.   2261   av. 87.0
              Scaevola 20 quaest.   530   av. 26.5

     Total   46 bks.   2791   av. 60.7 (7 sections)

     E 183–4   (i) Paul qu. 1–3   580 ⎫ 5 bks. 737
                 Scae. qu. 1–2   157 ⎭ av. 147.4
           (iii) Paul qu. 9–11   320 ⎫ 6 bks. 375
                 Scae. qu. 7–9   55 ⎭ av. 62.5
           (v) Paul qu. 15   168 ⎫ 2 bks. 211
                 Scae. qu. 13   43 ⎭ av. 105.5
         (vii) Paul qu. 21–26   218 ⎫ 8 bks. 224
                 Scae. qu. 19–20   6 ⎭ av. 28.0

     Total   21 bks.   1547   av. 73.7 (4 sections)
          Paul 13 bks.   1286   av. 98.9
          Scaevola 8 bks.   261   av. 32.6

     F 183–4   (ii) Paul qu. 4–8   671 ⎫ 9 bks. 875
                 Scae. qu. 3–6   204 ⎭ av. 97.2
          (iv) Paul qu. 12–14   205 ⎫ 6 bks. 224
                 Scae. qu. 10–12   19 ⎭ av. 37.3
         (vi) Paul qu. 16–20   99 ⎫ 10 bks. 145
                 Scae. qu. 14–18   46 ⎭ av. 14.5

     Total   25 bks.   1244   av. 49.8 (3 sections)
          Paul 13 bks.   975   av. 75.0
          Scaevola 12 bks.   269   av. 22.4

     (5 March 531–9 May 531: 2 barristers)

XXXIII 185–204 Call. 2 quaest.   242   av. 121.0
              Paul 23 resp.   1373   av. 59.7
              Scae. 6 resp.   1599   av. 266.4
              Valens 7 fid.   178   av. 25.4
              Ulp. 6 fid.   1403   av. 233.8
              Maecianus 16 fid.   526   av. 32.9
              Gaius 2 fid.   191   av. 95.5
              Paul 3 fid.   157   av. 52.3
              Pomp. 5 fid.   70   av. 14.0

     Total   70 bks.   5739   av. 82.0 (7 sections)

     E 185   (i) Call. 2 quaest.   242   2 bks. 242 av. 121.0
       188   (iii) Paul resp. 8–15   684 ⎫ 11 bks. 1773
       189   Scae. resp. 2–4   1089 ⎭ av. 161.2
       192   (v) Paul resp. 20–23   17 ⎫ 5 bks. 63
       193   Scae. resp. 6   46 ⎭ av. 12.6
       200– (vii) Maec. fid. 9–16   157 ⎫
        4   Val. fid. 5–7   57 ⎪
                Pomp. fid. 3–5   19 ⎬ 17 bks. 838
                Ulp. fid. 5–6   517 ⎪ av. 49.3
                Paul fid. 3   88 ⎭

Total		35 bks.	2916	av. 83.3 (4 sections)
		Callistratus 2 bks.	242	av. 121.0
		Paul resp. 12 bks.	701	av. 58.4
		Scaevola 4 bks.	1135	av. 283.7
		Maecianus 8 bks.	157	av. 19.6
		Valens 3 bks.	57	av. 19.0
		Pomponius 3 bks.	19	av. 6.3
		Ulpian 2 bks.	517	av. 258.5
		Paul fid. 1 bk.	88	av. 88.0

F 186	(ii)	Paul resp. 1–7	571 ⎫	8 bks. 853
187		Scae. resp. 1	282 ⎭	av. 106.6
190	(iv)	Paul resp. 16–19	101 ⎫	5 bks. 283
191		Scae. resp. 5	182 ⎭	av. 56.6
194	(vi)	Valens fid. 1–4	121 ⎫	
195		Ulp. fid. 1–4	886	
196		Maec. fid. 1–8	369 ⎬	22 bks. 1687
197		Gaius 2 fid.	191	av. 76.7
198		Paul fid. 1–2	69	
199		Pomp. fid. 1–2	51 ⎭	

Total		35 bks.	2823	av. 80.7 (3 sections)
		Paul resp. 11 bks.	672	av. 61.1
		Scaevola 2 bks.	464	av. 232.0
		Valens 4 bks.	121	av. 30.2
		Ulpian 4 bks.	886	av. 221.5
		Maecianus 8 bks.	369	av. 46.1
		Gaius 2 bks.	191	av. 95.5
		Paul fid. 2 bks.	69	av. 34.5
		Pomp. 2 bks.	51	av. 25.5

(9 May–15 Aug. 531: 2 barristers to 21 June, then 9)

XXXIV	205–15	Paul 5 sent.	882	av. 176.4
		Hermogenianus 6 iur. epit.	612	av. 102.0
		Gaius 1 cas.	39	av. 39.0
		(?) Scaevola 1 qu. fam.[19])	0	av. 0.0

Total		13(12) bks.	1533	av. 117.9 (6 sections)

E 205	(i)	Paul sent. 1 init.	170 ⎫	1½ bks. 339
206		Herm. iur. epit. 1	169 ⎭	av. 226.0
209	(iii)	Paul sent. 3	112 ⎫	2 bks. 187
210		Herm. iur. epit. 3	75 ⎭	av. 93.5
213	(v)	Paul sent. 5	342 ⎫	3 bks. 508
214		Herm. iur. epit. 5–6	166 ⎭	av. 169.3

Total		6½ bks.	1034	av. 159.1 (3 sections)
		Paul 2½ bks.	624	av. 249.6
		Herm. 4 bks.	310	av. 77.5

[19] One *liber singularis* should be inserted here if the principle of equality is to be respected. See above, p. 164.

F 207	(ii)	Paul sent. 1 fin., 2	223 ⎫	2½ bks. 377	
208		Herm. iur. epit. 2	154 ⎭	av. 150.8	
211	(iv)	Paul sent. 4	35 ⎫	2 bks. 83	
212		Herm. iur. epit. 4	48 ⎭	av. 41.5	
215	(vi)	Gaius 1 cas.	39 ⎫	2 bks. 39	
215a		? Scae. 1 qu. fam.	0 ⎭	av. 19.5	

Total	6½ (5½) bks.	499	av. 76.8 (3 sections)	
	Paul 2½ bks.	258	av. 103.2	
	Herm. 2 bks.	202	av. 101.0	
	Gaius 1 bk.	39	av. 39.0	
	? Scaevola 1 bk.	0	av. 0.0	

(15 Aug.–2 Sept. 531: 2 barristers)

XXXV	216–19	Venul. 19 stip.	282	av. 14.8
		Neratius 3 resp.	51	av. 17.0
		Paul 4 Nerat.	164	av. 41.1
		Tryph. disp. 1–12	809	av. 66.5

Total	38 bks.	1306	av. 34.4

E 216	Venul. 19 stip.	

Total	19 bks.	282	av. 14.8
	Venuleius 19 bks.	282	av. 14.8

F 217	Nerat. 3 resp.	
218	Paul 4 Nerat.	
219	Tryph. disp. 1–12	

Total	19 bks.	1024	av. 53.9
	Neratius 3 bks.	51	av. 17.0
	Paul 4 bks.	164	av. 41.1
	Tryphoninus 12 bks.	809	av. 66.5

(2 Sept.–25 Oct. 531: no barristers)

XXXVI	220–3	Paul 3 man.	174	av. 58.0
		Tryph. disp. 13–21	589	av. 65.4
		Paul 3 decr.	340	av. 113.3
		Gaius 3 reg.	6	av. 2.0

Total	18 bks.	1109	av. 61.6

E 220	Paul 3 man.	
222	Paul 3 decr.	
223	Gaius 3 reg.	

Total	9 bks.	520	av. 57.8
	Paul 6 bks.	514	av. 85.7
	Gaius 3 bks.	6	av. 2.0

F 221	Tryph. disp. 13–21	

Total　　9 bks.　　　　　　　　　　　　589　　av. 65.4
　　　　　Tryphoninus 9 bks.　　　　　589　　av. 65.4

(25 Oct.–19 Nov. 531: no barristers)

XXXVII　225–　　Paul 1 cogn.　　　　　　　　28　　av. 28.0
　　　　　38[20])　Paul 1 conc. act.　　　　　32　　av. 32.0
　　　　　　　　　Paul 1 usur.　　　　　　　46　　av. 46.0
　　　　　　　　　Paul 1 SC Turpill.　　　　16　　av. 16.0
　　　　　　　　　Marci. 1 SC Turpill.　　　101　　av. 101.0
　　　　　　　　　Paul 1 SC Lib.　　　　　　50　　av. 50.0
　　　　　　　　　Paul 1 SC Claud.　　　　　6　　av. 6.0
　　　　　　　　　Paul 1 poen. omn.　　　　　7　　av. 7.0
　　　　　　　　　Paul 1 poen. pag.　　　　　14　　av. 14.0
　　　　　　　　　Paul 1 reg. Cat.　　　　　　9　　av. 9.0
　　　　　　　　　Paul 1 form. test.　　　　　6　　av. 6.0
　　　　　　　　　Paul 1 inoff. test.　　　　28　　av. 28.0
　　　　　　　　　Paul 1 tac. fid.　　　　　14　　av. 14.0
　　　　　　　　　Paul 1 instr. signif.　　　23　　av. 23.0

Total　　14 bks.　　　　　　　　　　380　　av. 27.1

E 225　　Paul 1 cogn.
　226　　Paul 1 conc. act.
　227　　Paul 1 usur.
　228　　Paul 1 SC Turpill.
　229　　Marci. 1 SC Turp.
　230　　Paul 1 SC Lib.
　231　　Paul 1 SC Claud.

Total　　7 bks.　　　　　　　　　　　279　　av. 39.9
　　　　　Paul 6 bks.　　　　　　　　178　　av. 29.7
　　　　　Marcianus 1 bk.　　　　　　101　　av. 101.0

F 232　　Paul 1 poen. omn.
　233　　Paul 1 poen. pag.
　234　　Paul 1 reg. Cat.
　235　　Paul 1 form. test.
　236　　Paul 1 inoff. test.
　237　　Paul 1 tac. fid.
　238　　Paul 1 instr. sign.

Total　　7 bks.　　　　　　　　　　　101　　av. 14.4
　　　　　Paul 7 bks.　　　　　　　　101　　av. 14.4

(19 Nov.–9 Dec. 531: no barristers)

XXXVIII　239–44　Paul 1 SC Tert.　　　　　22　　av. 22.0
　　　　　　　　　Paul 1 SC Orf.　　　　　　12　　av. 12.0
　　　　　　　　　Paul 1 leg. Falc.　　　　152　　av. 152.0

[20] 224 Gai. 1 reg. transferred to group ix, 39a. Above, pp. 168, 262.

		Gaius 1 tac. fid.	7	av.	7.0
		Gaius 1 SC Tert.	3	av.	3.0
		Gaius 1 SC Orf.	3	av.	3.0
	Total	6 bks.	199	av.	33.2
E	239	Paul 1 SC Tert.			
	240	Paul 1 SC Orf.			
	241	Paul 1 leg. Falc.			
	Total	3 bks.	186	av.	62.0
		Paul 3 bks.	186	av.	62.0
F	242	Gaius 1 tac. fid.			
	243	Gaius 1 SC Tert.			
	244	Gaius 1 SC Orf.			
	Total	3 bks.	13	av.	4.3
		Gaius 3 bks.	13	av.	4.3

(9 Dec.–17 Dec. 531: no barristers)

XXXIX	245–7	Gaius 3 manum.	42	av.	14.0
		Gaius 3 verb. obl.	187	av.	62.0
		Gaius 6 leg. XII tab.	158	av.	26.3
	Total	12 bks.	387	av.	32.2
E	245	Gaius 3 manum.			
	246	Gaius 3 verg. obl.			
	Total	6 bks.	229	av.	38.2
		Gaius 6 bks.	229	av.	38.2
F	247	Gaius 6 leg. XII tab.			
	Total	6 bks.	158	av.	26.3
		Gaius 6 bks.	158	av.	26.3

(17 Dec. 531–3 Jan. 532: no barristers)

XL	248–62	Pomp. 2 enchir.	16	av.	8.0
		Pomp. 1 enchir.	452	av.	452.0
		Paul 1 iur. lib.	8	av.	8.0
		Paul 1 art. lib. caus.	8	av.	8.0
		Paul 1 iur. fact. ign.	63	av.	63.0
		Paul 1 iur. sing.	11	av.	11.0
		Paul 1 grad.	480	av.	480.0
		Paul 1 off. adses.	25	av.	25.0
		Paul 1 off. prae. vig.	58	av.	58.0
		Ulp. 1 off. prae. vig.	1	av.	1.0
		Ulp. 1 off. prae. urb.	72	av.	72.0
		Paul 1 off. prae. urb.	3	av.	3.0
		Arc. Char. 1 mun. civ.	101	av.	101.0

	Arc. Char. 1 off. prae. praet.	26	av. 26.0
	Ulp. 1 off. quaest.	29	av. 29.0
Total	16 bks.	1353	av. 84.6

E 248	Pomp. 2 enchir.	
249	Pomp. 1 enchir.	
250	Paul 1 iur. lib.	
251	Paul 1 art. lib. caus.	
252	Paul 1 iur. et fact. ignor.	
253	Paul 1 iur. sing.	
254	Paul 1 grad.	

Total	8 bks.	1038	av. 129.7
	Pomponius 3 bks.	468	av. 156.0
	Paul 5 bks.	570	av. 114.0

F 255	Paul 1 off. adses.
256	Paul 1 off. prae. vig.
257	Ulp. 1 off. prae. vig.
258	Ulp. 1 off. prae. urb.
259	Paul 1 off. prae. urb.
260	Arc. Char. 1 mun. civ.
261	Arc. Char. 1 off. prae. praet.
262	Ulp 1 off. quaest.

Total	8 bks.	315	av. 39.4
	Paul 3 bks.	86	av. 28.7
	Ulpian 3 bks.	102	av. 34.0
	Charisius 2 bks.	127	av. 63.5

(3–25 Jan. 532: no barristers)

XLI 263–6	Paul 6 imp. sent.	27	av. 4.5
	Q.Mucius 1 horon	20	av. 20.0
	Labeo 10 post. Iav. epit.[21])	374	av. 37.4
	Proc. 3 post. Lab.	11	av. 3.7
Total	20 bks.	432	av. 21.6

E 263	Paul 6 imp. sent.	
264	Q. Mucius 1 horon	
266	Proc. 3 post. Lab.	

Total	10 bks.	58	av. 5.8
	Paul 6 bks.	27	av. 4.5
	Q. Muc. 1 bk.	20	av. 20.0
	Proc. 3 bks.	11	av. 3.7

[21] This figure is reached by counting the texts with the inscription 'Labeo' rather than 'Iavolenus'. In fact F also excerpted the texts inscribed 'Iavolenus'. If these are assigned to him to total figures for the Papinian committee and for F are modified as in note 22 below.

F 265   Labeo 10 post. Iav. epit.

Total	10 bks.	374	av.	37.4
	Labeo 10 bks.	374	av.	37.4

(25 Jan.–22 Feb. 532: no barristers)

XLII 267–8

	Scae. 40 dig.	3190	av.	79.7
	Lab. 8 Paul epit.	299	av.	37.4
Total	48 bks.	3489	av.	72.7 (4 sections)

E 267

	(i) Scae. dig. 1–13	608	av.	46.8
	(iii) Scae. dig. 30–40	83	av.	7.5
Total	24 bks.	691	av.	28.8 (2 sections)
	Scaevola 24 bks.	691	av.	28.8

F 267
268

	(ii) Scae. dig. 14–29	2499	av.	156.2
	(iv) Lab. 8 Paul epit.	299	av.	37.4
Total	24 bks.	2798	av.	116.6 (2 sections)

(22 Feb.–30 April 532: no barristers)

XLIII 269–75

	Pomp. 20 epist.	258	av.	12.9
	Pomp. 5 SCC	103	av.	20.6
	Scae. 1 qu. pub. tract.	158	av.	158.0
	Val. 7 act.	6	av.	0.9
	Venul. 10 act.	51	av.	5.1
	Venul. 6 interd.	246	av.	41.0
	Fur. Anth. led.	15	av.	15.0
Total	50 bks.	837	av.	16.7

E 269
270

	Pomp. 20 epist.			
	Pomp. 5 SCC			
Total	25 bks.	361	av.	14.4
	Pomponius 25 bks.	361	av.	14.4

F 271
272
273
274
275

	Scae. 1 qu. pub. tract.
	Val. 7 act.
	Venul. 10 act.
	Venul. 6 interd.
	Fur. Anth. 1 ed.

Total	25 bks.	476	av.	19.0
	Scaevola 1 bk.	158	av.	158.0
	Valens 7 bks.	6	av.	0.9
	Venuleius 16 bks.	297	av.	18.6
	Furius 1 bk.	15	av.	15.0

(30 April–9 July 532: no barristers)

Summary of Papinian mass

Group	Books	Total lines	Average	E Books	Total lines	Average	F Books	Total lines	Average
XXXI	58	6603	113.8	29	3131	108.0	29	3472	119.7
XXXII	46	2791	60.7	21	1547	73.7	25	1244	49.8
XXXIII	70	5739	82.0	35	2916	83.3	35	2823	80.7
XXXIV	13	1533	117.9	6½	1034	159.1	6½	499	76.8
XXXV	38	1306	34.4	19	282	14.8	19	1024	53.9
XXXVI	18	1109	61.6	9	520	57.8	9	589	65.4
XXXVII	14	380	27.1	7	279	39.9	7	101	14.4
XXXVIII	6	199	33.2	3	186	62.0	3	13	4.3
XXXIX	12	387	32.2	6	229	38.2	6	158	26.3
XL	16	1353	84.6	8	1038	129.7	8	315	39.4
Total (main mass)	291	21,400	73.54	143½	11,162	77.78	147½	10,238	69.41
Appendix									
XLI	20	432	21.6	10	58	5.8	10	374	37.4
XLII	48	3489	72.6	24	691	28.8	24	2798	116.6
XLIII	50	837	16.7	25	361	14.4	25	476	19.0
Total (Appendix)	118	4758	40.32	59	1110	18.81	59	3648	61.83
Total (whole mass)	409[22]	26,158	63.96	202½	12,272	60.60	206½	13,886	67.24

Summary of whole Digest

	Books	Total lines	Average	A Books	Total lines	Average	B Books	Total lines	Average
Sabinian[22] mass	546	49,364	90.41	303	27,604	91.10	235	21,760	92.60
				C			D		
Edictal mass	573	37,779	65.93	300¾	20,097	66.82	261¼	17,682	67.68
				E			F		
Papinian[23] mass	409	26,158	63.96	202½	12,272	60.60	206½	13,886	67.24
Grand total	1528	113,301	74.15						

Key: A = Tribonian, B = Dorotheus, C = Theophilus, D = Anatolius, E = Constantinus, F = Cratinus.

[22] See note 8, above.

[23] If the changes indicated in n. 7, 21 above are made the figures read: 419 26,683 63.68 202½ 12,272 60.60 216½ 14,411 66.56.

APPENDIX TWO

List of words and phrases discussed in the text and footnotes. References are to chapters and notes: thus 3[69] refers to chapter 3, note 69.

APPENDIX THREE
Table of Legal Texts

References in the form 1[370] are to chapters and footnotes.
References in the form 36 are to pages.

Gaius *Institutes*
1.7: 1[370]
1.53: 9[90]
1.170: 3[366], 9[27]

4.30: 9[90]

Codex Theodosianus
1.1.5: 1[146], 2[92], 5[6, 74], 9[62]
1.1.6: 5[7]; – 6.1: 9[55]; – 6.2: 5[75]; – 6.3: 5[87], 9[55]
1.4.2: 5[1]; – 3: 2[103], 3[47]
1.5.13: 216
1.6.7: 216
1.9.1: 216
1.10.7: 216
1.11.1: 216; – 2: 216
1.12.5: 216; – 7: 216
1.14.1: 216

2.1.7: 217
2.8.26: 217
2.9.2: 217
2.10.3: 217
2.12.4: 217
2.16.2: 217
2.17.1: 217
2.19.1: 217; – 2: 217
2.26.5: 213; – 1: 217

3.1.4: 213
3.5.2.1: 213
3.6.1: 216
3.7.1: 216
3.8.2: 216
3.11.1: 216
3.13.3: 3[313], 213, 217

3.16.2: 213, 217; – 3: 3[313]
3.17.4: 213

4.3.1: 218
4.4.3: 3[37]
4.6.6: 218
4.10.1: 218; – 2: 218; – 3: 218
4.13.9: 218
4.14.1: 218
4.20.3: 3[425], 213
4.21.1: 218
4.22.3: 218, 222

5.1.8: 217
5.10.1: 217
5.18.1: 217

6.4.16: 218
6.5.2: 218
6.10.4: 2[38]
6.12.1: 218
6.17.1: 218
6.22.8: 2[38]
6.23.1: 218; – 3: 218
6.24.9: 218
6.26.8: 218; – 14: 218
6.28.4: 218
6.31.1: 218
6.32.2: 218
6.35.3: 218; – 13: 218

7.1.13: 218; – 15: 218; – 17 pr: 213, 218; – 17.1: 213; – 18: 213, 218
7.4.12: 219; – 26: 219; – 35: 219

7.8.2: 3[432], 213; – 8: 219
7.9.2: 219
7.13.11: 219
7.20.2: 219

8.1.16: 219
8.4.2: 219; – 15: 219; – 28: 219
8.5.2: 219; – 3: 219; – 22: 219; – 25: 219; – 35: 219; – 40: 219; – 41: 219; – 51: 219; – 57: 219; – 58: 219
8.7.7: 219; – 17: 219; – 18: 219; – 19: 219; – 20: 219; – 21: 219
8.8.6: 219; – 7: 219; – 9: 219
8.12.2: 219
8.13.1: 219; – 6: 219
8.18.1: 219; – 5: 219; – 7: 219

9.1.1: 220
9.2.3: 220
9.3.5: 220
9.7.7: 220
9.16.11: 220
9.19.1: 1[359]; – 2: 3[374], 213
9.25.2: 220
9.26.3: 220
9.28.1: 220
9.34.7: 220, 222
9.37.1: 220; – 2: 220; – 4: 220
9.42.1: 220; – 24: 220

CTh
9.43.1: 3[36]

10.10.30: 217
10.19.15: 217
10.20.1: 217; – 13: 217
10.21.2: 217; – 3: 217

11.1.14: 220; – 25: 220
11.8.1: 220; – 2: 220; – 3: 220
11.9.2: 220
11.13.2: 3[426]
11.13.3: 1[194]
11.16.6: 220; – 11: 220
11.30.1: 7[26], 220; – 2: 220; – 6: 220; – 16: 1[74]; – 30: 220
11.35.1: 220
11.36.4: 220; – 20: 7[26], 220; – 26: 220
11.37.1: 220

12.1.3: 1[359]; – 6: 222; – 51: 221; – 152: 7[178], 213, 221
12.3.1: 221
12.5.3: 221
12.6.2: 221; – 13: 221; – 30: 222
12.7.2: 214, 221

16.2.31: 214; – 45: 221
16.5.65: 221
16.6.6: 221
16.8.22: 221
16.9.2: 221
16.10.24: 221

Pre-Justinian *Novels*
Marjorian *Nov.*
2.7.: 1[195]
2.14: 1[191]

Valentinian *Nov.*
10.32: 1[195]
13.15: 1[190]
15.18: 1[195]

Prefaces to Justinian's *Codes*
C. Cordi: 1[176], 7[1]
pr: 1[227], 3[367], 449, 514, 545, 721, 722, 812
1: 2[134], 3[114], 387, 462, 5[24], 65
2: 2[2], 136, 141, 144, 3[208], 691, 782, 5[132], 8[150], 202
3: 3[40], 51, 107, 222, 305, 366, 404, 415, 460, 695, 731, 764, 793, 822
4: 1[298], 2[134], 3[172], 248, 404, 458, 539, 686, 731, 791
5: 5[65]
6: 3[343]

C. Dedôken: 41
pr: 42
9: 2[5], 5[100]
11: 2[5]
12: 2[87], 105, 5[23]
17: 2[5]

C. Deo auctore, see *CJ* 1.17.1

C. Haec: 2[36], 3[26], 7[1, 28]
pr: 1[146], 2[72], 158, 8[99], 104
1: 1[114], 2[2], 12, 37, 41 44, 3[26], 587, 5[76], 82, 120, 7[29], 8[102], 106, 122, 142, 153, 208
2: 8[102], 118, 120, 9[58], 87
3: 1[147], 2[72], 5[61, 62], 8[106]

C. Imperatoriam: 188
pr: 3[143], 383, 689, 770, 112
1: 3[164], 415, 416, 754, 774, 786, 112
2: 2[97], 3[204], 300, 545, 713, 112, 9[66]
3: 2[2], 3, 136, 3[364], 467, 514, 112, 5[138], 6[1, 5]
4: 2[2, 3]
5: 6[9, 24], 9[91]

6: 2[32], 77, 3[40], 712, 766, 6[13, 14]
7: 2[78], 3[207], 112, 6[7]

C. Omnem: inscr.: 5[86]
pr: 3[383], 431, 493, 759, 835, 113
1: 2[32], 3[40], 48, 282, 300, 341, 366, 394, 412, 526, 545, 739, 766, 778, 800, 829, 113, 5[150], 6[12, 14], 9[66, 68, 99]
2: 1[148], 2[2], 3, 3[74], 147, 157, 194, 317, 326, 394, 460, 545, 726, 734, 749, 831, 838, 113, 9[68]
3: 2[144], 3[210], 394, 514, 545, 757, 113
4: 2[82], 3[41], 48, 78, 89, 112, 149, 207, 209, 283, 339, 367, 416, 545, 780, 830, 113, 184
5: 1[354], 3[40], 48, 93, 112, 113, 6[12]
6: 2[2]
7: 2[28], 29, 3[75], 207, 545, 792, 113
8: 3[112], 511, 828, 113
9: 3[207], 326, 370, 113
11: 1[185], 352, 3[107], 415, 113, 9[91]

C. Summa: 3[26], 652, 7[1]
pr: 3[131], 752, 769, 8[102], 104, 106, 120, 122
1: 3[132], 133, 5[82], 8[102], 105, 106
2: 2[2], 12, 66, 158, 3[26], 5[120], 8[102], 143, 154
3: 3[50], 7[176], 8[102]
4: 8[104], 131
5: 8[106]
6: 1[315]

C. Tanta, see *CJ* 1.17.2

Codex Iustinianus
1.1.2.2: 8[55]; – 4: 3[267]; – 5: 1[269]; – 5.2: 1[106]; – 5.3: 1[106]; – 6: 1[269]; –

CJ

11; − 2.10: 3^{115}, 160, 168, 367, 370, 414, 538, 539, 797, 818, 113, 9^{47}, 61; − 2.11: 1^{353}, 2^{3}, 3^{51}, 114, 207, 242, 289, 290, 326, 361, 460, 525, 691, 720, 752, 808, 809, 113, 5^{14}, 6^{299}, 7^{24}; − 2.12: 2^{85}, 3^{413}, 515, 545, 771, 734, 842, 113, 5^{22}, 8^{122}; − 2.13: 1^{196}, 3^{51}, 172, 232, 366, 367, 405, 426, 798, 843, 113; − 2.14: 3^{160}, 370, 545, 113; − 2.15: 3^{205}, 113; − 2.16: 3^{367}, 369, 113; − 2.17: 1^{196}, 2^{3}, 3^{207}, 319, 366, 412, 426, 525, 545, 755, 775, 795, 800, 113, 5^{68}; − 2.18: 1^{298}, 299, 2^{114}, 249, 3^{41}, 162, 172, 183, 281, 310, 348, 404, 405, 407, 445, 447, 454, 538, 826, 113; − 2.19: 1^{185}, 2^{249}, 3^{128}, 385, 643, 747, 113, 9^{91}; − 2.20: 1^{350}, 3^{51}, 409, 514, 536, 113, 9^{9}, 66; − 2.20a: 3^{368}, 490, 727, 113, 9^{47}; − 2.21: 2^{249}, 3^{205}, 225, 230, 310, 333, 389, 394, 476, 477, 539, 545, 727, 736, 789, 835, 74, 113; − 2.22: 3^{74}, 394, 455, 493, 545, 810, 113; − 2.23: 3^{112}, 201, 297, 370, 538, 752, 113

1.18.1: 3^{238}
1.19.3: 7^{58}; − 5: 3^{416}
1.20.2: 3^{378}
1.21.1: 7^{155}
1.22.5: 3^{242}
1.27.1: 1^{268}, 3^{624}, 110; − 1.pr-4: 1^{11}; − 1.6: 1^{224}; − 1.8: 1^{266}; − 1.10: 3^{671}; − 1.12: 3^{671}; − 1.21: 3^{671}; − 2: 1^{268}, 3^{617}, 110; − 2.1: 3^{703}; − 2.2: 3^{703}; − 2.7: 3^{671}
1.28.3: 3^{259}
1.29.3: 8^{107}; − 5: 3^{127}, 368, 802, 116
1.30.1: 3^{158}; − 2: 3^{158}; − 3: 8^{24}

1.31.1: 7^{35}; − 5.1: 8^{56}, 8.5; − 5.2: 8^{64}
1.32.1: 7^{36}
1.33.2: 7^{37}
1.35.1: 7^{24}
1.37.1: 7^{41}, 84
1.39.1: 7^{76}
1.40.3: 3^{268}; − 6: 3^{193}; − 14: 3^{477}
1.49.1.2: 8^{44}
1.51.1: 3^{515}, 8^{51}; − 5: 3^{416}; − 6: 7^{101}; − 7: 3^{267}; − 14.pr: 3^{406}, 427, 106; − 14.1: 3^{412}, 106; − 14.2: 3^{206}, 237, 429, 106; − 14.3: 3^{325}, 453, 106
1.53.1.3: 8^{118}
1.54.3: 3^{166}; − 6: 8^{107}
1.55.9: 7^{149}; − 11: 8^{2}

2.7.26: 3^{673}, 831; − 26.pr: 8^{44}; − 26.1: 8^{32}; − 27: 8^{31}, 71; − 29.pr: 3^{231}, 382; − 29.1: 3^{416}
2.9.1: 6^{307}; − 3: 8^{124}
2.12.23: 3^{50}, 8^{121}
2.18.24.pr: 3^{168}; − 24.1: 3^{40}, 434, 5^{26}; − 24.2: 3^{172}, 173, 187, 237, 370, 400
2.19.2: 3^{542}
2.21.1: 8^{110}; − 13: 3^{372}
2.24.5: 3^{422}
2.40.5. pr: 3^{96}; − 5.1: 2^{114}, 3^{178}, 292, 414, 548
2.41.1: 3^{542}; − 2: 3^{51}, 168, 238, 386
2.44.1: 3^{346}, 8^{107}; − 2: 7^{63}; − 3: 8^{107}; − 4: 3^{550}
2.46.3.pr: 3^{161}, 169; − 3.1: 3^{303}; − 3.2: 3^{51}, 93, 122, 307, 367
2.50.8: 8^{124}
2.52.5.pr: 7^{62}; − 5.2: 3^{368}; − 6: 3^{446}; − 7.pr: 3^{152}, 165, 388, 417, 419, 420; 7.2: 3^{313}, 372
2.55.4.1: 3^{382}, 107; − 4.2: 3^{277}, 371, 107; 4.3: 3^{371}, 402, 107; − 4.5: 3^{51},

371, 107; − 4.6: 3^{166}, 417, 418, 107; − 4.7: 3^{411}, 435, 503, 542, 107; − 5.pr: 3^{113}, 367, 402, 408, 519; − 5.3: 3^{40}, 70, 294, 406, 533; − 6: 3^{172}, 176

2.58.1.pr: 3^{186}, 365, 371, 106, 8^{4}; − 2.pr: 3^{111}, 408, 514; − 2.2: 3^{371}; − 2.2a: 3^{172}; − 2.3a: 3^{371}; −2.4: 3^{112}, 126, 408, 424, 453, 505, 544; − 2.6: 3^{353}; − 2.8: 3^{371}; − 2.8a: 2^{114}, 3^{385}; − 2.9: 3^{514}; − 2.11: 3^{409}, 539; − 2.12: 3^{383}, 401

3.1.13.pr: 3^{495}; − 13.1: 3^{398}, 401; − 13.2: 3^{380}, 408, 486; − 13.2a: 3^{408}; − 13.2b: 3^{102}, 415, 7^{24}; − 13.2c: 3^{79}, 201, 416, 520; − 13.3: 3^{408}, 415; − 13.4: 3^{346}, 404, 408, 454; − 13.5: 3^{101}, 302; − 13.8: 3^{317}, 401; − 13.8a: 3^{220}, 378, 404; − 13.9: 3^{384}, 408, 423; − 13.11: 3^{544}; − 14.pr: 3^{70}, 490; − 14.1: 3^{107}, 222, 268, 431, 514; − 14.2: 3^{397}; − 14.3: 3^{193}; − 14.4: 3^{371}, 426; − 14.5: 3^{331}, 371; − 15: 3^{550}; − 16: 3^{146}, 159, 310, 384, 407, 449; − 17: 3^{410}; − 18: 3^{171}, 373, 384, 397

3.2.3.1: 3^{453}; − 4: 5^{182}; − 5: 5^{182}
3.4.1.2: 3^{333}
3.6.3: 8^{124}
3.10.2: 5^{182}; − 3: 2^{130}, 159, 191, 3^{192}, 656, 109
3.11.5: 8^{129}
3.13.1.pr: 8^{51}; − 1.1: 8^{116}; − 7.pr: 8^{2}, 5; − 7.1: 3^{516}, 83, 4, 6
3.15.2: 3^{388}
3.21.2: 3^{376}
3.22.5: 3^{376}; − 6: 3^{61}, 8^{132}, 235
3.24.1: 7^{131}; − 3: 3^{410}, 8^{130}
3.25.1.1: 3^{481}

CJ

3.27.1: 3[414]

3.28.1: 6[307]; – 3.1: 6[307]; – 27: 7[27, 64]; – 28: 3[172], 7[65]; – 30: 8[136]; – 30.pr: 8[99, 102]; – 30.1: 3[61], 7[176], 8[117, 129, 131]; – 31: 3[404], 8[117]; – 32: 3[61, 404], 8[132]; – 33.pr: 3[70, 186, 316, 367, 478]; – 33.1: 3[40, 42, 46, 153, 172, 173, 388, 452]; – 34.pr: 3[392]; – 34.1: 3[95, 156, 180, 264, 284, 404, 407, 426]; – 35.pr: 3[443]; – 35.1: 3[40, 425]; – 35.2: 3[404]; – 35.3: 3[517]; – 36.pr: 3[404]; – 36.1: 3[167, 313]; – 36.1a: 3[404]; – 36.1b: 3[355, 404]; – 36.1c: 3[168]; – 36.2: 3[40, 383, 416, 424]; – 36.2a: 3[269, 378, 528]; – 36.2b: 3[264, 284]; – 37.pr: 3[376]; – 37.1a: 3[367]; – 37.1d: 3[168]; – 37.1e: 3[169, 355, 366, 367]; – 37.1f: 3[396]

3.29.1: 3[453]

3.31.1.2: 8[112]; – 6: 7[24]; – 7.1: 3[425]; – 12.pr: 3[415]; – 12.1: 3[138, 376, 396]; – 12.2: 3[378]

3.32.12: 3[222]; – 19: 3[386]

3.33.12: 5[33]; – 12.pr: 1[188], 3[383, 392, 426], 5[26]; – 12.1: 1[188], 3[51, 177, 179, 366, 426, 473]; – 13: 5[36]; – 13.pr: 3[172, 374]; – 13.1: 3[181]; – 13.2: 3[399]; – 13.3: 3[259]; – 13.4: 5[65], 8[117]; – 14: 5[36]; – 14.pr: 3[167]; – 14.1: 3[249, 346, 386, 410], 5[26]; – 14.2: 3[87, 452]; – 15: 5[36]; – 15.pr: 3[515]; – 15.1: 3[40, 107]; – 15.2: 3[40, 172, 173, 178, 196, 245, 249, 272, 370], 5[26]; – 16: 5[36]; – 16.pr: 3[51, 168, 367, 410]; – 16.1: 3[388], 5[26]; – 16.2: 3[403]; – 17.pr: 3[41, 44, 168]; – 17.1: 3[390]; – 17.2: 3[542]

3.34.13: 3[374, 378, 417, 419, 425, 484]; – 14.pr: 3[40, 272, 273, 323], 109; – 14.1: 3[172, 173, 407, 730, 777], 109

3.36.25: 8[4]

3.38.1: 6[307]; – 3: 3[414]; – 3.1: 6[307]; – 12.pr: 3[89, 416, 546], 8[110, 112]; – 12.3: 3[89, 423]

3.39.6: 213
3.40.1: 3[425]
3.42.5: 3[29]; – 9: 3[172]
3.43.1: 5[186]

4.1.11.pr: 3[388, 416, 454], 106; – 11.2: 3[79, 244, 371, 416], 106; – 12.pr: 3[199, 293, 371, 392], 107; – 12.1: 3[371], 107; – 12.1a: 3[335, 371], 107; – 12.2a: 3[289]; – 12.2c: 3[397], 107, 8[130]; – 12.3: 2[114], 3[371], 107, 8[53]; – 12.4a: 3[371, 481], 107; – 12.4b: 3[371], 107; – 12.4c: 3[397], 101; – 12.4d: 3[371, 416, 422], 107; – 12.6: 3[404], 107; – 13.pr: 3[167, 365, 367]; – 13.1: 3[414]

4.2.3: 8[107]; – 17: 2[73], 8[109, 117, 136]

4.3.1.2: 3[60]
4.5.4: 3[483]; – 10: 3[45], 5[33]; – 10.pr: 3[168]; – 10.1: 3[40, 298, 504]; – 10.2: 3[40], 5[27]; – 11: 5[36]; – 11.pr: 2[115], 3[490]; – 11.1: 5[26]

4.6.1: 6[307]; – 8: 1[193]

4.10.12: 8[4]

4.11.1.pr: 3[242, 366, 386, 521]; – 1.1: 3[51]; – 1.2: 3[399, 489, 495]

4.13.3: 3[346]
4.16.4: 8[53]
4.18.2.pr: 3[172, 222]; – 2.1: 1[188], 3[51, 127, 367, 372, 378, 388, 407, 416, 424, 426]; – 2.1a: 3[490]; – 2.1c: 1[188]; – 2.1d: 3[51, 333, 515]; – 3: 3[550], 8[117]

4.19.23: 3[172]; – 25: 3[407]

4.20.5: 8[107]; – 7: 8[53]; – 9: 3[283]; – 17: 8[129]; – 18: 2[73], 8[136]; – 18.pr: 1[187], 3[426]; – 18.1: 7[176], 8[131]; – 19.2: 8[4, 105]; – 19.3: 3[302, 416]; – 20: 3[113, 366, 373, 386, 392, 416]

4.21.1: 3[796]; – 17: 2[73], 8[136]; – 17.pr: 8[102]; – 17.1: 8[117]; – 17.2: 8[118]; – 19.pr: 3[376, 483], 106; – 19.2: 3[401]; – 20.pr: 3[427]; – 20.2: 3[79, 93, 122, 317, 534]; – 20.3: 3[371, 397]; – 21.pr: 3[237, 254, 273, 416, 429]; – 21.2: 1[188, 196], 3[273, 416, 426]; – 21.4: 3[302, 388, 415, 416]

4.24.11: 3[172]
4.27.2: 5[8]; – 2.pr: 3[167, 355, 525]; – 2.1: 3[223, 541], 8[58]; – 2.2: 3[372, 475]; – 3.pr: 3[143, 417, 419]

4.28.7: 5[33]; – 7.pr: 3[51, 372, 386, 388], 5[26]; – 7.1: 3[372, 387, 417, 419]

4.29.19: 3[514]; – 21: 8[7, 224]; – 22.pr: 3[394]; – 22.1: 3[277]; – 23: 5[33]; – 23.pr: 3[342, 466, 500, 523]; – 23.1: 3[520]; – 24: 5[33]; – 24.pr: 5[26]; – 24.1: 3[305, 388]; – 25.1: 3[318]

4.30.5: 3[492]; – 10: 3[417]; – 13: 3[407], 8[53, 66, 229]; – 14: 2[73], 8[136]; – 14.pr: 3[131]; – 14.1: 8[120, 134]; – 14.2: 8[102, 111, 120]; – 14.3: 8[101]; – 14.4: 8[130]; – 14.6: 8[117]; – 15: 2[73], 8[137]; – 16: 3[417, 418, 492], 115

4.31.14.pr: 3[417, 419]; – 14.1: 3[281, 318, 388], 8[105]

4.32.26: 8[107]; – 26.pr: 3[388], 9[87]; – 26.2: 3[61]; – 26.3: 8[132]; – 26.5: 8[117]; – 28.pr: 3[366, 367, 406, 417, 418], 106, 9[34]; – 28.1: 3[407, 416, 516], 106

CJ

4.33.24: 8^4

4.34.11: 3^{625}; — 11.2: 3^{471}, 107; — 12: 3^{51}, 153, 367, 410, 417, 420, 115

4.35.19: 8^4; — 22: 8^2; — 22.3: 3^{60}, 8^3, 7, 11, 13; — 23.pr: 3^{147}, 172, 173, 365, 381, 115; — 23.1: 3^{741}, 798; — 23.2: 3^{237}, 429; — 23.3: 2^{112}, 3^{127}, 129, 367, 711, 8^{134}

4.37.6: 3^{51}, 169, 225, 355, 5^{48}; — 7: 3^{51}, 412

4.38.6: 8^3; — 15: 5^{33}; — 15.pr: 3^{376}, 515, 8^{109}; — 15.1: 5^{26}; —15.2: 1^{196}, 3^{97}, 150, 426, 447; — 15.3: 8^{117}

4.39.9: 3^{50}, 417, 419

4.43.2: 7^{55}

4.44.2: 3^{177}; — 5: 2^{13}; — 8: 3^{521}, 7^{19}

4.51.3: 3^{415}; — 7: 3^{550}

4.54.9. pr: 3^{51}, 168, 218; — 9.1: 3^{305}, 335

4.58.3.1: 1^{193}, 3^{426}

4.61.9: 7^{72}

4.65.10; 3^{415}; — 35: 3^{675}; — 35.pr: 3^{139}, 294, 317, 117; — 35.1: 3^{719}; — 35.3: 3^{232}

4.66.2.1: 3^{262}, 400, 106; — 3.pr: 3^{166}, 168, 262, 400; — 3.1: 3^{272}, 400, 453; — 3.3: 3^{400}, 541; — 3.5: 3^{262}, 400

5.2.1: 7^{42}

5.3.15.pr: 3^{51}; — 15.1: 213; — 19: 3^{26}; — 19.pr: 8^{58}, 228; — 19.3: 229; — 20.pr: 3^{461}, 115; — 20.1: 3^{366}, 414, 417, 115; — 20.3: 115; — 20.5: 8^{130}; —20.6: 3^{431}, 115; — 20.7: 3^{153}, 218, 381, 660, 756, 115; — 20.8: 8^{130}; — 20.9: 3^{51}, 115

5.4.6: 3^{29}; — 20.1: 3^{414}; — 23: 1^{78}, 10, 11; —

23.pr: 1^{89}, 137, 186, 3^{150}, 172, 426, 8^{52}; — 23.1: 1^{80}, 8^{50}, 229; — 23.1a: 229; — 23.1b: 3^{417}, 8^{56}, 229; — 23.2: 229; — 23.4: 1^{82}, 229; — 23.5: 3^{247}; — 23.5a: 229; — 23.7: 229; — 23.8: 8^{45}, 66, 229; — 24: 3^{545}; — 25: 5^{36}; — 25.pr: 3^{51}; — 25.2: 3^{40}, 56, 168; — 25.3: 3^{56}, 404, 5^{26}; — 26: 5^{36}; — 26.pr: 3^{168}; — 26.1: 3^{243}, 5^{26}; — 26.2: 3^{496}; — 27: 3^{707}; — 28.pr: 3^{40}, 167, 115; — 28.1: 3^{272}; — 28.2: 3^{283}, 444, 765, 833, 115; — 28.4: 3^{414}, 517, 115

5.5.2: 3^{164}, — 3.1: 7^{179}, 222; — 3.2: 8^4; — 4.1: 8^{55}; — 6.2: 3^{60}; — 7.1: 3^{319}; — 7.2: 1^{75}, 80, 3^{93}, 122; — 8: 3^{60}, 8^{132}

5.7.1: 7^{45}

5.8.1.pr: 3^{516}

5.9.1.2: 3^{101}; — 3: 7^{44}; — 5.6: 8^{130}; — 6.11: 8^{130}; — 9.pr: 3^{139}, 8^{99}, 102; — 9.1: 8^{113}; — 10.pr: 3^{403}, 407, 458, 106; — 10.2: 3^{488}, 106; — 10.3: 3^{516}, 106; — 10.5: 3^{219}, 311, 106; — 10.6: 3^{424}, 106

5.11.7: 5^{53}, 145; — 7. pr: 3^{51}, 168, 172, 173; — 7.1: 3^{490}; — 7.2: 3^{395}, 409, 469, 538; — 7.3: 3^{221}; — 7.5: 3^{303}, 477

5.12.1.2: 8^{116}; — 20: 3^{346}; — 29: 8^{122}; — 30.pr: 3^{172}, 213, 300, 452, 107; — 30.1: 3^{415}, 107; — 30.2: 3^{530}, 107; — 31.pr: 3^{309}; — 31.1: 8^{117}; — 31.2: 3^{433}; — 31.3: 3^{221}; — 31.6: 3^{290}, 388, 399; — 31.8: 3^{401}

5.13.1.pr: 3^{70}, 138, 383, 417, 419; — 1.1a: 3^{242}, 470; — 1.1b: 3^{294}, 387; — 1.1c: 3^{101}; — 1.1d: 3^{172}; — 1.2: 3^{172}, 402; —1.2a: 3^{78}, 107, 172,

174, 210; — 1.3: 3^{396}; — 1.3a: 3^{346}; — 1.5: 3^{230}; — 1.5a: 2^{114}, 3^{54}; — 1.6: 3^{172}; — 1.7: 3^{172}, 409; — 1.7a: 3^{368}; — 1.7b: 3^{378}; — 1.8: 3^{172}, 173; — 1.9: 3^{93}, 122, 172; — 1.10: 3^{172}; — 1.11: 3^{336}; — 1.13b: 3^{106}; — 1.13c: 3^{90}, 91; — 1.14: 3^{392}; — 1.14a: 3^{177}, 366, 541; — 1.15: 3^{492}; —1.15b: 3^{172}; — 1.15c: 3^{213}; — 1.16a: 3^{218}; — 1.16d: 8^{117}

5.14.4: 3^{434}; —8: 3^{366}; —9.1: 8^{130}; — 11: 5^{54}, 145; — 11.pr: 3^{167}; — 11.4: 3^{223}

5.15.3: 2^{73}, 8^{112}, 136

5.16.6.1: 3^{49}; — 24.1: 3^{172}; — 24.2: 7^{149}; — 25.1: 7^{176}; — 25.2: 7^{176}; — 26: 8^{125}; — 27: 5^{55}, 145; — 27.pr: 3^{367}, 416; — 27.1: 2^{114}, 3^{159}, 162, 507, 9^{20}

5.17.3.1: 3^{49}, 8^{120}; — 3.3: 3^{49}, 8^{120}; — 8.1: 3^{290}; — 8.3: 8^{130}; — 9: 8^{132}; — 10: 8^{112}; — 11: 2^{148}; — 11.1: 8^{130}; — 11.1a: 3^{355}, 398, 110; — 11.2: 3^{787}; — 11.2a: 3^{686}, 738, 8^{117}; — 11.2b: 3^{107}, 248, 800; — 12: 3^{59}

5.18.6.1: 3^{187}, 8^{124}; — 6.3: 3^{172}

5.19.1: 3^{313}, 7^{46}, 213

5.20.2: 3^{136}, 5^{33}

5.25.1: 8^{134}

5.27.1: 1^{75}, 80; — 2: 7^{68}; — 3.2: 3^{325}; — 6: 8^{23}, 225; — 7: 8^{31}; — 7.1: 8^{42}, 46; — 7.3: 8^{42}, 44, 50, 53, 54, 66; — 8: 8^{136}; — 8.pr: 3^{182}; — 8.2: 8^{116}, 133; — 9: 8^{136}; — 9.pr: 8^{102}; — 9.1: 8^{116}; — 9.2: 8^{101}; — 9.3: 7^{176}, 8^{131}; — 9.5: 8^{101}; — 9.6: 8^{117}; — 10: 206; — 10.pr: 3^{367}, 416,

CJ

6.27.2: 6[307]; — 4: 2[118], 5[39]; — 4.pr: 3[167]; — 4.1: 3[521]; — 4.2: 3[237], 386, 401, 5[27]; — 5: 1[115], 2[49], 110, 118, 189, 3[655], 5[48], 65; — 5.pr: 3[168]; — 5.1: 1[188], 3[51], 366, 376, 426, 495; — 5.1a: 3[410], 5[47], 65; — 5.1b: 3[100], 107, 178; — 5.1c: 3[51], 303, 329; — 5.1d: 3[51], 521; — 5.1e: 3[375]; — 5.3: 3[167], 169; — 5.3: 3[167], 169; — 5.3a: 3[414]; — 6: 2[118], 3[424], 5[65]

6.28.1.pr: 3[170]; — 3: 3[346], 389, 74; — 4: 2[118]; — 4.1: 3[172], 176, 367, 417; — 4.2: 3[139], 346, 417; — 4.3: 3[40], 442, 462; — 4.4: 3[367], 393; — 4.5: 3[112], 367, 404; — 4.8: 3[86], 341, 367, 368, 417, 419

6.29.3: 2[118], 5[39]; — 3.pr: 3[51], 168, 367, 392, 5[29]; — 3.1: 3[40], 141, 499; — 4: 2[118], 5[39]; — 4.pr: 3[376]; — 4.1: 3[112], 218, 343, 512, 5[27]

6.30.15: 7[128]; — 17: 9[86]; — 18.pr: 8[122]; — 18.3: 8[116]; — 19: 2[118]; — 19.pr: 3[40], 42, 46, 107, 401, 107; — 19.2: 3[378], 107; — 19.3: 3[378], 540, 107; — 19.4: 3[378], 520, 107; — 20: 2[49], 118; — 20.pr: 3[51], 167, 386, 398; — 20.1: 3[168], 392, 493; — 20.2: 5[30], 47; — 21: 2[49], 118; — 21.pr: 3[376]; — 21.1: 3[51], 205, 5[30], 47; — 21.2: 3[407], 422, 465; — 21.3: 3[370]; — 22: 2[118]; — 22.pr: 3[490]; — 22.1: 3[177], 189, 484; — 22.1a: 3[415]; — 22.1b: 3[190], 386, 407, 411, 537; — 22.2b: 3[223]; — 22.3: 3[345]; — 22.5: 3[388], 396; — 22.5: 3[455]; — 22.10: 8[101]; — 22.11: 3[378], 422; — 22.13a: 3[256], 304, 333, 378; — 22.14a: 3[326]; — 22.15: 3[381]; — 22.16: 3[238], 387

6.31.3: 3[386]; — 6.pr: 3[139], 367, 109; — 6.2: 3[708]

6.33.3: 2[118]; — 3.pr: 3[232], 385, 402, 404, 409; — 3.2: 3[376], 513; — 3.3: 3[378]; — 3.4: 3[346]

6.34.2: 8[107]

6.35.1.2: 8[170]; — 11: 2[118], 5[48]; — 11.pr: 3[51], 57, 107, 244; — 11.1: 3[367]; — 11.2: 3[57], 209, 392; — 11.3: 3[404], 530; — 12.pr: 3[51], 109, 8[118]; — 12.1: 3[275]

6.36.5: 3[473]; — 8.1: 3[464]; — 8.2: 8[130]

6.37.1: 3[389], 74; — 12: 3[29]; — 22: 3[377]; — 23: 2[118], 5[48]; — 23.pr: 3[51], 253, 355; — 23.1: 3[346], 407, 415; — 23.1d: 3[373]; — 23.2: 3[177], 416, 447; — 23.2a: 3[447], 5[26]; — 24: 2[118], 5[48]; — 24.pr: 3[167]; — 24.1: 3[416]; — 25: 2[118]; — 25.pr: 3[168]; — 25.1: 3[424]; — 26: 3[445], 109, 8[110]

6.38.3: 2[118], 3[389]; — 4: 2[118], 5[48]; — 4.pr: 3[168]; — 4.1: 3[160], 373, 410, 545; — 4.1a: 3[188], 243, 414, 425; — 4.1b: 3[356], 407; — 4.1c: 3[171], 272, 424; — 4.2: 3[521], 8[117]; — 5.pr: 3[231], 382, 821, 109; — 5.1: 3[177], 370, 768, 109

6.40.2: 2[118]; — 2.pr: 3[153], 346, 371, 385; — 2.1: 3[172], 176; — 2.2: 3[180], 217, 248, 371, 388, 415; — 3: 2[118]; — 3.pr: 3[114], 125; — 3.1: 3[327]; — 3.2: 3[40], 44, 107

6.41.1: 8[137]; — 61.pr: 9[87]; — 1.1: 1[196]

6.42.3: 3[300]; — 14.1: 3[819]; — 16.pr: 3[32]; — 22: 8[120]; — 30: 2[118], 3[40], 90, 339, 532; — 31: 2[118], 5[48]; — 31.pr: 3[167], 425; — 31.1: 3[188]; — 31.2: 8[117]; — 32: 2[118]; — 32.1: 3[371], 399,

405; — 32.3: 3[121]

6.43.1: 2[118], 207; — 1.pr: 3[225], 375, 411, 106; — 1.1: 3[54], 172, 106; — 1.2: 3[199], 416, 106; — 1.5: 3[534]; 106 — 2: 2[118]; — 2.pr: 3[371], 476; — 2.1: 3[89], 172; — 2.2: 3[172]; — 2.3: 3[102], 9[34]; — 3: 2[118]; — 3.pr: 3[51], 168; — 3.1a: 3[51], 168, 393; — 3.1b: 3[95], 378, 424; — 3.2: 3[197]; — 3.2a: 3[219]; — 3.3: 3[414]; — 3.3a: 3[367]

6.46.2.pr: 6[307]; — 6: 1[112], 2[99], 118, 5[48]; — 6.pr: 3[167], 475; — 6.1: 3[51], 385; — 7.pr: 3[168]

6.48.1: 207

6.49.6.3: 3[89]; — 7: 2[118]; — 7.pr: 3[40], 399; — 7.1b: 3[40], 51, 168, 392; — 8.pr: 3[167], 109

6.50.2: 8[114]; — 6: 3[300]; — 12: 8[114]; — 18.pr: 3[218], 404; — 19: 3[606]

6.51.1.pr: 3[495], 518, 796, 111; — 1.1: 3[415], 544, 111; — 1.1a: 3[415], 518, 111; — 1.1b: 3[239], 274, 367, 417, 841, 111; — 1.1c: 3[139], 495, 111; — 1.2: 3[242], 111; — 1.2a: 3[51], 172, 392, 111; — 1.3: 3[282], 367, 396, 111; — 1.3a: 3[242], 111; — 1.4: 3[335], 367, 111; — 1.5: 3[51], 113, 387, 111; — 1.6: 3[172], 174, 111; 1.6a: 3[172], 174, 111; — 1.7: 3[804]; — 1.8: 3[367], 111; — 1.9: 3[40], 100, 214, 290, 482, 111; — 1.9b: 3[355], 111; — 1.9c: 3[172], 111; — 1.9e: 3[455], 111; — 1.10: 3[292], 306, 387, 407, 537, 111; — 1.10a: 3[448], 746, 111; — 1.10b: 3[386], 111; — 1.10c: 3[448], 746, 111; — 1.10d: 3[745], 746; — 1.10e: 3[407], 745, 807, 111; — 1.11: 3[448], 111; — 1.11b: 3[146],

CJ

8.51.3.pr: 3^{395}; 106; — 3.1: $3^{164, 421}$, 106; — 3.2: 3^{416}, 106

8.53.24: 3^{346}; — 26: 7^{124}; — 33.pr: 8^{110}; — 33.2: 3^{61}, 8^{117}, 128; — 34.1b: 3^{244}, 107; — 34.2a: 3^{426}; — 34.2b: 1^{188}, 8^{130}, — 34.3: $3^{172, 174, 246, 267, 451}$, 107; — 34.3a: 3^{373}, 107; — 34.3b: 3^{319}; — 34.4: $3^{285, 373, 398, 402}$, 107; — 34.4a: 1^{188}, $3^{51, 80, 341, 373, 426, 427}$, 107; — 35.pr: $3^{248, 326}$; — 35.2: $3^{259, 409, 416}$; — 35.3: 3^{113}; — 35.3c: 3^{424}; — 35.4: 3^{403}; — 35.5e: 8^4; — 36.1: 3^{69}; — 36.2: 7^{21}; — 36.3: 3^{534}; — 37: $3^{230, 417, 419}$, 115, 9^{34}

8.55.1.2: 3^{480}; — 7.pr: 7^{125}; — 7.4: 3^{115}; — 9: 3^{346}, 7^{126}; — 10.1: 3^{194}, 416; — 10.2: 3^{514}

8.56.4: $3^{168, 372, 402}$, 425, 8^{122}

8.57.1.pr: 3^{60}

8.58.2: 3^{131}, $8^{110, 136}$

9.1.19: 3^{50}; — 21: 7^{70}

9.2.1: 8^{107}; — 9.2: 8^{130}; — 17.1: 3^{60}

9.3.2: 7^{132}

9.4.1.3: $3^{317, 416}$; — 4: 7^{133}

9.8.1: 3^{158}; — 2: 3^{527}; — 6: 8^{155}

9.9.9: 3^{158}; — 17.pr: 3^{333}; — 19: 3^{115}; — 27: 3^{449}; — 29: 7^{158}; — 29.1: 3^{102}; — 32: 7^{134}; — 34: 3^{313}, 7^{47}, 213; — 35.pr: 3^{445}, 110

9.12.8.2: 3^{459}; — 8.3: 3^{318}

9.13.1: 2^{148}; — 1.1: 3^{762}; — 1.1a: 3^{711}; — 1.1b: $3^{690, 733}$; — 1.1c: 3^{740}; —

1.3: 3^{113}, 110; — 1.3a: 3^{832}; — 1.3b: $3^{192, 736}$, 110; — 1.6: 8^{117}

9.17.1: 6.26

9.18.6: 3^{172}; — 7.pr: 3^{158}; — 9: 7^{135}

9.19.6: 1^{142}, 3^{127}, 8^{30}, 34, 35, 48, 58

9.22.1: 3^{542}; — 5: 3^{527}; — 11: 3^{34}; — 16: 3^{415}; — 22.2: 3^{374}, 213

9.23.1: 3^{389}, 74, 6^{307}

9.24.1.5: 3^{353}; — 2: 3^{248}

9.25.1: 3^{193}

9.26.1: 3^{46}, 7^{137}

9.28.1: 7^{138}

9.30.2: 3^{477}

9.31.1.1: 3^{330}

9.35.11: 3^{60}

9.36.2: 7^{139}, 8^{124}

9.39.1: 8^{107}

9.41.5: 8^{115}; — 7: 8^{114}; — 9: 8^{109}; — 11: 3^{35}; — 13: 8^{124}; — 18: 3^{421}, 106

9.42.2.pr: 3^{464}; — 2.1: 7^{140}

9.43.3.4: 3^{60}, $7^{141, 142}$

9.44.3: $8^{111, 121}$

9.45.6: 3^{238}

9.46.7: 3^{60}

9.47.3.1: 8^{120}; — 17: 3^{210}; — 23.1: 3^{416}

9.49.10: 7^{144}

9.51.13.2c: 3^{172}

10.1.4: 3^{161}; — 9: 8^{109}; — 10: 7^{48}

10.2.2.pr: 3^{530}; — 3.pr: 3^{300}

10.3.2: 3^{254}

10.4.3.1: 3^{223}

10.5.3: 3^{158}

10.10.5.1: 3^{403}

10.11.2.1: $3^{67, 158, 527}$; — 5: 3^{407}

10.15.1.1: 3^{192}

10.16.10: 7^{146}; — 12.3: 3^{158}; — 12.13: 8^{54}

10.20.1: $7^{147, 148}$

10.22.5: 2^{73}, 8^{136}

10.31.4: 5^{180}

10.32.14: 8^{54}; — 22: 7^{162}, 8^{107}; — 23: 3^{224}; — 48: 7^{118}; — 52: 7^{165}; — 64.1: 7^{178}; — 66: 8^{30}; — 67.1: 3^{208}; — 67.4: $3^{113, 244, 323}$, 108; — 67.6: $3^{93, 122, 367, 370}$, 108

10.34.1: 7^{164}; — 3: 3^{407}

10.35.2.1: 3^{472}; — 2.2: 3^{217}; — 3: 8^{136}; — 3.1: 3^{392}; — 3.2: 3^{407}, 7^{178}

10.40.9: 3^{94}, 7^{57}

10.41.3.1: 3^{416}

10.44.2: 3^{506}; — 4: $8^{107, 108, 125, 136}$

10.48.8: 7^{152}; — 9: 8^{110}; — 11: 8^{107}

10.52.6: 8^{107}

10.55.3.1: 9^{87}

10.60.1.1: 3^{386}

10.71.4: 3^{215}; — 7: 8^4

10.72.1: 7^{166}; — 5: 7^{167}; — 13.1: 7^{177}, 222

10.73.2: 7^{168}, 214

11.6.2: 9^{87}; — 6: 3^{272}, 8^{109}

11.7.7: 7^{49}

11.8.1: 7^{50}; — 10: 7^{51}; — 13: 3^{305}

11.9.2: 7^{52}; — 4: 7^{54}

11.10.6: 8^{107}; — 7.pr: 3^{158}; — 7.4: 3^{158}

11.12.1.1: 3^{158}

11.14.2.1: 7^{177}

11.19.1: 3^{416}

11.21.1.1: 7^{169}

11.24.1: 3^{158}

11.26.1: 3^{196}

11.28.1.1: 8^{55}

11.32.3.pr: 8^{130}

11.33.3.2: 3^{60}

11.41.3: 8^{107}

11.43.3: 8^{107}; — 7: 8^{101}; — 11: 225

11.44.1: 3^{516}

11.48.2.1: 3^{454}; — 4:

Novels

3^{224}, 118; – 4: 3^{398}, 118

24: 1^{177}; – pr: 4^{23}, 9^{37}; – 1: 9^{14}; – 2: 2^{114}, 9^{20}; – 4: 1^{151}, 4^{84}; – 5: 1^{151}, 286; – 6.1: 3^{45}

25: 1^{177}; – pr: 4^{23}, 9^{37}; – 1: 1^{151}, 4^{47}

26: 1^{177}; – pr: 1^{294}, 4^{23}, 9^{37}; – 1.1: 1^{151}; – 2.1: 4^{47}

27: 1^{177}, 9^{37}

28: $1^{177, 296}$; – pr: 1^{153}, 4^{80}, 9^{37}; – 2: 1^{306}; – 3: 1^{151}; – 4.1: 4^{62}; – 5.1: 1^{96}, 4^{86}

29: 1^{177}; – pr: 4^{23}, 9^{37}; – 2: 1^{151}; – 3: 9^{22}; – 4: 1^{96}

30: 1^{177}; – pr: 1^{386}, $4^{23, 24}$, $9^{36, 37}$; – 1: 4^{75}; – 2.6: 4^{62}; – 5.pr: 1^{151}; – 5.1: 1^{291}; – 6.pr: 1^{96}; – 6.1: 4^{53}; – 7: 4^{84}; – 9: $1^{217, 259}$; – 11.pr: 9^{20}; – 11.2: $1^{185, 223, 229}$

31: 1^{177}; – pr: 9^{12}; – 1.2: 1^{151}, 4^{62}; – 2: 4^{50}

32: 4^3; – 1: 9^{20}; – epil: $4^{40, 43}$

33: $3^{112, 738, 742, 791}$, 118, 4^{92}

34: $4^{3, 91}$; – pr: $3^{217, 349}$, 118; – 1: 3^{398}, 118; 9^{20}

35: $2^{3, 35, 151}$, 4^{95}, 225; – pr: 2^{65}, $3^{26, 303, 323}$, 118, 8^{147}; – 1: $3^{26, 505}$, 118, 8^{73}; – 2: 3^{416}, 118, 8^{148}; – 3: 3^{410}, 118, 8^{150}; – 4: 2^{168}, $3^{424, 449, 460}$, 118, 9^{65}; – 5: 3^{186}, 118; – 7: 3^{93}, 118; – 8: $2^{168, 170}$, $3^{90, 737}$, 118; – 9: 2^{170}; – 10: 2^{170}, $3^{90, 180, 388}$, 118

36: 1^{271}, 4^{89}; – pr: $3^{114, 164, 201, 303, 310, 312, 323, 452, 717}$, 117; – 2: $3^{317, 385}$, 117; – 2: $3^{317, 385}$, 117; – 4: $3^{187, 370, 386, 729}$, 117; – 5: $3^{370, 728}$, 117; – 6: 2^{232},

3^{64}; – epil: 117

37: 4^{89}; – pr: 1^{228}, $3^{457, 501}$, 118; – 3: $3^{188, 427, 811}$, 118; – 5: 3^{827}; – 6: 1^{250}; – 7: 2^{256}, $3^{122, 386, 449, 710}$, 118; – 8: 1^{250}, 3^{388}, 118; – 9: 3^{760}; – 10: 1^{250}, 3^{393}, 118; – 11: 3^{108}, 118; – 12: 3^{218}, 118

38. pr: 4^{84}, 9^{79}; – 3: 4^{84}; – 5: 4^{77}; – 6: $4^{62, 111}$; – epil: $4^{40, 43, 51}$

39.pr: 1^{298}, 2^{114}, $4^{16, 23, 70, 72, 84}$; – 2.pr: 1^{291}

40.pr: 2^{254}; – epil: 1^{185}

41: 4^{92}, 9^{79}

42: $1^{107, 214}$; – pr: $4^{16, 72}$; – 1.1: 4^{84}; – 1.2: 9^{28}; – epil: 4^{40}

43.pr: 1^{269}, 4^{109}; – 1.pr: $4^{62, 109}$; – 1.1: $4^{108, 112}$; – epil: $4^{40, 108, 109}$

44.pr: 2^{25}; – 2: 4^{72}; – epil: $4^{40, 43}$

45: 1^{214}; – 1: 1^{250}; – epil: 4^{20}

46.pr: $4^{19, 22}$, 9^{22}; – 2: 4^{72}; – epil: 4^{40}

47.pr: 4^{23}, 9^{79}; – epil: 4^{40}

48.pr: $4^{16, 72}$; – epil: 4^{40}

49.pr.pr: 1^{298}; – pr.1: 4^{21}, 9^{20}; – pr. 2: $4^{16, 72}$; – 1. pr: 4^{84}; – 1.1: 1^{306}; – epil: 4^{40}

50: 4^{94}; – inscr: 1^{151}; – pr: $4^{16, 72}$; – epil: 4^{43}

51.pr: $4^{16, 72}$; – 1: 4^{51}; – epil: 4^{40}

52.pr: 1^{293}, 4^{72}; – 2: 9^{22}

53: 2: 1^{62}, 4^{72}; – 3: 9^{20}; – 6: 9^{20}; – epil: $4^{40, 43}$

54.pr: 1^{233}; – epil: 4^{40}

55.epil: 4^{40}

56.pr: $4^{16, 43, 72}$; – 1: 1^{306}, 4^{51}

57.epil: 4^{40}

58: 4^{51}

59.pr: 4^{109}; – 2: 4^{109}; – 3: 4^{109}; – 5: $4^{62, 109}$; – 6: 4^{109}; – 7: $4^{109, 116}$; – epil: $4^{40, 108, 109}$

60.pr: 1^{299}, 2^{114}, 4^{27}; – 1.pr: 3^{59}; 125; – 1.1: 4^{51}

61: 1^{178}, 4^{25}; – 1.1: 4^{70}; – 2: 4^{84}; – epil: 4^{40}

62: 4^{88}, 4.13; – pr.pr: $3^{164, 751}$, 119; – 1.1: $3^{790, 825}$; – 1.2: $3^{315, 397, 801}$, 119; – 1.3: $3^{387, 735}$, 119; – 2.2: 3^{732}, 119; – 2.5: 3^{779}; – 5: $3^{272, 273}$

63.1: $4^{51, 70, 71}$; – epil: 4^{40}

64: 1^{246}; – 1: 4^{109}, 9^{22}; – 2: 1^{245}, $4^{51, 108, 109}$, 9^{12}

65: 4^{91}; – pr.pr: 3^{773}, 119; – pr.2: 3^{709}; – 1.5: $3^{272, 424, 803}$, 119

66: 4^{25}; – 1.1: 1^{151}; – 1.2: 2^{163}, 4^{52}; – epil: 4^{40}

67.2: 4^{71}

68: 1^{178}; – pr: $4^{16, 72}$; – 1.2: $1^{247, 248}$; – epil: 4^{40}

69. 1.1: 4^{71}; – 3: 4^{72}; – 4.2: 4^{111}; – 4.3: 4^{51}

70.pr: $4^{16, 72}$; – epil: 4^{40}

71.1: $4^{68, 70}$; – epil: 4^{40}

72.epil: 4^{40}

73.pr.pr: 1^{298}, 4^{72}; – pr.1: 1^{301}; – 3: 4^{76}; – 6: 4^{72}; – 8.2: 4^{71}; – epil: 2^{114}

74: 1^{178}; – pr.pr: 1^{298}, 3^{41}, 125; – pr.2: 4^{72}; – 1: 4^{84}, 9^{22}; – 4: 1^6, 4^{72}; – epil: 2^{114}, 4^{40}

75: 1^{177}, $2^{3, 22, 154}$, 4^{95}; – pr: 3^{806}; – 1: 3^{718}, 119; – 2: 2^{52}, $3^{207, 489, 782, 814}$, 119; – 3: 3^{816}, 119

76.epil: 4^{40}

77: 1^{139}

78. pr: 125; – 4.1: 1^{170}; – 5: 1^{306}, 125

79. 3: 4^{51}

80. 8: 4^{62}; – 10.pr:

General Index